THE PAPERS OF ULYSSES S. GRANT

THE PAPERS OF

ULYSSES S. GRANT

Volume 8: April 1–July 6, 1863
Edited by John Y. Simon

ASSISTANT EDITORS
John M. Hoffmann
David L. Wilson

——

SOUTHERN ILLINOIS UNIVERSITY PRESS

CARBONDALE AND EDWARDSVILLE

FEFFER & SIMONS, INC.

LONDON AND AMSTERDAM

Library of Congress Cataloging in Publication Data (*Revised*)

Grant, Ulysses Simpson, Pres. U.S., 1822–1885.
    The papers of Ulysses S. Grant.

    Prepared under the auspices of the Ulysses S. Grant Association.
    Bibliographical footnotes.
    CONTENTS: v. 1. 1837–1861—v. 2. April–September 1861.
—v. 3. October 1, 1861–January 7, 1862.—v. 4. January 8–March 31,
1862.—v. 5. April 1–August 31, 1862.—v. 6. September 1–December 8, 1862.—v. 7. December 9, 1862–March 31, 1863.—v. 8.
April 1–July 6, 1863.
    1. Grant, Ulysses Simpson, Pres. U.S., 1822–1885. 2. United
States—History—Civil War, 1861–1865—Campaigns and battles
—Sources. 3. United States—Politics and government—1869–1877
—Sources. 4. Presidents—United States—Biography. 5. Generals—
United States—Biography. I. Simon, John Y., ed. II. Ulysses S.
Grant Association.
E660.G756 1967   973.8′2′0924   67–10725
ISBN 0-8093-0884-3 (v. 8)

To Julia Grant Cantacuzène (1876–1975)

Contents

Maps and Illustrations

Introduction

During the opening months of 1863, Major General Ulysses S. Grant had been frustrated in every attempt to approach the Confederate stronghold of Vicksburg on solid ground. After exploring numerous ways in which Vicksburg could not feasibly be attacked, he sent Acting Rear Admiral David D. Porter's fleet past the batteries and marched troops overland to a point south of the formidable Confederate defenses. At the end of April, he finally established his army on the east bank of the Mississippi River at Bruinsburg, from which roads led to both the state capital of Jackson and to Vicksburg. Then he moved directly and rapidly toward a major victory.

As Grant moved inland, Jefferson Davis, who also regarded Vicksburg as the key to the Mississippi, sent General Joseph E. Johnston with reinforcements to take overall command. Grant moved with dazzling speed to isolate the Vicksburg garrison commanded by Lieutenant General John C. Pemberton. Instead of advancing directly on Vicksburg, the prize so long desired, Grant struck at Jackson, sending Johnston northward in some disarray, then turned toward Vicksburg, pushing Pemberton backward with victories at Champion's Hill and Big Black River. By May 18, Grant had driven Pemberton's army to Vicksburg and positioned his own force to prevent any cooperation between the two Confederate armies or to defeat each separately.

The campaign from Bruinsburg to Vicksburg showed Grant at his best. Disregarding the advice of Major General William T. Sherman, who had argued for resumption of the Mississippi Central campaign of the previous autumn, Grant moved with a speed which bewildered his opponents, dared to cut loose from his base of supplies, and developed plans from day to day as the nature of the country or Confederate moves dictated. Understanding both the strengths and limitations of his army of volunteers, Grant led an innovative campaign which astounded the North, although apprehension continued until the surrender of Vicksburg.

Repulsed in assaulting Vicksburg on May 19, Grant tried again on May 22, taking heavier casualties with no apparent benefit. With no loss of equanimity, Grant settled into a traditional siege. Throughout the campaign he exhibited the ability to learn from mistakes, to improvise, to maintain his sights on long-range goals. Steady pressure on Vicksburg for six weeks led to the surrender of Pemberton's entire army on July 4.

During the siege, Grant resolved his long-term problem with Major General John A. McClernand, his ambitious subordinate. During the assault of May 22, McClernand had sent reports of partial success which led Grant to commit more troops to a vain effort. After that, Grant simply sought the first opportunity to remove McClernand and found it when McClernand issued orders congratulating his own 13th Army Corps without first sending them to department headquarters. McClernand's removal on June 18 so neatly coincided with the arrival of his replacement, Major General Edward O. C. Ord, as to suggest that Grant used the military impropriety as an excuse.

By the close of the Vicksburg campaign, Grant was approaching the apex of his military career. Once he had crossed the Mississippi River, he "felt a degree of relief scarcely ever equalled since." Even with the army at Vicksburg intact and reinforcements pouring into the state, he saw his way clear to ultimate victory. This new burst of confidence infused his correspondence with an added measure of crispness, clarity, and self-assurance.

We are indebted to W. Neil Franklin, Karl L. Trever, and Richard E. Wood for searching the National Archives; to Barbara Long for maps; to Anita Anderson and Deborah Pittman for typing; to Harriet Simon for proofreading; and to Richard T. Boss, Michael H. Duffy, Kathy Heggemeier, Vernice Howard, Tamara Melia, and Christopher D. Morris, graduate students at Southern Illinois University, for research assistance.

Financial support for the Ulysses S. Grant Association for the period during which this volume was prepared came from Southern Illinois University and the National Historical Publications and Records Commission. The latter also provided the fellowship under which David L. Wilson served as assistant editor.

December 29, 1977 John Y. Simon

Editorial Procedure

---

1. Editorial Insertions

A. Words or letters in roman type within brackets represent editorial reconstruction of parts of manuscripts torn, mutilated, or illegible.

B. [. . .] or [— — —] within brackets represent lost material which cannot be reconstructed. The number of dots represents the approximate number of lost letters; dashes represent lost words.

C. Words in *italic* type within brackets represent material such as dates which were not part of the original manuscript.

D. Other material crossed out is indicated by ~~cancelled type~~.

E. Material raised in manuscript, as "4th," has been brought in line, as "4th."

2. Symbols Used to Describe Manuscripts

AD	Autograph Document
ADS	Autograph Document Signed
ADf	Autograph Draft
ADfS	Autograph Draft Signed
AES	Autograph Endorsement Signed
AL	Autograph Letter
ALS	Autograph Letter Signed
ANS	Autograph Note Signed
D	Document
DS	Document Signed

Df	Draft
DfS	Draft Signed
ES	Endorsement Signed
LS	Letter Signed

3. Military Terms and Abbreviations

Act.	Acting
Adjt.	Adjutant
AG	Adjutant General
AGO	Adjutant General's Office
Art.	Artillery
Asst.	Assistant
Bvt.	Brevet
Brig.	Brigadier
Capt.	Captain
Cav.	Cavalry
Col.	Colonel
Co.	Company
C.S.A.	Confederate States of America
Dept.	Department
Div.	Division
Gen.	General
Hd. Qrs.	Headquarters
Inf.	Infantry
Lt.	Lieutenant
Maj.	Major
Q. M.	Quartermaster
Regt.	Regiment or regimental
Sgt.	Sergeant
USMA	United States Military Academy, West Point, N.Y.
Vols.	Volunteers

4. Short Titles and Abbreviations

ABPC	*American Book-Prices Current* (New York, 1895–)
CG	*Congressional Globe* Numbers following represent the Congress, session, and page.

J. G. Cramer	Jesse Grant Cramer, ed., *Letters of Ulysses S. Grant to his Father and his Youngest Sister, 1857–78* (New York and London, 1912)
DAB	*Dictionary of American Biography* (New York, 1928–36)
Garland	Hamlin Garland, *Ulysses S. Grant: His Life and Character* (New York, 1898)
HED	*House Executive Documents*
HMD	*House Miscellaneous Documents*
HRC	*House Reports of Committees* Numbers following *HED, HMD,* or *HRC* represent the number of the Congress, the session, and the document.
Ill. AG Report	J. N. Reece, ed., *Report of the Adjutant General of the State of Illinois* (Springfield, 1900)
Lewis	Lloyd Lewis, *Captain Sam Grant* (Boston, 1950)
Lincoln, Works	Roy P. Basler, Marion Dolores Pratt, and Lloyd A. Dunlap, eds., *The Collected Works of Abraham Lincoln* (New Brunswick, 1953–55)
Memoirs	*Personal Memoirs of U. S. Grant* (New York, 1885–86)
O.R.	*The War of the Rebellion: A Compilation of the Official Records of the Union and Confederate Armies* (Washington, 1880–1901)
O.R. (Navy)	*Official Records of the Union and Confederate Navies in the War of the Rebellion* (Washington, 1894–1927) Roman numerals following *O.R.* or *O.R.* (Navy) represent the series and the volume.
PUSG	John Y. Simon, ed., *The Papers of Ulysses S. Grant* (Carbondale and Edwardsville, 1967–)
Richardson	Albert D. Richardson, *A Personal History of Ulysses S. Grant* (Hartford, Conn., 1868)
SED	*Senate Executive Documents*
SMD	*Senate Miscellaneous Documents*
SRC	*Senate Reports of Committees* Numbers following *SED, SMD,* or *SRC* represent the number of the Congress, the session, and the document.
USGA Newsletter	*Ulysses S. Grant Association Newsletter*
Young	John Russell Young, *Around the World with General Grant* (New York, 1879)

5. *Location Symbols*

CLU	University of California at Los Angeles, Los Angeles, Calif.
CoHi	Colorado State Historical Society, Denver, Colo.
CSmH	Henry E. Huntington Library, San Marino, Calif.
CtY	Yale University, New Haven, Conn.
CU-B	Bancroft Library, University of California, Berkeley, Calif.
DLC	Library of Congress, Washington, D.C. Numbers following DLC-USG represent the series and volume of military records in the USG papers.
DNA	National Archives, Washington, D.C. Additional numbers identify record groups.
IaHA	Iowa State Department of History and Archives, Des Moines, Iowa
I-ar	Illinois State Archives, Springfield, Ill.
IC	Chicago Public Library, Chicago, Ill.
ICarbS	Southern Illinois University, Carbondale, Ill.
ICHi	Chicago Historical Society, Chicago, Ill.
ICN	Newberry Library, Chicago, Ill.
ICU	University of Chicago, Chicago, Ill.
IHi	Illinois State Historical Library, Springfield, Ill.
In	Indiana State Library, Indianapolis, Ind.
InFtwL	Lincoln National Life Foundation, Fort Wayne, Ind.
InHi	Indiana Historical Society, Indianapolis, Ind.
InNd	University of Notre Dame, Notre Dame, Ind.
InU	Indiana University, Bloomington, Ind.
KHi	Kansas State Historical Society, Topeka, Kan.
MdAN	United States Naval Academy Museum, Annapolis, Md.
MH	Harvard University, Cambridge, Mass.
MHi	Massachusetts Historical Society, Boston, Mass.
MiD	Detroit Public Library, Detroit, Mich.
MiU-C	William L. Clements Library, University of Michigan, Ann Arbor, Mich.
MoSHi	Missouri Historical Society, St. Louis, Mo.
NHi	New-York Historical Society, New York, N.Y.

NIC	Cornell University, Ithaca, N.Y.
NjP	Princeton University, Princeton, N.J.
NjR	Rutgers University, New Brunswick, N.J.
NN	New York Public Library, New York, N.Y.
NNP	Pierpont Morgan Library, New York, N.Y.
OClWHi	Western Reserve Historical Society, Cleveland, Ohio.
OFH	Rutherford B. Hayes Library, Fremont, Ohio.
OHi	Ohio Historical Society, Columbus, Ohio.
OrHi	Oregon Historical Society, Portland, Ore.
PHi	Historical Society of Pennsylvania, Philadelphia, Pa.
PPRF	Rosenbach Foundation, Philadelphia, Pa.
RPB	Brown University, Providence, R.I.
TxHR	Rice University, Houston, Tex.
USG 3	Maj. Gen. Ulysses S. Grant 3rd, Clinton, N.Y.
USMA	United States Military Academy Library, West Point, N.Y.
ViHi	Virginia Historical Society, Richmond, Va.
ViU	University of Virginia, Charlottesville, Va.
WHi	State Historical Society of Wisconsin, Madison, Wis.
Wy-Ar	Wyoming State Archives and Historical Department, Cheyenne, Wyo.
WyU	University of Wyoming, Laramie, Wyo.

Chronology

APRIL 1–JULY 6, 1863

APRIL 1. After a reconnaissance on the Yazoo River with Act. Rear Admiral David D. Porter and Maj. Gen. William T. Sherman, USG decided against an attack on Haynes' Bluff, thus eliminating the last approach to Vicksburg from the north.

APRIL 3. Accompanied by his son, Frederick Dent Grant, USG went upriver to Milliken's Bend, La., to make arrangements to move his army to New Carthage, La., south of Vicksburg.

APRIL 7. U.S. naval forces unsuccessfully attacked Charleston, S.C.

APRIL 11. USG decided to attack Grand Gulf, Miss.

APRIL 16. USG and Julia Dent Grant watched seven gunboats, three steamboats, and some barges run the Vicksburg batteries. One steamboat was lost.

APRIL 17. USG at Richmond, La.

APRIL 17. Col. Benjamin H. Grierson began a cav. raid through Miss. which ended on May 2 when he arrived at Baton Rouge, La.

APRIL 18. USG at Smith's Plantation, La., and New Carthage.

APRIL 19. USG returned to Milliken's Bend.

APRIL 22. Six steamboats and twelve barges ran the Vicksburg batteries. One steamboat sank, one was totally disabled, one was badly damaged.

APRIL 24. USG reconnoitered Grand Gulf.

APRIL 27. USG's forty-first birthday.

xxi

APRIL 27. USG asked Sherman to distract C.S.A. attention by making a demonstration at Haynes' Bluff. Sherman did so on April 29.

APRIL 29. After Porter's gunboats engaged the batteries at Grand Gulf, USG decided to land troops below.

APRIL 30. USG landed troops at Bruinsburg, Miss.

MAY 1. Battle of Port Gibson, Miss., in which troops of Maj. Gen. John A. McClernand's 13th Army Corps pushed back the force of C.S.A. Maj. Gen. John S. Bowen to secure USG's bridgehead in Miss.

MAY 1–4. Battle of Chancellorsville, Va., which ended in disastrous defeat for Maj. Gen. Joseph Hooker's Army of the Potomac.

MAY 3. USG established a supply base at Grand Gulf, which C.S.A. forces had evacuated.

MAY 5. USG reached Hankinson's Ferry, Miss.

MAY 7. USG at Rocky Springs, Miss.

MAY 9. C.S.A. Gen. Joseph E. Johnston assigned overall command in Miss.

MAY 9–10. USG's forces skirmished near Utica, Miss.

MAY 10. USG at Cayuga.

MAY 12. USG at Fourteen Mile Creek.

MAY 12. USG's forces under Maj. Gen. James B. McPherson won a victory at Raymond, Miss.

MAY 14. USG occupied Jackson, Miss., pushing Johnston northward.

MAY 15. USG turned toward Vicksburg, concentrating at Edwards Station, Miss.

MAY 16. USG won the battle of Champion's Hill or Baker's Creek, Miss.

MAY 17. After an engagement at Big Black River Bridge, Miss., C.S.A. forces withdrew to Vicksburg.

MAY 18. USG besieged Vicksburg.

MAY 19. USG unsuccessfully assaulted Vicksburg.

MAY 21. U.S. forces under Maj. Gen. Nathaniel P. Banks besieged Port Hudson, La.

MAY 22. USG's second assault failed with heavy casualties. USG placed much blame on inaccurate reports from McClernand.

MAY 26. USG sent an expedition to Mechanicsburg, Miss.

JUNE 2. USG ordered a brigade under Brig. Gen. Joseph A. Mower to Mechanicsburg, and the next day sent another brigade under Brig. Gen. Nathan Kimball.

JUNE 6. USG started toward Satartia, Miss., and Mechanicsburg by river but turned back after learning of enemy action in the area.

JUNE 7. C.S.A. forces attacked the U.S. garrison at Milliken's Bend. Black troops, under fire for the first time, aided by gunboats, repulsed the attack and inflicted heavy casualties.

JUNE 15. Two divs. of the 9th Army Corps, commanded by Maj. Gen. John G. Parke, arrived to reinforce USG.

JUNE 18. USG removed McClernand from command, replacing him with Maj. Gen. Edward O. C. Ord.

JUNE 23. Maj. Gen. William S. Rosecrans opened the Tullahoma campaign, forcing Gen. Braxton Bragg southward.

JUNE 25. USG exploded a mine beneath the Vicksburg fortifications, denting but not breaking the C.S.A. lines.

JUNE 27. Maj. Gen. George G. Meade replaced Hooker as C.S.A. forces entered Pa.

JULY 1. Three days of battle began at Gettysburg, Pa.

JULY 1. USG exploded another mine under the Vicksburg fortifications.

JULY 3. USG and C.S.A. Lt. Gen. John C. Pemberton discussed the capitulation of Vicksburg.

JULY 4. Vicksburg surrendered.

JULY 4. Maj. Gen. Benjamin M. Prentiss repulsed an attack on Helena, Ark.

JULY 4. C.S.A. Gen. Robert E. Lee began to withdraw from Gettysburg.

JULY 5. Sherman began to advance toward Jackson and Johnston's army.

The Papers of Ulysses S. Grant
April 1– July 6, 1863

To Col. *William S. Hillyer*

Before Vicksburg April 1, 1863.

COL W. S. HILLYER
PROVOST MARSHAL GEN'L

You will have a commissioned officer at Memphis, whose special duty it shall be immediately on their arrival at Memphis, to board all Steamboats coming from South of Helena, and examine their cargoes, and seize and turn over to the Chief Quarter Master of the Department, or such Quarter Master as may be designated by him, all cotton and other property which is not permitted by authority from these Head Quarter. In all such cases, you will take duplicate receipts for such confiscated property, and forward one to these Head Quarters. When authority is granted by other than the Dept. Commander to ship cotton, the army Corps Commanders granting such authority, will state that it is done by authority of Department Commander

U. S. GRANT Maj Gen'

Copies, DLC-USG, V, 19, 30; DNA, RG 393, Dept. of the Tenn., Letters Sent.

To *Act. Rear Admiral David D. Porter*

Before Vicksburg, April 2d 1863.

ADMIRAL D. D. PORTER
COM'D'G. MISSISSIPPI SQUADRON.

After the reconnoissance of yesterday[1] I am satisfied that an attack upon Haines Bluff would be attended with immense sacrifice of life, if not with defeat.

This then closes out the last hope of turning the enemy by the right. I have sent troops through from Milliken's Bend to New Carthage to garrison and hold the whole route, and make the wagon road good.

At Richmond[2] a number of boats were secured which can aid in carrying subsistence from that point to New Carthage, and will also answer for ferrying any intermediate bayous. In addition to this I have a large force working on a canal from the river to Willow Bayou, in in clearing this latter out. With this done there will be good water communication from here to Carthage, for barges and tugs. I have sent to St. Louis and Chicago for barges and tugs, and ordered all empty barges here to be fitted up for the transportation of troops and artillery. With this appliances I intend to be able to move 20,000 men at one time. To morrow I shall have work commenced to prepare at least six Steamers to run the blockade.

Having then fully determined upon operating from New Carthage either by the way of Grand Gulf or Warrenton, I am of the same opinion as when I addressed you a few days since, that is that it is important to prevent the enemy from further fortifying either of these places.

I am satisfied that one Army Corps with the aid of two Gunboats, can take and hold Grand Gulf until such time as I might be able to get my whole army there, and make provision for supplying them. If necessary, therefore, I would send this number of troops as soon as the necessity for them was demonstrated.

I would, Admiral, therefore renew my request to prepare for running the blockade at as early a day as possible.

I shall go up to Milikens Bend to-morrow, but will be over to see you on this subject the day following.

U. S. Grant.
Maj. Gen.

P. S. I would respectfully request if it would not be well to send to Memphis for all the spare small boats belonging to your branch of service not otherwise in use.

U. S. G.

Copies, DLC-USG, V, 19, 30; DNA, RG 393, Dept. of the Tenn., Letters Sent; Alcorn Collection, WyU. *O.R.*, I, xxiv, part 3, 168; *O.R.* (Navy), I, xxiv, 521.

1. On April 2, 1863, USG telegraphed to Maj. Gen. Henry W. Halleck. "In two weeks I expect to be able to collect all my forces and turn Enemy's left   With present high water the extent of ground upon which troops could land at Haines Bluff is so limited that the place is impregnable   I reconnoitered the place yester-day with Adml Porter and Sherman"   Telegrams received (2), DNA, RG 107, Telegrams Collected (Unbound); copies, *ibid.*, Telegrams Received in Cipher; *ibid.*, RG 393, Dept. of the Tenn., Hd. Qrs. Correspondence; DLC-USG, V, 5, 8, 24, 94. *O.R.*, I, xxiv, part 1, 24. On March 31, USG had written to Maj. Gen. William T. Sherman. "To-morrow soon after breakfast Admiral Porter and myself will start up the Yazoo on a reconnoisance and would like to have your company. We breakfast here about 7 O'Clock but will wait until you arrive." ALS, DLC-William T. Sherman.

2. Richmond, La., on Roundaway Bayou about twenty miles west of Vicks-burg. On March 31, Maj. Gen. John A. McClernand wrote to USG. "I have just returned from Richmond, and have the pleasure to announce the fact that a detach-ment of this Corps now occupies that place   Taking with them, a few skiffs and yawls, the detachment pushed on to the Bayou on this side of Richmond, and while skirmishing with a detachment of the enemy, crossed the Bayou, paddling their craft with the butts of their guns, and entered the town   Two of the enemy were killed. No loss was sustained on our side   The Bayou is a broad stream of the kind, and flows with considerable current. Whether communication by land or water, with New Carthage, will be found most eligible, I am not yet able to say. I will further report on the subject at an early day. Col T. W. Bennett of the 69th Indiana is in command of the detachment, which consists of a Regiment of Infantry, and detachment of Cavalry & pioneers   The movement was rapid and so far completely successful"   ALS, DNA, RG 94, War Records Office, Union Battle Reports.

To Lt. Col. Charles A. Reynolds

Before Vicksburg, April 2d 1863.

LEIUT. COL. C. A. REYNOLDS,
CHIEF QUARTERMASTER.

Do not fail to send here without delay the material necessary for fitting up the barges here for the transportation of troops and artillery.

Telegraph Quartermaster at Smithland to know if Gen. Rose-crans will have Steamers enough, with those you are now sending him, to supply him. If not send some more. I presume it is a matter of the greatest importance that Gen. Rosecrans should have a large supply of stores during the present high water.

U. S. GRANT.
Maj. Gen'l.

Copies, DLC-USG, V, 19, 30; DNA, RG 393, Dept. of the Tenn., Letters Sent. On April 3, 1863, USG wrote to Maj. Gen. James B. McPherson. "Send down here all the empty Coal, Hay and all other barges you now have. As fast as barges are emptied send them down by any Steamers coming down." Copies, *ibid.*

To Maj. Gen. Stephen A. Hurlbut

———

Before Vicksburg, April 3. 1863.

MAJ. GEN. S. A: HURLBUT,
COM'D'G. 16TH ARMY CORPS

Your communication of the 1st is received. I heartily approve of the move you propose. I have ordered Washburne to take command of all the Cavalry in your command.[1] It may be organized into a Division of Brigades, composed according to your own judgement, with Gen. Washburne's Headquarters where you think the most appropriate.

I have ordered Prentiss to send you another regiment without delay,[2] and send one Steamer to him to facilitate its movements. You will also ask Admiral Porter to send the Marine Brigade up the Tennessee river, with instructions to report to Dodge, and cooperate with him.

U. S. GRANT.
Maj. Gen.

Copies, DLC-USG, V, 19, 30; DNA, RG 393, Dept. of the Tenn., Letters Sent. On April 1, 1863, Maj. Gen. Stephen A. Hurlbut wrote to USG. "The present situation of the enemies forces is submitted to you   Brig. Genl. S. A. Wood commanding North Alabama, Head Quarters: Florence. About 4000 men, mostly mounted   two Batteries of Artillery   Pickets along line of Bear Creek   Col. Barteaus Brigade of Cavalry lately reinforced, Head Quarters—Verona. Pickets to Baldwin. Next Ham and Faulkner, each a Regiment of Cavalry. extending along line of Tallahatchie, Pickets north of Holly Springs (Faulkner however is now at Panola) Brig. Genl. Chalmers commanding North Miss. Head Quarters at Panola. Ham, McGirk, Faulkner, Blythe & Richardson and all roving Bands are ordered to report to Chalmers. He has one six gun Battery at Panola and one behind the Tallahatchie near Abbeville On east side of the river, Cox, Roddy, and a portion of Van Dorns force are in Hardin Wayne and other counties. They are collecting stores and have flats in Horse creek and Duck rivers There is every indication of a raid to be made soon on our lines of communications I absolutely need another regiment of Cavalry at once—with that furnished me— ~~with~~ a good regiment with good horses, I will move from Corinth La Grange and this place, simultaneously sweeping round from Corinth to Pontotoc from La Grange straight down the Ridge with three regiments throwing one in above Oxford and cutting the Miss. Central—the other by Okalona and perhaps to Columbus now lightly guarded cutting that road while Grierson with his regiment would proceed by forced marches to Selma or Meridian. Both Selma and Meridian have few troops To break the Chunkey river or Pearl river bridge would be my object. Their Rolling stock is reduced and wearing out as. Barney informs me and they limit trains to ten miles an hour They are drawing supplies from Noxumbee and other counties of Miss. and conscripting relentlessly. As part of this movement I will send from La Grange on Holly Springs a Brigade of Infantry and some artillery and distroy the Tallahatchie bridge now being repaired and break up the car wheels and axles left there at the time of our withdrawal which are of vast service to them. I shall also move a force to the left of Panola from this place so as to keep Chalmers quiet or drive him back towards Grenada. I dislike to make this movement without more Cavalry for Dodge as his is the most exposed of any point. I therefore urgently request another Regiment to be sent me at once—If none can be spared from below I will go on with what I have as soon as I receive your orders" Copies, *ibid.*, Letters Received; *ibid.*, 16th Army Corps, Letters Sent. *O.R.*, I, xxiv, part 1, 26–27.

On April 1, Hurlbut wrote to Lt. Col. John A. Rawlins reporting information gathered by Forest Coburn concerning C.S.A. strength at Port Hudson, La., and Yazoo City and Greenwood, Miss. LS, DNA, RG 94, War Records Office, Dept. of the Mo. *O.R.*, I, xxiv, part 3, 166–67. On April 12, Lt. Col. William H. Thurston, inspector gen., 16th Army Corps, wrote to USG. "I am directed by the Major General Commanding, to say, that the bearer, F. Coburn, represents himself to be in the employ of Maj General Banks, and that he has a good knowledge of the Country below. He will give you such information as he has and then desires to be sent below. We know nothing of him, except his own Statement, as he claims to have lost all his papers from Maj Genl. Banks." Copy, DNA, RG 393, 16th Army Corps, Inspector Gen., Letters Sent.

On April 2, USG wrote to Hurlbut. "I understand that the 14th 12th 8th and 34th Iowa Regiments are under orders to report to me. You may direct the 14th to be left at Cairo, and the 35th now at Cairo to come here. The remainder of the Regiments send here also." Copies, DLC-USG, V, 19 (2), 30; DNA, RG 393, Dept. of the Tenn., Letters Sent. *O.R.*, I, xxiv, part 3, 169.

1. By Special Orders No. 93, Dept. of the Tenn., April 3. DS, Washburn Papers, WHi; McClernand Papers, IHi; copies, DLC-USG, V, 26, 27; DNA, RG 393, Dept. of the Tenn., Special Orders. *O.R.*, I, xxiv, part 3, 169. Maj. Gen. Cadwallader C. Washburn was assigned to duty by Hurlbut on April 9. *Ibid.*, p. 182.

2. By Special Orders No. 93, Dept. of the Tenn., April 3. DS, McClernand
Papers, IHi; Washburn Papers, WHi; copies, DLC-USG, V, 26, 27; DNA,
RG 393, Dept. of the Tenn., Special Orders.

To Maj. Gen. John A. McClernand

Head Quarters, Dept. of the Ten.
Before Vicksburg, Apl. 3d 1863.

MAJ. GEN J. A. McCLERNAND
COMD.G 13TH ARMY CORPS.
GEN.

Some time ago I gave a permit for H. L. Tibbetts[1] to move
North with his family and personal property. This permit was
given on representations satisfactory to me at the time but I
understand you have since arrested these people and seized their
property. If I have been deceived this is right but if not they are
entitled to take their property and go on the permit previously
given. I would be pleased to get a report in this case and would
also request that all the property seized be held secure until decided. Trade has not been opened south of Helena and therefore
I give no permits to ship any of the staples of the country North
of Memphis until the Treasury Dept. have decided upon them.

Very respectfully
U. S. GRANT
Maj. Gen. Com

ALS, McClernand Papers, IHi. On April 6, 1863, Maj. Gen. John A. McClernand,
Milliken's Bend, wrote to USG. "Herewith you will find a further partial report
made by the commission of Enquiry, of which *Col. Mudd* is President. As several
of his recommendations relates to points beyond my military jurisdiction I refer
them to you. I concur in his *first* recommendation, and would respectfully invite
your action to carry it into effect. I, also, concur in his *second* recommendation and
would respectfully suggest that the subject to which it relates be referred to Maj
Genl *McPherson* for his action   The *third* recommendation I will carry into effect,
so far as to turn the 142 bales of cotton over to Tibbatts or his representatives or
agents, leaving it to you, in your discretion to give permission for its shipment.
I, also, concur in the fourth recommendation and will carry it into effect with your

sanction; otherwise not." Copies, *ibid.*; DNA, RG 393, 13th Army Corps, Letters Sent.

1. Among the wealthy planters listed in the 1860 census of Carroll Parish, La., were Dr. Hiram B. Tebbetts or Thebbetts, aged forty-eight, born in Mass., who owned 121 slaves and a plantation valued at $71,250; and Horace B. Tebbetts or Thebbetts, aged fifty-two, born in Mass., who, with his wife Francis E. owned 262 slaves and plantations valued at $401,855. Joseph Karl Menn, *The Large Slaveholders of Louisiana—1860* (New Orleans, 1964), pp. 181–82. After the Civil War, Horace B. Tebbetts received more than $19,000 in compensation for cotton seized by the government. *HED*, 44-1-189, pp. 16, 28.

To Julia Dent Grant

Apl. 3d 1863,

DEAR JULIA,

Fred. and I have just returned from a trip fifteen miles up the river where we had quite a horseback ride. He enjoys himself finely and I doubt not will receive as much perminant advantage by being with me for a few months as if at school. He has written several letters since he arrived only one of them to you however. It is now so near time for the mail to start that he cannot write to-night.

Two days ago Fred. went up the Yazoo with me on a reconnoisance. We went as far on an ordinary steamer as it was safe to go and then took an Iron clad Gunboat. I left Fred. behind on the steamer. He was quite disappointed.

I sent to Buck by Capt Osband a lot of views taken at Hollysprings for him to look at through his sterioscope. I hope he has not left it behind. I believe I wrote you that my black coat is not in my trunk! Have you got it? It is hard to tell when the final strike will be made at Vicksburg. I am doing all I can and expect to be successful.

Staff are all well. You see so many people direct from here that you get all the news. How is Col. Dickey? I ought to write to him but I have so much of this to do, officially that I never write anything not absolutely necessary. Remember me to the Col.

Fred. and myself send love and kisses to all of you.

Good night dear Julia.

ULYS.

ALS, DLC-USG.

To Maj. Gen. Henry W. Halleck

———

Head Quarters, Dept. of the Ten.

Before Vicksburg, Apl. 4th 1863,

MAJ. GEN. H. W. HALLECK,

GEN. IN CHIEF, WASHINGTON, D. C.

GEN.

By information from the south, by way of Corinth, I learn that the enemy in front of Rosecrans have been reinforced from Richmond, Charleston, Savanna, Mobile and a few from Vicksburg. They have also collected a Cavalry force of 20.000 men. All the bridges Eastward from Savanna and North from Florence are being rapidly repaired. Chalmers[1] is put in command of North Miss., and is collecting all the Partizan Rangers and loose and independent companies of Cavalry that have been opperating in this Dept. He is now occupying the line of the Tallahatchie. This portends preparation to attack Rosecrans and to be able to follow up any success with rapidity; also, to make a simultaneous raid into West Tennessee, both from North Miss. and by crossing the Ten. river.

To counteract this, Admiral Porter has concented to send the Marine Brigade up the Ten. river to co operate with Gen. Dodge at Corinth.[2] I have also ordered an additional regiment of Cavalry from Helena into West Ten. I inclose with this a letter from Maj. Gen. Hurlbut giving a program which he wishes to carry out, and so much of it as to drive the enemy from the Tallahatchie and cuting the roads where they have been repaired, I think can be successfully executed. I will instruct him not to scatter his forces so as to risk loosing them.

I have placed one Division of troops on Deer creek with communication back to the Miss. river just above Lake Washington. The object of this move is to keep the enemy from drawing supplies from that rich region (and use them ourselves) and to attract the attention of the enemy in that direction. The navigation is ~~good~~ practicable for our Iron Clads and small steamers through to the Yazoo river by the route lately tried by Admiral Porter, with the exception of a few hundred yards in Deer Creek near Rolling Fork. This was obstructed by the enemy and they are now guarding and fortifying there. This move will have a tendency to make them throw in an additional force there and move some of their guns. My force had as well be there as here until I want to use them. A reconnosance to Haines Bluff demonstrates the impracticability of attacking that place during the present stage of water. The West bank of the river is densly wooded and under water. The East bank only runs up to the bluff for a short distance below the raft, then diverges, leaving a bottom widening all the way down in most part covered by water and all of it next to the bluffs so covered. The hill sides are ~~covered~~ lined with Rifle Pitts, with embrasures here and there for field Artillery   To storm this, but a small force could be used at the onset.

With the present batteries of the enemy, the Canal across the point can be of but little use.

There are a system of Bayous runing from Millikins Bend, and also from near the river at this point, that are navigable for barges and small steamers, passing around by Richmond to New Carthage. There is also a good wagon road from Millikins Bend to New Carthage. The dredges are now engaged cutting a canal from here into these bayous. I am having all the empty coal ~~barges~~ and other barges prepared for carrying troops and artillery and have written to Col. Allen for some more; and also for six tugs, to tow them.³ With these it would be easy to carry supplies to New Carthage and for any point South of that.

My expectation is for a portion of the Naval fleet to run the batteries of Vicksburg whilst the Army moves through by this new route. Once there I will move either to Warrenton or Grand Gulf, most probably the latter.⁴

From either of these points there are good roads to Vicksburg, and from Grand Gulf there is a good road to Jackson and the Black river bridge without crossing Black river.

This is the only move I now see as practicable, and hope it will meet your approval. I will keep my army together and see to it that I am not cut off from my supplies or beat in any other way than a fair fight. The discipline and health of this Army is now good, and I am satisfied the greatest confidance of success prevails.

I have directed Gen. Webster to commence the reconstruction of the rail-road between Grand Junction and Corinth.⁵ The labor will be performed by the Eng. regiment and Contrabands, thus saving additional expense. The streams will be crossed on piles. In this way the work should be done by the first of May.

> I am Gen. very respectfully
> your obt. svt.
> U. S. GRANT
> Maj. Gen.

ALS, Davenport Public Museum, Davenport, Iowa. *O.R.*, I, xxiv, part 1, 25–26. For the enclosure, see letter to Maj. Gen. Stephen A. Hurlbut, April 3, 1863.

1. James R. Chalmers, born in 1831 in Halifax County, Va., graduated from South Carolina College in 1851 and practiced law in Holly Springs, Miss., before the Civil War. Confirmed on Feb. 17, 1862, as C.S.A. brig. gen., he was assigned on April 3, 1863, to command in the two northern tiers of counties in Miss. east of New Albany, soon enlarged with command of the partisan corps in west Tenn. *O.R.*, I, xxiv, part 3, 659, 713, 746. On April 4, Maj. Gen. Stephen A. Hurlbut wrote to Lt. Col. John A. Rawlins. "Brig Genl L. Thomas Adj Genl. is here on a tour of inspection. I am gratified that so far as he has seen or expressed an opinion it is favorable. There has been a small picket affair on the line of the Nonconnah to day not yet over. Our cavalry pickets (2d Wisconsin) were struck about day light   two men wounded two captured. Col Stevens (2d Wis.) with about 100 men pursued crossed the Nonconnah & drove their pickets 6 miles when finding the enemy in force about from 600 to 800 cavalry & dismounted men and hearing

of a battery he fell back. I immediately ordered Lauman's 1st Brigade 4 Regiments and a Battery forward & pushed two Battalions 5th O. V. C over the Nonconnah. I have not yet heard from them nor do I think the enemy will wait for an attack. I think it was a ruse to draw a portion of our Cavalry out and surround them. If they come in before the Boat leaves I will report further, but think this is all— I scarcely believe that Chalmers would venture infantry & artillery so near us and think it is only a dash of mounted men." ALS, DNA, RG 94, War Records Office, Union Battle Reports. *O.R.*, I, xxiv, part 1, 512. On April 5, Hurlbut wrote to Rawlins. "The movement of yesterday appears to have been a dash merely of mounted men. Chalmers has moved up to Senatobia. Very considerable activity among the irregular Cavalry of the enemy is manifest along my southern front, especially South & East of Corinth. I have been anxiously waiting for cavalry horses from St Louis. Yesterday I received 350 which upon inspection are worthless. Genl Thomas went with me to look them over and sent a message to Col Allen to send no more, of that sort, but to send forward 1500 good cavalry horses for immediate use. I hope they may come and come soon. Dodge received a message from Rosecrans requesting him to move on Tuscumbia in combination with a movement on R's part on Florence. I have directed him to send the plan of the movement as I cannot well see how Rosecrans can reach Florence Except in heavy force. As however Dodge is strong enough to whip any thing on this side Tennessee River and yet cover Corinth—I shall have him move as requested. I have expected the 4th Mo. Cavalry but they have been sent to Nashville to Rosecrans. The enemys cavalry as previously reported are in force on the North & East sides of the Tennessee with some Artillery. Hence the necessity of an active Cavalry both from Jackson and Corinth—a hard service wearing to men & horses—I refer to my former letters on this subject" ALS, DNA, RG 393, Dept. of the Tenn., Letters Received. *O.R.*, I, xxiv, part 3, 174.

2. See following letter.

3. See letter to Col. Robert Allen, April 4, 1863.

4. On April 8, Maj. Gen. William T. Sherman wrote to Rawlins. "I would most respectfully suggest, for reasons which I will not name, that General Grant call on his corps commanders for their opinions, concise and positive, on the best general plan of campaign. Unless this be done, there are men who will, in any result falling below the popular standard, claim that their advice was unheeded, and that fatal consequences resulted therefrom. My own opinions are—1. That the Army of the Tennessee is far in advance of the other grand armies. 2. That a corps from Missouri should forthwith be moved from Saint Louis to the vicinity of Little Rock, Ark., supplies collected while the river is full, and land communication with Memphis opened via Des Arc, on the White, and Madison, on the Saint Francis Rivers. 3. That as much of Yazoo Pass, Coldwater, and Tallahatchee Rivers as can be gained and fortified be held, and the main army be transported thither by land and water; that the road back to Memphis be secured and reopened, and, as soon as the waters subside, Grenada be attacked, and the swamp road across to Helena be patrolled by cavalry. 4. That the line of the Yalabusha be the base from which to operate against the points where the Mississippi Central crosses Big Black, above Canton, and, lastly, where the Vicksburg and Jackson Railroad crosses the same river. The capture of Vicksburg would result. 5. That a force be left in this vicinity, not to exceed 10,000 men, with only enough steamboats to float and transport them to any desired point; this force to be held always near enough to act with the gunboats, when the main army is known to be near

Vicksburg, Haynes' Bluff, or Yazoo City. 6. I do doubt the capacity of Willow Bayou (which I estimated to be 50 miles long and very tortuous) for a military channel, capable of supporting an army large enough to operate against Jackson, Miss., or Big Black River Bridge; and such a channel will be very valuable to a force coming from the west, which we must expect. Yet this canal will be most useful as the way to convey coal and supplies to a fleet that should navigate the reach between Vicksburg and Red River. 7. The chief reason for operating solely by water was the season of the year and high water in Tallahatchee and Yala-busha. The spring is now here, and soon these streams will be no serious obstacle, save the ambuscades of the forest, and whatever works the enemy may have erected at or near Grenada. North Mississippi is too valuable to allow them to hold and make crops. I make these suggestions with the request that General Grant simply read them, and simply give them, as I know he will, a share of his thoughts. I would prefer he should not answer them, but merely give them as much or as little weight as they deserve. Whatever plan of action he may adopt will receive from me the same zealous co-operation and energetic support as though conceived by myself. I do not believe General Banks will make any serious attack on Port Hudson this spring." *O.R.*, I, xxiv, part 3, 179–80. For an explanation of the purpose of the letter, see *Memoirs of Gen. W. T. Sherman* . . . (4th ed., New York, 1891), I, 342–45. According to Adam Badeau, *Military History of U. S. Grant* (New York, 1868), I, 184–85, Rawlins handed this letter to USG, who read it without comment and never responded to Sherman. The two gens. had, however, already discussed the matter. *Ibid.*, pp. 183–84.

5. See letter to Maj. Gen. Stephen A. Hurlbut, March 29, 1863.

To Act. Rear Admiral David D. Porter

Head Quarters, Dept. of the Ten.
Before Vicksburg, Apl. 4th 1863.

ADMIRAL D. D. PORTER,
COMD.G MISS. SQUADRON.

ADMIRAL,

In view of information just received by way of Corinth of the movements of the enemy in North Mississippi and Middle Tennessee I would respectfully suggest the propriety of sending the Marine Brigade up the Tennessee river to defend that line.

The enemy are Massing large forces of Cavalry in front of Rosecrans and collecting all Partizan Rangers and loose companies of Cavalry on the line of the Tallahatchie. The road from Duck river   The road from Duck river to Savanna Ten. is being put in good order. Everything portends an attack upon Rosecrans with a powerful Cavalry force to follow up any success and a raid from North Miss. and Middle Ten. at the same time upon my forces and lines of communication in West Ten.

If this Brigade is sent I would suggest that Gen. Ellet be instructed to keep his fleet well together: destroy all rafts, flats, skiffs and everything that can facilitate the crossing of the river. If on arrival at the Mouth of Duck river it should be found safe to land with his small force he might to advantage proceed up that stream for some distance and destroy the ferries &c. that he would probably find.

I will instruct Gen. Dodge, Comd.g at Corinth, to have a watch at Hamburg Landing for the arrival of Gen. Ellet and from that time the two could co-operate to better advantage than either could act upon instructions given from here.

Very respectfully
U. S. Grant
Maj. Gen.

ALS, DNA, RG 45, Correspondence of David D. Porter. *O.R.* (Navy), I, xxiv, 76. For the resulting orders, see *ibid.*, pp. 76–77.

To *Act. Rear Admiral David D. Porter*

Head Quarters, Dept. of the Ten.
Before Vicksburg, Apl. 4th 1863.

Admiral D. D. Porter,
Comd.g Miss. Squadron,
Admiral,

I see by the Vicksburg papers an Advertisement calling upon planters to bring in all their small boats to be sold to the Govt. May this not be intended to make a raid upon our transports and burn at least a part of them? I suggest this as the guard boat has been withdrawn from below the fleet of transport.

> I am Admiral, very respectfully
> your obt. svt.
> U. S. GRANT
> Maj. Gen.

ALS, MoSHi. On April 4, 1863, Act. Rear Admiral David D. Porter wrote to USG. "I have received your note, A raid on the steamers with skiffs would be an impossibility—I think the object of Advertising for skiffs is to have them ready to catch our coal & provision barges as they go by, Vicksbug.—Also to have skiffs by which they can make little raids opposite Vicsburgs on our pickets. I will however have a guard-boat sent down at the usual place." LS, DNA, RG 393, Dept. of the Tenn., Letters Received.

To Maj. Gen. Stephen A. Hurlbut

> Headquarters Dep't. of the Tenn.
> Before Vicksburg, April 4, 1863.

MAJ.-GEN. S. A. HURLBUT, COMDG. 16TH ARMY CORPS.
GEN.—

I have ordered a regiment of cavalry from Helena to you and sent the steamer Illinois to take them.

At my request Admiral Porter has ordered the Marine Brigade up the Tenn. river to co-operate with Dodge. This brigade has boats, bullet-proof, and has an armament of Howitzers. When these troops pass Memphis you will be able to judge of about the time they will reach Hamburg Landing and can instruct Dodge to communicate with them there.[1]

> Very respectfully,
> U. S. GRANT, Maj.-Gen.

[Walter Romeyn Benjamin], "Before Vicksburg," *The Collector*, II, 17 (Jan., 1889), 73. Copies, DLC-USG, V, 19 (2), 30; DNA, RG 393, Dept. of the Tenn., Letters Sent. *O.R.*, I, xxiv, part 3, 172.

On March 30, 1863, Maj. Gen. Stephen A. Hurlbut wrote to USG. "I inclose last Telegram from Dodge. It is important that he should have another Regiment of Cavalry so as to relieve Cornyn. The other Cavalry with him is broken down in Horses—and I am yet unable with all my efforts to get a remount from St Louis. If there is any spare Cavalry below I wish to reinforce Dodge at Corinth & Kimball at Jackson so as to meet any movement across the Tennessee. With the amount of Cavalry now gathering on my front & left, it is important to meet them with their own arm and thus cover the R. Road by Cavalry Excursions"   ALS, DNA, RG 94, War Records Office, Dept. of the Tenn. *O.R.*, I, xxiv, part 3, 154–55; (incomplete) *O.R.* (Navy), I, xix, 685. Hurlbut enclosed a copy of a telegram of March 29 from Brig. Gen. Grenville M. Dodge, Corinth. "Midshipman Henry Travis of the Sloop of War Mississippi has arrived here on Parole.   he says that his ship run aground and that they fought her one hour afterwards then all hands made the shore   after firing the ship she floated down below and blowed up   they took with him forty six men and the captain of marines   the ship was not struck until after she got ashore   says the current turned their ship that the batteries did not do them any harm and that they could not depress their guns enough to do them much damage   the rest of officers and men are in Jackson   A Scout just in from Grenada road says only few militia at Grenada, but considerable force in Yazoo   that he heard cannonading up to Sunday night, and three (3) guns Monday   reports an increase of force on our front mostly mounted only few Infantry and says that determined efforts are to be made to break up our communication there is no doubt but what the increase of Cavalry is to break up our Rail Road, and the Infantry are to relieve from Rail Road guard duty. No troops have been moved out of Vicksburg up to Wednesday night except one Brigade that went towards Yazoo City   A great portion of the Army is now East of Big Black" Copy, DNA, RG 94, War Records Office, Dept. of the Tenn. *O.R.*, I, xxiv, part 3, 155; (incomplete) *O.R.* (Navy), I, xix, 685.

On March 30, Hurlbut wrote to Lt. Col. John A. Rawlins. "Yesterday a disgraceful incident occurred   The passenger train was seized about two miles this side of Moscow by *twelve* Guerrillas altho it had on board twenty five soldiers armed & three or five officers who yet made no attempt to defend themselves & the public property. The Engineer started his engine when he discovered the Guerillas with such suddeness as to break the coupling ran up to Moscow took down 100 Soldiers and saved the train. Passengers were robbed & the officers & soldiers carried off North. If they are returned under parole I do not intend to receive them. Pursuant to directions received in Jany from Genl Grant I am now preparing a list of ten families of seccessionist to be sent outside the lines selecting the most wealthy & prominent in position. A scout whome I sent out a few days since to Panola has just come in. Brig Genl Chalmers the two teirs of Northern counties in Miss. He has at Panola a Battery of six Guns, another at or below the Tallehatchie R. R. Bridge (M. C. R. R.) *no* Infantry. He is gathering in and organizing the irregulars—Faulkners Cavy has come up there from Oxford about 500 strong   He may be able to concentrate 1200 or 1500, every person is being conscripted, they have ammunition but few arms except pistols. It is unquestionably their intention to make a dash on some point of the R Road near Moscow or Lafayette as soon as organized say in a week or more—Their movements however depend on the success or failur[e] of the Yazoo Pass expedition of which I regret that I recieve no information. I do not know if will be possible to throw a force into his rear & cut off his battery from Helena   It is to long a move from here   they would be off before I had gone 15 miles. From Corinth I am informed that Brig Genl Wood with about 4000 men and two batteries is at Tuscumbia advance pickets on Bear creek. I think it a corps of observation only. The enemy appeared yesterday at Savannah seized all carpenters & carpenters tools & threw a few shells across the River at our Cavy scouts, rumors are that they propose to cross. I think this doubtful but they are closely watched. Genl Dodge deserves great credit for his vigilence and activity. I shall sent a Regt of Cavy to stay with Richardsons men who are banding again. I have their Muster Rolls. The city is quiet." Copy, DNA, RG 393, 16th Army Corps, Letters Sent. *O.R.*, I, xxiv, part 1, 485.

On April 1, Hurlbut wrote to Rawlins. "I desire through you to call the General's attention to the fact that all our transportation boats for forage & supplies have been sent down the River under orders. There are but two St Louis Boats remaining here. I cannot get horses to remount my Cavalry because of want of transportation as Col. Allen informs me—I cannot get forage for the horses I have for the same reasons & shall soon be out of rations. Less than Eight first class Boats will not be enough to supply this Depot, running regularly between here and St Louis. Three of our large Boats have been sent up the Cumberland, and there are none in the Upper Rivers. I think you must have more boats than you need below and it will soon be a very serious matter here, and if here, then to the whole army below. I urgently request immediate consideration to be given to this matter . . . P. S. I inclose extract of communication from Mr Wallace just in from Noxubee Co. Miss. . . . They (the rebels) are still massing their forces upon Rosecrans, determined to overwhelm him. Their Cavalry force is very large, fully twenty thousand and they are making every effort to swell it too twenty five thousand and to crush him by relentless pursuit if the advantage is with them. They are drawing forces to reinforce Johnson from Richmond, Charleston Savannah, Mobile, Vicksburg, although few have gone from Vicksburg. The force within supporting distance of Vicksburg, he estimates at from fifty to seventy five thousand men." ALS, DNA, RG 393, Dept. of the Tenn., Letters Received. *O.R.*, I, xxiv, part 3, 165–66. Also on April 1, Hurlbut wrote to Rawlins. "I send the above just received. Such preparations are to recross the Tennessee. I have sent this to day to Cairo to be telegraphed to Rosecrans. I respectfully and earnestly ask another Cavalry Regiment for Dodge at Corinth" Hurlbut copied a telegram of April 1 from Dodge. "The Enemy are repairing all the Bridges from Savannah East and from Florence North. They are also building a large number of Boats in several of the Creeks—They also guard the River from Florence to Duck River, and now have heavy bodies of Cavalry massed near Mount Pleasant. Three Gunboats have just gone up the River" ALS, DNA, RG 94, War Records Office, Dept. of the Mo. *O.R.*, I, xxiv, part 3, 166. See letter to Maj. Gen. Stephen A. Hurlbut, April 3, 1863.

1. On April 9, Hurlbut wrote to Rawlins. "I inclose copy of dispatch from Genl Rosecrans. I have answered that Dodge will be ready to cooperate with him with 3500 good troops. Brig Genl Ellet ran by this place yesterday without reporting—I do not know for what point. I have advised that he be sent to the Cumberland or Tennessee to aid in this movement. If it is possible for a force from Helena or Greenville to get in below Panola it would be advisable so to do. There is a rumor of the fall of Charleston not credited." ALS, DNA, RG 94, War Records Office, Dept. of the Mo. *O.R.*, I, xxiii, part 2, 224. For the telegram from Maj. Gen. William S. Rosecrans, see *ibid.*, p. 215.

To Maj. Gen. John A. McClernand

Head Quarters Dept. of the Ten.
Before Vicksburg, Apl. 4th 1863.

MAJ. GEN. J. A. McCLERNAND,
COMD.G 13TH ARMY CORPS,
GEN.

Your note of this evening is just received and read. As I shall move up to Millikins Bend to-morrow to remain it will not be necessary for me to enter into any particular directions. I will state however that it is no part of my present intentions to bring back the troops you have sent to Carthage ever by the route they went over. You can prepare therefore for supplying them where they are and also for sending the remainder of the Division so soon as you can see the way clear for supplying them. The canal from here into Walnut Bayou can be completed in a few days for the passage of small boats and in two weeks for tugs and barges. On the subject of sending boats below I will tell you my preparations to-morrow.

I am glad to hear of your success in reaching New Carthage and in finding such good roads.

You can be the judge of the necessity of sending Osterhaus'[1] other Brigade to him, but if they can be supplied it probably would be better to send it.

Very respectfully
U. S. GRANT
Maj. Gen. Com

ALS, McClernand Papers, IHi. On April 4, 1863, Maj. Gen. John A. McClernand, Milliken's Bend, wrote to USG. "I have occupied Richmond, approached within two miles of New Carthage, and pursued the enemy down Bayou Videl until he crossed it, seven miles below and I was arrested by the enemy's taking with him, or destroying, the means of crossing after him. He is understood to have sought refuge on St. Joseph Lake. The enemy referred to is a portion of Harrison's Cavalry troop, which, in all, is represented to consist of about seven Companies. Meantime I have built an excellent floating bridge, two hundred feet long across Roundaway bayou at Richmond. Yesterday evening, after some search, I found an old skiff, and made a reconnoissance from Smith's Plantation toward Carthage. A levee had extended along Bayou Videl from its junction with Roundaway—two miles—to Carthage. This levee is broken in three places. I crossed all the crevasses except the last, which brought me within a few hundred yards of Carthage, and in full view of that place and the Mississippi River. When I had approached so near the town, the enemy's picket fired upon me, and came very near hitting me. One of the balls whistled between the members of my little party, which consisted of Gen'l Osterhaus, Lieut. Col. Warmoth, and three or four Infantry men. The last crevasse intervened between us and the enemy's picket. Besides my forces here, I have two Regiments at Richmond, one at Home's plantation, about half way between Richmond and Smith's plantation; (in rear of Carthage,) and two regiments of Infantry, and some ten small companies of Cavalry, with four mountain howitzers at Smith's plantation   This is the present disposition of my forces covering a distance of some thirty miles. All this has been accomplished within three days. The communication by land from here to Smith's (two miles from Carthage) is good. To day I started small boats down Roundaway from ~~Carthage~~ Richmond to Smith's to ascertain the navigable capacities of the stream, but have not heard the result. Any number of troops could comfortably encamp within two miles of Carthage. *To overcome these two miles is the point.* If a steamer could pass through the mouth of Bayou Videl, or the mouth of Harper's bayou just above Carthage, or through the bayou still above from Duckport, to Smiths, and transport troops to Carthage, that would be one way. If piles could be driven, and a way ~~could~~ be made over the crevasses in the levee that would be another way. I have sent an engineer, today, to examine with reference to the latter, and write this communication, *specially*, to request you, if, upon this statement of the case you think proper, to send a small steamer either by the river, the canal, or the Duckport bayou to test the former. If you determine to send a boat, please, signal me to that effect. She should be accompanied by an armed vessel under instructions to shell Carthage; and the fire of the vessel should be obliquely up or down the river, so as to avoid the camp of my troops in the rear. Gen'l Osterhaus will recognize the whistle of the vessel to be sent, by replying with three shots from a mountain howitzer—two minutes interveening between the first two shots, and three minutes between the second and third shots. It is represented that there is but little more dry land than the levee affords, at Carthage and above and below for some miles; nevertheless, as I have already said, there is fine camping ground for an army back of Carthage, where it could wait for transportation to the river and across the river. My forces now near Carthage are drawing supplies from the adjacent country. If it is intended that they shall remain there for some days, or a longer time, please advise me, at once, so that I may order forward supplies. It is but just that I should bear ~~my~~ testimony to the activity and zeal displayed by General Osterhaus, Col. Bennett, and Capt. Pattersen of the Pioneers, and all the officers and men who have participated in the achievement of the results mentioned, and to the success that has attended their efforts. Col. Mather of my Staff will bear this to you, and give you any further explanations that you may need." LS, DNA, RG 393, Dept. of the Tenn., Letters Received. Incomplete in *O.R.*, I, xxiv, part 3, 170–71.

On April 5, McClernand wrote to USG. "I have this moment received a report from Genl. Osterhaus of this date. The party I sent down bayou Videl yesterday morning to get a ferryboat that had been hidden by the enemy on the opposite side of the bayou became a subject of sharp contest between a detachment of ~~the 2nd~~ our cavalry and a party of about one hundred rebel cavalry. Our cavalry drove the enemy away, got the boat and brought it up to Smith's plantation. Genl. Osterhaus further reports that a small reconnoitering party sent out in a skiff towards Carthage yesterday morning was fired upon by the enemy's picket, at Carthage, as they had fired upon my party the evening previous. He intended to send a stronger party over in the evening of the same day on the ferryboat referred to." ALS, DNA, RG 94, War Records Office, Dept. of the Tenn. *O.R.*, I, xxiv, part 3, 173. On April 7, McClernand wrote to USG. "I have the honor to enclose to you copies of reports received from Brig Gen Osterhaus and also of Capt Patterson in relation to the Capture of Carthage on the Miss" LS, DNA, RG 393, Dept. of the Tenn., Letters Received. The report of Brig. Gen. Peter J. Osterhaus, April 6, to McClernand is in *O.R.*, I, xxiv, part 1, 489–90. The report of Capt. William F. Patterson, Ky. Engineers and Mechanics, April 6, is *ibid.*, I, xxiv, part 3, 174.

On April 1, Lt. Col. John A. Rawlins had written to McClernand. "You will please detail at once two thousand (2.000) men of your command, with Shovels and Spades, to report to Capt. F. E. Prime, Chief Engineer for fatigue duty at 'Duck Point,' tomorrow, the 2nd inst. The detail will be in readiness at 7½ O'clock A. M. at Milliken's Bend, where Steamboats, will be in waiting to transport them to 'Duck Point,' and will be relieved each day at 6 O'clock P. M. and returned by Steamers to Milliken's Bend. This detail will continue daily until further orders." LS, McClernand Papers, IHi. On the same day, McClernand wrote to USG. "I have just returned from Richmond, and find your order instructing me to furnish a daily detail of two thousand men. Of course the detail will be furnished, but I think it probable, that you would not have ordered it with a fuller knowledge of my operations. I am forwarding the regiments of the 9th Division to Richmond, as fast as they can be crossed over Roundaway Bayou in small craft. By to morrow evening, I expect to have a floating bridge completed which will hasten the passage of the troops to that place; and hope by nightfall of the same day, to have pushed forward two regiments of infantry, and a strong detachment of cavalry, four miles on the road towards New Carthage, and next day, unless the road be found impracticable to Bayou Videl, within a mile or two of Carthage. A cavalry recconnoisance made to day, by a small cavalry party, that swam their horses over the bayou at Richmond, found the road practicable, about half the distance, from that place to Carthage. The same party captured the enemy's mail, and its carrier, going from Vicksburg, and discovered a detachment of eighty, or a hundred, of the enemy. The prospect is quite encouraging so far, perhaps more so, than that afforded by the Ducksport enterprise; and I hope you will find it consistent with your general views, to leave me to prosecute my present undertaking; with all the resources at my disposal. I am now repairing the roads, and bridges, between here and Richmond, a distance of twelve miles,—including a floating bridge, of two hundred feet in length, and will soon commence, repairing the road, from that place to Carthage and constructing barges, to ply between the same places, unless stopped by unknown obstacles. I would be pleased to accompany you, from this camp, to Richmond, that you might judge for yourself." ALS, DNA, RG 94, War Records Office, Dept. of the Tenn. *O.R.*, I, xxiv, part 3, 164.

Also on April 1, McClernand wrote to USG. "There are some 500 fugitive negroes upon my picket line. Many of them are now entirely destitute, and all must become so unless they are cared for. As you will perceive from the accompanying petition, they are regarded as an eliment of danger to the few whites still remaining in the vicinity. There are only four alternatives. 1.st to leave them as they are. 2.d to require them to work for such landed proprietors as may choose to hire them, upon such just terms of compensation and treatment as may be prescribed by the Military authorities. 3.d to deport or colonize them. 4.th to employ them under the direction of the Q. M. in providing for their own subsistance and in picking and ginning abandoned or forfeited cotton for the benefit of the U. S. upon the terms mentioned in the Q. M. report herewith inclosed or upon other terms to be prescribed by the Dept. or Corps. Commander As the case is one of urgent humanity—and also affects the discipline and police of my camp it needs to be acted upon without delay. My choice would be to colonize them, but as this disposition would involve protracted discussion and the necessity for legislation, and much delay, and as the system of granting permits to individuals to pick and gin cotton with hired negro labor has led to the most atrocious frauds and outrages upon the local inhabitants, the negroes, and the Gov't. I am left to prefer the latter alternative; that is, to employ the negroes refered to and those in like circumstances as mentioned, under the direction of the Q. M. In that event authority would have to be assumed to purchase necessary bagging and rope for bailing, at the expense of the U. S. or to apply a part of the proceeds of the cotton to indemnify the purchase of those articles, which would be virtually the same thing." Copies, McClernand Papers, IHi; DNA, RG 393, 13th Army Corps, Letters Sent.

On April 2, McClernand wrote to USG. "Among the letters found with the mail carrier, yesterday, is one signed by Sergeant A. Myott, and dated on the 27th Ulto at Vicksburg, in which the writer says that all the force lately at Vicksburg, except his own regiment, has gone up to Yazoo to meet the Yankees. This I think is proximately but not literally true. Since then doubtlessly several Regiments, have returned to Vicksburgh In the Vicksburg Whig of the 31st Ulto,' an order of the same date is noticed requiring all persons to bring all skiffs and other craft, to Vicksburg and deliver them to the military Authorities and obtain payment for the same. I mention this fact because it may import something desirable to be known." LS, *ibid.*, RG 94, War Records Office, Dept. of the Tenn. *O.R.*, I, xxiv, part 3, 169.

1. Peter J. Osterhaus, born in Prussia in 1823, came to the U.S. as a refugee revolutionist in 1849, settling eventually in St. Louis, where he was a bookkeeper for a hardware co. Joining the Mo. Vols. as a private at the outbreak of the Civil War, he was soon commissioned maj. (April 27, 1861), col., 12th Mo. (Dec. 19), then confirmed as brig. gen. on June 9, 1862.

To Maj. Gen. William T. Sherman

Head Quarters, Dept. of the Ten.
Before Vicksburg, Apl. 4th 1863,

Maj. Gen. Sherman,

Dear Sir;

You may send the boy captured on Deer Creek back to Vicksburg, and also the Confederate money.

I have no objections to a free exchange of prisoners, at this place, but unless required to do so I will not receive "paroled prisoners" to be exchanged hereafter unless the officers are allowed to accompany them.

You may if you please inform Maj. Watts of this.

Very truly yours
U. S. Grant
Maj. Gen

ALS, DLC-William T. Sherman. On April 4, 1863, Maj. Gen. William T. Sherman wrote to USG. "I enclose you a letter sent me by Maj Watts, agent for the exchange of Prisoners in Vicksburg, asking that we return a prisoner captured on Deer Creek. This prisoner is a large boy, dressed in a kind of uniform found with a Rifle which he attempted to conceal, and was confused in his statements at one time admitting himself to be a soldier and again denying it. With your consent I will send the boy home, as from the scare of his mother I think he will give us no further trouble. The package of money I showd you a few days ago was all Confederate money, that is no money at all. Also with your consent I would Lend it, as the Lendee is one of the most enthusiastic Kentuckyans I know." ALS, DNA, RG 94, War Records Office, Dept. of the Tenn. *O.R.*, II, v, 431–32. Sherman enclosed a letter of April 4 to him from Maj. N. G. Watts, Vicksburg, agent for prisoner exchange. "A Youth named D. Clark, was taken prisoner on Deer Creek, about the 22d Ulto :—and I am informed is now in charge of Colo Smith 8th Mo : Regt. I am also informed you are willing to Exchange him for Sergeant Stevens orderly to Colo: Smith Comg Brigade—Sergeant Stevens was sent by me to New Orleans on the 1st Day of this month, to be delivered over to the Federal Authorities as a prisoner of war—I have been compelled to adopt this way of delivering Federal prisoners, on account of Genl Grant's refusal to receive them —I hope General you will return the boy to me, that I may return him to his distressed Parents—" ALS, DNA, RG 94, War Records Office, Dept. of the Tenn. *O.R.*, II, v, 432. On the same day, Sherman endorsed this letter. "Respectfully referred to Genl Grant with letter of this date. I would recommend that this agent be notified we will exchange prisoners under the Cartel strictly officers bing included. It must be inconvenient to our prisoners to go to New Orleans, whence they could only reach us by a sea voyage." AES, DNA, RG 94, War Records Office, Dept. of the Tenn. *O.R.*, II, v, 432. On April 8, Sherman wrote to Lt. Col. John A. Rawlins discussing a lengthy interview with Watts. ALS, *ibid*. *O.R.*, II, v, 448–49.

To Col. Robert Allen

April 4th 1863.

Col. R. Allen,
Chief Q M. St. Louis Mo.
Col.

Gen. Sullivan[1] is going to Cairo Ill. on duty and I have concluded to send him on to St. Louis to see you in person on the subject of which I have written twice; that is for a supply of tugs and barges   Gen. Sullivan will explain the use to which they are to be put and the probabilities of success. I have been twice telegraphed by Gen. Halleck to send back boats. It must be that a great many boats are now in the Cumberland river. I have quite a number in the Yazoo. When they return I will be able to send back more. At present I could not move more than two Divisions of my forces at one time. I have instructed Col. Reynolds to turn back those brought from the Ohio and to see that sufficient are kept to do the Army business between St. Louis and Memphis.

At the time I telegraphed Col. Parsons for small boats I was expecting to make the move by Yazoo pass the main move on Vicksburg. They were so long coming however that this could not be done and may not have sucseeded had they been here in time.

Very respectfully
U. S. Grant
Maj. Gen.

ALS, Parsons Papers, IHi.

1. On March 20, 1863, Lt. Col. John A. Rawlins issued Special Orders No. 79, Dept. of the Tenn. "Brig. General J. C. Sullivan, is hereby relieved from duty

with the 16th Army Corps and will report in person and without delay to these Head Quarters for orders   Brig. Genl. Nathan Kimball will proceed immediately and without delay to Memphis, Tenn., and there report to Major General S. A. Hurlbut, Commanding 16th Army Corps, for assignment to duty." Copies, DLC-USG, V, 26, 27; DNA, RG 393, Dept. of the Tenn., Special Orders. On April 1, Rawlins issued Special Orders No. 91. "So much of Special Orders No. 79 of date March 20th 1863 from these Headquarters as relieve Brig Genl J. C. Sullivan from duty with the 16th Army Corps and directs him to report at these Headquarters is revoked, he will remain on duty with the 15th Army Corps" Copies, *ibid*. Also on April 1, Rawlins issued General Orders No. 23. "Colonel George P. Ihrie, U. S. A., Additional Aid de Camp, having been appointed Commissary of Musters for the Department, is relieved from duty as Acting Inspector General. Brig. Gen. J. C. Sullivan, U. S. Vol's, is hereby appointed Acting Inspector General of the Department, and will be obeyed and respected accordingly." Copies, DLC-USG, V, 13, 14, 95; (2) DNA, RG 393, Dept. of the Tenn., General and Special Orders. *O.R.*, I, xxiv, part 3, 165. Col. George P. Ihrie had been appointed commissary of musters in General Orders No. 19, March 23. Copies, DLC-USG, V, 13, 14, 95; (2) DNA, RG 393, Dept. of the Tenn., General and Special Orders. *O.R.*, I, xxiv, part 3, 135-36. On April 1, Rawlins wrote to Hurlbut. "There have been so many General officers ordered here that they cannot all be provided with commands. You will therefore place Brig. Gen. J. C. Sullivan on duty in your Army Corps." Copies, DLC-USG, V, 19, 30; DNA, RG 393, Dept. of the Tenn., Letters Sent. On April 2, USG wrote to Hurlbut. "I understand from Gen. Sullivan that many recruits can be got from loyal Tennesseeans, if notice was given that they would be received. You are authorized to give such notice, and to receive all who will enlist in the regiments now in the field." Copies, *ibid*.

To Maj. Gen. Stephen A. Hurlbut

Head Quarters, Dept. of the Ten.
Before Vicksburg, Apl. 5th 1863.

MAJ. GEN. S. A. HURLBUT,
COMD.G 16TH ARMY CORPS,
GEN.

I send three Steamers to be returned loaded with land transportation left at Memphis by the troops now in the field. I wish them to be sent down with as little delay as possible with from one hundred to one hundred & fifty wagons and harness complete, and so many of the mules as it may be convenient to load on the steamers.

Mules for all the wagons sent is not desirable as there is now a surplus on hands here and the country is full of them ready to go to work for the Union. About the only loyalty in this region is possessed by the mules and contrabands.

Very respectfully

U. S. GRANT

Maj. Gen. Com

ALS, DNA, RG 94, War Records Office, Military Div. of the Miss.

On April 5, 1863, Lt. Col. John A. Rawlins wrote to Lt. Col. Charles A. Reynolds. "The General commanding has directed Maj. Gen. McClernand to send and bring forward from Helena, Ark. here, all the wagons and mules that can be spared from that place, with harness complete, to each wagon, for six mules, and especially to bring the saddle and lead mules for each wagon, as the others can be supplied from the country. He has also written to Maj. Gen. Hurlbut in reference to sending wagons, mules and harness from Memphis to this place, a copy of which letter is herewith enclosed for your information. You will please see that the wagons, mules and harness mentioned in said letter, and to the full number mentioned therein, are sent here without delay. Collect all the barges that can be found at Memphis or Helena, no matter to whom they belong, and fit up and put them in condition for transporting horses, wagons ~~and~~ artillery and army stores and send them to this place as fast as possible. There must be no delay. Flat bottom barges with rakes at each end are preferable. At least forty such are required, but send any kind you can get suitable for the purposes indicated. You will also send forward at once, lumber and ~~the~~ materials for the repairing and putting in condition the barges now here. Leiut. Henry W. Janes, Act'g. Ass't. Quartermaster is hereby detailed to report to you for orders, to aid and facilitate the carrying out of the instructions herein contained, respecting the getting forward of the barges, and the material for repairing those here. Enclosed is a copy of a letter to Gen. Allen, St. Louis.   You will please telegraph to him, and hasten if possible the compliance with the requests it contains. Decked barges, used for coaling Steamers, and used for towing purposes by them, are peculiarly desirable. They can be procured along the river, at coal mines. If they have coal on them, buy the coal and send it with them. An Agent should be send to attend to this."

Copies, DLC-USG, V, 19, 30; DNA, RG 393, Dept. of the Tenn., Letters Sent.

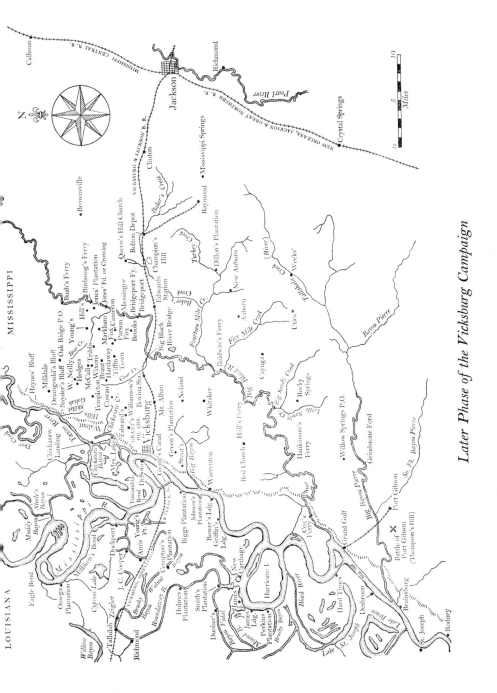

Later Phase of the Vicksburg Campaign

To Maj. Gen. John A. McClernand

Head Quarters, Dept. of the Ten.
Millikins Bend La. Apl. 6th/63

Maj. Gen. J. A. McClernand
Comd.g 13th Army Corps,
Gen.

To morrow I wish to inspect the two Divisions of your Corps now here, commencing with Gen. Carr's[1] at 10 a. m. & Gen. [*Andrew J.*] Smith's at 11 a. m.

I do not wish the troops to pass in review but merely to be drawn up in line so that I can ride by them and see the men.

Very respectfully
your obt. svt.
U. S. Grant
Maj. Gen. Com

ALS, McClernand Papers, IHi. On April 6, 1863, Maj. Gen. John A. McClernand wrote to USG. "I had arrangements already made for a review of one of my Divisions on the day after to-morrow; and if that will suit you as well, I will have the other ready for the same day. If you prefer however I will give orders for tomorrow as you request." LS, *ibid.* On the same day, Lt. Col. John A. Rawlins endorsed this letter. "Day after to-morrow will Suit as well" ES, *ibid.*

1. Eugene A. Carr of N. Y., USMA 1850, served mostly on the frontier and reached the rank of capt., 4th Cav., in the prewar army. Appointed col., 3rd Ill. Cav., in Aug., 1861, he served in Mo. and was appointed brig. gen. as of March 7, 1862, in recognition of his service at Pea Ridge. See James T. King, *War Eagle: A Life of General Eugene A. Carr* (Lincoln, Neb., 1963). On March 14, 1863, Carr, "Near Ste. Genevieve Mo.," wrote to Rawlins. "By orders of which the enclosed is a copy, I am directed to proceed on the arrival of transports to join the forces under Maj. Genl U. S. Grant. This command consists of a little over five thousand men with one Battery of rifled six-pounders, and two companies of cavalry forming my escort and Provost Guards. Capt. C. H. Dyer A. A. Gen'l. who bears this communication will present you with the Return for the last ten days, and give what other information may be required. This command is part of the force which has during the past winter been operating under Brig. Gen'l. Davidson in S. E. Missouri   It comprises the whole of his 1st Division under Brig. Genl. Wm. P. Benton, five Regt's. and one Battery, and half his 2d Division three Iowa Regiments under Col W. M. Stone 22d Iowa   The whole will form what I suppose would be a small Division in your army, but I do not like to reorganize, because I would in forming two Brigades be obliged to reduce Gen'l.

Benton's command, and I prefer to wait till I am permanently assigned in your army.—In the meantime Genl Benton's Division is thoroughly organized for any immedeate Service as is also the part of the Division under Col. Stone which really consists of his original Brigade. Gen'l. Benton's date is April 28th/62, mine is March 7th/62 The troops are in fine health and spirits, and pleased with the prospect of serving under Genl. Grant. Welfley's Battery 1st Mo. Art. belongs to this command, but has been detached to Cape Girardeau. Gen Davidson promised that it should be returned to me, but I think it doubtful whether I get it. I hope the General will send orders where to report by the return of Capt. Dyer" LS, DNA, RG 94, War Records Office, Dept. of the Tenn. On March 16, Carr, Cairo, telegraphed to USG. "I am under orders to join you with 5,000 troops of the Army of Southeast Missouri. If you have any orders in particular, please forward them to Memphis." *O.R.*, I, xxiv, part 3, 117. On March 20, Rawlins issued Special Orders No. 79 assigning Carr and his brigade to McClernand. DS, McClernand Papers, IHi; copies, DLC-USG, V, 26, 27; DNA, RG 393, Dept. of the Tenn., Special Orders. *O.R.*, I, xxiv, part 3, 122–23. On March 25, Maj. Gen. James B. McPherson wrote to Rawlins. "Brig Gen'l Bentons command (a part of Gen'l Carr's) consisting of four Regiments and a Battery, has just arrived here, under orders from Genl Prentiss at Helena to report at Lake Providence. Thinking there is some mistake, as I understood General Grant to say that Genl Carr would be assigned to Genl McClernand I have directed Gen'l Benton to disembark his men and horses as they have been on Boats over a week, leaving his Artillery Stores &c on board until I can hear from you." Copies, DNA, RG 393, 13th and 17th Army Corps, Letters Sent; *ibid.*, 17th Army Corps, Letters Sent. *O.R.*, I, xxiv, part 3, 145. On March 28, McClernand, Milliken's Bend, wrote to USG. "Genl. Carr, together with the following forces, except one regiment and part of another which are on the way, has arrived at this Camp. He will have eight regiments in all, one Battery and two Companies of Cavalry. These forces composed the 1st Division of the Army of South East Missouri and part of the 2d. I will organize the eight regiments into two Brigades, constituting one Division under command of Genl. Carr, unless you direct otherwise. Please advise me of the No. to be assigned to the Division." LS, McClernand Papers, IHi. On the same day, Rawlins endorsed this letter. "Maj Gen. McClernand will organize these forces as within proposed. The Division will constitute the 14th Inft. Division of the Army of the Tennessee. A copy of the organization will be forwarded to these Headquarters." ES, *ibid.*

To Julia Dent Grant

April 6th 1863.

DEAR JULIA,

Ten days will probably take me away from here and I hope then soon to have the river open. You may come down on the

Tigress if you wish and pay me a visit to return on the same boat. She will probably stay two days.

I am sorely afflicted at this time scarsely being able to sit, lay, or stand. Biles are the matter. If I have another one come I must try Dr. Kittoe's remedy.—Wont Mrs. Hillyer come down with you. I want you to bring the children along. It is very pleasant now and the trip down here and back will do you good. —I want besides very much to see you and the children.

Kisses for yourself and children. Weather is fine and roads good. Fred. enjoys himself hugely. His pony gets but little rest.

ULYS.

ALS, DLC-USG.

To Thomas W. Knox

———

Head Quarters, Department of the Tennessee,
Before Vicksburg, April 6th 1863.

THOMAS W. KNOX,
CORRESPONDENT NEW YORK HERALD.—
SIR.—

The letter of the President of the United States, authorizing you to return to these Head Quarters, and remain, with my consent, or leave if such consent is withheld,[1] has been shown me.

You came here first in positive violation of an order from General Sherman. Because you were not pleased with his treatment of Army followers, who had violated his order, you attempted to break down his influence with his command, and to blast his reputation with the public. You made insinuations against his sanity, and said many things which were untrue, and so far as your letter had influence, calculated to effect the public service unfavorably.

General Sherman is one of the ablest Soldiers and purest men in the country. You have attacked him, and been sentenced to expulsion from this Department for the offence. Whilst I would conform to the slightest wish of the President, where it was founded upon a fair representation of both sides of any question, my respect for General Sherman is such, that in this case I must decline unless General Sherman first gives his consent to your remaining.[2]

> I am, Sir,
> Yours &c.
> U. S. GRANT
> Maj. Gen.

Copies (certified by Lt. Col. John A. Rawlins), InFtwL; DLC-William T. Sherman; copies (uncertified), Sherman Papers, InND; DLC-USG, V, 19 (2), 30; DNA, RG 393, Dept. of the Tenn., Letters Sent. *O.R.*, I, xvii, part 2, 894. Thomas W. Knox, correspondent of the *New York Herald*, had written an account of the Chickasaw Bayou expedition which infuriated Maj. Gen. William T. Sherman. *Ibid.*, pp. 580–90. On Feb. 23, 1863, USG wrote to Brig. Gen. Lorenzo Thomas. "I have the honor to transmit herewith proceedings of Court Martial in the case of Thomas W. Knox, and copy of General Orders, No. 13. from these Head Quarters, publishing same." Copies, DLC-USG, V, 5, 8, 24, 94; DNA, RG 393, Dept. of the Tenn., Hd. Qrs. Correspondence. The proceedings of the court-martial (*ibid.*, RG 153, LL 554), in which Knox was charged with spying, giving intelligence to the enemy, and disobedience of orders, showed the prosecution somewhat embarrassed when Knox produced a pass from USG's hd. qrs. dated Dec. 16, 1862, prepared by Capt. Theodore S. Bowers, permitting Knox in the Dept. of the Tenn. The court gave a mixed verdict, finding Knox guilty only of disobedience of orders but sentencing him to expulsion from the dept., which was announced in General Orders No. 13, Dept. of the Tenn., Feb. 19. Copies, DLC-USG, V, 13, 14, 95; DNA, RG 393, Dept. of the Tenn., General and Special Orders. *O.R.*, I, xvii, part 2, 889–92. During the court-martial, numerous officers of Sherman's command signed a petition dated Feb. 10 addressed to USG praising Sherman's generalship. Copy, DLC-William T. Sherman. See John F. Marszalek, Jr., "The Knox Court-Martial: W. T. Sherman Puts the Press on Trial (1863)," *Military Law Review*, 59 (Winter, 1973), 197–214.

On Feb. 23, Sherman wrote to Rawlins. "General Orders no 13, from your Head Qrs of date Feb 19, 1863, involves certain principles that I think should be settled by the highest authority of our Government, and I beg most respectfully their reference through the Judge Advocate General to the Commander in Chief. The Findings on the 3rd charge, 1st specification are, 'the facts proven as stated but attach no criminality thereto,' viz that the accused knowingly and wilfully disobeyed the lawful command of the proper authority, by accompanying the Expedition down the Mississippi below Helena. The inference is that a commanding officer has no right to prohibit citizens from accompanying a Military Expedition; or if he do, such citizens incur no criminality by disregarding such command. The 'Findings' of the 1st specification 1st charge, Guilty except the words 'thereby conveying to the Enemy an approximate estimate of its strength in direct violation of the 57 Article of War,' involves the principle that publications of Army organisation and strength in a paper having the circulation South and North of the New York Herald, does not amount to an indirect conveyance of inteligence to an Enemy. I regard these two points as vital to our success as an Army, contending against an Enemy who has every advantage of us in position and means of inteligence. I do not expect any Court Martial, or any officer should do or attempt to do an unlawful act, but I do believe the Laws of Congress and of War clearly cover both these points, and believing that the true interests of the Government, and of our People demand a radical change in this respect, I avail myself of this means of to inviteing their earnest consideration of the issues involved. If a commanding officer cannot exclude from his camps the very class of men which an Enemy would select as spies and informers, and if to prove the conveyance of indirect information to the Enemy, it be necessary to follow that information from its source, to the very Armies arrayed against us, whose Country thus far our hundreds of thousands of men have been unable to invade, and yet whose newspapers are made up of extracts from these very Northern papers, then is it fruitless to attempt to conceal from them all the data they could ask for to make successful resistance to our plans, and to attack our detached parties and Lines of communication. To this cause may well be attributed the past reverses to our arms, and the exposition of almost any plan devised by our Generals. I believe this cause has cost us millions of money, thousands of lives and will continue to defeat us to the end of time, unless some remedy be devised." ALS, NHi. *O.R.*, I, xvii, part 2, 892–93. On Feb. 25, USG endorsed this letter. "Respectfully forwarded to Head Quarters of the Army, Washington D. C. for consideration of Judge Advocate" Copies, DLC-USG, V, 25; DNA, RG 393, Dept. of the Tenn., Endorsements.

1. Lincoln based his letter of March 20 on opinions of Brig. Gen. John M. Thayer, Maj. Gen. John A. McClernand, and other officers that Knox's offense "was technical, rather than wilfully wrong . . ." Lincoln, *Works*, VI, 142–43.

2. On April 6, Knox wrote to Sherman for his consent; on April 7, Sherman replied in a letter concluding: "My answer is—never—" Copies, InFtwL; Sherman Papers, InND; DNA, RG 94, War Records Office, Dept. of the Tenn. *O.R.*, I, xvii, part 2, 893–95. On April 8, Sherman wrote to USG. "I received last night the copy of your answer to Mr Knox's application to return and reside near your Head Quarters. I thank you for the manner and substance of that reply. Many regard Knox as unworthy the notice he has received. This is true but I send you his letter to me, and my answer. Observe in his letter to me sent long before I could have heard the result of his application to you, he makes the assertion that you had no objection but rather wanted him back and only as a matter of form required my assent—he regretted a difference of between a 'portion of the Army' and the Press. The insolence of these fellows is insupportable. I know they are encouraged: but I know human nature well enough & that they will be the first to turn against their patrons. Mr Lincoln of course fears to incur the enmity of the Herald, but he must rule the Herald, or the Herald will rule him, he can take his choice. I have been foolish & unskilful in drawing on me the Shafts of the Press—By opposing Mob Law in California I once before drew down the Press, —but after the smoke cleared off, and the People saw where they were drifting to, they admitted I was right. If the Press be allowed to run riot, and write up, and write down at their pleasure, there is an end to a Constitutional Governmt in America, and anarchy must result. Even now the real People of our Country

begin to fear & tremble at it, and look to our Armies as the anchor of safety, of order, submission to authority, bound together by a real Governmt and not by the clamor of a demoralized Press and crowd of demagogues." ALS, DNA, RG 94, War Records Office, Dept. of the Tenn. *O.R.*, I, xvii, part 2, 895. On April 12, USG wrote to Lincoln. "Enclosed please find copy of my letter, and also one from Gen. Sherman, to Thos. W. Knox, Correspondent of the New York Herald in reply to his application to be permitted to remain in this Dept. I send these knowing the propensity of persons to misrepresent grounds taken in matters when they are personally interested and fearing that, in this case, it might be represented that your wishes had not met with the respect due them. As stated in my letter the wish of the President will always have the force and respect of an order." ALS, InFtwL.

To James E. Yeatman

Apl. 7th 1863,

JAS. Y. YEATMAN
PRES. WESTERN SAN. COMMISSION.
SIR:

My special order No 98 of the 29th of March[1] assigning a steamer to the United States Sanitary Commission for the free transmission of sanitary stores from Cairo to the Army in the field under my command is not worded to give the meaning I intended, and as was expressly agreed between Mr. Olmsted[2] and myself. It was my intention that the Western Sanitary Commission should have exactly the same privileges as the United States Commission. The order will be changed to conform to this ruling.[3]

The object was to introduce to the Army all sanitary stores through some regular and organized channel and in such a way that the soldiers would get the full benefit of all contributions.

The great number of Sanitary Commissions that have been supplying troops here has led to great abuse and much trouble. Many persons desiring to visit the Army take advantage of this to get here, free, and are the most importunate persons for free passages to their homes, and for other favors. In some instances they bring a few articles to sell.

My attention was just to-day called to the particular wording of this order. I will repair it at once.

It is not necessary for me to assure you of my appreciacion of the good done both by the United States and the Western Sanitary Commissions and my desire to facilitate their opperations in every way consistent with the interests of service.

I am sir, your very obt. svt.

U. S. GRANT

Maj. Gen.

ALS, deCoppet Collection, NjP. James E. Yeatman, born in 1818 near Wartrace, Tenn., moved to St. Louis in 1842, where he eventually became a prominent businessman and president of the Merchants' National Bank. As president of the Western Sanitary Commission, Yeatman published a letter dated March 13, 1863, describing a recent visit to USG's army. *Missouri Democrat*, March 14, 1863.

On April 8, USG wrote three messages in behalf of Annie Wittenmyer, Iowa Sanitary Agent. "Col Abbott 30th Iowa Vols. is authorized to deliver to Mrs. Wittemeyer agt Volunteer Sanitary Commission twelve Bales of Cotton rescued by him from the river to be shipped north for the benefit of said Commission" "Mrs. Wittemeyer agt Volunteer sanitary commission is authorized to ship north twelve bales of Cotton rescued from the Miss River by the 30th Regt Iowa Vols below Vicksburg and use the same for the benefit of the soldiers of the army through the agency of said commission   A Treasury Permit will be required to ship north of Memphis." "The above permit extended to cover thirteen and one half bales of Cotton the amount actually rescued and saved by Col Abbott" Copies, DNA, RG 92, Letters Received by Capt. A. R. Eddy Relating to Cotton. In Annie Wittenmyer, *Under the Guns: A Woman's Reminiscences of the Civil War* (Boston, 1895), pp. 244–46, this transaction is inaccurately explained.

On April 10, Cordelia A. P. Harvey, Wis. Sanitary Agent, Memphis, wrote to USG. "After having consulted with the medical Authorties here, & from Washington, and knowing the feeling from personal observation of our sick, both in camp, & hospital, also the strong desire throughout our Western Army generally, that the same system of Furloughs be granted to the soldiers in your Deptment, that has been given, & acted upon with such signal success in the Army of the Potomac,—I presume to address you—trusting that you have not forgotten our recent introduction. That something of this kind will come from you sooner or later is the prevailing belief, but the speed with which it comes will materially affect its value. A good foundation for the *hope* of such a Furlough, would today improve the sanitary condition of your Army an hundred fold. I speak from the testimony of Army Surgeons. Dear Gen'l, you would by speedily issuing such an order save many valuable lives, & put new strength, & courage into many noble hearts. The Army of the West would bless you forever, & through them our *yet to be* glorious country. Trust to the honor of our people & believe me—they will return to you—fight under, with, & for you with more energy, & perseverance than ever before. Desiring *chiefly* that the Loyalty strength & efficiency of our Army be preserved." ALS, DNA, RG 393, Dept. of the Tenn., Letters Received.

1. Special Orders No. 88. Copies, DLC-USG, V, 26, 27; DNA, RG 393, Dept. of the Tenn., General and Special Orders; *ibid.*, Special Orders. *O.R.*, I, XXIV, part 3, 153–54.

2. Best known for his work as architect of Central Park, New York City, and his descriptions of the prewar South, Frederick Law Olmsted served as secretary of the U.S. Sanitary Commission. For Olmsted's meeting with USG in March, see Olmsted, "The Genesis of a Rumor," *The Nation*, VI, 147 (April 23, 1868), 328–29; Laura Wood Roper, *FLO: A Biography of Frederick Law Olmsted* (Baltimore and London, 1973), pp. 222–23. On April 21, Olmsted wrote to USG. "You may recollect that in an interview which I had with you, on the 26th ulto. you proposed to rescind previous orders authorizing free transportation of Sanitary stores, except as should be provided for by special order no 86. which was issued the next day. I asked you if this would not cause inconvenience to the Western Sanitary Commission adding that I should regret that my suggestions to you should lead to any such results. You answered that it would not affect them at all, as their means of transportation were independent. I expressed some surprise at this, but you reassured me. I am informed by Mr Yeatman that you were mistaken. The Western Sanitary Commission has no means of government transportation within your department, independently of your orders   Having acted under a misapprehension of the facts, I do not doubt that you will be disposed to meet the wishes of the Western Sanitary Commission to have their former priveleges restored." LS (press), DLC-Frederick Law Olmsted.

3. By Special Orders No. 101, April 11. Copy, DNA, RG 393, Dept. of the Tenn., General and Special Orders.

To Maj. Gen. Henry W. Halleck

———

Head Quarters Department of the Tennessee
Before Vicksburg, April 8th, 1863.

Major Gen. H W Halleck
Gen-in Chief
Washington D. C.,
Gen.

If it can be consistently done I would request that my Chief Quartermaster Lieut Col Reynolds be transferred to the same position on the staff of a Corps Commander, and some one better qualified for the very heavy business of the Department be given me. Col Reynolds is a very faithful officer, and I think can conduct the business of an Army Corps to the interests of the Public Service, but he is not quite up to his present duties

I will be satisfied to take any Quartermaster who you may think suitable, and available, but my choice would be between Lt Col. Ingalls,[1] Lt. Col. Bingham[2] and Capt Eddy, and in the order in which they are here named.

> I am, General, Very Respectfully
> Your Obdt Servant.
> U. S. GRANT
> Major General.

Copies, DLC-USG, V, 5, 8, 24, 94; DNA, RG 393, Dept. of the Tenn., Hd. Qrs. Correspondence. See letters to Maj. Gen. John A. McClernand, April 15, and to Lt. Col. Charles A. Reynolds, April 21, 1863.

1. Rufus Ingalls, USG's USMA classmate and associate at Fort Vancouver, continued as chief q. m., Army of the Potomac.
2. Judson D. Bingham of Ind., USMA 1854, 1st lt., 2nd Art. before the Civil War, then was appointed capt. and asst. q. m. He served as chief q. m., 17th Army Corps, with the *ex officio* rank of lt. col., before replacing Reynolds as chief q. m., Dept. of the Tenn.

To Maj. Gen. John A. McClernand

> Head Quarters, Dept. of the Ten.
> Millikin's Bend, Apl. 8th 1863,

MAJ. GEN. J. A. McCLERNAND,
COMD.G 13TH ARMY CORPS,
GEN.

The exploring party on Walnut Bayou found a Mill in good runing order on the banks of the bayou about four miles from Cooper's Plantation towards Richmond. There was about 2000 bushels of corn at the mill and enough more in the neighborhood to make it up to about 5000 bushels. The Mill was immediately set to work grinding the corn. Your troops at Richmond, and the contrabands with your command, can be at least partially supplied from there by sending either teams or boats after the Meal.

There are also a large number of Mules in the neighborhood which it would probably be well to save. Will you please direct your Quartermaster to look after them?

Very respectfully
U. S. Grant
Maj Genl

ALS, McClernand Papers, IHi.

To Brig. Gen. Napoleon B. Buford

Milliken's Bend, La. April 8th 1863.

Brig. Gen. W. B. Buford
Com'd'g. at Cairo, Ills.

Enclosed I send you extract of a telegraphic dispatch sent from Cairo to the Associated Press   This dispatch furnishes the enemy important news, and probably in time to defeat the consummation of our plans. A casemate battery is being erected in the position described. The work has been carried on at night, thus far without the enemy discovering it. It will yet take about four nights to complete these batteries, when the enemy is put in possession of a knowledge of its existence and position by this correspondent.

You will please cause the arrest of this man, and send him to the Provost Marshal at in Memphis, under guard, with instructions to keep him a close prisoner until I can prefer charges against him, and have him tried or otherwise disposed of.

U. S. Grant.
Maj. Gen'l.

Copies, DLC-USG, V, 19 (2), 30; DNA, RG 393, Dept. of the Tenn., Letters Sent. On April 17, 1863, Brig. Gen. Napoleon B. Buford wrote to USG. "Your letter of the 8th inst, was received yesterday directing me to arrest the correspondent of the Associated Press, who was the author of the enclosed Telegram, and send him to the Provost Marshall Gen at Memphis. I immediately ascertained the author to be L. W. Myers & have this day placed him in charge of Dr. J. H Murphy, Surgeon of the 4th Min: who is here with a guard going south, who will deliver him with your original letter and my letter to the Provost Marshall Gen: at Memphis. On examination I learn Mr Myers obtained his information from a Major who was passenger on the Boat which arrived arrived on the 3rd inst from below. His impression was that the Battery had been completed and opened fire at that date. He states the Major was communicative and uttered his news publicly. Mr Myers was innocent of of the intention to do the service injury, but is now convinced of his great imprudence. On that day I was sick, but had given orders to have the Telegram sent to my room   Lieut W. M. Cooper, an acting A. D. C. who is inexperienced, took upon himself to approve the telegrams, to save me from interruption—I deeply deplore the event. As I believe Mr Myers to be a truthful Patriotic man, who committed this grave offence not apprehending its consequences; I respectfully ask that he be pardoned. I shall personally examine all telegrams, but the mail is only 48 hours in communicating news to St Louis and 16 to Chicago. The officers of the Army are much to blame"   LS, *ibid.*, Letters Received. For the dispatch see *Illinois State Journal*, April 4, 1863.

To Maj. Gen. Stephen A. Hurlbut

Head Quarters, Dept. of the Ten.
Millikin's Bend, La, Apl. 9th/63

MAJ. GEN. S. A. HURLBUT,
COMD.G 16TH ARMY CORPS,
GEN.

Suppress the entire press of Memphis for giving aid and comfort to the enemy by publishing in their columns every move made here by troops and every work commenced. Arrest the Editors of the Bulliten and send him here a prisoner, under guard, for his publication of present plans via New Carthage & Grand Gulf.

I am satisfied that much has found its way into the public press through that incoragibly gassy man Col. Bissell of the Eng. Regt. I sent him to you[1] thinking he could not do so much harm there as here. His tongue will have to be tied if there is anything going on where he is which you dont want made public. I feel a strong inclination to arrest him and trust to find evidence against him afterwards.

> Very respectfully
> U. S. GRANT
> Maj. Gen Com

ALS, PPRF. On April 8, 1863, Lt. Col. John A. Rawlins wrote to Maj. Gen. Stephen A. Hurlbut. "You will require the publishers of all Newspapers in Memphis to present to you for your perusal a copy of all news from below Memphis, whether obtained from Northern papers or otherwise before printing, and prohibit the publication of any news relating in any manner, however remotely to army movements here" Copies, DLC-USG, V, 19 (2), 30; DNA, RG 393, Dept. of the Tenn., Letters Sent. On April 12, Hurlbut wrote to Rawlins. "I this day received orders from the Major Genl. to suppress the entire press of Memphis and send the Editors of the Bulletin down under guard, which orders have been fully complied with. Messrs Nabers & Hough the Editors of the Bulletin will go down under guard on the Boat which bears this communication. I regret to say that many officers from below, in fact almost all seem to consider it their duty to avoid Head Quarters here, even when bearers of dispatches, and to occupy themselves in stating to newspaper men & others what they know or imagine in reference to movements below. As dispatches sent to me are not marked with the name of the bearer, and almost invariably come after delay of one or two days by the Post Office I cannot check this pernicious course. For example I received to day order of 3d April for sending down Mules Harness & Wagons which order was executed two days ago by sending 150 wagons &c complete, on a copy furnished me by Lt. Col. Reynolds" ALS, *ibid.*, Letters Received. For the order suppressing the newspapers of Memphis, see *O.R.*, II, v, 476. On April 13, Hurlbut wrote to Rawlins. "Upon examination I find that Mr R. Hough whose name appears in the Bulletin as one of the Editors & Proprietors, has nothing to do with the paper. As he is Surveyor of the Port I have relieved him from the order. Mr Nabers is under orders to go down. Mr Bingham the news editor is not here but at St Louis" ALS, DNA, RG 109, Union Provost Marshals' File of Papers Relating to Two or More Civilians. See letter to Maj. Gen. Stephen A. Hurlbut, April 23, 1863.

On April 20, C. Melson, Memphis, wrote to USG. "In making this communication I am influenced only by a desire to see our government administered by honest, true, & loyal men. I have no ends of my own to subserve, no private malise to gratify, no favors to ask of any officer of the government, but to the point. R. Hough Surveyor of this port—his oath of office to the contrary notwithstanding—has been directly giving aid and comfort to the enemy. During the winter of 61-62 he was engaged in smuggling Pistols, Quinnine, Cotton Cards &c &c into the rebel states, he had associated with him T. Tomeny late a candidate for Congress, W. G. Carleton, Madison bet Main & Front sts. Mr Kelsey who is, or was, in Mr Hough's office, an Irish levee contractor whose adress can be obtained from J. G. McBain, 4 Union st. and most likely some of his present assistants, whose mouths he has thus sealed. Mess M Hawks & F. Y. Carlyle, offices in same building as Carleton, know of this fact, and can be made to give other names, that would fasten the thing beyond a doubt. It is also a notorious fact that Jews get permits for goods when no one else can, and darkly hint that said permits cost 'vera mooch monish' I think one of them—Sugarman—took a car load of goods to Bolivar Tenn a few days ago. A Good Detective—not such as they have in Memphis—but one with the appearance and address of a gentleman could trace him up. Hoping you may deem this of sufficient importance to demand attention." ALS, DNA, RG 393, 16th Army Corps, Letters Received. On April 23, Rawlins endorsed this letter to Hurlbut. ES, *ibid.*

1. See letter to Maj. Gen. Stephen A. Hurlbut, March 29, 1863, note 1.

To Maj. Gen. William T. Sherman

Millikens, Bend La April 9, 1863

MAJ GEN W. T. SHERMAN
COMM'DG 15TH ARMY CORPS.

To equalize the Artillery, between Army Corps I will have to transfer one battery from you to General McClernand. The General expresses a prefference for Hoffmans Battery.[1]

I do not want to select your best battery or one for which you have a preference but if you would as soon send this one, do it, if not, Send any other battery.

The Division to which this battery will be attached will move from here in a day or two. I wish therefore you would send it up as soon as possible. I will direct the Quartermaster to furnish the transportation to-morrow

U. S. GRANT
Maj. Gen.

Copies, DLC-USG, V, 19 (2), 30; DNA, RG 393, Dept. of the Tenn., Letters Sent.

1. 4th Ohio Battery Light Art., Capt. Louis Hoffmann.

To Maj. Gen. Stephen A. Hurlbut

Millikens, Bend La April 10, 1863

MAJ GEN S. A. HURLBUT
COMM'DG 16TH ARMY CORPS

The movements spoken of previously and now in your letter of the 7th, brought by Gen Lee you may make so as to effectively cooperate with Rosecrans, and without reference to movements here.

At the present Stage of water it is impossible to make any move from Hellena or here to go in South of Ponola   Your movements will therefore be somewhat independent of anything here. I could be ready to move here in four days but for the Stage of Water. One foot lower would enable me to keep the wagon road open from here to New Carthage over which to march my troops and Artillery. As it is, I fear when the water is let into the canal now ready, the water will cover this road.

The Marine Brigade was not directed to report at Memphis but to proceed to Hamburg on the Tennessee and cooperate with Genl Dodge. I thought my letter to you explained this. It was my meaning that when this Brigade passed Memphis, you could form a better opinion of the time when they would likely reach Hamburg, than I could, and inform Genl Dodge so that he might have some one on the look out for them.[1]

U. S. GRANT
Maj Gen.

Copies, DLC-USG, V, 19, 30; DNA, RG 393, Dept. of the Tenn., Letters Sent. On April 7, 1863, Maj. Gen. Stephen A. Hurlbut wrote to USG. "Brig Genl A. L. Lee being still within this command and being the ranking officer of the Cavalry service I have directed him to visit you & confer upon the movement of Cavalry which I had the honor to propose in my letter of April 1. Every arrival confirms me in the information & belief that the line of Roads below is lightly guarded. I deeply regret the culpable neglect at St Louis by which I am crippled in horses at this juncture. I wish Genl Lee to get your views fully so that there may be the most accurate timing possible for the contemplated movement, to connect as nearly as can be done with your investment of Vicksburgh"   ALS, ibid., Letters Received. USG endorsed this letter "Answered"   AE, ibid.

On April 6, Hurlbut had written to Lt. Col. John A. Rawlins. "The dash on our front here has proved to be solely a cavalry (irregulars) movement. I inclose copy of message from Genl Rosecrans to Dodge which indicates an important movement not only for his Corps but necessarily for this force. If this movement goes on it will very materially aid my contemplated Cavalry dash on the Rail Road below for it will draw off their Cavalry force into Alabama & leave my field clear. They draw now most of their supplies from Noxubee & neighboring Counties in Miss. The line of this Corps is now well maintained and the troops in good order & fine spirits. Horses now is the only thing I now require to be ready for a movement. This Cavalry dash I desire to time so as to cooperate with what I suppose to be your plan, to land below Vicksburgh on south side Black River, silencing the Grand Gulf batteries   By cutting the Road I shall as I think materially aid in the movement, as well as by shoving the head of Infantry Columns as low as the Tallahatchie" ALS, *ibid.* O.R., I, xxiii, part 2, 214. For the enclosures, see *ibid.*, pp. 214–15.

On April 8, Hurlbut wrote to Rawlins. "I have the honor, herewith, to transmit, statements made by sundry refugees and others, received by Brig. Gen. W. S. Smith. It is rumored that Tilghmans' command has recently gone to Mobile, probably en route for Chattanooga and Tullahoma. The report lacks confirmation. Husseys statement as to the movement of troops to re-inforce Bragg is corroborated by other statements." LS, DNA, RG 94, War Records Office, Dept. of the Mo. The enclosed statements are *ibid.*

On April 12, Hurlbut wrote to USG. "The enemy are now running the Rail Road from Decatur to Tuscumbia carrying off supplies to Johnson's Army. Dodge informs me that he expects Rosecrans force to shew itself on the Tennessee about Wednesday next. I have ordered the 7th Kansas to move tomorrow to Corinth supplying their place at Germantown with the 9th Ills. This will give Dodge the two most effective Regiments of Cavalry that I can furnish him the 10th Mo & 7th Kansas & place the whole under command of Cornyn. It is reported that Pontoon Bridges are in construction above Florence, and that the enemys left in Meddle Tennessee is heavily reinforced with a strong massing of troops near Harpeth's shoals. This may hinder or delay Rosecrans movement in combination with which Dodge is to move—But whenever this movement does take place which I think will be this week—the dash below will be attempted. The withdrawal of the Yazoo Pass Expedition will leave a force which I think will be used to reinforce Chalmers at Panola if they really intend to move up. I am in doubt about this but the balance of my judgment is that Chalmers is merely a cover for obtaining supplies. I have delayed starting on the actual construction of the Memphis & Charleston R Road until the front is thoroughly cleared   meanwhile am accumulating materials & supplies for the work at LaGrange. Lawler has come in from a ride with the 18th Ills   reports 1. Lt. Col. 2 Captains—3 Lieuts & 38 Privates prisoners. I regret to lose the 15th Regulars from the Fort but must supply their place as I best can   There is no news of any special import about this point & all is quiet along the south Front of the line. It is currently believed below that the attack on Vicksburgh will be abandoned. A man from Port Hudson reports to me that they are preparing Boats in Red River to carry the Hartford by boarding acknowledging that it will be a heavy loss of life but determined to do it"   ALS, *ibid.*, RG 393, Dept. of the Tenn., Letters Received. *O.R.*, I, xxiv, part 3, 189–90.

On April 13, Hurlbut wrote to USG. "I send you the following dispatch, just received: MURFREESBOROUGH, *April* 11, 1863. My expedition leaves Nashville to-day by river. It will probably reach Hamburg six days hence. Dodge should move as soon as your orders can reach him. Should communicate with my force by messenger at Hamburg, so that each may know the whereabouts of the other. My force will probably land at Eastport. W. S. ROSECRANS. General Dodge will move on Wednesday, as agreed." *Ibid.*, p. 191.

On April 14, Hurlbut wrote to USG. "I enclose you the copies of dispatches received from Corinth, La Grange, and Murfreesboro. It would seem as if the enemy had got notice of Rosecrans intended movement on the Tennessee   I have ordered Dodge to take five thousand men with two batteries from District of Corinth, open communications at Hamburgh with Rosecrans, and as soon as their mutual whereabouts is known to move rapidly on Tuscumbia, cutting by Cavalry, if possible, the Rail Road from Decatur to Tuscumbia—This will take place on Wednesday or Thursday if Rosecrans succeeds in getting up the River—The Marine Brigade has not reported yet—If Ellet has gone up the Tennessee as directed he will be in time to co-operate—If not he should be cashiered for running by me without reporting—His assistance would be invaluable at this time, provided his command is of any use at all, which I do not know—If Rosecrans moves with Convoy he can break through—If not I doubt his getting down the Cumberland and up the Tennessee—Under cover of this movement I shall sweep down with Cavalry, and expect no difficulty in getting to Meredian—I am still horribly crippled for want of horses, by the gross neglect of Quarter Masters in St Louis —I have only received two hundred, with which I have mounted the 7th Kansas, and sent them to Dodge. No further news of moment." Copy, DNA, RG 393, 16th Army Corps, Letters Sent. *O.R.*, I, xxiv, part 3, 193.

On April 15, Hurlbut wrote to USG. "The enemy have been reinforced at Tuscumbia and its neighborhood, and line the East Bank of the Tennessee from Savannah up. They are about 5600 strong principally cavalry with 11 pieces of Artillery. Capt Spencer A. A. G for Genl Dodge has been to Tuscumbia & returned with full information, for which act he deserves great credit. Nothing has yet been heard of Rosecrans expedition or from Ellet. Dodge moves tomorrow with 5000 men and good artillery with instructions to proceed to Iud Iuka and await Rosecrans [ordering] to East Port. If Rosecrans fails to get up to make a reconnoissance in force, to be converted into a heavy attack if it looks feasible, Oglesby is ordered to support him with 2000 from Jackson and local garrisons, if required. They are not to assume any serious risk unless to carry out Rosecrans movement. I feel the most abundant confidence in Dodge and have no doubts of the result. On Friday or Saturday the Cavalry from LaGrange will move, & I shall throw by Rail Road to Holly Springs or below there three Regiments of Infantry & a Battery to march rapidly thence to Panola getting in rear of Chalmers if possible   He is now on Coldwater. In twelve hours after this expidition gets off I shall move two of my old Regiments & a battery with Cavalry from this place to Coldwater to attack in front on Chalmer's position & hope to be able by hard marching to catch his battery. Glendale east of Corinth was attacked yesterday but Enemy were expelled & heavily pursued"   ALS, DNA, RG 393, Dept. of the Tenn., Letters Received. *O.R.*, I, xxiv, part 3, 195–96.

On April 17, Hurlbut wrote to Rawlins. "Rosecrans telegraphs to day that his expedition 2000 strong picked men left Palmyra on Monday last and should be off Hamburgh to night. They are not yet heard of nor is Ellet. Dodge was at Bear Creek yesterday, has not been heard from to day as yet. Grierson's cavalry expedition started at day light from LaGrange   I do not expect to hear from him for 15 or 20 days unless from Southern papers. Genl Smith started to day with three Regiments and a Battery for Panola by Holly Springs going down on Rail Road. Thence by land in North side Tallahatchie to Panola. Three Regiments & a Battery of Lauman's with 200 Cavalry move tomorrow morning direct on Cold Water & Panola   These various movements along our length of line will I hope so distract their attention that Grierson's party will get a fair start & be well down to their destination before they can be resisted by adequate force. God speed him for he has started gallantly on a long and perilous ride. I shall anxiously await intelligence of the result." ALS, DNA, RG 393, Dept. of the Tenn., Letters Received. *O.R.*, I, xxiv, part 3, 202.

On April 18, Hurlbut wrote to Rawlins. "In January last while I commanded the District of Memphis—I received a letter from Genl Grant on the subject of the Charleston & Memphis Rail Road, with instructions to give notice to all persons of the results of interference with the Road. This notice was given in General Order No 10 of the District of Memphis & fully published in the papers. An attack was made by a party of Guerillas living North of the Road, of the most gross & cowardly nature. This band of 20 or 25 are not even part of Richardson's command, but simply plunderers who when caught claim organization but are not enrolled or subject to any military authority. I proceeded to carry out the notice previously given the terms of which notice are taken almost word for word from Genl Grant's letter—for I do not believe it is wise to threaten and not perform. The families sent out are eight in number and are prominent secessionists. This memorial is now presented. There is no name to it of any man of acknowledged loyalty, and nearly every man on the list ought to be sent South. I forward it as in duty bound for the consideration of the Major General Comg, with this remark only that I believe the banishment has done good not harm. I have long been of the opinion that no *sympathiser* should be allowed within our lines"   AL (signature clipped), DNA, RG 94, War Records Office, Dept. of the Tenn. *O.R.*, I, xxiv, part 3, 206. See letter to Maj. Gen. Stephen A. Hurlbut, Jan. 3, 1863. In a lengthy undated petition to USG, received on April 12, William K. Poston and others of Memphis protested this expulsion policy. DS, DNA, RG 393, Dept. of the Tenn., Letters Received. On April 18, Hurlbut wrote to Rawlins. "Since closing my last letter I learn from Oglesby that Capt Fitch U. S. N with four Gun boats is between Hamburgh & Eastport as advance of Rosecrans expedition. If any thing new turns up before the Boat leaves I will send it"   ALS, *ibid.*, RG 94, War Records Office, Dept. of the Tenn. *O.R.*, I, xxiv, part 3, 206; *O.R.* (Navy), I, xxiv, 61.

On April 20, Hurlbut wrote to Rawlins. "Owing to the prolonged delay of Rosecrans Expeditionary forces in coming up and reporting, Genl. Dodge has been compelled to have a brisk skirmish beginning at Bear Creek and continued to Caney Creek to which the enemy fell back in a disordered retreat. Dodge reports our loss One Hundred, the enemy's much heavier, as he found their dead & wounded abandoned on the line of Retreat. Capt Fitch with his Gun boats came up and Col. Straight with 1900 picked men has joined Dodge before this time. I have ordered Dodge reinforced with 2000 men from Corinth and have moved up a Garrison ~~from~~ for Corinth from Jackson & Bolivar. The enemy are no doubt strongly reinforced with Infantry. Rosecrans telegraphed to me to move Dodge on Wednesday which I did. His Expedition was delayed and did not make its appearance at Hamburgh until Sunday morning. Ellet's Marine Brigade are at

Hamburgh, having wilfully delayed at Cairo five days as I am informed by Genl Sullivan. His boats are reported too deep to go up to Tuscumbia or even Eastport. I have directed Dodge not to attack Tuscumbia unless the movement will be a success (which it would have been last week) but to shew front strongly on Bear Creek Keeping open Communications with Corinth—and to let Straights Expedition move in his rear by Verona and Tupelo thence across the Country to their destination, and then drop back to Corinth. I suggest this course because my Cavalry from LaGrange have before this destroyed the Rail Road below and near Tupelo and in the confusion they may get fairly started across Alabama before they are known. If however with the reinforcements he is sure of driving the enemy from Tuscumbia he will attack strongly. I have telegraphed to Rosecrans and recommended a strong demonstration on left of Johnson's line in aid of the Tuscumbia movement. The line works now to Columbus. I rejoice exceedingly in the success of the passage of the batteries, it will tend to stop the mouths of the croakers at home, and of the *Newspaper officers* in the Army. I look now for the occupation of Grand Gulf and the abandonment or surrender of Vicksburgh Grierson will cut the R Road if he lives at or near Chunkey Bridge about Wednesday night or Thursday. No news here of any moment"   ALS, DNA, RG 94, War Records Office, Union Battle Reports. *O.R.*, I, xxiv, part 3, 214–15.

On April 21, Hurlbut wrote to Rawlins. "I send you last dispatch from Corinth also written report from Col. Bryant 12th Wisconsin as to movement on Coldwater. The River at Coldwater Station proved impassable, our troops fell back to Hernando. I have just had verbal report from Bryant. Major Hayes 5th O. V. Cavy has died of his wound. His conduct was most gallant. With forty men he captured 65 prisoners. We have 80 in all. Fearing that Chalmers might be reinforced from Greenwood, I have sent this morning the 14th & 46th Illinois & one battery, with orders if they hear Smith's guns to force a passage by bridging or otherwise and join him. I have just received a dispatch from LaGrange that a woman just in from Holly Springs reports heavy cannonading south of Holly Springs on yesterday. If this is so, Smith has run across some other band or force for Chalmers has not moved yet I think from Coldwater. Smith has 1500 good Infantry and a good battery and although I am somewhat anxious about his not appearing in their rear at or about Senatobia before our men left Coldwater on Monday noon I think he is strong enough to work his way back or forward, against any thing but a movement in force from below, of which I have no intelligence. Dodge is I am satisfied careful as well as brave & will hold the line of Bear Creek as long as necessary"   ALS, DNA, RG 94, War Records Office, Union Battle Reports. *O.R.*, I, xxiv, part 1, 554; *ibid.*, I, xxiv, part 3, 217. On April 26, USG endorsed this letter. "Respectfully forwarded to Hd Qrs. of the Army & attention called to reports of Col. Bryant and Col. Grierson." AES, DNA, RG 94, War Records Office, Union Battle Reports. For the enclosures see *O.R.*, I, xxiv, part 1, 554–55, 556.

On April 25, Hurlbut wrote to Rawlins. "The Expedition against Chalmers suffered the misfortune of most combined movements. Genl. Smith did not get into the rear in time, and from high water in Coldwater River, & the slowness and extreme caution of Col. Bryant of 12th Wisconsin, who led the force from here, that part of the expedition did not force the passage of the River. As Smith came up on Wednesday—Chalmers broke into small squads and ran off to Panola, burning all bridges. I have had nothing from Dodge for three days, but his base is firm at Eastport; on the line of Bear Creek. I sent you copy of letter from

Grierson, near Pantotoc. I have not heard from his main column since. The 2d Iowa cavalry has burned Okalona, destroyed the Road and Barracks; also large amount of provisions, &c., at Tupelo, either by themselves or by the enemy in fear of them This is reported by two of that Regiment who were cut off & came into Corinth. The Country Cavalry is hanging around them, but I think they will work their way in. There is nothing else here of news—As soon as I get news from any of these expeditions I will forward it" ALS, DNA, RG 94, War Records Office, Union Battle Reports. *O.R.*, I, xxiv, part 1, 555.

On April 26, Hurlbut wrote to Rawlins. "I learn from Dodge that he occupied Tuscumbia on 24th and proposed to take Florence on 25th, quite a brisk skirmish on Little Bear Creek, loss not reported if any—Johnson sent word to troops at Tuscumbia, that he could not reinforce Great consternation from the belief that Dodge is the head of a column to attack Johnson in flank and rear. Col Straight pushes out to day on his trip—Dodge feels confident of his position—The Column under Gen Smith dispersed chalmers, capturing many small arms, principally shot guns, 230 Horses and Mules, and a number of wagons of provisions and supplies— Our troops are now all at their stations—Nothing further from Grierson. The 2d Iowa Cavalry, is reported to have destroyed barracks, stores and Rail Road at Okalono and Tupelo, and at other points. They are not in yet, and may have some trouble, but Hatch will take care of himself and his men—Everything so far as I can learn is moving well on this line, though Chalmers may make a dash to pass our R Road, or capture a train—The men are in splendid health. Hospitals much reduced and room enough for patients from below" Copy, DNA, RG 393, 16th Army Corps, Letters Sent. *O.R.*, I, xxiv, part 3, 237.

On April 27, Hurlbut wrote to Rawlins. "I send you copy of dispatch just received—Col Hatch deserves great credit for his dashing movement—especially when it is known that from the neglect at St Louis, in furnishing cavalry horses, the force was most wretchedly mounted—I will send full reports—I have no doubt of Grierson's full success." Copy, DNA, RG 393, 16th Army Corps, Letters Sent.

On April 28, Hurlbut wrote to Rawlins. "Asboth reported night before last that Cape Giradeau now garrisoned by McNeile was attacked by Marmaduke— I directed him to send two Regiments of Infantry there from Columbus with a section of Artillery and squadron 4th Mo Cavalry which has been done. They are to return to Columbus as soon as troops come down from St Louis. I am now temporarily mounting the 6th Iowa Infy on horses & mules captured in the Chalmers Expedition and shall send them with 2d Iowa Cavalry and 4th Illinois —to meet Grierson on his return and disperse any force that may be gathering to annoy or impede him. Grierson has the 6th & 7th Ills and is I think strong enough to come through. Loring has moved to Grenada from Greenwood but I think not in time to interfere with Grierson" ALS, *ibid.*, Dept. of the Tenn., Letters Received. *O.R.*, I, xxiv, part 3, 246.

On April 29, Hurlbut wrote to Rawlins. "I have just received the enclosed telegram. 'Anticipating a gathering to oppose Grierson's return, I had mounted the 6th Iowa Infantry, and sent them with the 2d Iowa Cavalry and 4th Illinois this morning, towards Okalona to relieve Grierson. I think he will come in above Okalona and toward Corinth—I have full faith that he can cut through any force they can raise' " Copy, DNA, RG 393, 16th Army Corps, Letters Sent. *O.R.*, I, xxiv, part 1, 519–20.

On May 3, Hurlbut wrote to Rawlins. "I have the honor to report that Gen Dodge and his command have returned to Corinth—Gen Dodge furnished to Col

Straight five hundred horses, and the latter named officer proceeded upon his mission pursuant to instructions already furnished to you" Copy, DNA, RG 393, 16th Army Corps, Letters Sent. *O.R.*, I, xxiv, part 3, 269.

On May 5, Hurlbut wrote to Rawlins. "I enclose herewith a short statement from Maj Gen Oglesby of the results of Dodge's expedition. You will perceive that it has been thoroughly a success, so far as this command is concerned. There is more doubt of the success of the expedition from Rosecrans. The chief cause of failure in this, (if it fails) will have been in the delay of a week which intervened from the time they were to report. By referring to my previous communications you will perceive that the several movements indicated in them to be carried on by this command, have been performed with a reasonable degree of accuracy, and with a very brilliant success, in the main attempt to pierce the enemys country. The movement on Tuscumbia on the one side drew attention and gathered their Cavalry in that direction, while the movement on Cold water and Panola drew Chalmers and his band in the other—Thus our gallant soldier Grierson proceeded with his command unchallenged, and has splendidly performed the duty he was sent upon—I very earnestly support his claim for promotion earned by long and meritorious service, and now crowned by this last achievement—I trust he will be able to join the main army below Grand Gulf, if not he will go to Banks. In either event he will be a gain to the part of the army he may join. If it be practicable, I strongly request that he and his command, may be sent to me—" Copy, DNA, RG 393, 16th Army Corps, Letters Sent. *O.R.*, I, xxiv, part 3, 276.

1. See letter to Maj. Gen. Stephen A. Hurlbut, April 4, 1863, note 1.

To Maj. Gen. John A. McClernand

Head Quarters, Dept. of the Tenn.
Millikens Bend, La. Apr. 11th 1863

MAJ GENL. JNO. A MCCLERNAND
COMD'G. 13TH ARMY CORPS.
GENERAL

A dispatch just received from Admiral Porter informs me that he has received ord[ers] from Washington which compel him to run below the Vicksburg batteries sooner than he had contemplated. He desires me to have troops enough at Carthage to take down and possess Grand Gulf at once before the enemy can take away their guns and plant them elsewhere.[1] I have been pushing the preparatio[ns] on the transports to run the blockade, with all dispatch.

Will go down to-day to see how many of them can be got off.

The transports will have aboard from sixty to one hundred thousand rations each.

With this the force necessary to take can be supplied until our new route is opened. I will go down to Young's Point directly and in the earliest mome[nt] these boats can be got off, their number etc. and on my return write out the necessary instructions.

The great amount of both land and water transportation that is required to move the 1st Infantry, I would direct that they be left behind to go when preparations are more complete

> Very respectfully
> U. S. GRANT
> Maj. Gen. Comd'g.

Copy, DNA, RG 393, 13th Army Corps, Letters Received. On April 11, 1863, Maj. Gen. John A. McClernand, Milliken's Bend, wrote to USG. "I have availed myself of all means within my power to forward ammunition to Carthage. Would it not be advisable for you to send an additional supply by the first safe opportunity. One brigade of Genl. Carr's Division went forward as a detail to day, to work on the road between here and Richmond. The remaining brigade will leave in the morning for Richmond. This Division, as quick as it can be made available, will releive the detachments from Genl Osterhaus' Division stationed between Richmond and and Smiths, so as to enable the latter to embark as soon as practicable after the transports reach Smiths   A deficiency of waggons for the transportation of ammunition &C may cause some delay. If I find I can obviate this impediment by the use of boats on the Roundaway bayou I will do so. I think it important that the supporting Division should have sufficient time to put itself in readiness, immediately, to follow the advance Division. The two field batteries with the advance Div are scarcely sufficient to meet all contingencies. May I not order forward the Seige train, if I find I can send it through without delay?" LS, *ibid.*, Dept. of the Tenn., Letters Received. *O.R.*, I, xxiv, part 3, 186. On the same day, USG wrote to McClernand. "I think it advisable that the Heavy Guns be left behind, until the result of letting the water into the canal upon the dirt road has been ascertained. If they should be got across and any unforseen accident should make it necessary to bring them back, it might be difficult to do so. I will see you in the morning." LS, McClernand Papers, IHi.

1. Also on April 11, Act. Rear Admiral David D. Porter, Yazoo River, wrote to USG. "I have received a Communication from the Department which will compel me to go below the batteries with the fleet, sooner than I anticipated. I would like to know if the transports will be ready to go with me, and how many. I would also urge the importance of throwing as many troops as possible, without delay, into Grand-Gulf, that we may capture the guns there, and not let them mount them some where else. I can take ~~them~~ the troops all, in the at Carthage and be upon the rebels at Grand Gulf before they know it, shell them out, and let the troops land and take possession." LS, DNA, RG 94, War Records Office, Dept. of the Tenn. *O.R.*, I, xxiv, part 3, 186; *O.R.* (Navy), I, xxiv, 600.

To Maj. Gen. Frederick Steele

Millikins, Bend, La. April 11, 1863.

MAJ GEN. F STEELE
COMM'DG 11TH DIV. ARMY OF THE TENN.

Remain with your Division at Greenville for further orders. It is a better place for your troops, than your old camp, and to some extent may serve to keep the enemy from getting provisions from the Deer Creek Country.

Rebellion has assumed that shape now that it can only terminate by the complete subjugation of the South or the overthrow of the Government   it is our duty therefore to use every means to weaken the enemy by destroying their means of cultivating their field, and in every other way possible.

All the negroes you have you will provide for where they are issuing their necessary rations, until other disposition is made of them. You will also encourage all negroes, particularly middle aged males to come within our lines.

Gen L Thomas is now here,[1] with authority to make ample provision for the negro.

I will direct Col McFeely[2] to make arrangements for sending your rations.

Whilst at Greenville, destroy or bring off all the corn and beef cattle you possibly can.

The 150 bales of cotton you speak of may be brought in and 100 additional bales if they can be taken from either neighbors to the Douglass plantation,[3] or persons holding office und the Confederate Government.

U. S. GRANT
Maj Gen.

Copies, DLC-USG, V, 19 (2), 30; DNA, RG 393, Dept. of the Tenn., Letters Sent. *O.R.*, I, xxiv, part 3, 186–87. On April 10, 1863, Maj. Gen. Frederick Steele, Greenville, Miss., wrote to USG. "My command has just returned to this Place having pursued the Rebels under Col. Furguson about 42 miles down Deer Creek.   their precise strength I could not ascertain, but they had six pieces of artillery and from six hundred to a thousand Cav. & Inf. At Dr Thomas' planta-tion they received from Rolling Fork rëenforcements, including 2 ten pound Parrotts. Here they drew up in Line of battle and opened on us with their artillery. It was in an open field between us, and I advanced upon them in Line and using all my artillery. They fled before the Inf. became engaged. My Troops had made a fatiguing march and we encamped on the place the enemy had just left. The next morning I sent out a force to ascertain where the enemy was. They had moved towards Rolling Fork, where it was said they were to receive large rëenforce-ments. For reasons which I will explain in my official Report to Genl. Sherman. I then started back to this Place, bring about a thousand head of stock, horses, mules and beef cattle. There are also a number of ox wagons, carts buggies &c. A great many negroes have followed the command. I wish you would send up six boats to carry the stock &c. I advised all the negroes that asked my advice to stay on the plantations where they belonged; except two engineers & a blacksmith. Please send me instructions as to what shall be done with these poor creatures. In many instances our men burned up every thing there was to eat on the planta-tion, in spite of all my endeavors to prevent it. It is estimated by some of the officers that we burnt five hundred thousand bushels of corn. There were twenty five thousand bushels known at Thompsons' which the negroes said was destined for Vicksburg. We has lost a considerable number of stragglers, some of whom were taken because they wished to be, no doubt. One man of my escort was killed and one other Cavalry man wounded. The enemy made his appearance on our rear to-day while we were bridging Black Byou at Frenches' plantation but were soon dispersed with the loss of one man on our part. We have one Lieutenant and two privates prisoners. I send this dispatch by Major Peterson. Please send me orders in regard to my future movements. I am told that there are 150 bales of cotton 7 or 8 miles from here belonging to a Mr. Miller; rebel. I could probably get it in to the river, if it would be proper to mark it S. A Douglass. The enemy have 5 or six boats on Bogue Philiah and a landing about 2 miles from Deer Creek high up, a good road leading a cross, and several bridges." ALS, DNA, RG 94, War Records Office, Dept. of the Tenn. *O.R.*, I, xxiv, part 1, 501–2.

On April 19, Maj. Gen. William T. Sherman wrote to Lt. Col. John A. Rawlins. "Enclosed I send a Report from Genl Steele. I think the Deer Creek Country has been afflicted enough to make them in the future dread the Yankee's visit, and would therefore request that General Steele be required to destroy the Grist Mill he describes and return to his Camp. Extra steamers might be sent him to bring off any extra stock & Forage he may have collected. or if you desire to afflict that Region more, you might order him to go up the River a little higher, and visit Williams Bayou. I observe by the Rebel papers they are uneasy about the Hush-puck-a naw, or sunflower. Some maps represent Williams Bayou as the head of the Sunflower but mine make the sunflower a large River rising in the Mississipi about 10 miles below the Yazoo Pass. If you still desire to dis-tract attention some men from Helena might find the head of sunflower and follow it a few miles. I visited the Battery at the Point this morig, and found Capt Phillips who represented the embrasure gorges as too low, not admitting the Guns to an elevation enough to reach the Courthouse. I have sent to the Engineer Capt Kossack the tools & men needed to make the alterations during the night. I reached the Levee with the Armenia so that I now feel better satisfied as to our means of communication. I have a guard of 100 men with the Battery and a chain of sentinels to my Quarters, so that I could send relief in case the Battery is threatened. If the Enemy has boats, he may attempt to spike guns calculated to do such mischief. If you think prudent I will increase the Guard. Water in my Camps remains status quo." ALS, DNA, RG 94, War Records Office, Union Battle Reports. *O.R.*, I, xxiv, part 3, 208–9. Sherman enclosed a letter of April 18 from Steele. "The expedition up William's Bayo did not reach its destination on account of Ferguson's having burnt the Bridge across Black Bayo and flooded the country by cutting the Levee. They succeeded however in bringing back some mules and negroes. It is becoming a perfect mania with the colored population to become yankees; and most of the men express their willingness to fight for their freedom. We brought in 37 bales of cotton today; and I shall send it and about 120 mules down on the boat tonight. Also a few horses. I sent 74 bales to Genl. Grant on the comsy. boat.   Yesterday I sent 100 mules with Mr L. Dent on Genl. Grant's order   it was a first rate lot. My A. A. Q. M. took down 257 in the first lot. We have several teams hauling Forage and cotton; and several yokes of oxen employed in the same way. We have an immense quantity of corn meal. If your A. C. S. will send up sacks or barrels he can have enough to issue to the whole corps. A deserter who came in last night says Jeff. Davis has issued an order that any officer or man of this expedition who is caught, shall be hung. Our men have treated these people too roughly to suit my taste, and they are encouraged in it by many officers. There are some widows who have large families of young children or girls, and no sons who have been stript of nearly every thing they had to eat and of all means of making crops. In such cases, it is my intention to give up teams &c sufficient to prevent distress. Am I right? Our people have also taken a quantity of old carriages, buggies &c which can be of little or no use to us. I have excluded citizens from my lines, and ladies are constantly writing me for permission to lay their complaints before me. I would rather fight a battle than encounter them. A negro came in today just from Rolling Fork. I will enclose some papers he brought, which makes it probable that his story is correct. He says they are making Forts on both sides of the Fork by putting cotton bales two side by side at the bottom and heaping them up with earth. These Forts he says are about 100 yards on from Deer Creek; on the other side of the branch that runs into Steele's Bayo. He says he met Ferguson with 7 pieces of artillery and a lot of foot soldiers 8 miles this side of Rolling Fork, on their way to the Fork. He thought they had about 800 soldiers at the Forts when he left there. The people throughout this whole country, he says are running their negroes to Jackson, and taking their property to Rolling Fork. They have a cavalry camp at Courtney's plantation, about 7 miles from here; and send out squads all over the country to prevent the negroes from running off. I intend to pay them a visit tomorrow and make an expedition on the other side of Deer Creek. They destroy our bridges as soon as we leave them, which causes us a great deal of labor. The two deserters who came in first, wish to enlist in Landgraebers Battery. They are Germans and one of them has a brother, an officer in our service, so that the information they gave me was undoubtedly correct. . . . P. S. There is an old gentleman here Mr. Hunt who claims to be a union man, and who has testimonials from some of our officers in K. Y. wishes to get permission to ship his cotton to Memphis in order to get something to keep him from starving" ALS, *ibid.*, RG 393, Dept. of the Tenn., Letters Received.

1. On April 1, Brig. Gen. Lorenzo Thomas, Cairo, wrote to USG. "I have the honor to report that I have arrived within your command to make inspections

under special instructions of the Secretary of War. I shall after a time visit you. Enclosed please find a Special order of this date which the good of the service rendered imperative" ALS, *ibid*. The enclosed orders dismissed most of the officers of the 128th Ill. for failure to maintain discipline and prevent desertion. Copy, DLC-USG, V, 105. *Ill. AG Report*, VI, 532. On April 10, Rawlins wrote to Maj. Gen. John A. McClernand. "You will please cause to be fired a salute on the arrival of Brigr. General L. Thomas Adjutant General of the Army, corresponding to his rank." LS, McClernand Papers, IHi.

2. See letter to Brig. Gen. Lorenzo Thomas, April 16, 1863.

3. On April 5, Steele wrote to Sherman. "General Grant directed me to endeavor to get through to Deer Creek from Mrs. Smith's plantation, and to get out the cotton belonging to the S. A. Douglas plantation. The cotton had been burned a few days since, and that route to Deer Creek was impracticable, on account of the water. . . ." *O.R.*, I, xxiv, part 3, 173. See letter to Maj. Gen. Edward R. S. Canby, Dec. 20, 1864.

To Mrs. S. F. Bricker

Millikins Bend La.
April 11th 1863.

Mrs. S. F. Bricker,
My Dear Madam,

I have just this moment read your letter of the 10th of March in relation to your two sons in the 120th regt. Ohio Vols. This regiment is now on the Mississippi river below Vicksburg and I cannot see your sons immediately as you request but I will take the very first opportunity of doing so and do all in my power to cheer them up.

I regret exceedingly that your husband was not permitted to visit them after he had got so near as Memphis. My orders are against citizens visiting the army in general but I would always make an exception in favor of those who have children in the service.

Truly Yours
U. S. Grant
Maj. Gen.

ALS, ICHi.

To Maj. Gen. Henry W. Halleck

Head Quarters, Dept. of the Tennessee,
Milliken's Bend, La. Apl. 12th 1863.

MAJ. GEN. H. W. HALLECK,
GEN. IN CHIEF, WASHINGTON,
GEN.

There is nothing in the way now of my throwing troops into Grand Gulf, and destroying the works there; then sending them on to Port Hudson to co-operate with Gen. Banks in the reduction of that place, but the danger of overflowing the road from here to New Carthage, when the water is let into the new canal connecting the river here with the bayous coming out at Carthage. One Division of troops is now at Carthage and another on the way. By turning in the water to the canal water communication can be opened between the two places in a very few days for barges and tugs. Of the former I have but fifteen, as yet, and of the latter but three, suitable for this navigation. To use this route therefore it is absolutely necessary to keep open the wagon road to take over Artillery and to march the troops.

In about three nights from this time Admiral Porter will run the Vicksburg batteries with such of his fleet as he desires to take below and I will send four steamers, the machinery protected from shot by hay bales & sand bags, to be used in transporting troops and in towing barges.

The wagon road by filling up the lowest ground (this work must now be nearly completed) will be about twenty inches above the water in the swamps. The river where it is to be let into the canal is $4\frac{9}{10}$ ft. above the land. This however is fifteen miles by the river below where the dirt road starts out. Had I seen nothing of the effect of crevasses upon the back country I should not doubt the effect would be to overflow the whole country through which we pass. But there has been a large crevasse just below where this canal leaves the river, for a long time, through which the water has been pouring in great volume. I cannot see that this additional crevasse is going to have much other effect than to increase the breaks in the bayou levees so as to make the discharge equal to the supply. I will have a map of this section made to send you by next mail which will make this more intelligible. The embarrassments I have had to contend against on account of extreme high water cannot be appreciated by anyone not present to witness it. I think however you will receive favorable reports ~~from~~ of the condition and feeling of this Army from every impartial judge, and from all who have been sent from Washington to look after its welfare.

> I am Gen. very respectfully
> your obt. svt.
> U. S. GRANT
> Maj. Gen. Com

ALS, IHi. *O.R.*, I, xxiv, part 1, 29. On April 11, 9:00 A.M., USG had telegraphed much of this information to Maj. Gen. Henry W. Halleck. "The Yazoo Expedition has reached the Mississippi. My forces in a few days will all be concentrated here. Grand Gulf is the point at which I expect to strike and send an Army Corps to Port Hudson to co-operate with Genl. Bank's. Will reach the Mississippi at New Carthage now in my possession with wagon road & canal & bayous navigable for tugs & barges between here & there." Telegram received, DNA, RG 107, Telegrams Collected (Bound); *ibid.*, Telegrams Collected (Unbound); copies, *ibid.*, RG 393, Dept. of the Tenn., Hd. Qrs. Correspondence; DLC-USG, V, 5, 8, 24, 94. *O.R.*, I, xxiv, part 1, 28.

To Col. John C. Kelton

Head Quarters Department of the Tennessee
Millikens Bend La., April. 12th, 1863,

COL. J. C. KELTON
ASSISTANT ADJUTANT GENERAL,
WASHINGTON D. C.,
COLONEL,

Herewith I send you reports of Major General Sherman, and the Division and Brigade Commanders under him, of the late reconnoisance through Steele and Black Bayous', and Deer Creek made by them in conjunction with a portion of Admiral Porters fleet, commanded by himself in person. The object of the expedition was to find a practicable passage to the Yazoo river without passing the enemy's batteries at Haines Bluff; to liberate our fleet and troops then held above Greenwood, and, if found sufficiently practicable to enable me to land most of my forces east of the Yazoo at some point from which Haines Bluff and Vicksburg could be reached by high land. The accompanying reports show the impracticability of the route.

This expedition, however, was not without its result. It carried our troops into the heart of the granary from which the Vicksburg forces are now being fed. It caused great alarm among the enemy, and led them to move a number of their guns from from batteries on the river. The citizens fled from their plantations and burnt several thousand bales of cotton; some not burned was brought away by the Gun-boats. Much of their beef, bacon, and poultry was consumed by our troops and distributed by the negroes. A scow loaded with bacon for the enemy was destroyed, and probably 200,000 bushels of corn in the crib was burned up. several hundred negroes also returned with the troops.

The recent expedition of Gen. Steele to the neighborhood of rolling Fork, shows that the enemy are still holding that position. He also destroyed several hundred thousand bushels of corn and brought off about 1000 head of stock and a number of the laboring class.

　　　　　　　　　　Very Respectfully
　　　　　　　　　　Your obt Servt.
　　　　　　　　　　U. S. Grant
　　　　　　　　　　Major General.

Copies, DLC-USG, V, 5, 8, 24, 94; DNA, RG 393, Dept. of the Tenn., Hd. Qrs. Correspondence. *O.R.*, I, xxiv, part 1, 28–29. For the enclosures, see *ibid.*, pp. 431–54.

To Maj. Gen. John A. McClernand

Milliken's, Bend, La. April 12 1863

MAJ GEN. J. A. McCLERNAND
COMM'DG 13TH ARMY CORPS

I was anxious to have seen you and and had a conversation upon present movements before your leaving if I could have done so. I will however probably go over to New Carthage before you get away.

On Tuesday[1] or Wednesday night Admiral Porter will run the Vicksburg batteries, and I will send at the same time four Steamers and all the barges then ready, probably twelve. If these all get through safely you will have 300,000 rations aboard and transportation by close packing for two batteries and from six to eight thousand men. It is desirable that you should take all the men possible with the transportation at your hands at the start.

It is my desire that you should get possession of Grand Gulf at the earliest practicable moment. Concentrate your entire corps there with all rapidity and as soon as transportation can be got through for them, move down the river to Bayou Sara. From there you can operate on the rear of Port Hudson in conjunction with Banks from Baton Rouge.

I will write to General Banks to be sent down by the Gunboats informing him of present plans and timing our movements as near as possible.

It is expected that Genl Banks will garrison Port Hudson with a few troops and with the remainder of his effective force come up to cooperate in the reduction of Vicksburg. This will give us increased facilities for moving troops from New Carthage to Grand Gulf.

I wanted particularly to see you about the facilities for getting troops from Smith's plantation to New Carthage and the chances for embarking them. Also to consult upon the probable effects of letting the water into the canal upon the Levees between Richmond and Carthage.[2]

The water will be let in on Monday or Tuesday   You will want to have your men guard against all contingences. As water is now flowing through the same channells in great volume, from various crevasses, commencing just below the canal, I cannot see that this new cut is going to have much effect. We must be prepared for the effects however, whatever it may be. I have been more troubled to know how to supply you with amunition until water communication is established than on any other subject, If roads hold good there will be no difficulty, but without them there will be. It is not safe to send by the river as we do coal

U. S. Grant

Maj Gen

Copies, DLC-USG, V, 19, 30; DNA, RG 393, Dept. of the Tenn., Letters Sent; *ibid.*, 13th Army Corps, Letters Received; Alcorn Collection, WyU. *O.R.*, I, xxiv, part 3, 188–89. On April 12, 1863, Maj. Gen. John A. McClernand, Smith's Plantation, wrote to USG. "I am at this place, two miles from Carthage. It is reported that the enemy have a force of, some, twelve or fifteen hundred men, including a battery of *four* 6 pdr. and *two* 12 pdr. guns, at the lower end of St. Joseph Lake. By reference to the map of Mississippi, you will see that there is a road leading from Grand Gulf to Warronton which crosses the Big Black a short distance above its mouth—and another leading, back, by Willow Spring, to Warrenton, which crosses the Big Black higher up. Whether my forces should ~~disembark~~ ascend the Big Black and disembark at the crossing of the first or second road mentioned; or on the Mississippi shore near Grand Gulf, is a question upon which I am not advised. As I have none but imperfect maps, please, furnish me a complete one, with all other information you can afford; also; guide if you can. A messenger will be found at my Head Quarters, at the Bend, to bring anything you may wish to send. I will order the seige pieces forward, with your permission. Genl. Benton, to whose brigade they are attached, says he can bring them. Small craft are, today, bringing commissary stores from Richmond to this place. As soon as they return they will bring ammunition. I have ordered the 9th and 14th Divisions of my Corps to hold themselves in readiness for concentration there, preparatory to embarkation. As my means of supplying my forces with ammunition and other requisite stores are limited and not altogether reliable, I must trust to you to assist me. . . . P. S. I may find it useful to return, to morrow, to Richmond and the Bend." ALS, DNA, RG 393, Dept. of the Tenn., Letters Received. *O.R.*, I, xxiv, part 3, 188. On April 13, 4:00 a.m., McClernand, Smith's Plantation, wrote to USG. "Your dispatch of the 12th inst, is recd   I will return to the Bend in the morning. As I have sent orders for the removal of Genl Smiths Division; is it not important that another Corps should be immediately ordered forward to maintain the communication between Millikens Bend and this place?" Copies (2), McClernand Papers, IHi; DNA, RG 393, 13th Army Corps, Letters Sent.

1. April 14.

2. On April 12, USG signaled to Col. Lionel A. Sheldon, 42nd Ohio, Richmond, La. "as there will probably be a rise in the bayou, put a [. . . .] by which you can assertain the rise by to morrow at 8 o clock   Keep a correct record of it" Signal received, DLC-James M. McClintock. On April 13, 7:10 A.M., Sheldon signaled to USG. "The bayou ~~arose~~ arose one and three eights inches during the 11 hours preceeding 8 oclock this morning." Signal received, *ibid.*

To Maj. N. G. Watts

Milliken's Bend, La April 13 1863.

MAJ N. G. WATTS.

AGENT OF EXCHANGE OF PRISONERS, C. S. A.

On consultation with the Adjutant General of the Army as to the propriety of receiving prisoners of war, for exchange without the Officers accompaning them, he advises me to receive them.

The Dix-Hil cartel requires that officers and Soldiers taken prisoners by either party should be sent to one of the two places agreed upon for exchange within ten days after their capture. The order of Mr Davis to hold Officers, I looked upon as a violation of this Cartel or at least a revocation of it. And that I had a right to make exchanges on any other basis without direct instructions to do so from the Government.

Gen Thomas informs me that notwithstanding this order to return offercers they are exchanging them in the East and that he has no doubt but that all will be exchanged   I will therefore receive all prisoners you may please to send, and will return to you the same class of prisoners as they fall into my hands.

U. S. GRANT
Maj Gen.

Copies, DLC-USG, V, 19, 30; DNA, RG 393, Dept. of the Tenn., Letters Sent. *O.R.*, II, v, 476.

On April 12, 1863, Maj. Gen. William T. Sherman wrote to USG. "A Flag of Truce brought me the family of Mrs Mary M Tompkins of California, who wishes to go to San Francisco, via New York City. She understands her obligations and duties and I have promised she may with your approval pass to New York and San Francisco provided she respect the Laws of propriety whilst passing through our Territory. She has two daughters with her Lilly and Rose, 13 & 11. Please give the necessary passes. I send papers sent me by Maj Watts, and have a message that in the Gunboat attack the Montauk was sunk—Maj Watts sent me word that the attack on Charleston had been renewed. He says he has many prisoners he would like to deliver up, but his orders remain the same as before as to officers. Captain Brown has given his parole and gone up to Memphis from Jackson. If Mr Dana wants an excuse to see some secession officers; and if you have any distinct proposition to make for the exchange of prisoners, send them down and I will go on with the Flag—Mr Dana can go along. He asked me to notify him the first chance. General Thomas may advise you if it be proper to receive Prisoners of War, under the old Cartel. I see in northern papers so many notices of the renewal of exchanges, that I believe there must be some truth in it, though Major Watts told me distinctly he had orders not to exchange officers, and sent me word today that he had nothing new on this subject." ALS, DNA, RG 94, War Records Office, Dept. of the Tenn. *O.R.*, II, v, 471.

To Col. John C. Kelton

Head Quarters, Department of the Tennessee,
Before Vicksburg, April. 13th 1863,

Col. J. C. Kelton
Assist Adjt. General,
Washington D, C.,
Colonel,

I have the honor to acknowledge the receipt of a copy of a communication of Maj. Gen Lewis Wallace to Maj. Genl Halleck of date March 14th 1863, relative to his failure to participate in the first days fight at Pittsburg landing, and submitted to me for my remarks.[1]

Instead of making a detailed report myself in answer to said communication, I called on Maj. Gen. J. B. McPherson, Leiut Col Jno A Rawlins and Major W. R. Rowley all of whom were members of my staff at that time, and were cognizant of the facts, for their statements in reference to the same, and these I respectfully transmit[2]

All these reports are substantially as I remember the facts, I vouch for their almost entire accuracy. And from these several statements separate and independent of each other, too, a more correct judgement can be derived than from a single report. Had Gen. Wallace been releived from duty in the morning, and the same orders been communicated to Brig Gen Morgan L. Smith (who would have been his successor) I do not doubt that the Division would have been on the field of battle and in the engagement, before one o'clock of that eventful 6th of April. There is no estimating the difference this might have made in our casualties.

> I am Colonel
> Very Respectfully
> Your Obdt Servant
> U. S. GRANT
> Major Gen Vols

Copies, DLC-USG, V, 5, 8, 24, 94; DNA, RG 393, Dept. of the Tenn., Hd. Qrs. Correspondence. *O.R.*, I, x, part 1, 178. See endorsement to Maj. Gen. Henry W. Halleck, April 25, 1862. On June 27, 1863, Maj. Gen. Lewis Wallace, Cincinnati, wrote to USG. "While in Washington three or four months ago, I filed in the office of the Gen. in Chief an official explanation of my march during the first day of the battle of Shiloh. I intended sending a copy of it to you; but on my return to Cincinnati I found the original had been misplaced. Since then I have ascertained that the paper was, with others, carried home, so that if you care about it, I can, by writing there, immediately forward it to you. The explanation was filed solely with a view to relieve myself from aspersions which had been circulated to my great injury. I did not know at the time that you had any erroneous impressions about my conduct that day. No reflections of any kind had been reported to me as coming from you; nor did I intend my paper to contain any against you. Afterwards, however, I saw for the first time the endorsement with which you sent up my official report of the battle. In all probability you recollect that endorsement. It would be uncandid for me to deny that the sight of it mortified quite as much as it astonished me, and that it left me at loss whether to ask a Court of Enquiry or attempt privately to satisfy you that you were mistaken. I advised with General Ord on the subject during the winter, and lately with Gen. Burnside, both of whom seemed to think that I had only to state the facts to you to obtain a complete acquittal at your hands. And such is now my opinion. My confidence in my ability to satisfy you is equal to my confidence in your justice. If you have done me injury through a wrong impression, you can certainly have no motive for refusing to right me as far as you can. Your simple statement of satisfaction on the points would, as far as public opinion is concerned, relieve me entirely. I regret not having a copy of the endorsement alluded to by me, as it would be better to give it entire. Enough of it is reccollected, however, to answer the purpose. In it you say that at 11 o'clock in the forenoon I recieved your order to march to Pittsburg Landing; that, not arriving in time, you sent an officer to hurry me up: that still later you sent Capt. Rawlins to hurry me &c. Now, that statement that I recieved an order from you *to march to Pittsburg Landing*, is the key to the misunderstanding. Since you say you sent it to me, I have no doubt that you did. Having in your passage up the river from Savannah directed me to be ready to move at a moment's notice, you had a right to believe I would be ready, and that I would arrive at Pittsburg Landing, only six miles distance, in two hours from the time of recieving the order. Moreover I do not doubt that you calculated I would recieve the order at 11 o'clock. Then, with all these admissions on my part, evidently strengthening your impressions, why did I not march straight to Pittsburg Landing? What occasioned my delay until nightfall, the time I did arrive? The explanation I have to give in answer is very simple, and affords a solution without impinging your official statement or mine either: it is that, while you sent me an order to *march to Pittsburg Landing*, the order I actually recieved by the hand of Capt. Baxter at 11:30 A. M. directed me to *march and form a junction with the right of the army, without specifying that any change of its position had occurred.* I beg your attention while I now explain the feeling with which I recieved that order, and its effect. From the statements of Col. Knefler and Lts. Wane and Ross, you will see that before you passed up the river and communicated with me at Crump's Landing, I had taken measures to concentrate my division that it might be ready to move instantly. Their statements, coupled with Col. Strickland's, furnish proofs that I was both anxious to recieve your order to march and impatient at not recieving it. I feared you would defeat the rebels without giving me a chance to be present; and that fear was strengthened by Capt. Baxter's news, to the effect that you were repulsing them all along the line. About disaster he said not a word. It happened, also, that through the reports of my cavalry, I knew exactly where the right of the army had been resting, and that they could guide me by a direct road to the exact point. Besides that, I made no doubt that your intention was for me to proceed by the direct route instead of by Pittsburg Landing, as the latter would require a march of nearly ten miles before effecting the junction, while the former would require one of only six miles. Being anxious and impatient to get up, as stated, and never doubting that the fight was going all right, and fully of opinion that I would find the army on the ground it occupied in the morning when the attack begun, I moved off at exactly twelve o'clock with my cavalry in advance, proceeding by the directest road to the precise place indicated in the order Baxter gave me. From this statement of mine, taken in connection with those of the officers named, and which I enclose for the purpose of corroboration, it will be apparent, I think, that there was a mistake committed, and that the mistake was neither yours nor mine, but Capt. Baxter's, who, while liable for the consequences, is to be excused, since he took pains to convey the order correctly, as is proven by the fact that he attempted to reduce it to a memorandum, and gave it to me in that shape, though unsigned. It is greatly to be regretted, especially by myself, that the memorandum was not preserved. Its production would have made it unneccessary for me to send you the statements I feel it my duty to enclose herewith. That mistake is the solution I rely on. I believe it furnishes a satisfactory explanation of everything in the way of blame that has been attached to my movements that day: thus, it explains why I was so long in coming up; why it became neccessary to send officers to hurry me; why Capt. Rowley found me marching away from Pittsburg Landing when I should have been marching to it; why Capt. Rawlins at so late an hour in the afternoon found me so far from the field; finally, it explains why my command marched sixteen miles instead of six, consuming in the operation the precious hours of that bloody afternoon. I am quite sure, however, that, even in your opinion, my actions under that mistake justify my assertion that, far from intentionally disobeying, I was earnestly striving to execute literally as possible what I thought to be your order. In connection with the above, as a further explanation,

I beg leave to call your attention to one other point. If I had recieved an order to march to Pittsburg Landing, I could have had but two motives in disobeying it: one a wish to see you defeated and ruined, the other cowardice. I ask you to consider these in the light of the facts. First, the theory that I was governed by such base and guilty motives must presume that simultaneously with the reciept of your order I knew you were losing the battle: on this head Colonel Knefler's statement shows that the same messenger who brought the order informed us that you were gaining the battle. Next, if I had believed that you were being defeated, and that by moving up with my command I could have retrieved the day, yet hung back from a desire to see you overwhelmed, how easily I could have sat still, and based a justification on the lack of signature to the order? But I did not sit still: on the contrary, never questioning the validity of the order, I marched promptly to obey it. This fact ought, it seems to me, to be conclusive as to the disposition actuating me. As to the second motive, if I had known you were losing the battle, fear would have held me where I was or dictated a march to Savannah. Instead of either, I marched for the battle field. Consider also the direction of my march. I was actually going to a position which would have carried me, with a little column of five thousand men, alone and unsupported in the rear of ~~Bragg's~~ Beauregard's whole army. I appeal to you, General, was that a position which a coward would have voluntarily sought? Would the instincts of fear have pointed it ought as the place of safety? A few days ago I requested permission to visit Vicksburg, partly to observe your seige operations, now become very interesting, but chiefly to see you in person about this business. As the permission was refused me, I am compelled to adopt this less satisfactory mode of communication. I hope, however, it will be all I intend it—an exoneration of myself in your opinion. If it so proves, I further hope you will answer me to that effect." ADfS and copy, Wallace Papers, InHi. On July 18, Wallace wrote a protest to Secretary of War Edwin M. Stanton in which he requested a court of inquiry. ADfS (dated July 17), *ibid*. *O.R.*, I, x, part 1, 188–89. On Sept. 16, Wallace wrote to Stanton to request that action on the court of inquiry be suspended since Wallace hoped to settle the matter with USG. *Ibid*., pp. 189–90. See letter to Lewis Wallace, March 10, 1868.

1. Copy, Rowley Papers, IHi. *O.R.*, I, x, part 1, 174–77.
2. On March 30, 1863, USG wrote to Capt. Algernon S. Baxter, Chicago. "You will please send me Statement at your earliest possible convenience, of the time and circumstances at and under which you delivered my order to Maj Genl Lewis Wallace at Crump Landing, to move to the field of battle at Pittsburg Landing on the 6th day of April 1862 and the time as nearly as you can remember that I passed Crup Landing on my way to Pittsburg Landing   This is necessary to the answering of inquiries made by Genl. Wallace of Genl. Halleck." Copies, DLC-USG, V, 19, 30; DNA, RG 393, Dept. of the Tenn., Letters Sent. No reply by Baxter is known, but he described the orders in 1886. Robert Underwood Johnson and Clarence Clough Buel, eds., *Battles and Leaders of the Civil War* (New York, 1887), I, 607. On March 27, 1863, Maj. Theodore S. Bowers wrote to Maj. William R. Rowley asking for a statement of facts concerning Wallace's conduct on the first day of Shiloh. ALS, Rowley Papers, IHi. The statements of Rowley, Maj. Gen. James B. McPherson, and Lt. Col. John A. Rawlins are in *O.R.*, I, x, part 1, 178–88. See letter to Col. John C. Kelton, April 20, 1863.

To Maj. Gen. John A. McClernand

Millikens Bend, La April 13, 1863

MAJ GEN J. A MCCLERNAND
COMM'DG 13TH ARMY CORPS

I am having a complete map of the East bank of the Mississippi made for you, showing all the Streams and roads from Port Hudson to Vicksburg. I sent you a guide yesterday.

Instructions which I sent to your Headquarters and which you could not yet have received answers most of your note. It is not desirable that you should move in any direction from Grand Gulf, but remain under the protection of the Gunboats and free all the transportation for the concentration of troops at that place. The present plan if not changed by the movements of the enemy will be to hold Grand Gulf. Send a force to co,operate with Banks to effect the reduction of that place and then move upon Vicksburg either by reaching Big Black Bridge or Jackson Miss.

If you should not return to the Bend, I will endeavor to see you at Carthage before you leave.

Make every facility you can for moving troops from Smiths plantation to Carthage and for shipping them there   get all the ammunition you can through   Until water communication is open with Carthage there will be more difficulty in getting through this supply than any other. I have explained in a former communication that provisions will be sent by the transports that run the blockade

U. S. GRANT
Maj Gen.

Copies, DLC-USG, V, 19, 30; DNA, RG 393, Dept. of the Tenn., Letters Sent; *ibid.*, 13th Army Corps, Letters Received; Alcorn Collection, WyU.

On April 13, 1863, Maj. Gen. John A. McClernand, Milliken's Bend, wrote to USG. "I think the contemplated expedition ought not to take less, than three hundred rounds of ammunition per man—which would give, a total of six million, rounds, for a force of twenty thousand men. Deducting from this sum, sixty rounds per man to be carried by the soldier, the balance would be four million, eight hundred thousand rounds. To transport this amount of ammunition, thirty five miles, by land, from here, to Carthage, would require three days in the present miry state of the roads, and three hundred wagons. Not having more than one hundred and fifty wagons that can be made available, it would require eight days to transport it, including two for one return trip. To transport three hundred rounds, per gun, for ten six gun batteries of different calibre's, would require three days, and at least ninety wagons, making in all, for the transportation of, both, infantry, and artillery, ammunition, thirteen days, including four days, for two return trips. To obviate this delay, and to hasten the important movement in view, I would earnestly reccommend, that the estimated supply of ammunition for all arms, be sent down in one or more gunboats. If the gunboats cannot be made available, then I would reccommend, that a transport be laden with ammunition, and sent down. To avoid accidents, I would place, two barges filled with wetted baled cotton, so as to shield the bow, the exposed side, and the stern of the transport. And if notwithstanding, this precaution, the cotton should be ignited by the fire of the enemy, the transport might be cut loose, and thus enabled to escape destruction. . . . P. S. I would also enquire whether some of the transports intended to run the blockade might not be used to carry camp and Garrison Equippage, and thus further relieve the land movement across to Carthage, (over the worst possible roads since the recent rains,) of encumbrance and delay?" LS, DNA, RG 393, Dept. of the Tenn., Letters Received. *O.R.*, I, xxiv, part 3, 190.

To Maj. Gen. Cadwallader C. Washburn

Millikins Bend La.
April 13th 1863.

MAJ. GEN. C. C. WASHBURN
DEAR SIR:

Lieut. Col. Wilson of my Staff informs me that you are anxious to get an Asst. Adj. Gen. who is well qualified for the position. I am able to help you out if you are not already supplied with either of two men I now think of. One is Samuel Ferguson, private in the 11th Ia Vols. He has been a clerk in the A. Gen. Office now for eighteen months, First under Gen. C. F. Smith and since his death with me. He is thoroughly acquainted with the duties of the office, is a young man of unimpeachable character & habits and of strong good sence. I would infinitely prefer him myself for that office to the very great majority of those now filling it.

The second is Capt. Wm Wilkins A. A. Gen. to Brig. Gen. A. Williams of the Eastern Army and son of Judge Ross Wilkins of Detroit Michigan. He is a man of about 38 years of age and as fine tallent as any in his state. I have not seen much of him since /51 but first knew him in Mexico as a Lieut. and I believe Adj. of a Michigan Regt. He became fond of the service and tried hard to get in the regular Army for a number of years. In /55 when there was an increase in the Army he was tendered the position of Captain in a new regiment. But his practice as a lawyer had become too well established to quit it. On the breaking out of the rebellion he accepted the position of A. A. Gen. on the Staff of Gen. Williams. He now writes to me that he wants to get West and get promotion, or in other words wants to get with a Maj. Gen.

Of these two I do not know which to recommend the most highly. The first named my acquaintance with is present and with the latter it was years back.

Your letter relative to the move up the Ark. was received.[1] The move would be a most excellent one if it could be made without interfering with opperations here. My instructions nor the expectations of the public would admit of a diversion from the main object now. I think everything promises favorably here at this time.

Yours Truly
U. S. Grant
Maj. Gen

ALS, WHi.

1. On April 6, 1863, Maj. Gen. Cadwallader C. Washburn, Helena, wrote to USG. "Yesterday an intelligent young man accompanied by three ladies reported himself at my head quarters from Little Rock, which place he left on the 1st inst, having come through on a forged pass. He reports that Gen. Hindman had gone to the east side of the Miss river, and that Genl. E. Kirby Smith, & Holmes & Price were at Little Rock. He says that there are about 8,000 troops at Little Rock and four or five thousand at Pine bluffs, that they were in a most wretched condition until Price came, since which time matters have much improved, and the deserters from the army are rapidly returning, Gen. Price having issued a proclamation stating that all deserters would be pardoned if they immediately returned. He says that it was understood at Little Rock that Price was

soon to make a move towards Missouri—He says that several small boats are plying on the Arkansas and that quite a large amount of Supplies such as corn & pork are now at Little Rock. That a few days before he left, the Steamer Bracelet went down to the 'Post of Ark' and fished up from a well in which it was thrown by our troops, a large siege gun, & brought it to Little Rock. That there are no ~~siege~~ fortifications at Little Rock or Pine bluffs, but that the rebels are fortifying a Bluff between Pine Bluff & Little Rock. He further says that the Arkansas river is still very high, & the largest class of boats can reach Little Rock. He says that there are a large number of Union citizens at Little Rock, and that they were greviously disappointed that our troops did not go there after taking the 'Old Post—' To day two ladies were brought to my head quarters who left Camden on the Washita River nine days ago. One of them is a Connecticut lady and is trying to get back to that state. She informed me that Genl. Price came to Camden on a steamer one week before she left, & proceeded to Little Rock. He had a good many soldiers with him, & many steam Boat loads had come up the Washita as far as Camden since then & proceeded to Little Rock to join him. She also said that the deserters were flocking to his standard in great numbers, & that they ~~soldiers~~ worshipped him. That at Little Rock she was told that Price would move towards Missouri very soon. Camden is a place of nearly 4000 inhabitants and has a foundry where the rebels are making Cannon & cannon balls constantly, and that at this time boats of a pretty large size can go there. I give you this information for what it is worth. To disperse this army now at Little Rock & Pine Bluff would be but a small job, but if Smith & Price are allowed to reorganise it, it may give us a good deal of trouble hereafter." ALS, DNA, RG 94, War Records Office, Dept. of the Mo.

To Brig. Gen. Lorenzo Thomas

Head Quarters, Dept of the Tenn.
Milliken's Bend, La. April 14, 1863.

BRIG. GENL. L. THOMAS
ADJUTANT GENERAL, OF THE ARMY,
WASHINGTON D. C.
GENL:

I have the honor to acknowledge the receipt of the communication of Col. Silas Noble of the 2nd Regt Ills. Cavalry to the Hon. Owen Lovejoy, Member of Congress from Illinois of date, Chicago, Ills. Jany 26th 1863. and referred to me by your order of date Febry 28th 1863. relative to my action toward him while he was subject to my orders,[1] and for your information to respectfully submit the following statement.

The 2nd Regt Illinois Cavalry, Col. Silas Noble, Commd'g. reported to me at Cairo, Ills. while I was in command of the District of South East Missouri in the fall of 1862, and detachments of it were sent to Paducah, Ky. Caledonia and Metropolis, Ills. and part of it stationed at Cairo, Ills. and its dependencies. Col. Noble remained in the immediate command of that portion of his regiment remaining at Cairo, and in my official and social intercourse I found him an excellent gentleman. From Cairo he was ordered to Paducah, Ky. and assumed the command of his Regiment there. Brig Genl (late Major Genl) C. F. Smith in command of Paducah reported the name of Col. Silas Noble, for incompetency, for examination before a Board of Examiners convened by order of Major Genl. Halleck, Commdg. the Dept of the Missouri, at Cairo, Ills. and ordered to Paducah, Ky. But the movement of the expedition against Forts Henry and Donelson broke up the Board before his examination. Although only two companies of said regiment accompanied said expedition, Col. Noble was ordered by Genl. Smith to go in command of them for the reason that if he was left with the main body of his Regiment at Paducah, as the ranking Officer he would be entitled to the command of the Post, a position Genl. Smith deemed him unfit to fill. After the fall of Fort Donelson, on his own application, I permitted him to return to Paducah. When Genl. Sherman moved from Paducah to join the expedition up the Tennessee River in March. 1862. Col. Noble was left in command of that Post, it having been previously transferred from my command. I knew no more of him officially until the District of West Tennessee was extended by order of Major Genl. Halleck. to take in the Districts of Cairo and Miss. which again placed Col. Noble under my orders; Soon after a petition was forwarded to me direct from the Company Officers of his regiment asking for a board of examiners to examine and inquire into the qualifications and fitness for their positions, of all the Field Officers of said Regiment, which petition was returned to be forwarded through the proper Military channel. Sometime afterwards several of the company officers and one of the Field Officers of said Regiment called my attention to the fact of such a petition having been sent me and that nothing had been heard of it, and when informed of the direction it had taken they said Col. Noble would never permit it to pass through him for it was expressly with a view to his examination the board was asked, that all the Field Officers were named in it for the reason that while they knew and felt his incompetency for the position he held, they regarded him as a loyal and patriotic gentleman and desired to save his feelings. I thereupon ordered a Board of Examiners to meet at Bolivar, Tenn. in pursuance of Special Orders, No 230. issued from Headquarters, District of West. Tennessee, a copy of which is herewith enclosed, and sent in his name with the names of other other Officers equally high in rank, for examination before said Board. Immediately after the convening of said Board he applied for a leave of absence which was not granted him. But before his case was reached for examination the movement of my forces against the enemy on the Tallahatchie again broke up the Board of Examiners. In this latter move so much depended upon the Cavalry, Col Noble was the ranking Officer, and being satisfied of his inefficiency, I deemed it my duty to remove him to some point where his rank would not interfere with the proper command of it. and accordingly ordered him to Paducah, Ky. a Post I supposed perfectly secure. He seemed at the time and I have no doubt was well pleased with his orders. He had not been long in the command of Paducah until serious complaints came from there of his officious interference in matters over which the civil authorities had jurisdiction, and to avoid further complaints I published an order of which the enclosed is a copy.[2] This however had not the desired effect and being now fully satisfied that he was as unfit to command a Post as he was incompetent to command his Regimen[t] in the field, I ordered him on Recruiting Service to the State of Illinois in which service I hoped, from his acquaintance and influence he might be able to do something in the line of a Soldier, for his country. On the 31st of Dec. 1862. I received an application from several of the Officers of his Regiment asking that he might be dismissed the service for incompetency, inefficiency and indolence which application I approved and forwarded to Headquarters of the Army, Washington, D. C.[3] Before reading the communication of Col. Noble to the Hon. Owen Lovejoy I did not know what were his politics. In the selection of my Staff, and in the recommendation of officers of my command for promotion it has been with a view to their competency and without reference to their present or previous party politics.

> I have the honor to be, Genl,
> Very Respectfully.
> Your Ob't. Servant.
> U. S. GRANT
> Major Genl. Commdg.

LS, DNA, RG 94, Vol. Service Division, N756 (vs) 1862.
　　On April 18, 1863, USG endorsed a letter of April 15 of Col. John J. Mudd, 2nd Ill. Cav. "Respectfully forwarded to Head Quarters of the Army, Washington D. C., for further information information in case of Colonel S Noble, of the 2nd Ill. Cav Vols." Copies, DLC-USG, V, 25; DNA, RG 393, Dept. of the Tenn., Endorsements.

　　1. On Jan. 26, Col. Silas Noble, Chicago, wrote to U.S. Representative Owen Lovejoy of Ill. "I am, as I suppose you remember, Colonel of the Second Illinois Cavalry—the oldest Cavalry Colonel in service from our State. As I ranked all the cavalry officers there, I was Acting Chief of Cavalry at Grand Junction, in Tenn., near the Mississippi state line, for some time. When Genl Grant came there, Col Dickey, of Ottawa, of the 9th Ills Cavalry, came with him. Col Dickey asked me to concede rank to him so that he might be Chief of Cavalry. This of course I would not do. The next day I received an order from Genl Grant to leave my Regiment and go to Paducah and take charge of that Post, which of course I did. I had commanded there before, and the Secesh had no love for me. They charged me with being a negro stealer, a black abolitionist, &c. They got one or two men who claim to be Union to go to Genl Grant and ask my removal. They accomplished their purpose, and I received orders to report at Springfield on recruiting service. The real Union men of Paducah immediately sent a man on to Washington to see the President and request that I be reinstated. The President told him that if the Union men would get up a petition that I be reinstated and send it to him, he would forward it to Genl Grant with a recommendation that I be put back in command of the Post. A delegation has also gone to Genl Grant to ask the same thing. The result of that mission I have not heard. I learn from one of my Captains, a man of unquestionable truth and veracity, that Genl Grant asked a disaffected officer in my Regiment to get the officers of the Regiment to sign a paper to have me dismissed from the service—for what cause I have never learned. Only five of my twelve companies were with Genl Grant then, and in these are all the disaffected officers of the Regiment. The sole cause of this disaffection, so far as I know, was failure to be promoted. I could not promote all, and I

selected for promotion those I believed most deserving. My Lieut Col, Quincy McNeil, of Rock Island, has resigned. John J. Mudd, the First Major of the Regiment will be McNeil's successor, I suppose. He is an exceedingly ambitious man, and wishes to be Colonel of the Regiment, and will be so if I am got out of the way. He has Genl Grant's ear, and acts constantly as a common informer. Genl Grant does not hesitate to talk about me before everybody—my officers included —in such a manner as is calculated to destroy my reputation as an officer and as a man of common sense. Ever since I have been under him he has spared no pains to annoy me. I do not care so much about his opinion of me, for I know just what it is worth, and the reason of it; but when he so far comes down from the position he occupies as the commanding General of a great and victorious army, as to encourage disaffection among the officers of a Regiment, he must, it seems to me, lower himself in the estimation of all patriots. By such course he could seriously affect the harmony and efficiency of any Regiment in his command. The position I occupy as the oldest Cavalry officer from our state is rather an important one. It should bring me upon the staff of Genl Grant, or very near him. I know he does not desire this, nor do I. I am a strong and earnest Republican. He has none such about him, and I think he does not wish to have any. I have not had my Regiment together since I left the state, nor have I had a separate command for an hour; but, on the contrary, Genl Grant has kept me where I could make no reputation, and where I could have no chance to prove whether I have any capacity as a military man. About my military capacity I have nothing to say, for I have never had a military education; but I claim that I can command a military Post as well as anybody, and that I am possessed of common sense. My commission was voluntarily tendered to me by our state authorities. I never intimated that I desired it, and hesitated long before I would consent to accept it. My desire to do my whole duty to my country influenced me, and I finally entered the service, anxious to do some good, and willing to make any and every sacrifice for the Administration and my country. I am yet willing to do anything in my power to uphold and support the Government; and, now, if I can no longer do any good in the army, I am willing to step aside and let some other man take my place. I have already proposed to Gov Yates, Dubois, and others, that I would resign, but they object to my doing so, and insist upon my remaining in service. If I can do anything for *our* cause, and the cause of humanity and universal liberty, by retaining my connection with the army, I should like to do so; but I have no disposition to do so if I am to be treated worse than a traitor, and constantly insulted by a man who has no claims in patriotism, moral principle, or intellectual endowments, over me—in a word, I don't propose to remain and be treated as I have been, so far, by Genl Grant. During my whole life, before going into the army, I have been treated as a man and a gentleman. I hear that Genl Grant recommends that I be dismissed from the service, but I do not learn that any charges have ever been made against me. I shall be sorry to leave my Regiment, for it is entitled to a position it cannot have under any other officer. It is under good discipline, is well armed and mounted, and has always done its full duty whether in squads or in battalions. This gives it the right to an honorable position in the service. But, more than this, it is the oldest Cavalry Regiment from the state—the First, Col Marshall, having been mustered out of service more than a year ago. If I leave it, and another Colonel is appointed, it will, of course, be ranked by nearly every other Regiment in the service. I desire to save my men in this respect, if I can. Now, if my friends feel any interest in this matter, and will see that I and my

Regiment have justice done us, I will stay in the service and do my duty—as I ever have done—to my country and the men under my command. If not, I will resign and go home to my business—which certainly requires my attention, and to the friends who know I have done my duty faithfully and honestly, and understand the motives that have influenced me in all this matter." ALS, *ibid.*, RG 94, Vol. Service Division, N756 (vs) 1862. On Feb. 28, Maj. Thomas M. Vincent, AGO, endorsed this letter. "Respectfully referred to Major General Grant, Comdg Dept of the Tennessee" AES, *ibid.*

On Jan. 6, Noble, Paducah, wrote to U.S. Senator Lyman Trumbull of Ill. that USG was unduly influenced by Maj. Gen. John A. Logan and Col. T. Lyle Dickey. "There is not, among all his Generals, that I know of, one single leading Republican." ALS, DLC-Lyman Trumbull. On Jan. 24, Noble, Chicago, wrote to U.S. Representative Elihu B. Washburne of Ill. another letter strongly critical of USG. ALS, DLC-Elihu B. Washburne.

2. On Dec. 7, 1862, Lt. Col. John A. Rawlins issued Special Field Orders No. 16. "Whereas the State of Kentucky has fulfilled all the requirments of the constitution of the United States and of the laws of Congress, by choosing Union Men to fill all officies of State both for enacting and executing her laws, the Military Authorities within this Department and in the State of Kentucky are prohibited from any interference in such execution. The Military cannot be used in enforcing the civil authority of the state, except to surpres riot and mob resistance to law, but in no case will it be permitted to interfere with its execution. All Civil Authority that can be legally executed in the absence of Military Authority will be permitted at Military Posts." DS, DNA, RG 94, Dept. of the Tenn., Orders and Special Orders; copies, *ibid.*, Vol. Service Division, N756 (vs) 1862; *ibid.*, RG 393, Dept. of the Tenn., Special Orders; *ibid.*, General and Special Orders; DLC-USG, V, 26, 27, 91.

3. See letter to Maj. John J. Mudd, Dec. 31, 1862. On March 18, Noble wrote to President Abraham Lincoln. "If you will revoke the order dismissing me from the service I will go to the Regt settle up my business & resign   I must go there to settle my accts & get my horses & other things I left there—I will feel much obliged if you will do so—" ALS, DLC-Robert T. Lincoln. On March 23, Lincoln wrote to Secretary of War Edwin M. Stanton asking that Noble be appointed an additional paymaster. Lincoln, *Works* (*Supplement*), p. 183. On the same day, Noble wrote to Lincoln declining the appointment. LS, DLC-Robert T. Lincoln.

To Brig. Gen. Lorenzo Thomas

Head Quarters, Dept. of the Ten.
Millikins Bend La. Apl. 14th/63

Adj. of the Army,
Washington D. C.
Sir:

Enclosed I send you copy of a telegraphic dispatch from J. T.

Bolinger of Paducah Ky.[1] to Green Adams[2] or Hon. S. L. Casey,[3] Washington City, intercepted by the opperater at Cairo and sent to me. I would be pleased to have this dispatch laid before the President and Sec. of War.

The regiment which Col. Daugherty belongs to is not in my department and I do not know by what authority he is at Paducah. I have relieved him from command and ordered him to join his regiment.[4]

Of the character of the parties named in this dispatch, or their particular interests, I know nothing except by hearsay. Trimble[5] was the Union Candidate two years ago in that Dist. for Congress but I have heard him discribed as an unscrupulous trader who would as leafe supply munitions of war to the enemy as to the Government if the proffit was a little greater. I do not even know the occupation of Duke[6] or his standing with his neighbors. Bolingers character is represented to me as being even more unscrupulous than Trimbles and his loyalty much more doubtful. I am not aware that I ever saw the man.

This dispatch evidently discloses the fact that Daugherty is a tool in the hands of Bolinger & Co. and they must keep him there for a purpose.[7] I will endeavor to place a man in command at Paducah who can be used neither by Bolinger Casey & Co. or Trimble, Duke & Co. now that I learn such companies exist.

> Very respectfully
> your obt. svt.
> U. S. GRANT
> Maj. Gen

ALS, DNA, RG 108, Letters Received.

1. The telegram was dated April 2, 1863. "I got here last night and greatly to my surprise found bills had been struck calling a District Convention. I suppressed it for a time at least, until Casey could get things fixed up at Washington and then return home at once. We must have our policy foreshadowed before a convention is held. This Department must at once be taken from under Genl Grant. His every act has been in sympathy with Trimble, Duke & Co. Make Casey's District a seperate one and give Col. Dougherty full control over it. Capt. Harry Bartling Co. "I," 2nd Ills. Cavalry who has been here for six months, a great favorite with Casey's friends, has been ordered off to Vicksburg. Have an

order to have him transferred back to this Department immediately. I wrote you at length yesterday. Do your part and we will be certain to do ours." Copies, *ibid.*; *ibid.*, RG 393, Dept. of Ky., Letters Received; *ibid.*, Dept. of the Tenn., Hd. Qrs. Correspondence; DLC-USG, V, 5, 8, 24, 94. For a possible clue to USG's hostility to J. T. Bollinger, see Lincoln, *Works* (*Supplement*), p. 114.

2. Green Adams, born in Barbourville, Ky., in 1812, was a Whig lawyer-politician who served as U.S. Representative (1847–49, 1859–61), the second time for the American Party. During most of the Civil War he was Treasury Dept. Auditor for the Post Office Dept.

3. Samuel L. Casey, born in Union County, Ky., in 1821, served in the Ky. House of Representatives (1860–62) and as U.S. Representative (1862–63). He then engaged in southern trade, facilitated by his status as a former congressman and his relationship with James F. Casey, USG's brother-in-law. See letter to William H. H. Taylor, Oct. 6, 1863.

4. On March 13, USG had endorsed a letter of Capt. Samuel Johnson, 22nd Ill., reporting Col. Henry Dougherty absent without leave. "Respectfully returned to Head Quarters of the Army. I never knew by what authority Col. Daugherty was in command at Paducah, but supposed the authority was derived from the War Department. Col. Daugherty is a gallant officer who has lost a leg in the service of his country. He is well able to command a Post and may not be able to command a Regiment in the field." Copies, DLC-USG, V, 25; DNA, RG 393, Dept. of the Tenn., Endorsements. On April 10, Lt. Col. John A. Rawlins issued Special Orders No. 100 ordering Dougherty to report to Maj. Gen. William S. Rosecrans for duty with his regt. Copies, DLC-USG, V, 26, 27; DNA, RG 393, Dept. of the Tenn., Special Orders.

5. Lawrence S. Trimble, born in Fleming County, Ky., in 1825, practiced law in Paducah, served as judge (1856–60) and as president of the New Orleans and Ohio Railroad Co. (1860–65). Unsuccessful in his campaign for election to Congress in 1863, he was elected to the three succeeding Congresses.

6. For Thomas A. Duke of Paducah, unsuccessful candidate for Congress in 1863, see Duke to Abraham Lincoln, July 6, 1863, ALS, DLC-Robert T. Lincoln.

7. On April 14, Dougherty wrote to USG. "This will introduce to you Mr. Thomas Redd, a Loyal man of this city. He visits you on business of vital importance to the Union Men of this ~~County~~ community Any thing he may communicate I can vouch for as true." ALS, *ibid.*, RG 94, War Records Office, Dept. of the Mo. On April 26, Rawlins endorsed this letter. "Respectfully returned to Maj Gen. S. A. Hurlbut, comdg 16th Army Corps who will take immediate steps to ascertain the true condition of affairs at Paducah, and other portions of Kentucky in his command and afford to the Union men of that state all the protection possible consistent with the interest of the service" ES, *ibid*. On May 13, Maj. Gen. Stephen A. Hurlbut wrote to Lt. Col. William H. Thurston, inspector gen., 16th Army Corps, ordering him to Paducah. "On arriving at Paducah you will examine fully into the conduct of Col Henry Dougherty while commander of that Post, especially in relation to his connection with any movements looking toward future elections to office in the District, and ascertain whether the weight and influence of his official position has been lent to any particular candidates or citizens. Also whether or not he has been connected with any attempt at insubordination in seeking the removal of the General Commanding Department or any other conduct of like nature. . . ." Copy, *ibid.*, RG 393, 16th Army Corps, Letters Sent. In the meantime, Hurlbut had received a telegram of April 30 from Brig. Gen.

Alexander Asboth, Columbus, Ky., transmitting a telegram from Col. James S. Martin, 111th Ill., commanding at Paducah, discussing efforts to detach Paducah from USG's dept. and restore Dougherty to command. Telegram received, *ibid.*, Dept. of the Tenn., Letters Received. On April 18, Dougherty wrote to USG. "From what I daily see and hear in, and about this Post, I feel it my duty—in justice to you, the loyal men of Ky.,—our cause and myself to write you a few lines. Genl. the Courts here are corrupt, the Authorities in many instances miserable Traitors: while the Loyalests are ground down by an insufferable injustice perpetrated against them continually. I have looked on often without the power to interfere when I felt that was my duty to do so. Among other tricksters we have to contend with here, stands conspicuous our all, (the more noted than honest), Dr. Duke. This man has been, and is active in the circulation of reports very detrimental to your reputation. He told me with great gusto that you told him to write any thing ~~you~~ he desired for your Field Order No. 16.),—leaving the Negro out and that you would sign it. He tells it to great effect in about these words— viz. 'Genl. Grant just told me to set down and write any thing I desired   He did not care a damn what it was so I left the Negro out. And—that he would sign it.' He then goes on to boast that he is the '*Author* of Genl. Grants Special Field Order No. 16' (placing the civil authority in the ascendency.) This man is known to be a traitor under the cover of that eternal song—'Constitution.' Dr. Duke swears he will go to Genl Grant and have me removed a man ordered to the Command of this Post who will work to suit him and his party. As to this Genl. all I can say is,—that I have aimed to do my duty and I well know that I could not do this here. and be upheld by the designing enemies of our cause. This same Duke swears that had Col Noble removed twice; that he can have you do his bidding   He is surely a dangerous man; and altho' the Loyal men here feel that he imposed upon you by letters and false representations yet they feel that if they present their case to you, you will by quick to render them that aid which they most need. I am sure Genl. that none of the men whose names are signed to the petition which will be handed you by Mr _____ are aspiring to Office, or even desire Office. I am sure further that their representations are correct: And when you see the state of things here in this part of your department—and learn that Duke, and a class of such men are not only seeking office, but are trying to break down every barrier in the way of their treasonable plots and crimes,—I say when these things are shown to you as we see them here, I doubt not that you will do all in your power to the aid and support of these men whom I know to be good Loyal, unconditional Union men. As to their humble, poor and perhaps improper petition all I will say is that I am sure it was gotten up by that sincerity of purpose such the true patriot always feels in such times, as they are now passing through. And all they ask, or all that I ask for them is only justice. I ask nothing for myself, still in view of the coming election, and the aims of the *secesh*—in this election, I am sure that a change of Commandant at this post, until after the election would be a death blow to the hopes of the Loyalests,   The main object of the petitioners, is to have none but unconditional, uncompromising and unyielding men elected to any office of honor, trust or profit; and also for power sufficiently delegated to the local Commander of this part of Ky.—in your command to relieve our Rebel civil officers of their present positions; from these considerations: (first,) some of theire terms of office do not expire for six years and none of them in less than two. Second there is at least two millions of dollars worth of property here subject to confiscation, and if the present civil officers are permitted to remain in power, it will be impossible for the Government to secure its rights—they are already at work covering up the property of Rebels subject to confiscation by Act of Congress—for they are in arms against the United states. I have written much more than I designed, still many pages might be written on this subject: so Genl. Hoping you will favarably consider this letter and your humble petitioners'' ALS, *ibid.*, RG 94, War Records Office, Dept. of the Mo.

On May 2, Dougherty wrote to USG at length, repeating and expanding his denunciation of Duke. Copy, *ibid.*, RG 393, 16th Army Corps, Letters Received. Dougherty enclosed a copy of a letter of April 29 from Bollinger to USG. "I have learned that Col. Dougherty has been releived from Command of this post, in consequence of a Telegraphic Despatch sent from here to Washington, by me, to the Hon. Mr. Casey, & Judge Adams of Kentucky. The Telegram was sent under the following circumstances, viz. When at Louisville on the 18th of March, attending the Union Convention, I met the above named gentlemen with the ballance of the delegates from this Congressional District in Caucus. The policy for our district was discussed and it was agreed that this district should all be placed under the same command, from the reasons that last summer before our election took place we had very great confusion—from the fact that different policy was pursued in each command, and Traitors elected to office. The elections to come off next August, are much more important. A. Governer, and Representative for Ky to be elected also Members to Congress, and as pretended Union who have at one time been known as Union men, are now showing their true positions. And as such men are to be used as tools for Traitors, to vote for and put in office, Union men were anxious that a policy should be adopted, that would give us Union men for all offices to be filled, and more especially a Member of Congress who would vote any amount of money and any number of men to carry on the war; and who would throw no obsticles in the way. I had learned that the entire state of Kentucky would be placed under one command. Soon after reaching home the Union men began to complain at Mr Casey because it was not done, and talked of holding a convention to put on the track some other man   I felt that this was unjust to Mr Casey who had given his whole influence to carry on the war, and wishing him to do something to satesfy his constituency and also to change affairs in this district which every Union man desired. Under thise and many other considerations I hurriedly wrote out the despatch, and sent it off. I stated to Col. D. that I wished to send a Telegram to Washington, to Mr. Casey in regard to his election,   I did not think at the time that there was any thing wrong about it, or any thing that would be offensive to any one, as I knew none was interested. My friends all will bear witness to the fact, that I never spoke of you in any other way than respectfully. But have beleived that you have been deceived by false representations of Duke and judge Trimble, who at the beginning of the War were regarded as Union men, But are not now. Duke was elected to the state senate by Rebel votes & his associations and votes while at Frankfort were with Traitors,   His associations here are with Traitors. And I now say that not a single Union man in Paducah will indorce him as a Union man. He cannot get a single Union vote in this District for Congress, and today was on the street, denouncing the Government much to the delight of a crowd of secesh. Judge Trimble made a speech ten days ago in my town (Mayfield) and for 1½ hours abused the President and war policy, and had no word of abuse for Traitors. I called him out and asked him if he would vote men & money to carry on the war against Traitors? His answer was: not a man or dollar. These are the

men who were anxious for your Order No. 16. to be issued for the purpose of
making friends with Traitors, by getting over 100 negroes out of the lines some
belonging to Traitors, and some of them to men in the Southern Army. Also to
prevent the military authorities from punnishing traitor officers who were useing
their Offices to oppose Union men, by summonsing all Traitors to act as Grand
Jurors. This order was also intended by these Traitors to plaice one or the other
in Congress by preventing the Union men from calling on the Military for assistance. Dr. Duke claims the credit for having had Col. Noble removed. If he did
he did not do it by telling the truth, and the Union men in this district will sustain
me in what I say if you will have the matter investigated. Col. Dougherty came
here with predjudice against Union men, but he soon found out who were true
friends to the Govt., and who were the enemies of the same, and has given Union
men all the prevelages over Traitors that he could. Every Union man here is for
Col. Dougherty and would be glad to see him restored, as all know that he is
above intrigue against any superior officer: and in case of Telegram I sent; after
I sent it, I went home to Mayfield and when the telegram came asking that Col.
Dougherty indorse it: he done so from the fact the he knew that I was a union
man and did not think any thing was wrong in it. If you will investigate the
matter you will find that every true Union man in this district will indorse me,
The Union men in my County indorsed me last summer by electing me County
Clerk. I am the only man in the district that denounced Traitors in the canvass   I
am the first Union man in Kentucky that was Robbed or imprisoned by Rebels.
I hate them, I despise them, I denounce them and will continue to do so as long
as I live. I am the must Ultra Union man in the District, and ~~suffered~~ am hated
more than any Union man in the district, and I defy any man to show how I have
ever said or done any thing against my country. Yet men and Federal Officers
who today are bording with traitors, have tried to make the impression that I am
untrue to the Government. There cannot be found in Paducah a man, Traitor, or
Union who will not say on oath that my Union sentiments are above suspicion.
I have written this letter in justice to Col. Dougherty. If any wrong was done I
alone have done it in my anxiety to have traitors defeated and a man sent to
Congress from this District who would sustain the War." Copies, *ibid.*; *ibid.*,
Dept. of Ky., Letters Received; McClernand Papers, IHi. Dougherty also enclosed in his letter of May 2 a petition of April 9 addressed to USG. "We the
undersigned, a portion of the *unconditional* and *uncompromising Union* men of
Paducah and surrounding country embraced in your command in this state, most
humbly beg the privilege—of respectfully representing to you—that false statements were—used to induce your Special Field Order No. 16.—which sais.
'Whereas, the State of Kentucky has fulfilled all the requirements of the Constitution of the United States, and of the laws of Congress, by choosing Union men
to fill all offices of State, both for enacting and executing the laws, the military
authority within this Department, and in the state of Kentucky, are prohibited
from any interference in such execution.' Now Genl. allow us most respectfully,
yet in candid—and unquallified terms, to state that the contrary is true. Sir this
County (McCracken), our Sherriff, County Clerk, Circut Court Clerk, County
Judge, County Attorney, Mayor of the city Police Judge and all minor offices
with but one or two exceptions are filled with men who have been—and are now
disaffected—men of Rebel sentiments some of whom have been identified with
the Rebellion, and all of whom are now Revel sympathizers. Marshall, Hickman,
—and we might say the other Counties in Ky., under your control—stand in the

same category,—And as matters now stand, there is continual conflict ~~with~~ between the civil and Military in this part of the Department. The civil resisting and evading all orders issued by the Military; therefore in order to forward peace and Harmony in this part of the state,—(in your command;) and that truely loyal men may not be imposed upon any longer by the mockery of civil law in this part of the country—and that they find protection from harm, and redress to repeeted wrongs, in the Military Authority which they have, and ever will gladly support —We do each, and all most earnestly and humbly pray that you will *Countermand* your special field order No. 16.—restoring the civil authority. There are other greater reasons—Genl than those stated above, for our interest, and earnest prayer in this matter, which we will give in as few words as passible. Our general elections comes off in August next, when we elect Governor, Lieut. Gov., Attst. Genl., Congressman, Legislators—&c.   if some thing is not done for the Union men of Ky., especially this part of the state, ~~and~~ west of the Tennessee River in your command—all the offices will be filled ~~with~~ by secessionests and those who sympathize with the Rebels—infact we already have candidates for the various offices; whom we regard as Traitors; While the only hope, or remedy we have in the premises—is the restoration of the Military authority. So far at least as the election is concerned: we would respectfully suggest that you order that no man within your command—shall stand for office, vote, trade, carry on commerce —until they subscribe to some such oath as the following *viz.* 'I do swear solemnly and willingly—that I will maintain, support and defend the Constitution and the Government of the United States against all enemies *foreign* or domestic—and further that I will vote for no man for office, or sustain any man in office—who is not in favor of appropriating men and money, until this present causless rebellion is put down, and peace and union reestablished so help me God.' We would not wish to be understood as dictating the policy you should pursue: but only to let you know our wants, and what our grievance are: and will be if the Rebels succeed in carying the elections coming on. We also beg leave to state that we are aware that you were actuated by the best of motives, when you issued your Field Order No. 16. We know the men who misrepresented the states of affairs in your command in Ky., and we will now state they are not regarded as Union men at home where they are best known. In evedence of the facts stated above, we will respectfully refer you to documents from our Post. Commander Col. Dougherty, accompanying this petition all of which is humbly and most respectfully submitted to your careful consideration beleiving, and hoping you will do something for the Union men of Ky in this part of your Command." DS, DNA, RG 393, 16th Army Corps, Letters Received.

To Maj. Gen. Stephen A. Hurlbut

Head Quarters, Dept. of the Ten.
Millikins Bend, La. Apl. 14th 1863,
MAJ. GEN. S. A. HURLBUT,
COMD.G 16TH ARMY CORPS,
GEN.

Enclosed I send you copy of a dispatch intercepted by the opperator at Cairo and sent to me.

This discloses the fact that there are two parties, Trimble Duke & Co, on the one side, and Bolinger Casey & Co. on the other, each striving for the ascendency and each endeavoring to gain it through their influance with the commanding officer. I know nothing of the merits of these two parties but have heard Trimble and Bolinger discribed as unscrupulous persons who did not set half the value upon the restoration of the Union they do upon the accomplishment of their own ambitious ends. I know nothing about this however myself nor what their seperate interests may be. But I want you to place a commanding officer at Paducah who will do his duty irrespective of influance from outsiders.

Very respectfully
U. S. GRANT
Maj. Gen. Com

ALS, MH. See preceding letter.

To Maj. Gen. James B. McPherson

Millikens Bend, La. April 14 1863
MAJ GEN J B MCPHERSON
COMM'DG 17TH ARMY CORPS

Has any arrangements been made to bring Quimby's Division

here? I naturally supposed that the transports which brought him out of the Pass would bring him down here. If nothing has been done, direct him to stop all boats except Mail Boats going up until he gets enough to bring him down.

Commence moving one Division of your command to this place. Boats to move the entire Division cannot be sent all at once, but let the troops come on what boats there are and the same boats can return for the balance. The boats that takes this can be sent directly on for Quimby to be released and go North if Quimby does not require it.

U. S. GRANT
Maj Gen.

Copies, DLC-USG, V, 19, 30; DNA, RG 393, Dept. of the Tenn., Letters Sent.

To Brig. Gen. Lorenzo Thomas

Head Quarters Dept. of the Tennessee
Millikens Bend, La. April 15th 1863.

BRIG. GENERAL L. THOMAS.
ADJUTANT GENERAL OF THE ARMY.
GENERAL.

On the 5th Inst I detached 1st Lieut Kilburn Knox, 13th U. S. Infantry, from his Regement with orders to report to Major General James B McPherson, commanding 17th Army Corps, for assignment to duty as asst. Commissary of Musters of the 3rd Division, Army of the Tennessee, but having no Officer in his Army Corps available for duty as Commissary of musters for the Corps, Major General McPherson assigned him as Corps Commissary of Musters, Major Daniel Chase, of the 13th U. S. Infantry, who is well advanced in years, is now available for the latter position, but as the order of detail of Lieut. Knox has gone forward to Washington he cannot be relieved without authority from your office. I would therefore respectfully ask that such authority be granted so that Lieut Knox can be detailed as Assistant Commissary of Musters for said 3rd Division and Major Chase as Commissary of Musters for the 17th Army Corps.

There are so few officers in this Department available for the Commissary and Asst. Commissaries of Musters, under General Orders Number 48, from your office, that every one who can possibly be spared from his command has to be detailed on such duty. I hope however to get along without requiring them to be sent me from other commands.

> I am, very Respectfully
> Your obt Servant
> U. S. GRANT
> Major General.

LS, DNA, RG 94, Letters Received. On April 16, 1863, Brig. Gen. Lorenzo Thomas, Milliken's Bend, wrote to USG. "As requested by your letter of yesterday's date, you are authorized to assign Major D. Chase, 13th Regt. of Infty., as Commissary of Musters of the 17th Army Corps, and 1st Lieut. K. Knox, 13th Regt. of Infty., as Asst. Commissary of Musters of the 3d Division, Army of the Tennessee." LS, *ibid.*

On April 7, Maj. Thomas M. Vincent, AGO, wrote to USG about the importance of remedying "the deficiency of officers for mustering duty . . ." Copies, DLC-USG, V, 105; DNA, RG 393, Military Div. of the Miss., War Dept. Correspondence.

To Maj. Gen. John A. McClernand

Milliken's Bend, La. April 15 1863

MAJ GEN. J A. McCLERNAND.
COMM'DG 13TH ARMY CORPS

Admiral Porter informs me that he can take in each of his vessels about 250 Infantry. This will enable you to take about one Division in addition to what the transportation sent around will take. There has been great delay and neglect in the Quarter masters Department, in getting ready the barges and the reports of progress I have recieved I find on a personal inspection have not been realized. There is not more than five barges ready to carry artillery on. In addition to this you will have about three suitable for transporting Infantry.

In loading troops on barges to be towed by Steamers great caution should be infused into the men to keep cool and to avoid getting too much on one side or in other words to keep the barges trimmed.

It may possible be that these vessels will not run the blockade to night. If they do not they will go to-morrow night certain

U. S. GRANT
Maj Gen.

Copies, DLC-USG, V, 19, 30; DNA, RG 393, Dept. of the Tenn., Letters Sent; *ibid.*, 13th Army Corps, Letters Received; Alcorn Collection, WyU. *O.R.*, I, xxiv, part 3, 194; *O.R.* (Navy), I, xxiv, 565.

On April 14, 1863, USG had written to Maj. Gen. John A. McClernand. "The Gunboat fleet and transports will run the blockade to-night. Should they get through securely you will want to concentrate your forces at Smith Plantation as rapidly as possible" Copies, DLC-USG, V, 19, 30; Alcorn Collection, WyU; DNA, RG 393, Dept. of the Tenn., Letters Sent; (dated April 15) *ibid.*, 13th Army Corps, Letters Received. On April 15, 6:35 P.M., McClernand telegraphed to USG. "I am at Richmond   I find that the rise in the bayou is decreasing. I shall be at Smiths plantation to night." Telegram received, DLC-James M. McClintock.

Also on April 15, Act. Rear Admiral David D. Porter wrote to USG. "I was in hopes we would have gotten off last night, but no transports reported. Looking at them this morning I see they have made but little progress since yesterday at four o'clock. I would like to get off as soon as possible, for the longer we delay, the more guns and troops they will have at Grand Gulf. I am sure they know all about our move. The cars were running constantly all day yesterday and they are throwing troops some where, or else bringing them in. Will you let the transports report to me if possible, at 4 o'clock this afternoon, so that I can let the Captains see the orders on which they will go down River; and get away tonight if it is possible." LS, DNA, RG 393, Dept. of the Tenn., Letters Received.

On April 16, USG telegraphed to McClernand. "In leaving here you left 1000 sick and straggling with out any provision either of tents or Medical attendance. Great difficulty has been experienced in providing for them." Telegram received, DLC-James M. McClintock; copies, DLC-USG, V, 19, 30; DNA, RG 393, Dept. of the Tenn., Letters Sent; *ibid.*, 13th Army Corps, Letters Received. *O.R.*, I, xxiv, part 3, 198. On the same day, McClernand wrote to USG. "Dr. Holston, my Medical Director, applied to get my sick into into the hospital steamers for want of notice, I did not feel at liberty to publish my military movements, nor to delay them on account of the sick. Dr. Holston was directed to provide for them. I hope the stragglers will be sent forward and that the sick will be admitted into the Hospitals. Details were left in charge of them,—and Division Commanders used every effort to have them admitted into the Hospitals.

I do hope the Hospitals will be sufficient to hold and accommodate them." Copies, McClernand Papers, IHi; DNA, RG 393, 13th Army Corps, Letters Sent. On April 18, McClernand wrote to USG. "I have the honor to enclose herewith copies of communications from the several Medical Directors of the 9th, 10th, 12th & 14th Divisions, and from the Medical Director of the 13th Army Corps— in relation to the sick left at Milliken's Bend by them,—referred to in your communication of the 16th inst. If Medical Director Mills made any such statement to you—that any part of the sick of this Army Corps were abandoned or left uncared for, and unprovided with rations, medicine, shelter and medical attendance,—who needed either,—it is untrue in fact, as you will see by these communications. Complaints on this account, if made by him, must have been made because I had expressed indignation at his refusal to receive the sick of my command until forty eight hours notice had been given. I deemed it unwise to announce the military movements of my command two days before it was made. Although he got eleven hospital tents from my Corps Quarter Master—all he had,—yet he complained with petulence to my A. A. Gen'l. at not finding the Quarter Master at the Steamer, and the refusal of the clerks to deliver the tents to him, without a requisition,—compelling him to return to his office, to make a requisition before he could get the tents. The wants of the soldiers are constant and unremitting,— especially the sick,—but I have the satisfaction to believe that the officers and surgeons of this Army Corps, devote themselves cheerfully and constantly to supply their wants and alleviate their suffering,—and I feel called upon to vindicate them against such unjust and unwarrantabe charges of inhuman treatment." Copies, *ibid.*

On April 16, McClernand, "near New Carthage," wrote to USG. "I am concentrating all my Corps, except one regiment, to be left temporialy at Richmond, between Holmes Plantation and New Carthage—six miles—. I will forward the regiment to be left at Richmond, as soon as you can relieve it by ordering forward other troops. The Cavalry, I have charged with patroling the levee between here and Richmond. A detachment of three or four hundred of the enemy —ferrying and wading bayous, made a dash at the levee and our lines, three miles from here, Yesterday morning, but were driven back in hasty flight, with the loss of two men Captured and perha[ps] others wounded. I would emphasize the opinion, previously communicated, of the importance of your ordering other troops forward, immediately, to hold the line from here to Richmond, and the bend, Two of Genl Osterhous' Regiments are already transfered to the Miss levee at Carthage—the balance of his Division, will follow to the same place, as rapidly as small Craft, (in the absence of the expected transport will permit. No Gunboats, here yet" Copy, *ibid. O.R.*, I, xxiv, part 3, 197. On the same day, Lt. Col. Walter B. Scates, adjt. for McClernand, Smith's Plantation, wrote to Lt. Col. John A. Rawlins reporting a skirmish near Dunbar's Plantation. LS, DNA, RG 393, Dept. of the Tenn., Letters Received. *O.R.*, I, xxiv, part 1, 496–97.

On April 17, McClernand wrote to USG. "At seven Oclock this morning, the wreck of the Steamer 'Henry Clay' was seen floating past New Carthage, on fire. At the same time, three barges were seen passing. Without any other than small craft; I sent these into the stream and succeeded in bringing to shore two of the largest,—one partially laden with coal—the other laden with camp equipage, which had been put on board at Milliken's Bend, on the 15th inst. The third barge, laden with coal, passed on, but was scuttled, it being out of my power to bring her in. Besides these, a number of sacks of grain; bales of hay et cet, were brought to. About 12 Oc[l]ock M. eight gunboats, which had also run the blockade, at Vicksburg, came to. Boarding the first arrival, I notified the commander, Capt. Howell, that there was a rebel camp at Perkin's plantation, about five miles below Carthage, and requested him to push forward and shell it, while a detachment of my forces should pursue the fleeing enemy. He referred me to Rear Admiral Porter, whom he said would soon arrive in the gunboat Benton. Soon after, Rear Admiral Porter arrived on the Benton. I immediately called on him, and requesting him to do so, he sent forward the gunboat 'Tuscumbia' to shell the hostile camp, which was done. In the meantime, Genl Osterhaus sent forward a detachment of the 9th Division, to pursue and harrass the enemy, but with what effect has not yet been reported. I also informed the Admiral, that a vessel, supposed to be a hostile one, was seen at Perkin's plantation, the evening before, and that it would be advisable to cruise the river for a distance below Carthage. And pointing out to him the hulk of the 'Indianola,' I suggested to him the importance of an examination, to ascertain whether she could not be raised and made sea worthy." LS, DNA, RG 393, Dept. of the Tenn., Letters Received; DfS, McClernand Papers, IHi. *O.R.*, I, xxiv, part 3, 200–201.

To Brig. Gen. Lorenzo Thomas

Head Quarters, Dept. of the Ten.
Millikins Bend, La. Apl. 16th 1863,

Brig. Gen. L. Thomas,
Adj. Gen of the Army,
Gen.

The following are the changes which I asked to have made in staff officers and which you were kind enough to tell me you would make, subject to the approval of the Sec. of War or President as ~~they~~ may be required.

Lieut. Col. Robt. Macfeely[1] Chief Com.y 15th A. C. to be Chief Com.y of the Dept. of the Ten. vice Lt. Col. Hawkins appointed Brig. Gen.[2]

Lieut. Col. J. H. Wilson Asst. Inspect.r Gen. 10th A. Corps. ~~to be~~ and transfered to the Dept. of the Ten. to fill an original vacancy.

Gen. Gorman I understand has reported for duty at Helena and concluded not to avail himself of his leave.[3]

> Very respectfully
> your obt. svt.
> U. S. GRANT
> Maj. Gen.

ALS, DNA, RG 94, ACP, A98 CB 1863. On April 17, 1863, Brig. Gen. Lorenzo Thomas, Milliken's Bend, issued Special Orders No. 11 making the staff appointments requested. Copy, DLC-USG, V, 105.

1. Robert Macfeely of Pa., USMA 1850, held the rank of 1st lt. when the Civil War began, then was assigned to the Commissary Dept. He entered the Dept. of the Tenn. on Jan. 1, 1863, as chief commissary, 15th Army Corps, with the rank of lt. col. On April 15, Maj. Gen. William T. Sherman wrote to Rawlins. "Lt Col McFeely, ACS to my Corps having been transferred to Department HeadQuarters, I ask that you approve this my application that Adjutant General Thomas now here, make appointments as follows to complete my staff Capt J Condit Smith Corps Quarter Master with rank of Lieut Colonel. Capt Charles A. Morton CS. Corps A. C. S. with rank of Lieut. Colonel. Lieut Stephen. C. Lyford Ordnance Corps to be Aid-de-Camp with the present Rank of Major, and with the premise to exchange him to be the Inspector General of the Corps as soon as Major Sawyer arrives, and consents as I know he will to the transfer." ALS, DNA, RG 94, ACP, S309 CB 1863. On April 17, USG endorsed this letter. "I would respectfully recommend the appointments asked in this communication be made." AES, *ibid.* On the same day, Thomas issued Special Orders No. 11 making these changes. Copy, *ibid.* Secretary of War Edwin M. Stanton subsequently endorsed Sherman's letter disapproving the transfer of 1st Lt. Stephen C. Lyford from the Ordnance Dept. AES, *ibid.*

2. On April 13, Thomas issued Special Orders No. 8. "Lieut Col J. P. Hawkins Commissary of Subsistence is hereby appointed a Brigadier General in the United States Army. He will be relieved from his duties in the Subsistence Department to at once enter upon the important duties of organizing the troops of African descent to form his command." Copy, DLC-USG, V, 105.

3. On April 13, Maj. Gen. Benjamin M. Prentiss, Helena, wrote to Lt. Col. John A. Rawlins. "I have the honor to report that Brig. Gen. W. A. Gorman, Post Commandant, having returned from a visit to Department Head Quarters, and reported to me officially that he did not design at present to avail himself of the leave of absence granted him by the Department Commander, but that he reported for duty, I have assigned him to duty and issued orders accordingly. Should he desire hereafter to take his leave of absence, I will endorse upon it the day he leaves the post as the commencement of his leave, provided such action on my part will be acceptable to the Commanding General." LS, DNA, RG 393, Dept. of the Tenn., Letters Received. See letter to Maj. Gen. Benjamin M. Prentiss, April 21, 1863.

To Maj. Gen. Henry W. Halleck

Apl. 17th 1863.

Maj. Gen. Halleck, Washington.

Seven Gunboats & three transports run the Vicksburg batteries last night. The crew of steamer Henry Clay excepting the pilot deserted soon after geting under fire, ~~excepting the pilot,~~ ~~and~~ The boat took fire and burned up. One other transport slightly damaged. One man killed & three wounded on the Benton. No further casualties reported. A number of barges were also sent.

U. S. Grant
Maj. Gen.

ALS (telegram sent), DNA, RG 107, Telegrams Collected (Bound); telegram received, *ibid. O.R.*, I, xxiv, part 1, 30. This telegram was received at Washington on April 19, 1863, 11:50 p.m. On April 17, USG again telegraphed to Maj. Gen. Henry W. Halleck. "I go to Carthage today   If possible will occupy Grand Gulf within ~~ten~~ four (4) days" Telegrams received (2), DNA, RG 107, Telegrams Collected (Bound); *ibid.*, Telegrams Collected (Unbound); copies, *ibid.*, Telegrams Received in Cipher; *ibid.*, RG 393, Dept. of the Tenn., Hd. Qrs. Correspondence; DLC-USG, V, 5, 8, 24, 94. This telegram was received at Washington on April 20, 12:50 a.m. On April 17, Lt. Col. John A. Rawlins issued Special Orders No. 107. "Capt. O. H. Ross, A. d. C., will proceed by 1st Steamer North to Cairo, Illinois, as bearer of dispatches, to be telegraphed from there to Washington. He will await at Cairo one day for answers. The Military Authorities at Memphis and Cairo, will furnish every facility necessary to the prompt execution of this order." Copies, DLC-USG, V, 26, 27; DNA, RG 393, Dept. of the Tenn., Special Orders.

On April 17, USG signaled to Maj. Gen. William T. Sherman. "What is the Success of running the Blockade last night." Signal received, ICarbS. On April 19, Sherman wrote to Rawlins. "As it may be a matter of interest to the General in Command to know I have to report that the fate of the three Transports sent past the Vicksburg Batteries during the night of April 17 is as follows. Silver Wave, Capt McMillan, manned by officers and soldiers of Gen Ewings Brigade passed the Batteries safely without loss or damage. Forest Queen, Capt Conway, manned by her regular Crew, was struck in the hull, and was disabled by a round shot cutting a steam pipe—wheel Rope & wheel also cut away and otherwise cut up. She drifted down opposite our lower picket station where the Gunboat Tuscumbia, Capt Shirk took her in tow and landed her just above the crevass—on this shore. I have ordered all the materials & workmen needed for her repairs, and Capt Conway reports to me that he will move tomorrow night by the Warrenton Batteries and join the fleet at Carthage. The Henry Clay Capt Rider became disabled and was in a sinking condition soon after coming within Range of the Upper Batteries. She had in tow a Barge with some soldiers in which was cast loose & floated down stream and is supposed to be safe. The boat itself took fire and burned to the waters edge and floated down stream a burning mass. I was in person in a Boat at our Briggs Picket station and my Boat picked up the pilot Taylor floating near the Burnig wreck. He told a wonderful story by no means consistent in all its parts, but asserting positively that every human being had left the Boat, save himself before he discovered her on fire. Several of the crew have come in from whom I gather the following particulars. The Boat had two yawls, which received on board the crew & hands with certain exceptions noted below, which yawls pushed off & landed at Desoto, when they landed and hid behind an old Levee during the cannonade. After it had ceased they began to make their way through the submerged swamp towards our Camp, and all on board the yawls have reached camp, except the Barkeeper & Chambermaid (white) and one Deck hand named Henry, also a white man— . . . Capt Rider was last seen by John Kennedy on the Hurricane Deck, but is unaccounted for. Watchman Mets, same as Capt Ryder. The Boats Carpenter, and the 2nd Cook are represented to have gone into the Hold & closed the Hatches, in which case they are surely lost. This is the most accurate account I can obtain of their fate. There was manifestly great Consternation & Confusion on board all the time." ALS, DNA, RG 393, Dept. of the Tenn., Letters Received. *O.R.*, I, xxiv, part 3, 207–8.

On April 16, USG signaled to Capt. Edwin D. Phillips, 1st Inf. "you will Commence firing from your Casemate Batteries as soon as the mist Clears up in the morning.   direct your firing as pr previous Instructions through Capt Prime and fire Leisurely Reporting the result of your firing. A surgeon will Be sent down Early in the morning"   Signal received, ICarbS. On April 17, 3:00 P.M. and 11:30 P.M., Phillips signaled to USG.   "our fire is not very effective but it must be ~~very~~ anoying   I have discontinued firing on the Court House on account of the damage to the Embrasures   Range range is very much   the Enemy have not returned fire"   "our firing has not Ben good   the shots fall short, though aimed at the highest Elevation the casemates would allow   Will try again ~~in the morning~~ tomorow." Signals received, *ibid.* On April 18, Lt. Col. John A. Rawlins wrote to Phillips. "Captain Kossack has instructions from Captain F. E. Prime to examine and make any changes in the casements, necessary to give you the required elevation for your guns. You will fire slowly, with a view simply to the annoyance of the enemy, and the ascertaining of the effectiveness of your fire and the range of your guns." Copies, DLC-USG, V, 19, 30; DNA, RG 393, Dept. of the Tenn., Letters Sent.

On March 30, Phillips had written to Rawlins. "I have the honor to report for the information of the General, that I am in Camp with my Company, on the east side of the Cut in the Canal, (nearest Vicksburg).—The Guns and Carriages are 'dismounted,' and would not be observed at the distance of a few yards. At this point the Guns may be mounted, and moved down the road, to the work now in progress there, with much facility. A small Boat is much needed here to enable me to communicate with the opposite bank of the Canal." ALS, *ibid.*, Letters Received. On April 8, Rawlins wrote to Phillips. "You will please place in the casements Battery before Vicksburg the two thirty pounder Parrott Guns in your charge to morrow night"   Copies, DLC-USG, V, 19 (2), 30; DNA, RG 393, Dept. of the Tenn., Letters Sent. On April 22, Phillips wrote to Rawlins. "I have the honor to report for the information of the Commanding General, that pursuant to instructions, on the seventeenth instant I commenced firing upon the 'Court house,' and the 'Railroad Depot' in Vicksburg, with two thirty pounder Parrott Rifles, placed in Casemate Battery opposite the town. The firing was continued at introvals during the day light, until the night of the twentieth, with very unsatisfactory results on the first and second [d]ays, the projectiles having been thrown with much inaccuracy, and having mostly fallen short of the town. On the third, the firing was better; and on the fourth day, though little effective, it was excellent; the shells apparently bursting at the height and distance of the dome of the Court house, and at the very centre of the ridge pole of the Depot, the elevations used being fifteen and ten degrees respectively. Still the result of the firing, as that of Siege Artillery, has not been effective. The Enemy seems to have quitted the use of the Depot on the third day. In the night of the twentieth, pursuant to instructions, I removed to the landing; and so soon as a steamer arrived, the Detachment with the Guns, Ammunition &c. were embarked and reached the First Infantry Camp this morning. I wish to say that I highly appreciate the efforts of Captain W. Cossack, of the Vol: Engineers whose strong Casemates, could they have been tested would have shown that they were skillfully planned and executed with great judgement and labor." ALS, *ibid.*, RG 94, War Records Office, Union Battle Reports. *O.R.*, I, xxiv, part 3, 222–23.

On April 17, 8:00 P.M., USG signaled to Act. Rear Admiral David D. Porter. "Bring gun boats and mortars, and shell the city all night, till 10½ o clock to morow." Signal received, DLC-James M. McClintock. On the same day, Porter signaled to USG. "I am moving mortar boats close. Will be ready early tomorrow" Signal received, *ibid.*

To Lt. Col. John A. Rawlins

Richmond Louisiana
April 17th 1863.

Lt. Col. J. A. Rawlins
A. A. Gen Dept. of the Ten.
Col.

Riding along the bayou through which a channel must be made teaches that much more work is to be done to make it navigable. Instruct Prime & Pride to call for all the force they can possibly work and distribute them to the best advantage. Call on McPherson to ride over the road himself and put that in the best order he can and also give every assistance to clearing

out the bayou. Pride should have every saw that it is possible to
rig at work with men enough to keep them constantly going.

Very respectfully

U. S. GRANT

Maj. Gen. Com

ALS, PPRF. On April 17, 1863, Lt. Col. John A. Rawlins endorsed this letter to
Maj. Gen. James B. McPherson. ES, *ibid.*

To Maj. Gen. John A. McClernand

Smiths Plantation La. April 18th 1863.

MAJ GEN J. A. McCLERNAND,
COMM'DG 13TH ARMY CORPS.

I would still repeat former instructions, that possession be
got of Grand Gulf, at the very earliest possible moment. Once
there no risk should be taken in following the enemy until our
forces are concentrated. Troops first there should entrench themselves for safety, and the whole of your corps concentrated as
rapidly as our means of transportation will permit. Genl.
McPherson will be closing upon you as rapidly as your troops
can be got away and rations supplied.[1]

I see that great caution will have to be observed in getting
barges past the crevasse near Carthage and I apprehend a loss
of some Artillery may be encountered

I will send over at once the Pontoon train with men to lay it.
It can at least be thrown across Bayou Videl opposite your Head
Quarters to enable troops and Artillery to march a good portion
of the way to Carthage. If it can possibly be laid so as to cross
the levee crevasse near Carthage, it would be of much greater
service. Should we succeed in getting Steamers past Vicksburg
they will bring you a further supply of rations   In the meantime
all the wagons, including all the regimental trains, should be kept
constantly on the road between here and Millikens Bend. The

number of wagons available is increasing daily. Troops guarding the different points between here and Richmond should gather all Beef Cattle and forage within reach of them and destroy no more than they can use.

I will be over here in a few days again and hope it will be my good fortune to find you in safe possession of Grand Gulf.

You do not want to start however without feeling yourself secure in the necissary transportation

U. S. GRANT

Maj Gen

Copies, DLC-USG, V, 19, 30; DNA, RG 393, Dept. of the Tenn., Letters Sent; *ibid.*, 13th Army Corps, Letters Received; Alcorn Collection, WyU. *O.R.*, I, xxiv, part 3, 205. On April 18, 1863, Maj. Gen. John A. McClernand, Smith's Plantation, La., wrote to USG. "I have the honor to call your attention to, and most earnestly urge upon your consideration the very great importance of placing at once, below Vicksburg, a sufficient number of transports, to carry my whole command at once. This Corps has now gained a position, that will enable us to capture Grand Gulf, and cooperate in the reduction of Fort Hudson. With these points in our possession, the Mississippi open to New Orleans—with the combined efforts of both armies, and gunboat fleets, we shall be able to attack Vicksburg in front and rear, and soon it must fall into our hands—and with its fall, a virtual end will be put to the war in the South West—and a hopeful prospect of putting a speedy end to the rebellion. But to use the advantages we have gained in taking our present position—no time must be allowed the enemy, to prepare to meet us, on the line of our present advance. A short delay here, may endanger the certainty of our success—which must attend a rapid forward movement at this time. The loss of a dozen steamers, in running the blockade, will be nothing in comparison to what we may lose in the advantage we have now gained, the sickness of the men, & the loss of the campaign, which must be made in the next six weeks. With ~~the Ferry boat Williams, and~~ a steam tug or two—the Quarter Master, Commissary, & ordnance stores could be towed down in flats from Richmond, in a very few days—as it would shorten the hauling one half. These boats would be invaluable at this time. The gunboats, not being under your control, cannot be relied on, for the transportation of troops—while at the same time, they can render more valuable service, than in transporting the Army. In every point of view then, the importance of placing a number of Transports below Vicksburg, immediately, cannot be over-estimated—and I submit that a sufficient number should at once be sent down." LS, DNA, RG 393, Dept. of the Tenn., Letters Received. *O.R.*, I, xxiv, part 3, 204–5.

On April 19, McClernand wrote to USG. "My present movement, if properly sustained, ought, and I believe, will, eventuate in the extinguishment of the Rebellion in the Gulf States, and limit it in the East. Please give me a dozen good transports—They are necessary to enable me to move my forces rapidly, and to strike the enemy before he can fortify. They will be worth untold millions to our cause—not only in money—but in momentous military results. Without them, delay and approaching hot weather may ensue to jeopardize everything. Without them, Grand Gulf may become another Vicksburg or Port Hudson. The loss of a few transports in running the blockade are not worthy to count anything in the opposing scale—Earnestly sympathizing in your plans and purposes, no effort or personal sacrifice, on my part, will be spared, to give them complete success Meanwhile, although the process of transferring troops to the Mississippi levee in skiffs and other small craft, must necessarily be tedious and slow, yet it will be diligently and energetically prosecuted— . . . P. S. It is desirable that supplies should—particularly commissary stores—should be sent on the transports." ALS, DNA, RG 393, Dept. of the Tenn., Letters Received. *O.R.*, I, xxiv, part 3, 207. See letter to Maj. Gen. John A. McClernand, April 20, 1863.

1. On April 15, Maj. Gen. James B. McPherson, Lake Providence, wrote to USG. "The advance of Genl. Quinby's Division reached here last night consisting of Col: Sanborn's & Boomer's Brigades. Col: Holme's Brigade with the Genl. is expected today—I supposed of course Genl. Quinby would come down immediately on getting out of the '*pass*,' but some of the Boats were so badly damaged that he found it necessary to delay a short time at Helena for repairs—Logan's & McArthurs Divisions are all ready to move and Comr. Graham informs me that Boats will be sent up immediately—I shall forward the Troops as fast as I can get boats to take a Brigade—. . . P. S. I will come down as soon as the 1st Brigade of Genl. Logan's Division is started" ALS, DNA, RG 393, Dept. of the Tenn., Letters Received. On April 18, Lt. Col. John A. Rawlins issued Special Orders No. 108. "Major General James B McPherson, Commanding 17th Army Corps, will move forward, at once, two Regiments of his Command, to Richmond, La., They will take with them three days rations" Copies, DLC-USG, V, 27, 28; DNA, RG 393, Dept. of the Tenn., Special Orders. *O.R.*, I, xxiv, part 3, 205.

To Maj. Gen. Henry W. Halleck

Head Quarters, Dept. of the Ten.
Millikins Bend La. Apl. 19th 1863.

MAJ. GEN. H. W. HALLECK,
GEN IN CHIEF, WASHINGTON,

I returned last night from New Carthage, at and near which is laying Admiral Porters fleet, of ~~seven~~ six Iron Clads, and the ram "Gen. Price," together with two Divisions of Gen. McClernand's Army Corps. The whole of Gen. McClernands Corps is between Richmond and New Carthage.

I had all the empty barges here prepared for the transportation of troops and Artillery, and sent ten of them by the Vicksburg batteries with the fleet. Whilst under the guns of the enemy's batteries, they were cut loose and I fear some of them have been permitted to run past New Carthage undiscovered. They were relied upon to aid in the transportation of troops to take Grand Gulf.

The wagon road from here to within two miles of New Carthage is good for Artillery. From that point on the bayou levee is broken in a number of places, making cross currents in the bayou and hence it is difficult to navigate with barges. I think, however, steamers will be able to run from where the wagon road ends to the river.

By clearing out the timber from the bayous there will be good navigation from here to New Carthage for tugs and barges, also small stern wheel steamers. This navigation I think can be kept good by using our dredges constantly until there is a twenty-feet fall. On this subject, however, I have not taken the opinion of an Engineer officer nor have I formed it upon sufficient investigation to warrant me in speaking possitively.

Our experiment of runing the batteries of Vicksburg I think has demonstrated the entire practicability of doing so with but little risk. On this occasion our vessels went down even slower than the current, using their wheels principally for backing. Two of the steamers were drawn into the eddy and run over a part of the distance in front of Vicksburg three times. I shall send six more steamers by the batteries as soon as they can possibly be got ready. I sent a dispatch to Gen. Banks that I thought I could send an Army Corps to Bayou Sara to cooperate with him on Port Hudson by the 25th.[1] This now will be imposs[ible.] There shall be no unnecessary [de]lay, however, in my movements. I hope very soon to be able to report our possession of Grand Gulf with a practicable and safe route for furnishing supplies to the troops. Once there, I do not feel a doubt of success in the entire clearing-out of the enemy from the banks of the river.

At least three of my Army Corps Commanders take hold of the new policy of arming the negroes and using them against the rebels with a will. They at least are so much of soldiers as to feel themselves under obligations to carry out a policy (which they would not inaugerate) in the same good faith and with the same zeal as if it was of their own choosing. You may rely on my carrying out any policy ordered by proper authority to the best of my ability.[2]

> I am Gen. Very respectfully
> your obt. svt.
> U. S. GRANT
> Maj. Gen.

ALS, CSmH. *O.R.*, I, xxiv, part 1, 30–31.

1. On April 14, 1863, USG wrote to Maj. Gen. Nathaniel P. Banks. "I am concentrating my forces at Grand Gulf. Will send an Army Corps to Bayou Sara, by the 25th to co-operate with you on Port Hudson. Can you aid me and send troops after the reduction of Port Hudson to assist at Vicksburg?" Copies, DLC-USG, V, 5, 8, 24, 94; DNA, RG 393, Dept. of the Tenn., Hd. Qrs. Correspondence. *O.R.*, I, xxiv, part 3, 192. On April 30, Banks twice wrote to USG, first from "Steamer 'Sykes,'" then at 6:00 A.M. from Brashear City. "It is of the utmost possible importance, that you should send a force to the Red River immediately to cooperate with the Army and Navy now here.—We have the Atchafalaya and the mouth of the Red River. An addition to my force now will give us the whole country west of the Mississippi. Please give me all information of your movements in this direction" Copy, DNA, RG 393, Dept. of the Tenn., Unregistered Letters Received. *O.R.*, I, xv, 711. "I modify my dispatch sent by the Admiral so far as to recommend the union of our forces on the Bayou Sara. My fear was that our supplies could not be made secure, but upon further reflection, I am satisfied that with the force you propose to send and my own we can march directly to the rear of Port Hudson and thus open communication by the way of Baton Rouge for all Supplies. In this view the Bayou Sara Route is the most feasible We are anxious to hear from you. There is no news here." Copy, DNA, RG 393, Dept. of the Tenn., Unregistered Letters Received. *O.R.*, I, xv, 711; *ibid.*, I, xxiv, part 3, 247; *O.R.* (Navy), I, xx, 69.

On May 3, noon, Banks, Opelousas, La., wrote to USG. "If you can forward by the Black River the Corps mentioned in your despatches we can expel the enemy from Louisiana, and holding between us, the country west of the Mississippi—you by the Tensas and Black, and I by the Atchafalaya River, Vicksburg and Port Hudson must fall. Both depend upon the country west. Can you not forward these troops now? It is of the most vital importance that we should be strong here now, when the enemy is panic stricken. I send information received here of the movements of Kirby Smith. Can you inform me of the forces in Arkansas. I shall move in the direction of Alexandria tomorrow morning to ascertain the enemy's force and intentions in that quarter. This will determine my immediate movements." Copies, DNA, RG 94, War Records Office, Union Battle Reports; *ibid.*, RG 393, Dept. of the Tenn., Unregistered Letters Received; *ibid.*, Dept. of the Gulf, Letters Sent. *O.R.*, I, xv, 309; *ibid.*, I, xxiv, part 3, 265.

On May 5, Banks received USG's letter of April 14. On May 6, Banks wrote to USG. "By the twenty fifth, probably,—by the first, certainly,—we will be there." Copy, DNA, RG 94, War Records Office, Dept. of the Tenn. See *O.R.*, I, xv, 313–14. This message reached USG on May 10. DLC-USG, V, 22; DNA, RG 393, Dept. of the Tenn., Register of Letters Received. See letter to Maj. Gen. Nathaniel P. Banks, May 10, 1863.

On May 8, 8 :00 A.M., Banks, Alexandria, La., wrote to USG. "My command reached Alexandria yesterday, without opposition, the advance entering the town early in the afternoon. Admiral Porter with his fleet and several of Admiral Farragut's Boats took possession of the town yesterday morning without resistance. I have stated to him that I can furnish his fleet, that of Admiral Farragut, and your transports with coal, and your army partially with provisions, by the Atchafalaya and Red River. But it will be difficult. If Port Hudson is reduced all this can be done direct from New Orleans, and our future operations will proceed without interruption from want of supplies and with certain success. In answer to your despatch received in cypher, I answered I could co-coperate with you on the 25th instant or the 1st of June, our successful march here enables me to do this on the 25th May. I shall have 15.000 (fifteen thousand) good men all told. We can move by the Bayou Sara to the rear of Port Hudson, get our supplies from Baton Rouge, where Major General Augur can join us with *four thousand* men. The fleet of Admiral Porter above, that of Admiral Farragut below, and our forces in the rear, or so many of yours as you can spare, the fall of the Post will be *instant and certain*. I beg your most favorable consideration to this matter. Lt. Colonel Irwin, my adjutant, will explain my views more in detail." Copy, DLC-Nathaniel P. Banks. *O.R.*, I, xv, 720; *ibid.*, I, xxiv, part 3, 281.

2. On March 30, Maj. Gen. Henry W. Halleck wrote to USG. "It is the policy of the government to withdraw from the enemy as much productive labor as possible. So long as the rebels retain and employ their slaves in producing grains, &c, they can employ all the whites in the field. Every slave withdrawn from the enemy, is equivalent to a white man put *hors de combat*. Again, it is the policy of the government to use the negroes of the South so far as practicable as a military force for the defence of forts, depots, &c. If the experience of Genl Banks near New Orleans should be satisfactory, a much larger force will be organized during the coming summer; and if they can be used to hold points on the Mississippi during the sickly season, it will afford much relief to our armies. They certainly can be used with advantage as laborers, teamsters, cooks, &c. And it is the opinion of many who have examined the question without passion or prejudice, that they can also be used as a military force. It certainly is good policy to use them to the very best advantage we can. Like almost anything else, they may be made instruments of good or evil. In the hands of the enemy they are used with much effect against us. In our hands we must try to use them with the best possible effect against the rebels. It has been reported to the Secretary of War that many of the officers of your command not only discourage the negroes from coming under our protection, but, by ill-treatment, force them to return to their masters. This is not only bad policy in itself, but is directly opposed to the policy adopted by the government. Whatever may be the individual opinion of an officer in regard to the wisdom of measures adopted and announced by the government, it is the duty of every one to cheerfully and honestly endeavour to carry out the measures so adopted. Their good or bad policy is a matter of opinion before they are tried; their real character can only be determined by a fair trial. When adopted by the

government it is the duty of every officer to give them such a trial, and to do everything in his power to carry the orders of his government into execution. It is expected that you will use your official and personal influence to remove prejudices on this subject, and to fully and thoroughly carry out the policy now adopted and ordered by the government. That policy is, to withdraw from the use of the enemy all the slaves you can, and to employ those so withdrawn, to the best possible advantage against the enemy. The character of the war has very much changed within the last year. There is now no possible hope of a reconciliation with the rebels. The union party in the south is virtually destroyed. There can be no peace but that which is enforced by the sword. We must conquer the rebels, or be conquered by them. The north must either destroy the slave-oligarchy, or become slaves themselves,—the manufacturers—mere hewers of wood and drawers of water to southern aristocrats. This is the phase which the rebellion has now assumed. We must take things as they are. The government, looking at the subject in all its aspects, has adopted a policy, and we must cheerfully and faithfully carry out that policy. I write you this unofficial letter, simply as a personal friend, and as a matter of friendly advice. From my position here, where I can survey the entire field, perhaps I may be better able to understand the tone of public opinion, and the intentions of the government, than you can from merely consulting the officers of your own army." ADfS, DNA, RG 94, Generals' Papers and Books, Letters Sent by Gen. Halleck, Drafts and Copies; LS (dated March 31), *ibid.*, War Records Office, Dept. of the Mo. *O.R.*, I, xxiv, part 3, 156–57. On April 22, Lt. Col. John A. Rawlins issued General Orders No. 25. "Corps, Divisions and Post Commanders will afford all facilities for the completion of the Negro Regiments now organizing in this Department, Commissaries will issue supplies, and Quartermasters will furnish stores on the same requisitions and returns as are required from other troops. It is expected that all Commanders will especially exert themselves in carrying out the policy of the Administration, not only in organizing colored regiments and rendering them efficient, but also in removing prejudice against them." Copies, DLC-USG, V, 13, 14, 95; (2) DNA, RG 393, Dept. of the Tenn., General and Special Orders. *O.R.*, I, xxiv, part 3, 220.

On April 10, Maj. Thomas McGrain, Jr., 53rd Ind., Memphis, submitted his resignation "on account of the Emancipation policy and the arming of the slaves." DLC-USG, V, 21; DNA, RG 393, Dept. of the Tenn., Register of Letters Received. On April 23, USG endorsed this letter. "Respectfully forwarded to Head Quarters of the Army with the request that this Officer be dismissed the service" Copies, DLC-USG, V, 25; DNA, RG 393, Dept. of the Tenn., Endorsements. On April 10, Capt. Seth Daily, 53rd Ind., Memphis, submitted his resignation for the same reason. After Maj. Gen. Stephen A. Hurlbut recommended a dishonorable discharge, USG endorsed the resignation on April 23. "Recommendation of General Hurlbut approved and respectfully forwarded to the Head Quarters of the Army, Washington, D. C." Copies, *ibid.* Capt. Henry M. Howard, 1st Kan., also objected "to arming the Negroes." On April 27, USG endorsed his letter of resignation. "Respectfully forwarded to Head Quarters of the Army with the recommendation that this officer be dismissed the service with forfeiture of all pay and allowance" Copies, *ibid.*

To Col. John C. Kelton

Head Quarters, Department of the Tennessee,
Millikens Bend, La., April 20th 1863,

COL. J. C. KELTON
A. A. GEN., WASHINGTON, D. C.,
COL:

Herewith I have the honor to enclose reports of Maj: Gen. Mc.Pherson, Lieut Col. Rawlins, and Major Rowley, called for by endorsement on Maj. Gen L. Wallace's letter of the 14th of March, accounting for his tardiness in reaching the field of battle, on the 6th. day of April 1862.

Instead of making this report myself, I called upon these officers, all of whom were on my staff at the time, and cognizant of the facts, and all being separated when called upon for their reports. A more correct judgement will be derived probably than from a single report.

All these reports are substantially as I remember the facts. I can vouch for their almost entire accuracy. Had Gen. Wallace been relieved from duty in the morning, and the same orders communicated to Genl. Morgan L. Smith, who would have been his successor, I do not doubt but the Division would have been on the field of battle, and engaged, before 1 o'clock of that eventful 6th. of April. There is no estimating the difference this might have made in our casualties

I am, Col. Very Respectfully
Your obt servant,
U. S. GRANT
Major General. Vols.

Copies, DLC-USG, V, 5, 8, 24, 94; DNA, RG 393, Dept. of the Tenn., Hd. Qrs. Correspondence. See letter to Col. John C. Kelton, April 13, 1863, note 2.

On Aug. 27, 1863, Maj. Gen. William T. Sherman wrote to Brig. Gen. John A. Rawlins. "Confidential—I have a long & very proper letter from Genl Lew Wallace speaking in terms of great respect for Genl Grant but evidently restrained from expressing them direct. What do you think of my answering him in a kind tone & holding out to him a hope of again serving with modified notions.

at Shiloh he was laggard but has he no good qualities which with proper cultivation might Save his honor & be of use to the Service" Telegram received, DNA, RG 94, War Records Office, Dept. of the Tenn.; copy, *ibid.*, RG 393, Dept. of the Tenn., Telegrams Sent. *O.R.*, I, xxx, part 3, 183–84.

To Maj. Gen. John A. McClernand

Milliken Bend, La April 20th 1863.

MAJOR GENL J. A MCCLERNAND
COMMDG 13TH ARMY CORPS.

Six Steamers I hope will be ready to run the Enemy's batteries to night the cotton and hay for barracading a greater number is not on hand at present. These boats are now loaded and loading with 6.00 thousands rations and a very considerable quantity of forage Barges will enter the Bayou to day with the expectation of getting through to Carthage by Tuesday night. A large number of yawls, barges and tugs, must be here in a day or two In addition to this there are some twelve steamers here that will be able to run the bayou when the work of clearing them out is completed.

General McPherson will keep close upon you but recollect that all the transportation of his army corps, as well as your own, is now being used to get through your supplies. I think no more wagons should be taken through except for transportation of Ordnance Stores the Steamers that run the Blockade have about, 160,000 rations on board and some forage, more will be going to night. Direct the teams to stop at Richmond and establish Depots of supplies there

U. S. GRANT.
Maj. Genl.

Copies, DLC-USG, V, 19, 30; DNA, RG 393, Dept. of the Tenn., Letters Sent; *ibid.*, 13th Army Corps, Letters Received; Alcorn Collection, WyU. *O.R.*, I, xxiv, part 3, 212.

On April 20, 1863, Maj. Gen. John A. McClernand, Smith's Plantation, La., twice wrote to USG. "The 'Forest Queen' arrived last night in a shattered condition. I am unloading the Commissary and Quartermaster's stores from her.

General Osterhaus' Division will be on the Mississippi levee to-night. He is moving his Division down to Perkin's plantation, for the purpose of making room for the disembarkation of Gen'l Carr's, which will commence being crossed over in the morning. I have just brought to this place one large barge, and expect to bring others in the morning, which will hasten the transfer of Gen'l Carr's Division—I sent Col. Wright, and Lieut. Haine, Engineer, down the Vidal this morning, to examine whether a land route might be found from here to the Mississippi river, at, or below, Perkin's plantation. Col. Wright, this moment, reports, that, by throwing a bridge across Gilbert Bayou, and another across ~~Bridge~~ Mound Bayou, with one or two other small structures, the Mississippi may be reached, by, land, at Perkin's. If I become satisfied that this can be done, I will move a portion of my corps by land, while the balance is being crossed over in small boats, to Carthage—I have ordered forward the detachment of this corps left at Richmond—learning that the detachment ordered by you from Gen'l McPherson's had reached there. I expect to move upon Grand Gulf so soon as two Divisions shall have been placed, *in hand*, upon the levee—Having just returned from Holme's Plantation, I learn that what was supposed to be a white flag, is shown on the Mississippi shore opposite to Carthage. I have sent Lieut. Col. Mudd to enquire and report concerning the matter—Details are working upon the road from here to Richmond, and the road is rapidly drying—Cattle are being brought in, which supply my corps with fresh meat—Nothing is omitted that will hasten the earliest practicable forward movement—Your dispatch to Rear Admiral Porter is this moment received and forwarded—I am anxiously hoping for the arrival of additional transports—At this point, your despatch of this date comes to hand. I am rejoiced at its contents. I will cause the 'Forest Queen' to be held ready to afford any assistance that may be found necessary in bringing to any of the transports that may be disabled in running the blockade. I will request the Admiral to hold his boats in readiness to do the same—" ALS, DNA, RG 393, Dept. of the Tenn., Letters Received. *O.R.*, I, xxiv, part 3, 211–12. "I have ordered, through Liut Col. Dunlap, Corps Quartermaster, a quantity of rope, to be used in the construction of two bridges: one across Bayou Videl, and an other across Mound Bayou, with the design of securing land transportation to the bank of the Mississippi river, said to be practicable. If Col Dunlap has not the rope required, please afford him facilities for procuring it,—" Copy, DNA, RG 393, 13th Army Corps, Letters Sent.

On April 21, Lt. Col. John A. Rawlins wrote to McClernand. "In addition to the fleet of Steamers that will be sent down the river to-night, six barges and one tug will be sent" Copy, *ibid.*, Letters Received. On the same day, McClernand wrote twice to USG. "I learned from Gen'l Osterhaus last night, that he found a rebel cavalry picket at Perkins, which he drove away, and that their Infantry, which has been operating between here and St Joseph's lake, has crossed over to Grand Gulf—" ALS, *ibid.*, Dept. of the Tenn., Letters Received. *O.R.*, I, xxiv, part 3, 215–16. "Brig Genl Smith will send you two men—Mr Hall, a citizen of Minnesota and Mr Delano an overseer from Tensas Parish. Mr. Hall claims to have been pressed into the rebel army, and served a short time at Vicksburg, and to be now on his way home. They bring but little information of importance, except that from Perkin's plantation, six miles south of New Carthage, there is a good dry route along the river bank to a point opposite Natchez. The route lies through a rich and highly cultivated Country. A report which he brings, that, the enemy intend making a demonstration against New Orleans, may or may not be worthy of attention. It is more than two months, since he heard it from his Comd'g Officer." LS, *ibid.*, RG 109, Union Provost Marshals' File of Papers Relating to Two or More Civilians; DfS, McClernand Papers, IHi.

On April 20, Rawlins issued Special Orders No. 110. "The following orders are published for the information and guidance of the 'Army in the Field,' in its present movement to obtain a foot-hold on the East bank of the Mississippi River from which Vicksburg can be approached by practicable roads. 1. The 13th Army Corps Maj. General John A. McClernand Commanding will constitute the right wing. 2. The 15th Army Corps Maj General. W. T. Sherman Commanding will constitute the Left Wing. 3. The 17th Army Corps, Maj. General James B. McPherson, Commanding, will constitute the Center 4. The order of march to New Carthage will be from right to left. 5. Reserves will be formed by Divisions from each Army Corps, or an entire Army Corps, will be held as a reserve, as necessity may require. When the reserve is formed by Divisions, each Division will remain under the immediate Command of its respective Corps Commanders unless otherwise specially ordered, for a particular emergency. 6. Troops will be required to bivouac, until proper facilities can be afforded for the transportation of Camp Equipage. 7. In the present movement, one tent will be allowed to each Company for the protection of rations from rain, one wall-tent for each Regimental Headquarters, one Wall-tent for each Brigade Headquarters, and one wall-tent for each Division Headquarters. Corps Commanders having the books and blanks of their respective Commands to provide for, are authorized to take such tents as are absolutely necessary, but not to exceed the number allowed by General Orders, No. 160, A. G. O. series of 1862. 8. All the teams of the three Army Corps, under the immediate Charge of the Quartermasters bearing them on their returns will constitute a train for carrying supplies and ordnance, and the authorized Camp Equipage of the Army. 9. As fast as the 13th Army Corps advances, the 17th Army Corps will take its place, and it, in time, will be followed in like manner, by the 15th Army Corps. 10. Two regiments from each Army Corps, will be detailed by Corps Commanders, to guard the lines from Richmond to New Carthage 11. General Hospitals will be established by the Medical Director, between Duckport and Miliken's Bend. All sick and disabled soldiers will be left in these Hospitals. Surgeons in charge of Hospitals will report Convalescents, as fast as they become fit for duty. Each Corps Commander will detail an intelligent and good Drill officer, to remain behind to charge of the convalescents of their respective Corps: Officers so detailed will organize the men under their charge into squads and Companies, without regard to the Regiments they belong to, and in the absence of Convalescent Commissioned Officers to command them, will appoint non-commissioned officers or Privates. The force so organized will constitute the guard of the line from Duckport to Miliken's Bend. They will furnish all the guards and details required for General Hospitals, and with the Contrabands that may be about the Camps, will furnish all the details for loading and unloading boats. 12. The movement of troops from Miliken's Bend to New Carthage will be so conducted as to allow the transportation of ten day's supply of rations, and one half the allowance of ordnance required by previous orders. 13th Commanders are authorized and enjoined, to collect all the beef-Cattle, Corn, and other necessary supplies on the line of march, but wanton destruction of property, taking of articles, useless for Military purposes, insulting citizens, going into and searching houses without proper orders from Division Commanders, are positively prohibited. All such irregularities must be summarily punished. 14. Brig. Gen'l J. C. Sullivan, is appointed to the command of all the forces detached for the protection of the line from here to New Carthage. His particular attention is called to General Orders, No. 69, from Adjutant General's Office, Washington of date March 20th 1863." Copies, DLC-USG, V, 27, 28; DNA, RG 393, Dept. of the Tenn., Special Orders; Alcorn Collection, WyU. *O.R.*, I, xxiv, part 3, 212–14. General Orders No. 69 provided for the formation of "Invalid Detachments" at hospitals for limited duties.

To Surgeon Madison Mills

Millikin Bend La April 20th 1863.

SURG MADISON MILLS
MEDICAL DIRECTOR

A gradual movement of troops f. will take place from here to New Carthage leaving sufficient guards along for. the protection of the line. All troops will be removed from below the new canal or Duck Point: hence it will be necessary to bring to this side of the canal all Hospitals   As the river will be guarded at the canal and also at Milliken Bend any point or as many points between the two places, may be taken for Hospitals as you may deem necessary. These Hospitals should be at once established: as the troops will not be permitted to carry with them their tents, any number of them can be obtained that may deemed necessary. by calling on the Officer who will be left behind in charge of them. One officer will be left, from each Army Corps, to take charge of public property belonging to their several Corps, and to take charge of convalescents to organize them into companies, and to make them perform Military duty. Surgeons in charge of these Hospitals should be instructed to report all patients to officers so detailed as rapidly as they are restored to sufficient health to do duty. I shall move my Head Quarters to New Carthage on Wednesday but as I will be likely be there for a week or more it will not be necessary for the Medical Director to go there until he is satisfied with the arrangments for sick left behind

U S. GRANT
Maj. Genl.

Copies, DLC–USG, V, 19, 30; DNA, RG 393, Dept. of the Tenn., Letters Sent.

To Julia Dent Grant

———

Millikin's Bend La.
April 20th 1863.

Dear Julia,

I want you to go to St. Louis and stay there until you get the deed from your brother John for the 60 acres of land *where our house* is, and have it recorded. Also get the deed for 40 acres where your brother Lew's. house is and have it recorded.[1] Be shure and have this done right. Then lease out the farm to some good and prompt tenant, for five years, giving them the privilege of taking off every stick of timber and puting the whole place in cultivation. Bind them to take care of the house, fences and fruit trees.[2] Place Bass Sappington[3] or Pardee in charge to collect the rent and when all is done say to your father that the house is for his use as long as he wants it and the rents are to go to him for the other place.

If John Dent wants to go to Calafornia you may offer him $1600 for 40 acres adjoining the 60 acres. If he desires this have this deed recorded also before you leave. I want it distinctly understood however that I do not desire this trade and only make the offer to enable him to go and look after other property he has. If it was not that I am poor and have not a dollar except my savings in the last two years I would not hesitate to furnish him all the necessary money without any other guarantee than the conciousnous that I had done him a favor.

In case you make this trade it will be necessary for you to go to Galena to get the money. You can explain to Orvil that I have purchased property and paid $3000 on it and have to pay $1600 more. You can settle the difference they make out against me at the store but try and have Lank. who kept the books, to make up the account. Ask Orvil how brother Simps estate was settled.

Inform him that I should never have mentioned it in the world but some of them are seting so much higher merit upon money than any other earthly ~~consid~~ consideration that I feel it a duty to protect myself. If you go to Galena be patient and even tempered. Do not expose yourself to any misconstruction from a hasty remark. Be firm however. Give up no notes except what you get cashed unless they pay the whole with the interest accrued. In that case you can allow them for what they say I owe with the same interest upon the debt they pay you. Should you however get but a part of the money give only the notes they pay. Tell Orvil that on final settlement I will allow the same interest that I receive. So long as they hold money of mine they need not be afraid to trust me.

This business all settled you can visit any of your friends until you hear that I am in Vicksburg when you can join me as soon as possible. Try and engage a Governess to teach the children, one who speaks German if possible. Do not make a possitive bargain however until you write to me.

U. S. GRANT

ALS, DLC-USG.

1. When Joseph W. White defaulted on his deed of trust for USG's Hardscrabble farm, ownership reverted to Frederick Dent, who had never formally transferred the property to USG. In the meantime, Dent had defaulted on notes mortgaging his land, and these notes had been acquired by his son, John C. Dent. White Haven abstract, Mr. and Mrs. Delbert Wenzlick, St. Louis County, Mo. On May 7 and 8, John Dent conveyed to Julia Grant the Hardscrabble farm, another tract of twenty acres, and still another forty acres, the last presumably including Wish-ton-wish, the house of Lewis Dent once occupied by USG. *Ibid.*

2. On July 13, Julia Grant leased the Hardscrabble farm to White for two years beginning the previous March 1 for $100 yearly. Papers in the case of Ulysses S. Grant and Julia B. Grant vs. Joseph W. White, Circuit Court, Twenty-second Judicial Circuit of Missouri, St. Louis, Mo. See letters to Julia Dent Grant, May 10, 1861, note 11; June 29, 1863.

3. Sebastian Sappington, who owned land adjacent to the White Haven estate across Gravois Road and had served as justice of the peace, became USG's agent for his St. Louis County property.

To Maj. Gen. Henry W. Halleck

———

Millikin's Bend La. [*April*] 21. [*1863*]

MAJ. GEN. H. W. HALLECK,
GEN-IN-CHIEF

I move my Hd. Qrs. to Carthage tomorrow.

Every effort will be exerted to get speedy possession of Grand Gulf and from that point to open the Mississippi.

If I do not under estimate the enemy my force is abundant with a foothold once obtained to do the work. Six transports will run the Vicksburg batteries tonight.

U. S. GRANT.
Maj. Genl

Telegram received, DNA, RG 107, Telegrams Collected (Bound); *ibid.*, Telegrams Collected (Unbound); copies, *ibid.*, Telegrams Received in Cipher; *ibid.*, RG 393, Dept. of the Tenn., Hd. Qrs. Correspondence; DLC-USG, V, 5, 8, 24, 94. *O.R.*, I, xxiv, part 1, 31. This telegram was received in Washington on April 24, 1863.

To Act. Rear Admiral David D. Porter

———

Millikins Bend La.
April 21st 1863.

ADMIRAL.

The boats we expected to run the blockade with to-night failed to get ready in time. They however will be ready to go through to-morrow night.[1] I sent a party yesterday to burn the houses on the point opposite Vicksburg but they found it impossible to get to them without great difficulty and under a fire from short range of the enemy's batteries. They stuck to it until they drew seventeen shots and then gave up the job to try it at night. The night attempt was made and failed. The enemy were found to occupy these houses with a strong guard and our troops were compeled to withdraw with a loss of one man wounded.[2]

It is evident that our boats cannot run the blockade without the river being lit up to expose every steamer to full view.

Under these sircumstances we may meet with a heavy loss. I would suggest Admiral the propriety of sending a gunboat up to-morrow night to watch below the batteries to give such aid as they may require.

A fleet of our barges has arrived and one of the tugs. I will send some of these with the fleet.

We have got a small steamer and some barges into Walnut Bayou. Hope to get them through to Carthage by Thursday.

I move my Hd Qrs. to Carthage on Wednesday.

Yours Truly
U. S. Grant
Maj. Gen.

To Admiral D. D. Porter
Comdg Miss Squadron

P. S. Your note with sketch of passes to Smith's Plantation[3] is received. I have ordered through a saw to cut down the trees mentioned in your note as being in the way of navigation.

U. S. G.

ALS, USMA. *O.R.*, I, xxiv, part 3, 215; *O.R.* (Navy), I, xxiv, 602. On April 20, 1863, Act. Rear Admiral David D. Porter, "Flag Ship 'Benton' New Carthage," wrote to USG. "I sent the Tuscumbia and Price down to Grand Gulf to reconnoitre today, and destroy flat boats, and the following is the result—The Rebels are at work fortifying, three guns are mounted on a bluff, 100 feet high, pointing up river. Two deep excavations are made in the side of the hill (fresh earth)—it cannot be seen whether guns are mounted on them or not. About 30 tents only could be seen, but a heavy dust on the Road leading along Big Black—covered wagons were traveling on the road.—4 boats 12 miles up Big Black at a bridge which stops the way—they are small boats. The officers landed on the Louisiana side where they found horses, cattle, mules, fowls and provisions of all kinds in great abundance—large amount of forage, plenty of negroes. 300 beef cattle on one plantation—people running in all directions, and driving off the negroes and cattle. My opinion is, that they will move heaven and earth to stop us if we dont go ahead. I could go down and settle the batteries, but if disabled would not be in condition to cover the landing when it takes place, and I think it should be done together. If the troops just leave all their tents behind, and take only provisions we can be in Grand Gulf in 4 days. I dont want to make a failure and am sure that a combined attack will succeed beautifully. I think ten thousand good men landing in Vicksburg the other night, would have taken it, we can do this easier. This move has demoralized these fellows very much, dont give them time to get over it. I wish twenty times a day that Sherman was here or yourself, but I suppose we cannot have all we wish. I have been working hard on barges, got the tug up to Smiths landing with a fine one to day; picked up another last night which will go up tomorrow, and will also send the largest one of all to Smiths before sundown. We can with the steamers and barges, land 6000 men, if you think that enough—if we can get more transports it will be better. The best way to send them down is to let them drift under low fires, and push by, one at a time, half an hour apart, if they build no fires to light up   the boats should not be too close together. I would not pack them with cotton, but with wet ~~heavy~~ hay, which proved an excellent defence. You will find volunteer[s] enough in my squadron, if you have any trouble, and the steamer men can come down afterwards." LS, DNA, RG 94, War Records Office, Military Div. of the Miss. *O.R.*, I, xxiv, part 3, 211; *O.R.* (Navy), I, xxiv, 600–1.

On April 21, Lt. Col. John A. Rawlins issued Special Orders No. 111. "The following will be the order of running the Vicksburg batteries by the Steamers designated for that purpose. At 9 o'clock P. M. to night all the boats designated will Steam down the river to the mouth of the Yazoo river, each taking one barge in tow, where they will remain in the Channel until signaled to leave. Geo. W. Graham, Master of Transportation, will designate the Signal to be used and also the order in which the boats will run. On the Signal being given, the first boat named will drop down with the current and each six minutes thereafter, each boat in the order designated, will be signalled to follow. No. Steam will be used unless absolutely necessary for the management of the Steamers until arriving near the upper batteries of Vicksburg. From that point all Steam will be put on until the last battery is run. On arrival opposite the Pickets below Vicksburg the boats will all round to and report to Col. Abbott in Command of Pickets. Should any of the boats become disabled and unmanageable, Engineers will stop the Engines and permit their boats to float past the batteries, when they will be taken in tow by those still in running condition   Colonel C. B Lagow having volunteered for the service is put in the immediate Command of the Steamer 'Tigress,' and of the entire fleet. He will be obeyed and respected accordingly. After reporting to Col. Abbott the fleet will proceed down the river to New Carthage, and report to Maj Gen'l J. A. McClernand. Col. Lagow will see that no barges or boats are permitted to be lost through negligence of Steamboat Commanders." Copies, DLC-USG, V, 27, 28; DNA, RG 393, Dept. of the Tenn., Special Orders. *O.R.*, I, xxiv, part 3, 216–17.

1. The word "to-night," erroneously entered in USG's letterbooks, is printed in the *O.R.* text.

2. On April 21, Maj. Gen. William T. Sherman wrote to USG. "The party of men sent to burn the houses on the point immediately in front of Vicksburg returned unsuccessful. The whole Point was under water, and the only means of reaching the houses was along an old levee with many breaks in it, through which the water sets in a strong current. On both sides of that Levee the fallen abattis is impassable. The houses ordered to be destroyed are within 1000 yards of the heaviest Vicksburg Batteries, and the officer sent drew 17 shots before he gave it up. In the night I despatched another party who found the place picketed strong. The party was fired on, having one man wounded, and returned. The enemy has too great an advantage there, and I doubt if we can destroy the buildings in ques-

tion without a great cost of life. Spite of all we can do they can light up this shore, and Steamboats runing the Blockade must reckon on this as one of the certain attendig dangers. A Gunboat should be below Vicksburg to haul out of danger crippled boats, else the loss will be heavy, but I suppose this is impossible now." ALS, DNA, RG 393, Dept. of the Tenn., Letters Received. *O.R.*, I, xxiv, part 3, 216. On the same day, USG wrote to Sherman. "A steam fleet will run the Vicksburg batteries to-night leaving the mouth of the Yazoo about 10½ P. M. They have been directed to round to when opposite Col. Abbotts pickets and report to him. Please inform Col. Abbott of this fact and instruct him to put out a signal light soon after he hears the batteries open." ALS, Dr. and Mrs. Robert L. Alznauer, Los Angeles, Calif. *O.R.*, I, xxiv, part 3, 216; *O.R.* (Navy), I, xxiv, 601. On the same day, "5½," USG wrote to Sherman. "The boats detailed to run the blockade will not be ready to go to-night. They will go to-morrow night certain." ALS, DLC-William T. Sherman.

3. On April 19, Porter wrote to USG. "I send you a sketch of a new route just above where we went in. I had it sounded, and you see the result in figures— it wants but one or two trees removed—the light drafts could go through now— as far as every thing is concerned—the ~~least~~ least water is 15 feet from Smiths plantation to the Mississippi—If you get any sized steamer to Smiths, there will be no trouble the rest of the way—the current is rather strong. I see nothing like work here yet.   the 'Silver Wave' is at Smiths. Landing"   LS, DNA, RG 94, War Records Office, Military Div. of the Miss. The enclosed map showed an alternate route from the Mississippi River into Bayou Vidal.

To Maj. Gen. Benjamin M. Prentiss

Head Quarters, Dept. of the Ten.
Millikin's Bend La. Apl. 21st 1863.

MAJ. GEN. B. M. PRENTISS,
COMD.G DIST. E. ARK.
GEN.

Send to this place with as little delay as practicable two regiments of Cavalry with their equipage generally except tents. Only one tent will be allowed to each company to protect rations and ammunition and one wall tent to regimental Hd Qrs. One Hospital tent to each regiment will also be allowed. Steamers will be sent from here to bring this Cavalry.

Very respectfully
U. S. GRANT
Maj. Gen. Com

ALS, DNA, RG 393, District of Eastern Ark., Letters Received.

On April 25, 1863, Maj. Gen. Benjamin M. Prentiss, Milliken's Bend, wrote to USG. "After congratulating you upon your success in getting transports below, permit me to apologize for my being here today. I trust however you will excuse me as it was my intention to converse with you concerning matters of interest to the service. I therefore took first boat down, and regret to find that I will not have time to come and see you, as I will leave for Helena in the morning.—General, Some two weeks ago General Gorman obtained leave of absence from you,—but upon returning to Helena, he was not disposed to avail himself of it, and was assigned to duty as commandant of the Post,—Being the senior Brig. General there, he commands the troops.—I must say that he and I can agree in every thing military except Policy.—He is not in favor of using negroes as soldiers—I am. —He differs with me as to keeping our lines closed. I am not willing to permit persons outside to have supplies.—In short, personally we agree, but with the present policy of the Government in view, it would be better to have him either in the field or in some other Dept. As for myself, I shall be content wherever I am sent or kept by you. True, my preference is to be wherever I can do most for our success. The rebels at Little Rock are bold in their declarations as to going to Missouri, and I sometimes think this may be a ruse—and have heard from some they intended coming to the river at Helena. My opinion is, the number of troops I have there is too small. If the rebels do go to Missouri, a column should start from Helena to Little Rock, getting in their rear. I mention this with the full knowledge that you have not the troops to spare; but could they not be obtained at other points above. I wanted to see Genl. Thomas concerning the new organizations; but I find he has left to join you.—The two regiments of Cavalry ordered from Helena were in readiness to leave when I left, and will soon be with you.— I feel deeply interested in your success, and await with anxiety the result of present moves. I leave in the morning for Helena. . . . P. S.—In case you deem it well to increase the force at Helena, I suggest that that command hereafter report direct to your Head quarters, instead of thro' the Army Corps." ALS, *ibid.*, Dept. of the Tenn., Letters Received. On April 27, Lt. Col. John A. Rawlins issued Special Orders No. 117. "Brig Gen W. A Gorman is hereby relieved from duty in this Department, and will report in person, immediately and without delay, to Maj-Genl. Irvin McDowel, President of the Military Commission now in session at St Louis, Mo. and from there he will report by letter to the adjutant General of the army, Washington D. C. for orders." Copies, McClernand Papers, IHi; DNA, RG 94, Letters Received.

On May 5, USG wrote to Prentiss. "You will send, without delay, immediately after the receipt of this order, all the cavalry in your district, except two regiments, to report to Maj. Gen. S. A. Hurlbut, commanding the Sixteenth Army Corps, at Memphis, Tenn. Lieut. Col. J. D. Bingham, chief quartermaster, has been directed to instruct all steamers leaving Milliken's Bend to report to you, to assist in transporting the troops to Memphis." *O.R.*, I, xxiv, part 3, 273. See letter to Maj. Gen. Benjamin M. Prentiss, May 25, 1863.

To Lt. Col. Charles A. Reynolds

Milliken Bend La April. 21st 1863

Lieut Col C A Reynolds
Chief Quarter Master

In view of the expected fall in the river and possibly the difficulty that may be encountered in reaching Walnut Bayou through the canal,[1] I think it advisable to put through at once, all the barges now ready to receive freight &c to Cooper plantation. Should the water then fall the distance would not be great to haul supplies to reach the bayou, which will be navigable with a great fall of water   should the river still keep up the barges can be brought back to the mouth of the canal to receive their loading. This should not be delayed longer than to morrow

U S Grant
Maj Genl.

Copies, DLC-USG, V, 19, 30; DNA, RG 393, Dept. of the Tenn., Letters Sent; Alcorn Collection, WyU.
    On April 21, 1863, Lt. Col. John A. Rawlins issued Special Orders No. 111 in which section xii relieved Lt. Col. Charles A. Reynolds as chief q. m., Dept. of the Tenn.; section xiv, however, revoked section xii. Copies, DLC-USG, V, 27, 28; DNA, RG 393, Dept. of the Tenn., Special Orders. On April 22, Reynolds wrote to Rawlins. "I respectfully request, that I be relieved from duty as the Chief Qr-Master of the Department of the Tennessee, and ordered to report to Genl. L Thomas Adjt General U. S. Army for orders. I regret that I am obliged to ask this of the General Commanding and especially so, at this time, but self respect compels me to this course, in view of complaints that have been made, censuring my course in the discharge of the duties, of the Chief Qr. of the Department. I would briefly state to the Genl, Commanding that the position of Chief Qr Master was not of my own choosing, but having accepted the same, I have endeavored to perform my whole duty honestly and faithfully, and I am not aware wherein I have failed. I must say I have been embarrassed in the discharge of my duty, by the inexperience and in some cases—the perfect incapacity of some of the subordinates assigned to me, in fact the Department of the Tennessee has been in many respects a school for new Quartermasters." ALS, *ibid.*, RG 94, Staff Papers, Reynolds. On the same day, Rawlins issued Special Orders No. 112 relieving Reynolds. Copies, DLC-USG, V, 27, 28; DNA, RG 393, Dept. of the Tenn., Special Orders.

    1. On April 22, USG wrote to Maj. Gen. John A. McClernand. "Direct Capt. Patterson to work as many of his men as he can spare in cleaning out the

Bayou from Richmond to the river. Maj. Tweedale, on Walnut Bayou will give him all necessary instructions." Copies, *ibid.*, 13th Army Corps, Letters Received; McClernand Papers, IHi. On the same day, McClernand, Smith's Plantation, La., wrote to USG. "Your dispatch, of this date, ordering me to 'direct Cap't. Patterson to work as many of his men as he can spare in clearing out the bayou from Richmond to the river,' is received. I hasten to reply, that Cap't Patterson is now moving his corps, (except a party building a signal tower at Holme's,) some seven miles below here, on Vidal, for the purpose of building a bridge across that bayou—Gen'ls Hovey and Osterhaus, and Lieut. Haine, Engineer, report the scheme to be entirely practicable; and Gen'l Osterhaus says he will have his portion of the work done tomorrow evening. With such a route two or three such structures, you will have but little trouble, or delay, in moving your whole army, by land, to Perkin's plantation, some fifteen miles above Grand Gulf. I am sending a barge down to Gen'l Hovey, to be used in constructing one of the bridges. Having left to my discretion what portion of the Pioneer Corps may be spared, and believing it to be consistent with what I take to be the spirit of your order, and what you would have ordered yourself, upon full knowledge of the facts, I have not interfered to change the order above mentioned in regard to the Pioneer Corps. above mentioned—If, Gen'l, in this I have erred, it only remains to so advise me, and whatever portion of the corps you may direct, will be sent to report to Maj. Tweedale. I have made very good progress, today, in transferring Gen'l Carr's Division to the Mississippi levee—I will send the 'Forest Queen,' up the river tonight, to watch for the expected transports, and to give them any needed assistance. I start a courier, in haste, with this dispatch." ALS, DNA, RG 393, Dept. of the Tenn., Letters Received. *O.R.*, I, xxiv, part 3, 220–21. Also on April 22, McClernand wrote to USG. "I have had many obstacles to encounter, particularly, in the want of boats, in sufficient numbers to transfer my forces to the river. These obstacles are aggravated by the heavy rain that fell during the past night. Still, however, by unceasing effort, I have succeeded passably well. Genl. Osterhaus' Division is over. One brigade of Carr's is nearly over:—and a regiment of another is just leaving the landing at this place. I have established commissary depots here,—at Jame's and Perkin's Plantations, and have sent my Ordnance Officer over to establish an Ordnance depot at Perkin's. The officers sent have not been able to assure me of the practicability of the land route from here to Perkin's; but are still investigating the matter, under instructions to report upon the subject at the earliest practicable moment. I hope the rope sent for is on the way. If it is possible, run a tug through for use as 'tow.' I find I cannot get the Admiral's 'tow' except occasionally." LS, DNA, RG 393, Dept. of the Tenn., Letters Received.

To Jesse Root Grant

———

Millikins Bend La
April 21st 1863.

Dear Father,

Your letter of the 7th of April has just this day reached me. I hasten to answer your interogitories.

When I left Memphis with my past experiance I prohibited trade below Helena. Trade to that point had previously been opened by the Treasury Department. I give no permits to buy Cotton and if I find any one engaged in the business I send them out of the Department and seize their Cotton for the Government. I have given a few families permission to leave the country and to take with them as far as Memphis their Cotton. In doing this I have been decieved by unprincipled speculators who have smuggled themselves along with the Army in spite of orders prohibiting them and have been compelled to suspend this favor to persons anxious to get out of Dixie.

I understand that Govt has adopted some plan to regulate geting the Cotton out of the country. I do not know what plan they have adopted but am satisfied than any that can be adopted, except for Government to take the Cotton themselves, and rul[e] out speculators altogether will be a bad one. I fee[l] all Army followers who are engaged in speculating off the misfortunes of their country, and really aiding the enemy more than they possibly could do by open treason, should be drafted at once and put in the first forlorn hope.

I move my Head Quarters to New Carthage to-morrow. This whole country is under water except strips of land behind the levees along the river and bayous and makes opperations almost impossible. I struck upon a plan which I thought would give me a foot hold on the East bank of the Miss. before the enemy could offer any great resistance. But the difficulty of the last one & a half miles next to Carthage makes it so tedious that the enemy cannot fail to discover my plans. I am doing my best and am full of hope for complete success. Time has been consumed but it was absolutely impossible to avoid it. An attack upon the rebel works at any time since I arrived here must inevitably resulted in the loss of a large portion of my Army if not in an entire defeat. There was but two points of land, Hains Bluff & Vicksburg itself, out of water any place from which troops could march. These are thoroughly fortified and it would be folly to attack them as long as there is a prospect of turning their position. I never expect to have an army under my command whipped unless it is very badly whipped and cant help it but I have no idea of being driven to do a desperate or foolish act by the howlings of the press. It is painful to me as a matter of course to see the course pursued by some of the papers. But there is no one less disturbed by them than myself. I have never saught a large command and have no ambitious ends to accomplish. Was it not for the very natural desire of proving myself equal to anything expected of me, and the evidence my removal would afford that I was not thought equal to it, I would gladly accept a less responsible position. I have no desire to be an object of envy or jealousy, nor to have this war continue. I want, and will do my part towards it, to put down the rebellion in the shortest possible time without expecting or desiring any other recognition than a quiet approval of my course. I beg that you will destroy this letter. At least do not show it.

Julia and the children are here but will go up by the first good boat. I sent for her to come down and get instructions about some business I want attended to and see no immediate prospect of being able to attend to ~~attend~~ myself.

Ulysses

ALS, IC.

    Richardson (p. 293) quotes a letter from USG to his father, apparently written about this time. "The Government asks a good deal of me, but not more than I feel fully able to perform." This may be a paraphrase of the confidence expressed in USG's letter of April 21.

To Maj. Gen. Henry W. Halleck

Youngs Point Apr 23rd 1863

Maj Gen H. W. Halleck
Gen in Chief

Six Boats and a number of Barges ran the Vicksburg Batteries last night. All the boats got by more more or less damaged. The "Tigress" sunk at 3. A. M and is a total loss. Crew all safe— The "Moderator" was much damaged. I think all the Barges went through safely   Col Logan [*Lagow*] of my Staff was on the "Tigress" in command of the fleet. Casualties so far as reported two men mortally wounded and several (number not known) wounded more or less severely. About five hundred shots were fired. I look upon this as a great success. At the Warrenton Batteries there was heavy firing but all the Boats were seen to go past   What damage done these is not known

U S. Grant
Maj Genl

Telegram received, DLC-Robert T. Lincoln; DNA, RG 107, Telegrams Collected (Bound); copies, *ibid.*, Telegrams Received in Cipher; *ibid.*, RG 393, Dept. of the Tenn., Hd. Qrs. Correspondence; DLC-USG, V, 5, 8, 24, 94. *O.R.*, I, xxiv, part 1, 31. This telegram was received in Washington at 7:20 p.m., April 25, 1863. See letter to Brig. Gen. Montgomery C. Meigs, Aug. 10, 1863.

To Maj. Gen. Stephen A. Hurlbut

Head Quarters Dept. of the Ten.
Millikins Bend, La. Apl. 23d 1863.

Maj. Gen. S. A. Hurlbut
Comd.g 16th Army Corps,
Gen.

It appearing that the proprietor and Editor of the Bullitin has been absent for some time, and the controll of his paper out of his hands, you are authorized to permit its issue for the publication of the letter list and such Northern news as you may deem proper to be published.

Neighbors, one of the former proprietors, I regard as one of the most dangerous as well as most disloyal citizens of Memphis. I would advise a close watch to be kept over him and on the slightest deviation from a correct course I would expell him from our lines.

> Very respectfully
> U. S. GRANT
> Maj. Gen. Com.

ALS, ICHi. *O.R.*, I, xxiv, part 3, 226. See letter to Maj. Gen. Stephen A. Hurlbut, April 9, 1863.

On Aug. 14, 1863, USG wrote to Hurlbut. "Two gentlemen have spoken to me for the privilege of opening a daily newspaper in Memphis. I have no objection to any number of papers being established there under just such restrictions as you may deem advisable to establish." AL (signature clipped), DNA, RG 393, 16th Army Corps, Letters Received.

To George G. Pride

> Head Quarters, Dept. of the Ten.
> Milliken's Bend La. Apl. 23d 1863.

COL. G. G. PRIDE
CHIEF ENG. MIL. R-ROADS,
COL.

It is with regret that I learn ~~that~~ you can stay no longer in this Dept. in the Government service. Your services have been of a kind that I had no one about me who could have performed with any sort of satisfaction to me or advantage to the service.

Besides the general valuable services you have rendered whilst serving on my Staff there has been three several times when I acknowledge myself under special obligations to your energy and practical knowledge of what you undertake. First; at Pittsburg Landing on that memorable 6th of April 1862 when our men by being forced back from their first line were left without ammunition, except the supply in cartridge boxes, by your forsight and energy in superintending in person you kept up the supply with wagons, from a single Ordnance boat, and over roads almost impassable. Second; After the Van Dorn & Forest raids upon our lines of communication last December, when it became necessary to open the road from Memphis to Grand Junction you by your energy, and skill in that branch of Engineering, opened up that road to the public service almost as fast as guards could be put upon it for public service. This was of inestimable value to the Government.—Third; in the construction of the last canal at this place no so nearly ready for practial use I feel that all is due to you for the progress made. It was at your suggestion and by your personal efforts that the dredge boats, without which the canal could not have been made, were obtained. To your indefatigable personal attention to their working am I, and the country, indebted for the skillful use made of them.

It affords me the greatest pleasure to offer this slight testamonial of appreciation of your services and regret only that I have not the power to make it more substantial.

Very Truly Your Friend
U. S. Grant
Maj. Gen.

ALS, MoSHi.

To Maj. Gen. John A. McClernand

———

April 24th, 1863,

Maj Gen. J. A McClernand
Comdg 13th. Army Corps.
General,

I would like to have Gen Ousterhaus make a reconnoisance, in person, to a point on the Mississippi opposite the mouth of

Bayou Peirre, and a short distance below, to where there is a road leading from the river to Grand Gulf. The map shows such a road. It is desirable to learn if there is a landing at that point, and if it can be done by inquiry to learn also the condition of the road on the opposite side. If a landing cannot be made in front of Grand Gulf it may be necessary to reach there by this route. The maps show this road, and also a road from the same point to Port Gibson. It is also important to know if there is a road on the west bank of the river from here to a point below Grand Gulf. Should any of our Gunboats get below the Gulf and not be able to return it could be used in communicating with them.

Very Respectfully

U. S. Grant

Major General.

Copies, DLC–USG, V, 19, 30, 98; DNA, RG 393, Dept. of the Tenn., Letters Sent; *ibid.*, 13th Army Corps, Letters Received; Alcorn Collection, WyU.

On April 23, 1863, Maj. Gen. John A. McClernand, Smith's Plantation, wrote to USG. "I have the honor to report that I received a dispatch from Rear Admiral Porter, last night, stating that the enemy was constructing works at Grand Gulf. He bombarded their works within range, but could not reach those upon the hill. He intends renewing the bombardment to-day, and requests an infantry force to co-operate. I have ordered all the available forces to move—yet with due caution in landing—and to remain under the protection of the Gunboats. You will please forward the pontoon train as soon as possible, as a bridge across the bayou, below, would add greatly to the means of reaching the river—" LS, DNA, RG 393, Dept. of the Tenn., Letters Received. *O.R.*, I, xxiv, part 3, 226; *O.R.* (Navy), I, xxiv, 605. The letter from Act. Rear Admiral David D. Porter is in *O.R.*, I, xxiv, part 3, 222; *O.R.* (Navy), I, xxiv, 603. Also on April 23, McClernand wrote to USG. "I have the honor to inform you that 5 Steamers have arrived safely—& one was sunk. General Osterhous Division were embarked—8 Regiments Infantry & two Batteries & are ready to start for Grand Gulf at 10 oclock A. M. this day" Copy, DNA, RG 393, 13th Army Corps, Letters Sent. *O.R.*, I, xxiv, part 3, 227.

On April 23, Porter, "Off New Carthage," wrote to USG. "Feeling that something was going on at Grand Gulf that should be stopped, I went down with the whole squadron to reconnoiter. A strong fort (at present mounting three guns only) pointing up the river was a part of the extensive works now under way. I went down in the Lafayette and drove the workers out; that fort did not fire at us, but one below it did; also one lower still. Three rifled shot went over the Lafayette after I left. The rebels had a steamer (the Charm) down, bringing supplies. We drove her away before she had time to land them. These forts are only partly finished; in a week they will be formidable. I found a preacher (half Union man), who was just from Grand Gulf. He told me all about the fortifications and the number of troops. They are throwing in troops from Vicksburg as fast as they can by land, and bringing down guns, &c., as fast as they can by water. There are four forts in all, well placed, and mounting twelve large guns. They have been preparing this place six weeks, and have known all about this move; expected it sooner. I would have attacked had there been but two forts. I made my plans to do so, but considered it unwise to put myself in a position where I might be separated from the army, which might have happened under present circumstances. They have 12,000 troops at Grand Gulf, and still increasing the number. My informant tells me that they have plenty of beef and corn meal. They seem to have about 500 contrabands at work. I could see no more. My idea was to attack the forts at once and land troops at the same time, but I think we should have superior numbers, for the position is a very strong one. If the troops can get by, we can land them below, and land on a road leading to the fort, or go up Bayou Pierre, which leads to the Port Hudson Railroad. As you know your own plan, I won't pretend to offer any suggestions. I merely give you the information I have obtained. I send you a little plan of the place." *Ibid.*, pp. 225–26; *O.R.* (Navy), I, xxiv, 605–6.

On April 24, McClernand wrote three letters to USG. "At 11 o'clock, P. M., of the 22nd inst, I received a communication from Admiral Porter, informing me that he had been reconnoitering during the day, near Grand Gulf, and had found that the enemy had built extensive works there which were occupied by guns, and that if left to himself he would make the place impregnable. He added that he had driven the enemy out of the principal work, but that the others was out of range, and could not be attacked without bringing on a general engagement, for which he (the Admiral) was not prepared. He further advised me, that he would attack the forts in the morning, and requested that I should send a land force to hold them, in case he should succeed in accomplishing their reduction; closing by saying, that it was a case in which dispatch, and a dash, was important, and might save everything. Although not prepared to make a sustained movement against the place, and inadequately supplied with ammunition, I sent an order to Genl. Osterhaus, six miles in advance, to embark his division, with all the artillery and ammunition he could make available, on such boats as he could find, and hold himself in readiness to follow the gunboats, and to co-operate in attacking the enemy's position at the Gulf, and to hold it. Many obstacles remained to encounter: the collection of boats, which were deficient in number; difficulty of communicating, across the flooded bayous and swamps, with officers, and muddy roads,—Yet by 11 o'clock, A. M., on the 23d, the General had embarked his division, including two batteries, and was awaiting the movement of the gunboats. At 12 o'clock, Admiral Porter, (whom I called on,) advised me that he had just returned from the Gulf, and that he had found the situation, there, different. That he had discovered two more forts—in all, four—and a land force, estimated at 12,000, and that he had concluded to delay the attack upon the place— at all events, until he could confer with me. Only having some 3000 men embarked, and immediately available for the movement, I determined at once, to make a reconnoisance of the Gulf; and accordingly asked the use of the ram 'Price,' which was furnished me by the Admiral for the purpose. In an hour and a half I was within some two miles of the enemy's position,—a rough sketch of which I exhibited to you last night. The 'Price' threw two shots, one of which struck the foot of the bluff near the enemy. I saw no great activity of any kind, displayed by the enemy; nor did I see any formidable display of batteries or forts. Indeed; it was questionable, in my mind, whether the enemy had any entrenchments; yet others asserted that they had seen both riflepits and earthworks, for the protection of infantry and artillery, and it may be so. I am satisfied, however, that there are no extensive or very strong works; though the position in itself is one of the stronged I ever saw.—Upon my return, I met with Admiral Porter, and told him that I could see no activity on the part of the enemy; and that I thought it important that the gunboats should so annoy him as to prevent him from entrenching. I cannot too strongly urge that it be done now. The enemy should be at once driven away from the crest and river slope of the bluffs; and I believe the gunboats can easily do it. When I have concentrated my Corps, and have it in readiness for embarkation upon such transports as can be furnished—and a footing has been secured for me by the gunboats; I will take the place against any force now there; probably against any likely to be there. With the increased facilities promised in the boats which run the blockade the other night, and those understood to be coming, I will soon have my corps on the Mississippi levee, only fifteen miles from the Gulf." "If the Black river cut-off is navigable, ~~our~~ my forces might ascend to some eligible landing on the Black river, and promptly gain the rear of the enemy at Grand Gulf, and thus cut off his escape   If that line should be found impracticable, another might be adopted in marching some twenty-five miles across the country to a point opposite the mouth of Bayou Pierre, which may probably be accomplished in forty-eight hours. Arrived at that point, I would have to rely on gunboats, (unless transports run the blockade at Grand Gulf,) to cross my command to the East bank of the Mississippi, and, if necessary, to take them to an eligible landing on the Bayou. Gen'l Williams, last year, ascended the same bayou nearly to the point at which the railroad from Grand Gulf to Port Gibson, crosses it. Provisions and forage, could, doubtless, be found on this line. Another plan is, a front attack, and the reduction of the enemy's fortifications, on the bold promontory overlooking the mouth of Big Black, the Mississippi, and the town of Grand Gulf, below, by the gunboats. Possessed of such a footing, the Infantry can do the balance. But they must have this footing; and it can only be obtained by the gunboats; as frail transports, laden with men and munitions of war, could not be advanced, under the hostile fire, to the shore. The gunboats ought to be able to do this. They can do it. These three plans, severally, may be found practicable, and two or more of them are capable of being combined. All are respectfully submitted for your consideration." LS, DNA, RG 393, Dept. of the Tenn., Letters Received. *O.R.*, I, xxiv, part 3, 227–29. "According to your order, I have directed Genl Osterhous to make an armed reconnoisance to, and, if necessary, to the object in view below the mouth of Bayou Pierre and to report with out delay, the result of his observations so that it may be determined whether it will be best to recall him from his destination, or for the rest of my Corps to follow." Copy, DNA, RG 393, 13th Army Corps, Letters Sent. *O.R.*, I, xxiv, part 3, 229.

To Maj. Gen. William T. Sherman

——————

Head Qrs. Dept. of the Tennessee
In the Field, April 24th, 1863,

Major General W. T. Sherman
Comdg. 15th. Army Cops
General,

In company with Admiral Porter, I made to day a reconnoisance of Grand Gulf. My impressions are, that, if an attack
can be made within the next two days, the place will easily fall.
But the difficulty from getting from here, (Smiths Plantation) to
the river are great.

I foresee great difficulties in our present position, but it will
not do, to let these retard any movement. In the first place, if a
battle should take place, we are necessarily very destitute of all
preperations for taking care of wounded men. All the little extras
for this purpose, were put aboard of the Tigress, the only boat
that was lost. The line from here to Millikens Bend is a long one
both for the transportation of supplies and to defend; and an
impossible one for the transportation of wounded men. The water
in the bayous is falling very rapidly, out of all proportion to the
fall in the river, so that it is exceedingly doubtful whether, they
can be made use of for purposes of navigation. One inch fall in
the river, diminishes the supply of water to these bayous to a
very great extent, whilst their capacity for carrying it away
remains the same.

Should the river fall sufficiently to draw of all the water on
the point where you are encamped, our line will have to be by
wagons across to below the Warrenton batteries. Whilst there
I wish you would watch that matter, and should the water fall
sufficiently make the necessary roads for this purpose. You need
not move any portion of your Corps, more than is necessary for
the protection of the road to Richmond until ordered. It may
possibly happen, that, the enemy may so weaken his forces about

Vicksburg and Haines Bluff as to make the latter vulnerable particularly with a fall of water to give a more extended landing.

I leave the management of affairs at your end of the line to you.

I shall send Surgeon Hewitt the Bend to morrow to consult with the Medical Director about the best policy to pursue for caring for our sick and wounded.

Very Respectfully

U S. GRANT

Major General.

Copies, DLC-USG, V, 19, 30, 98; DNA, RG 393, Dept. of the Tenn., Letters Sent; Alcorn Collection, WyU. *O.R.*, I, xxiv, part 3, 231. On April 26, 1863, Maj. Gen. William T. Sherman wrote to USG. "Your letter of Apl 24 is this moment received. I feared the difficulties you now experience and went myself yesterday and examined the new Canal from Duckport to Willow Bayou. I sounded it in its whole length—it is near three miles long, the 1st mile is comparetively good—the middle mile is bad—has not an average depth of one foot, and the last mile has 3 ft. 2 ft. and nothing. 200 yards at Willow Bayou is dry. I made a rude estimate and allowing for four dredges, (I only found two employed,) will take near 50 days work to make a canal 8 feet deep. Your tugs draw 7½ feet. All my orders were out to march in the mornig, but I have this moment countermanded them. Steeles Division is at Millikens Bend and I will leave him there to guard that point and the Road back to Richmond. Tuttle is at the Canal. I will at once make him go to work to build a wagon Road back along the Canal to the Bayou, as auxiliary to the one from Millikens Bend—I examined it as I was sounding the Canal & think it can be done. Blairs Division I will hold here, and proceed to make the examinations you suggest, but I am already familiar with evry avenue possible. Though the water in the River has fallen 2 feet, and retired from the Plains where my present camp is, still there is enough water in the woods back & in the ditches for a boat to navigate from here to the Biggs place. Between Biggs and Bedford place opposite Warrenton there is an old crevasse and the cut is wide, deep, & impassable   Still I will make further examination of it. I do not believe it will be possible for an empty wagon to proceed from here to any point below Warrenton for 2 weeks. I do not believe the new canal will be available in one month. I think I can make a wagon Road back from Tuttles Camp to Richmond which will be separate & distinct from the one now used, and to that extent available to your purposes. I may also with plank make a Road across to the Hecla place from Youngs Point. I have an excellent map, but have today furnished my Division Commanders all but the original   I will enclose a sketch with this illustrating the Road I propose to assist you in. To haul hence via Biggs & the Bedford place below Warrenton is simply impossible. We did corduroy 2 miles of it once, but there are 4 feet of water now and even should the water retire it will remain a pulpy quagmire for a month. I believe you have good Bayou Navigation from Carthage up to Richmond, and our best course is to push Road to Richmond, and if possible the Canal & Bayou above Richmond. The Tug Rumsey should have run the Batteries last night, but she did not go. She will start tonight, and it is favorable, being rainy & dark. She has two barges in tow. Graham is here at this moment & will carry this up to Millikens Bend & despatch it to you." ALS, DNA, RG 94, War Records Office, Dept. of the Mo. *O.R.*, I, xxiv, part 3, 234–35.

To Maj. Gen. John A. McClernand

Head Qrs. April, 25th 1863

MAJ. GEN. JNO. A. MCCLERNAND
COMMANDING 13TH A. C.
GENERAL.

Lt. Col. Wilson goes to-day to explore the East bank of the river for the purpose of ascertaining if it is possible to reach the high lands of Mississippi from any point above Black River. He will require one Regt. of troops, and the use of a Steamer. You will please furnish these.

No Steamer capable of navigating the Bayous will be taken

Very respectfully
U. S. GRANT,
Maj. Gen. Comd'g.

Copy, DNA, RG 393, 13th Army Corps, Letters Received.

To Maj. Gen. James B. McPherson

Head Quarters, Dept. of the Tennessee
In the Feild, April 25th, 1863,

MAJOR GENL. MCPHERSON
COMDG 17TH, ARMY CORPS,
GENERAL,

I have instructed that all the barges now through the canal be run down the bayou to the most convenient point for loading them, from Millikens Bend. The Chief Quartermaster is also instructed to set his teams to work, as many of them as he can to hauling out stores to them. Direct Bingham where to have three barges placed, and put a sufficient guard over them for their protection. You can also direct what particular supplies had better be brought first. Commissary stores, Ordnance and Medical supplies however should be brought more particularly than anything else

> Very Respectfully
> U. S. GRANT
> Maj. Gen

Copies, DLC-USG, V, 19, 30, 98; DNA, RG 393, Dept. of the Tenn., Letters Sent; Alcorn Collection, WyU.

Also on April 25, 1863, USG wrote to "Com'dg Officer Advance of 17th Army Corps." "For the present, until other troops advance to take your place, you will encamp one Regiment on the Road between Richmond and Smiths Plantation, at such place as Capt. Prime, Chief Engnr, may dictate. You will direct the regiment so left to commence immediately clearing out the drift and all obstructions to navigation. Inform Gen McPherson of what you are doing so that you may be relieved by other troops as they come up." Copy, DLC-USG, V, 98.

To Lt. Col. Judson D. Bingham

Head Quarters, Department of the Tennessee,
Smiths Plantation, La., April 25th, 1863,

LT COL. BINGHAM
CHIEF QUARTERMASTER
COLONEL,

I understand a number of barges are now in the Canal. Call on Capt. Prime to have them shoved forward to the best point, to have them loaded by hauling from Millikens Bend. Gen McPherson can inform you what point this will be. Then set a portion of the teams, as many as possible, to hauling there subsistence stores, ammunition &c.,   By the time these boats can be loaded, the bayous will be navigable to the river, on this side.

I will instruct Gen. McPherson to place a guard with three boats to remain as long, as stores are left to be guarded.

Very Respectfully

U S Grant

Maj Genl.

Copies, DLC-USG, V, 19, 30, 98; DNA, RG 393, Dept. of the Tenn., Letters Sent. On April 26, 1863, Lt. Col. Judson D. Bingham, Milliken's Bend, wrote to USG. "I have the honor to report that Fifteen Barges have been passed through the new Canal, and are at Cooper's plantation, ready for use. Four Barges, not yet decked over, are at Cooper's, with the necessary materials & mechanics to prepare them for use, making a total of Nineteen (19) now in the Bayou. The work of passing them through the Canal was delayed by the falling of the water, and the Agents in charge of the work at first not acting with sufficient energy. Three Barges are now aground, and cannot be brought back or sent forward. The Officer that I sent to Cooper's plantation represents that the Barges should be sent below that point, as the water is falling very rapidly there. I have directed that details be applied for from Gen. Tuttle's command to assist the mechanics in keeping the Barges afloat at Cooper's plantation." ALS, *ibid.*, Letters Received. On April 27, Bingham wrote to USG. "I have the honor to acknowledge the receipt of your letter of the 25th inst. this morning. I sent orders early this morning, to push the Barges forward to the point indicated by Gen. McPherson, Zeigler's plantation. The officer whom I placed in charge of the work has exhibited much energy during the last three days, and I think the Barges will be pushed forward as rapidly as possible. I gave orders yesterday to the Corps Quartermasters, to push forward supplies to Ziegler plantation, in the order indicated by Gen McPherson, and directed them to send agents to the same place to receive and forward the supplies by Barges. All the Barges that could be hauled through the Canal are now in the Bayou. All the available teams are employed in hauling forward supplies, and I am hitching up more as fast as I can get mules." ALS, *ibid.*, RG 94, War Records Office, Dept. of the Tenn. On April 29, Bingham wrote to USG. "I have the honor to report that in consequence of the rapid falling of water in the Bayou, I have directed all the materials &c in the Canal to be collected at Duckport and held in readiness for removal. I have been forwarding supplies to Ziegler's plantation for several days, and in accordance with your instructions, received to-day, have sent a Quartermaster to establish a Depot for supplies at Perkin's Plantation, and have given orders for the organization of trains in each Corps for the purpose of hauling supplies to that place. I respectfully request to be informed if you desire me to continue the erection of Storehouses on the River bank, near the entrance to the Duckport Canal." ALS, *ibid.*, RG 393, Dept. of the Tenn., Letters Received.

To Maj. Gen. Henry W. Halleck

———

Near Grand Gulf Miss
April 27th 1863.

MAJ. GEN H. W. HALLECK
GEN IN CHIEF

Moving troops from Smith's Plantation has been a tedious operation, more so than it should have been. I am now embarking troops for the attack on Grand Gulf. Expect to reduce it tomorrow

U. S. GRANT
Maj Gen Comdg

Telegram received, DNA, RG 107, Telegrams Collected (Bound); copies, *ibid.*, Telegrams Received in Cipher; *ibid.*, RG 393, Dept. of the Tenn., Hd. Qrs. Correspondence; DLC-USG, V, 5, 8, 24, 94. *O.R.*, I, xxiv, part 1, 31. This telegram was sent from Memphis on May 2, 1863, 9:00 P.M., and received at Washington on May 3, 1:15 A.M.

On April 26, USG wrote to an unnamed correspondent. "I am happy to say the admiral and myself have never yet disagreed upon any policy." Adam Badeau, *Military History of Ulysses S. Grant* (New York, 1868), I, 190.

To Maj. Gen. John A. McClernand

———

Head Quarters Department of the Tenn.
Perkins Plantation La April 27, 1863

MAJ. GENL. JNO A MCCLERNAND
COMMDG 13TH ARMY CORPS
GEN.

The amount of transportation being to limited for the number of men it is desirable to take to Grand Gulf I especially intended that no horses except what was necessary for drawing the Artillery should be taken. Should we effect a landing and I feel but little doubt of the result the steamers can return for the Officers horses. It would not be desirable to have them in making a sudden charge to secure the capture of the heights

Do not send troops down the river until it is known that they can get through. That fact I suppose will be known by morning All repairs that can be made to night to the Un Seaworthy transports should be made by Details from the Divisions to which they are assigned. Commanders of the "Tuscumbia" and the "Price" will give such assistance as they can by application to them. Medical Directors to Divisions should have brought with them every thing for the comfort of the sick and wounded without Wagons from Smiths Plantation. If they have left any thing back they should go back to night in Small boats and get these articles here by 8. o'clock tomorrow.

> Very respectfully
> U. S. GRANT
> Maj. Gen.

Copies, DLC-USG, V, 19, 30, 98; DNA, RG 393, Dept. of the Tenn., Letters Sent; *ibid.*, 13th Army Corps, Letters Received; Alcorn Collection, WyU. On April 27, 1863, Maj. Gen. John A. McClernand wrote to USG. "I have the honor to acknowledge the receipt of your order in relation to taking on board the transports baggage and horses. Strict orders will be given. But the wording of your note would exclude the horses of Field, Brigade, Division & Corps officers horses. Please advise me if this was your intention, before I issue orders to Division Commanders." DfS, McClernand Papers, IHi; copies, DNA, RG 393, 13th Army Corps, Letters Sent. On the same day, USG wrote to McClernand. "Whilst embarking most stringent orders should be given against the loading of unauthorized baggage. and Suitable officers should be appointed to each boat to see that nothing is taken on but what is strictly authorized. Horses, except for Artillery, should be possitively prohibited and all excess of officers baggage." ALS, McClernand Papers, IHi.

To Maj. Gen. John A. McClernand

Head Quarters Department of the Tennessee
Perkins Plantation La. April 27, 1863. 11. P. M.
MAJ GEN'L J A McCLERNAND
COMDG 13TH ARMY CORPS
GEN.

The position now occupied by the enemy at Choctaw Bayou

is one from which they can be easily driven, if not captured, by sending a force to engage them in front whilst the majority of the force take the road leading by the North east side of Bruins Lake This latter road seems to be the one t[he] mass of the troops should take to reach the river bank near to and below Grand Gulf,

If you are satisfied that Smiths Division will not find transportation here they should start early in the morning by this route. Logans Division will also follow them tomorrow. The Troops of Osterhaus now out cannot be brought back until releived by other troops, and that will be too late for them to take part in the present movement with their Division. You might if the Transportation at hand will justify it, leave one Brigade of Smiths Division to act with Osterhaus, until the Troops can all be brought together and direct Smith to take command of the Two regiments on the road when he comes up with them.

This force of Bowens[1] should be driven entirely out of the country or captured.

> Very respectfully
> U. S. GRANT
> Maj Gen.

Copies, DLC-USG, V, 19, 30, 98; DNA, RG 393, Dept. of the Tenn., Letters Sent; *ibid.*, 13th Army Corps, Letters Received. *O.R.*, I, xxiv, part 3, 239.

On April 27, 1863, Maj. Gen. John A. McClernand wrote several times to USG. "I have the honor to enclose suggestions of Colonel Mudd as worthy of your attention" Copies, McClernand Papers, IHi; DNA, RG 393, 13th Army Corps, Letters Sent. "I have the honor to enclose herewith the promised sketch illustrating the Lake road to St. Joseph and Hard Times in the west bank of the Mississippi River. The sketch sent is a copy of the original furnished by Genl. Osterhaus." DfS, McClernand Papers, IHi; copies (2), DNA, RG 393, 13th Army Corps, Letters Sent. "Being busily engaged in preparing orders for the impending movement, I send Col. Mudd and Lieut. Tunica, Engineer of 9th Division, to make explanations in connection with the map I sent you this evening, and the reconnoisance being made towards Grand Gulf. For reasons which these officers will explain, it appears that the reconnoitering force cannot safely go further without reinforcement. That force consists in part, of two regiments of Gen'l Osterhaus' Division, which, it was intended, should join him below, at 'Hard Times,' in the impending conflict. By ordering Gen'l Smith forward, I can enable the regiments to go on, if there be a road, but still fear that by waiting for reinforcements they might reach Hard Times too late to join their command. I await your direction whether I shall recall the detachment or send Gen'l Smith to reinforce it, and protect the line of communication until Gen'l McPherson comes up—" "Gen'l Osterhaus expects a report, this evening from Col. Kegwin, comd'g expedition in the direction of Grand Gulf. That report will determine the question of the practicability of reaching a point near that place by land. Until that question is determined, I will, unless you direct otherwise, postpone ordering any portion of my command in that direction. Gen'l Osterhaus reports that some of the transports assigned to him are at present unseaworthy. Gen'l Carr reports the same in regard to one of the transports assigned to him. The constant use of such of the boats as passed Vicksburg since their arrival, in bringing troops, &c., through a narrow bayou to this place, has increased their unseaworthiness, and has left no time for repairing them—I fear more time will be required to make them seaworthy than will be agreeable to either of us. I have assigned to Gen'l Hovey the two barges that came down this morning, in addition to the steamer 'Horizon;' but one of them is represented to be, at most, almost, in a sinking condition, and will require to be repaired. Your order of the 24th inst., prohibiting the wagons from being brought over from Smith's, on boats, has left behind dispensing wagons and ambulances. Division commanders make this explanation of the absence of both, and, in turn, I make it to you. I have, however, the Corps Hospital wagon along." ALS, *ibid.*, Dept. of the Tenn., Letters Received. *O.R.*, I, xxiv, part 3, 238–39.

Also on April 27, Lt. Col. John A. Rawlins issued Special Orders No. 117. "One Division of the 17th. Army Corps will be pushed as rapidly as possible, (taking five days rations with them,) to Purkins Plantation and south, if a practicable road is found, to a point on the river near or below Grand Gulf. One more Division of the 17th Army Corps, will be moved to the Mississippi river at Prkins Plantation, and the third held in reserve between Richmond and Smiths Plantations. The 15th Army Corps will supply all the guards necessary to hold the line to Richmond, including the latter place. It will be the duty of Commanding Officers of troops on the road to, see that all the teams of the different Army Corps are kept constantly on the road bringing supplies, and that the roads are kept in repair. The two Regiments of Cavalry now expected from Helena will report for duty, temporarily, to Major General Sherman. Major General Sherman will detail a competent officer to take general supervision of all the supply trains of the Army, and put as much Cavalry at his command, as he may deem necessary to enable him to perform his duties efficiently. It will be the duty of the officer in charge of the Wagon-train to see that all the teams are kept constantly on the road, and that all stores are properly delivered at Perkins' Plantation on the Mississippi River. The Chief Quartermaster will collect together as rapidly as possible teams to add to the general supply train. He will select an Assistant or Acting Assistant Quartermaster to take charge of the depot at Perkins Plantation The chief Commissary of subsistince, will detail a Commissary to take charge of all supplies pertaining to his Department at the same place. Lieut Col. W S. Oliver of the 7th Missouri Infantry Volunteers is hereby appointed Master of Transportation for the transport fleet below Vicksburg He will see that all the steamers, barges, and small boats are kept properly employed, and that none of them are lost, or allowed to go to destruction. Army Corps Commanders will furnish Lt. Col Oliver such details of men as he may require for the efficient working of his fleet without further orders from these Head Quarters." DS, McClernand Papers, IHi. On April 30, Rawlins wrote to Lt. Col. William S.

Oliver, 7th Mo. "You are hereby releived from duty as Master of Transportation and will resume the command of your regiment. In making this order the Major General Commanding directs me to return you his thanks for the gallant manner in which you ran the blockades at Vicksburg and Grand Gulf and the efficiency with which you have discharged the duty of your recent position At the request of Colonal Logan and Stevenson who say your regiment cannot do without you this order is made." Copies, DLC-USG, V, 19, 30, 98; DNA, RG 393, Dept. of the Tenn., Letters Sent.

On April 28, McClernand wrote to USG. "The members of my Staff have just finished a reconnoisance. They found a good road, from this landing, two miles across the Point, to the Miss, below Grand Gulf. There is a fine camping ground where the road strikes the Miss, and the town, some 2½ miles above, is in full view. There is a fine landing at the same place. No activity on part of the enemy was discovered. I have sent anoth[er] reconnoitering party, accompanied by a topographical Engineer, in a skiff, to sketch the enemys position. The result of their observations will be reported." Copy, *ibid.*, 13th Army Corps, Letters Sent.

1. All other copies read "Harrison's," referring to C.S.A. Maj. Isaac F. Harrison, 15th Battalion, La. Cav., then harassing U.S. forces. See letter to Maj. Gen. John A. McClernand, May 4, 1863.

To Maj. Gen. John A. McClernand

Head Quarters Department of the Tennessee
Perkins Plantation La. April 27, 1863

MAJ GEN. J. A. MCCLERNAND.
COMMANDING 13TH ARMY CORPS.
GEN:

Commence immediately the embarkation of your Corps or so much of it as there is transportation for. Have put aboard the Artillery, and every article authorized in orders, limiting baggage, except the men, and hold them in readiness, with their places assigned to be moved at a moments notics.

All the troops you may have, except those ordered to remain behind, send to a point nearly opposite, Grand Gulf, where you will see by special orders of this date General McPherson is ordered to send one Division

The plan of attack will be for the Navy to attack and silence all the Batteries commanding the river. Your Corps will be in the river ready to send to and debark on the nearest elligable land below the promontory first brought to view, passing down the river. Once on shore have each Commander instructed before hand to form his men the best the ground will admit of and take possession of the most commanding point, but avoid seperating your command so that it cannot support itself. The first object is to get a foothold where our troops can maintain themselves until such time as preparations can be made and troops collected for a forward movement.

Admiral Porter has proposed to place his boats in the position indicated to you a few days ago, and to ferry over with them such troops as may be below the city after the guns of the enemy are silenced.

It may be that the enemy will occupy positions back from the river out of range of the Gunboats, as to make it desirable to run past Grand Gulf and land at Rodney, in case this should prove the plan a signal will be arranged and you duly informed for indicating when the transports are to start with this view. Or it may be deemed expedient for the boats to run past, but not the men, in this case. Then the transports would have to be brought back to where the ~~river~~ men could land, and move by forced march to below Grand Gulf, reimbark rapidly and proceed to the latter place.

There will be required then three signals, one to indicate that the transports can run down and debark the Troops at Grand Gulf one that the transports can run by without the troops and the last that the transports can run by with the troops on bourd.

Should the men have to march all Baggage and Artillery will be left to run the Blockade

If not allready directed require your command to keep three days ration in their Haversack not to be touched until a movement commences

> Very respectfully
> Your obedient Servt
> U. S. GRANT
> Major General

Copies, DLC-USG, V, 19, 30, 98; DNA, RG 393, Dept. of the Tenn., Letters Sent; (2) *ibid.*, 13th Army Corps, Letters Received; McClernand Papers, IHi; Alcorn Collection, WyU. *O.R.*, I, xxiv, part 3, 237–38. On April 26, 1863, Maj. Gen. John A. McClernand wrote to USG. "Many persons say, I could march my Corps to Hard Times, three miles above Grand Gulf I have sent a detachment to-day, to reconnoitre, and officially report upon the subject The detachment sent to Bayou Pierre, are somewhat retarded in their progress, by reason of the enemy's burning the bridges, behind them, as they retreat I am starting over to Mound Bayou, to see what progress Genl Hovey has made in bridging Vidal and Mound Bayous It is said that he is at work on the last bridge Several gentlemen represent that as they came down to this landing yesterday, they saw a wagon train moving South. Others say, they had opportunities of seeing the same, but did not. It is rather probable that the enemy are re-inforcing the garrison at the Gulf—hence the importance of the suggestion I ventured to make, the other day—that at least a feint should be made upon Warrenton and Haines' Bluff—a feint to be pushed to bold attack, if circumstances favor." ALS, DNA, RG 393, Dept. of the Tenn., Letters Received. *O.R.*, I, xxiv, part 3, 234. On the same day, Col. William S. Hillyer wrote to McClernand. "You will immediately embark as many of your forces as possible, on all steamboats and barges not actually used in navigating the Bayou's. Have all your picks and shovels put aboard, and your artillery and ammunition. There are several barges in the Bayou which you will have brought out as soon as possible, to be used for landing troops." Copies, DLC-USG, V, 19, 30, 98; DNA, RG 393, Dept. of the Tenn., Letters Sent; *ibid.*, 13th Army Corps, Letters Received; (attributed to USG) Alcorn Collection, WyU.

On April 27, McClernand wrote to USG. "Rear Admiral Porter requests a detail of Sergt. James M. Totten Co. "D" 23d Ind. Vol. Infty, in Genl. Logan's Division, as a pilot is needed for the present movement." DfS, McClernand Papers, IHi; copy, DNA, RG 393, 13th Army Corps, Letters Sent. On the same day, Lt. Col. Walter B. Scates wrote to McClernand. "In obedience to your order; I have personally examined the transports and barges, as far as practicable. The estimates are above the views of the officers of the Steamers generally. The Steamers Forest Queen, Cheeseman, & Moderator; together with four barges, Lake Erie, Dinrual, Aurora No 28, and Auroro No 29, will be assigned to the 14th Divn, Genl Carr Comdg. The Steamers Genl Price, Empire City and Silver Wave and four barges—W. H. B.—a large decked barge, a large hay barge, and a small barge (the latter three without names) will be assigned to the 9th Division, Brig Genl Osterhaus The Steamer Horizon will be assigned to Brig Genl Hovey I do not think it possible to put even three, much less four, Divisions on the boats at hand. Several of the boats need some trifling repairs which should be done immediately by the divisions to which they are assigned The remaining portion of the Corps might be marched as far in direction of the point to be attacked, as the route may be practicable and of ready access to the river, if there be such a route, whence the delay in bringing them into action would be less than from our present location. On return of the transports from first trip; the boats assigned to Brig Genl Carrs Division will report to Brig Genl Hovey, and those assigned to the Division of Genl Osterhaus, will report to Brig Genl Smith to transport their respective Divisions to the scene of action." ALS, *ibid.*, Dept. of the Tenn., Letters Received. On the same day, McClernand endorsed this letter to USG. "I have had all the boats collected here, during the past night and this morning. I have assigned them according to the within report, and have ordered Genls. Carr & Osterhaus to embark immediately, at the landings assigned to each. I have ordered Genl Hovey to embark as much of his Command as possible, and have ordered Genls Carr and Osterhaus to send the transports bearing their commands back for the purpose of bringing up the remainder of the Corps. I have systemized everything and ~~started to as~~ ordered the immediate embarkation. Shall the remainder of my Corps wait here for the return of the transports, or march down to a landing nearer the field?" AES, *ibid.*

On April 28, McClernand wrote to USG. "Having been informed by Admiral Porter that the Price was at my disposal for the transportation of troops, and as the Flag Ship of the fleet of transports, I write to inform you that I have published her in my orders to Division Commanders, as the Flag Ship of the fleet and that, until we shall have reduced Grand Gulf, it is important that I should have control. By arrangement her movements of the other transports. I should state that in the estimate of the capacities of vessels to carry troops the Price was set down at 1200   I am informed that she will only carry 250 and, with even that small number, she would be unable to use her guns   Genl Carr is embarked: so is Genl Osterhous except the Brigade from Genl Smith. General Smith is under orders to remove with the rest of his Division to a point opposite to or below, and as near as may be to Grand Gulf, and take with him the detachment from Genl Osterhous now on the way. As yet, it does not appear that the limited number of small and inferrier transports at my disposal will enable me to take more than two Divisions,—excluding Genl Hovey's, which I was very anxious to take. Cant the GunBoats take it or a large portion of it, down to Hard Times, three miles above Grand Gulf and put it out there until the other transports are unloaded and can come back for it. This would place a good Division under an able officer in supporting distance of the advance." Copy, *ibid.*, 13th Army Corps, Letters Sent. *O.R.*, I, xxiv, part 3, 242. On the same day, USG wrote to McClernand. "In disembarking Carrs Division at Hard Times leave his Artillery on board the transports: and when Hoveys Division moves let it be with Infantry only. Carrs Artillery will operate with Hovey till his own can be brought forward   This arrangement will save time"   Copies, DLC-USG, V, 19, 30, 98; DNA, RG 393, Dept. of the Tenn., Letters Sent; *ibid.*, 13th Army Corps, Letters Received; Alcorn Collection, WyU. *O.R.*, I, xxiv, part 3, 242. On April 29, McClernand wrote to USG. "Generals Hovey and Osterhaus' Divisions are in hand and ready to move against the Gulf. General Carr's is in condition readily to fall in, when transports can be made available, and so the 2d Illinois Cav'y." Copy, DNA, RG 393, 13th Army Corps, Letters Sent.

To Maj. Gen. William T. Sherman

Smith's Plantation La.
April 27. 1863

MAJOR GENERAL W. T. SHERMAN
COMD'G. 15TH ARMY CORPS
GENERAL—

If you think it advisable, you may make a reconnoissance of Haine's Bluff, taking as much force and as many Steamers, as you like.—Admiral Porter told me, that he would instruct Capt. Breese to do as you asked him with his Fleet.

The effect of a heavy demonstration in that direction would be good, so far as the enemy are concerned, but I am loth to order it, because it would be so hard, to make our own troops understand that only a demonstration was intended, and our poeple at home would characterize it as a repulse.—

I therefore leave it to you, whether to make such a demonstration.—

If made at all, I would advise, that you publish your Order beforehand, stating, that a reconnoissance in force was to be made for the purpose of calling the enemy's attention from movements South of Vicksburg, and not with any expectation of attacking.—

I shall probably move on Grand Gulf tomorrow.—

Truly yours
U. S. GRANT
Major General

Copies, DLC-USG, V, 19, 30; DNA, RG 393, Dept. of the Tenn., Letters Sent; *ibid.*, RG 45, Mississippi Squadron, Letters Received; MoSHi; Alcorn Collection, WyU. *O.R.*, I, xxiv, part 3, 240, (incomplete) 244; *O.R.* (Navy), I, xxiv, 591. On April 28, 1863, Maj. Gen. William T. Sherman twice wrote to USG. "I received your letter of the 27th last night and early this mornig went to see Capt Breese and agreed with him as to the demonstration on Haines Bluff, the moment the Choctaw arrives. She was at Memphis last Saturday, & should be here today. I will take 10 steamers & 10 Regiments and go up the Yazoo as close to Haines as possible without putting the transports under the Rifled guns of the enemy. We will make as strong a demonstration as possible. The troops will all understand the purpose and will not be hurt by the repulse. The People of the Country must find out the Truth as they best can. It is none of their business. You are engaged in a hazardous enterprise and for good reason wish to divert attention. That is sufficient to me and it shall be done. I will be all ready at day light and shall embark the men the moment Capt Breese notifies me he is ready. I have urged Gen Tuttle in person to push the Wagon Road from Duckport back to Walnut Bayou, and will let him have no peace till it is done, and will put a train of about 100 of my Regimental wagons on it. Another train of my wagons from Steels division will travel the Road by which McPherson went out. For Forage & Provisions we might run the Batteries on some of the Boats that are now useless on account of the decline in the Waters of Walnut Bayou. The Road from Youngs Point to Briggs & Bedford below Warrenton is out of the question. Dismiss it from your calculations. The only Roads are via Walnut Bayou, and that Bayou Can only be reached from Millikens Bend and Duckport. All is well here but the rains have made the Road as you know, muddy & full of ruts." "Gen Tuttle will finish the Road tomorrow across to Walnut Bayou along the new Canal, and my Quarter Master in Cooperation with Col Bingham Chief Qr Master will put on it a train of 100 wagons collected from my Regimental trains which can be kept constantly hauling to Richmond. Another train of about 80 wagons from Steeles Division including my Division & Head Qr teams will be put on the Road from Millikens Bend to Richmond. I think you had better leave Col Bingham to control the movement of supplies from the River to Richmond and leave your teams to haul them to Perkins plantation. Col Bingham can appoint a Quarter Master at Richmond to load wagons arriving there, or to ship by barge from that place. The teams from your end and those here, should be equalized and meet at Richmond. I have ordered Steele who Commands at Millikens Bend to place two Regiments at Richmond to guard that point looking to the direction of the Tensas. Also two Regiments to be employed as a working party on the Road from Millikens to Richmond. As soon as the Cavalry arrives I have ordered Steele to cause it to patrol the Road between the Bend & the Tensas. The Choctaw has arrived. We have heard some cannonading in the direction of Grand Gulf. I hope you are in possession of that place. Tomorrow I will take ten Regiments and go up the Yazoo. I will feel Chickasaw Bayou, and the next day draw the fire of Haines Bluff. I will hang about Benson Blakes about where the Tuscumbia turned back when we reconnoitered there, and make such a demonstration as will force the enemy to reinforce heavily at that place and to that extent draw from Black River. I will use troops that I know will trust us and not be humbugged by a Repulse. The men have sense and will trust us. As to the Reports in newspapers we must scorn them, else they will ruin us and our country. They are as much enemies to Good Government as the secesh, and between the two I like the secesh best, because they are a brave open enemy & not a set of sneaking croaking scoundrels. I believe a diversion at Haines Bluff is proper right and will make it, let whatever Reports of *Repulse* be made. The Chochtaw is here, and you will hear Cannonading at Haines Bluff tomorrow & the day after." ALS, DNA, RG 94, War Records Office, Dept. of the Tenn. *O.R.*, I, xxiv, part 3, 242–44; (1-incomplete) *O.R.* (Navy), I, xxiv, 596.

On April 30, USG wrote to Col. William S. Hillyer. "Write to Sherman and say that I have received his letter since sending directions for him to bring two divisions of his corps here, that is, if he can effect a lodgment at Haines Bluff, and I would rather see him succeed in it than any other man living . . . I do not expect him to find an opportunity of making an attack but regard it barely as one of the possibilities that may exist in consequence of my move on Grand Gulf and the further possibility of the truth of the report I now hear that Black River bridge has been burned . . ." American Art Association, Jan. 21, 22, 1926, No. 337. Hillyer forwarded USG's letter to Sherman with an endorsement that the letter required no further explanation. See letter to Maj. Gen. William T. Sherman, April 29, 1863.

To Julia Dent Grant

Perkins, Plantation La.
April 28th 1863

DEAR JULIA,

I have been fretting here for several days to get ready to attack Grand Gulf with weather roads and water all against me. I will however be ready to-day and possibly make the attack. Tomorrow morning at furthest will see the work commenced.

I feel every confidance of sucsess but may be disappointed. Possession of Grand Gulf too I look upon as virtual possession of Vicksburg and Port Hudson and the entire Mississippi river.

Myself, Staff & Fred will be off in a little tug witnessing the Naval attack upon land batteries and the debarkation of troops to carry the hights. I feel very well but a goodeal disgusted. The want of a servant to take care of my things and pack up when we leave any place has left me now about bare of some necessary articles. I am always so much engaged on starting from anyplace that I cannot look after things myself. Did you think to send Nicholas?

Besure and attend to the business you went on as I directed. I hope John will not want to take $40 per acre for 40 acres more land because it is more than it would bring, for cash, and I do not want it. Then too there is still an encumbrance on the whole place that may have to be paid some day and is atleast a defect in the title.

Give my love to all at your house. I have been intending to write to Emma for some time but somehow I am either too lazy or have too much to do. Tell her I think just as much of her as though I wrote every week.

You had better not return to Memphis until you hear of me in Vicksburg. You can then come on at once. After your business is finished in St. Louis you might make Nelly a short visit and then go to Galena or any place you like best. I do not like you to be at the Gayoso House without me.

Good bye
ULYS.

ALS, DLC-USG.

To Maj. Gen. Henry W. Halleck

Near Grand Gulf.
April 29th 1863

MAJ GEN H. W HALLECK
GEN IN CHIEF

The gunboats engaged Grand Gulf Batteries from 8 A. M until 1 P M and from dusk until 10 P M   The Army and transports are now below Grand Gulf. A landing will be effected by the east bank of the river tomorrow   I feel that the battle is now more than half won

U S. GRANT
Maj Genl

Telegram received, DNA, RG 107, Telegrams Collected (Bound); copies, *ibid.*, Telegrams Received in Cipher; *ibid.*, RG 393, Dept. of the Tenn., Hd. Qrs. Correspondence; DLC-USG, V, 5, 8, 24, 94, 98. *O.R.*, I, xxiv, part 1, 32. This telegram was received in Washington at 3:00 P.M., May 8, 1863.

To Maj. Gen. James B. McPherson

> Head Quarters Dept. of the Tenn
> Near Grand Gulf April 29. 1863.

MAJOR GENL. MCPHERSON
COMMDG 17TH ARMY CORPS
GEN'L

Now that all the gun boats are below Black river there is danger that some of the transports might come out with Artillery aboard and do us much damage between here and James Plantation

I wish you to instruct one of the Companies of Artillery of Logans Division improvise a gunboat out of the Empire City by putting a section on board and to place the remainder of the Artillery left behind in Battery. Boats all come through without damage

> Respectfully
> U. S. GRANT

Copy, DLC-USG, V, 98. Entered as written by Lt. Col. John A. Rawlins, *ibid.*, 19, 30; DNA, RG 393, Dept. of the Tenn., Letters Sent; Alcorn Collection, WyU. The style strongly indicates USG's authorship.

On April 30, 1863, Col. Clark B. Lagow wrote to Maj. Maurice Maloney, 1st Inf., Perkins' Plantation, La. "You will immediatly move your thirty pound parrott guns down to the Bank of the river and put them in Battery. All the Gun boats and Transports except the Empire City are below Grand Gulf and it is barely possible the rebels may send some of their boats down Black River and up the Mississippi to Perkins and James Plantations to try and distroy our stores The object in putting your heavy guns in Battery on Perkins Plantation is to prevent any thing of this kind being done." Copies, *ibid.*

To Maj. Gen. William T. Sherman

Head Quarters Dept of the Tenn
Below Grand Gulf La. April 29. 1863

Maj. Genl. W. T. Sherman
Commanding 15th Army Corps
Gen.

We have had terrific cannonading most of the day. without silencing the Enemys Guns. finding the position so Strong late in the day. I decided to run the Blockade which being successfully done, I shall be able to effect a landing tomorrow morning either at the lower end of Grand Gulf, or below Bayou Pierre with all of McClernands Corps that can be landed next day. Move up to Perkins Plantation with two Divisions of your Corps as rapidly as possible, Leave the other Division for the present to occupy from Youngs point. to Richmond and to Hasten up Supplies and Ordnance Stores under the directions sent a few days ago. between Mcfeely Bingham. the public teams, and bayous rations ought to get along to supply the Army. The cavalry can collect beef Cattle and grain for some little time Direct the two regiments of Cavalry brought from Helena to move forward on this line, one to occupy from Richmond to Smiths Plantation and the other to come on to Perkins Plantation.

Yours truly
U. S. Grant
Maj. Gen.

Copies, DLC-USG, V, 19, 30, 98; DNA, RG 393, Dept. of the Tenn., Letters Sent; Alcorn Collection, WyU. *O.R.*, I, xxiv, part 3, 246. On May 1, 1863, Maj. Gen. William T. Sherman, "on board *FlagShip Black Hawk*, below Haines" wrote to USG. "Am this momt in recpt of yours from below Grand Gulf. have sent orders for Steeles & Tuttles Divisions to move to Perkins and shall follow tomorrow. We will be there as soon as possible. Tuttle will move by the New Road & Steele by Richmond. Yesterday the New Chocktaw followed by all the other Gunboats and our transports approached the Bluff. We kept up a heavy fire which was returned by the Enemy. The Choctaw was struck 53 times but her injuries are not in any vital part Strange to say no one was hurt—The DeKalb also was uninjured—the Tyler caught one shot on her water line which is repaired.

I disembarked the Command at Blakes negro quarters and made disposition as for attack which was kept up till after dark, drawing heavy fire. Today I have felt all the paths & levees back, the ground Except the Levees beig all under water still, and at 3 P M we will open another Cannonade to prolong the Diversion and keep it up till after dark, when we shall drop down to Chickasaw and so on back to Camp. Tomorrow I will move Blairs Division up to Millikens bend just below your Head Quarters and with Steeles & Tuttles Divisions will obey your order and reach Perkins. I hear the enemy has crossed over to Briggs Plantation in Yawls, doubtless to see what we are about—They will not find out much. The Road to Richmond cant be reached from Biggs on account of the overflow. All our Regimental wagons must be on the Road, which will leave me without wagons but I will get to Perkins some how. Steele will write you all of interest from Millikens. All well with us here, and I do not apprehend any serious loss in the Cannonade proposed for this P M. I want to prolong the Diversion as much as possible in yr favor." ALS, DNA, RG 94, War Records Office, Dept. of the Tenn. *O.R.*, I, xxiv, part 1, 576–77; (incomplete) *O.R.* (Navy), I, xxiv, 598–99.

To Lt. Col. Judson D. Bingham

Head Quarters Dept of the Tenn
Near Grand Gulf April 30. 1863

Col Bingham
Cheif Qr. Mr
Col:

Prepare two tugs to run the Blockade with two barges each in tow.

Col Macfeely will have the barges loaded to nearly their full capacity, with rations and then fill up with oats and Hay so as to cover the Tugs, as near as possible.[1] Do this with all expedition in 48 hours from receipt of orders if possible. Time is of immense importance. Should their crews decline coming through, Call on the commanding officer for Volunteers and discharge the crews. Those Volunteering will be continued in charge after running the Blockade.

Respectfully &c
U. S. Grant
Major General.

Copies, DLC-USG, V, 19, 30, 98; DNA, RG 393, Dept. of the Tenn., Letters Sent; Alcorn Collection, WyU. *O.R.*, I, xxiv, part 3, 248. On May 5, 1863, Lt. Col. Judson D. Bingham, Milliken's Bend, wrote to USG. "I have the honor to report that your instructions of April 30th, were received at 11 o'clock, A. M. May 1st in relation to sending two Tugs with four Barges down the River. I immediately commenced the execution of your instructions, and at 7 o'clock A. M. May 2d the four largest and best Barges that I could obtain were loaded with subsistence Stores. I made a written application to the Commander of the troops here (Maj. Gen. Steele) for a detail to assist in loading the Barges, and preparing them for the trip; Capt. Gaster, A. Q. M. who had immediate charge of the preparations, by my direction, also made an application for a detail. None was furnished, and the loading and preparations were made by the mechanics employed in the Quartermaster Department, and a few Negros that I had collected. The force was so small that it was compelled to work night and day until the Barges were ready. On the evening of May 2d, I heard that our troops had evacuated Young's Point, and that the enemy had landed near the abandoned camps. I then consulted with Maj. Gen Sherman, who advised me to wait until the next night (3d), and he would send a force to occupy the Point, to prevent the capture of the Boats from the Louisiana shore, in case the Tugs were compelled to land, to repair any damages that might be sustained. I followed the advice of Gen. Sherman, and delayed the departure of the Boats until 10' o'clock P. M. of the 3d. On the morning of the 3d only two of the Barges were in condition to start; one was stuck to the Guards, and another leaking, and would not sustain enough Hay to protect the Tug. I was therefore compelled to send only one Tug with two Barges, as I could not prepare another two in time. At 10 o'clock. P. M. of the 3d, the Tug with two Barges was started down the River, with crew complete, and a detail of the commissioned Officer and fifteen armed men to repel boarders. Soon after the Tug rounded the Point I saw several flashes from Guns, but heard only two or three reports. The firing did not seem to be from very heavy guns. Soon after the firing commenced I saw a light which I supposed was made by the enemy on the Louisiana shore; but it passed down the River so rapidly as to satisfy me that the Barges were on fire. Our troops hold possession of a portion of the Point, and rescued one man from the wreck, whose statement I enclose herewith. I am now preparing two large Barges, and can send them down the River at any time, but do not consider it advisable to do so without further instructions, as they are almost sure of destruction unless we can send them on a dark night. In about three or four days the moon will be more favorable for the purpose. I am using every exertion to forward supplies in wagons, and have sent to Memphis for more transportation. It should be here in a day or two." ALS, DNA, RG 94, War Records Office, Dept. of the Tenn. *O.R.*, I, xxiv, part 1, 687–88.

On April 30, Lt. Col. John A. Rawlins issued Special Orders No. 120. "Colonel Wm. S. Hillyer, A. D. C., is assigned to the duty of Superintending the transportation and supplies to the Army below Grand Gulf. He is authorized to take charge of all transportation both land and water and generally to exercise such authority in the name of the General Commanding as he may think necessary for the purpose of keeping the Army promptly supplied. Army Corps Commanders, will direct their Chief Quartermasters, to seize for the use of the Army in the field, during the ensuing campaign, such wagons and teams, as may be necessary for transportation, belonging to the inhabitants of the country through which they may pass." DS (incomplete), McClernand Papers, IHi; copies,

DLC-USG, V, 27, 28; DNA, RG 393, Dept. of the Tenn., Special Orders.

1. On April 30, USG wrote to Lt. Col. Robert Macfeely. "Immediately after the receipt of this the cheif Quartermaster will turn over to you four barges, which you will load to nearly their full capacity, with Commissary Stores, using all possible dispatch in getting them ready to run the blockade   You will consign them to Lieut. Col. Taggart at Hard Times landing near Grand Gulf   The Cheif Q: M. will arrange the details for transportation." Copies, DLC-USG, V, 19, 30, 98; DNA, RG 393, Dept. of the Tenn., Letters Sent; Alcorn Collection, WyU. On the same day, Rawlins wrote to Lt. Col. Grantham I. Taggart. "You will issue to the troops of your command without provision returns for their subsistence during the next five days, three rations, keeping an accurate account of the same in order that the issues may be covered by proper authority hereafter." Copies, *ibid.*

To Act. Rear Admiral David D. Porter

———

Hd Qrs Field of battle
Near Port Gibson. Miss.
May 1st 10.15 A M '63

ADMIRAL PORTER,

We have driven the enemy handsomely, taken 150 prisoners at least several guns—Bowen himself is here—therefore I wish you would send up and attack the batteries as soon as possible. If there is still a division of troops left at the landing, send them up to assault the works on the South Side, after you have silenced the guns.

I send an order to McPherson to give you all assistance
Very Respectfully
U. S. GRANT
Maj. Gen

LS, MdAN.

To *Act. Rear Admiral David D. Porter*

Near Port Gibson, Miss
May 1st 1863, 8.30 P. M.

ADMIRAL,

I have to request that you will take charge of the prisoners captured to day, (from 300 to 500)[1] and issue rations ~~till~~ to them till they can be sent north   I am compelled to request this owing to the lack of provisions with my command in the field.

Will you also be kind enough to have rolls made of them; I have no one now who can attend to this matter; we expect to take more prisoners to morrow.

Our day's work has been very creditable; we have *six* guns, 3 to 500 prisoners, killed Genl. Tracy[2] and utterly routed the enemy. Our forces are on the move, and will lie very close to Port Gibson tonight—.ready for early action tomorrow.

Grierson of the cavalry, has taken the heart out of Mississippi—[3]

Very Respectfully
U. S. GRANT
Maj. Gen

LS, MdAN.

1. C.S.A. losses at Port Gibson, according to brigade reports, were 60 killed, 340 wounded, 387 missing. *O.R.*, I, xxiv, part 1, 668. U.S. losses were 131 killed, 719 wounded, 25 missing. *Ibid.*, pp. 583–85. For slightly different totals, see letter to Col. John C. Kelton, July 6, 1863. On May 9, 1863, Maj. Gen. John A. McClernand wrote to USG reporting 13th Army Corps casualties for the battle of Port Gibson at 112 killed, 655 wounded, 2 missing, 8 "Since Died." Copy, DNA, RG 393, 13th Army Corps, Letters Sent.

2. Edward D. Tracy, born in Macon, Ga., in 1833, was a lawyer-politician of Huntsville, Ala., before the Civil War. Entering the Civil War as capt., 4th Ala., he rose to lt. col., 19th Ala., ranking from Oct. 12, 1861, and commanded this regt. at Shiloh. Appointed brig. gen. as of Aug. 12, 1862, he commanded the 2nd Brigade, Maj. Gen. Carter L. Stevenson's Div., at Port Gibson, where he was killed in battle.

3. See telegram to Maj. Gen. Henry W. Halleck, May 3, 1863.

To Maj. Gen. John A. McClernand

———

Head Quarters Dep't of the Tenn
May 1st 1863.

MAJ. GEN. McCLERNAND
GEN.

Push the enemy with ~~keep~~ skirmishers well thrown out, till it gets too dark to see ~~them~~ him. Then place your command on elegible ground where night finds you. Park your Artillery so as to command the surrounding country and renew the attack at early dawn and if possible push the enemy from the field or capture ~~them~~ him. No camp fires should be allowed unless in deep ravines and to the rear of the troops.

U. S. GRANT
Maj. Gen'l.

Copies, DLC-USG, V, 19, 30, 98; DNA, RG 393, Dept. of the Tenn., Letters Sent; (2) *ibid.*, 13th Army Corps, Letters Received; Alcorn Collection, WyU. *O.R.*, I, xxiv, part 3, 260.

On April 30, 1863, Maj. Gen. John A. McClernand twice wrote to USG. "I beg to suggest whether, by concentrating the fire of the gunboats upon the batteries on the side of the promontory, they might not be silenced and a footing at once gained for the Infantry, to the left and behind the promontory?" Copy, DNA, RG 393, 13th Army Corps, Letters Sent. "I am pushing forward the 13th Army Corps, with the hope of seizing the bridge across Bayou Pierre, near that place. Please cause all that belongs to the Corps in the rear to follow rapidly." Copy, *ibid. O.R.*, I, xxiv, part 3, 248.

To Brig. Gen. John S. Bowen

———

Head Quarters Dept of the Tenn
Port Gibson Miss, May 2. 1863.

BRIG. GEN. J. S. BOWEN.
SIR:

Your note of this date asking twenty four hours suspension of Hostilities and privilege of sending officer and men, to look

after wounded and bury dead is just recieved   Although always
ready to extend any consistent courtesy to alleviate suffering I
cannot comply with your wish in this matter. A dispatch now in
my possession shows that you are expecting reinforcements and
additional munitions of war.[1] I deem therefore the request un-
reasonable and one you could not expect me to comply with. I
will state however that your dead and wounded are receiving the
same attention that my own are. Further that when hostilities
for the present have ceased, I will extend every privilege consistent with my duties and that it may be in my power to extend
looking to the relief of suffering soldiers

Very respectfully

U. S. GRANT

Maj. General

Copy, DLC-USG, V, 98. On May 2, 1863, C.S.A. Brig. Gen. John S. Bowen,
Grand Gulf, wrote to "Comdg of U. S. Forces at or near Port Gibson Miss."
"I have the honor to request that you will allow a suspension of Hostilities between
our forces for the period of 24 Hour, and extend to me the usual privilege of
burying my dead, and looking after my wounded. I would ask that one field
officer be allowed to go from each Brigade and one officer of the line with ten
men from each regiment   Lieut Frank Carter A. D. C. the bearer of this despatch
is fully authorized to arrange any terms that may be deemed avisable"   ALS,
DNA, RG 94, War Records Office, Dept. of the Tenn. *O.R.*, I, xxiv, part 3, 263.

1. On May 1, 6:30 P.M., Bowen telegraphed to Lt. Gen. John C. Pemberton.
"I am falling back across Bayou Pierre. I will deavor to hold that position until
reinforcements arrive. I have had as much meat carried over as I could. The rest
will be burned to-night, as will the corn stored here. There will be very little to
eat here for my own command or the reinforcements. The want of ammunition is
one of the main causes of our retreat   The men did nobly, holding out the whole
day against overwhelming odds. The town will be in possession of the enemy in
a few hours, and communication cut off"   (Galena) *Weekly Northwestern Gazette*,
June 2, 1863; copy, DLC-USG, V, 98. Printed as sent at 5:30 in *O.R.*, I, xxiv,
part 1, 660. The *Gazette* printed Bowen's telegram with a letter of U.S. Representative Elihu B. Washburne, Port Gibson, May 2, to the editor stating that he
was enclosing the original document found in the telegraph office when the town
fell. A telegram from Washburne to his wife, May 3, announcing the fall of Port
Gibson had been endorsed "Approved" by USG. *Ibid.*, May 12, 1863.

To Act. Rear Admiral David D. Porter

Port Gibson May 2d/63

DEAR ADMIRAL,

Our forces entered this place at an early hour this morning.[1] Found all the rebels gone and bridges burned.[2] The bayou is not fordable for many miles up   consequently we will be delayed until the stream is bridged. I think this will be completed by 2 O'Clock. I will then move immediately to Grand Gulf with two Divisions of McPhersons Corps and send McClernand to Willow Springs.

I do not anticipate any resistence unless the enemy are materially reinforced. They however have several batteries and a Division of troops on the opposite bank of the river as if a stand was to be made.

I think to-morrow at 10 O'Clock my advance may be looked for at the Gulf. Would it not be well to have most of the Gunboats there at the same time?

Very respectfully
U. S. GRANT
Maj. Gen Com

ALS, Bixby Collection, MoSHi.

1. On May 2, 1863, USG wrote to Maj. Gen. John A. McClernand. "Place Guards immediately about the town and require troops to be kept near their colors. The men are now running riot in the most disorderly manner"   Copies, DLC-USG, V, 98; (2) DNA, RG 393, 13th Army Corps, Letters Received. On the same day, Lt. Col. John A. Rawlins sent an identical message to Brig. Gen. Alvin P. Hovey. Copies, DLC-USG, V, 19, 30; DNA, RG 393, Dept. of the Tenn., Letters Sent; Alcorn Collection, WyU.

2. Also on May 2, Col. Clark B. Lagow wrote to McClernand. "One Battery of 20 pdr Parrot guns, of Genl. Osterhaus' Division has been to report to Maj. Genl. Jno. A. Logan—temporarily for purpose of shelling enemy's positions at the ruins of bridge below here." Copy, DNA, RG 393, 13th Army Corps, Letters Received. On the same day, 9:15 A.M., Rawlins wrote to Maj. Gen. James B. McPherson. "You will detach a strong Brigade to proceed by the ford 3 ms at the town under the guidance of the Black boy, sent herewith. Send also a Staff officer to return and report to me concerning it   Let the Brigade push across the Bayous and attack the enemy in flank now in full retreat thro Willow Springs—

demoralized and out of Ammunition   Gen. Jno E. Smith with his Brigade will execute this order"   Copies, DLC-USG, V, 19, 30, 98; DNA, RG 393, Dept. of the Tenn., Letters Sent; Alcorn Collection, WyU. *O.R.*, I, xxiv, part 3, 262.

To Maj. Gen. Henry W. Halleck

Grand Gulf
May 3rd 1863

MAJ GEN H W HALLECK
GEN IN CHIEF

We landed at Boulinsburg April 30th moved immediately on Port Gibson—met the enemy eleven thousand strong four miles south of Port Gibson at 2. A. M. on the First and engaged him all day entirely routing him with the loss of many killed and about five hundred prisoners besides the wounded   Our loss about one hundred killed and five hundred wounded   The Enemy retreated towards Vicksburg destroying the Bridges over the two forks of Bayou Pierre   These were rebuilt and pursuit continued until the present time   Besides the heavy artillery at this place, four field pieces were captured, some stores and the Enemy driven to destroy many more.

The country is the most broken and difficult to operate in I ever saw   Our victory has been most complete and the Enemy thoroughly demoralized

Very Respectfully
U S GRANT
Maj Gen Comdg

Telegram received, DNA, RG 107, Telegrams Collected (Bound); *ibid.*, Telegrams Collected (Unbound); copies, *ibid.*, Telegrams Received in Cipher; *ibid.*, RG 393, Dept. of the Tenn., Hd. Qrs. Correspondence; DLC-USG, V, 5, 8, 24, 94, 98. *O.R.*, I, xxiv, part 1, 34. This text was telegraphed from Memphis on May 7, 1863.

To Maj. Gen. Henry W. Halleck

Grand Gulf, Miss.
3 May 1863

MAJ. GEN. HALLECK,
GEN'L IN CHIEF
WASHINGTON.

I learn that Col. Grierson with his cavalry, had been heard of first ten days ago, in Northern Mississippi. He moved thence and struck the railroad 30 miles east of Jackson at a point called Newton Station. He then moved Southward toward Enterprise, demanded the surrender of the place—gave one hour grace during which Gen'l Loring arrived.[1] He left at once and moved toward Hazelhurst on the new orleans & Jackson Railroad   At this point he tore up the track, thence to Bahala ten miles further South on the same road. Thence Eastward on the Natchez road where he had a fight with Wirt Adams' Cavalry.[2] From this point he moved back to the N. O. & J. R. R. to Brookhaven ten miles south of Bahala. When last heard from he was three miles from Summit ten miles South of the last named point, supposed to be making his way to Baton Rouge   He has spread excitement throughout the State, destroyed railroads, trestle works, bridges, burning locomotives & rolling stock taking prisoners destroying stores of all kinds. To use the expression of my informant "Grierson has knocked the heart out of the State."

U. S. GRANT.
Maj. Gen'l.

Telegram received, DNA, RG 107, Telegrams Collected (Unbound); (dated May 6, 1863) *ibid.*, Telegrams Collected (Bound); (undated) *ibid.* Misdated May 6 in *O.R.*, I, xxiv, part 1, 34. USG's text reached Memphis on May 7 and was telegraphed from Cairo on May 8. On May 5, Col. Benjamin H. Grierson, Baton Rouge, wrote a lengthy report of the entire expedition to Lt. Col. John A. Rawlins. ALS, DNA, RG 94, War Records Office, Union Battle Reports. *O.R.*, I, xxiv, part 1, 522–29.

1. William W. Loring, born in N. C. in 1818, was a lawyer-politician in Fla. before appointment as capt., Mounted Rifles, as of May 27, 1846. Remaining

in the army, he resigned as a col. on May 13, 1861. Appointed C.S.A. brig. gen., and promoted to maj. gen. on Feb. 17, 1862, he was sent west after a bitter quarrel with Thomas J. "Stonewall" Jackson. Sent to Meridian, Miss., to intercept Grierson, Loring went to Enterprise in response to a feint; Grierson moved in the opposite direction. *Ibid.*, pp. 544–45.

2. William Wirt Adams, born in 1819 in Frankfort, Ky., served briefly in the army of the Republic of Tex. (1839), and before the Civil War was a planter, banker, and state legislator in Miss. After declining appointment as C.S.A. postmaster-gen., he raised and commanded Wirt Adams' Miss. Cav. Ordered to intercept Grierson's cav., Adams reported that: "I found it impossible, to my great mortification and regret, to overhaul them." *Ibid.*, p. 533.

To Maj. Gen. Henry W. Halleck

————

Head Quarters Dept. of the Ten.
Grand Gulf Miss. May 3d/63

MAJ. GEN. H. W. HALLECK,
GEN. IN CHIEF, WASHINGTON,
GEN.

On the 29th of April Admiral Porter attacked the fortifications at this place with seven iron clads, commencing at 8 O'Clock a. m. and continued until half past one engaging them at very close quarters, many times not being more than one hundred yards from the enemy's guns. During this time I had about 10,000 troops on board transports, and in barges along side, ready to land them and carry the place by storm the moment the batteries bearing on the river were silenced so as to make the landing practicable.

From the great elevation the enemy's batteries had it proved entirely impracticable to silence them from the river, and when the gunboats were drawn off I immediately decided upon landing my forces on the Louisiana shore and mach them across the point to below the Gulf. At night the gunboats made another vigerous attack and in the din the transports safely ran the blockade. On the following day the whole of the force with me was transfered to Bruinsburg, the first point of land below Grand Gulf from which the interior can be reached, and the march immediately commenced for Port Gibson. Gen. McClernand was in the advance with the 13th Army Corps. At about 2 A. M. on the 1st of May, when some four miles from Port Gibson, he met the enemy. Some little skirmishing took place before daylight but not to any great extent.

The 13th Army Corps was followed by Logans Division of McPhersons Corps which reached the scene of action as soon as the last of the 13th was out of the road.

The fighting continued all day and until after dark over the most broken country I ever saw. The whole country is a series of irregular ridges divided by deep and impassable ravines, grown up with heavy timber, undergrowth and cane. It was impossible to engage any considerable portion of our forces at any one time. The enemy were driven however from point to point towards Port Gibson until night closed in under which it was evident to me they intended to retreat. The pursuit was continued after dark until the enemy was again met, by Logans Division, about two miles from Port Gibson. The nature of the country is such that further pursuit, in the dark, was not deemed prudent or advisable. On the 2d our troops moved into the town without finding any enemy, except their wounded. The bridge across bayou Pierre, about two miles from Port Gibson on the Grand Gulf road, had been destroyed and also the bridge immediately at Port Gibson on the Vicksburg road. The enemy retreated over both these routes leaving a battery and several regiments of Infantry at the former to prevent a reconstruction of the bridge.

One Brigade under Gen. Stevenson was detached to drive the enemy from this position, or occupy his attention, and a heavy detail set to work under Lt. Col. Wilson & Capt. Trissilian[1] to reconstruct the bridge over the other. This work was accomplished, a bridge and road way over one hundred & twenty feet long made and the whole of McPhersons two Divisions marched over before night. This corps then marched eight miles, to North Fork of bayou Pierre, rebuilt a bridge over that stream and was on the march by 5½ O'Clock this a. m[2]   Soon after crossing the bayou our troops were opened on by the Artillery of the enemy. It was soon demonstrated that this was only intended to cover the retreat of the main Army.—On arriving at Willow Springs Gen. McPherson was directed to hold the position from there on to the Big Black, with one Division, and Gen. McClernand, on his arrival, to join him in this duty. I immediately started for this place with one Brigade of Logan's Division and some twenty Cavalry men. The Brigade of Infantry was left about seven miles from here, contrabands and prisoners taken having stated that the last of the retreating enemy had passed that point.

The woods between here and the crossing of the Big Black is evidently filled yet with detachments of the enemy and some of the Artillery. I am in hopes many of them will be picked up by our forces.

Our loss will not exceed one hundred & fifty killed and five hundred wounded. The enemy's loss is probably about the same. We have however some five hundred of their men prisoners and may pick up many more yet. Many stragglers, particularly from the Missouri troops, no doubt have fallen out and will never join their regiments again.

The move by Bruinsburg undoubtedly took the enemy much by surprise. Gen. Bowen's, the rebel Commanders defence was a very bold one and well carried out. My force however was too heavy for his and composed of well discipilined & hardy men who know no defeat and are not willing to learn what it is.

This army is in the finest health and spirits. Since leaving Millikins Bend they have marched as much by night as by day, through mud and rain, without tents or much other baggage, and on irregular rations, without a complaint and with less straggling than I have ever before witnessed. Where all have done so nobly it would be out of place to make invideous distinctions.

The country will supply all the forage required for anything like an active campaign and the necessary fresh beef. Other supplies will have to be drawn from Millikin's Bend. This is a long and precarious route but I have every confidance in succeeding in doing it.

I shall not bring my troops into this place but immediately follow the enemy, and if all promises as favorably hereafter as it does now, not stop until Vicksburg is in our possession.

Admiral Porter left here this morning for the Mouth of Red River. A letter from Admiral Farragut says that Banks has defeated Taylor and captured about 2000 prisoners.[3] ~~E. H. Smith~~

Col. Griersons raid from La Grange through Mississippi has been the most successful thing of the kind since the breaking out of the rebellion. He was five miles south of Pontotac on the 19th of April. The next place he turned up was at Newton about thirty miles East of Jackson. From there he has gone south touching at Hazelhurst Bahala and various other places. The southern papers and southern people regard it as one of the most daring exploits of the War. I am told the whole state is filled with men paroled by Grierson.

> Very respectfully
> Your obt. svt.
> U. S. GRANT
> Maj. Gen.

ALS, DNA, RG 94, War Records Office, Union Battle Reports. *O.R.*, I, xxiv, part 1, 32–34.

1. Stewart R. Tresilian, a private of Co. A, 49th Ill., acted as engineer and aide to Maj. Gen. John A. McClernand at the battle of Shiloh and as engineer for Maj. Gen. John A. Logan's 3rd Div., 17th Army Corps, during the Vicksburg campaign, without, apparently, receiving any commission. For his report on the bridge at Port Gibson, see *ibid.*, I, xxiv, part 2, 204.

2. The suspension bridge at Grindstone Ford crossed the North Fork of Bayou Pierre approximately eight miles from Port Gibson on the road to Willow Springs. Repair of the bridge is described *ibid.*, I, xxiv, part 1, 129.

3. See letter to Maj. Gen. Nathaniel P. Banks, March 22, 1863.

To Maj. Gen. John A. McClernand

Head Quarters Dept of the Tennessee
6:55. A. M. May 3rd 1863.

MAJ. GEN. J. A. MCCLERNAND
COMMDG 13TH ARMY CORPS
GENERAL:

By working all night the Bridge at this crossing was got ready by the troops at Sunrise   Before one brigade had finished crossing the enemy opened on the head of the column with artillery   It is also stated by Contrabands that the enemy were reinforced during the night. Under these circumstances I deem it prudent to guard all the roads to the rear. You will therefore leave one Brigade of your reserve division at the crossing of Bayou Peirre, on the direct road from Port Gibson to Grand Gulf. Direct them to keep pickets far down the river to watch the enemies movements in that direction. The Brigade so left can furnish the guard for the new bridge at Port Gibson. Leave the remainer of the reserve Division at the forks of the road where you turn directly to the left to reach this place and about seven miles from Port Gibson. This is the second place where you take the left hand road to reach this place.

Very respectfully
U. S. GRANT
Major General

Copies, DLC-USG, V, 19, 30, 98; DNA, RG 393, Dept. of the Tenn., Letters Sent; *ibid.*, 13th Army Corps, Letters Received; Alcorn Collection, WyU. *O.R.*, I, xxiv, part 3, 265–66.

To Maj. Gen. John A. McClernand

———

Head Quarters Dept of the Tenn
May 3. 1863.

MAJ GEN'L MCCLERNAND

Some of our men who have just come in took the left hand
road about half a mile this side of the bridge at Port Gibson, and
run into an Alabama regiment. Make a reconnoisance in that
direction with a part of one division. The Enemy may be prac-
tising a sharp game to get in our rear, with a force to distroy all
we have   When every thing in the forks of the river is cleared
out and ferries distroyed the troops engaged in it will join their
division.

Very respectfully
U. S. GRANT
Maj Genl

Copies, DLC-USG, V, 19, 30, 98; DNA, RG 393, Dept. of the Tenn., Letters
Sent; (2) *ibid.*, 13th Army Corps, Letters Received; Alcorn Collection, WyU.
On May 3, 1863, Maj. Gen. John A. McClernand wrote repeatedly to USG, first
from "Near Port Gibson." "Your two despatchs are recd. I have left one Brigade
of Genl Carrs Divn at Port Gibson and ordered the 2nd Brigade of his Division
to halt at the second turn of the road to Willow Springs. The balance of my corps
is on the way to Willow Springs, or to any point, you may desire to have them
halted. I have thrown two Regiments out to the left to feel for any enemy on my
left flank" "I am closed up in the rear of the long train attached to the 17th
Army Corps   If that Corps is able of itsself to go on, there is no occasion for its
train to get out of my way; but if you think I should be in supporting relation to
it ~~the train of it~~ the train should be ordered to one side. The enemy, from the
best accounts, were massed at and near the lower bridge at Port Gibson expecting
that we would move on the direct road to Grand Gulf   The flank movement now
being executed I think is rapidly drawing him in the direction of the crossing of
Big Black   Had you not better be careful, lest you may, personally, fall in with
the enemy on your way to Grand Gulf" ALS, DNA, RG 393, Dept. of the Tenn.,
Letters Received. *O.R.*, I, xxiv, part 3, 266–67. "North Branch of Bayou Pierre."
"I have just recd word from General Carr. He threw skirmishers across Bayou
Pierre on the burning ruins of the Rail Road bridge and found that the Enemy
had retreated   He commenced retreating at 1. O. C. last night expecting that
we would move on the direct road from Port Gibson to Grand Gulf. He had
brought up 8000 men as a reinforcement had had fortified at the Rail Road bridge
and all the heights to Grand Gulf but seeing our flank movement Pemberton who
was in command said that he must fall back & accordingly (as I have already said)

is doing so" ALS, DNA, RG 393, Dept. of the Tenn., Letters Received. *O.R.*,
I, xxiv, part 3, *266.* "Willow Ford." "My Corps will be out of rations tomorrow.
I am as you are aware without means of Transportation. I ask that you will cause
rations to be sent out immediately in charge of some officer instructed to report
to me. Liut Col Taggart is behind collecting what articles of subsistance he can
but the troops in advance left scarcely any thing: I would suggest a fact which
may become very important in connection with the subject of this communication.
It is this; ten miles farther on the Jackson road the Big Black can be reached at
Halls ferry within two miles. The Big Black might be navigated to that ferry"
Copy, DNA, RG 393, 13th Army Corps, Letters Sent. *O.R.*, I, xxiv, part 3, *266.*

To Maj. Gen. William T. Sherman

Head Quarters, Dept. of the Tenn.
Grand Gulf, Miss.
May. 3d, 1863.

Maj. Genl. W. T. Sherman,
Comdg. 15th Army Corps.
Gen'l.

My base is now at this point, and in executing your orders for
joining me, you will govern yourself accordingly.

I wish you to collect a train of one hundred and twenty (120)
wagons, from those now in use between Milliken's Bend, and
Perkin's place, send them to Grand Gulf and there load them
with rations as follows: *One hundred thousand* pounds of bacon,
the balance, coffee, sugar salt and hard bread. For your own use
on the march from Grand Gulf, you will draw three days rations
and see that they last *five days*.

It's unnecessary for me to remind you of the overwhelming
importance of celerity in your movements.

On the 1st instant at 2 A. M. we met the rebels 11.000 or
12.000 men, under Bowen, with Green,[1] Baldwin[2] and Tracy, in
a very strong position near Port Gibson, four miles south, and
engaged them hotly all day, driving them constantly—One victory was complete; we captured 500 prisoners, four guns, killed
General Tracy, and a large number of the enemy. Our own loss
will not exceed 150 killed and 500 wounded.

The Country is extremely broken and therefore very difficult to operate in.

Yesterday we pushed into Port Gibson, by 8 o'clock to find the enemy gone, and all the bridges across Bayou Pierre destroyed. The bridge was rebuilt, and our troops pushed onto Willow Springs—found the fine bridge over the North Fork of Bayou Pierre destroyed—repaired it, and by 5 o'clock this morning, were in motion again; by 9 we were at "Willow Springs," having met the enemy's skirmishers just beyond the bayou. Logan is now on the main road from here to Jackson, and McPherson closely followed by McClernand is pursuing on the branch of the same road from "Willow Springs.

The enemy is badly beaten, greatly demoralized and exhausted of ammunition. The road to Vicksburg is open; all we want now are men, ammunition and hard bread—we can subsist our horses on the country, and obtain considerable supplies for our troops.

> Very Respectfully,
> U. S. GRANT
> Maj. Genl. Comdg

LS, PPRF. *O.R.*, I, xxiv, part 3, 268–69.

1. Martin E. Green, born in Fauquier County, Va., in 1815, settled in Lewis County, Mo., where he operated a sawmill. In 1861 he organized and commanded Green's Mo. Cav., Mo. State Guard. Confirmed as C.S.A. brig. gen. on Sept. 30, 1862, he commanded the 2nd Brigade, Brig. Gen. John S. Bowen's Div., at the battle of Port Gibson, and was killed during the siege of Vicksburg, June 27, 1863. His report of the battle of Port Gibson is *ibid.*, I, xxiv, part 1, 672–75.

2. William E. Baldwin, born in Statesburg, S. C., in 1827, had a book and stationery business in Columbus, Miss., before the Civil War. As col., 14th Miss., he was captured at Fort Donelson, then after exchange, confirmed as brig. gen. on Oct. 3, 1862. Baldwin's report of the battle of Port Gibson, where he commanded the 1st Brigade, Maj. Gen. Martin L. Smith's Div., is *ibid.*, pp. 675–78.

To Brig. Gen. Jeremiah C. Sullivan

Head Quarters Dept of the Tenn
~~Near~~ Grand Gulf May 3. 1863

BRIG. GEN. J. C. SULLIVAN
COMMDG TROOPS BETWEEN MILLIKEN BEND AND SMITHS
PLANTATION,
GENERAL:

You will give special attention to the matter of shortening the line of Land Transportation from above Vicksburg to the steamers below   as soon as the river has fallen sufficiently you will have a road constructed from Youngs point to a Landing just below Warrenton, and dispose of your troops accordingly Every thing depends upon the promptness with which our supplies are forwarded

Very respectfully
U. S. GRANT
Maj Gen

Copies, DLC-USG, V, 19, 30, 98; DNA, RG 393, Dept. of the Tenn., Letters Sent; *ibid.*, 15th Army Corps, 2nd Div., Letters Received; Alcorn Collection, WyU. *O.R.*, I, xxiv, part 3, 268. On May 4, 1863, Brig. Gen. Jeremiah C. Sullivan endorsed this letter. "Respectfully forwarded to Major-General Blair. I have no troops with whom to execute this order. Major-General Blair having assumed command at this point, and having control of all the forces, is, therefore, the proper officer to execute the provisions of this order." *Ibid.* Sullivan, Milliken's Bend, wrote an undated letter—received on May 3—addressed to Lt. Col. John A. Rawlins. "This afternoon I was informed by Maj. Genl. Blair that he was ordered to turn over the command of this place to me—Leaving here but two Regiments, —I can obtain no information as to the Number of Convalescents, their Camps or their ability for Service—The duties required of me will call for a much better organized force than I find here. I will however do the best I can, but for the present will consider myself fortunate, if, with the entire absence of discipline and organization, I am able to keep the line of our present transportatio[n] open— The proposed road across Youngs Point I think can be built,—Can I have an order for Two Hundred and Fifty Negroes—*Enlisted* at Helena—?" ALS, DNA, RG 393, Dept. of the Tenn., Letters Received.

On May 3, USG twice wrote to the commanding officer, Perkins' Plantation, La. "Will cause all of the troops belonging to this command on the Louisiana side of the Mississippi below perkins plantation to be collected at Grand Gulf by steamers and will constitute a guard at his place. The two regiments of Cavalry will be sent forward on the Jackson road with the utmost dispatch to report at these Hd Qrs. See that this order is promptly communicated to the commanders of Detachments and that in the execution of it all public property is transferred to Grand Gulf." "Send as soon as soon as practicable under proper escort to Millikens Bend the accompanying prisoners of war, also diliver the letter herewith sent to their proper addresses." Copies, DLC-USG, V, 19, 30, 98; DNA, RG 393, Dept. of the Tenn., Letters Sent; (1) Alcorn Collection, WyU.

On May 8, Sullivan wrote to Rawlins. "After consultation on the report made by Capt. Prime. T. E. I have decided to build the wagon road from Duck Port Along the lower side of canal to Amis. Plantation—4 miles from there to Comptons—3 miles—thence to Holmes 2 miles—The objection to the road across *Youngs Point* is that the wagon train would be under fire nearly the entire distance —The Engineers report that 'Steele's Road is impassible, and that it is 'perfectly useless to try and build a road there for at least ten days'—I have received no orders as to the disposition to be made of the Prisoners sent here from Port Gibson—I will detain them until I hear from you—" ALS, DNA, RG 393, Dept. of the Tenn., Letters Received. On the same day, 7:00 P.M., Sullivan wrote to USG. "I have just returned from opposite Warrenton—and find the road perfectly *practicable*, I will be able to furnish you rations on the River 2 miles below Warrenton Batteries by Saturday evening—I will move every thing from this Depôt by Saturday Morning—There are rumors of *raids* being '*threatened*' about Richmond—I will answer for the safety of the line—No boats have arrived from above, and we have no news from Greenville—" ALS, *ibid.*

On May 9, Brig. Gen. Lorenzo Thomas, Milliken's Bend, wrote to USG. "Brig. General Sullivan, under your orders was disposed to entirely abandon this position, and concentrate his force at Youngs point, and also withdraw the troops from Richmond: This would open these positions to the guerillas, ~~what~~ who, now, that the waters are subsiding, are becoming troublesome They would undoubtedly come in to this position if abandoned, and in a very short time break up all our plantations even to Lake Providence The General agrees with me in my views, and will leave here the Regiment now at Richmond, and also keep his cavalry actively employed in arming the country. In the mean time we will rapidly arm the blacks, and thus gather a force to secure the line of the river. I think it highly important that General Sullivan should be in command of the entire district including the troops under General Reed at Lake Providence. A guerilla force is operating near that place at the present time. The active operations of the army have necessarily retarded the filling of negro Regiments It is important for protection here that the Regiments in course of organization be rapidly filled. I would suggest therefore that you authorize the Recruiting officers to enlist the negroes in the several Regiments where there seem to be so many in excess as waiters and hangers on to those who are not authorized to have them. This course will rid you of a good many mouths to feed, when it is so difficult to provide for a large army. I make this suggestion for your consideration. I shall proceed this evening to Lake Providence. Hoping soon to learn that you have again soundly thrashed the rebels." ALS, *ibid.*

On May 12, Lt. Col. Judson D. Bingham, Young's Point, wrote to USG. "I have the honor to report that the road from Sherman's landing to Griffins landing, about five miles below Warrenton, was completed yesterday; and the advance supply train, following immediately behind the construction party, crossed the last bridge as soon as completed, and delivered supplies on the new landing on the arrival of the Steamer from below. The round trip can be made in one day; and as soon as a sufficient supply for the army for fifteen or twenty days is delivered at Griffin's landing, I will forward a large number of teams to the front. I sent a Barge, containing about fifteen thousand Bushels Coal, down the River, on the night of the 10th, and it arrived safely below. I have placed an officer in charge of the Depot at Grand Gulf, who will facilitate the transportation of supplies beyond that place. . . . P. S. Troops commenced arriving from Memphis yesterday." ALS, *ibid.*

To *Julia Dent Grant*

Grand Gulf Miss.
May 3d 1863,

DEAR JULIA,

I have just got in here after a battle fought and won by us. I have been on horseback since early this morning, rode in here leaving my army fifteen miles in the country, have written dispatches and a report for Washington and have to go back tonight. This will keep me up until 12 o'clock tonight. Fred is very well, enjoying himself hugely. He has heard balls whistle and is not moved in the slightest by it. He was very anxious to run the blockade of Grand Gulf. My victory at this place, over Bowen, is a most important one. Management I think has saved us an imense loss of life and gained all the results of a hard fight. I feel proud of the Army at my command. They have marched day and night, without tents and with irregular rations without a murmer of complaints. I write in very great haste. Mr. Washburn is here with me. He is immensely delighted as is also Gov. Yates. Jim Casey is here but I have had no opportunity of talking to him yet.

Good buy dear Julia,
ULYS.

ALS, DLC-USG.

To Maj. Gen. John A. McClernand

May 4. 1863

Maj. Gen. Jno. A. McClernand
Commdg 13th Army Corps
Gen:

There will be no general movement of the troops before the cool of the evening if at all to day

You can therefore collect for your command such supplies as the country affords. Reconnoitre the Jackson road and ascertain if any of the enemy have retreated in that direction, and if so whether any considerable portion of them.

Grand Gulf is now the base of supplies   All troops and stores south of Perkins Plantation have been ordered to that point.

Very respectfully
U. S. Grant
Maj. Gen'l.

Copies, DLC-USG, V, 19, 30, 98; DNA, RG 393, Dept. of the Tenn., Letters Sent; *ibid.*, 13th Army Corps, Letters Received; Alcorn Collection, WyU. On May 4, 1863, 8:45 A.M., USG, "Black River Crossing," wrote to Maj. Gen. John A. McClernand. "I have ordered everything between Bruinsburg and Port Gibson, forward—When the rear arrives at Port Gibson, the brigade at that place, you will order to join its division; and the brigade at the forks of the Jackson and the willow springs road, you will order forward at once its division." Copies (2), DNA, RG 393, 13th Army Corps, Letters Received.

On May 4, McClernand, Willow Springs, frequently wrote to USG. "Col Clark Wright informs me that he drove Harrisons forces to VanBuren Bayou, seven miles back of St Joseph, and captured fifteen prisoners, some mules & horses   A portion of the Cavalry under his command has just arrived: the balance he will bring over to Grand Gulf and thence, push forward to join me. I hope every facility will be afforded to hasten the transportation of his command, with ~~his~~ its camp and garrison equipage, and teams across the river." LS, *ibid.*, RG 94, War Records Office, Dept. of the Tenn. *O.R.*, I, xxiv, part 3, 270. "Unless you can furnish the transportation to remove the arms collected on the Battle Field they will have to be left behind or destroyed, as you are aware I am without the means of moveing them" "Your dispatch of this date is received—I wrote to you yesterday directing the letter to Grand Gulf, that my Corps was without the means of transportation and would be without rations to day, except as far as it could gather them in the rear of the 17th Army Corps and requesting that rations be sent out. I infer that you did not receive the communication. I repet the request that it contains   The teams belonging to this Corps are as you are aware behind

and cannot be brought here unless water transportation is afforded to bring them
across the river—I have sent 3 officers successively to look after this matter but
of course their efforts will avail nothing unless transports can be made available
temporary use. I reconnoitered ahead on the Jackson road last night and found
nothing. A rebel force variously estimated force two Regiments of ten thousand
men, are reported by different spectators to have passed Westerly yesterday
morning on the Jackson Road to the forks of Vicksburg and Grand Gulf road and
to have returned a short distance and turned to the left to cross the Big Black at
the crossing of the Vicksburg road. This counter movement no doubt was caused
by our advance to the Willow Springs. You are aware that I have left a Brigade
at Port Gibson and another at the first turn of the roads, West of the bridge across
the north branch of Bayou Pierre. Shall I not order them to join me follow me when
I move?" "The signal officer loaned me by Admiral Porter has returned. Cant
you return me Liut H. G. Fisher & Liut Edge and there party. These are the same
officers brought by Genl Morgan from Cumberland Gap   One of the officers
Liut McClintock was lately promoted in other service. If his place could be supplied by an other officer it would be desireable"   "I have the honor to report that
General Osterhaus has reconnoitered along the Jackson road six miles. No portion
of the enemy retreated on the road beyond General Osterhous present Camp. The
portion that retreated as already reported turned to their left to make their way
to Hankins Ferry, which is whare, I understand your Head Qurs are. An Irish-
man, who deserted from the enemys transports crew last night at Halls Ferry,
reports that there are four Steamers at Halls Ferry, which the enemy has ordered
to be destroyed upon our appearance. Halls Ferry is 11½ miles from here and 1½
miles from the Jackson road. Shall I make make an effort by a night march to
seize them. Please answer at once." "No trains or provisions have yet arrived
from Grand Gulf—The officer in charge of transports has given preference to the
17th Army Corps in everything. The bagage of that Corps is being sent forward
to the exclusion of ammunition and provisions for the 13th Army Corps   Priority
is even given to forage over necessary supplies for the 13th Army Corps. Only
three of the wagons of my Corps had been crossed over the river, up to this morning. I am convinced that your order to send out provisions and ammunition with
any teams that may be found at Grand Gulf has failed to chalange obediance.
Without necessary provisions & ammunition of course, I cannot answer for results
—early this morning, I sent a strong detachment consisting of cavalry Infantry
& Artillery to Halls ferry to seize if possible any boats there. I went five miles
on the way myself"   Copies, DNA, RG 393, 13th Army Corps, Letters Sent.
The second, fourth and fifth of these messages are in *O.R.*, I, xxiv, part 3, 269–70.

To Maj. Gen. James B. McPherson

————

Head Quarters Dept of the Tenn
May 4. 1863

MAJ GEN. McPHERSON
COMDG 17TH ARMY CORPS
GENL:

There will be no march made before the cool of the evening if to day at all. I wish you would have a reconoisance made of the roads near the river up and down. My information is that there is no crossing below where you now are until you get below the mouth of the Bayou leading from the Miss to Black river. I would like to be as far satisfied as possible of this fact. There are Steamers on the river the capture of which would be of great assistance to us. see if their whereabouts can be ascertained.

Very resply
U. S. GRANT Maj Gen

Copies, DLC-USG, V, 19, 30, 98; DNA, RG 393, Dept. of the Tenn., Letters Sent; Alcorn Collection, WyU.

On May 6, 1863, USG, "Hankinsons Ferry," wrote to Maj. Gen. James B. McPherson. "Move one Division of your command to Rocky Springs to-morrow, leaving the other to occupy from your present Head Quarters to the Ferry. On the approach of Sherman's advance order up the second." ALS, NjR.

To Maj. Gen. William T. Sherman

————

Head Quarters, Dept. of the Ten.
Big Black Crossing, May 4th/63

MAJ. GEN. W. T. SHERMAN,
COMD.G 15TH ARMY CORPS,
GEN.

Order forward immediately your remaining Division leaving only two regiments, (to garrison Richmond,) as required in previous orders. Have all the men leave the West bank of the river with three days rations in haversacks and make all possible dispatch to Grand Gulf.

Very respectfully
U. S. GRANT
Maj. Gen. Com

Leave one Brigade at Millikins Bend and Youngs Point until troops ordered from Hurlbuts command reach there to relieve them. Four regiments have been ordered down.

U. S. G.

ALS, Washington University, St. Louis, Mo.

On May 5, 1863, USG, "Hankinsons Ferry," wrote to Maj. Gen. William T. Sherman. "As soon as landed at Grand Gulf march immediately for this place You will find two roads about seven miles from Grand Gulf, well beaten by the travel of our wagons, the left hand one coming to this ferry and the direct road leading to Willow Springs" Copy, DLC-USG, V, 98.

To Maj. Gen. Stephen A. Hurlbut

———

Head Quarters, Dept. of the Ten
Hankinsons Ferry, May 5th 1863.

MAJ. GEN. S. A. HURLBUT
COMD.G 16TH ARMY CORPS,
GEN.

Send Laumans Division to Millikin's Bend to be forwarded to this army with as little delay as practicable. Let them move by brigades as fast as transportation can be got.

This Division will bring with them all their camp and garrison equipage and transportation.

I am ordering to you all the Cavalry from Helena except two regiments.[1] You can further strengthen your Southern line by bringing troops from the District of Columbus. The completion of the road from Grand Junction to Corinth will enable you to draw off all the troops North of that road. Make such disposition of the troops within your command as you deem advisable for the best protection of lines of communication.

When the road to Corinth is completed put in there as fast as possible sixty days supply of provisions and forage.

This order for Lauman's Division is in addition to the four regiments ordered a few days since.[2]

You will have a large force of Cavalry. Use it as much as possible for attracting attention from this direction. Impress upon the Cavalry the necessity of keeping out of peoples houses, or taking what is of no use to them in a Military point of view. They must live as far as possible off the country through which they pass and destroy corn, wheat crops and everything that can be made use of by the enemy in prolonging the war. Mules and horses can be taken to supply all our wants and where it does not cause too much delay agricultural implements may be destroyed. In other words cripple the rebellion in every way without insulting women and children or taking their clothing, jewelry &c.

Very respectfully

U. S. GRANT

Maj. Gen Com

P. S. The leave of absence given Col. Johnson is extended until such time as his Brigade may reach the Army in the field.

U. S. G.

ALS, DNA, RG 393, 16th Army Corps, Letters Received. Incomplete in *O.R.*, I, xxiv, part 3, 274–75.

On May 5, 1863, Maj. Theodore S. Bowers, Milliken's Bend, wrote to Maj. Gen. Stephen A. Hurlbut. "Recent attempts have demonstrated the impossibility of sending supplies by the Vicksburg Batteries during these moon-light nights. The Army is therefore dependent upon land transportation for supplies. The distance to be waggoned to a point from which stores can be sent to Grand Gulf by steamboats is 44 miles, and since Gen Grant has advanced into the interior from Grand Gulf, it is feared that with the present limited land transportation it will be impossible to keep the Army from suffering. The advancing force has only two wagons to a Regiment with which to carry 5 days rations, ammunition and other stores. All other teams have been thrown into the General Supply Train, which is still inadequate. Under these circumstances the chief Commissary and Quartermaster here request me to advise you of the facts, and ask you to please send forward all teams that can possibly be spared from your Command. They will be returned to you as soon as the present emergency passes away. Gen Grant is in the advance and cannot be consulted on the subject of this letter, but the great importance of keeping the army supplied, induces me to present these facts for your consideration. If you can spare any teams it is of the highest importance that they be sent at once. Capt Eddy is unable to furnish them." ALS, DNA, RG 393, 16th Army Corps, Letters Received. *O.R.*, I, xxiv, part 3, 275–76.

On May 9, Hurlbut wrote to USG. "Yesterday evening at 7.20 p. m. I received your dispatches. General Veatch was notified at once, and sends four regiments of Infantry to Milliken's Bend. The 4th Division, Brig. Gen. Lauman commanding is ready to embark by Brigades as soon as transportation is furnished. I send you this division complete and only regret that I am not there to fight it. I call in to day four regiments from Corinth and two from Columbus to fill vacancies. I hope you will sweep out the rabble especially as I learn that mischief makers are looking after you with hopes based upon your downfall. I will keep this line, and be able to spare troops after awhile. It is hard to part with my men, but I know you will give them a chance" LS, DNA, RG 393, Dept. of the Tenn., Letters Received. On Sunday, May 10, Hurlbut wrote to Lt. Col. John A. Rawlins. "I received by Col Riggin, on Friday evening at 7 P. M. orders for five Regiments to be sent to Millikens Bend. They were on the boats before 10 P. M. on Saturday. I also received orders for movement of 4th Division. They are ready, and await transportation. To supply the vacuum at Memphis I have ordered down two Regiments from Columbus now on their way, and a few from Corinth which will be here to day or tomorrow. As I have a very strong interest in my old Division and know their preference—I respectfully ask of the Maj General commanding to attach them to General Sherman's Corps, as they and I have the fullest confidence and largest acquaintance with him and his command   I send them with their entire Regimental and Division train, as I suppose they will be needed for public service. I enclose copy of dispatch from Dodge as to the doings of his Cavalry near okalona—Hatch had been down in that neighborhood three days before, and I think I shall keep up a succession of Cavalry movements in that corner of the State, until I hear from Straights expedition about which I am anxious. I hope you will be able to send this Division back across the country from Vicksburgh. I hope they are not to be permanently separated from this command" Copy, *ibid.*, 16th Army Corps, Letters Sent. *O.R.*, I, xxiv, part 3, 291. On May 16, Hurlbut wrote to USG. "The last Brigade of the 4th Divn leaves tonight or in the morning having been detained for want of Boats to move them. I have directed the Division to Milliken's Bend where I suppose they will find orders. If no orders are there they will push forward an officer to receive orders from you. Two Companies of the 15th Ills Cavalry and three Batteries accompany & make part of the Division. Marmaduke with his force is on Crawley's Ridge near Wittburgh —Price is reported to have sent half his force to Kirby Smith at Monroe and to be on his way to join Marmaduke with the residue. He left Little Rock on 11th May —Prentiss' Cavalry had a sharp conflict with them at Wittburgh. Under these circumstances I have directed Prentiss to hold the Cavalry destined for this point. Rebel Cavalry in considerable force are gathering at Okalona intention not known, but I presume to cover North Mississippi. Chalmers with his force was on Friday near Coldwater N. W. of Holly Springs—probably 1500 strong. A movement in this direction may possibly be attempted if they can gather strength enough   No news of any kind from Washington" ALS, DNA, RG 393, Dept. of the Tenn., Letters Received. Dated May 17 in *O.R.*, I, xxiv, part 3, 321.

1. On May 5, USG wrote to Lt. Col. Judson D. Bingham. "Please order all

boats leaving Millikens Bend for northern ports to report to Maj. Genl. B. M. Prentiss, at Helena, for the purpose of transporting troops from that point to Memphis. You will also discharge such boats as you can spare from public Employment." Copies, DLC-USG, V, 19, 30, 98; DNA, RG 393, Dept. of the Tenn., Letters Sent; Alcorn Collection, WyU.

2. On May 4, Rawlins wrote to Hurlbut. "You will order four regiments of your command to Millikens Bend La. with the utmost dispatch. Take them from Those Troops most convenient for transportation and replace them by drawing from the forces at Columbus" Copies, *ibid*. On May 12, Brig. Gen. Jeremiah C. Sullivan, Young's Point, wrote to Rawlins. "Four Regiments, Col J. B. McCown, comd'g have reported here from Memphis. Brigr Genl Ewing Comd'g 3d Brig. 2d Div. 15th A. C. has been ordered to report, with his command, to Maj. Genl Blair, for duty." ALS, DNA, RG 393, Dept. of the Tenn., Letters Received.

To Col. William S. Hillyer

Head Quarters, Dept. of the Ten.
Hankinson's Ferry, May 5th 1863.

Col. W. S. Hillyer A. D. C.
Col.

See that the Com.y at Grand Gulf loads all wagons presenting themselves for stores with great ~~great~~ promptness. Issue any order in my name that may be necessary to secure the greatest promptness in this respect. Let Sherman detail an officer to do your duty in the La. shore until stores can be got out here. If necessary for promptness relieve the present Com.y and call on Sherman for an officer to take his place.

Movements here are delayed for want of Ammunition and stores. Every days delay is worth two thousand men to the enemy. Give this your personal attention.

Yours &c
U. S. Grant
Maj. Gen. Com

ALS, OClWHi. On May 5, 1863, USG wrote to the commissary of subsistence, Grand Gulf. "The Comy of Subsistence in charge of Stores at Grand Gulf will load all teams presenting themselves for rations with promptness and dispatch regardless of requisitions or provision returns, There must be no delay on account of either lack of Energy or formality on the part of the C. S. at Grand

Gulf." Copies, DLC-USG, V, 19, 30, 98; DNA, RG 393, Dept. of the Tenn., Letters Sent; Alcorn Collection, WyU.

Also on May 5, USG wrote to Col. William S. Hillyer. "The Provost Marshal General will pay to the bearer, J. M. Seeds, for services rendered the Government in obtaining information, and for long confinement suffered at the hands of the rebels whilst engaged in such service, One thousand (1000) dollars." ALS, PPRF. On the same day, USG prepared a pass. "Pass the bearer, Mr. J. M. Seeds, to Grand Gulf and North on all Government transports free of charge. Mr. Seeds is authorized to remain at any Military post during his pleasure." ANS, DNA, RG 94, Letters Received, 40C 1867. After the Civil War, James M. Seeds presented a series of claims for additional compensation for services as a scout, which began in Oct., 1861. On Feb. 10, 1866, USG endorsed an application of Seeds. "James M. Seeds voluntay vacated his position as pilot & sought employment in the secret service branch of the Army. He was employed for certain duty, knowing full well the risks he assumed & the emoluments he abandoned in engaging in the service. Having been captured and long detained as a prisoner of war losing his money and articles of value, he also, lost his time; and no reason exists why the Govt should re imburse him for the money and valuables he lost, and pay him the wages of a pilot (a position he vacated of his own accord) during the season of his detention as a prisoner in the south" Copy, DLC-USG, V, 58. On Jan. 28, 1867, Col. Daniel H. Rucker wrote to USG about Seeds, and summarized USG's rather unsympathetic response in a letter of Feb. 2 to Bvt. Maj. Gen. Edward D. Townsend. Copies, DNA, RG 94, Letters Received, 40C 1867. On June 7, 1872, Seeds wrote to USG about his claims. LS, *ibid.* For attempts by Seeds to receive $5,775 from Congress, see *HRC*, 43-2-24; *Congressional Record*, 44-1, 653, 3769.

To Col. William S. Hillyer

———

Head Quarters Dept of the Tenn
Hankensons Ferry Miss May 5th 1863

Col W. S. Hillyer A. A. D. C.

Col.

We will risk no more rations to run the Vicksburg Batteries. the river falling will enable us to contract our lines so as to give but eight miles of Land transportation to bring them from Youngs point to below Warrenton Batteries The road has been commenced on this route and will probably be finished in a day or two.

When this is done all the troops this side of Richmond can join their Divisions & Corps in the field—so direct them. All the Hay Forage Stores and cotton brought by us should be brought to Grand Gulf in anticipation of this move, as soon as possible. To prevent any misunderstanding I will state that the troops to come here are two Brigades of Gen. McArthurs Division, Two brigades of Blairs[1] the third of his to follow when reinforcements arrive from Memphis and one regiment of Cavalry   The two regiments of McClernands Corps can remain at Grand Gulf to constitute the Garrison there, also a Squadroon of the Cavalry and one of Logans Batteries, now behind at Perkins Plantation. All other Forces are to return to Youngs point.

> Yours truly
> U. S. Grant
> Maj. Gen.

Copies, DLC-USG, V, 19, 30, 98; DNA, RG 393, Dept. of the Tenn., Letters Sent. *O.R.*, I, xxiv, part 3, 275.

1. Francis P. Blair, Jr., resigned in July, 1862, as U.S. Representative from Mo. to serve in the army. Ordered by President Abraham Lincoln to Helena, Ark., on Nov. 17, he arrived a month later to command a brigade. Lincoln, *Works*, V, 498–99. On March 12, 1863, he was confirmed as both brig. gen. and maj. gen., although he had been reelected to Congress. On April 4, Blair was appointed by Maj. Gen. William T. Sherman to command the 2nd Div., 15th Army Corps, in place of Brig. Gen. David Stuart.

On March 21, Stuart asked to be relieved from duty because the Senate had refused to confirm his appointment. On March 29, Sherman endorsed this letter to USG. "Request that Gen. Stuart be ordered to Cairo, or the limits of the Dept there to await the action of the President in his case, viz: the rejection of the Senate of his nomination. I would be pleased if in the order favorable mention would be made of one who has patiently & assiduously done his duty"   Copy, DNA, RG 393, 15th Army Corps, Endorsements Sent. On April 2, Lt. Col. John A. Rawlins issued Special Orders No. 92. "The Senate having adjourned without confirming the appointment of Brigadier General David Stuart, made by the President he is hereby relieved from the Command of the 5th Division, Army of the Tennessee, and will proceed to Memphis, Tenn, from whence he will report by letter to the Adjutant General of the Army, Washington D. C. for orders   In thus relieving Brig. Gen. Stuart, from duty the General Commanding deems it but justice to a brave, intelligent and patriotic Officer to express his deep regret at the loss to the country of his valuable services in the Field, where, by meritorious action, he won the right to the position the favor of the President had conferred." Copies, DLC-USG, V, 26, 27; DNA, RG 393, Dept. of the Tenn., Special Orders. On April 7, Sherman endorsed to USG a petition of officers of the 2nd Div. concerning Stuart. "The paper hereto attached, ~~seemingly~~ being the spontaneous action of the officers of the 2nd Division of this Corps, though in seeming violation of an old and well established Military Rule, is not actually a violation of the Army Regulations which prohibits similar papers conveying praise or censure of officers in the Military service. General Stuart is not now in the Military Service. He has commanded the 2nd Division of this Corps, since Dec. 28, until notice of his non confirmation by the senate of the United States, and for a year prior to that time was either a Colonel or Brigadier with the Regiments that Compose the Division. This manifestation of the love, esteem and high respect of his fellow soldiers and officers is General Stuarts chief reward for faithful and Gallant services. These services have been acknowledged again and again by all his Commanders, and though I have seen Gen Stuart daily through this eventful period, watched him by day & night and seen in his every act the evidence of an accomplished Gentleman, a refined heart, a brave and manly soldier, enthusiastic in the Great Cause to snatch our Country's Governmt from the abyss of anarchy and dissolution that threatened and still threatens it; though willing to do him all honor & praise: and to cement the kindly feelings that now so properly ~~come to~~ exist between him & his command, I ought not to join in this Petition further than to say that General Stuart possesses my personal & official confidence, and I will ever hail his restoration to service in whatever Capacity the President in his judgment may think fit to assign him. As an officer and citizen I submit my own judgment to that of the appointing power, and the senate of the United States upon which body no one can reflect, and I must cheerfully abide their action. But if the Senate has from any cause been misled, I will do all I can as a soldier and Gentleman, to bear evidence to the truth of facts, which may aid General Stuart, should he desire to vindicate his character ~~against unseen foes, by~~ and to renew~~ing~~ his Military Career. With these remarks I forward the Petition to the HeadQrs of the Dept." ADfS, DLC-William T. Sherman; copy, DNA, RG 393, 15th Army Corps, Endorsements. Sherman later stated that Stuart was not confirmed "by reason of some old affair at Chicago." *Memoirs of Gen. W. T. Sherman . . .* (4th ed., New York, 1891), I, 341. Stuart had been charged as corespondent in a celebrated 1860 divorce case. Theodore Calvin Pease and James G. Randall, eds., *The Diary of Orville Hickman Browning* (Springfield, Ill., 1925), I, 435–42.

To Lt. Col. Judson D. Bingham

                                        Head Quarters Dept of the Tenn
                                        Hankinsons Ferry May 5. 1863

LT. COL. BINGHAM
CHEIF QR. MR
COL,

Send an Asst Q. M. Capt Gaster[1] if possible to report for duty at Head Quarters. Send him without delay   Release all boats that can possibly be spared. Send all Canal Boats and Barges worth the Towage back to the Quartermaster at Cincinnati. The Tugs still left above Vicksburg retain there for such service as you may find for them.

> Respectfully &c
> U. S. GRANT
> Maj Gen

Copies, DLC-USG, V, 19, 30, 98; DNA, RG 393, Dept. of the Tenn., Letters Sent; Alcorn Collection, WyU.

On May 8, 1863, Lt. Col. Judson D. Bingham, Milliken's Bend, wrote to USG. "I have the honor to report that all the teams have been engaged in transporting supplies to Perkin's Plantation. I have sent Officers and Agents over the Road frequently, to report to me the manner in which the work of pushing forward supplies has been performed, and also to keep me advised of the condition of the Road. They have all reported, that the trains are kept constantly running; that they have been unloaded promptly at Perkin's Plantation, and returned to this place, and that the road has been good, except for a few hours after the rain. I directed Lt. Janes, in charge of supplies at Perkin's Plantation, to forward stores across the River to Grand Gulf as rapidly as possible, and reports show that he has been prompt in the execution of the order. All wagons on the Richmond Road will return here, and cross from Young's Point to a landing about three miles below the Warrenton Batteries, a distance of about 9 miles. I have been over a portion of the Road from Young's Point to Howland's Plantation to-day, and an Officer went through to Johnson's Crevasse. The road is practicable, and the necessary supplies of Commissay Stores, Ordnance Stores, and Medical stores can be forwarded in one hundred wagons. Every exertion will be made, and I have no doubt but that the necessary supplies can be delivered at an accessible point on the River below the Warrenton Batteries." ALS, DNA, RG 393, Dept. of the Tenn., Letters Received.

1. William Gaster of Ohio was appointed capt. and asst. q. m. as of April 14, 1862.

To Lt. Commander Elias K. Owen

> Head Quarters Dept of the Tennessee
> In Field Hankensons Ferry Miss. May 5/863

CAPT. E. K. OWEN.
U. S. NAVY
CAPT.

Place the Flag Ship (your's) in the mouth of Black River to watch any movement of the enemy in that stream. Leave Capt.

Murphys vessel[1] in front of Grand Gulf to guard stores to convey any steamer that require it.

This will enable Capt. Murphy to Carry out Admiral Porters wish to have a survey made of Grand Gulf and surroundings. Send the remaining Iron Clad to the neighborhood of Warrenton to watch the movement of the enemy there and to prevent them from sending troops across the river to interrupt our lines from Millikins Bend and Youngs Point.

Very respectfully
U. S. GRANT Maj Gen

Copies, DLC-USG, V, 19, 30, 98; DNA, RG 393, Dept. of the Tenn., Letters Sent; Alcorn Collection, WyU. *O.R.*, I, xxiv, part 3, 272. Elias K. Owen joined the U.S. Navy as a midshipman in 1848 and attained the rank of lt. commander as of July 16, 1862. When Act. Rear Admiral David D. Porter left for the Red River on May 3, 1863, he placed Owen, commanding the U.S.S. *Louisville*, in charge of the Vicksburg gunboats. *O.R.* (Navy), I, xxiv, 627.

1. John McLeod Murphy, who had resigned from the U.S. Navy as midshipman in 1852, was appointed act. lt. as of Dec. 4, 1862, and assigned to command the U.S.S. *Carondelet*.

To Maj. Theodore S. Bowers

Head Quarters Department of the Tenn.
Hankensons Ferry Miss. May 5 1863

MAJ T. S. BOWERS

The moment a practicable road is constructed across from Youngs Point directing the Commanding officer to draw on to that line, and abandon every every place between Millikens Bend and Grand Gulf.

As soon as this is done McArther can join his Corps will [*with*] all the troops of his Division now on the line to be abandoned.

I ordered two Brigades of Blairs Division to be sent here at once but hear nothing of the order having been recieved. The

Third Brigade is to follow as soon as four regiments ordered from the 16th Army Corps arrived.

The Tuscumbia will go up as soon as she can to the terminus of our line below Warrenton. Direct Bingham to send immediately to Memphis for One hundred more wagons and teams. He must send an Officer to see that they are brought promptly. Let him call at Helena, and if all or any of them can be brought from there bring them.

> Yours &c.
>
> U. S. Grant
>
> Maj. Gen.

P. S. Order one regiment of the Cavalry that came from Helena immediately Here

> U. S. G.

Copy, DLC-USG, V, 98.
On May 5, 1863, Capt. Frederick E. Prime, Milliken's Bend, wrote to Lt. Col. John A. Rawlins. "An examination of the road from Genl Sherman's old Hd Qrs to the Biggs Plantation renders it advisable not to attempt to repair that road at present. Genl Blair proposes to land supplies below the entrance of the canal, wagon across the point & the dam at mouth of canal & thence to Brigg's Plantation and thinks that a bridge can be thrown across Johnson's crevasse—barges to run the blockade to build this bridge if necessary—I shall go down via that road to-day & examine into the practicability of that plan— . . . P. S. Capt Jenney, one company of pioneers and two regts will be at work to-morrow afternoon repairing & renewing the road from Milliken's Bend to Richmond—in compliance with instructions received by Genl Blair." ALS, DNA, RG 393, Dept. of the Tenn., Letters Received.

To Commanding Officer, Milliken's Bend

────────

> Head Quarters Dept of the Tenn
> Hankensons Ferry May 5, 1863

Commanding Officer
Millikens Bend La.
Sir:

I understand the enemy have established a Battery below Greenville   If so renew my request to Capt. Breese of the navy to send one Iron Clad to dislodge them, and send at the same time sufficient force to drive the enemy across Deer Creek or capture them

You will be the judge of what force will be necessary for this purpose & if they can be spared from so inform Capt Breese and request him to go above and remain as long as deems advisable and to make such dispositions as he may think will prevent a recurrence of the Blockade

Very respectfully
U. S. GRANT Maj Gen

Copies, DLC-USG, V, 19, 30, 98; DNA, RG 393, Dept. of the Tenn., Letters Sent. On May 5, 1863, USG wrote to Lt. Commander K. Randolph Breese. "I understand the enemy have placed a battery below Greenville which defies the Tin Clads. If so I would request that you send one of the Iron Clads to drive them out. The Commanding officer at Youngs Point or Millikin's Bend will send troops to push the rebels beyond Deer Creek." ALS (facsimile), *The Flying Quill: Autographs at Goodspeed's* (Sept., 1973), p. 2.

To Maj. Gen. Henry W. Halleck

Head Q'rs In the Field
May 6th 1863.

MAJ GEN H. W. HALLECK
GEN IN CHIEF

Ferrying and transportation of rations to Grand Gulf is detaining us on the Black river. I will move as soon as three 3 days rations received and send wagons back to the Gulf for more to follow. Information from the other side leads me to believe the Enemy are bringing forces from Tullahoma Should not Gen Rosecrans at least make a demonstration of advancing?

U S. GRANT
Maj Genl

Telegram received, DNA, RG 107, Telegrams Collected (Bound); copies, *ibid.*, Telegrams Received in Cipher; *ibid.*, RG 393, Dept. of the Tenn., Hd. Qrs. Correspondence; DLC-USG, V, 5, 8, 24, 94, 98. *O.R.*, I, xxiv, part 1, 35. This telegram was received in Washington at 1:30 A.M., May 13, 1863.

To Maj. Gen. Stephen A. Hurlbut

———

Head Quarters, Dept. of the Ten.
Hankinsons Ferry, May 6th 1863.

MAJ. GEN. S. A. HURLBUT,
COMD.G 16TH ARMY CORPS.
GEN.

Telegraph to Gen. Halleck direct the forces I have drawn from you and should reinforcements be necessary to hold your District let him know it. Whilst Head Quarters are so distant communicate direct with Washington in all important matters but keep me advised at the same time of what is going on.

Everything here looks highly favorable at present. The only thing now delaying us is the ferriage of wagons and supplies across the river to Grand Gulf. We hold the bridge across Black river at this place and have had troops within seven miles of Warrenton. Also command the next crossing some fifteen miles higher up the river from which another road leads direct to Vicksburg. Rations now are the only delay.

Very respectfully
U. S. GRANT
Maj. Gen. Com

ALS, DNA, RG 393, 16th Army Corps, Letters Received. *O.R.*, I, xxiv, part 3, 279.

General Orders No. 32

———

Head Quarters, Department of the Tennessee,
In Field, Hawkinson's Ferry, Miss., May 7. 1863.

GENERAL ORDERS NO. 32.

SOLDIERS OF THE ARMY OF THE TENNESSEE!

Once more I thank you for adding another victory to the long list of those previously won by your valor and endurance. The triumph gained over the enemy near Port Gibson on the 1st inst., is one of the most important of the war.

The capture of five cannon, and more than a thousand prisoners; the possession of Grand Gulf, and a firm foothold upon the highlands between the Big Black and Bayou Pierre, from whence we threaten the whole line of the enemy, are among the fruits of this brilliant achievement.

The march from Milliken's Bend, to a point opposite Grand Gulf, was made in stormy weather, over the worst of roads; bridges and ferries had to be constructed; moving by night as well as by day, with labors incessant and extraordinary, privations have been endured by men and officers as have rarely been parallelled in any campaign. Not a murmur nor a complaint has been uttered.

A few days continuance of the same zeal and constancy will secure to this Army the crowning victory over the rebellion.

More difficulties and privations are before us. Let us endure them manfully.

Other battles are to be fought. Let us fight them bravely.

A grateful country will rejoice at our success, and history will record it with immortal honor.

U. S. GRANT
Major General Commanding.

Copies, DLC-USG, V, 13, 14, 95; DNA, RG 393, Dept. of the Tenn., General and Special Orders; Dodge Papers, IaHA; (printed) USGA. *O.R.*, I, xxiv, part 1, 35.

To Maj. Gen. John A. McClernand

Head Quarters Dept of the Tenn
Rocky Springs Miss. May 7. 1863

MAJ GEN. J. A MCCLERNAND
COMDG 13TH ARMY CORPS.
GEN.

If your rations are up so as to give you three or more days on hand Move in the morning to Auburn with at least one division and the remainder between that and Baldwin   you have a direct road to Auburn and also to Baldwin

I do not yet know if there is intermediate roads   If there are, move one division on each of the roads named and the other two on the intermediate roads

Should there be but the two roads move the four Divisions so as to bring them well up on the line connecting the two places

General McPherson will move on a road south of you so as to be well up.

Send all the teams you can spare after putting three days rations in mens Haversacks, back to Grand Gulf for rations and ammunition.

Shermans Forces being in the rear will protect our trains for one more trip if they move promptly   Send me a statement of the amount of rations and ammunition you have on hand and on the way between Grand Gulf & your Camp

Very respectfully

U. S. GRANT

Maj. Gen.

P. S. Trains should not go interely unguarded but should be accompanied by at least two men to each wagon

U. S. G

Copies, DLC-USG, V, 19, 30, 98; DNA, RG 393, Dept. of the Tenn., Letters Sent; *ibid.*, 13th Army Corps, Letters Received; Alcorn Collection, WyU. *O.R.*, I, xxiv, part 3, 280.

On May 6, 1863, Maj. Gen. John A. McClernand, Willow Springs, twice wrote to USG. "I send herewith a prisoner by the name of Kelly; formerly, a resident of Williamson County, Illinois. He estimates the rebel force at Vicksburgh at 80.000, but says, that is far under the reported number   He says that the rations, in hand, at Vicksburgh are reported to be equal to the subsistence of the army there for eight days; but he believes, that they will not last more than five days. This, however, is an inference on his part   He furthermore says, that neither Edwards Station, nor Jackson, are fortified. These are the principal points upon which I interrogated him. Kelly represents himself as a Kinsman, by marriage, of Genl Logan. Nineteen ambulances, with wounded men, have arrived here this morning from Port Gibson. They came, as I understood, because some one (I don't know who) had ordered the wounded at Port Gibson to be taken to Grand Gulf (of course *via* Willow Springs) and because of an apprehension that they would have been captured, if they had tried to go back to Grant Hospital.

You are aware that five ambulances were captured by rebels at the Battlefield last night. There is no suitable place for the wounded, here,   It would be dangerous to send them back to Grant Hospital; hence, I would advise that they be immediately conveyed to Grand Gulf and that the ambulances which belong to this corps be returned. The wounded brought here belong to Genl Smith's command. The Medical Director for the Dept will know whether any still remain at Port Gibson   if so; ought they not to be rescued from the danger of capture? My Medical Director is absent under orders from Dr Hewitt"   LS, DNA, RG 393, Dept. of the Tenn., Letters Received. "Col Taggart, Chf Commissary of the 13th Army Corps, calls to see you this morning. His object is to get an order placing a hundred wagons, of the 17th Army Corps, or any wagons, at his disposal, for the purpose of bringing rations to the men of the 13th corps. He will explain the necessity for it. Gen'l Osterhaus reports that he learns that the main force of the enemy on the east side of the Big. Black, has retreated towards Edward's Station, on the railroad, and east of the Black. The detachment encountered by General Osterhaus yesterday were a corps of observators sent out to watch our approach. The cavalry with Gen'l Osterhaus is now occupying all the roads North, East, and South of the cross roads, near Cayuga. Reconnoitering parties have been sent from the same vicinity towards Utica and Gallatin. A corps of observation has been sent out towards Edward's Station; while still another party has been sent ~~out towards~~ up the river in pursuit of the rebel steamers." ALS, *ibid. O.R.*, I, xxiv, part 3, 277.

On May 7, McClernand, Rocky Springs, wrote to USG. "My whole Corps is up to, or beyond, this point. I rode forward early this morning to the front and within a short distance of Hall's Ferry. The enemy has planted a battery (probably) of three guns on the West bank of Big Black for the purpose of commanding the Ferry. My pickets are close up, on the East side of the river. Genl Osterhaus has bivouacked one brigade of his command, with a section of Artillery, on the far side of Big Sandy, the remainder of his command is on the near side of the same creek   Genl Carr has bivouacked his Division to the right of Genl Osterhaus and has placed his seige guns in position.—Genl Hovey is moving forward to take position to the left of Genl Osterhaus.—General Smith is in reserve, on the little Sandy, about a mile & a half in the rear, and besides holding himself ready to support the front, will hold, and guard, the approach by the Utica road —I understand that Genl Sherman has seized the river transports, and thus, longer delayed the wagons upon which I am relying to bring adequate supplies of food and ammunition. The enemy are fortifying at Edward's Station, and fugitive negroes report, that he is rapidly concentrating re-inforcements at that place, and West of there, by rail. I think the enemy is in strong force. Is it not important that the Army of the Tennessee should be fully supplied and put in the best fighting order? The political consequences of the impending battle will be momentous. ~~in their political consequences.~~ I am still causing the country to be scoured. The 'Forest Queen' is said to be the only boat now available to cross men and material of war. Would not the exigency justify the risk of running the blockade with additional transports? Genl Logans Division is up to Rocky Springs." ALS, DNA, RG 393, Dept. of the Tenn., Letters Received. *O.R.*, I, xxiv, part 3, 279–80.

To Maj. Gen. William T. Sherman

————

Head Qrs. Dept. of the Tn.
Hankinsons Ferry May 7th 1863.

MAJ. GEN. SHERMAN,
COMDG 15TH A. C.
GEN.

Bring one Division of your Corps here and releive the last of the 17th. Whilst here they will guard the bridge over Black river keeping pickets well on the North bank. The others of your corps will save distance and come on to the same road at Rocky Springs by moving directly to Willow Springs. So direct them.

Should I fail to direct it hereafter I want the bridge at this place totally destroyed when the last of your forces leave the place.

Very respectfully
U. S. GRANT
Maj. Gen

P. S. I move my Hd Qrs. to Rocky Springs to-day.

ALS, James S. Schoff, New York, N. Y.

To Col. William S. Hillyer

————

Head Quarters, Dept. of the Ten.
Hankinson's Ferry May 7th 1863.

COL. W. S. HILLYER,
A. A. D. C.
COL.

Send me a report of about the number of rations on hand and sent forward from Grand Gulf. Send also to Mackfeeley & Bingham and remind them of the importance of rushing forward rations with all dispatch. The road across to below Warrenton ought now to be completed. If so rations can be got over by that route very rapidly. The disabled boats could be taken above and loaded as rations arrive and when loaded could be towed down and issued from. Having two of these boats it would be easy to to bring all the rations from near Warrenton that is required and keep the other steamers comparitively free.

Yours Truly

U. S. GRANT

Maj. Gen. Com

Send word to Mcfeeley and Bingham that I look to them to make their Departments efficient and to see that supplies reach Grand Gulf.

U. S. G.

How many teams have been loaded with rations and sent forward? How many have gone to the 13th Army Corps? I want to know as near as possible how we stand in every particular for supplies. How many wagons have you ferried over the river? How many are still ready to bring over? What teams have gone back for rations?

U. S. G.

Direct Mackfeeley to send two rations of bread, salt & coffee to one of meat and sugar and to send no other rations until a full supply of these are on hand.

U. S. G.

ALS, ICarbS. On May 7, 1863, Capt. Edward Tittmann, commissary, Grand Gulf, wrote to Col. William S. Hillyer reporting the quantities of foodstuffs on hand and those sent forward. ALS, DNA, RG 393, Dept. of the Tenn., Letters Received.

On May 6, USG had written to Hillyer. "If not allready done have every man that will bear transportation from the Hospital back of Bruinsburg to Grand Gulf near which which a Hospital should be established for their accomodation" Copies, DLC-USG, V, 19, 30, 98; DNA, RG 393, Dept. of the Tenn., Letters Sent.

To Maj. Gen. Henry W. Halleck

Rocky Springs Miss
May ~~12th~~ 8th [*1863*]

MAJ GEN H W HALLECK
GEN IN CHIEF

Our advance is fifteen (15) miles from Edwards Station on Southern Rail Road   All looks well. Port Hudson is undoubtedly evacuated except by a small garrison and their heavy Artillery.

U. S. GRANT
Maj Gen Comdg

Telegram received, DNA, RG 107, Telegrams Collected (Bound); copies, *ibid.*, Telegrams Received in Cipher; *ibid.*, RG 393, Dept. of the Tenn., Hd. Qrs. Correspondence; DLC-USG, V, 6, 8, 24, 94, 98. *O.R.*, I, xxiv, part 1, 35. This telegram was received in Washington at 7:20 P.M., May 14, 1863.

To Maj. Gen. John A. McClernand

Head Quarters Dept of the Tenn.
Rocky Springs May 8th/63

MAJ GENL MCCLERNAND
COMD'G 13TH ARMY CORPS
GENL:

The change of route ordered for the march of your Corps was on the strengt[h] of reports made by one of the Engr officers from Head Quarters who went beyond Cayuga to-day. He reports that the telegraph runs to Edwards Station and that it diverges from the Auburn road one half mile beyond Cayuga. I want your direction to be toward Edwards Station and intended my note only as information about the route.

Do not move until your wagons come up. If they arrive in time however I wou[ld] like you to push on a few miles tomorrow. Camp [at] the stream beyond Cayuga. This would give you a good opportunity of reconnoitering the roads beyond.

Very Respectfully

U. S. GRANT

Maj Genl

Copy, DNA, RG 393, 13th Army Corps, Letters Received. Earlier on May 8, 1863, USG wrote to Maj. Gen. John A. McClernand. "The road to Edwards Station leaves the Auburn Road about one half mile beyond Cayuga. The Telegraph follows this road. Instead of going to Auburn as I previously directed you can move on this latter or the telegraph road." Copies, DLC-USG, V, 19, 30, 98; DNA, RG 393, Dept. of the Tenn., Letters Sent; *ibid.*, 13th Army Corps, Letters Received; Alcorn Collection, WyU. On the same day, 7:00 P.M., McClernand, Big Sandy, wrote to USG. "Your dispatch of this date, modifying previous instructions relative to the route of my contemplated march is rec'd. You say you understand the telegraph road leading from the Raymond or Jackson road to Edward's Station diverges a half mile beyond Carthage Cayuga. Is there not some mistake about this? I have with me an intelligent negro, who has been driving a team, at intervals, for fourteen years, from Port Gibson to Edward's Station. He says the telegraph road to Edward's Station, diverges from the road leading from here to Raymond seven miles beyond Cayuga, and about two miles beyond Auburn. The point of divergence is at Barrow's plantation. Gen'l Osterhaus has consulted a map found by him, today, and is of the same opinion. This telegraph roads forms part of the main road leading from Port Gibson to Edward's Station. Sixty wagons, laden with ammunition, are reported to half left Grand Gulf at 2 o'clock P. M. They should be here in the morning. Herewith will be found a statement of the strength of the several Divisions of the 13th Army Corps, and the supply of provisions on hand. Col. Taggart is expecting to be able to supply the whole with three days rations in the morning. If you wish me to move my Corps before the expected supplies of ammunition and rations come up and are issued, please so advise me. Three deserters crossed the Big Black this evening, near Hall's Ferry, and came into my camp. They report the enemy to be concentrating between the bluffs on the East west side of the Big Black, and Bolton, on the East side of Big Black. Edward's station is about the centre of this line. They are burning cotton on the west side of Big Black, and declare they will leave nothing valuable between that stream and Vicksburg. If I am not ordered to move in the morning, I will direct Gen'l Osterhaus to send a detachment of one or two companies to Hall's Ferry, and feel the enemy, if he be there—" LS, DNA, RG 393, Dept. of the Tenn., Letters Received.

To Maj. Gen. William T. Sherman

Head Quarters Dept of the Tenn
Rocky Springs May 8, 1863

GEN W. T. SHERMAN
COMDG 15TH ARMY CORPS
GEN:

Troops moving on the road I have not deemed it necessary heretofore to send escorts with trains passing back and forth   If however all your forces have left Grand Gulf it will not be intirely safe to send them so any longer. I would direct therefore that you leave one Brigade at the forks of the roads when they divide, one branch going to Willow Springs the other to Hankinsons Ferry, until wagons now behind are all up.

I will direct Hillyer to load all the wagons he can tomorrow and send them up to your Brigade to be escorted by it.

After that to send no more but load them to have them ready until troops are coming to escort them.

Very respectfully
U. S. GRANT
Maj. Gen.

Copies, DLC-USG, V, 19, 30, 98; DNA, RG 393, Dept. of the Tenn., Letters Sent; Alcorn Collection, WyU. On May 9, 1863, 4:00 A.M., Maj. Gen. William T. Sherman, Hankinson's Ferry, wrote to USG. "Yours of May 8 is received. It came too late to halt one of my Brigades at the Forks of the Road, but I will send orders for Tuttle to remain at Willow springs which will cover the same point, and I advise you to issue some General order and send it to all points—prescribing, just how many wagons shall be to each Regm't—how many to each Brigade &c on this march   There are 500 wagons across the River and with each is an officer pressing to have it cross over as the absolute safety of the Army depends on that wagon.—Make some uniform & just Rule and Send some body back to regulate this matter as your Road will be crowded, & jammed unless it be done. McArthur is ready to cross over and can escort trains out. Blair will be their today or morrow & should remain at Hard Times till you have all the wagons & provisions you aim to secure. It is useless to push out men here till their supplies are regulated, unless you intend to live on the Country. Hilyer is doing his best; but each Corps and Division & Brigade Commander is there urging for ward the particular wagon, and the steamboats can only bring wagons in a particular ratio. The Rule I adopted was   1st 2 wagons per Regm't of troops   2nd. Wagons exclusively loaded with provisions & ammunition 3rd. According to the discretion of the officer, in charge—I left Col Stone at Hard Times, but Blair will be there tonight. Please make a General order on this subject at once, publish it to all Corps, Divisions, & Brigades, and let Hilyer enforce it—stop all troops till your army is partially supplied with wagons and then act as quick as possible, for this Road will be jammed as sure as life if you attempt to supply 50000 men by one single Road. I will halt Steeles Division here, Tuttles at Willow Springs and Blairs at Hard Times, each ordered to keep supplied with Beef & corn, and as much bread, sugar & coffee as possible. Gen Crocker moves to the front today." ALS, DNA, RG 94, War Records Office, Dept. of the Tenn. *O.R.*, I, xxiv, part 3, 284–85. See letter to Maj. Gen. William T. Sherman, May 9, 1863.

To Col. William S. Hillyer

Head Quarters Dept of the Tenn.
Rocky Springs Miss. May 8. 1863

COL. W. S. HILLYER.

COL:

I have directed Sherman to leave one Brigade at the forks of the road seven miles from Grand Gulf to escort all wagons that come up tomorrow night and before

All other wagons you may have loaded up ready to forward when ever troops are coming up but do not send them out otherwise.

Hereafter I will send escorts whenever trains are going back. If possible so arrange as to send the greatest possible amount of hard Bread salt and coffee with all forces of troops coming this way

Yours &c

U. S. GRANT

Maj Gen.

Copies, DLC-USG, V, 19, 30, 98; DNA, RG 393, Dept. of the Tenn., Letters Sent; Alcorn Collection, WyU. On May 8, 1863, Lt. Col. Robert Macfeely, Milliken's Bend, wrote to USG. "I have the honor to report that since the 2d inst. I have forwarded by Wagons, to Perkins plantation and Grand Gulf, over three hundred thousand rations of Hard Bread Coffee, Sugar, & Salt, 225.000 rations of Salt meat and 130.000 of soap. The other parts of the ration not being considered essential, only a small amount was sent, for issue to Hospitals. The above Statement does not include the amount forwarded to day, as the reports of the day have not yet been handed to me. There has been no delay in sending forward stores from this place. The Commissaries working night & day when there was any to be loaded. There is now on hand at this place nearly two millions Complete rations: Invoices have been received of half million more rations en route. On relieving Col Hawkins I directed Col. Haines to keep constantly on hand at this place three millions complete rations. This amount I expect to have in the course of a week. I will use every exertion to keep your army supplied. I have just seen your letter to Col Hillyer in relation to the parts of the ration you desire sent: These instruction will be strictly complied with. No more meat will be forwarded until ~~until~~ a proportionate quantity of Hard Bread has been sent The new road across Young's point will, I am informed, be placed in good condition in a day or two. There will then be no. difficulty in supplying your army. The rations are here and all that is required, are the means of transportation to get them forward"   ALS, DNA, RG 94, War Records Office, Dept. of the Tenn. *O.R.*, I, xxiv, part 3, 281–82. On May 8, USG wrote two other letters to Col. William S. Hillyer. "The limitation of transportation prescribed by Sherman will not carry ammunition alone, I want as you suggest all the wagons brought from the other side of the river except what can be advantageously used ~~for~~ there   All wagons coming out to be loaded with Ammunition and Commissary Stores." "I send with Escort some prisoners civilians picked up by Colonel Wright from the vicinity of where our ambulances were picked up. Send them all back to Bruinsburg and release them after swearing them to abstain from taking any part in the rebellion either by giving information to the enemy or other wise   Should any of them refuse to ~~do~~ give such a pledge, send them to Millikins Bend by first opportunity, to be detained for further orders"   Copies, DLC-USG, V, 19, 30, 98; DNA, RG 393, Dept. of the Tenn., Letters Sent.

Also on May 8, 8:00 A.M., Col. Clark Wright, "Junction of Grand Gulf & Port Gibson Roads," wrote to Lt. Col. John A. Rawlins. "I arrived at this point last night. My rear vedetts were firing during the night & morning, with the advance of the Enemy. His main force fell back to Port Gibson during the evening & night. I am still unable to give reliable information of who the Infantry are or where they come from. I am Induced to believe However that we see their entire force, which could not exceed one thousand or twelve Hundred men with 5 pieces of artilery. If Such is the fact, that force might have been at Fayette and been ordered up by Adams to drive me out instead of coming from Port Hudson, as reported by contrabands. I will moove back in that direction to day and acertain if possible, the true state of affairs,   Surgeon Kernan, & three of my men were captured in the charge yesterday, I had no other loss. My force is about 300 men & Four Howitzers. I took one days Rations from a train this morning for them; nothing in the vicinity in the way of subsistence. I will report immediately any other information obtained"   ALS, *ibid.*, RG 94, War Records Office, Dept. of the Mo. *O.R.*, I, xxiv, part 3, 283. On the same day, Rawlins wrote to Wright. "You will hold the Enemy in check as much as possible and fall slowly back upon the Grand Gulf road which is protected by General Shermans forces now moving out. Send reports from time to time of the condition of things with you." Copies, DLC-USG, V, 19, 30, 98; DNA, RG 393, Dept. of the Tenn., Letters Sent.

To Capt. Frederick E. Prime

———

Head Quarters Dept of the Tenn.
Rocky Springs Miss May 8th 1863

CAPT F. E. PRIME
CHEIF ENGR DEPT OF THE TENN.
CAPT.

If you have not already passed Grand Gulf lay out Defensive works there for a Garrison of say 2000 men,   What I want is defences on the hill to protect our stores at the landing from an attack from inland. I do not expect to have at any time to have a large force there nor do I want at present any works commenced that will take a great while in the execution. Contrabands can be sent from here to do the labor and you can select who you please to superintend the work,

Yours &c
U. S. GRANT
Maj Gen

Copies, DLC-USG, V, 19, 30, 98; DNA, RG 393, Dept. of the Tenn., Letters Sent; Alcorn Collection, WyU.

To Maj. Gen. John A. McClernand

———

Head Qrs. Dept. of the Ten.
Rocky Springs, Miss.
May 9th 1863 9. P. M.

MAJ. GENL. J. A. McCLERNAND,
COMDG. 13TH ARMY CORPS,
CAYUGA P. O.
GENL.

Move your command tomorrow on the Telegraph road, to five mile Creek. Instructions have been given to Genls. McPherson[1] and Sherman to move so as to continue on the same general front with you.

Have all the laterals roads leading from your line of march, carefully examined, to facilitate communication with the other corps, in case of necessity.

Please send a competent officer to Perkin's plantation to superintend the transportation of your remaining camp and garrison equipage to Grand Gulf, and the storage thereof at that point.

> Very Respectfully,
> U. S. Grant
> Maj Gen

Copies, DLC-USG, V, 19, 30, 98; DNA, RG 393, Dept. of the Tenn., Letters Sent; *ibid.*, 13th Army Corps, Letters Received; Alcorn Collection, WyU. *O.R.*, I, xxiv, part 3, 284. On May 9, 1863, 9:40 p.m., Maj. Gen. John A. McClernand, Big Sandy, wrote to USG. "Your dispatch of this date is this moment received. A train, with a limited quantity of ammunition & rations, came up late this evening. It will take some time to sort & issue the ammunition; also, to issue the rations. I hope to have all done by, or before, nine O'clock in the morning, and to take up the line of march, at least by that hour, for five mile creek, which is about ten miles from here.—The reconnoitering party sent out by me this morning, & of which I advised you, went to five mile creek and have returned. A reconnoitering party of the enemy had come as far in this direction as Cayuga, but had returned just before my party reached that place. Please advise me what relations Genls Shermans and McPhersons Corps will bear—during the advance—to mine. I send an orderly to bring any information you may be pleased to give me on that point." ALS, DNA, RG 393, Dept. of the Tenn., Letters Received. *O.R.*, I, xxiv, part 3, 284.

Earlier on May 9, McClernand wrote to USG. "I have just ordered a party forward, accompanied by the Engineer of this corps, to reconnoitre the road to and beyond Cayuga. I will report the result as soon as possible. Upon examination, I think it best to have Gen'l Smith's Division where it is until I move my whole corps. He is only about 1½ miles behind Big Sandy." LS, DNA, RG 393, Dept. of the Tenn., Letters Received. On the same day, Lt. Col. John A. Rawlins wrote to McClernand. "Brig. Gen. Tuttles Division 15th Army Corps have been directed to move forward to night to the point now occupied by Brig. Gen. A. J. Smiths Division of your army Corps   You will therefore please order the latter to move up to the Big Sandy." Copies, DLC-USG, V, 19, 30, 98; DNA, RG 393, Dept. of the Tenn., Letters Sent; *ibid.*, 13th Army Corps, Letters Received; Alcorn Collection, WyU. *O.R.*, I, xxiv, part 3, 283. On the same day, McClernand wrote to USG. "Two fugitive negroes from the immediate vicinity of Utica came on this morning   They report the arrival of Ten thousand rebels troops within a mile and a half of that place and that they understood others were Coming   I think the report an exaggeration, yet it is not improbable that there is some foundation in it." Copy, DNA, RG 393, 13th Army Corps, Letters Sent.

1. On May 9, 7:00 P.M., USG wrote to Maj. Gen. James B. McPherson. "March your command tomorrow, to water beyond Utica, provided you can find it within six or seven miles of that place, on the direct Raymond road." LS, NjR. On May 9, 7:30 P.M., "Camp at Cross Roads, 7 miles from Utica—" McPherson wrote to USG. "Genl. Crockers' Division arrived here and went into Camp at 2 P. M. Genl. Logans' Division is just coming up—Col: Wright's Cavalry are in Utica & have had some little skirmishing with the Enemy, I enclose his report. The information that I have been able to obtain thus far is very indefinite, I sent Capt. Foster to the point where 'Newlands Mills' used to be—there are no such mills in Existence having been destroyed a few years since—He saw or heard nothing of the Enemy, Col: Strong & Lieut. Gile with a few orderlies went through from this point to *Cayuga*. A short time before they reached the Town, Fifty rebel Cavalry were there, about half of them left and went towards Jackson, and the remainder went towards Utica—Some of the Citizens in the Vicinity of Utica say *Beauregard* is at or near Jackson—I may be able to get some more authentic information before morning, If so will send it to you immediately— Please find a sketch of my Camp—and a Vicksburg paper of the 6th inst—" ALS, DNA, RG 393, Dept. of the Tenn., Letters Received. *O.R.*, I, xxiv, part 3, 287. The map remains with the letter.

To Maj. Gen. William T. Sherman

Head Quarters, Dept. of the Ten.
Rocky Springs, May 9th 1863.

MAJ. GEN. W. T. SHERMAN,
COMD.G 15TH ARMY CORPS,
GEN.

I do not calculate upon the possibility of supplying the Army with full rations from Grand Gulf. I know it will be impossible without constructing additional roads. What I do expect however is to get up what rations of hard bread, coffee & salt we can and make the country furnish the balance.

We started from Bruinsburg with an average of about two days rations and received no more from our own supplies for seven days. Abundance was found in the mean time. Some corn-meal, bacon and vegitables was found and abundance of beef and mutton.

A delay would give the enemy time to reinforce and fortify. If Blair was up now I believe we could be in Vicksburg in seven days. The command here has an average of about three days rations which could be made to last that time.

You are in a country where the troops have already lived off the people for some days and may find provisions more scarce but as we get upon new soil they are abundant particularly in corn and cattle.

Bring Blairs two Brigades up as soon as possible. The advance will move to-day to about three miles beyond Cayuga and also on the Utica road.

Your Division at Willow Springs should also move to this place.

Yours truly
U. S. GRANT
Maj. Gen. Com

P. S. In puplishing the order limiting the transportation I have designated Conduit Smith to take charge of the general supply train. I done this because I know no one but him, now with the Army, and available, who is capable. I hope you will not regard this as an interferance with your Corps. It will be but a few days that his services will be required in this service at furthest.

U. S. G.

ALS, IHi. Incomplete in *O.R.*, I, xxiv, part 3, 285–86.

To Brig. Gen. Michael K. Lawler

Head Quarters Dept of the Tenn
Rocky Springs Miss May 9, 1863

BRIG GEN. M. K. LAWLER
GEN:

Two prisoners have now reported to me with paroles granted by you.

This entirely unauthorized. General Orders #49 War Department notifies our own troops and the southern authorities that prisoners can only be paroled at the places agreed upon in the Dix-Hill Cartel, any other parole is void[1]   Besides this prisoners running loose throug[h] our camp is giving the enemy an advantage which they pay men for risking their lives to obtain. I want no more liscenced spies within our lines.

Very respectfully

U. S. GRANT

Maj. Gen.

Copies, DLC-USG, V, 19, 30, 98; DNA, RG 393, Dept. of the Tenn., Letters Sent. On May 9, 1863, USG wrote to Brig. Gen. Jeremiah C. Sullivan. "Keep all prisoners sent to Millikins Bend for further orders   If they are sent north they will be sent east for exchange. I prefer keeping them where they are until the fate of Vicksburg is settled and then paroling them at the nearest southern Military Post to us. To releive them now they might be able to give information of value to the enemy." Copies, *ibid.*

On April 15, Lt. Col. James Harrison Wilson had written to Brig. Gen. Michael K. Lawler. "Allow me to congratulate you on your well earned promotion. I do it with all my heart for personal as well as public reasons. You are confirmed to date from Novr. 29th 1862; enclosed you will find an Official extract— Containing the names of those in *Our* Army. I am directed by Col. Rawlins to say your promotion gives complete satisfaction to every body at Hd. Qrs. from the General down. The General and I discussed the list last night and I can say he heartily joins in the sentiment. You are ordered to report without delay to these HeadQuarters and at Genl. McClernand's request will be assigned a command in his corps. The order will doubtless reach you by this mail. . . ." ALS, Lawler Papers, ICarbS. On the same day, Lt. Col. John A. Rawlins issued Special Orders No. 105. "Brigadier General Michael K. Lawler, U. S. Vols., will report to Major General John A. McClernand, Comdg. 13th Army Corps, for duty." DS, *ibid.*

On May 24, Lawler wrote to Brig. Gen. Lorenzo Thomas. "I am one of the Brigadiers appointed to take rank from the 29th November 1862.—If seniority is awarded as we are placed in the list it would place me among the juniores. I was the senior Colonel from the West and would be gratified to have rank with the new appointments as we stood before, and according to regulations—" LS, DNA, RG 94, ACP, L516 CB 1863. On May 29, USG endorsed this letter. "Respectfully referred to Head Quarters of the Army, Washington, D. C.   Brig. Gen Lawler as colonel, ranked most of the Brigadier Generals who have been recently appointmented in this Department. He has always been one of my best officers in the field, and in recent battles greatly distinguished himself" ES, *ibid.*

1. On March 28, USG wrote to "Commanding Officer Confederate Forces." "Herewith enclosed find a number of copies of General Orders. No 49 present series from Hd Quarters of the Army Washington D. C. It is due that this order should have as great a circulation as possible among southern commanders. I

respectfully request that you will give the copies sent that circulation" Copies, DLC-USG, V, 19, 30; DNA, RG 393, Dept. of the Tenn., Letters Sent. *O.R.*, II, v, 400. AGO General Orders No. 49, Feb. 28, which established rules with regard to paroles, specified that copies would be sent to the "opposing forces." *Ibid.*, pp. 306–7. On May 20, Col. William Hoffman, commissary gen. of prisoners, wrote to USG. "The Secretary of war directs that, unless specially authorized no Confederate prisoners of war, will be released on condition of taking the Oath of Allegiance." LS, DNA, RG 393, Dept. of the Tenn., Letters Received. *O.R.*, II, v, 669. On the same day, Hoffman wrote to USG quoting at length his letter to C.S.A. Lt. Col. William H. Ludlow on the same subject. LS, DNA, RG 94, War Records Office, Dept. of the Tenn. *O.R.*, II, v, 670.

To Col. William S. Hillyer

Head Quarters, Dept. of the Ten
Rocky Springs, May 9th/63

Col. W. S. Hillyer,

What you have done is just right. It seems that fewer wagons would have done to have sent back but they can be brought up here after if necessary. I feel somewhat uneasy for our trains that are out now but hope they will get through all right. Sherman received my orders after his troops had all far passed the point where I directed him to leave a Brigade. Send no more trains without an escort but follow previous instructions to send all the supplies of Ammunition and provisions you can with every body of troops coming this way.

You have had my instructions about the troops that are to come here from the line of our present route to Millikin's Bend? Also that every thing brought by us, even to McClernands Camp equipage, is to be brought to Grand Gulf?

Write to Lyford, by order, to send 100 rounds of ammunition for 50.000 men and 100 rounds for all Artillery in the field.

I hope the hospital will turn out all right.

Yours Truly
U. S. Grant
Maj. Gen Com

ALS, deCoppet Collection, NjP.

To Col. *William S. Hillyer*

————

Head Quarters Dept of the Tenn
Rocky Springs Miss May 9, 1863

Col. W. S. Hillyer

If there is any scarcity of wagon on the west side of the river cross no more to this side. Also direct McFeely to reduce the meat ration to one quarter to the whole ration of bread coffee and salt and to drop the sugar altogether

There has evidently been a great deal of pulling and hauling among Division to get the advantage in transportation.

Has a regiment of Cavalry crossed the river yet? There services are much needed here.

Yours truly
U. S. Grant
Maj. Gen.

Copies, DLC-USG, V, 19, 30, 98; DNA, RG 393, Dept. of the Tenn., Letters Sent; Alcorn Collection, WyU.

To Maj. *Theodore S. Bowers*

————

Head Quarters Dept of the Tenn
Rocky Springs Miss May 9. 1863

Major T. S. Bowers
J. A. Genl. A A A Gen
Hd Qrs Dept Tenn.
Major:

What I have wished to impress upon the Generals remaining on the Louisiana side of the Mississippi is that the wagon road from Millikens Bend to Perkins plantation should be shortened by every possible means and that when circumstances will admit of it, it shall run from Youngs Point to a point below Warrenton.

Meanwhile all possible execution should be made to keep the army supplied, by the present route.

Hard Bread, Coffee & salt, should be kept up any how—and then the other articles of the rations as they can be supplied. Has either of the Regiments of Cavalry from Helena reported.[1] As soon as they arrive send one of them forward with all despatch

Very respectfully
U. S. GRANT
Maj. Gen.

Copies, DLC-USG, V, 19, 30, 98; DNA, RG 393, Dept. of the Tenn., Letters Sent; Alcorn Collection, WyU. *O.R.*, I, xxiv, part 3, 285. Also on May 9, 1863, USG wrote to Lt. Commander Elias K. Owen, U.S. Navy. "A road is now about completed across the point from Young's Point to below the Warrenton Batteries. This will shorten the route over which supplies have to be drawn, to about eight miles and enable me to abandon the route across by Richmond. I would request that you keep the Tuscumbia at the depot below Warrenton; keep one of the other Gunboats at Grand Gulf, and with the other two keep the river clear between the two points." Copies, DLC-USG, V, 19, 30, 98; DNA, RG 393, Dept. of the Tenn., Letters Sent. On May 10, Owen, U.S.S. *Louisville*, wrote to USG. "The 'Mound City' is now or should be at the Depot below Warrenton—the Tuscumbia, disabled, is at James' Landing guarding the Naval Hospital—I will despatch the 'Carondelet' at once to assist Capt Shirk, and then to watch the river above—Our coal is getting very short, and the blockade at Vicksburg seems to be more efficient, as no supplies have come down safely. The fleet below will require a larger amount than we now have on hand. At James' Landing there are some five thousand bushels on the bank, which I should like to get off, if that post is to be abandoned—I would require one of the empty barges, and the crews of the 'Carondelet and Tuscumbia,' or a sufficient number of contrabands, to fill it—also to have all the coal brought down to this place." ALS, *ibid.*, Letters Received.

1. On May 9, 9:00 P.M., USG wrote to the commanding officer, 4th Iowa Cav., Grand Gulf. "Immediately after the reception of this order you will march your command to Willow Springs, where you will rest, till tomorrow morning; then move on, to this point and report at these headquarters for further orders. In making this move tonight, you will have in view the potection of the wagon trains, now on the road." Copies, DLC-USG, V, 19, 30, 98; DNA, RG 393, Dept. of the Tenn., Letters Sent; Alcorn Collection, WyU.

To Julia Dent Grant

Rocky Springs Miss.
May 9th 1863.

DEAR JULIA

I move in the morning to Auburn Miss. Two days more, or Teusday next, must bring on the fight which will settle the fate of Vicksburg. No Army ever felt better than this one does nor more confidant of sucsess. Before they are beaten they will be very badly beaten. They look for nothing of the kind and could not be brought to a realizing sense of such a ~~thing~~ possibility before the fact. Important news will no doubt follow close upon this.

I am very well camping in the forests of Mississippi. People all seem to stay at home and show less signs of fear than one would suppose. These people talk a greatdeel about the barbarities of the Yankees but I hear no complaints where the Army has been of even insults having been offered.

I have before told you to start to join me as soon as you hear of the Army being in Vicksburg. I do not know what I may be called on for next, supposing that I am sucsessful here, but you can at least join me until I am compelled to go elswhere. Give my love to all your friends. Fred. is very well, so is Jess. and Miss' pony. Kisses for yourself and the children.

Good night dear Julia

ULYS.

ALS, DLC-USG.
    On May 17, 1863, 12:30 P.M., Maj. Theodore S. Bowers, Steamer *Groesbeck*, Young's Point, wrote to Julia Dent Grant. "I have just rec'd a letter from the General, written from Jackson Miss. on the 15th. He was quite well and in most excellent spirits. He met the enemy, under Gen. Joe Johnson, on the 14th inst. and after a severe fight of over three hours, routed them and took possession of Jackson. The General has established his Headquarters in the State House. The Boat is about leaving and I must close." ALS, *ibid*.

To Maj. Gen. Nathaniel P. Banks

———

Head Quarters, Dept. of the Ten.
Rocky Springs Miss. May 10th/63

MAJ. GEN. N. P. BANKS,
COMD.G DEPT. OF THE GULF.
GEN.

My advance will occupy to-day Utica, Auburn and a point equally advanced towards the Miss. Southern rail-road between the latter place and the Big Black. It was my intention on gaining a foothold at Grand Gulf to have sent a sufficient force to Port Hudson to have insured the fall of that place, with your co-operation, or rather to have co-operated with you to secure that end. Meeting the enemy however as I did, South of Port Gibson, I followed him to the Big Black and could not afford to retrace my steps. I also learned, ~~too~~, and believe the information ~~to~~ be reliable, that Port Hudson is almost entirely evacuated.

This may not be true but it is the concurrent testimony of deserters and contrabands.

Many days cannot elapse before the battle will begin which is to decide the fate of Vicksburg, but it is impossible to predict how long it may last. I would urgently request therefore that you join me, or send all the force you can spare, to cooperate in the great struggle for opening the Miss. river.

My means of gaining information from Port Hudson are not good but I shall hope, even before this reaches Baton Rouge, to hear of your forces being on the way here.

Grierson's Cavalry would be of imense service to me now and if atal practicable for him to join me I would like to have him do it at once.

For fear of this accidentally falling into the hands of the enemy I will not communicate to you my force.

I am Gen. very respectfully
your obt. svt.
U. S. GRANT
Maj. Gen.

ALS, OClWHi. *O.R.*, I, xv, 315–16; *ibid.*, I, xxiv, part 3, 288–89. On May 12, 1863, 8:00 A.M., Maj. Gen. Nathaniel P. Banks, Alexandria, La., wrote to USG. "Your despatch of the 10th inst., I received by the hand of Captain Effers this morning at 6.30. I regret to say that it is impossible for me to join you at Vicksburg in time, or with force to be of service to you in any immediate attack. I have neither water nor land transportation to make the movement by the River or by land. The utmost I can accomplish is to cross for the purpose of operating with you against Port Hudson I could cross my infantry and artillery—without transportations—receiving supplies from Baton Rouge, in the rear of Port Hudson. That is the utmost I can accomplish on the other side of the Mississippi, above Port Hudson. Were it within the range of human power I should join you, for I am dying with a kind of vanishing hope to see two armies acting together against the strong places of the enemy. But I must say without qualifications, that the means at my disposal do not leave me a shadow of a chance to accomplish it. I have been making preparations to join your Corps at Bayou Sara, and though this would have laid all my trains and supplies open to the enemy's cavalry, I should have risked it. We believe that a force of about 7.000 of the enemy has left Arkansas River to join Kirby Smith at Shreveport, leaving the Washita at Pine Bluff, near Monroe; then to come down the Red River to Grand Ecore above Nachitoches, where they are fortifying in strong position. There is undoubtedly a Texan column on the road to join them. My advance is now sixty miles above Alexandria. The only course for me, failing in co-operation with you, is to regain the Mississippi and attack Port Hudson, or to move against the enemy at Shreveport. Port Hudson is reduced in force, but not as you are informed. It has now ten thousand men, and is very strongly fortified. This is the report of Admiral Farragut, whose fleet is above and below the works. I regret very much my inability to join you. I have written Colonel Grierson that you desire him to join you & have added my own request to yours. Captain Effers goes to Baton Rouge to communicate with him. Wishing you all possible success, and feeling that you have all the prayers of our people." Copies, DNA, RG 94, War Records Office, Union Battle Reports; *ibid.*, RG 393, Dept. of the Gulf, Letters Sent; *ibid.*, Dept. of the Tenn., Unregistered Letters Received. *O.R.*, I, xv, 317–18; *ibid.*, I, xxiv, part 3, 298–99; (incomplete) *O.R.* (Navy), I, xx, 185.

On May 13, Banks wrote twice to USG. "More complete investigation of the country on the red and Mississippi Rivers, leads me to believe that it is possible for me to join you. I shall make every sacrifice, and hazard everything to accomplish this object. My advance will move to Semmesport, Red River to day. I hope to move my command from Semmesport by the aid of transport and Naval vessels to Grand Gulf; in which event 10 or 12 day's will accomplish the movement. I am now 350 miles distant from you. Nothing will be allowed to delay our movements I will keep you advised of our progress from day to day. I can add about 12.000 to your column." "I have sent subsequent to the dispatch of yesterday, transmitted by Captain Gibbs, a note of this date informing you of my determination to join you at all hazards; with as little delay as possible There are great difficulties in the way of our movement, but we shall overcome them all. my belief is that your first suggestion of sending a force to co-operate with us against Port Hudson is best. Port Hudson can be reduced without delay, and with perfect certainty, if you can assist us with from 10.000, to 20.000 men, we can then aid you by a force of 25.000, and if Hunter joins us, with still stronger number's, and furnish supplies, ammunition, and everything necessary for the support of your army and our own, from New Orleans without trouble or delay. I earnestly urge upon you the consideration of this subject in this light; but should it be impossible for you to conform with it, I shall move to you as soon as possible with the force that I have stated. At best the movement against Port Hudson can delay us but a few days, and will not only give you our co-operation, but will free your Cavalry from the difficulties which now prevent its return. My Head Quarters will be at Semmesport to-morrow. The moral effect of the reduction of Port Hudson, upon Vicksburg and the junction of our forces after that, will be inappreciably great." Copies, DNA, RG 393, Dept. of the Tenn., Unregistered Letters Received; *ibid.*, Dept. of the Gulf, Letters Sent. *O.R.*, I, xv, 731–32; *ibid.*, I, xxiv, part 3, 303–4. The second letter is incomplete in *O.R.* (Navy), I, xx, 185–86. These letters reached USG on May 26. *Memoirs*, I, 544.

An undated document, "Memoranda upon the military movement for May 1863" addressed to USG appears in Banks's letterbook between letters dated April 23 and 24, but content suggests preparation in May. "Let me again earnestly press upon your consideration these advantages in reducing Port Hudson first 1st Enabling me to aid you at Vicksburg with 25.000 men at least, instead of 12000. 2nd The certain and immediate reduction of Port Hudson, and the immense moral effect produced thereby both on our troops, and on those of the enemy at Vicksburg. 3rd Perfect security for my communications with New Orleans & for procuring ample supplies of provisions and ammunition for both armies from New Orleans; also coal for both fleets and transports 4th Should Hunter's troops join me, as promised and expected—the additional aid of these troops. 5th A secure line of retreat for all the forces in case of disaster 6th Facilitating the rejoining your command by Colonel Grierson's Cavalry" Copy, DNA, RG 393, Dept. of the Gulf, Letters Sent. *O.R.*, I, xv, 732; *ibid.*, I, xxiv, part 3, 304.

On May 14, Act. Rear Admiral David D. Porter, Grand Gulf, wrote to USG. "I entered Alexandria La. on the 6th, having taken possession of Forts De Russy, heavy works half way up the river. General Banks arrived in Alexandria 24 hours after I did. Your despatches to him, met me on Red River, and he received them 12 hours afterwards on the 11th. I don't think you will get any assistance from that quarter, at least for some time—he expects you to cooperate with him. General Hunter I heard had arrived in N. Orleans with a large force. I am pretty sure they are evacuating Port Hudson, they have no provisions" LS, DNA, RG 94, War Records Office, Dept. of the Tenn. *O.R.*, I, xxiv, part 3, 309; *O.R.* (Navy), I, xxiv, 648, 650.

To Maj. Gen. John A. McClernand

Head Quarters Dept of the Tenn.

Cayuga, Miss. May 10th 1863. 4. P. M. 1863

Maj. Gen. J A. McClernand
Comdg 13th Army Corps
General:

Your note written at 9. A. M. is just received. My Head Quarters will remain here to night and be removed to Auburn in the Morning. You need not move tomorrow except to better your position on five mile creek.

Sherman whose rear will not be able to pass this place to night, will move up so as to be about the same distance from the Vicksburg and Jackson Railroad as your self. McPherson will also move on to about the same east and west line starting from Utica.

Your note complains of want of transportation. I have passed one and a part of another of your Divisions. I am satisfied that the transportation with them, to say nothing of the large number of mules mounted by Soldiers, would carry the essential parts of five days rations for the Command to which they belong if releived of the Knapsack, Officers, ~~and~~ Soldiers and negros now riding.

You should take steps to make the means at hand available for bringing up the articles necessary for your Corps

Equal facilities have been given each of the Army Corps in all respects   No special order having been given to favor any one except to give the first thirty wagons to the 13th Army Corps

Very resply

U. S. GRANT

Maj Gen.

Copies, DLC-USG, V, 19, 30, 98; DNA, RG 393, Dept. of the Tenn., Letters Sent; *ibid.*, 13th Army Corps, Letters Received; Alcorn Collection, WyU. *O.R.*, I, xxiv, part 3, 289. On May 10, 1863, Maj. Gen. John A. McClernand, Cayuga, Miss., wrote to USG. "The head of my column is arrived at this place. Its advance guard is at five mile creek. Various rumors of the enemy's crossing detachments of Cavalry and Infantry over Big Black are afloat, but are as yet unauthenticated. I beg to remind you again that my corps is supplied with a very small number of teams, and that their cooking utensils, in large part, are behind   It is but just both to you and myself that this fact should be stated." ALS (dated May 9), USG 3; copy (dated May 10), DNA, RG 393, 13th Army Corps, Letters Sent. Dated May 10 in *O.R.*, I, xxiv, part 3, 289. McClernand apparently misdated his letter, then USG misread the date as the time.

To Maj. Gen. James B. McPherson

Head Quarters, Dept. of the Ten.
Cayuga Miss. May 10th 1863

Maj. Gen. J. B. McPherson,
Comd.g 17th Army Corps,
Gen.

Gen. McClernand is now on Five Mile creek, on the telegraph road to Edwards Station. He is directed to move no further to-morrow but to reconnoiter the roads to Fourteen mile creek. Sherman will not get much past this place to night. In the morning he will move forward to Auburn and if he meets with no resistance will throw his advance forward to Fourteen mile creek, on the Raymond road.

Move your command forward also so as to occupy something near the same East & West line with the other Army Corps. Let me know what point you move to.

Send your Cavalry out to watch the movements of the enemy as far to the Southeast as you can.

Very respectfully
U. S. Grant
Maj. Gen Com

ALS, NjR. *O.R.*, I, xxiv, part 3, 289–90. On May 10, 1863, Maj. Gen. James B. McPherson, "Weeks Plantation 4 miles east of Utica," wrote to USG. "Enclosed please find a sketch of my position. The road is very dry and dusty, following the 'divide' between the Big Black and north Fork of 'Bayou Pierre.' there are no streams on the road and the Troops have suffered some for water. On my arrival in Utica about noon, I found Col Wright with his Cavalry, who reported considerable skirmishing with the enemy, but as no one was hurt, the skirmishing amounted to very little. There were probably one hundred Rebel Cavalry in our front, and a small force reported at the Bridge across Tallahala creek, north fork of Bayou Pierre on the road to 'Chrystal Springs.' I immediately dispached Col Wright with his whole Cavalry force in a S. E. direction crossing the creek lower down than where this force was said to be stationed, and then proceed up on the south side and cut them off if possible. He was also instructed to learn all he could of the whereabouts of the enemy, & as it is only 18 to twenty miles to the Miss Central R. R. and probably not many Troops in that direction, to make a dash over that way and destroy the Telegraph and Rail Road Track if he should find it practicable. A forward movement of about five miles will bring me on an east and west line with auburn, and near one of the branches of 14 mile Creek. I had to be guided to day in selecting camp somewhat by the chances of getting water." LS, DNA, RG 393, Dept. of the Tenn., Letters Received. *O.R.*, I, xxiv, part 3, 290. The sketch map is attached to the letter. On May 11, Col. Clark Wright, Roach's Plantation, wrote to Lt. Col. John A. Rawlins. "I left this place at 6 a. m. this morning, and by a circuitous route reached the Jackson and New Orleans Railroad, with some 200 men, 1½ miles north of Crystal Springs, distant 25 miles. I at once placed one-half of the command in the best position for defense that the circumstances would admit, and with the other half proceeded to destroy the telegraph line and railroad. I took out 1½ miles of wire, and burned it on top of three bridges I destroyed. I cut the road by tearing up the rails at three points. I burned out one culvert, and warped the rails materially at two points by building large fires on them. In the aggregate, 1½ miles of road is destroyed, and will require at least five or six days to repair it. I burned some one hundred and twenty-five bales of cotton, marked C. S. A., paroled 18 citizens, and captured 15 prisoners and a number of mules and horses brought to camp. I learned that some 4,500 troops had passed up to Jackson from Port Hudson within the last four days, on the railroad, and about the same number by land, or marching. Within the last ten days they have called in all the forces to Jackson from the surrounding country. I am now in the same camp I left this morning. Have marched 50 miles to day, in addition to the labor performed and above specified. My command is worn down by incessant labor for the last twenty days and nights, and would respectfully ask permission to rest men and horses for one day." *Ibid.*, I, xxiv, part 1, 701.

To Lt. Herman A. Ulffers

Head Quarters Dept of the Tenn
Rocky Springs, May 10th 1863

LT. H. A. ULFFERS
ASST ENG.R

You will proceed immediately with dispatchs for General Banks

The Tug. Ramsey will be put at your disposal and will take you to Admiral Porters fleet; You will consult with Admiral Porter as to the best means of reaching Gen Banks or Baton Rouge and adopt such measure as may be deemed best to effect the desired communication.

As soon as you have delivered your dispatches you will if

practicable, return to these Head Quarters using the safest and most rapid route.

It may be that Greirsons Cavalry will return and that that may be the quickest way.

Very respectfully

U. S. GRANT.

Maj Gen.

Copies, DLC-USG, V, 19, 30, 98; DNA, RG 393, Dept. of the Tenn., Letters Sent; (misdated May 9) Alcorn Collection, WyU. On May 10, 1863, USG wrote to Col. William S. Hillyer. "Please direct the Captain of the tug 'Ramsey' to take on board Lieut H. A. Ulffers. Asst Eng.r bearer of Dispatches to general Banks and proceed under his directions without delay to Admiral Porters fleet. The tug will return to Grand Gulf with Admiral Porters fleet without waiting for Lieut Ulffers." Copies, DLC-USG, V, 19, 30, 98; DNA, RG 393, Dept. of the Tenn., Letters Sent. Herman A. Ulffers, born in Westphalia, involved in engineering in the U.S. before the Civil War, served as a topographical engineer as early as 1861, but held no regular appointment until confirmed as capt., asst. adjt. gen., on March 18, 1864.

To Maj. Gen. Henry W. Halleck

Cayuga Miss

May 11th 1863.

MAJ GEN H W. HALLECK

GEN IN CHIEF

My forces will be this evening as far advanced towards Fourteen Mile Creek—the left near Black River and extending in a line nearly East and west—as they can get without bringing on a general engagement. I shall communicate with Grand Gulf no more except it becomes necessary to send a train with heavy escort. You may not hear from me again for several days.

U S. GRANT

Maj Genl

Telegram received, DNA, RG 107, Telegrams Collected (Bound); DLC-Robert T. Lincoln; copies, DLC-USG, V, 6, 8, 24, 94, 98; DNA, RG 393, Dept. of the Tenn., Hd. Qrs. Correspondence; *ibid.*, RG 107, Telegrams Received in Cipher. *O.R.*, I, xxiv, part 1, 35–36. This message did not reach Washington until May 18.

To Maj. Gen. John A. McClernand

Head Quarters Dept of the Tenn
Cayuga Miss May 11th 8:15 P. M. 1863
MAJ GEN JNO. A. MCCLERNAND
COMDG 13TH ARMY CORPS
GENERAL:

In accordance with my verbal instructions this afternoon You will move your Command at daylight tomorrow.On the Auburn and Edwards Station road, and if practicable a part, of one Division, by the road to the westward of the one just mentioned.

Move cautiously but as rapidly as convenient and so that your entire corps will arrive on the Fourteen mile creek simultaneously and in a compact line. It is also important that your Corps reach the creek at or about the time that Sherman does, he having to move only about seven miles.

I shall pass to the front early tomorrow and go to Raymond if I can from that place   I shall return on the road to a convenient point for Head Quarters in the vicinity of Fourteen mile creek

Very resply
Your obt Servt
U. S. GRANT
Maj. Gen.

Copies, DLC-USG, V, 19, 30, 98; DNA, RG 393, Dept. of the Tenn., Letters Sent; *ibid.*, 13th Army Corps, Letters Received; Alcorn Collection, WyU. *O.R.*, I, xxiv, part 3, 296.

On May 11, 1863, Maj. Gen. John A. McClernand wrote to USG. "On the map enclosed is traced a new road, now being opened from Baldwins Ferry to intersect the Hall's Ferry & Cayuga Road somewhere between the two last named places. This road is referred to in the communication of the rebel scout Russell to Genl Loring. Negroes coming in this morning report that the enemy expect to throw a force upon our rear. This road may form part of the route by which, with the aid of their Steamers they may attempt to flank us, and fall on our rear. Would it not be advisable for some Corps in the rear to send forward strong detachments to hold Hall's and Baldwin's Ferrys, and frustrate this probable design?" LS, DNA, RG 94, War Records Office, Dept. of the Tenn.; DfS, McClernand Papers, IHi. *O.R.*, I, xxiv, part 3, 293. The enclosed letters are printed *ibid.*, p. 294. On the same day, USG wrote to McClernand. "You will have to guard Baldwins Ferry, and the Black river in your flank from your command. I will direct other troops to guard Hall's Ferry" Copy, DNA, RG 393, 13th Army Corps, Letters Received.

Also on May 11, McClernand wrote frequently to USG, each time from Five Mile Creek. "I venture to make a suggestion which, of course, will be only estimated according to its value. Reports, and what should be the policy of the enemy, combine to warn us that he will attempt to cross the Big Black in our rear, and isolate us by cutting our communication. Having steamboats at his disposal, he could rapidly cross troops for that purpose. In view of this danger, I would enquire: whether it would not be advisable for us to shift our advancing columns further to the left—resting our left flank upon the Big Black. By so doing, we could prevent the descent of the enemy's steamers; could effectually guard the river, and avoid the disadvantage of detaching forces to command both Hall's and Baldwin's Ferries. If this approach should be adopted, and I should continue on the left, I could move, by two roads, to Fourteen Mile Creek—from Cayuga to Baldwin's Ferry, and from Old Auburn to a point on the road from New Auburn to Baldwin's Ferry. The (rebel) map, sent this morning, will illustrate these roads. Gen'l Sherman's Corps could move to the intersection of Fourteen Miles Creek by the road leading from the vicinity of Old Auburn to Edward's depot; and Gen'l McPherson could move still to the right of Gen'l Sherman. If the object of the movement so far to the right, is to threaten or destroy the railroad in the direction of Jackson, could not that be done by a detachment suddenly thrown in that direction? Indeed, would not the movement more to the left, by drawing the enemy's attention in that direction, facilitate that result?" LS, *ibid.*, Dept. of the Tenn., Letters Received. *O.R.*, I, xxiv, part 3, 292. "I sent forward a detachment of two regiments of Infantry, three companies of Cavalry and a section of Artillery at 4 Oclock A. M. to day, to reconnoitre towards fourteen mile creek, with reference to the Enemy's movements and designs, and to positions favorable for encampments. Upon the return of the detachment I will advise you of the result." LS, DNA, RG 393, Dept. of the Tenn., Letters Received. "Osterhous has just returned from the reconnoitering force sent forward this Morning. One Regiment of that force is now at the Forks of the Raymond and Edwards Station road Detachments of Cavalry are sent forward from that point under instructions to proceed upon both of those Roads to Fourteen Mile Creek and return with such information as they may be able to obtain. Water was found in the vicinity of New Auburn but only so scanty supply Beyond the divergance of the Edwards Station Road and New Auburn. Genl Sherman might find water on a branch of the Fourteen Mile Creek" Copy, *ibid.*, 13th Army Corps, Letters Sent. *O.R.*, I, xxiv, part 3, 293. To Lt. Col. John A. Rawlins. "The Cavalry sent out this morning to reconnoiter on the road leading to Edwards Station & to Raymond have returned. The party going to Edwards Station, found the enemy in half a mile of fourteen mile Creek in too strong force to allow the party to proceed further. Negroes informed the officer in Command, that the enemy intended to offer obstinate resistance at that Creek. Still I do not think he is in Strong force there You heard this morning the result of the reconnoisance on the Raymond road our party fell in with the enemy's pickets who ran. There is little, or no, water between here and Fourteen mile Creek. So we will probably have to fight for the water of that stream. I think of sending Genl Smiths Division from Cayuga to Baldwins Ferry, and from there to the right, on the road leading from Baldwins

Ferry to New Auburn; until his right forms a junction with the left of the balance of the Corps,—instructing him to leave such a force to guard Baldwins ferry as he may think expedient. Cavalry, only can reach Baldwins to night, and I have only one company to send; the balance being worn out for the present" Copy, DNA, RG 393, 13th Army Corps, Letters Sent. *O.R.*, I, xxiv, part 3, 292.

Also on May 11, USG wrote to McClernand. "The 15th Army Corps is here with six Brigades and but four Batteries, and all of them smooth Bore guns. To equalize the Artillery it will be necessary to retransfer the Battery given to you from that corps, whilst at Millikins Bend and also to temporarily detach a section of 20 pd parrotts for the ensuing Battle   Four Twenty pd parrotts are enough to handle in the timbered Country, and these two guns will help the 15th army corps in action very materially" Copies, DLC-USG, V, 19, 30, 98; DNA, RG 393, Dept. of the Tenn., Letters Sent; *ibid.*, 13th Army Corps, Letters Received. *O.R.*, I, xxiv, part 3, 295. On the same day, Maj. Gen. Frederick Steele, New Auburn, Miss., wrote to Rawlins. "With the sanction of Genl. Sherman I write to inform the Genl. Comdg. that Genl. McClernand has sent a Battery of four guns deficient in men and amunition to take the place of Grifiths Battery taken from my Division. I would rather have Grifith's Battery, if it is not expedient to send it back, ~~I would rather not have any~~ or some one which is well appointed. I would rather not have any, as it is not practicable for me to drill men and get ammunition for the one designated by Genl. McClernand. Grifith's Battery is still maned in part by men from my Inf. Regiments." ALS, DNA, RG 393, Dept. of the Tenn., Letters Received. Rawlins drafted his letter to McClernand on the docket sheet of Steele's letter. "The Battery you were expected to send to Maj Genl W. T. Sherman Comdg 15th Army Corps, in pursuance of directions of the genl comdg of this date was the 1s Iowa Bat Capt Griffith Comdg, formerly with Genl sherman   You will therefor order the ~~Iwa~~ 1s Iowa Battery Capt Griffith comdg to report immediately to Maj Genl W. T. Sherman. The one you have ordered will be returned to you" ADf, *ibid.*; LS, Rawlins Papers, ICHi. *O.R.*, I, xxiv, part 3, 295. Also on May 11, McClernand twice wrote to USG. "Your dispatch respecting the Griffith Battery is received. That particular battery was not transferred to Genl Sherman, because it was one of the only two which belonged to Genl Carrs Division   The one transferred to Genl Sherman was from Genl Hoveys Division, which had four batteries. To have transferred Griffiths would have involved a second transfer and consequent delay and confusion—The one transferred to Genl Sherman I have every reason to believe is quite as effective as Griffiths   With this explanation, of course, your order will be literally obeyed, unless you direct otherwise" "The Battery has gone forward from Genl Hovey's Division, and cannot be recalled tonight. The transfer of Capt Griffith's Battery will be made as soon as my command reaches Genl Sherman's on tomorrow" LS, DNA, RG 393, Dept. of the Tenn., Letters Received.

To Maj. Gen. James B. McPherson

Head Quarters, Dept. of Tenn.
Cayuga, Miss.
1 P. M. May 11th 1863.

MAJ. GENL. MCPHERSON,
COMDG, 17TH ARMY CORPS,
4 MILES BEY.D UTICA.
GENERAL,

Move your command tonight to the next cross roads three or four miles to your front, if you can find water; and tomorrow push with all activity into Raymond.

At the latter place you will use your utmost exertions to secure all the subsistence stores, that may be there, as well as in the vicinity. We must fight the enemy before our rations fail, and we are equally bound to make our rations last as long as possible. Upon one occasion you made two days' rations last seven; we may have to do the same thing again. I look to you to impress the necessity of this upon your division and brigade commanders, and through them upon the troops. One train of wagons is now arriving and another will come with Blair, but with all there remains the necessity of economy in the use of the supplies we have, and activity in gathering others from the Country. Sherman is now moving out on the Auburn and Raymond Road and will reach Fourteen mile creek tonight. When you arrive at Raymond he will be in close supporting distance.

I shall move McClernand to Fourteen Mile Ck. early tomorrow so that he will occupy a place on Sherman's left.

I will either see you myself tomorrow at Raymond or send you further instructions at that place.

Very Respectfully.
U. S. GRANT
Maj. Genl. Comdg

LS, NjR. *O.R.*, I, xxiv, part 3, 297. On May 11, 1863, 4:45 P.M., Maj. Gen.

James B. McPherson, "Camp at Cross Road 5 miles E. Utica," wrote to USG. "Dispatch just received—Will move forward immediately about 3½ or 4 miles which gives me [— — — —] ind I can find to [— — — —] ill bring me near [— — — —] of 14 mile creek—I am impressing on my command the great necessity of economy in the use of rations, and am collecting all I can from the Country. In meats we can do well enough but it is very difficult to get hold of bread Stuffs. With regard to Teams for a General Supply Train I have none in the command—I left Millikens Bend with 5 to a Regt. and some of these have never come across the River or at least have not reached their Regts. The Transportation is barely sufficient to haul the Camp & Garrison Equipage Extra Ammunition & other necessary supplies—We tried several wagons picked up from the country but they have most invariably broken down"   AL (mutilated), DNA, RG 393, Dept. of the Tenn., Letters Received.

To Maj. Gen. William T. Sherman

Cayuga Miss May 11. 1863

MAJ. GEN. W. T. SHERMAN
COMDG 15TH A. C
GEN.

It will be necessary to guard Halls Ferry with a regiment of Infantry, and a company of Cavalry until our positions are fully taken, after which Cavalry alone can watch the rear.

McClernand is directed to guard Baldwins Ferry.[1] I will direct Tuttle to send a regiment for this duty, so that you need not make any farther detail until you want his regiment releived by some other troops.

A company or Squadroon of the Iowa Cavalry with you should be sent back this evening to stay with the Reg. Regiment at Halls Ferry.

Yours &c
U. S. GRANT
Maj. Gen.

Copies, DLC-USG, V, 19, 30, 98; DNA, RG 393, Dept. of the Tenn., Letters Sent; Alcorn Collection, WyU. *O.R.*, I, xxiv, part 3, 296.

1. See letter to Maj. Gen. John A. McClernand, May 11, 1863. On May 12, Lt. Col. Jefferson Brumback, 95th Ohio, Baldwin's Ferry, wrote to USG. "Col

McMillen is just now absent for a short time on a scout to examine roads &c in this vicinity. This regiment moved pursuant to your directions from Cayuga last evening. The road you pointed out brought us here, Baldwin's Ferry, and not to Hall's Ferry, the place that we were to reach according to our understanding. This is the first public ferry across the Big Black below the rail road bridge. It is six miles from Cayuga to this point. From this place one road leads back to Cayuga, another to Old Auburn on the Natches Trace. From the last road about 1½ miles from here a road takes off to the left which leads as we are informed to Edwards' depot on the R R. Day before yesterday a small force of rebel cavalry was on that road and came down to the ferry here. It is said to be 9 miles from here by road to Edwards depot, about 6 in a direct line. to the bridge We drove a small picket across the river when we came here. The enemy have pickets in sight on the other side of the river, and either two or three brigades a short distance back. A citizen here in whom we have much confidence says that two days ago a rebel scout was at his house & said that as our army moved northerly the Confederates would move Southerly on the other side of the B Black & cross a strong force either at Halls Ferry which is 6 or 7 miles below here, or at another ferry still lower (Handelman's I think) to get in our rear & cut our communications, our pickets think that from sounds heard last night the enemy were moving northerly perhapse in considerable force early this morning. We have ~~rumorrs~~ rumors of a military road on the other side of the B Black running nearly parallel with the stream from the R R down the river. We understand that there are no pickets or guards at the lower ferries & that a small force of the enemy was across the river at Hall's Ferry & on this side last night. There are roads between the river & Natches Trace by which the enemy might throw forces in our rear either from a point on the rail road above, or from one of the ferries below." ALS, DNA, RG 393, Dept. of the Tenn., Letters Received.

To Maj. Gen. William T. Sherman

8.15 P. M.
Head Quarters, Dept. of the Ten.
Cayuga Miss. May 11th 1863.

MAJ. GEN. W. T. SHERMAN,
COMD.G 15TH ARMY CORPS,
GEN.

McClernand is ordered to move up by the telegraph road and also a road to the left of that to Fourteen mile creek, starting at daylight. McPherson is directed to move on to Raymond.

I will go forward to-morrow probably as far as Raymond and return in the evening to near Fourteen mile creek for Head Quarters.

Col. Hillyer writes that about 200 wagons are loaded and will leave for the front to-day escorted by two regiments.

very respectfully
U. S. GRANT
Maj. Gen. Com

ALS, IHi. *O.R.*, I, xxiv, part 3, 296. On May 11, 1863, Maj. Gen. William T. Sherman, Auburn, Miss., wrote to Lt. Col. John A. Rawlins. "I am halted on the ground at Auburn near the pond of water described by Capt Prime. I have ridden forward a mile or so and water is very scarce to 14 mile creek and when we cross it we should push on to Raymond 11 miles distant. If McClernand moves on the telegraph Road he should reach 14 mile creek 8 miles in front of his present camp at the same time that I do   I shall await orders here   I sent you two letters back through Col Scates we found in the Post office here dated May 10, speaking of assemblig many million Rations in Vicksburg for *the Seige*. Also one from Condit Smith. The messenger who brought it met the wagons I had sent back in anticipation of that very event. These wagons all belong to my corps, and is and will be the reason of my beig short of provisions and ammunition but I foresaw that there would be no teams at Millikens Bend, & therefore I ordered back the wagons of my Corps which were acting as a supply train after having deposited their provisions at Perkins. I know of no provisions at Perkins but those brought by my train, but Smith will now push them forward as fast as possible. I think he will have about 150 wagons, which if pushed will make 300 tons, or one steamboat load a day, which would soon make provisions abundant at Grand Gulf. I think it very prudent to cover Halls Ferry, and note the fact that one of Tuttles Regiments is detached to that point: I send a company of Cavalry to report to the officer commanding the Infantry Regm't. I shall expect orders in the course of the night, prepared to move at daybreak." ALS, DNA, RG 94, War Records Office, Dept. of the Tenn. *O.R.*, I, xxiv, part 3, 296–97.

To Maj. Gen. John A. McClernand

Head Quarters Dept. of the Tennessee
Fourteen Mile Creek 11. A. M. May 12. 1863

MAJ. GEN JNO A MCCLERNAND
COMDG 13TH ARMY CORPS.
GENERAL:

Sherman has gained the crossing at this place with a little skirmishing with a loss of six or eight men killed or wounded He will probably succeed in following out original inten~ten~

tions of going in advance of this place to the cross roads. Gain the creek with your command if possible and hold it with at least one Division thrown across.

Reconnoitre the roads in advance and also in this direction so as to open communication with Sherman and myself;

If bridges are distroyed make fords if possible.

> Very respectfully
> U. S. GRANT.
> Maj. Gen.

Copies, DLC-USG, V, 19, 30, 98; DNA, RG 393, Dept. of the Tenn., Letters Sent; *ibid.*, 13th Army Corps, Letters Received. *O.R.*, I, xxiv, part 3, 299. On May 12, 1863, Maj. Gen. John A. McClernand, Fourteen Mile Creek, wrote to USG. "After a sharp skirmish, in which a few of our men were wounded, (number not yet ascertained) I seized the main Crossing of 14 Mile Creek. Genl Hoveys Division accomplished this result at 11 oclock A. M. inst, and an outpost was immediately established on the opposite side of the Creek. I am now reconnoitering with the view to throw a division across and in advance, when the rest of my Corps Comes up. If this cannot be done without bringing on a general engagment, I will advise you and ask further direction—believing that this course will meet with your approbation. The message I sent by your aid-de-Camp relative to Genl Osterhous danger turns out to be without foundation. The Messenger who brought it to me is repudiated by Genl Osterhous   So all is well with him. I have heard from Genl Smith, who is some three miles distant"   Copy, DNA, RG 393, 13th Army Corps, Letters Sent. *O.R.*, I, xxiv, part 3, 299. McClernand's letterbooks contain a letter to USG dated May 11, Fourteen Mile Creek, which appears to be a draft of the letter dated May 12 and could not have been drafted until May 12, when McClernand reached Fourteen Mile Creek. Copy, DNA, RG 393, 13th Army Corps, Letters Sent. *O.R.*, I, xxiv, part 3, 293.

To Maj. Gen. John A. McClernand

————

> Head Quarters Dept of the Tenn
> Dillons Plantation Miss. 9:15 P. M. May 12/863

MAJOR GEN. JNO A MCCLERNAND
COMDG 13TH ARMY CORPS
GEN:

McPherson gained Raymond this afternoon after a severe fight of several hours in which we lost four or five hundred killed and wounded   The enemy was driven at all points leaving most of his wounded and over one hundred prisoners in our hands.

He retreated towards Clinton and no doubt to Jackson   I have determined to follow and take first the Capitol of the state Accordingly McPherson is ordered to move at daylight from Raymond towards Clinton and Jackson. Sherman leaves here at 4 A. M. in the morning in the same direction. You will start with three of your Divisions as soon as as possible by the road north of Fourteen mile creek by this place and on to Raymond   The road is plain and cannot be mistaken. A supply train left Grand Gulf yesterday and Blairs Division with an additional train to day.

Under present instructions these trains will divide at the forks of the road where ~~wh~~ you and Sherman Seperated this Morning. I would direct therefore that your fourth Division goes back to old Auburn, and wait until these trains arrive, both of them, and conduct them after the army on the Raymond Road until they recieve further orders from these Head Quarters.

Very respectfully

U. S GRANT

Maj. Gen.

Copies, DLC-USG, V, 19, 30, 98; DNA, RG 393, Dept. of the Tenn., Letters Sent; *ibid.*, 13th Army Corps, Letters Received; Alcorn Collection, WyU. *O.R.*, I, xxiv, part 3, 300. On May 13, 1863, Maj. Gen. John A. McClernand, "Crossing of 14 Mile Creek," wrote to USG. "Your dispatch instructing me to move by the road north of Fourteen Mile Creek to Dillons plantation and thence to Raymond is recd., and will be promptly executed; and so your instructions in regard to the guarding of the excepted supply train. I enfer that Genl Blairs Division will also escort the supply train   In moving by the road north of Fourteen mile Creek to Dillons, my flank and rear may be exposed to attack from the enemy's line between Edwards, Station and Bolten; nevertheless, I will try and protect myself to the best advantage." Copy, DNA, RG 393, 13th Army Corps, Letters Sent. *O.R.*, I, xxiv, part 3, 307.

To Maj. Gen. James B. McPherson

———

10:45 a. m.
Head Quarters, Dept. of the Ten.
14 Mile Creek, May 12th 1863

MAJ. GEN. J. B. MCPHERSON,
COMD.G 17TH ARMY CORPS,
GEN

Sherman has gaine[d] the crossing at this place with a little fighting for it, the enemy having destroyed the bridge first however. McClernand is West from here on the Telegraph road with three Divisions and one throw[n] around by Baldwin's Ferry. No news from him yet but firing reported in that direction. If you have gained Raymond throw back forces in this direction until communication is opened with Sherman. Also feel to the North towards the rail-road and if possible destroy it and the telegraph.

If the road is opened I will ride over to see you this evening but I cannot go until I know McClernand is secure in his position.

Very respectfully
U. S. GRANT
Maj. Gen

ALS, NjR. *O.R.*, I, xxiv, part 3, 300–1. On May 12, 1863, 9:15 P.M., USG, "Dillons Plantn," wrote to Maj. Gen. James B. McPherson. "Move on to Clinton and Jackson at daylight in the morning. Sherman will leave here at 4 a. m to follow and support you. McClernand will also follow from his position which is about four miles Northeast from here." ALS, NjR. *O.R.*, I, xxiv, part 3, 301.

On May 12, 2:30 P.M., McPherson, "2½ mils from Raymond," wrote to USG. "We have met and engaged the enemy at this point 1000 strong. Thus far we have apparently the advantage, though the battle is not yet ended—Woods, ravines prvent the effective use of our Artillery." LS, DNA, RG 94, War Records Office, Union Battle Reports. On the same day, McPherson, Raymond, wrote twice more to USG, the second time at 11:00 P.M. "We met the enemy about six thousand strong, commanded by Brig General Gregg, at a point two and a half miles west of this place, where they were posted and fully prepared to receive us. After a sharp and severe contest of about Three hours duration, in which Maj. Genl. Logan's Division was chiefly engaged, the enemy were driven back and retreated precipitately, passing out of this Town, on the Jackson Road, Edwards Depot Road and Gallatin Road. The rough and impracticable nature of the

Country, filled with ravines and dense undergrowth, prevented anything like an effective use of Artillery or a very rapid pursuit. Our loss has been pretty severe in Genl John E. Smith's and General Dennis' Brigades, though I think two hundred and fifty will cover the total killed, wounded and missing. The loss of the enemy is fully as heavy if not more so than ours. There are Eighty of their wounded in town; besides the number left on the 'Battle Field' and picked up by our men. We disabled two of the enemy's guns, one by bursting which fell into our possession, and captured about one hundred prisoners. We have to mourn the loss of Col Richards of the 20th Ills. who was killed while gallantly encouraging his men. Col Ed McCook 31st Ills was wounded in the foot. These as far as I know are the only casualties in the Field Officers. As soon as the returns, are in, I will give you full particulars   Two Rebel Colonels are known to have been killed"   Copies, *ibid.*, RG 393, 13th and 17th Army Corps, Letters Sent; *ibid.*, 17th Army Corps, Letters Sent. *O.R.*, I, xxiv, part 1, 704–5. "It is rumored but with how much truth I have not been able to ascertain, that heavy reinforcements are coming to the Enemy from Jackson to night, and that we may expect a Battle here in the morning,   I shall try and be prepared for them if they come—" ALS, DNA, RG 94, War Records Office, Dept. of the Tenn. *O.R.*, I, xxiv, part 3, 301.

On April 14, McPherson had written to Lt. Col. John A. Rawlins. "Col Elias S. Dennis of the 30th Illinois Volunteers received his commission of Brigadier General of Volunteers to rank from the 29th of November Yesterday. In the absence of Brig Genl Leggett I have assigned him to the command (temporarily) of the 2d Brigade 3d Division"   Copies, DNA, RG 393, 13th and 17th Army Corps, Letters Sent; *ibid.*, 17th Army Corps, Letters Sent.

To Maj. Gen. William T. Sherman

Head Quarters Dept of the Tenn.
9:15 P. M. Dillons Plantation Miss. May 12 1863
MAJ. GEN. W. T. SHERMAN
COMDG 15TH ARMY CORPS
GENERAL:

After the severe fight of today at Raymond and repulse of the enenemy towards Clinton and Jackson, I have determined to move on the latter place by way of Clinton, and take the Capitol of the state and work from there westward. McPherson is ordered to march at day light to Clinton. You will march at 4. A. M. in the morning and follow McPherson. McClernand will follow you with three Divisions, and send his fourth back to old Auburn, to

await the arrival of trains now on the road, and Blairs Division
to conduct them after the Enemy.

>Very respectfully
>U. S. GRANT
>Maj. Gen.

Copies, DLC-USG, V, 19, 30, 98; DNA, RG 393, Dept. of the Tenn., Letters
Sent. *O.R.*, I, xxiv, part 3, 300.

To Maj. Gen. John A. McClernand

———

>Head Quarters Dept. of the Tenn
>Dillons Plantation Miss. May 13th 1863

MAJ. GEN. JNO A. MCCLERNAND
COMDG 13TH ARMY CORPS
GENERAL:

One Division of Genl Sherman Corps is north or west of
Turkey Creek the other between Fourteene mile Creek and
Turkey Creek. Tomorrow he will move North and strike the
Railroad between Bolton and Edwards Station. McPherson is
undoubtedly in Raymond and has had from the amount of firing
heard, had a hard fight. He also will move onto the railroad
towards Bolton.

Edwards Station is evidently the point on the railroad the
enemy have most prepared for recieving us, therefore I want to
keep up appearances of moving upon that place, but want to get
possession of less guarded points first. You will then move tomorrow to keep up this appearance a short distance only from
where you now are, with the three advanced Divisions, leaving
the fourth or Smiths, about in its present position. From my map,
there seems to be two creeks from one to two miles in advance
of your present position towards Edwards Station which you

might reach. Gen. Steele has sent one regiment down the north side of Fourteen mile Creek to communicate with you.

Very respectfully

U. S. Grant

Maj. Gen.

Copies, DLC-USG, V, 98; DNA, RG 393, 13th Army Corps, Letters Received. *O.R.*, I, xxiv, part 3, 299–300. Copies (dated May 12), DLC-USG, V, 19, 30; DNA, RG 393, Dept. of the Tenn., Letters Sent; Alcorn Collection, WyU.

To Maj. Gen. John A. McClernand

Head Qrs. Dept. of the Tenn

Raymond Miss. May 13th/63

Maj. Gen. J. A. McClernand

Comd.g 13th Army Corps.

Gen

Col. Duff will point out to you where you can separate your command and march to this place in two columns. McPherson moves directly on Clinton. Sherman takes a right hand road about one mile from town and moves towards Jackson. I want you to place one Division at the point of divergence of the two advance Corps and leave the balance in town and back towards my camp of last night. It would be well to leave one Division back at or near Dillon's plantation. This is where Sherman camps last night.

Very respectfully

U. S. Grant

Maj. Gen. Com

ALS, PPRF. *O.R.*, I, xxiv, part 3, 305. On May 13, 1863, USG again wrote to Maj. Gen. John A. McClernand. "Please detail a Regiment from your advanced Division to act as Provost Guard of this town. Charge the Provost Marshal to releive all the guards now on duty here by new details—to see that prisoners and hospitals are properly protected—and that soldiers are required to conduct themselves in an orderly manner, and prevented from entering and pillaging houses."

Copies, Miss. Dept. of Archives and History, Jackson, Miss.; DNA, RG 393, 13th Army Corps, Letters Received.

Also on May 13, McClernand, "Camp at Dillons Plantation," wrote to USG. "I have the honor to acknowledge the receipt of your dispatch of this date. In pursuance of your instructions, I set my Army Corps in motion at 6 o'clock A. M. and arrived at this place about 3. P. M. I sent Genl Osterhaus Division forward to Raymond, but upon reaching the creek 4 miles this side, I am just informed by him—he found Genl Steele's Wagontrain just starting, and may not be able to reach Raymond tonight in consequence. If not, he will be at Raymond at 5½ o'clock A. M. tomorrow. He is instructed—upon reaching Raymond, to make a detail of one Regiment, and to fully execute your orders, in relation to guards—hospital—and police discipline of soldiers to prevent the pillaging of houses. According to your instructions of yesterday—I sent Genl Smith's Division to guard from New Auburn to Raymond, the ammunition and provision trains, on their way from the Gulf, together with the train of the 13th Army Corps. The latter only has arrived. The other Divisions, I moved on the North side of Fourteen Mile Creek. In order to effect this movement safely, and to make a demonstration as directed by you, I threw Genl Hovey's Division forward within two & a half miles of Edward's Depot, and drew it up in line of battle, until the 9th and 14th Divisions had Crossed Baker's Creek, which was attended with some delay on account of having to explore the road and construct a ford—the bridge having been destroyed. In consequence of this delay, Genl Hovey's Division did not arrive until 4½ oclock P. M. I am happy to be able to report *that this movement has been safely effected without loss, although the rear guard was attacked, and we had to skirmish with the enemy, whom we dispersed, on withdrawing the Division from its position.* I had anticipated trouble in effecting the change of position in so delicate a matter with flank and rear exposed. I hope the threatening demonstration against Edward's Station held by my command for several hours today may have so far divided the attention of the enemy, as to have furthered your plan in the main movement against Jackson. I enclose copy of order to Genl Osterhaus for your information. The mail train from the Gulf has just arrived safely. Genl Blair's Division is near. Genl Smith burned the bridge at his encampment on 14 Mile Creek before leaving. He is encamped tonight, near Old Auburn." LS, *ibid.*, Dept. of the Tenn., Letters Received. Incomplete in *O.R.*, I, xxiv, part 3, 305.

To Maj. Gen. John A. McClernand

Head Quarters Dept of the Tenn.
Raymond Miss. 7:30. P. M. May 13. 1863

MAJOR GENL JNO A MCCLERNAND
COMDG 13TH ARMY CORPS
GENL:

Move one division of your ~~Division~~ Corps through this place to Clinton, charging it with the duty of distroying the R. R. as far as possible to a point on the Direct Raymond and Jackson road   Move another Division three our four miles beyond Mississippi Springs, and eight or nine miles beyond this place, and a Third to Raymond ready to support either of the others:

Also direct your thirty pdr seige guns to follow close behind the advance guard of the Division, which takes post beyond Mississippi Springs, on the main Jackson road. You will begin your movements at 4 A. M. tomorrow.

McPherson reached the Railroad at Clinton at three oclock P. M. without encountering any serious opposition.[1]

Very respectfully

U. S. GRANT

Maj. Gen.

Copies, DLC-USG, V, 19, 30, 98; DNA, RG 393, Dept. of the Tenn., Letters Sent; *ibid.*, 13th Army Corps, Letters Received; Alcorn Collection, WyU. *O.R.*, I, xxiv, part 3, 305–6.

1. On May 13, 1863, Maj. Gen. James B. McPherson, Clinton, wrote to USG. "The advance reached this place about 3 P. M., meeting with no opposition except a little skirmishing with cavalry—captured three of his dispatches from Pemberton of this date, and about 250 sacks of corn, etc." J. H. Wilson, "A Staff-Officer's Journal of the Vicksburg Campaign, April 30 to July 4, 1863," *Journal of the Military Service Institution of the United States,* XLIII (July, 1908), 103. McPherson enclosed an undated letter from Lt. Gen. John C. Pemberton to Maj. Gen. William W. Loring, Bovina, Miss., ordering him to take a defensive position at Edward's Depot, a letter of May 12 from Pemberton to Brig. Gen. John Gregg, Raymond, ordering him to attack if U.S. forces were engaged at Edward's Depot or Big Black Bridge, and a letter of May 13 from Pemberton, Bovina, to Gregg, Clinton, ordering him to fall back to Jackson. *Ibid.*, pp. 103–4. The letters to Gregg are in *O.R.*, I, xxiv, part 3, 862, 873. On May 13, USG wrote to McPherson. "Move at early dawn upon Jackson. Sherman will move at the same hour by the direct Raymond & Jackson road. McClernand will be brought up to this point with his rear and his advance thrown on the two Jackson roads." AL (signature clipped), DNA, RG 94, War Records Office, 17th Army Corps. *O.R.*, I, xxiv, part 3, 307–8.

To Maj. Gen. William T. Sherman

Head Quarters Dept of The Tenn.
Raymond Miss May 13th 1863

MAJ. GEN. W. T. SHERMAN
COMDG 15TH ARMY CORPS
GENERAL:

Move directly towards Jackson, starting at early dawn in the morning. McPherson will start at early dawn from Clinton which place he reached at 3. P. M. today without difficulty.

Two of McClernands Divisions will be thrown forward one by the Clinton road and one by the road where by you.

Very respectfully
U. S. GRANT.
Maj. Gen.

Copies, DLC-USG, V, 19, 30, 98; DNA, RG 393, Dept. of the Tenn., Letters Sent; Alcorn Collection, WyU. *O.R.*, I, xxiv, part 3, 307. On May 13, 1863, Maj. Gen. William T. Sherman, Mississippi Springs, wrote to USG. "Your orders are received as per Enclosed Envelope. An officer has been over to me from Genl. McPherson, and I have sent two messengers to him. We are abreast and I have sent him word that I will move at (before) 6 a m. We will communicate across country durig the march. I send an East Tennesseean, who talks well and has been to Port Hudson, Jackson and at the Fight at Raymond. I send him not as a Prisoner because he gave himself up, but as one who will inform you. Be careful to have McClernand bring forward his 20 lbs. Parrott Guns,—viz Foster's Wisconsin Battery. Also if possible a couple or more of the 30s. I have ɴᴏ no doubt we will find rifle pits and redoubts.—We must cut the Bridge across Road as quick as possible, and fight the sooner the better. I suppose you will come up. McClernand might be sure of an open Road by taking the lower Mississippi Springs Road. Still I will keep out of his way on this." ALS, DNA, RG 393, Dept. of the Tenn., Letters Received.

To Maj. Gen. Henry W. Halleck

Raymond Miss.

12 10 P. M. May 14th 1863.

Maj. Gen. H. W. Halleck
Genl-in-Chief

McPherson took this place on the twelfth (12th) after a brisk fight of more than two (2) hours.

Our loss fifty one (51) killed, and one hundred and eighty (180) wounded. Enemy's loss seventy five (75) killed, buried by us, and one hundred and eighty six (186) prisoners, besides wounded.[1]

McPherson is now at Clinton. Sherman on the direct Jackson road & Genl McClernand bringing up the rear.

I will attack the State Capital today.

U. S. Grant

Maj. Genl.

Telegram received, DLC-Robert T. Lincoln; DNA, RG 107, Telegrams Collected (Bound); copies, *ibid.*, Telegrams Received in Cipher; *ibid.*, RG 393, Dept. of the Tenn., Hd. Qrs. Correspondence; DLC-USG, V, 6, 8, 24, 94, 98. *O.R.*, I, xxiv, part 1, 36. This telegram, sent via Memphis, reached Washington on May 18, 1863, 5:40 P.M.

1. USG later revised upward his figures for losses at the battle of Raymond to 69 killed, 341 wounded, 32 missing. *O.R.*, I, xxiv, part 1, 59. The compilers of the *O.R.* put C.S.A. losses at 73 killed, 251 wounded, 190 missing. *Ibid.*, p. 739.

To Maj. Gen. Francis P. Blair, Jr.

Head Quarters Dept of the Tenn.

Jackson Miss May 14. 1863.

Major. Gen. F. P. Blair
General.

This place was carried at about 3 P. M. this day, the Garrison retreating north towards Canton under command of Gen. Jo.

Johnson. Their design is evidently to cross the Big Black and pass down the Peninsula between the Black and Yazoo rivers. We must beat them. Turn your troops immediately to Bolton, take all the trains with you, Smiths Division and any other troops now with you ~~Smiths~~ will go to the same place. If practicable take parrallel roads so as to divide your troops and train.

> Very respectfully
> U. S. GRANT
> Maj. Gen.

Copies, DLC-USG, V, 19, 30, 98; DNA, RG 393, Dept. of the Tenn., Letters Sent; Alcorn Collection, WyU. *O.R.*, I, xxiv, part 3, 311. Earlier on May 14, 1863, USG, "near Jackson," had written to Maj. Gen. Francis P. Blair, Jr. "Do not on any account leave the Wagon train behind you until it reaches Raymond. Fearing that a single Division would not be sufficient guard between Auburn and Raymond I sent Gen. Smith back with his Division to strengthen you." Copies, DLC-USG, V, 19, 30, 98; DNA, RG 393, Dept. of the Tenn., Letters Sent; Alcorn Collection, WyU.

On May 13, 8:40 P.M., C.S.A. Gen. Joseph E. Johnston, Jackson, wrote to Lt. Gen. John C. Pemberton. "I have lately arrived, and learn that Major-General Sherman is between us, with four divisions, at Clinton. It is important to re-establish communications, that you may be re-enforced. If practicable, come up in his rear at once. To beat such a detachment would be of immense value. The troops here could co-operate. All the strength you can quickly assemble should be brought. Time is all-important." *O.R.*, I, xxiv, part 1, 261; *ibid.*, I, xxiv, part 3, 870. Johnston sent three messengers with copies of this letter to Vicksburg, one of whom was a spy who delivered it to Maj. Gen. James B. McPherson. Adam Badeau, *Military History of Ulysses S. Grant* (New York, 1868), I, 252; *Memoirs*, I, 507–9. Acting on this information on May 14, USG concentrated troops at Bolton. On Jan. 30, 1874, Pemberton wrote to USG asking whether it was true that his correspondence with Johnston had been intercepted. Copy, DNA, RG 109, Pemberton Papers. On Jan. 31, Levi P. Luckey wrote to Pemberton to confirm the story. Copy, DLC-USG, II, 2. In response to a letter of Feb. 2 from Pemberton to USG asking permission to make the information public, Luckey responded on Feb. 11 that the information was available in Badeau's book and that USG had no objection to Pemberton's use of it. ALS, DNA, RG 109, Pemberton Papers.

To Maj. Gen. John A. McClernand

Head Quarters Dept of the Tennessee
Jackson Miss. May 14th 1863

Maj. Gen. Jno A. McClernand
Commdg 13th Army Corps
General:

Our troops carried this place about three o.clk this p. m. after a brisk fight of about three hours The Enemy retreated north towards Canton Johnson in command It is evidently the design of the Enemy to get north of us and cross the Black river and beat us into Vicksburg. We must not allow them to do this Turn all your forces towards Bolton Station and make all dispatch in getting there. Move troops by the most direct road from wherever they may be on the receipt of this order.

Sherman and McPherson will immediately retrace their steps, only detaining a force to distroy the Railroads North & East.

Very respectfully
U. S. Grant.

Copies, DLC-USG, V, 19, 30, 98; DNA, RG 393, Dept. of the Tenn., Letters Sent; *ibid.*, 13th Army Corps, Letters Received; Alcorn Collection, WyU. *O.R.*, I, xxiv, part 3, 310. On May 14, 1863, Maj. Gen. John A. McClernand, Raymond, twice wrote to USG. "Colonel R. Owens 60th Indiana and Colonel Vance 96th Ohio were left at Perkins' Plantation to do guard and fatigue duty under command of Col Owens. I had expected they would be releived and replaced by Regiments from other commands as they arrived, and these Regiments permitted to rejoin General Smith's Division. Such has not been done, however, and I am constrained to ask that they be ordered forward, as I know that Genl's Smith & Burbridge as well as Cols Owens and Vance are extremely anxious to have these regiments with the Divisions. Detaching two regiments from one Division has reduced it below the common average strength of others. They have been ordered to the Gulf, I understand, to replace two regiments left there. I hope they may in turn be releived by others. Col Owens writes asking instructions in relation to giving written protections to persons who are willing to take an oath of allegiance. He also asks instructions in relation to his powers and duty in feeding the destitute families of colored as well as whites, not in government employment. Again he inquires, is Grand Gulf a post in the sense of army Regulations, that empowers Commanders of Posts to order a General Court Martial. Cases have occurred demanding one. He also inquires in relation to the Hospital at James' Plantation. There are 800 patients in it, and will soon be 1000 who will be left without protection from guerrillas by the withdrawal of the forces at Perkins' and the abandonment of the communication by way of Richmond and Smiths Plantation. Please be good enough to give me your instructions upon each one of these questions." LS, DNA, RG 393, Dept. of the Tenn., Letters Received. "I have the honor to report that Gen'l Osterhaus reached here last night about 1 o'clock A. M. The head of Gen'l Carrs Division, reached here about 6½ o'clock, A. M., and has gone forward on the Jackson road. It will probably encamp to-night, four miles beyond the Mississippi Springs—the point designated by you. The head of Gen'l Hovey's Division reached here at 9¾ o'clock A. M., and may not be able to go further on the Clinton road than ———— Creek, which is four miles from here. He is instructed to destroy the railroad westward. I have instructed Genls. Carr and Hovey to open communication with each other. The positions assigned to them, respectively, I take to be about six miles apart. Gen'l Smith reported to me last ~~night~~ evening that he was at Old Auburn; and again, before day, that the train from the Gulf was near him. Report also brings Blair within a few miles of Smith. In accordance with what I understood to be your instructions, and because it would have exposed it to capture or dispersion, I instructed Gen'l Smith to withdraw the detachment he had left behind to watch Baldwin's Ferry—Everything seems to be going on well, though the tremendous rainstorms of last evening and today have made the march laborious and less expeditious than it would have been under more favorable circumstances. Unless you direct otherwise, I will instruct Gen'l Osterhaus to send part of the supply train on the Jackson road and part on the Clinton road, retaining part here—Reports are pretty rife that the enemy are in strong force at Edward's Depot; yet, if so, it is surprising that he did not attack my rear, yesterday, more vigorously than he did. As this place is more readily accessible to the different parts of my command, (which, agreeably to your instructions, is divided over a considerable space,) than any other now known to me, I will remain here for the present. Hence, any orders you may wish to send will find me here, or be forwarded to me—" LS, *ibid.*; ADf, McClernand Papers, IHi. *O.R.*, I, xxiv, part 3, 310–11.

On May 15, 1:15 A.M., McClernand, Raymond, wrote to USG. "I have ordered Generals Carr, Hovey, and Osterhaus to concentrate their divisions upon Bolton, and Genl Smith to move his division towards Edwards Station, and contingently to Bolton—each with all possible dispatch—" LS, DNA, RG 393, Dept. of the Tenn., Letters Received. Misdated May 14 in *O.R.*, I, xxiv, part 3, 311. On May 15, 4:45 P.M., USG, Clinton, wrote to McClernand. "Move your command early tomorrow towards Edwards Depot—marching so as to feel the force of the enemy, should you encounter him, and without bringing on an engagement unless you feel entirely able to contend with him. Communicate this order to Maj. Genl Blair—who will move with you" LS, McClernand Papers, IHi. *O.R.*, I, xxiv, part 3, 313. On the same day, McClernand, Bolton, wrote to USG. "Osterhous seized Bolton this morning at 9 oclock, taking several prisoners. Soon after, General Hovey arrived by the way of Clinton. Reports were rife, that the enemy were moving in strong force upon me, by the Edwards Station and Bolton Road, and particularly by the Edwards Station and Raymond road. Rapidly disposing my scanty forces to meet him, I pushed forward reconnoisances in every direction toward Edwards Station and Brownsvill Skirmishing at intervals, occurred throughout the day, and just before sunset the enemy undertook to feel my position and force. He was promptly met and repelled. We are now resting upon our arms. General Carr came up to Raymond this evening and I moved him

out a mile and a half to the road leading to Edwards Station, in supporting distance
of Osterhous, and to Cover the main road to Edwards Station. I will move him
in the morning by the middle road. Blair is at Raymond and I will move him on
the road now held by Carr. Smith is probably at or near Dillons to-night. I will
move him if I can in immediate co-operation with Blair, Hovey having the right,
and resting his right near the rail road—Osterhous and Carr centre, and Blair &
Smith the left   I will move forward by 6 oclock in the morning and at least feel
the enemy. It is very desirable that McPherson should at the same time move
forward upon Edwards Station on the north side of the rail road and Cut off the
enemy if I should drive him from his position. Broken bridges may delay the
movement on both sides of the rail road   I have heard nothing of the general
supply train. May I rely on it, or shall I send back the entitled teams of the Regiments to Grand Gulf   If so, will there be troops on the way to protect them?
Genl Osterhous has just Captured a letter written by a Rebel Captain in Vicksburg in which he says that on the 10th Inst the rebel force there was 40,000, and
estimates our force at 70,000"   Copy, DNA, RG 393, 13th Army Corps, Letters
Sent. *O.R.*, I, xxiv, part 3, 313–14.

To Maj. Gen. James B. McPherson

12:15 a. m.

Near Jackson, May 14th/63

MAJ GEN. MCPHERSON,

Sherman is in advance of this place to within 2½ miles of
Jackson. The enemy opened very heavily with Artillery but soon
after our skirmishers advanced the firing seased.—Sherman will
push on as rapidly as possible. Send me word how you are progressing; we must get Jackson or as near it as possible to-night.

Sherman will send a Brigade or more towards you, or to the
left of this road immediately.

> Yours Truly
> U. S. GRANT
> Maj. Gen Com

ALS, NjR.

To Maj. Gen. William T. Sherman

———

Head Quarters Dept of the Tennessee
Jackson Miss May 14th 1863

Maj Gen. W. T. Sherman
Comdg 15th Army Corps
General:

Designate a Brigade from your Command to guard the city. Collect stores and forage and collect all public property of the enemy. The Division from which such Brigade may be selected will be the last to leave the city. You will direct them therefore to commence immediately the effectual distruction of river Railroad Bridge and the road as far east as practicable   Also distroy North & south. The 4th Iowa and a Brigade of Infantry should be sent east of the river with instructions for the Cavalry to go on east as far as possible. Troops going east of the river should burn all C. S. A cotton and stores they find.

Very respectfully
U. S Grant
Maj. General.

Copies, DLC-USG, V, 19, 30, 98; DNA, RG 393, Dept. of the Tenn., Letters Sent; Alcorn Collection, WyU. *O.R.*, I, xxiv, part 3, 312.

To Col. William S. Hillyer

———

Head Quarters Dept of the Miss.
Jackson Miss May 14 1863

Col. Hillyer A. D. C
Grand Gulf Miss
Colonel:

Col. Pughs Brigade of General Laumans Division will form the garrison at Grand Gulf. The Brigades are to remain at Grand

Gulf until ~~all arrive~~ the Division shall have arrived. You will so direct. Forward despatches with all possible Haste.

> Very respectfully
> U. S. GRANT
> Maj. Gen.

Copies, DLC-USG, V, 19, 30, 98; DNA, RG 393, Dept. of the Tenn., Letters Sent; Alcorn Collection, WyU.

On April 27, 1863, Col. William S. Hillyer wrote to Brig. Gen. Lorenzo Thomas resigning in order to attend to his law practice and real estate holdings in St. Louis, and to settle the estates of three members of his wife's family. ALS, DNA, RG 94, ACP, H256 CB 1863. On April 27, USG endorsed this letter. "Approved and respectfully forwarded. Col. Hillyer has been with me from my first appointment as Brig. Gen. he has served faithfully and intelligently first as Aid de Camp and then as Provost Marshal Gen. In every position he has given entire satisfaction and I am lothe to loose him. Being personally acquainted with the facts set forth as grounds for this resignation I approve it." AES, *ibid.* On the same day, Thomas issued Special Orders No. 17 accepting the resignation as of May 15. Copy, DLC-USG, V, 105.

On June 30, Hillyer, St. Louis, wrote to USG. "I have been home for ten days and this is the first time I have attempted to write more than my signature. The rheumatism in my arm, with which I was afflicted when I left you, increased in painfulness until it became perfectly excruciating and made my trip up the river the most miserable journey I ever experienced. When under the treatment of the most severe remedies I got relief from the pain my arm was left paralyzed and even now I am unable to raise my right hand to my head and can neither dress or wash myself or cut my food. I can use my hand now but no other portion of my right arm—This will be a sufficient apology to you for my long delay in writing. My general health is good except weakness from the use of powerful medicines —I could not express to you General the day I left my heart felt appreciation of your uniform kindness to me and I have found since that you may have thought strange of my somewhat abrupt leaving—But bodily pain is apt to make a man forgetful of the courtesies and proprities of life and I was suffering very much. I found out here and in Memphis that your enemies and mine were disposed to attribute my leaving the army to misunderstandings and dissatisfactions between us—and I have taken every occasion to make known the fact that there never had been an unkind word thought or expression between us, (so far as I know), during the whole of our official intercourse—that I have never had a truer, firmer, friend than you, and that there was no man living for whom I have a higher respect or as warm an affection—that the only regret I had in leaving the army was in leaving you—and that if I ever rejoined the army my highest ambition would be to rejoin your staff—If I can at any time serve you in any possible way, General, it will afford me the utmost pleasure to do so and do not hesitate to command me—I rode out with my family to Mr Dent's yesterday, to see Mrs Grant. We found her and the children in the best of health and spirits—I learned that Col lagow had been spending a week there and had just left for Springfield. It was the first I knew of Lagows being in the neighborhood supposing he had started down to rejoin you—He will probably be with you by the time you get this—Mr Dent is looking very well and is an intense rebel—I left Willie out there to spend the week with Buck—Every thing looks gloomy in the East—I cannot understand the movements of our army—It may be too deep for me—Hooker is relieved— What do you think of Gen Meade? Cant you hurry up Vicksburg and spare a few of your troops for Pennsylvania—I often hear the expression 'I wish Grant was there.' I have no fixed plans for the future now—I shall start east in about two weeks and will then determine what to do—my great object now is to regain the use of my arm—I wish you would send me over your own signature a permit to come to your head quarters and pass to any part of your Department—I testified before the Military Commission last week—McDowell is evidently tired of the business and anxious to have as little more testimony as possible   He confined me to answering questions which he propounded in regard to my Department and wouldn't permit me to disclose some memphis matters which I thought ought to be made. I had told him in conversation that you had promised me to send a court of enquiry to Memphis after the fall of Vicksburg and I suppose he preferred that that court should dispose of these matters. There is one matter I expect you had better provide for—My testimony shows that Hurlbut and Dodge have had a large amount of scout service money—I was asked to whom if anybody they reported the disbursement of this money—I could not tell. The Court seemed to put some stress on this point and I think you had better make some order requiring the Generals who have received this money from the Pro Mar Dept to report to you what they have done with it. I suggest this so that you may be relieved from any criticism   My testimony seemed to be entirely satisfactory to the Court— I met McClernand at the Planters House last week—He looked very abject. I never saw a man so cut down—He is making a strong effort to make a newspaper sympathy for him—What was the immediate cause of his removal? Give my regards to the staff—" ALS, USG 3. Hillyer's testimony is in DNA, RG 159, Proceedings of the Court of Inquiry, II, 547–51.

To Maj. Gen. Henry W. Halleck

Jackson Miss May 15. [*1863*]

MAJ. GEN. H. W. HALLECK
GENL-IN-CHIEF

This place fell into our hands yesterday after a fight of about three (3) hours.

Joe. Johnston was in command. The enemy retreated north, evidently with the design of joining the Vicksburg forces.

I am concentrating my forces at Bolton to cut them off if possible. A dispatch from Gen. Banks showed him to be off in Louisiana, not to return to Baton Rouge until the tenth 10. of May. I could not lose the time.

I have taken many prisoners from Port Hudson, who state that but one brigade was left there. Port Hudson will be evacuated on the appearance of troops in the rear. I sent a Special Messenger to Gen. Banks giving him the substance of the information I had, and asking him to join me as soon as possible. This message was sent on the tenth 10.

U. S. GRANT. M. G.

Telegram received, DNA, RG 107, Telegrams Collected (Bound); DLC-Edwin M. Stanton; copies, DNA, RG 107, Telegrams Received in Cipher; *ibid.*, RG 393, Dept. of the Tenn., Hd. Qrs. Correspondence; DLC-USG, V, 6, 8, 24, 94, 98. *O.R.*, I, xxiv, part 1, 36. This telegram was received in Washington at 5:00 P.M., May 20, 1863. On May 11, 11:00 A.M., Maj. Gen. Henry W. Halleck telegraphed to USG. "If possible the forces of yourself & of Genl Banks should be united between Vicksburg & Port Hudson so as to attack these places separately with the combined forces. The same thing has been urged upon Genl Banks. Genl Hooker recrossed to the north of the Rappahannock, but he inflicted a greater loss upon the enemy than he recieved himself." ALS (telegram sent), DNA, RG 107, Telegrams Collected (Bound); telegram received (in cipher), *ibid.*, RG 393, Dept. of the Tenn., Telegrams Received. *O.R.*, I, xxiv, part 1, 36. Also on May 11, Halleck wrote to Maj. Gen. Nathaniel P. Banks. "The Quartermaster-General has sent you additional steam transportation to supply your present wants, and it is hoped you will unite with General Grant so as to attack Vicksburg and Port Hudson separately. If within your power to operate between the two places, and with your combined strength to attack a divided enemy, your success will be almost certain. By attacking Port Hudson from below or Vicksburg from above you enable the enemy to unite his forces upon the point attacked. . . ." *Ibid.*, I, xv, 725. In his *Memoirs* (I, 524), USG stated that Halleck's letter to Banks of May 11 was shown him on May 17, just prior to the assault on Big Black River Bridge. This letter "ordered me to return to Grand Gulf and to co-operate from there with Banks against Port Hudson, and then to return with our combined forces to besiege Vicksburg." Having dismissed the officer who brought the letter without, apparently, making a copy, USG probably recollected the contents incorrectly. See Bruce Catton, *Grant Moves South* (Boston and Toronto, 1960), pp. 447–48, 533–34.

On May 20, Lt. Col. John A. Rawlins wrote to Maj. Theodore S. Bowers. "You will forward by special Boat and Messinger the Accompanying dispatch to W. S. Fuller Esq Supt. of Military Telegraph at Memphis Tenn. Direct the Master of Transportation to send a steamer at once as it is of the utmost importance." Copies, DLC-USG, V, 19, 30, 98; DNA, RG 393, Dept. of the Tenn., Letters Sent. The message was transmitted through a telegram of May 23 from Maj. Gen. Stephen A. Hurlbut to President Abraham Lincoln. "The Army of the Tennessee landed at Bruinsburg on thirtieth April   on 1st May fought battle of Port Gibson   defeated rebels under Bowen whose loss in killed wounded & prisoners was at least 1500   loss in artillery 5 pieces   On 12th May at the battle of Raymond Rebels were defeated with a loss of 800. On the 14th defeated Joseph E Johnson Captured Jackson with loss to the enemy of 400 besides immense stores

& manufactories & 17 Pieces artillery   On the 16th fought the Bloody & decisive battle of Bankers Creek in which the entire Vicksburg force under Pemberton was defeated with loss of 29 pieces of Artillery & 4000 men. On the 17th defeated same force at Big Black bridge with loss of 2600 men & 17 pieces of Artillery   On the 18th invested Vicksburg closely. Today—Gen Steele carried the rifle pits on the north of the city   The right of the army rest on the Mississippi above Vicksburg." Telegram received, *ibid.*, RG 107, Telegrams Collected (Bound); *ibid.*, Telegrams Collected (Unbound); DLC-Robert T. Lincoln. *O.R.*, I, xxiv, part 3, 344.

To Maj. Gen. Francis P. Blair, Jr.

———

Headquarters Department of the Tennessee,
In the Field, May 16, 1863.

MAJ. GEN. F. P. BLAIR,
COMMANDING DIVISION FIFTEENTH ARMY CORPS:
GENERAL: Move at early dawn toward Black River bridge. I think you will encounter no enemy by the way. If you do, however, engage them at once, and you will be assisted by troops farther advanced. Sherman left Jackson to-day and is moving by forced march. He will join us by 10 a. m. to-morrow, after which you will receive orders from him.

Very respectfully,
U. S. GRANT,
Major-General.

O.R., I, lii, part 1, 358.

To Maj. Gen. Francis P. Blair, Jr.

———

Hd Qrs Dept of the Tennessee
Clinton Miss May 16th 1863

MAJOR GENL BLAIR
COMDG DIVISION
Information received indicates that the enemy have moved out to Edwards Station and are still pushing on to attack us with

all their force. Push your troops on in that direction as rapidly as possible: If you are already in the Bolton road continue so, but if you still have choice of roads take the one leading to Edwards Depot—Pass your troops to the front of your train, except a rear guard, and keep the ammunition wagons in front of all others.

I sent you orders of the 14th to move directly from wherever you might be to Bolton: Did you receive the order?

Very Respectfully

U S. Grant

Major General.

P. S. If you take the Edwards Depot road you will want to communicate with the troops along the rail road by all cross roads after having advanced to west of Bolton

Be cautious in approaching Bakers Creek, Before doing so know where friend. & enemy both are

U S. G.

Copies, DLC-USG, V, 19, 30, 98; DNA, RG 393, Dept. of the Tenn., Letters Sent; Alcorn Collection, WyU. *O.R.*, I, xxiv, part 3, 319. On May 16, 1863, Maj. Gen. Francis P. Blair, Jr., had written to USG. "I received an order last evening from Gen McClernand to take the road from Raymond to Edwards Depot which I accordingly did and am now at 9.50 a. m, within 1½ miles from Bakers Creek   Gen A. J. Smiths Division is with me. We are feeling the enemy cautiously skirmishing and I have sent to ascertain the exact whereabout of Osterhaus, Carr, and Hovey. We shall ~~probably~~ attack as soon as we can develop the enemys position and ascertain that of our friends"   ALS, DNA, RG 94, War Records Office, Dept. of the Tenn. *O.R.*, I, xxiv, part 3, 319.

To Maj. Gen. John A. McClernand

———

Head Quarters, Dept. of the Tenn.
Clinton Miss. May 16th 1863
5.40.—A. M.

MAJ. GEN. J. A. McCLERNAND
COMMANDING 13TH ARMY CORPS.
GENERAL.

I have just obtained very probable information, that the entire force of the enemy has crossed the Big Black, and was at Edwards Depot at 7 o'clock last night. You will therefore disencumber yourself of your trains, select an eligible position, and feel the enemy.

Our whole force is closely following you, and orders have been issued, requiring the utmost celerity in the march towards Edwards Depot.

Don't bring on a general engagement till we are entirely prepared. Draw your troops closely to-gether and notify Blair what to do. I will leave here for the front at 8 A. M.

Very respectfully your obedt. Servt.
U. S. GRANT, Maj. Gen. Comd'g.

Copy, DNA, RG 393, 13th Army Corps, Letters Received. Maj. Gen. John A. McClernand endorsed this letter. "This dispatch must have been misdated the 16th instead of the 15th, as it reached me on the 15th." Copy, *ibid*. USG's related early morning letters of May 16, 1863, to Maj. Gen. James B. McPherson and to Maj. Gen. William T. Sherman indicate that USG could not have written this letter to McClernand on May 15, and the chronology is further established by USG's report of his movements. See letter to Col. John C. Kelton, July 6, 1863.

To Maj. Gen. John A. McClernand

Hd. Qrs Dept of The Tennessee.
Near Bakers Creek May 16th 63.

Maj Genl Jno A McClernand
Comdg 13th Army Corps
General

    From all information gatherd from citizens and prisoners the mass of the Enemy are south of Hoveys Division   McPherson is now up to Hovey and can support him at any point   close up all your other forces as expeditiously as possible but cautiously. the enemy must not allowed to get to our rear.   if you can communicate with Blair and Ransom[1] do so and direct them to come up to your support by the most expeditious route

Yours

U S Grant

Maj Genl

Copies, DLC-USG, V, 19, 30, 98; DNA, RG 393, Dept. of the Tenn., Letters Sent; *ibid.*, 13th Army Corps, Letters Received; Alcorn Collection, WyU. *O.R.*, I, xxiv, part 3, 317–18. On May 16, 1863, Maj. Gen. John A. McClernand, "Before Edwards Station," twice wrote to USG. "At 9¾ o'clock A. M., Gen'l Hovey had advanced on his road about four miles—Finds the enemy strongly posted in his front, showing two pieces of artillery at the distance of some four hundred yards. The Gen'l has taken fifteen prisoners, who represent the enemy to be from 50,000 to 60,000 strong. Osterhaus must be some four miles from Edwards Station. Gen'l Smith is about the same distance. McPherson, I think, should move up to the support of Hovey—who thinks his right flank will encounter severe resistance. Shall I hold, or bring on an engagement— ? Gen'l Hovey thinks the enemy has passed a large force towards Raymond, and to our rear, but an aide from Genl. Smith knows nothing of it." ALS, DNA, RG 393, Dept. of the Tenn., Letters Received. *O.R.*, I, xxiv, part 3, 316–17. "You dispatch relative to Blair and Ransom is rec'd. I have to report that Gen'l Blair has been with my forces all day, and is now only about a mile south of Osterhaus, and in the rear of Smith. I sent for Ransom to come up to the lateral road leading from Osterhaus road to Smith's, at 11½ o'clock A. M. The greatest space between any of my columns is between Gen'l Hovey and Gen'l Osterhaus. If Hovey could take space to the left, and let McPherson in on his right and rear, I think it would be better. Both Smith and Osterhaus have advanced since my last dispatch. I hear a sharp engagement to my right, doubtless between Hovey and the enemy. I am glad to be assured that McPherson is well up to Hovey." ALS, DNA, RG 393, Dept. of the Tenn., Letters Received. On the same day, 12:35 P.M., USG, "4 miles from Edwards'

Depot," wrote to McClernand. "As soon as your command is all in hand throw forward skirmishers and feel the enemy and attack him in force if an opportunity occurs. I am with Hovey & McPherson and will see that they fully cooporate." ALS, McClernand Papers, IHi. *O.R.*, I, xxiv, part 3, 318.

Early on May 16, Lt. Col. John A. Rawlins had written to McClernand. "You will direct Major Genl Blair to move with his Division to the support of Genl Osterhaus as soon as possible, moving on the same line by the 1st Latteral road leading into the one on which Osterhaus is now marching. Establish communication between Blair and Osterhaus at once and keep it up, moving forward cautiously" Copies, DLC-USG, V, 19, 30, 98; DNA, RG 393, Dept. of the Tenn., Letters Sent; *ibid.*, 13th Army Corps, Letters Received; Alcorn Collection, WyU. *O.R.*, I, xxiv, part 3, 317.

1. On May 16, Rawlins wrote to Brig. Gen. Thomas E. G. Ransom. "You will move your command so as to join our forces north of you by the first road leading northward. Enemy are reported as having sent a column to our left and rear. avoid being cut off" Copies, DLC-USG, V, 19, 30, 98; DNA, RG 393, Dept. of the Tenn., Letters Sent; Alcorn Collection, WyU.

To Maj. Gen. James B. McPherson

Head Quarters, Dept. Tenn.
Clinton, Miss.
May 16th. 5.45. A. M. 1863.

Maj. Genl. J. B. McPherson,
Comdg. 17th Army Corps.
General,

I have just received information that the enemy has crossed Big Black with the entire Vicksburg force. He was at Edwards Depot last night and still advancing—

You will therefore, pass all trains and move forward to join McClernand with all possible dispatch. I have ordered your rear brigade to move at once. and given such directions to other commanders as will secure a prompt concentration of our forces.

Very Respectfully
U. S. Grant
Maj. Genl. Com

LS, NjR. *O.R.*, I, xxiv, part 3, 320.

On May 15, 1863, Maj. Gen. James B. McPherson twice wrote to USG, the second time at 10:00 P.M. from "Jones' Plantation 2 miles from Bolton." "It is reported that the train of cars which left here yesterday is still five miles East, and that the train contains the specie of the Banks, and other valuables. There are said to be also five Engines near & with the train—These reports come by a contraband who states that the train was there two hours ago. There is a small force of the Rebels protecting the train—" "Genl. Logans Division is En-camped on Baker's Creek at this point immediately in rear of Hovey's Division. Two Brigades of General Crocker's Division are Encamped about three miles in rear of this, the remaining Brigade being with you in Clinton. I have just sent forward to Genl. Hovey to know if there is any thing important & Enclose his answer—" ALS, DNA, RG 393, Dept. of the Tenn., Letters Received. Brig. Gen. Alvin P. Hovey replied to McPherson. "No news from the front since last evening about sun down—Our pickets at that time were driven by the enemy—" ALS, _ibid_.

On May 16, 6:00 A.M., McPherson, "Jones' Plantation," wrote to USG. "I think it advisable for you to come forward to the Front as soon as you can" ALS, _ibid._, RG 94, War Records Office, Dept. of the Tenn. _O.R._, I, xxiv, part 3, 320. On the same day, Lt. Col. William T. Clark, adjt. for McPherson, wrote to USG. "In the absence of Gen'l McPherson, Col Wilson requests me to inform you of the positions of the different Divisions of Gen'l McClernand's Command as far as can be ascertained. 1st Gen'l Hovey is just in advance of Gen'l Logan across 'Baker's Creek. 2d Gen'l Osterhous is about three miles to left and front of Gen'l Hovey. (I think he must be four miles away) 3d Gen'l Carr passed through Raymond after two o'clock yesterday in the direction of Bolton—4th Gen'l Blair encamped eight miles to the rear of Raymond, night before last—the Genls Aid (Captain Steele) was informed that Gen'l Blair rec'd orders to turn to the left and advance towards Edwards' Depot—His precise position, could not be ascertained— . . . P. S. The General has gone to the front to reconnoiter—" ALS, DNA, RG 393, Dept. of the Tenn., Letters Received.

To Maj. Gen. William T. Sherman

> Head quarters, Dept. of the Tenn.
> Clinton, Miss.
> May 16th 1863
> 5.30 A. M.

MAJ. GENL. W. T. SHERMAN,
COMDG. 15TH ARMY CORPS.
GENERAL,

Start one of your divisions on the road at once with its ammu-nition wagons—and direct it to move with all possible speed till it comes up with our rear beyond Bolten.

It is important that great celerity should be shown in carrying out this movement, as I have evidence that the entire force of the enemy was at Edwards Depot 7 o'clock yesterday evening and still advancing.

The fight may be brought on at any moment—we should have every man on the field. The other division will follow as soon as possible.

> Very Respectfully,
> U. S. GRANT
> Maj. Gen. Com

LS, ICHi. Incomplete in *O.R.*, I, xxiv, part 3, 319.

To Maj. Gen. William T. Sherman

───────

> Near Bakers Creek, Miss.
> May 16th 1863

MAJ GEN. SHEARMAN,
COMD.G 15 ARMY CORPS,
GEN.

We met the enemy about four miles East of Edwards station and have had a desperate fight. The enemy were driven and are now in full retreat. I am of the opinion that the battle of Vicksburg has been fought. We must be prepared however for whatever turns up.

McClernand & McPherson are in full pursuit and will continue until night closes in. I want you to advance as far as possible tonight and start early in the morning again. When opposite Bolton turn North and get on to the Vicksburg road North of the rail-road and follow that.

We took to-day about 1500 prisoners and three batteries. Loss in killed & wounded heavy on both sides.[1]

Get to Black river as soon as possible.

Yours Truly

U. S GRANT

Maj Gen

ALS, ICHi.

1. At the battle of Baker's Creek, better known as Champion's Hill, U.S. losses were 410 killed, 1844 wounded, 187 missing. *O.R.*, I, xxiv, part 2, 7–10. C.S.A. losses have been estimated at 381 killed, 1800 wounded, 1670 missing. Thomas L. Livermore, *Numbers & Losses in the Civil War in America: 1861–65* (Boston and New York, 1900; reprinted Bloomington, Ind., 1957), p. 100.

To Maj. Gen. William T. Sherman

12 O'Clock 16th & 17th May/63

GEN.

Our advance is beyond Edwards Station   All start as soon as it is light enough to see in the morning. The enemy have lost to-day most severely probably from 7 to 10 thousand killed wounded and missing besides large numbers were no doubt cut of from geting back across Black river the way they come. Your moving North of the rail-road may enable you to get across at Bridgeport whilst the enemy are engaged at the bridge.

Blair has been well up all day to the right of A. J. Smith. I have given him instructions for his movement in the morning and notified him that he would probably find you at Blackriver when he would receive further instructio[n] from you.—The number of prisoners taken to-day will probably reach 3000, killed & wounded about 2000 on each side. The enemys loss may be greater.

Yours

U. S. GRANT

Maj. Gen

Your trains are up with provisions and I supposed you would come in contact with them about where you turned from the southern Vicksburg road. Cant [you have] some one to take to [give a few] loads of provisions?

U S G

ALS, ICHi.

To Brig. Gen. George F. McGinnis

Hd Qrs Dept of the Tennessee
In Field Champion Hills, Miss,
May 16th 1863.

BRIG GENL McGINNIS
COMDG BRIG. OF HOVEYS DIVISION
GENERAL.

You will remain with your Brigade and one from Crockers Division in possession of the Battle field.   see that the killed of both sides are burried keeping an account of the number of Rebils.   collect all Arms and materials left. You will also take from the supply train of your own Division two days supply of rations.

You will receive all prisoners now in our possession, enrol them on duplicate lists and remain here till further orders.

Very Respectfully
U S. GRANT
Major General

Copies, DLC–USG, V, 19, 30, 98; DNA, RG 393, Dept. of the Tenn., Letters Sent; Alcorn Collection, WyU.

To Maj. Gen. Francis P. Blair, Jr.

8.15
Edwards' Station Miss
May 17th 1863

Maj. Gen. F. P. Blair.
Genl.

Sherman is ordered to Bridgeport with his Corps. He will probably arrive there at about 10 this morning. Move to the same point with your Division and take the Pontoon train with you. Capt. Freeman is in charge of the train and will guide you.[1]

Very respectfully
U. S. Grant
Maj. Gen Com

ALS, DNA, RG 393, 15th Army Corps, 2nd Div., Letters Received.

1. On May 16, 1863, USG, "Champion Hills," wrote to Capt. Henry C. Freeman and 1st Lt. Christian Lochbihler. "Move the Pontoon train to night towards Edwards Depot pushing as close to Black River as the position of our troops will allow" Copies, DLC-USG, V, 19, 30, 98; DNA, RG 393, Dept. of the Tenn., Letters Sent; Alcorn Collection, WyU.

To Maj. Gen. William T. Sherman

---

8 a m
Edwards Station Miss.
May 17th 1863

Gen.

McClernand has engaged the enemy at their works about one mile East of the rail-road bridge. I have ordered the Pontoon train with Blairs Division to go to ~~Edward's Station~~ Bridgeport. I will endeavor to hold the enemy where he is to give you time to cross the river if it can be effect. The moment the enemy begin to give way I will endeavor to follow him so closely that he will not be able to destroy the bridge. Let me hear from you the hour you expect to arrive at Bridgeport.

Yours

U. S. GRANT

Maj. Gen Com

ALS, IHi. *O.R.*, I, xxiv, part 3, 322. On May 17, 1863, 10:30 A.M., USG wrote to Maj. Gen. William T. Sherman. "Lawlers Brigade stormed the enemy works a few minuets since, carried it capturing from 2000 to 3000 prisoners, 16 guns so far as heard from and probably more will be found. The enemy have fired both bridges. A. J. Smith captured 11 guns this morning with teams men and ammunition   I send you a note from Col. Wright"   ALS, S. H. M. Byers Papers, IaHA. On the same day, 2:00 P.M., Sherman, "Bridgetown," wrote to USG. "Blairs & Steels Divisions are here. I found a picket on the other side threw a few shells and the Picket of 1 Lt & 10 men surrendered. I now have a Regm't across and the Pontoons ought to be done in a couple hours   I expect to be on the High land back of Vicksburg by night. One of Tuttles Brigades is broke down by the march will be left at this Bridge   You may count on my being across in 3 hours. Shall I push into the City or secure a point on the Ridge"   ALS, DNA, RG 94, War Records Office, Dept. of the Tenn. *O.R.*, I, xxiv, part 3, 322.

To Maj. Gen. William T. Sherman

Head Quarters, Dept. of the Ten.

Black River, May 17th 1863,

MAJ. GEN. W. T. SHERMAN,

COMD.G 15TH ARMY CORPS,

GEN.

Our bridges here will not be ready to cross before daylight in the morning. Secure a commanding position on the West bank of Black river as soon as you can. If the information you gain after crossing warrants you in believing that you can go immediately into the city do so. If there is any doubt in this matter throw out troops to the left after advancing on to a line with the rail-road bridge to open communications with the troops here. We will then move in three columns, if roads can be found to move on, and either have Vicksburg or Hains Bluff tomorrow night.

The enemy have been so terribly beaten yesterday and today that I cannot believe that a stand will be made unless the troops are relying on Johnstone arriving with large reinforcements; nor that Johnstone would attempt to reinforce with anything at his command if he was atal informed of the present condition of things.

Yours,
U. S. GRANT
Maj. Gen. Com

ALS, Ritzman Collection, Aurora College, Aurora, Ill. *O.R.*, I, xxiv, part 3, 321–22. Also on May 17, 1863, USG wrote to Maj. Gen. William T. Sherman. "I have directed Col. Johnson who is ~~ackn~~ acting on my staff to collect as much Cavalry as possible and go towards Brownsville; to ascertain if he can the position and intentions of Jo Johnson. Please direct the Cavalry with you to go subject to the Colonels orders. If you have any information of the whereabouts of Jo. please inform The Colonel" Copies, DLC-USG, V, 19, 30, 98; DNA, RG 393, Dept. of the Tenn., Letters Sent.

To Brig. Gen. George F. McGinnis

Head Quarters Dept of the Tenn
Black River, Miss. May 17./63

BRIG GENL. MCGINNIS
COMMDG. RESERVE
GENERAL:

When Surgeon Mills Medical Director reports that all wounded are collected and cared for, bring your command forward to Edwards Station. All prisoners except such as the Medical Director may require as attendants for the rebel wounded will be brought along with you.

Parole all prisoners left behind & let the parole state, That they were wounded or nurses to ~~of~~ wounded prisoners.

Call on Surgeon Mills to inform you when he will be ready
to release your command.

Very respectfully

U. S. GRANT

Maj General.

Copies, DLC-USG, V, 19, 30, 98; DNA, RG 393, Dept. of the Tenn., Letters
Sent; Alcorn Collection, WyU. On May 17, 1863, Col. Clark B. Lagow wrote
to Brig. Gen. George F. McGinnis. "I am directed by Maj. Genl Grant Commanding, to say That in moving your command forward, you will see that all
arms, guns, and ordnance, are brought forward. You will call on the Quartermaster
to furnish you with such teams as you may need. They will be empty by issue of
provisions" Copies, DLC-USG, V, 98. Altered and entered as written by USG
ibid., V, 19, 30; DNA, RG 393, Dept. of the Tenn., Letters Sent.
    On May 18, McGinnis, "Champion Hills," wrote to Lt. Col. John A. Rawlins.
"It will be impossible for me to move forward my command today, Dr. Mills
informs me he cannot be ready until at least tomorrow. We have about 5 or 6
hundred rebel wounded (most of them badly) to parole and have to copy each one
with a pen as we have no printed blanks—We are collecting Arms & accoutrements as rapidly as possible and have now on hand at least 8 or 10 wagon loads
and will probably have as many more today, we have also 7 pieces of Artillery
with a number of caissons and have no animals or harness to haul them forward
—We succeeded in getting but one days rations for our men and about enough
for one meal for the prisoners last night and no prospect of getting more today—
will you please instruct me what to do and how I am to get the Artillery forward"
LS, *ibid.*, Letters Received. On the same day, USG wrote to the officer commanding provost guard, Edwards Station, Miss. "As soon as you learn that all troops
and trains have passed the bridge, you will march your command with all prisoners
in your charge, on the Vicksburg road as far as Mt Albans and there await further
orders." Copies, DLC-USG, V, 19, 30, 98; DNA, RG 393, Dept. of the Tenn.,
Letters Sent; Alcorn Collection, WyU.

To Lt. Col. Grantham I. Taggart

Head Quarters Dept of the Tenn

Black River Bridge Miss May 17, 1863

COL. TAGGART:

CHF C. S. 13TH ARMY CORPS

COLONEL:

Detach two teams loaded with provisions to go back to Jackson for our wounded. Major Bush[1] goes in charge. Also detach

twenty teams loaded with provisions for Shermans Corps. These latter will be sent immediately to Bridgeport.

They need not be sent under any escort, but go on the same road taken by Blairs Division this Morning.

U. S. GRANT
Maj. Gen.

Copies, DLC-USG, V, 19, 30, 98; DNA, RG 393, Dept. of the Tenn., Letters Sent. On Feb. 26, 1863, Maj. Gen. John A. McClernand wrote to USG. "Capt Grantham I. Taggart, now acting Chief Com'y of this Corps, whose promotion to Lt. Col. and assignment to this Corps, I asked sometime since, is today notified that he is so promoted and assigned to the 16th Army Corps. His services here are at present, are almost indispensible. I have written again requesting his assignment to this Corp, and ask that you will order him to remain on duty with it, until further advised from Washington." ADfS, McClernand Papers, IHi; copies, *ibid.*; DNA, RG 393, 13th Army Corps, Letters Sent.

On May 17, USG wrote to Surgeon Henry S. Hewit. "I send Major Bush to Jackson under Flag with provisions for our wounded. You will have to try and procure such articles as are necessary and cannot be sent from here, giving Vouchers which I see paid on presentation. We have had a hard fight with the Enemy yesterday at Bakers Creek and today at the Bridge. Major Bush who goes with this can give you particulars." Copies, DLC-USG, V, 19, 30, 98; DNA, RG 393, Dept. of the Tenn., Letters Sent.

1. Maj. Daniel B. Bush, Jr., 2nd Ill. Cav. See *Calendar*, Aug. 30, 1862.

To Maj. Gen. John A. McClernand

Head Quarters Dept of the Tenn
Black River May 18, 1863

MAJ GEN JNO A MCCLERNAND
COMDG 13TH ARMY CORPS
GENERAL:

Move your Corps as early as possible, taking the direct road as far as Mount Albans.

From that point reconnoitrer well as you advance. If a parralel road can be found within three miles of the direact Road—take it.

No teams will be allowed to cross the river until all the troops are over; except Ambulances and ammunition wagons. One

Brigade will be left to guard the Bridge and trains, and to bring the latter over after the troops have all passed.

Very respectfully
U. S GRANT
Maj. Gen.

Copies, DLC–USG, V, 19, 30, 98; DNA, RG 393, Dept. of the Tenn., Letters Sent; *ibid.*, 13th Army Corps, Letters Received; Alcorn Collection, WyU. *O.R.*, I, xxiv, part 3, 324. On May 18, 1863, 7:00 A.M., Maj. Gen. John A. McClernand, "Big Black river," wrote to USG. "Your dispatches recd. and I have the honor to in[form you] that its contents ~~were anticipate~~ as to [the order] of moving my forces and trains were anticipated by a corresponding order communicated to division commanders last night. I will commence crossing over the river within twenty minutes. You say take a parallel road if I find one. I suppose you mean to divide my forces on two roads if I can. If I am mistaken please correct me. Can you inform me the distance from the bridge to ~~St Alb~~ St Albans?" Copies, McClernand Papers, IHi; DNA, RG 393, 13th Army Corps, Letters Sent. *O.R.*, I, xxiv, part 3, 324.

On May 18, USG again wrote to McClernand. "Gen. Gorman having been relieved from duty at Helena and Gen. Ross having tendered his resignation you will designate a Gen. Officer from your command immediately to report to Gen. Prentiss to take the place of these officers." ALS, McClernand Papers, IHi. For the resignation of Brig. Gen. Leonard F. Ross, see letter to Maj. Gen. Stephen A. Hurlbut, Aug. 5, 1863.

To Maj. Gen. James B. McPherson

Hd Qrs Dept of the Tenn
Black River. Miss. May 18. 1863

MAJ. GEN. J. B. MCPHERSON
COMDG 17TH ARMY CORPS
GENERAL:

Start your column at the Earliest practicable moment

Their road—you being in the centre will be the direct Vicksburg Road.

No teams will be allowed to pass over the road until all the troops and Artillery have passed except Ammunition Wagons and Ambulances. One Brigade will be left to guard the Bridge and wagon trains and to pass the latter over as soon as all the troops are out of the way.

> Very respectfully
> U. S. G RANT
> Maj Gen.

Copies, DLC-USG, V, 19, 30, 98; DNA, RG 393, Dept. of the Tenn., Letters Sent; Alcorn Collection, WyU. *O.R.*, I, xxiv, part 3, 324. On May 18, 1863, USG again wrote to Maj. Gen. James B. McPherson. "Dispatches received. Sherman is now getin into position. You will follow the main V.Burg road and take position mostly to the left of the road." ALS, NjR.

Special Field Orders No. 134

> Head Quarters Dept of the Tenn
> Near Vicksburg, Miss. May 19th 1863
> 11.16 A. M.

S PECIAL F IELD O RDERS N O [*134*]

Corps commanders will push forward carefully, and gain as close positions as possible to the enemy's works untill 2 o'clock P. M. At that hour they will fire three volleys of artillery from all the peices in position. This will be the signal for a general charge of all the corps along the whole line.

When the works are carried, guards will be placed by all Division commanders to prevent their men from straggling from their companies

> By order of Maj Genl U. S. Grant
> J NO A R AWLINS
> Asst Adjt Genl.

DS, Rawlins Papers, ICHi; copies, Alcorn Collection, WyU; (designated Special Orders No. 134) DLC-USG, V, 27, 28; DNA, RG 393, Dept. of the Tenn., Special Orders. *O.R.*, I, xxiv, part 3, 329.

On May 19, 1863, Lt. Col. John A. Rawlins wrote to Maj. Theodore S. Bowers, Young's Point. "All troops of General Laumans Division at Youngs Point or that may arrive there you will please order to the Chickasaw Bayou Landing, from which place the Commanding Officer will report to the General commanding in person, in the rear of Vicksburg for orders. No more troops will go to Grand Gulf and all troops at Grand Gulf except the Garrison which consists of one Brigade of Infantry and one Battery of Artillery, of General Laumans Division ~~will be~~ you will ~~ordered~~ back to Chickasaw Bayou. require prompt compliance with this order" Copies, DLC-USG, V, 19, 30, 98; DNA, RG 393, Dept. of the Tenn., Letters Sent; Alcorn Collection, WyU. On the same day, Bowers wrote three letters to Brig. Gen. Jacob G. Lauman, the second at 4:00 P.M., the third at 8:00 P.M. "Col. Pugh's Brigade will proceed without delay from the lower landing to Bowers Landing, below Warrenton, from whence they will go to Grand Gulf by Steamers, and remain at that place as the permanent garrison. Camp and Garrison equippage and baggage of every description will be left at the Convalesent Camp, opposite the lower landing in charge of an officer and small guard. No baggage will be taken that can possibly be dispensed with. Land Transportation will be regulated according to instructions furnished by Col Bingham, Chief Q. M. You will proceed yourself immediately to Grand Gulf, and organize the troops and wagon train at that place, and immediately upon the arrival of Col Pugh's Brigade, you will proceed with Col. Hall's and Col. Johnson's Brigades, and the Brigade of McArther's Division now garrisoning Grand Gulf to Headquarters of the Army in the front, taking with you such supply train as may be got ready at Grand Gulf." "Please return to this place immediately for the purpose of taking the troops now here up Yazoo River. Gen Grant is investing Vicksburg and directs that all troops and Gun boats come to his assistance immediately up Yazoo. The troops here are being got ready. Come at once. I have ordered all troops at ~~Grand~~ Bowers Landing to return here by forced march. Please send the same orders" "You will proceed with all of your Command, now at this place on Steamers to be assigned you by Liut Col Bingham Chief Quartermaster, to Chickasaw Bluffs, and there debark, and proceed to the Army in the field. After debarking you will make a reconisance to ascertain the position of the enemy, if in the vicinity, and open Communication with Gen Steele, who is supposed to occupy the left of our line, and report the result of ~~your~~ Same to Col Bingham, Chief Q. M. at the Landing. The main body of your Command will be held in readiness to escort the supply train which will be in readiness to go forward with you. Take with you all your wagons, and load them with supplies at the point of debarkation. No baggage will be taken, of any kind. You will vary the details of this order, as in your judgement, circumstances may require" ALS, DNA, RG 94, War Records Office, 16th Army Corps. The last two are in *O.R.*, I, xxiv, part 3, 327.

On May 20, USG wrote to Bowers. "Send McArthur to Warrenton and Lauman to Haines Bluff." Copies, DLC-USG, V, 19, 30, 98; DNA, RG 393, Dept. of the Tenn., Letters Sent. On the same day, USG wrote to Lauman. "Remain at Haines Bluff. Keep Scouts far out to the north and east to report any movement of the Enemy." Copies, *ibid.* Also on May 20, USG wrote to Maj. Gen. John A. McClernand. "Lauman is at Haines Bluff McArthur is about crossing to Warrenton Mortar Boats will soon be playing on the city." Signal received, ICarbS; copies, DLC-USG, V, 19, 30, 98; DNA, RG 393, Dept. of the Tenn., Letters Sent; *ibid.*, 13th Army Corps, Letters Received. On the same day, USG wrote to Act. Rear Admiral David D. Porter. "A Gunboat playing on the second water battery would materially help us. ~~The up~~ The first water battery is in our possession." ALS, MoSHi.

Also on May 20, McClernand wrote frequently to USG. "I have the honor to communicate the following, viz: In my front I have met a formidable line of earthworks, chiefly square redoubts or lunettes, connected together by a line of rifle pits, and the whole line in a very commanding position. Moreover, I am informed from various sources, that they have two lines of defense in the rear of the one I am now attacking. I do not think the position can be carried with our present extended lines. In my opinion, a change of the plan of attack, and the concentration of our forces on some particular point or points, would give better assurance of success. Otherwise, perhaps, a seige, becomes the only alternative—" ALS, *ibid.*, Dept. of the Tenn., Letters Received. *O.R.*, I, xxiv, part 3, 332. "I have suffered considerable loss but am pressing for a sharp engagement up to the enemys works. I hear nothing on the right or centre." "General Smith is within some hundred yards of the works. He says McPherson should advance on his right" Copies, DNA, RG 393, 13th Army Corps, Letters Sent. *O.R.*, I, xxiv, part 3, 332. Also on May 20, USG wrote to McClernand. "McPherson is within fifty yards of the main fort and can see Genl. Smith's men." Copy, DNA, RG 393, 13th Army Corps, Letters Received. On the same day, USG wrote to Maj. Gen. James B. McPherson. "If you intend assaulting the fort in front of your position send word to Sherman as long before the hours as possible. He will engage the enemy on the right so as to keep them from concentrating on you." ALS, NjR.

To Act. Rear Admiral David D. Porter

Rear of Vicksburg, Miss.
May 19th 1863.

DEAR ADMIRAL,

My forces are now investing Vicksburg. Sherman's forces run from the Miss. river above the city two miles East. McPherson is to his left and McClernand to the left of McPherson. If you can run down and throw shell in just back of the lower part of the City it would aid us and demoralize an already badly beaten enemy. The enemy have not been able to return to the City with one half of his forces. We beat them badly on the 16th near Edwards station and on the 17th at Black river bridge taking about 6000 prisoners besides a large number killed and wounded. Two Divisions were also cut off from their retreat and have gone Eastward many of their men throwing down their Ar[ms] and leaving. The enemy only succeeded [in] getting back three pieces of Artillery.

I have instructed my Qr. Mr. [and] Com.y to send up boats

to Lakes Landing with fora[ge and] provisions. Will you please
se[nd a convoy.]

> Your[s]
> U. [S. GRANT]
> M[aj. Gen.]

Please send a boat up to Hain's Bluff. I think it is evacuated.
Our cavalry have gone up to s[ee.]

> U. S. G[.]

ALS (torn), MoSHi. *O.R.*, I, xxiv, part 3, 326–27; *O.R.* (Navy), I, xxv, 15–16.
On May 20, 1863, Act. Rear Admiral David D. Porter, "Hayne's Bluff," wrote
to USG. "I received your letter about 4. P. M. yesterday, and hurried up provisions & troops to you as soon as possible. Gen'l Lauman's Division is here. Gen'l
Sullivan is here with stores. I congratulate you with all my heart, on your splendid
success. I suppose with Hayne's Bluff in our possession, and Warrenton, the city
must fall in a day or two. Gen'l McArthur ~~to~~ is going to pass over his troops at
Warrenton. I have ordered the gun boats to ferry them over. The mortars will
be in position to day and will commence early. As soon as I saw your artillery on
the hills yesterday, I pushed the gun boats up the Yazoo. The 'De Kalb' took possession of the forts, the enemy ran, and left every thing behind them—a few who
did not mind being taken prisoners, staid and delivered up every thing, even the
powder. I start the boats up the Yazoo as soon as I can clear away the raft. Best
wishes to Genl's sherman & steele. I rec'd both of their letters, and did all I could
to expedite matters. Your provisions should have gone last night." ALS, DNA,
RG 393, Dept. of the Tenn., Letters Received.

On May 19, USG wrote to Maj. Gen. James B. McPherson. "Sherman has
possession of several of the enemy's batteries. His right is now on the Miss. river.
I have sent to Malfuley [*Macfeely*] to bring up a load of supplies to Lake's Landing . . ." Anderson Galleries Sale No. 2146, March 16, 1927, p. 6. On the same
day, USG wrote to Lt. Col. Judson D. Bingham. "Send a boat with forage to
Mouth of Chickasaw bayou Lakes landing as soon as possible. Tell McFeeley to
send Comy stores also. I want you and Macfeeley to come along and take charge
of your departments in the field. I will ask Admiral Porter to send a convoy."
ALS (typescript), John M. Taylor, Washington, D. C.

To Maj. Gen. John A. McClernand

May 19th 1863

GEN.

Shermans right is now on the Miss river at the upper end of
the city some of the enemys batteries being in our possession. I

have sent for forage and supplies to be sent to Lake's Landing at the mouth of Chickasaw bayou Sherman's Qr. Mr. has been directed to empty teams and take them down after provisions for the army at once. Send some Qr. Mr here to take charge of wagons for your command.

> Yours.
> U. S. GRANT
> Maj Gen.

To MAJ. GEN. McCLERNAND

ALS, McClernand Papers, IHi. On May 19, 1863, Maj. Gen. John A. McClernand wrote to USG. "I am My Skirmishers are near the enemy's works, and my lines (not yet completed) advancing. I have opened artillery on the to enemy's works. Your dispatch by Col. Lagow is recd." ADfS, *ibid.*; copy, DNA, RG 393, 13th Army Corps, Letters Sent. *O.R.*, I, xxiv, part 3, 327. In addition, on the same day, McClernand wrote to USG reporting the positions of his troops and his instructions to div. commanders. DLC-USG, V, 22; DNA, RG 393, Dept. of the Tenn., Register of Letters Received.

Also on May 19, Lt. Col. John A. Rawlins wrote to Brig. Gen. Alvin P. Hovey. "You will move your Division to the west side of the Big Black River and there take up your position so as to best guard the two lower Bridges. The upper or Cotton Bale Bridge you will effectually distroy. All other troops with the prisoners of war and public property you will send immedeately forward. Let there be no delay in the execution of this order as it is of the highest importance that the crossings on the Big Black be properly defended and that the prisoners and public property be got over to Youngs Point La. with which place we now have full communication Rations will be sent you at once from here." Copies, DLC-USG, V, 98; DNA, RG 393, 13th Army Corps, Letters Received.

On May 20, McClernand wrote to USG. "I have the honor to report that General Hovey, with his Division is now about two miles from here. The General himself is here. My order to him was written in ignorance of your order to him to remain at Big Black, but reaching him after your order reached him, he understood it to be a revocation, by your authority, of your previous order. Taking it for granted, that he would be controlled by the order directly emanating from you, I did not deem it necessary to write to him in explanation. Even if I had done so, it would not have availed to stop him, as he had come some distance in this direction, before I received notice of your order. I think, however, from the General's representation, that no hostile movement threatens our rear. He knew of none, besides, he left two companies behind at the railroad bridge. Cannot his Division, or a part of it, be permitted to take part in the assault tomorrow? He awaits your order, an officer being sent back to halt his command until you are heard from. Any communication you may be pleased to send, will be forwarded to him. General Hovey suggests that only one bridge should be preserved at Big Black, and that, the one nearest to the Railroad bridge. I am close up to the enemy's works all along my line—have lost in killed and wounded, a number of men today, but have silenced most all of his guns in my front. I propose to assault the enemy's works in the morning, and have made arrangements with that view.

... P. S. Please answer immediately as Genl Hovey is waiting to be advisd"
LS, *ibid.*, RG 94, War Records Office, Dept. of the Tenn. *O.R.*, I, xxiv, part 3,
331–32. On the same day, 11:50 P.M., Rawlins wrote to McClernand. "Your
communication of to day in regard to Genl Hovey is received   send back one
Brigade of his Divisions to Big Black Bridge and allow the others to advance   let
all of the Bridges be effectualy destroyed except the one at smith Ferry nearest
the Railroad   this one will be preserved and defended   Col Wright with his
Cavalry will report to the officer in command of the rear Brigade at the Big Black
bridge   Genl Hoveys Commissary has been directed to load his wagons with
Subsistence Stores"   Copies, DLC-USG, V, 19, 30; DNA, RG 393, Dept. of the
Tenn., Letters Sent; *ibid.*, 13th Army Corps, Letters Received; Alcorn Collection, WyU.

Also on May 20, Rawlins wrote to Hovey. "Col. Wright of the 6th Missouri
Cavalry has been ordered to report to you at once. You will have reconnoisances
made of the several approaches to the Big Black Crossing especially of those at
and nearest the Railroad Bridge. The two lower Bridges you will not distroy
unless it becomes necessary for the defence of your position. The upper one distroy as per instructions of last evening." Copies, DLC-USG, V, 19, 30, 98; DNA,
RG 393, Dept. of the Tenn., Letters Sent. On the same day, Hovey wrote to
USG. "Since receiving your order to defend the bridges, (which arrived this
morng), I have just this instant (4 o,clock P M) receved an order from Gen
McClernand to hasten my Division to the front. *I am bound to presume that this
is in accordance with your Orders* and I shall be with Gen McClernand before midnight. This leaves the bridges entirely unguarded. Col Wright of the Cavalry
ordered by you to report to me has up to this time failed to do so. Before receivng
your order I sent my Cavalry Escort out to make a reconnoissance down Big
Black but they have not yet returned"   ALS, *ibid.*, RG 94, War Records Office,
Dept. of the Tenn. *O.R.*, I, xxiv, part 3, 331.

On May 21, McClernand wrote to USG. "I have the honor to inform you
that General Hovey has destroyed the upper bridge over Big Black, and an officer
has been sent to the cars to destroy the enemy's ammunition at Edwards Depot.
Major [Henry P.] Hawkins has just reported that there is no rebel force in the
rear, except one brigade in the neighborhood of Raymond. That force is so demoralized that many threw away their arms, swearing they would fight no more. The
last seen of them they were 12 or 14 miles east of Big Black, on their way to
Jackson. One hundred and sixty-nine head of beef-cattle have been collected and
left at the hospital for the wounded, but they were short of other parts of rations."
Ibid., p. 336.

To Brig. Gen. George F. McGinnis

Head Quarters Dept of the Tenn.
Near Vicksburg May 19: 1863

GENL. MCGINNIS.

Send all the prisoners in your command immediately forward.
We have possession of the Miss. above Vicksburg and can send

them to Youngs Point if we are not in possession of the city when they arrive. Send with the prisoners an escort of ~~an Escort~~ at least one Regiment who will not return to you.

Yours,

U. S. GRANT.

Maj. General.

Copies, DLC-USG, V, 19, 30, 98; DNA, RG 393, Dept. of the Tenn., Letters Sent. On May 19, 1863, USG wrote to the "Officer in Charge of prisoners Edwards Station Miss." "Come immediately forward with all the prisoners in your charge. Bring all prisoners between Edwards Station and Vicksburg with you" Copies, *ibid.*

On May 24, Lt. Col. John A. Rawlins issued Special Orders No. 139. "Colonel Clark B. Lagow, A. D. C., U. S. A. will immediately proceed to Memphis, Tenn., with the prisoners of War, captured in recent battles and now at or in the vicinity of Young's Point, La.,   He will deliver one certified list or roll of said prisoners to Island, No., 10, and furnish strong guards for them, until he can communicate with the General-in Chief of the Army as to the disposition to be made of them. One Roll or list of said prisoners will be retained by Maj. Bowers Judge Advocate. The Troops now guarding the prisoners will accompany them to guards to Memphis from where they will immediately return to this place. The prisoners will not be debarked at Memphis but sent immediately on to Island No. 10. Lieut. Colonel J. D. Bingham, A. Q. M. will furnish the necessary transportation. Col. Lagow will request Admiral D. D. Porter, to furnish a Gunboat escort the transports conveying prisoners" Copies, DLC-USG, V, 27, 28; DNA, RG 393, Dept. of the Tenn., Special Orders. *O.R.*, II, v, 695–96. On the same day, Maj. Theodore S. Bowers, Young's Point, issued Special Orders No. 130. "Lieut. Colonel Graham 22nd Iowa Infty. Vols. (Paroled) is appointed to take charge of paroled prisoners at this place and will report to Lieut Col. L. Kent, Provost Marshal for instructions." Copies, DLC-USG, V, 27, 28; DNA, RG 393, Dept. of the Tenn., Special Orders. *O.R.*, II, v, 695. See telegram to Maj. Gen. Henry W. Halleck, May 22, 1863.

To Commanding Officer, Confederate Forces

Head Quarters Dept of the Tenn.

Near Vicksburg Miss May 21, 1863

COMMANDING OFFICER

CONFEDERATE FORCES, JACKSON RAYMOND EDWARDS
    STATION AND INTERMEDIATE PLACES.

SIRS:

Capt Durbin[1] Asst Qr. Mr. U. S. Army goes with supplies

for wounded men of the two armies who from the nature of their wounds would not bear removal after the late engagements near the places named.

As soon as practicable, I will be pleased to get all the wounded men within our lines where they can receive care and attention, without being a tax upon the communities where they are. If the places named have been garrisoned so as to make it improper for me to send Flags of Truce with provision trains, I will be pleased to know it and will conform with any plan for the relief of such wounded as were necessarily left near the Battle feild as may be agreed upon.

My only desire is to know that there is no unnecessary suffering among the unfortunate wounded.

This I will feel satisfied of the moment I know they are in the hands of a Military Commander or that I am free to look after them.

> Very respectfully
> Your obdt Servant
> U. S. GRANT
> Maj General.

Copies, DLC-USG, V, 19, 30, 98; DNA, RG 393, Dept. of the Tenn., Letters Sent. *O.R.*, II, v, 685–86. See letter to Commanding Officer, Edwards Station, Miss., June 4, 1863.

On May 21, 1863, Lt. Col. John A. Rawlins wrote to Lt. Col. Judson D. Bingham. "Will furnish transportation for 30.000 rations, and such Sanitary Stores as the Medical Director may designate to Champion Hill, Raymond and Jackson Miss for our sick and wounded and the Rebel wounded prisoners, at those places. 18.000 of said rations will be left at Champion Hills Hospital, 6000 at Raymond and 6.000 at Jackson. Said Transportation and rations will be placed in charge of a Competent A. Q. M. to be designated by him. He will also send an Ambulance and team to report to Dr. H. S. Hewitt at Jackson." Copies, DLC-USG, V, 19, 30, 98; DNA, RG 393, Dept. of the Tenn., Letters Sent. On the same day, Rawlins wrote to Lt. Col. Robert Macfeely. "Will issue 30.000 complete rations with the exception of meat of which he will issue half rations, substituting for the remainder of the meat ration, Desicated Vegetables &c. if he has them, for our wounded at Champion Hills, Raymond and Jackson Miss. and the rebel wounded prisoners. The cheif Quartermaster has been directed to furnish Transportation and designate an officer to take charge of them." Copies, *ibid.*

On May 26, C.S.A. Maj. Gen. William W. Loring wrote to USG. "I have the honor to acknowledge the receipt of your communication under of 21st inst. I am directed by the General commanding the Army of Mississippi to assure you that the sick and wounded Federal officers and soldiers who have fallen, or who by the casualties of war may hereafter fall into our hands, will receive all the attention we can bestow. There can be no possible objection to the military authorities of the United States bringing or sending supplies and medicines for their sick and wounded in our possession *to outposts* where military operations have recently taken place. I avail myself of this opportunity to state that the friends and relatives of Major J. W. Anderson, the Chief of Artillery of Gen. Stevenson's Division, who was wounded in the recent engagement at Baker's Creek, would be grateful for any information respecting him—whether wounded, & if a prisoner in your hands." ALS, *ibid.*, RG 94, War Records Office, Dept. of the Tenn. *O.R.*, II, v, 709. On May 27, Brig. Gen. Peter J. Osterhaus wrote to USG. "I have the honor to send you by Captain J Carnahan of my staff a despatch just received under flag of truce from Major General Loring Rebel army. The rebel officer bearing the despatch is outside of my pickets, awaiting there your reply; In not permitting him to pass my lines, I hope to meet the approval of the General . . ." ALS, DNA, RG 393, Dept. of the Tenn., Letters Received. On the same day, Rawlins wrote to Osterhaus. "Your communication of this date, enclosing dispatch by 'flag of Truce from Maj Genl Loring of the Confederate Army is received   Your action in requiring the Confederate Officer, bearing the dispatch to remain outside of our lines is approved; You will please acknowledge the receipt of it, and say that the Major General Commanding the Army of the Tennessee knows nothing of Maj J. W. Anderson, about whom enquiry is made, that steps will be immediately taken to ascertain if he is in our lines a prisoner, and his condition. If any information should be obtained relative to him it will be communicated to his friends, add anything else in answer you may deem proper, a Copy of the Dispatch of General Loring to be answered is herewith enclosed" LS, *ibid.*, 13th Army Corps, 9th Div., Letters Received; copies (dated May 28), DLC-USG, V, 19, 30; DNA, RG 393, Dept. of the Tenn., Letters Sent. Dated May 27 in *O.R.*, II, v, 714.

On May 28, Lt. Col. Walter B. Scates, adjt. for Maj. Gen. John A. McClernand, telegraphed to Rawlins. "Dispatch Just recd from Gen Osterhaus reports that Capt Durbin met Genls Loring & Morgan near Jackson & Estimates forces with them at Seven thousand 7000   does not know what direction they were moving   rebel messenger with answer to Gen Grants despatch was stopped at Genl O's Pickets with option to enter or Stay outside the picket line until Genl Grants answer was returned or to returned & leave answer to be Sent under a flag" Telegram received, DNA, RG 94, War Records Office, Dept. of the Tenn. See *O.R.*, I, xxiv, part 2, 211.

1. Greene Durbin appointed 1st lt., 13th Ind., as of Dec. 7, 1861, then capt., asst. q. m., as of June 30, 1862.

General Field Orders

[*May 21, 1863*]

GEN FIELD ORDER

A simultaneous attack will be made to-morrow, at 10 o'clock

a m by all the Army Corps of this Army. During to-day Army Corps Commanders will have examined all practicable routes over which troops can possibly pass. They will get in position all the Artillery possible and gain all the ground they can with their Infantry and skirmishers. At an early hour in the morning a vigerous attack will be commenced by the Artillery & skirmishers. The Infantry with the exception of reserves & skirmishers, will be placed in Column of plattoons, or by a flank if the ground over which they may have to pass will not admit of a greater front, ready to move forward at the hour designated. Promptly at the hour designated all will start at quick time, with bayonetts fixed, and march immediately upon the enemy, without firing a gun until the outer works are carried.

The troops will go light carrying with them only their Ammunition, Canteens and one days rations.

The skirmishers will advance as soon as possible after Heads of Columns pass them and scale the walls of such works as may confront them.

If prossecuted with viger it is confidantly believed this course will carry Vicksburg in a very short time and with very much less loss than would be sustained by delay. Every days delay enables the enemy to strengthen his defences and increases his chances for receiving aid from outside.

ADf (by USG), CSmH; DS (by Lt. Col. John A. Rawlins), Rawlins Papers, ICHi. *O.R.*, I, xxiv, part 1, 171; *ibid.*, I, xxiv, part 3, 333–34.

To *Act. Rear Admiral David D. Porter*

———

Near Vicksburg, May 21st/63

Dear Admiral,

I expect to assault the City at 10 a m to-morrow. I would request, and urgently request it, that you send up the Gunboats below the City and shell the rebel intrenchments until that hour and for thirty minuets after.

If the Mortars could all be sent down to near the point on the
Louisiana shore and throw in shells during the night it would
materially aid me. I would like at least to have the enemy kept
annoyed during the night.

Yours Truly

U. S. GRANT

Maj. Gen

To ADM.L D. D. PORTER
COMD.G MISS. SQUADRON

ALS, MoSHi. *O.R.*, I, xxiv, part 3, 333; *O.R.* (Navy), I, xxv, 21.

To Maj. Gen. William T. Sherman

Head Quarters, Dept. of the Ten.

Near Vicksburg, May 21st 1863

MAJ. GEN. W. T. SHERMAN,
COMD.G 15TH ARMY CORPS,
GEN.

The advance pickets near the Jackson road in front of Mc-
Pherson's Corps report massing of troops since dark in their
front and that the rebels are coming outside of their works. This
would indicate a night attack. Notify your command and be prepared, if any unusual commotion should be heard towards the
Center, to take advantage of it and go into the rebel works and
fall upon the enemys flak and rear. A night attack would certainly indicate, I think, a disposition to cut out.

Yours &c

U. S. GRANT

Maj. Gen.

P. S. Make a feint of a night attack at 1 a. m. by firing a few
rounds of artillery. McPherson & McClernand are notified that
you will do so.

U. S. G.

ALS, ICHi.

On May 21, 1863, 11:00 P.M., USG wrote to Maj. Gen. John A. McClernand. "Skirmishers in front of McPhersons line report evidences of an attempt to make a night attack on them. Every preparation is made to receive it if made. Notify your command to be specially watchful, and if any commotion is heard towards the centre, be prepared to push immediately into the city and fall upon the rear of the enemy" Copy, DNA, RG 393, 13th Army Corps, Letters Received.

To Brig. Gen. John McArthur

Head Quarters Dept. of the Tenn.
Near Vicksburg Miss May 21. 1863

BRIG. GENL. MCARTHUR
GENERAL:

Enclosed you will find orders for the three Army Corps here. Your command being Detached will necessarily have to act indipendently. I want you to move with your entire force on the Vicksburg road towards the city. Move cautiously and be prepared to receive an attack at any moment. Penetrate as far into the city as you can. Should you find the city still in possession of the enemy, hold as advanced a position as you can secure yourself upon.

Very respectfully
U. S. GRANT
Maj. Gen.

Copies, DLC-USG, V, 19, 30, 98; DNA, RG 393, Dept. of the Tenn., Letters Sent; Alcorn Collection, WyU. *O.R.*, I, xxiv, part 3, 334.

On May 21, 1863, Lt. Col. John A. Rawlins wrote to Maj. Gen. John A. McClernand. "McArthurs Division has been ordered to Warrenton. You will establish communication at the earliest possible moment and when established draw your supplies from Warrenton In the meantime you will obtain these from 'Chickasaw Bayou.' " Copies, DLC-USG, V, 19, 30, 98; DNA, RG 393, Dept. of the Tenn., Letters Sent; Alcorn Collection, WyU. On the same day, 8:00 A.M., USG signaled to McClernand. "McArthur has not yet Reached Warrenten Will Be there this Eavning Come to My Hd Qrs on Receipt of this" Signal received, ICarbS.

To Maj. Gen. Henry W. Halleck

Near Vicksburg May 22d 1863

Maj. Gen. Halleck, Washington,

Vicksburg is now completely invested. I have possession of Hains Bluff & the Yazoo consequently have supplies. Today an attempt was made to carry the City by assault but was not entirely sucsessful. We hold possession however of some of the enemy's forts and have skirmishers close under all of them. Our loss was not severe.[1] The nature of the ground about Vicksburg is such that it can only be taken by a siege. It is entirely safe to us in time, I would say within one week, if the enemy do not send a large Army upon my rear. With the railroad destroyed to beyond Pearl river I do not see the hope the enemy can entertain of such relief. I hear that Davis has promised if the garrison can hold out for fifteen days he will send 100 000 men if he has to evacuate Tennessee to do it. What shall I do with the prisoners I have.[2]

U. S. Grant
Maj. Gen.

ALS (telegram sent), CSmH; telegram received, DNA, RG 107, Telegrams Collected (Bound). *O.R.*, I, xxiv, part 1, 37. This message was telegraphed to Washington by Maj. Gen. Stephen A. Hurlbut, Memphis, at 10:30 P.M., May 25, 1863. See *ibid.*, I, xxiii, part 2, 365.

1. U.S. losses in the May 22 assault on Vicksburg were 502 killed, 2550 wounded, 147 missing. *Ibid.*, I, xxiv, part 2, 160–65.
2. On May 25, Maj. Gen. Henry W. Halleck telegraphed to Hurlbut a message intended for USG. "No confederate officers will be paroled or exchanged till further orders. They will be kept in close confinement & be strongly guarded. Those already paroled will be confined." ALS (telegram sent), DNA, RG 107, Telegrams Collected (Bound); telegram received, *ibid.*, RG 393, Dept. of the Tenn., Telegrams Received. *O.R.*, II, v, 696. The same message went to other commanders. On May 26, Halleck telegraphed to Hurlbut. "Tell Genl Grant to send captured officers to Sanduskey & soldiers up the river for Camp Douglas or Fort Delaware; I will tell you which place to-morrow. Officers and men should be immediately separated." ALS (telegram sent), DNA, RG 107, Telegrams Collected (Bound); telegram received, *ibid.*, Telegrams Collected (Unbound); *ibid.*, RG 393, Dept. of the Tenn., Telegrams Received. *O.R.*, II, v, 706. On May 27, Hurlbut wrote to USG. "I have the honor to forward you the enclosed dispatch received 4 p. m. this date   Every thing is quiet here. We wait anxiously

but hopefully for news from you." Copy, DNA, RG 393, 16th Army Corps, Letters Sent. On May 29, Hurlbut wrote to Lt. Col. John A. Rawlins. "I have the honor to report that Col. C. B. Lagow A. D. C reported to me early this morning with 4408 prisoners. Pursuant to your orders the Guard was relieved about 12. M to day and Col. Lagow was verbally directed by me to send his Guard down at once. Col. Lagow does not appear to have paid any attention to this duty or to have taken any care of the officers and men under his charge nor even to have known how many men constituted the Guard. He informed me that they were about 1000—and were to go below on the Emerald. Although I considered 1000 —a very heavy load for the Emerald still I thought it might be done. Three Boats left here to day the Champion, the Courier and another with state authorities Sanitary Stores &c any of which could have taken 250 men & would have been thus guarded. Col. Lagow leaves for Vicksburgh himself and Col. Mansfield 54th Indiana reports to me for orders having received none. He reports 1400 men. I have ordered all that can go on the Emerald, to go on that Boat—the remainder await transportation at Fort Pickering. Col Mansfield also reports that the Prisoners have suffered for want of Provisions. I send them by order of Genl Halleck officers to Sandusky men—half to Indianapolis and half to Fort Delaware"   ALS, *ibid.*, RG 94, War Records Office, Dept. of the Tenn. *O.R.*, II, v, 718–19.

To Act. Rear Admiral David D. Porter

Head Quarters, Dept. of the Ten.
Near Vicksburg, May 22d/63 8 30 p. m.

ADMIRAL,

Your note dated 2 p. m. is just received.[1] I had sent you a dispatch stating that the assault at 10 a. m. was not sucsessful although not an entire failure. Our troops sucseeded in gaining positions close up to the enemy's batteries which we yet hold, and in one or two instances in getting into them.

I now find the position of the enemy so strong that I shall be compelled to regularly besiege the city. I would request therefore that you give me all the assistance you can with the Mortar & Gunboats.

McArthur has been ordered to join McClernand but I wish to countermand the order if it has not already been executed.

I have no means of communicating with Gen. McArthur at

present except by way of Youngs point. Will you do me the
favor to forward to him the accompanying.

Very Truly Yours

U. S. GRANT

Maj. Gen.

P. S. If the Gunboats could come up and silence the upper water
battery, and clear the Southern slope of the second range of hills
from the Yazoo bottom it would enable Sherman to carry that
position and virtually give us the city. The Mortar boats I think
could be brought with security to within one mile, or less, of the
Bluffs on the Miss. shore from which they could rain shells into
the city. Let me beg that every gunboat & every Mortar boat
be brought to bear upon the city.

U. S. G.

ALS, MdAN. *O.R.*, I, xxiv, part 3, 337–38; *O.R.* (Navy), I, xxv, 31. Earlier on
May 22, 1863, USG signaled to Act. Rear Admiral David D. Porter. "Our troops
now occupy some of the forts; no shells thrown yesterday or last night reached
them. Will you please bombard again to night." Copies, DLC-James M. McClintock; ICarbS.

1. On May 22, 2:00 P.M., and "Evening," Porter, U.S.S. *Tuscumbia*, wrote
to USG. "I attacked the batteries this morning at 8 o'clock with the gun boats,
after they had been playing on them all night. We silenced all the hill batteries,
and then attacked the water batteries at short range,—the enemy's fire slackend
considerably, but not enough to induce me to continue the action, the men being
very much fatigued. Continued the action an hour and a half longer than you
requested, and I wished to keep ammunition enough on hand in case you hove in
sight. In the meantime McArthur's division were seen straggling along the top
of the hills near the deserted batteries—the enemy perceiving they were unaccom-
panied by Artillery, got one or two field pieces in one of the batteries we had
silenced—I immediately got under way with two of the gunboats, and shelled
them out. Could General McArthur have known the state of things he could have
gone into the forts without any trouble, and can do so now. I will write to him
and inform him of the fact. It is an important position, and commands all the
batteries down to the water batteries. There is only one gun an the battery opposite the Marine Hospital. We disabled the big rifle gun above the canal, after a
short action with it, and we now hold the river, within 1800 yards of the batteries,
in front of the Marine Hospital." "I wrote to you today that we had commenced
an attack with all the gunboats on the forts on the hills, which we silenced, and
then proceeded to the water battery in front of the Hospital, in hopes of silencing
that. We found it a hard nut to crack, and fought it two hours, with apparantley
no damage to men, fort, or guns, which is not very strange, considering it stands
back from the river—none of it is above ground, and we never saw a man. The

vessels were a good deal cut up, but fortunately no one was killed. one of the hill batteries, after we had dismounted the gun, went to work to repair damages, and got a field piece in the fort, which we found out, and shelled the people away. Gen'l McArthur's troops which were landed at Warrenton this morning, went straggling along that way, and were fired at by this field piece—it is a pity they did not assault, for they would have taken the place without any trouble, as there were not twenty men in it—it is the most important fort along that range of hills —commands the big rifle gun fort, which we damaged and silenced, and the latter commands the rest of the batteries. I thought it would be well to let you know this, also that all the left of Vicksburg is open for the enemy to go out, or in, as he likes. Today, before Gen'l McArthurs came up, a large number of rebel cavalry went out, and a short time after a company of our Cavalry came in looking for Warrenton, and they never even met each other. McArthur has only 3000 men; if he had 5000, he could block up all that range of hills. If he will assault these forts, with the aid of the gunboats he will take them all. They are poorly manned, still he must have ladders as the ditches are deep. Our men are much used up, but we will bombard all we can. There is no danger of our firing into you, as we know exactly where you are. Most of our shell fall beyond the Court House, and none to the left of the fort which Gen'l Sherman has been working at today." LS, DNA, RG 94, War Records Office, Dept. of the Tenn. *O.R.*, I, xxiv, part 3, 337–38; *O.R.* (Navy), I, xxv, 29–30.

To Maj. Gen. John A. McClernand

————

May 22d 1863
2''30' P. M.

GEN.

I have sent a dispatch to you saying that McArthur left Warrenton last night. Was about half way to the city this morning at 1 a. m. Communicate with him and use his forces to the best advantage.

McPherson is directe to send Quinby's Division to you if ~~they~~ he cannot effect a lodgement where he is. Quinby is next to your right and you will be aided as much by his penetrating into the enemy's lines as by having him to support the Columns you have already got.

Sherman is geting on well.

Yours
U. S. GRANT
Maj. Gen

ALS, McClernand Papers, IHi. *O.R.*, I, xxiv, part 1, 173.

On May 22, 1863, 1:30 A.M., Lt. Col. Walter B. Scates, adjt. for Maj. Gen. John A. McClernand, wrote to Lt. Col. John A. Rawlins. "The Major Genl Commanding directs me to say that he has adopted his lines, taken his positions and is prepared   He had determined also upon a feint upon the left. In case of the feint or attack he will instruct Division Commanders to take & press every opportunity and advantage that offers. He is prepared ~~for~~ to begin a canonade at day-light this ~~thi~~ morning . . . P. S. The Major Genl Commanding further directs me to inform Major Genl Grant that he was very much annoyed on yesterday, by one of the enemy's batteries on his right, which poured a cross-fire upon his lines. He desires that Genl McPherson may concentrate his fire upon this battery as far as possible —early this morning"   ALS, DNA, RG 393, Dept. of the Tenn., Letters Received. *O.R.*, I, xxiv, part 1, 172. On the same day, 11:15 A.M., McClernand signaled to USG. "I am hotly engaged. The enemy are pressing me on the right and left. If McPherson would attack it would make a diversion." Signal received, ICarbS; DNA, RG 94, War Records Office, Military Div. of the Miss.; copies, *ibid.*, RG 393, 13th Army Corps, Letters Sent; McClernand Papers, IHi. *O.R.*, I, xxiv, part 1, 172. At 11:50 A.M., USG signaled to McClernand. "If your advance is weak strengthen it by drawing from your reserves or other parts of the lines" Copies, McClernand Papers, IHi; DNA, RG 393, 13th Army Corps, Letters Received. *O.R.*, I, xxiv, part 1, 172. McClernand then wrote to USG. "We have gained the enemy's entrenchments at several points, but are brought to a stand   I have sent word to McArthur to reinforce me if he can   Would it not be best to concentrate the whole or a part of his Command on this point . . . P. S. ~~Me~~ I have received your despatch—my troops are all engaged, & I cannot withdraw any to re-inforce others"   ALS, DNA, RG 393, Dept. of the Tenn., Letters Received. *O.R.*, I, xxiv, part 1, 56, 172. According to Adam Badeau, *Military History of Ulysses S. Grant* (New York, 1868), I, 324, USG endorsed this letter to Maj. Gen. James B. McPherson, sending Rawlins to deliver it, asking him to send Brig. Gen. Isaac F. Quinby's div. to McClernand. The original letter, however, has no such endorsement although further correspondence shows that the orders were somehow transmitted. At noon, McClernand wrote to USG. "We are hotly engaged with the enemy. We have part possession of two Forts, and the stars and stripes are floating over them. A vigorous push ought to be made all along the line." Copies (2), McClernand Papers, IHi; DNA, RG 393, 13th Army Corps, Letters Sent. *O.R.*, I, xxiv, part 1, 172, 176. Later USG signaled twice to McClernand. "Sherman and McPherson both are pressing the enemy, if one portion of your troops are pressed reinforce them from another. Sherman has gained some successes—"   "McArthur advanced from Warrenton last night; he is on your left.—Concentrate with him and use his forces to the best advantage." Signals received, ICarbS; copies, McClernand Papers, IHi; DNA, RG 393, 13th Army Corps, Letters Received. *O.R.*, I, xxiv, part 1, 173.

At 3:15 P.M., McClernand wrote to USG. "I have received your dispatches in regard to Genl Quinby's Division and Genl McArthur's Division. As soon as they arrive I will press the enemy with all possible speed and doubt not that I will force my way through—I have lost no ground—My men are in two of the enemys forts but they are commanded by rifle pits in the rear. Several prisoners have been taken who intimate that the rear is strong. At this moment I am hard pressed" ALS, DNA, RG 393, Dept. of the Tenn., Letters Received. *O.R.*, I, xxiv, part 1, 56, 173.

Also on May 22, McClernand wrote to USG. "I have had a hotly contested field all day, beginning with Artillery at day light, and Infantry at 10 'o'clock, when a general charge was made upon the enemy's lines. The casualties are considerable, including in the list of killed Col. Boomer, Lt. Col. Dunlap and several other commissioned officers,—and several field and line officers wounded, and many privates killed and wounded. Genl. Quimby's Division came too late to be applied in the engagement today. Genls. Osterhaus, Carr and Hovey report to me that their men are exhausted by fatigue and a want of sufficient food and rest. Genl. Quimby also says his men are very much fatigued. I doubt if a considerable portion of their commands will be qualified for efficient action tomorrow. Genl. McArthur's troops have not arrived, although I understand that his camp is within two miles and his Head Qrs. within one. I sent him some Artillery today, and heard firing from it this evening. On the receipt of your order, I instructed him to bring forward his division, if there was no. public property at Warrenton to protect,—otherwise one brigade only, and have just learned that he probably had but one brigade with him. I still think that to force the enemy's works, we will have to mass a strong force upon some one or two points of his defences. The enemy made two sorties this evening, but were repulsed. He seems disposed to turn my right flank. Indeed I this moment learn that he is attempting to pass between McPherson and me. I have some doubts, however, on this point. In order, however, to guard against this danger, I would suggest that Genl. McPherson immediately extend his line by Infantry or a strong picket until it joins my picket. In the morning I could relieve any force thus moved in this direction by a brigade of Genl. McArthur's Division, which I now understand to be on the way here." LS, DNA, RG 393, Dept. of the Tenn., Letters Received; DfS, McClernand Papers, IHi. *O.R.*, I, xxiv, part 3, 339. On May 23, Rawlins wrote to McClernand. "Your dispatch of last night is received. Any further assault on the enemys works will, for the present, cease. Hold all the ground you have acquired: get your Batteries in position, and commence regular approaches against the city. Order General Quimby to his former position on your right to report to his Corp Commander. Send McArthurs whole force back to the Big Bayou Crossing of the Warrenton and Vicksburg road with instructions to hold that crossing and adjacent highlands. Keep all roads ~~leading~~ south of you leading to the city well watched. There are plenty of supplies at Chickasaw Bayou Landing. Direct your Commissary to get up full rations for your men, and your ordnance officer full supplies of ammunition from there until they Can be had at Warrenton" Copies, DLC-USG, V, 19, 30, 98; DNA, RG 393, Dept. of the Tenn., Letters Sent; Alcorn Collection, WyU. *O.R.*, I, xxiv, part 3, 343.

On May 23, McClernand wrote to USG. "There are many killed & wounded of my Army Corps & Command lying on the field, under fire of the enemys rifle pits, & forts, which cannot be attended to, without a cessation of hostilities. Will you send a flag of truce in order to bury the dead & recover the wounded?" ALS, DNA, RG 393, Dept. of the Tenn., Letters Received; copy (dated May 24), *ibid.*, 13th Army Corps, Letters Sent.

On April 27, 9:00 A.M., Special Commissioner Charles A. Dana wrote to Secretary of War Edwin M. Stanton that the concentration of troops at New Carthage had been "somewhat delayed" because one boat carried "General McClernand's wife, with her servants and baggage." Dana further complained that instead of embarking troops, McClernand held a review of Ill. troops addressed by Governor Richard Yates, followed by an art. salute that violated

USG's orders to conserve ammunition. This telegram reached Washington on May 4, 6:00 P.M. *O.R.*, I, xxiv, part 1, 80–81. On May 6, Stanton wrote to Dana. "General Grant has full and absolute authority to enforce his own commands, and to remove any person who, by ignorance in action or any cause, interferes with, or delays his operations. He has the full confidence of the Government, is expected to enforce his authority, and will be firmly and heartily supported, but he will be responsible for any failure to exert his powers. You may communicate this to him." Copies, Ralph Geoffrey Newman, Inc., Chicago, Ill.; DLC-USG, V, 5, 8, 24, 94; DLC-Edwin M. Stanton; DNA, RG 393, Dept. of the Tenn., Hd. Qrs. Correspondence. Dated May 5 in *O.R.*, I, xxiv, part 1, 84. One copy was endorsed by Stanton on April 10, 1867. "This being a confidential despatch I think it should not be published by Badeau" AES, Newman. In fact, Adam Badeau did state that USG about May 14, while at Jackson, received authority to remove McClernand, quoted part of the message inaccurately, but omitted any indication of either sender or recipient. *Military History of Ulysses S. Grant* (New York, 1868), I, 364. On May 24, 1863, 7:00 P.M., Dana telegraphed to Stanton. "Your dispatch of the 5th instant was received at Jackson and communicated to General Grant according to your direction. Yesterday morning he had determined to relieve General McClernand, on account of his false dispatch of the day before stating that he held two of the enemy's forts, but he changed his mind, concluding that it would be better on the whole to leave McClernand in his present command till the siege of Vicksburg is concluded, after which he will induce McClernand to ask for leave of absence. Meanwhile he (General Grant) will especially supervise all of McClernand's operations, and will place no reliance on his reports unless otherwise corroborated. . . ." *O.R.*, I, xxiv, part 1, 87. See letter to Maj. Gen. John A. McClernand, June 17, 1863.

To Maj. Gen. William T. Sherman

May 22d 1863.

GEN.

Would it not be advisable to mine and blow up the salient near where you now have the flag planted on the enemy's parapet? I am sending after powder and expect to have it here some time during the night.

U. S. GRANT
Maj. Gen

MAJ. GEN. SHERMAN
COMD.G 15TH A. C.

P. S. The Cavalry sent from Hains Bluffs yesterday report that they hear of a body of rebel troops in the neighborhood of

Brownsville. That a messenger from Pemberton to Johnstone got through our lines with a message stating that he, Johnstone, had better not come in lest he should be defeated.

U. S. G.

ALS, deCoppet Collection, NjP. On May 22, 1863, Maj. Gen. William T. Sherman wrote to USG. "We have had a hard days work & all are exhausted. I leave Ewings & Giles Smiths Brigades close up to the Enemys works, ~~near~~ with Ransoms Brigade on their left—two of Tuttles Brigades in rear of the Batteries, and two Brigades in Reserve. I have ordered all to construct Breast works and have a thousand picks & shovels for that purpose   From Ewigs position a sap may be made to reach the high Bastion and it may be we can under mine & blow it up. My Men are too exhausted to do all this tonight   Steele also assauted but failed and after dark will withdraw behind the first hills. If Admiral Porter will send two of his best Gun boats along this shore and with his heavy artillery at close range clear the hill in front of my Right on the immediate Bank of the River, we may secure that flank of the Enemys works and thereby turn them. I think you had better send a staff officer to admiral Porter and convey to him the fact that the Enemy and his works are stronger than we estimated and that he should bring to bear on Vicksburg every Gun at his command. A Gunboat fleet should attend each flank of our army cooperating with it, and his mortars should come within easy range and drop shells by the thousand in the city. I think his mortar boats may safely come down this shore within 1000 yards of Steeles Right." ALS, DNA, RG 94, War Records Office, Dept. of the Tenn. *O.R.*, I, xxiv, part 3, 341.

To Brig. Gen. John McArthur

Head Quarters Dept of the Tenn
Near Vicksburg May 22. 1863.

BRIG. GEN. MCARTHUR:
GENERAL:

I authorized General McClernand to call for your troops to support him   If you have not allready complied with his order to do so you need not now go to him.

I am not sufficiently acquanted with the ground about Warrenton to direct you positively what to do. I would say though hold the Warrenton and Vicksburg road at the crossing of Big Bayou and also the adjacent high lands.

I think it possible General Banks may arrive at Warrenton

by tomorrow and with your combined forces you may suceed in securing a passage into Vicksburg.

> Very Respectfully
> U. S. GRANT
> Maj. Gen.

Copies, DLC-USG, V, 19, 30, 98; DNA, RG 393, Dept. of the Tenn., Letters Sent; Alcorn Collection, WyU.

To Act. Rear Admiral David D. Porter

> Head Quarters, Dept. of the Ten.
> Near Vicksburg, May 23d 1863

DEAR ADMIRAL,

Your note of this date is just received. I am satisfied you are doing all that can be done in aid of the reduction of Vicksburg. There is no doubt of the fall of this place ultimately but how long it will take is a matter of doubt. I intend to loose no more men but to force the enemy from one position to another without exposing my troops. I have information that the forces under Johnstone, who have been threatening me, have gone back to Calhoun on the Miss. Central rail-road. There is but about 8000 of them much demoralized. A force is collecting at Yazoo City which numbers now about 2000 men. Does this expose your boats now up the Yazoo? If so I will send Lauman to disperse them although I do not like to detach any force until this job here is closed out.

One week is as long as I think the enemy can possibly hold out.

> Very Truly Yours
> U. S. GRANT
> Maj. Gen. Com

ALS, MdAN. *O.R.*, I, xxiv, part 3, 343; *O.R.* (Navy), I, xxv, 31–32. On May 23, 1863, Act. Rear Admiral David D. Porter wrote to USG. "Yours of May 22d has been received. I am doing all with the mortars, and gun boats that can be done—I attacked all the batteries yesterday as high is the water batteries at Hospital, but I found it impossible, with our slow vessels to get beyond that point, the current was so strong; we were perfect targets for the enemy—The 'Tuscumbia' was soon disabled, and the other boats cut up between wind and water, and we had to haul out of action to repair damages. I fought the batteries one hour and a half longer than you asked me to do—I do not think it possible to get the gunboats up to the point you speak of without sacrifising every vessel and man on board, but I am feeling my way along with the mortars and drop them down a little every day. Depend that I am doing every thing that can be done with my small means.—I think we lost a fine chance yesterday, on your left of going into the fort on that range of hills. Those hills as I told you had no one on them—I forwarded your letter to General McArthur—Hope you will soon finish up this Vicksburg business or these people may get relief—I wrote to Genl Hurlburt four days ago, telling him that I thought you would thank him for every man he or any one else could send you. General Banks is not coming here with his men; he is going to occupy the attention of Port Hudson and has landed at Bayou Sara using your transports for that purpose   If the people in the batteries now in our possession see us sending coal barges by, it would be well to fire on any boats sent the enemy may send out to destroy them—" LS, DNA, RG 94, War Records Office, Dept. of the Tenn. *O.R.*, I, xxiv, part 3, 342–43; *O.R.* (Navy), I, xxv, 32.

On May 23, 8:00 P.M., Porter wrote to USG. "Yours of this date has just been received. The expedition I sent up the Yazoo River has returned, having met with great success. They destroyed two powerful rams; one nearly completed that would have cleaned us all out—destroyed a battery at Drury's Bluff—burnt up a fine navy Yard at Yazoo City and over two millions worth of property; some fine machine shops, and every thing in fact for carrying on an extensive naval establishment. All engines and boilers were tumbled into the river, and every thing destroyed that could help the rebel cause. There are no troops at all at Yazoo City, and no guns were found except [—] small [—] pounders the negroes report that they were all taken to Fort Pemberton. A surgeon belonging to that fort reports that in the first attack of the naval forces, the enemy had 19 killed by our guns, and 11 by a torpedo they were fooling with, and many wounded. The fort laid 9 hours without any ammunition—whipped and waiting for us to take possession. The gun boats found one battery of field pieces on the way up, and had one man killed—but cleaned out the battery. They start up again tomorrow to gather up all the steamers that have gone up sunflower and cannot escape. I am sorry to say that the Rebels have got the big rifle gun up again that we dismounted yesterday but the gunboats have gone at it again, and will try and dispose of it. All those hill batteries could be taken by a sudden assault and few lives lost—there are not many men in them. They should be attacked by the gunboats first, and then assaulted from the river side, their weakest side. There are reports that a large army is coming from the East, but I expect you are well posted on that subject. Johnson has only 7000 men with him. I shall have 10 mortars in position by morning and will keep up a continuous fire. Our shell are doing good execution—annoying the rebels very much—they tried to stop them with their rifled guns but cant touch them. I sincerely hope you will be successful. Col. Graham who was taken in the assault yesterday, came over today paroled. They put him in jail yesterday, and one of our shell fell through the roof, and gutted the roof building. I sent you all the powder I had, today and 200 feet of safety fuse. If you want more, telegraph and I will send it. I communicate easily with General Sherman. I hope when you assault the town, you will show them no quarter—they deserve none."

LS (press), DNA, RG 45, Correspondence of David D. Porter, Mississippi Squadron, General Letters.

To Brig. Gen. Jacob G. Lauman

Head Quarters Dept of the Tenn
In Field Rear of Vicksburg May 23/863

Brig Gen. Lauman
Comdg 4th Div. 16th A. C.
General:

Start tomorrow morning with your command for Warrenton by land. In marching down strike the Vicksburg and Bridgeport road so as to avoid the great press of teams on the direct road.

It is not my intention to place you at Warrenton but as near to Vicksburg as possible on the road leading South. You will receive more particular directions when you reach my Head Quarters

Very respectfully
U. S. Grant
Maj. General.

Copies, DLC-USG, V, 19, 30, 98; DNA, RG 393, Dept. of the Tenn., Letters Sent. On May 23, 1863, Brig. Gen. Jacob G. Lauman, "Haines Bluff," wrote to USG. "Enclosed I send you a copy of Major Wilsons report. from it you will see that he heard nothing very reliable of Johnsons Army—we have had various rumours varying with each relator as numbering from Eight Thousand to forty thousand men—The Guns left in the works at this point have all been spiked—" ALS, *ibid.*, Letters Received. On the same day, Maj. James Grant Wilson, 15th Ill. Cav., wrote to Lauman. "In accordance with your orders I proceeded with two companies of my regiment towards the town of Brownsville on the afternoon of the 21st. Resting our right at a plantation, I proceeded at an early hour on the morning of the 22d towards the Bird Song Ferry on the Big Black River. From there the command returned and advanced towards Cox's Ferry in which locality I met with what I deem reliable information in regard to Genl. Johnston's force. His army, said to number about Eight thousand and much disorganized and demoralized is at Calhoun Station, about thirty miles from the Big Black river, and not far distant from Canton Miss. I also learned that there is a confederate force assembling at Yazoo City, which already numbers two thousand men. During the expedition I captured one hundred and ninety-two head of cattle belonging to the Rebel government. Being unable to take them into Vicksburg for which place they were intended they were being marched to Yazoo City. I also captured about twenty-five horses and mules, and several Rifles and muskets. I met with many deserters in the woods and on the roads on which I passed, all of whom were much broken in spirit and tired of the war. The command returned without loss and reached your head quarters at 9 P. M. Friday the 22d inst. . . . P. S. A courier passed through the village of Oak Ridge Warren Co. yesterday morning, who escaped from Vicksburg the previous night bearing a message from Pemberton, *not to come* to the relief of Vicksburg as he was too late to do any good and would inevitably be captured by the Federal forces" ALS, *ibid.*

On May 26, USG signaled to Lauman. "I will send you picks in the morning." Signal received, ICarbS.

To Maj. Gen. Henry W. Halleck

Head Quarters, Dept. of the Ten.
Near Vicksburg Miss. May 24th/63

MAJ. GEN. H. W. HALLECK,
GEN IN CHIEF, WASHINGTON,
GEN.

My troops are now disposed with the Right, Sherman's Corps, resting on the Miss. where the bluffs strike the water, we having the first crest and the upper of the enemy's water batteries. McClernand is on the Left with his Corps his right having about one Brigade North of the rail-road, the rest South of it. One Division occupies the roads leading South & Southeast from the City.

The position is as strong by nature as can possibly be concieved of and is well fortified. The garrison the enemy have to defend it I have no means of knowing but their force is variously estimated from ten to twenty thousand. I attempted to carry the place by storm on the 22d but was unsucsessful. Our troops were not repulsed from any point but simply failed to enter the works of the enemy. At several points they got up to the parapets of the enemy's forts and planted their flags on the outer slope of the embankments where they still have them. The assault was made simultaneously by the ~~the~~ three Army Corps at 10 o'clock a. m.

The loss on our side was not very heavy at first but receiving repeated dispatches from Gen. McClernand saying that he was hard pressed on his Right & Left and calling for reinforcements, I gave him all of McPherson's Corps but four Brigades and caused Sherman to press the enemy on our right which caused us to double our losses for the day. The whole loss for the day ~~would~~ will probably reach 1500 killed & wounded. Gen. McClernands dispatches misled me as to the real state of facts and caused much of this loss. He is entirely unfit for the position of Corps Commander both on the march and on the battle field. Looking after his Corps gives me more labor, and infinitely more ~~labor~~ uneasiness, than all the remainder of my Dept.

The enemy are now undoubtedly in our grasp. The fall of Vicksburg, and the capture of most of the garrison, can only be a question of time. I hear a greatdeel of the enemy bringing a large force from the East to effect a raising of the siege. They may attempt something of the kind but I do not see how they can do it. The rail-road is effectually destroyed at Jackson so that it will take thirty days to repair it. This will leave a march of fifty miles over which the enemy will have to subsist an army & bring their Ordnance stores with teams. My position is so strong that I could hold out for several days against a vastly superior force. I do not see how the enemy could possibly maintain a long attack under these circumstances. I will keep a close watch on the enemy however.

There is a force now at Calhoun Station about six miles North of Canton on the Miss. C. R. R. This is the force that escaped from Jackson augmented by a few thousand men from the Coast Cities, intended to reinforce the latter place before the attack but failed to reach in time. In the various battles from Port Gibson to Black River Bridge we have taken near 6000 prisoners besides killed and wounded and scattered a much larger number. The enemy sucseeded in returning to Vicksburg with only three pieces of Artillery. The number captured by us was 74 guns besides what was found at Hain's Bluffs.

From Jackson to this place I have had no opportunity of communicating with you. Since that this army fought a heavy battle near Bakers Creek, on the 16th, beating the enemy badly killing & capturing not less than four thousand of the enemy besides capturing most of his Artillery. Lowring's Division was cut off from retreat and dispersed in every direction. On the 17th the Battle of Black River Bridge was fought the enemy again loosing about 2000 prisoners, 17 pieces of Artillery and many killed and wounded. The bridges & ferries were destroyed. ~~This detained me twenty four hours~~. The march from Edwards Station to Black River Bridge was made, bridges for crossing the Army constructed and much of it over in twenty-four hours. On the 18th the march to this place was made and the City invested. When I crossed the Mississippi river the means of ferriage was so limited, and time so important, that I started without teams and an average of but two days rations in haversacks. Our supplies had to be hauled about sixty miles from Millikin's Bend to opposite Grand Gulf, and from there to wherever the Army marched. We picked up all the teams in the Country and free Africans to drive them. Forage and meat were found in great abundance through the country so that although not over five days rations were issued in twenty days yet there was neither suffering nor complaint witnessed in the Army. As soon as reports can be got from Corps Commanders I will send in a report embracing the Campaign from Millikins Bend to the investment; if not the Capture, of Vicksburg. When I crossed the Miss. river it was my intention to detach an Army Corps, or the necessary force, to co-operate with Gen. Banks to secure the reduction of Port Hudson and the union of the two Armies. But I rec'd a letter from Gen. Banks stating that he was in Louisiana and would return to Baton Rouge by the 10th of May. By the reduction of Port Hudson he could add only 12 000 to my force. I had certain information that Gen. Jo Johnstone was on his way to Jackson and that reinforcements were arriving there constantly from Port Hudson and the Southern cities. Under this state of facts I could not afford to delay. Beating the enemy to near Port Gibson I followed him to Hankerson's Ferry on the Black River. This placed my forces fifteen miles on their way from Grand Gulf to this place, Black River Bridge or Jackson whichever I might turn my attention to. Altogether I am satisfied that my course was right and has given us with comparitive ease what would have ~~caused~~ cost serious battles by delay.

This Army is in the finest possible health and spirits.

> I am Gen. Very respectfully
> your obt. svt.
> U. S. Grant
> Maj. Gen.

ALS, DNA, RG 94, War Records Office, Union Battle Reports. *O.R.*, I, xxiv, part 1, 37–39.

To Act. Rear Admiral David D. Porter

---

12 A. M., from Hdqr Signal Station. Vicksburg
[*May 24, 1863.*]

To Admiral Porter,

Genl Steele with sharpshooters can keep the upper water battery from firing. With his battery he can silence the guns from the top of the second range of hills. If one or two gun boats will then move down and enfilade the southern slope of the second range Genl Steele can secure that height.

> U. S. Grant
> Maj Genl

Signal sent, DLC-James M. McClintock; signal received, DNA, RG 45, Letters from Officers, Mississippi Squadron; *ibid.*, RG 111, Vicksburg Signal Book. *O.R.* (Navy), I, xxv, 33. On May 24, 1863, 2:30 p.m., Act. Rear Admiral David D. Porter signaled to USG. "I have but one Gunboat here.   she is unfit for the purpose   The Carondolet below is unfit to go into a fight. Tuscumbia disabled and it would be too small a force to pass up by the Batteris: I will write you on the Subject: In the mean time I will open all the Mortars on that Spot." Signal sent, DNA, RG 94, War Records Office, Military Div. of the Miss.; signal received, DLC-James M. McClintock. *O.R.*, I, xxiv, part 3, 345; *O.R.* (Navy), I, xxv, 33.

On May 25, Porter wrote to USG. "I received your signal despatch, and was sorry not to be able to comply with your request. I brought the Choctaw down, intending to see what could be done with her in the way of enfilading the battery you spoke of, but on rounding to, she broke her machinery, and became useless. she would not do for the purpose you spoke of unsupported by other vessels, as she is so unmanageable in a current. The 'De Kalb' would have done, but she has leaked so badly since the last fire she was under that I was afraid to risk her, besides she had her steam pipe damaged on her expedition up river, and was in the hands of the machinists. I expect a monitor down every minute, and am packing the Cincinnati, (which arrived this morning) with logs, so that she can engage the batteries with her stern down stream. If General Sherman will send an officer up here to show us which battery he holds, and which he wants enfiladed, we could operate without any mistake—as it is we are doubtful—where we would have to fire—we might do damage to our friends. I enclose you a letter from General McArthur. I thought it strange he did not take advantage of our success—but he explains the reason. Great rejoicing at the north over the success of the Army here." LS, DNA, RG 393, Dept. of the Tenn., Letters Received. The enclosed letter of May 23 from Brig. Gen. John McArthur to Porter explained that orders from Maj. Gen. John A. McClernand to move McArthur's command prevented him from capturing the batteries. Copy, *ibid*. USG added an undated endorsement to Porter's letter. "Refered to Gen. Sherman who will please send an officer to point out to Admiral Porter the position of the battery which he wishes to have silenced by the Navy." AES, *ibid*. Maj. Gen. William T. Sherman also added an undated endorsement. "I got a signal dispatch to Same effect about two hours ago and ordered Genl Steele to send an officer down. I will go to the Right in the morig & display flags so that no mistake can occur. I am just in receipt of another signal despatch which I send you. I answered 'no appearances of a surrender, quite the reverse.'—The admiral must suppose me down at the Bluff, Else he would not signal me." AES, *ibid*.

To Maj. Gen. John A. McClernand

———

Head Quarters Dept of the Tenn
Near Vicksburg May 24. 1863

Major General Jno A McClernand
Commdg 13th Army Corps.

General:

Warrenton being the base from which your supplies will be drawn, it will be necessary for you to keep a guard there. Laumans is now on his way to McArthurs position and will hold the roads leading south from Vicksburg: hence there will be no necessity for a large force. One of your Regiments that has suffered severely will answer or you can send your cavalry to the rear of your Corps and pick up stragglers enough to form the garrison. Lake Landing Garrison was formed in this way.

Immediate measures should be adopted to bring up the stragglers. I have directed that measures be taken to secure this end on the Right and Centre.

Very respectfully

U. S. GRANT.

Major General.

Copies, DLC-USG, V, 19, 30, 98; DNA, RG 393, Dept. of the Tenn., Letters Sent; *ibid.*, 13th Army Corps, Letters Received. On May 24, 1863, Maj. Gen. John A. McClernand wrote to USG. "Your note in relation to the establishing a garrison at Warrenton, is this moment received. I have no available Cavalry at present. Two companies of the Cavalry of this Corps reported to you yesterday evening. Three companies left early this morning, as an escort for a train going to Warrenton.—one company this morning to Hall's Ferry,—and my body guard went to Baldwin's Ferry.—I have one brigade at Big Black,—two regiments at Perkin's Plantation,—and hold my present position by a force much diminished and weakened by the casualties of battle and the fatigues of the campaign. It is hardly safe to weaken it further by detachments from it. Would it not be better for McArthur or Lauman to garrison Warrenton, until one of the regiments from Perkin's Plantation comes up? Or would it not be better to garrison it by the troops now at Grand Gulf, or would it not be still better to make a depot on the River opposite McArthur's left flank and construct a new road from it, or by his present encampment,—to these Head Qrs. which would save a distance of five or six miles,—and supersede the necessity of a garrison. If this is not satisfactory, I will immediately send a Regiment there as a garrison." Copies (signed John A. McArthur), *ibid.*, Dept. of the Tenn., Letters Received; (signed McClernand) *ibid.*, 13th Army Corps, Letters Sent. *O.R.*, I, xxiv, part 3, 345. Also on May 24, Lt. Col. John A. Rawlins wrote to McClernand. "Order the regiments at once from Perkins Plantation to join their Divisions and send some of the Regiments of your Corps, that has suffered most in recent battles, to garrison Warrenton. it may be found practicable to open a road to the river, from McArthurs left, but for immediate supplies Warrenton will necessarily be the Depot." Copies, DLC-USG, V, 19, 30, 98; DNA, RG 393, Dept. of the Tenn., Letters Sent; *ibid.*, 13th Army Corps, Letters Received.

To Lt. Gen. John C. Pemberton

—

3.30 P. M.
Head Quarters, Dept. of the Ten.
Near Vicksburg, May 25th 1863

LT. GEN. J. C. PEMBERTON,
COMD.G CONFEDERATE FORCES
VICKSBURG MISS.
GEN.

Your note of this date proposing a cessation of hostilities for 2½ hours for the purpose of giving me an opportunity of collecting the dead and wounded is just received. As it will take some time to send word to all my forces to avail themselves of the opportunity afforded, and to return this to you so that notice may be given to your troops of the cessation of hostilities, I will name 6 O'Clock P. M to-day as the hour when we will commence collecting any wounded or dead we may have still upon the field. From that hour for two & a half hours all hostilities shall sease on our side.

Very respectfully
your obt. svt.
U. S. GRANT
Maj. Gen. Com

ALS, DNA, RG 109, Pemberton Papers. *O.R.*, I, xxiv, part 1, 277. On May 25, 1863, Lt. Gen. John C. Pemberton wrote to USG. "Two days having elapsed since your dead and wounded have been lying in our front, and as yet no disposition on your part of a desire to remove them being exhibited: in the name of humanity I have the honor to propose a cessation of hostilities for 2½ hours, that you may be enabled to remove your dead and dying men. If you can not do this, on notification from you that hostilities will be suspended on your part for the time specified, I will endeavor to have the dead buried and the wounded cared for" Copy, DNA, RG 109, Dept. of Miss. and East La., Letters Sent. *O.R.*, I, xxiv, part 1, 276–77. For orders implementing the truce, see *ibid.*, I, xxiv, part 3, 348; *O.R.* (Navy), I, xxv, 33.

On May 18, Pemberton had written to USG. "I have the honor to send with your consent Surgeons Coffey, Leary, Leonard, and Merrill, C. S. A. to attend to our wounded in the engagements of Baker's Creek & Big Black bridge: and to request that such courtesies be extended to them as are customary in civilized warfare; and that they be allowed to return as soon as their services are no longer needed; or if your Surgeon's attentions have rendered their presence with our men unnecessary" Copy, DNA, RG 109, Dept. of Miss. and East La., Letters Sent. Since there is no record of the receipt of this letter or any action in response, Pemberton may have decided against sending it.

On May 25, Maj. Gen. John A. McClernand wrote to USG. "During the pending of the truce this afternoon, a Confederate Commissary of Subsistence was introduced within the lines by Maj Platt, of the 11th Wis; stupidity, on the part of the Major, induced him to bring the officer to Genl Lawlers Hd Qrs, to obtain an interview with Col Lindsy, and, having seen our defences; I deem it unsafe to permit his return and have determined (if approved by you) to send him North, to be sent through our lines at Lexington Ky, or other convenient point. I say Lexington, because the officer is from that place. Will you signify your will in the matter?" LS, *ibid.*, RG 393, Dept. of the Tenn., Letters Received. See letter to Maj. Gen. John A. McClernand, May 26, 1863; *Missouri Democrat*, June 4, 1863.

To Maj. Gen. Henry W. Halleck

Near Vicksburg
May 25th 1863

MAJ GEN H. W. HALLECK
GEN IN CHIEF

There is evidence ~~that~~ of a force collecting near Black River north east of here about thirty miles I have ordered all the force that can be spared from West Tennessee and communicated with Gen Banks asking him to come with all the force he can. I can manage the force in Vicksburg and an attacking force on the rear of thirty thousand but may have more to contend against. Vicksburg will have to be reduced by regular siege.[1] My effective force here is about fifty 50 thousand and can be increased ten 10 thousand men from my own command

U S. GRANT
Maj Gen Com'dg

Telegram received, DNA, RG 107, Telegrams Collected (Bound); *ibid.*, Telegrams Collected (Unbound); copies, *ibid.*, Telegrams Received in Cipher; DLC-USG, V, 98. *O.R.*, I, xxiv, part 1, 39.

1. On May 25, Lt. Col. John A. Rawlins issued Special Orders No. 140. "Corps Commanders will immediately commence the work of reducing the enemy by regular approaches. It is desirable that no more loss of life shall be sustained in the reduction of Vicksburg, and the capture of the Garrison. Every advantage

will be taken of the natural inequalities of the ground to gain positions from which to start mines, trenches, or advance batteries. The work will be under the immediate charge of Corps Engineers, Corps Commanders being responsible that the work in their immediate fronts, is pushed with all vigor. Captain F: E Prime, Chief Engineer of the Department, will have general superintendence of the whole work. He will be obeyed and respected accordingly." DS, Rawlins Papers, ICHi; copies, DLC-USG, V, 27, 28; DNA, RG 393, Dept. of the Tenn., Special Orders. *O.R.*, I, xxiv, part 3, 348.

To Maj. Gen. Nathaniel P. Banks

Head Quarters Dept of the Tenn
Near Vicksburg May 25 1863

MAJOR GENERAL N. P. BANKS.
COMDG DEPT OF THE GULF.
GENERAL:

I send Col. Riggin of my staff to communicate with you on the subject of cooperation, between our respective forces in the effectual opening of the Miss River

Col Riggin can give you all the particulars of our present situation more ~~particularly~~ minutely than can well be done in a short communication.

I now have Vicksburg invested and draw my supplies from the Yazoo above Vicksburg and from Warrenton below the city.

I feel that my force is abundantly strong to hold the enemy where he is or to whip him if he should come out. The place is so strongly fortified however that it cannot be taken without either a great sacrifice of life or by regular seige. I have determined to adopt the latter course and save my men.

I can get no accurate information as to the number of men the enemy have the amount of provision or ordnance stores. They are evidently deficient in Artillery.

The greatest danger now to be apprehended is that the enemy may collect a force outside and attempt to rescue the garrison. My cavalry force is insufficient to guard properly against this but with what I have I am doing the best I can.

The railroad is effectually broken at Jackson, so that an army to come here within the next twenty days would have to haul their supplies and ordnance stores with teams at least fifty miles. The rebels set such a value upon the possession of a foothold, on the Miss. River, however, that a desperate effort may be made to hold this point. For this reason I deem it advisable that as large a force be collected here as possible. Having all my available force that can be spared from West Tenn. and Helena here, to get any more I must look outside of my own Department

You being engaged in the same enterprise I am compelled to ask you to give me such assistance as may be in your power.

When I commenced writing this it was my intention to propose sending to you if you could furnish the transportation, eight or ten thousand men to co operate with you on Port Hudson. But whilst writing a courier came in from my Cavalry stating that a force of the enemy are now about 4̶0̶ thirty miles north east of here   They may be collecting there for the purpose of making an attack. At present therefore I do not deem it prudent to send of any men I have, or even safe, without abandoning the advantages already gained. I would be pleased Gen. to have you come with such force as you are able to spare   you can be supplied with every thing from Young's point. The road is now good across the point opposite Vicksburg, and with your transports the ferriage can be made   I am in Hopes this letter will find you in possession of Port Hudson and therefore a much larger force to bring to this place than you could otherwise detach.

Col. Grierson would be of immense value to me now. If he has not already started, will you be kind enough to order him here immediately. He should come up o̶n̶ the Louisiana Shore to avoid delay

> I am General
> Very respectfully
> Your Obt Servt
> U. S. Grant
> Maj. Gen.

Copies, DLC-USG, V, 19, 30, 98; DNA, RG 393, Dept. of the Tenn., Letters Sent. *O.R.*, I, xxiv, part 3, 346–47.

On May 28, 1863, Maj. Gen. Nathaniel P. Banks wrote to USG. "Upon the receipt of the report of General Dwight, who visited you lately, my command moved from Semmesport for Port Hudson, landing at Bayou Sara at 2. O'clock on the morning of the 22nd. We reached Newport on the 23rd and moved upon Port Hudson. Several combats were had with the enemy in which we were successful—outside of his entrenchments he has no power,—and yesterday we made a combined assault upon his works. They are more formidable than have been represented, and his forces are Stronger The fight was very bitter and our losses severe, the enemy's losses are large but not in comparison with ours. On either side we pushed our troops close to the line of his fortifications, and on the right our forces occupied the opposite faces of the same parapet with the enemy. But we have not strength enough yet to carry their works. There are five thousand troops that I can bring to my support in three days. It is necessary that the enemy should be prevented from reinforcing the Garrison. I hope that he will be so occupied as to make it impossible for him to do so. Next to that it is essential that you should assist us if you can. We have ammunition, provisions, Artillery, and Cavalry, and want nothing but men. We shall be grateful for any aid however slight. Our solicitude for your safety is tempered with the strongest hopes that your good fortune and signal ability, will establish perfect success of all your plans. The garrison of the enemy is five to Six thousand men. The works are what would ordinarily be styled impregnable. They are surrounded by ravines, woods, valleys, and Bayous of the most intricate and labyrinthic character, that makes the works themselves almost inaccessible. It requires time even, to understand the Geography of the position. They fight with determination, and our men after a march of some five or Six hundred miles, have done all that could be expected or required of any similar force. I send this by an Officer of my Staff and hope that information may be recieved from you without delay. . . . P. S.—With the Gun Boat that takes this communication to you I send back the Steamers Forest Queen, and Moderator that you sent for the transportation of my troops. If it be possible I beg you to send to me at least one Brigade of four or five thousand men. This will be of vital importance to us, we may have to abandon these operations without it" Copies, DNA, RG 393, Dept. of the Gulf, Letters Sent; *ibid.*, Dept. of the Tenn., Unregistered Letters Received. *O.R.*, I, xxiv, part 3, 353–54; *ibid.*, I, xxvi, part 1, 519–20. On May 29, Banks wrote to USG. "The enclosed letter I had written to be sent to you at the moment yours of the 25th was presented to me by Col. Riggin. I regret it does not find me in condition to go to your support with all my force, without abandoning Port Hudson altogether, it will be impossible for me to do so, and then the aid I can give you must be very little. My force is far less than you imagine, and with such detachments from it as would be necessary to protect New Orleans. While Port Hudson, Mobile, and Kirby Smith, are within a few day's movement of New Orleans, my assistance would be insignificant—not enough to counterbalance the disadvantage occasioned by such movements of the enemy in this quarter, as would follow the withdrawal of my troops. I can only send you men. The material of my army will be without transportation. I can use only such boats as can come through Grand Lake which allows only at this Stage of the water five or Six feet—and they are few in number. Colonel Riggin will inform you what my force is—how much less than you imagine—and how slight the aid must be that it is in my power to give you.—When I came to Port Hudson it was with the understanding from General Dwights Report that you could assist us in its reduction, if it did not fall before my force alone—It is unexpectedly strong.—not stronger than I had supposed, but stronger than any body here would for a moment, admit. We can reduce it, if uninterrupted in the course of a week or ten days, with ten thousand men, in addition we could carry it in three days   If we hold Murfreesboro, Vicksburg, and Port Hudson at the same time, the enemy will beat us all in detail, and the Campaign of the West will end like the Campaigns of the East,—its utter and disgraceful defeat before an inferior Enemy. I cannot move my force to you in time or Strength to be of service for want of transportation. If you can aid me by the assistance of Eight or ten thousand men for a few days only I shall be relieved. This I am confident is the only method of obtaining Success.—It is in accordance with your original proposition and the view upon which I have made all my movements. I had expected to meet your troops here on the 25th May in accordance with your letter and dispatch, and had I been so fortunate, should now have been on my way to Vicksburg—What is required at this juncture of our affairs is a bold action on one side or the other. That which promises greatest results at the least cost of time and Strength is for you to aid us. You can hold your position for a few day's against any enemy—or if obliged to bend your line a little—to give and take—you will recover at once and destroy the enemy thus reduced to your camp. Unless we succeed on the River the war goes over to another Year. By the concentration of our forces,—even at some risk—we shall succeed.—That concentration is absolutely dependent upon the fall of Port Hudson. I beg you to consider this and render us your aid.—Do not send a few thousand men because it costs time. Let us have ten thousand and we will rush to you with all our power. I can furnish the transportation because we want nothing but the men and muskets, and can use for this purpose the Vessels of the fleet. The decision should be immediate—Colonel Griersons Cavalry is of great importance. It is now the only Cavalry force we have. He has rendered us great service and his immediate departure will entirely cripple us—I hope to avoid a seperation from him, by joining you at the same time he moves upon the plan I have suggested—I enclose a memorandum of the heavy artillery I can bring with my Corps—if relieved here in addition to the 15.000 men I can give you, much exhausted and ill. I feel I have not stated as I ought the Strength of my case but I am sure you will feel its importance though it be not clearly expressed—''   Copy, DNA, RG 393, Dept. of the Tenn., Unregistered Letters Received. *O.R.*, I, xxiv, part 3, 359–60. See letter to Maj. Gen. Nathaniel P. Banks, May 31, 1863.

To Maj. Gen. Benjamin M. Prentiss

Head Quarters, Dept. of the Ten.
Near Vicksburg, May 25th 1863,

MAJ. GEN. B. M. PRENTISS,
COMD.G DIST. S. E. ARK.
GEN.

The taking of Vicksburg is going to occupy time contrary to my expectations when I first arrived near it. To watch the enemy and to prevent him collecting a force outside near enough to attack my rear I require a large Cavalry force. If therefore you have not sent off the Cavalry ordered to West Tennessee send them at once to report to me on the Yazoo River. If you are certain that you can maintain your position with fewer forces than you now have send me all the Infantry & Cavalry you can spare.

Very respectfully
your obt. svt.
U. S. GRANT
Maj. Gen. Com

ALS, DNA, RG 94, War Records Office, Union Battle Reports. *O.R.*, I, xxiv, part 3, 349. On May 29, 1863, Maj. Gen. Benjamin M. Prentiss, Helena, Ark., wrote to USG. "I received, yesterday, your communication of the 25th inst, and take pleasure in being able to say in reply thereto, that I shall send you the 5th Ill. Cavalry, as soon as transports can be secured,—and these I am momentarily expecting from Memphis, whither Chief Quartermaster Hatch has gone. I also received a communication from Lt. Lyfords Senior Ordnance Officer, requesting me to send you four 24 Pdr Seige Guns, with carraiges, implements and ammunition. I had these gun in position, but by dint of hard labor succeeded in getting them to the levee last night, and will forward them by first boat. I cannot, General, with a due regard to the safety of this place, send away any of my infantry regiments. You will certainly do me the justice to believe that nothing short of what seems, to me at least, to be an absolute necessity, would induce m[e] to withhold a single man, or omit to do anything left to my discretion, that could by any possibility be of any assistance to you. I trust you will not deem it out of place, General, for me to congratulate you on the triumphat success which has thus far attended your operations against Vicksburg. I need not to assure you that the eyes of the nation and almost its last hope are centered in you and the gallant army you have so long and so successfully commanded. I am free to admit that

I feel altogether sanguine and confident of the result. My only regret is that I am not permitted to be with you, where, I am vain enough to believe, I could render you more efficient service, and thus do more to maintain and uphold the cause in which all our hopes are centered and upon the triumph of which depend not alone our national honor, but our national existence as well." Copy, DNA, RG 393, District of Eastern Ark., Letters Sent. *O.R.*, I, xxiv, part 3, 362–63. On May 30, Prentiss wrote to USG. "From information received I am led to believe that you have in your [*possession*] a Surplus of Artillery. In view of this belief and from the fact that owing to frequent calls the force at this post has become very much reduced, and, for the further reason that we are continually threatened with attack, I would respectfully request that at an early moment, you send me four Six pounders and two twelve pound Howitzers. I deem this, General, important if it is possible for you to Spare them." ALS, DNA, RG 393, 16th Army Corps, Letters Received. *O.R.*, I, xxiv, part 3, 365. On June 2, Lt. Col. John A. Rawlins endorsed this letter. "Respectfully referred to Maj. Gen. S. A. Hurlbut, Commanding 16th Army Corps who will supply Maj. Gen. Prentiss with the Artillery he requires. One of the six gun or two of the four gun Batteries of Gen. Smith's Division can be left at Helena." ES, DNA, RG 393, 16th Army Corps, Letters Received. *O.R.*, I, xxiv, part 3, 365. See letter to Maj. Gen. Stephen A. Hurlbut, June 3, 1863.

On May 25, Rawlins wrote to Maj. Gen. Stephen A. Hurlbut. "You will, if you have not already done so, send a heavy cavalry force as far south as Grenada. Every available man of your Infantry force that can be possibly spared from their present position, you will send forward at once to this place. Judging from the returns, the garrison for the District of Columbus can be considerably reduced without danger. Contract everything on the line from Memphis to Corinth, and keep your Cavalry well out, south of there; by this means you ought to be able to send here, quite a large force. The forces of Joe Jhonston, from six to ten thousand, are reported west of the Big Black, and about thirty miles north-east of here. From this force no serious danger is apprehended, but they may re-inforce it, until it becomes formidable. The investment of Vicksburg is complete, and supplies for our Army are drawn from Chickasaw Bayou on the Yazoo, above, and Warrenton on the Mississippi below the city. Send General Kimball if he can be possibly be spared in command, of the re-inforcements for this place." LS, DNA, RG 393, 16th Army Corps, Letters Received. *O.R.*, I, xxiv, part 3, 349–50. On the same day, Hurlbut wrote twice to USG. "We in the rear & the Country behind us are watching with unspeakable pride the glorious track of the Army of the Tennessee. Every sort of gratulation for the glory already won & the crowning victory to come. I can't write business fashion as yet in the reality of the past and the anticipation of the future. I send the 'Luminary' with a full cargo of ammunition reducing me to 100 rounds per man—I hope it will not be needed for Vicksburgh but it will be in the future. Johnson has called off all troops from above. Anticipating this I had ordered Col Hatch of the 2d Iowa Cavalry to take all the mounted men outside of Memphis & look up Chalmers. I have just heard from their first interview. Hatch found him in Senatobia Swamp charged at once— killed 9—drove the others into Panola across the Tallahatchie, except such as fled toward Helena—Chalmers is reported to have had 2000 regulars and 1000 conscripts. Hatch has 1700—1200 Cavalry—500 mounted Infantry—4 mountain Howitzers—one section 6 prs. My Cavalry will be at work all the time as far as I can reach   As yet I have not called up the Cavalry from Helena—as Prentiss has some fears for his place—The entire line here is now quiet" ALS, DNA, RG 393, Dept. of the Tenn., Letters Received. *O.R.*, I, xxiv, part 3, 350. "I enclose within dispatches—It would appear that they have news of the fall of Vicksburgh, at Washington, and Springfield, as yet it is only known here by GrapeVine, and the sad confession of the 'secesh'—Although left in the rear, I am very, very proud of belonging to the army of the Tennessee." Copy, DNA, RG 393, 16th Army Corps, Letters Sent.

On May 29, Hurlbut wrote to USG. "Your dispatch was recd at 11.30 P. M. last night. I have ordered four Regiments of Infantry from Columbus District and 8 Regiments from Jackson & Corinth to be pushed forward with all dispatch. They will be ready to move down as soon as Boats can be furnished. Jackson & that line will be temporarily abandoned up to Bolivar. I have also ordered all the detached Cavalry in District of Columbus here. My Cavalry has just returned from Panola breaking up Chalmers force. I shall send the entire mounted force toward Grenada, except such as are necessary to threaten Okalona & keep them from closing in rear of our Expedition. I am waiting orders from Washington as to disposition of the prisoners and have relieved the Guard. I find many officers & some soldiers coming up from below. All that are not unfit for service & not under orders from your Head Quarters I order back as I do not consider it a fit time for any indulgence" ALS, *ibid.*, Dept. of the Tenn., Letters Received. *O.R.*, I, xxiv, part 3, 363. On May 30, Hurlbut wrote to USG. "It is reported to me from a source believed to be reliable that heavy reinforcements are now on the way to Johnson, twenty thousand being drawn from Braggs Army, and others from Mobile and Port Hudson. I have informed Rosecrans for two weeks past that all my information pointed to heavy drafts from the force opposed to him— Up to this time he has refused to credit it—It is almost an impossibility to procure water Transportation to send my troops down—Four Regiments are ordered down from District Columbus and eight are now here or on their way from the Jackson command—I have boats for four Regiments which leave tomorrow— General Kimball will command the provisional Division. This reduces me considerably unless Rosecrans will move, in which case I shall be much relieved. Forrest has gone to Grenada with his command, it is said five thousand. I shall push my Cavalry as far south as they can go. We are exceedingly anxious for the army below." Copy, DNA, RG 393, 16th Army Corps, Letters Sent. *O.R.*, I, xxiv, part 3, 366. On May 31, Hurlbut wrote to Rawlins. "I send this by Brigadier-General Kimball, who goes below with a division of twelve regiments of infantry, in obedience to orders from you. I cannot very safely spare any more from this line until Rosecrans does something. Forrest with his cavalry is reported to have gone south, and I am of opinion that Johnston must have something like 30,000 men. He is said to expect D. H. Hill with 18,000 men from Virginia. The prisoners sent up have gone, under General Halleck's orders, to Indianapolis and Fort Delaware; half to each; officers to Sandusky. The enemy near Grenada are too strong for my cavalry to attack, but as they move below to Canton and Jackson, I shall push down. A gunboat should be kept on station between Helena and this place, as a battery is likely to be established at or near Austin. Steamboats have been very difficult to procure, and, if larger reenforcements are required, it would be advisable to send boats up from below, as there is a terrible delay in procuring transportation." *Ibid.*, p. 369.

On May 25, Governor Richard Yates of Ill. telegraphed to USG. "The news of your glorious [*victories*] recd.   guns firing now   Ten thousand (10000) ~~pris~~

or, more prisoners can be accommodated at Chicago" Telegram received, DNA, RG 107, Telegrams Collected (Unbound); *ibid.*, RG 393, Dept. of the Tenn., Telegrams Received.

To Maj. Gen. William T. Sherman

Head Quarters, Dept. of the Tenn.
Near Vicksburg, Miss., May 25th 1863.
MAJ. GEN. W. T. SHERMAN
COMDG. 15TH ARMY CORPS.
GEN.

I send you report of Col Johnson who was out in command of the Cavalry expedition to burn the Black River Bridge. I have now ordered Col Johnson to move by the Jackson road to get east of Black River, and then strike north and ascertain the numbers and intentions of the enemy, if possible, and to burn the bridge he first started out for if he can. This will leave Haines Bluff without a garrison   I deem that point of so much importance, that I am willing to weaken our force here rather than to leave it unoccupied. I would direct therefore that one Brigade from your command be sent there with as little delay as possible to hold that place.

Yours &c.,
U. S. GRANT
Major General.

Copies, DLC-USG, V, 19, 30, 98; DNA, RG 393, Dept. of the Tenn., Letters Sent; Alcorn Collection, WyU.
On May 25, 1863, USG wrote to Col. Amory K. Johnson. "Move with the Cavalry force at your Command by way of Black River Bridge on the Jackson Road until you get east of Black River   From there strike out through or near Brownsville and learn all you can of the movements of the enemy, Their numbers &c. If possible to reach the bridge you first started for, do so. When you return, report from Black River before bringing in your Cavalry." Copies, DLC-USG, V, 19, 30, 98; DNA, RG 393, Dept. of the Tenn., Letters Sent. See letter to Col. Amory K. Johnson, May 26, 1863.

To Maj. Gen. John A. McClernand

Head Quarters Dept. of the Tenn.
Near Vicksburg May 26. 1863

MAJOR GENERAL J. A. McCLERNAND
COMMDG 13TH ARMY CORPS:
GENERAL:

Your ordnance officer can obtain Heavy Artillery either naval guns or some of the captured ones, by calling on Lieut. Lyford, Chf of Ordnance at the Yazoo Landing.

Lieut Lyford, has sent to Helena and Memphis for seige guns which on their arrival will be distributed so that they shall occupy the points best adapted for their use.

Very respectfully
U. S. GRANT.
Maj Gen.

Copies, DLC-USG, V, 19, 30, 98; DNA, RG 393, Dept. of the Tenn., Letters Sent; *ibid.*, 13th Army Corps, Letters Received; Alcorn Collection, WyU. On May 26, 1863, Maj. Gen. John A. McClernand wrote to USG. "I have the honor to inform you that Genl. Lawler finds it inconvenient to keep in his camp, the rebel Major of whom I wrote you as having come into our camp during the suspension of hostilities yesterday. I have just directed that he be taken blindfolded to your Head Qrs. to await your decision. I am in great need of some more heavy guns. Among the guns captured at Big Black, six 12 pdr. bronze Howitzers and six 10 pdr. Parrott rifled guns. I should be pleased to know where these guns are,— and whether I can find them" LS (by Lt. Col. Walter B. Scates), DNA, RG 393, Dept. of the Tenn., Letters Received.

On May 25, 6:00 P.M., 1st Lt. Stephen C. Lyford, Lake's Landing, wrote to USG. "Admiral Porter offers to furnish as many heavy guns as you may need at any time, mounted on Naval carriages—I thinks 32's might be transported to your front—I have sent to Helena for 4-24 pdr seige guns and to Memphis for 4-30 pdr Parrotts   Those from Helena at the request of Gen'l Sherman—Our Infantry ammunition will hold out in abundance till a further supply arrives—" ALS, *ibid.* Also on May 25, Lt. Commander James W. Shirk, U.S.S. *Tuscumbia*, wrote to Brig. Gen. John McArthur. "I have received an order to deliver you a 14 inch Gun.   not having a pound of coal to carry me from this point to Warrenton, for the purpose of delivering the same—I would propose you send a transport to carry it from my vessel to Warrenton—You will find here a pair of timber wheels, which would aid you in your transportation of it from Warrenton—forward—" LS, *ibid.* On the same day, McArthur endorsed this letter. "The within communication in answer to a request of mine was received just before leaving this morning. at the request of Brig Gen Lauman it is respectfully referred to the Gen Comd. Dept. Gen Lauman has no artillerists acquainted with handling such a gun and suggests that Capt. Shirk be requested to send the necessary ammunition and gunners to work it. He will give all assistance required in getting it to position and guarding it. I am satisfied that with such a gun it would add materially to the reduction of the place, as from the positions that can be obtained along the Bluffs leading from Warrenton to Vicksburgh it enfilades the town and Water Batteris as well as the whole camp of the enemy. I would recommend that the gun be obtained and put in position" AES, *ibid.*

On May 26, Lt. Col. John A. Rawlins wrote to McClernand. "A deserter from the enemy in Vicksburg just in, states that it was agreed last night by the enemy to attack our lines and cutt their way out, that the signal was actually given, but was not responded to by the men. The same thing they say is to be attempted to night. Notify Your troops occupying the front to be extra Vigilant and those in support to sleep on their arms" Copies, DLC-USG, V, 19, 30, 98; DNA, RG 393, Dept. of the Tenn., Letters Sent; *ibid.*, 13th Army Corps, Letters Received. On the same day, USG signaled to McClernand. "All are advancing as fast as possible" Copy, *ibid.* On May 27, McClernand wrote twice to USG, first at 2:00 P.M. "Front comparatively quiet.—work progressing." Copy, *ibid.*, Letters Sent. "Col Whiting Comdg at Warrenton, rep[orted] Genl Johnson, with three or four thousand men, building [a] bridge across Big Black, from twelve to twenty mil[es] off. My Cavalry are now reconnoitering towards Bal[d]wins and Halls. I have no corroboration of the report. [I] will send word to Genl. Lauman. A gun boat should wat[ch] Warrenton." Copy, *ibid.* Dated [May 20] in *O.R.*, I, xxiv, part 3, 333. On the same day, Maj. Wright Rives, aide to McClernand, wrote to Rawlins. "The general directs me to inform you that the enemy in front of us, was moving wagons all last night, and that their railroad cars were also employed. Their object, no doubt is to move their heavy guns from the city to their lines of troops here. Maj Brady of the 8th Ind Infy reports that he could hear the wagons and cars plain, moving to our left. He also states that he saw signal lights during the night and beleives that they are making another line of works in rear of their present line. Would it not be well for our gun—and mortar boats to keep up a constant fire, so as to prevent this movement, by making them employ their guns on the river. Captain Foster (1st Wisconsin Battery) reports that late yesterday afternoon he blew up a magazine or caisson of the enemy's." LS, DNA, RG 393, Dept. of the Tenn., Letters Received. Also on May 27, McClernand wrote to Rawlins. "The forces now at Warrenton consist of the 114th Regt. O. V., Lt. Col. Kelly, Comdg. and a detachment of six companies of 87th Ills. Col. Whiting Comdg.,—in all not five hundred effective men, and not more than the place actually needs. If Genl. Grant has no objections I will retain Col. Whiting there. I have already directed Col. Whiting to strengthen his position, and take efficient measures to make the public stores safe,—as there are some apprehensions of trouble from guerillas and detached bodies of the enemy's cavalry. Would it not be advisable for the Gunboats to open communication with Warrenton so as to assist in case an attack should be made the place? I understand that there is one Gunboat lying about two miles above this point where the Young's Point road intersects the river." LS (by Scates), *ibid.*

To Brig. Gen. Peter J. Osterhaus

———

Head Quarters, Dept. of the Ten.
Near Vicksburg, May 26th 1863

BRIG. GEN. OSTERHAUS
COMD.G U. S. FORCES, BLACK RIVER BRIDGE,
GEN.

Direct Col. Johnson, if he has not already passed, to go by way of Bolton and destroy all the cars, confederate cotton grain & provisions in store there. If Johnson has passed send some of the cavalry still left to accomplish the same purpose.

Have your teams bring in all the cotton in the entrenchments opposite you and as your teams are coming into the river after supplies let them bring in the cotton with them.

Let the cavalry destroy all the rail-road bridges as far out as they go beyond the Black.

All forage beyond Black River that can be reached should be destroyed. All negroes, teams & cattle should be brought in and every thing done to prevent an Army supplying itself coming this way.

U. S. GRANT
Maj. Gen. Com

ALS, DNA, RG 393, 13th Army Corps, 9th Div., Letters Received. *O.R.*, I, xxiv, part 3, 351. On May 26, 1863, Brig. Gen. Peter J. Osterhaus, Big Black River Bridge, wrote to Lt. Col. John A. Rawlins. "I have the honor to acknowledge the receipt of the letter of Major Genl. Grant Comg Dept., instructing me to destroy certain Stores u. s. v   Col A. K. Johnson not having passed at this point yet and his movements being unknown to me, I hastened to execute these instructions as far as my means go; I ordered Captain Campbell and Ca. 60 men 3d Ills Cavalry to proceed at once to Edwards—& Bolton stations, following the Rail-Road if possible, and to destroy all conf. Stores, Cotton etc he may find there, burn all R. R. bridges and all means of subsistence for an Army in his reach; further-more to Collect all Cattle and male negroes and bring them to this (West) side of the big Black. I exspect the Captain to return to morrow morning, when I shall report on his success. Small as the Captains force is, I did not hesitate, to send him out, as I had intelligence from the Comdg officer of my pickets in that direction up to Noon, which assure me 'that he had scoured the Country on every road, and that there are no armed rebels this side of Clinton and Raymond' The Cotton in the intrenchments I also had collected (about 200 bales) and will forward it to morrow morning to the River landing. There are over 600 Sick and Wounded in the hospitals at Champion hill, half of them able to be transported; could I have them brought within our lines? These at Smith's plantation (Big Black fight) I had all transferred to this side; paroling at the same time 39 Rebel Soldiers in hospital there. Colonel Wright has not yet reported!.—" ALS, DNA, RG 393, Dept. of the Tenn., Letters Received.

On May 25, Maj. Gen. John A. McClernand twice wrote to USG. "I have the honor to inform you that Col. Clark Wright has not responded to Genl. Osterhaus, and refuses to do so, having no orders to do so, as he says, and under orders that conflict with it. He also asks for two 12 pdr. Howitzers. I most respectfully ask that Col. Wright may be ordered by you to report to Genl. Osterhaus. Genl. Osterhaus reports that the wounded, Surgeons, and nurses left at Raymond have been captured by the enemy and parolled. He thinks there is no great force at present in the rear, but the enemy is fortifying Jackson and collecting large numbers of negroes there. His scouts found a small mounted picket at the crossroad west of Brownsville. It is rumored that Johnson is near with a force, and that the enemy intended visiting the Hospital at Champion Hills to day to capture and parole the wounded and sick there. In consequence of this rumor, all who were able left the Hospital for his Head Qrs. He is wholly unable to keep pickets on all the routes and patrol the roads and country without more cavalry. I earnestly hope you will supply him. It is understood that the 54th Inda, left as guard at Raymond, was afterwards sent by you as a guard of prisoners to the river,—if so will you be pleased to order them to join their brigade at the Big Black?" LS, *ibid. O.R.*, I, xxiv, part 3, 347–48. "I have just received a communication from Col. Taggart, who says there are 1200 sick and wounded at James Plantation,—and some ammunition. Cotton, and forage at Perkins Plantation. The 60th Ind. and 96th Ohio were left at the latter place. I sent an order yesterday or the day before to these Regiments to report to me here. Shall the sick and all property be brought to Warrenton, or above, or shall the order be countermanded for moving one or both these Regiments.—I await your advice and further directions in the matter." Copy, DNA, RG 393, 13th Army Corps, Letters Sent.

Also on May 25, Col. Clark Wright, "Edwards Plantation Bridgeport Road," wrote to Rawlins. "I have Just completed a Reconizance by the way of Raymond to Clinton, Another by way of Brownsville to vicinity of Clinton no Rebel forces found or herd of in the vicinity of either route. A Rebel deserter Captured near Clinton reports, (And with a fair degree of Frankness) that Gen Lorings Command is greatly demoralized, & that some 4 000 of them have deserted & are now lying in the Swamps along the Miss. he further states that, Generls Loring & Gregg are making desperate efforts to concentrate thier scattered forces at various points from Canton to Yazoo Citty. he knows of no other forces having arrived from any other point, although they say they are looking for them. he says the Forces at Vixburgh Cannot be less than 45 or 50 000 he thinks thier policy will be (when there is no other alternative) to mass thier troops upon some one point & cut out rather than surrender." ALS, *ibid.*, Dept. of the Tenn., Letters Received.

On May 27, Rawlins wrote to Wright. "You will immediately report in person for orders to Brig Gen Osterhaus Comm'dg 9th Division at his camp at the Railroad crossing of the Big Black river on the Jackson road to whom has been assigned the guarding and watching of the several crossings on the Big

Black including that at Bridgeport." Copies, DLC-USG, V, 19, 30; DNA, RG 393, Dept. of the Tenn., Letters Sent; *ibid.*, 13th Army Corps, Letters Received. A telegram dated [June] 7 from McClernand to Rawlins appears more likely to have been sent May 24–25. "General Osterhaus has just reported that his cavalry force is too small. Colonel Mudd is using the Second Illinois on the Hall's Ferry and Baldwin's Ferry roads and the lateral roads connecting these with Big Black, and cannot well be spared from there. The Sixth Missouri, or some other detachment of cavalry, should be ordered to report to General Osterhaus." *O.R.*, I, xxiv, part 3, 388.

To Col. Amory K. Johnson

Head Quarters Dept of the Tenn
Near Vicksburg Miss May 26. 1863

COL. A. K. JOHNSON
COMMDG CAVALRY EXPEDITION
COL:

Since ordering you to proceed north on the east side of Black river I have determined to send a large Infantry and Artillery force to clean out any force the enemy may have between the Black and the Yazoo river. You will not go therefore as directed but join with the cavalry the main expedition

Three Brigades will start from the 17th Army Corps by the oak Ridge road, and an equal number from the 15th Army Corps, by way of Haines Bluffs all to unite near Sulphur Springs. They will probably get started this evening. You will join them with your cavalry force, and report to the Commanding Officer of the Expedition for orders

U. S. GRANT
Maj General

Copies, DLC-USG, V, 19, (incomplete) 30, 98; DNA, RG 393, Dept. of the Tenn., Letters Sent; Alcorn Collection, WyU. *O.R.*, I, xxiv, part 3, 351. See letter to Maj. Gen. Francis P. Blair, Jr., May 29, 1863, note 1.

To Maj. Gen. John A. McClernand

Head Quarters Dept of the Tenn
Near Vicksburg May 28 : 1863

Major General Jno A. McClernand
Commdg 13th Army Corps
General:

Two steamers have arrived loaded with ammunition All kinds are now in great abundance except 6 pdr. smooth bore and 12 pdr Howitzer ammunition. These will be here in a few days. There is also a sling cart for moving heavy artillery and all the appliances for repairing any defective pieces.

Admiral Porter kindly offers to furnish us any of his heavy artillery we may require. If you have any place where you would like to place Heavy Artillery you can have it by sending your cheif of Artillery to Lieut Lyford at the Chickasaw Bayou Landing.

Very respectfully
U. S. Grant
Maj. Gen.

Copies, DLC-USG, V, 19, 30, 98; DNA, RG 393, Dept. of the Tenn., Letters Sent; *ibid.*, 13th Army Corps, Letters Received. On May 28, 1863, USG wrote to Maj. Gen. James B. McPherson. "Two Steamers have arrived loaded with Ammunition &c so that their is an abundant supply of all kinds in hand except 6 pdr smooth bore and 12 pdr howitzer. Of these their will be an abundant supply in a few days. Lyford has also got a Sling Cart. If you require any heavy guns you can get them from the Navy. Lyford will have them moved for you." Copies, DLC-USG, V, 19, 30, 98; DNA, RG 393, Dept. of the Tenn., Letters Sent.

On May 29, 2:30 P.M., USG telegraphed to Maj. Gen. John A. McClernand. "Open your Artillery at five O'clock for half an hour" Copy, *ibid.*, 13th Army Corps, Letters Received. On the same day, McClernand wrote to USG. "I have the honor to inform you that I have been diligently engaged in preparing a report, in compliance with your order to report the operations of this Army Corps from the time it left Milliken's Bend up to the 28th inst.—But not having yet received reports from Division Commanders, and amid the duties of the field and camp, I have found it impossible to make it to-day. It will be finished at the earliest possible moment and forwarded. Our firing this morning burned some buildings in the city,—as a very large smoke was seen in that direction." LS, *ibid.*, Dept. of the Tenn., Letters Received.

To Brig. Gen. Jacob G. Lauman

———

Head quarters, Dept. of the Tenn.
In rear of Vicksburg, Miss.
May 28th 1863.

BRIG. GENL. LAUMAN,
COMDG. 4TH DIVN. 16TH A. C.
GENERAL,

You will immediately place your division in camp on the Hall's ferry road, on the south side of the creek near the large Hospital, its left resting on the road and right extending towards McClernand's left.

Strong grand guards, advance posts and pickets will be thrown out on the various approaches to Vicksburg, leading from your front and between it and the Mississippi, and every precaution be taken to prevent surprise from front or rear, or the enemy from communicating in any manner upon these roads. Every means will be resorted to in order to harrass the rebels.

You will also, without delay open a good road over the nearest practicable route to McClernand's left.

Very Respectfully.
U. S. GRANT
Maj. Genl. Com

LS, DNA, RG 94, War Records Office, Military Div. of the Miss. *O.R.*, I, xxiv, part 3, 356. This letter is entered in USG's letterbooks as written by Lt. Col. John A. Rawlins.

On May 28, 1863, Rawlins issued Special Orders No. 143. "Army Corps Commanders and Commanders of detached forces before Vicksburg, will picket all roads immediately in rear of their respective positions by which their camps or the City of Vicksburg can be approached, and prohibit all persons coming into or going out of our lines, without special authority from the Corps or Commanders of detached forces, whose pickets they desire to pass, or the authority of the General Commanding. The pickets will be placed sufficiently far out as to prevent surprise from any raid the enemy may attempt to make, and each commander will notify the others, of the position of his pickets." DS, Rawlins Papers, ICHi; copies, DLC-USG, V, 27, 28; DNA, RG 393, Dept. of the Tenn., Special Orders; Alcorn Collection, WyU. *O.R.*, I, xxiv, part 3, 356–57. On May 29, Rawlins issued Special Orders No. 144. "Army Corps Commanders and Commanders of detached forces will take immediate steps to obstruct and render impassible for troops all roads leading into the rear of their respective Commands and into Vicksburg, except the main Jackson road, via the Big-Black railroad bridge, and the different roads to Haines Bluffs. On the Bridgeport road and on all the roads south of it except the main Jackson road the obstructions will be commenced as far out as the Big Black river; and on all others to be obstructed as far out as possible, every bridge on them will be destroyed and at favorable points the timber cut across the roads in towards the City and up to our rear Pickets. The main Jackson road via Big Black Railroad bridge and the different roads to Haine's Bluffs will be unmolested" Copies, DLC-USG, V, 27, 28; DNA, RG 393, Dept. of the Tenn., Special Orders; Alcorn Collection, WyU. *O.R.*, I, xxiv, part 3, 363. On May 29, Maj. Gen. John A. McClernand wrote to USG. "Do you intend that the road to Warrenton shall also be obstructed?" Copy, DNA, RG 393, 13th Army Corps, Letters Sent.

To Maj. Gen. Henry W. Halleck

Near Vicksburg May 29. 1863.

The Enemy under Johnson are collecting in large force to attack me and rescue the garrison of Vicksburg. I have had my Cavalry and six Brigades of Infantry out looking after them and they confirm the report of a large force being collected at Canton.

The number is reported to be 45.000 but may not be so large. If Banks does not come to my assistance I must be re-inforced from elsewhere,   I will avoid a surprise and do the best I can with all the means at hand.

U. S. GRANT.
Maj. Genl.

Telegram received, DLC-Edwin M. Stanton; DNA, RG 107, Telegrams Collected (Bound); copies, *ibid.*, Telegrams Received in Cipher; DLC-USG, V, 98. *O.R.*, I, xxiv, part 1, 40. This telegram was sent from Memphis by Maj. Gen. Stephen A. Hurlbut, May 31, 1863, 1:00 P.M., and received in Washington June 2, 12:55 A.M. On June 2, 6:30 P.M., President Abraham Lincoln telegraphed to USG. "Are you in communication with Gen. Banks? Is he coming towards you, or going further off? Is there, or has there been any thing to hinder his coming directly to you by water from Alexandria?" ALS (telegram sent), RPB; telegram received, DNA, RG 94, War Records Office, Dept. of the Tenn. *O.R.*, I, xxiv, part 1, 40. Lincoln, *Works*, VI, 244. Also on June 2, 12:30 P.M., Maj. Gen. Henry W. Halleck telegraphed to USG. "Yours of 29th is recieved. I will do all I can to assist you. I have sent despatch after despatch to Genl Banks to join you. Why he does not, I cannot understand. His separate operation upon Port Hudson is in direct violation of his instructions. If possible send him this despatch. My last despatch from him was May 4th." ALS (telegram sent), DNA, RG 107, Telegrams Collected (Bound); telegram received, *ibid.*, RG 94, War Records Office, Dept. of the Tenn. *O.R.*, I, xxiv, part 1, 40.

To Act. Rear Admiral David D. Porter

Lake's Landing, Miss.
May 29th 1863.

REAR ADMIRAL PORTER,
COMDG. MISS. SQDRON
ADMIRAL,

Will you have the kindness to order the Marine Brigade to Hains' Bluff, with instructions to disembark at that point and remain in occupation till I can releive them by other troops.[1]

I have also to request you to put at the disposal of Maj. Lyford, Chief of Ordnance *two* 9 inch guns, implements and ammunition, complete, to be placed in battery in the rear of Vicksburg. After they are in battery and ready for use I should be pleased to have you man them by crews from your fleet.[2]

Very Respectfully
U. S. GRANT
Maj. Genl. Com

LS, MoSHi. *O.R.*, I, xxiv, part 3, 361; *O.R.* (Navy), I, xxv, 49–50. On May 29, 1863, Act. Rear Admiral David D. Porter, *Black Hawk*, wrote to USG. "The Brigade will leave for Hayne's Bluff early in the morning—I have not a nine inch gun here not anything larger than a 32 pounder (long ranges) excepting one ten inch gun with shell   this would require too much work to mount it on account of pivot bolts &c—I am fitting it on a mortar boat to throw shells into the pits, in front of sherman—I ordered two 9 inch guns sent to Gen'l McArthur, at Warrenton   they are there now on board the 'Tuscumbia' ready to be delivered. The difficulty will be in hauling them so far, tho' perhaps they may be in a better place for your purposes. I have six 8 inch guns on the 'Manitou' which vessel is now up at Yazoo City. The moment she arrives I will direct her Commander to land the guns, and send to Cairo at once for more 9 inch guns—" LS, DNA, RG 94, War Records Office, Dept. of the Tenn. *O.R.*, I, xxiv, part 3, 361; *O.R.* (Navy), I, xxv, 50.

On May 27, USG had written to Porter. "Gen Lauman on our left informs that your firing to-day did good execution but several shots were too far to the left—your right—going into his camp." Copies, DLC-USG, V, 30; DNA, RG 393, Dept. of the Tenn., Letters Sent. *O.R.* (Navy), I, xxv, 37. Dated May 26 in DLC-USG, V, 19.

1. On May 30, noon, Brig. Gen. Alfred W. Ellet, Marine Brigade, Haynes' Bluff, signaled to USG. "I have arrived here with my command and find no force to relieve. My force for duty is eight hundred. Will wait orders." Signal received, DNA, RG 94, War Records Office, Military Div. of the Miss. On May 31, USG wrote to Porter. "Will you please direct the Marine Brigade to debark at Haines Bluff and send all their steamers or as many of them as possible to Memphis to bring down reenforcements. I have ordered the troops but it is a difficult matter to get transportation. I would specially request that any of these steamers that can be spared be got off at the earliest possible moment" Copies, DLC-USG, V, 19, 30; DNA, RG 393, Dept. of the Tenn., Letters Sent; Alcorn Collection, WyU. *O.R.*, I, xxiv, part 3, 368; *O.R.* (Navy), I, xxv, 53. Probably on June 1, USG signaled to Porter. "where has the marine brigade been ordered to" Copy (undated), DNA, RG 111, Vicksburg Signal Book. Probably on the same day, Porter signaled to USG. "marine Brig was ordered to memphis to bring down troops—left early this morning" Copy (undated), *ibid*. See Warren D. Crandall and Isaac D. Newell, *History of the Ram Fleet and the Mississippi Marine Brigade* . . . (St. Louis, 1907), pp. 297–98.

2. On May 29, 11:40 A.M., Maj. Gen. James B. McPherson wrote to USG. "I would like two 9 inch guns to put in the battery where the two 30 p'r Parrotts are. Will you please direct Lyford to have them got up for me, with the necessary ammunition, implements &c, and if possible I would like to have the Navy furnish a few men to take charge of each gun. I will have the places prepared, and every thing ready as soon as they arrive." Copies (2), DNA, RG 393, 17th Army Corps, Letters Sent. On May 30 or 31, USG wrote to Maj. Gen. William T. Sherman a message telegraphed to the others. "Gens McClernand, Sherman & McPherson, open all your Artillery on the enemy at for half an hour commencing at 3 in the morning. Throw shell near the parapets and well into the city also." ALS (undated, docketed May 23), DLC-William T. Sherman; copies (dated May 30, 9:00 P.M.), DNA, RG 393, 13th Army Corps, Letters Received; (dated May 31) *ibid*., Dept. of the Tenn., Letters Sent; DLC-USG, V, 19, 30. *O.R.*, I, xxiv, part 3, 368.

To Act. Rear Admiral David D. Porter

Near Vicksburg May 29th/63

DEAR ADMIRAL,

A force of the enemy having driven our Cavalry in from about thirty-five miles Northeast from here I sent out a force of about

12 000 men on the evening of the 26th. This force is commanded by Maj. Gen. Blair and are instructed to clean out the enemy between the Black & Yazoo Rivers and, if possible, destroy the Miss. Central rail-road bridge over Black river. There is great danger of the enemy crossing Black river in rear of this force and cutting them off from their return to this place. I have instructed Gen. Blair in case of this kind to strike for the Yazoo River by which route a way back can be easily opened.

If you can send one or two Gunboats to navigate the Yazoo as high up as Yazoo City I would think it highly advisable at least until Blair is heard from.

Yours Truly
U. S. GRANT
Maj. Gen

To ADMIRAL D. D. PORTER
COMD.G MISS. SQUADRON

ALS, MdAN. *O.R.*, I, xxiv, part 3, 361; *O.R.* (Navy), I, xxv, 49.

To Maj. Gen. Nathaniel P. Banks

———

Head Quarters. Department of the Tenn.
Near Vicksburg. May. 29. 1863

MAJ. GEN. N. P. BANKS
COM'D'G DEPT. OF THE GULF.
GEN.

I send Mr. C. A. Dana, Inspector of the Pay Dept.[1] to urge the same suggestions made by me in the communication of which Col. Riggin was bearer.

I have nothing further to add since my last that Mr. Dana cannot communicate more fully than can well be done in a written statement.

The enemy are now concentrating a force near Canton, Miss. With an additional force here I could detach everything but about

25.000 men and go with the balance and capture or disperse him, leaving the State of Mississippi an easy prize to our Armies.

Hoping Gen. this may find you in possession of Port Hudson, and all the Mississippi River below here I remain,

Very truly, Your Obt. Servt.
U. S. Grant
Major General.

Copies, DLC-USG, V, 19, 30, 98; DNA, RG 393, Dept. of the Tenn., Letters Sent. *O.R.*, I, xxiv, part 3, 359. For evidence that this letter was never delivered, see *ibid.*, I, xxiv, part 1, 91, and *O.R.* (Navy), I, xxv, 147.

1. Charles A. Dana, born in N. H. in 1819 into a poor family, was largely self-educated before attending Harvard College (1839–41). He began his writing career during five years at Brook Farm, later becoming an editor of Horace Greeley's *New York Tribune* (1847–62). Appointed to investigate claims at Cairo (*PUSG*, 4, 83n–84n), Dana first met USG on July 4, 1862, at Memphis (*ibid.*, 5, 383). Entering into a partnership to purchase cotton, he arrived at Memphis in Jan., 1863, with a letter of introduction from Secretary of War Edwin M. Stanton to USG. Dana, *Recollections of the Civil War* (New York, 1898), p. 17. On Jan. 22, USG issued a pass. "Mr. Chas. A. Dana is authorized to pass through all parts of this Military Dept. including river . . . Good until countermanded." Goodspeed's Catalogue No. 378 (June, 1944), p. 16. On the preceding day, Dana had written Stanton a denunciation of current practices in the cotton trade, and he soon abandoned his own enterprise. Dana, *Recollections*, pp. 18–20. In March, Stanton appointed Dana a special commissioner of the War Dept., ostensibly to investigate the pay service, actually to report everything possible about military affairs along the Mississippi River. *Ibid.*, pp. 21–22. Stanton gave Dana a letter of introduction of March 11 addressed to USG and other gens. Copy, DLC-Edwin M. Stanton. Dated March 12 in *O.R.*, III, 3, 63–64. Dana's reports to Stanton, March 20–July 4, numerous, detailed, insightful, are *ibid.*, I, xxiv, part 1, 63–117.

To Maj. Gen. Francis P. Blair, Jr.

Head Quarters Dept. of the Tenn.
Near Vicksburg May 29. 1863

Maj: General F. P. Blair
Commdg Expedition
General:

Not hearing from you Since you left[1] I have become some

what uneasy lest the enemy should get some portion of his force in your rear. This you will have to look out for closely; should the enemy succeed in getting a force in your rear to strong for you to contend against strike for the Yazoo river, and get a courier to me by the west bank or any other way you can. I will ask Admiral Porter to send one or more gunboats to Yazoo City Let me hear from you by the bearer.

> Very respectfully
> U. S. GRANT.
> Maj. Gen.

Copies, DLC–USG, V, 19, 30, 98; DNA, RG 393, Dept. of the Tenn., Letters Sent; Alcorn Collection, WyU. On May 29, 1863, Maj. Gen. Francis P. Blair, Jr., "Mechanicsburgh," wrote to USG. "I am just in receipt of your communication of this date. I despached ten cavalry with a despatch to you last night & two this morning with the same intelligence but as your courier met both parties near Vicksburgh it will not be necessary to repeat it here. I found no enemy on my way here of any consequence. My advance came up with about four or five hundred of the enemy at this place about 1½ P M today.—They were driven back after a slight resistence & have fled beyond the Black River. Col Johnson has scoured the country pretty thoroughly on both sides of the route & along the Big Black as far down as Cox's ford, but finds only stragglers who are ~~mostly~~ all going over the river & concentrating at Canton where Johnson is understood to be. From all the intelligence I can obtain it appears that Genl Johnson is organizing an army at or near Canton, & I feel pretty well assured that no considerable force is on this side of the Black river. The route I have passed over contained but little or no forage or provisions but such as there was I destroyed or seized. I shall return tomorrow by a route which the bearer will name and on which I will be free from any flank attack. I shall seize everything on the road necessary for my troops & destroy the residue. The enemy who met my advance to-day ~~have~~ crossed the Big Black at Kibby's Ferry" ALS, DNA, RG 94, War Records Office, Dept. of the Tenn. *O.R.*, I, xxiv, part 2, 435.

1. On May 26, Lt. Col. John A. Rawlins issued Special Orders No. 141. "Three Brigades will be immediately detached from the 15th and 17th Army Corps, each, including the Brigade at Haines Bluff. The whole will be under the temporary command of Maj. Genl. F. P. Blair. The troops from the 15th Army Corps will proceed immediately to Haines Bluffs, those from the 17th Army Corps, will move by the Oak Ridge road to Sulphur Springs. At or near the latter place a junction will be formed between all the forces, when they will be moved upon, and drive out the enemy now collecting between the Black and Yazoo rivers. The expedition will carry in Haversacks and Wagons, seven days rations of Bread, salt, and coffee, and one-hundred and fifty rounds of ammunition including that in Cartridge boxes" DS, Rawlins Papers, ICHi; copies, DLC–USG, V, 27, 28; DNA, RG 393, Dept. of the Tenn., Special Orders; Alcorn Collection, WyU. *O.R.*, I, xxiv, part 3, 352.

To Maj. Gen. Francis P. Blair, Jr.

May 29. 1863

MAJ. GEN. F P. BLAIR
COMDG ADVANCE EXPEDITION
GEN

Yours of the 28th enclosing report of ~~the 28th~~ Col. Johnson is just recieved. it is so important that we should save all our troops to act together that I would direct that you take no risks whatever either of a defeat or of being cut off.

If you are satisfied of the presence of a large force at Canton and north of there return immediately leaving Mowers Brigade at Haines Bluff If you deem Haines Bluff in danger of an early attack you may also leave McArthurs with the Brigade of his Division. Returning distroy all the Forage and stock you can and obstruct all roads behind you by burning bridges falling timber and in all possible ways. I requested Admiral Porter yesterday to send a Gunboat or two up the river to cruise until you return

You may rest at Haines Bluff with your entire command until you receive further orders from me. Such information may be received from the enemy, and sufficient reinforcements arrive here as to make it advisable to send out an army large enough to clean out Jo Johnston, and his party

Very respectfully
U S GRANT
Maj. Gen.

Copies, DLC-USG, V, 19, 30, 98; DNA, RG 393, Dept. of the Tenn., Letters Sent; Alcorn Collection, WyU. *O.R.*, I, xxiv, part 3, 361–62. On May 28, 1863, Maj. Gen. Francis P. Blair, Jr., "Halls Plantation," wrote to USG. "I enclose a report from Col Johnson Comdg the Cavalry whom I have since seen. He has no doubt of the entire correctness of the statement with the exception that he believes the numbers are greatly exaggerated. I have not as yet determined upon the course to be taken by me, but will do so early in the morning upon consultation with Division & Brigade Comdgs If I shall determine to push on & it shall be found that the enemy are in the force represented or anything like it, it will be necessary for me to go over to the Yazoo River, & rejoin you by that route, if you can send up transportation for me under convoy of a gunboat. If you hear nothing more

from me in the next few days you may conclude I have taken this course. If however I should determine that I am not justifyed in pushing forward & seperating
myself farther from your army I will endeavor by a forced march to reach Haines
Bluffs in one days march"   ALS, DNA, RG 94, War Records Office, Dept. of
the Tenn. *O.R.*, I, xxiv, part 3, 354–55. For the enclosure see *ibid.*, p. 355.

On May 29, Blair, "Harts Plantation 35 miles from Vicksburg," wrote to
USG. "I wrote you last night & sent a copy of a note from Col Johnson, a duplicate of which I enclose. Upon further conversation with Col J he thinks the statement that Hill was in Jackson ten days incorrect & the language refers to Johnson
but he thinks that Hill is there or has been recently. I shall push to day & try &
carry out your instructions but if the statements should be corroborated I will
govern myself accordingly & not make the gap much wider between us. If you
do not hear from me soon, send Gunboats & transports up the Yazoo to enable
me to join by that route"   ALS, DNA, RG 393, Dept. of the Tenn., Letters
Received. On May 31, Blair, "Camp at Dramgooles Bluff," wrote to USG. "I
arrived here this evening at 1. Oclock with the Head of my column by what is
called the valley road from Satartia in the Yazoo to Haine's Bluff. I received your
orders to return here just as I had commenced my march to this point on yesterday morning. The enemy followed us with perhaps 20 or 30 cavalry or mounted
Infantry, but the valley was so open & clear that they dared not approach and
gave us no annoyance whatever—when they fired on us as they did yesterday &
to-day we knew exactly what force was necessary to repulse & drive them & did
not have to delay our march. The valley of the Yazoo is one of the most fertile
spots I ever saw and we found supplies & forage sufficient to supply Jo Johnsons
army for a month, if he has 40,000 men. I used all that we could & destroyed the
rest.   we must have burned 500,000 bushels of corn and immense quantities of
bacon most of which was concealed by its owners but discovered & either appropriated or destroyed by my order. I destroyed every grist mill in the valley and
have driven in to this place about 1,000 head of cattle. I brought with me an army
of negroes nearly equal to the number of men in my command and the Cavalry &
Infantry have seized & brought in two or three hundred head of mules & horses.
I also ordered the empty waggons to load with cotton & I think they have brought
30 or 40 bales. I burned all the balance of the cotton I found except a small quantity within our picket lines which can be secured for the Government if it is
desired. Jo Johnston will find very little for his army in the country between the
Black River & Yazoo for 45 miles north of Vicksburg. I consider Mechanicksburg
as the great straget point between the two Rivers—you can reach it by three
different & parellel roads from Vicksburg and you can supply an army there by
means of the Yazoo from which it is only 3 miles distant at the town of Satartia.
It is situated at the narrowest place between the two Rivers & communicates by
good & direct roads with Benton, Yazoo City, Kibbys Ferry & Cox ferry on the
Black River & also with Bridgeport on the Black River. I have no doubt that Jo
Johnson is collecting a considerable force now at Canton & other places beyond
the Black River. Every man we picked up was going to Canton to join him. The
negroes that say their masters have joined him there and those who were too old
to go or who would escape on any other pretext told us the same story. I consider
it very certain that he has a considerable force & is using every effort to increase
it & the hopes of relief from that quarter is all that delays the surrender of Vicksburg . . . I wish you would send an order here to turn over to E. M. Joel Capt &
A Q M all the ~~captured~~ mules, horses, cattle, cotton [—] captured by this com-

mand for the use of the Govt. The command is composed of officers who belong to so many differnt corps that I would prefer your giving the orders to giving it myself which I shall however do if is necessary." ALS, *ibid.*, RG 94, War Records Office, Dept. of the Tenn. *O.R.*, I, xxiv, part 2, 435–36.

To Brig. Gen. Peter J. Osterhaus

Head Quarters, Dept. of the Ten.
Near Vicksburg, May 29th 1863,

BRIG. GEN. OSTERHAUS,
COMD.G AT BLACK RIVER BRIDGE,
GEN.

Burn up the remainder of Black River Bridge. Make details from the Negroes collected about your camp, and also from the troops and have as much of the road taken up, East of the river, as you can. Pile the ties up and lay the rails across them and burn them up. Wherever there is a bridge, or trestle work, as far East as you send troops have them destroyed. Effectually destroy the road, and particularly the rails, as far East as you can.

Very respectfully
U. S. GRANT
Maj. Gen. Com

ALS, DNA, RG 393, 13th Army Corps, 9th Div., Letters Received. *O.R.*, I, xxiv, part 3, 362. On May 29, 1863, Brig. Gen. Peter J. Osterhaus wrote to USG. "Your Order of to day to burn the R. R. bridges and track east of here is just received and I take immediate Steps to execute them most effectually! I had the honor before, to report, that I had almost every bushel of Corn destroyed along the R R. line and the public road as far as Bolton; since then I did the same thing as far North and South of the R R. as my limited Means allowed it and Col Wright with the 6th Mo Cavalry is out at present to look around at and near Bridgeport. The following articles of Contraband were collected on these raids, and shipped to *Major Garber A. Q M* 13th A. Corps   53 Mules.   14 horses   152 bales of Cotton   to *Com. of Subsistence* 13th A. Corps 118 head of beef Cattle   *there are now on this side* ready for Shipment 330 bales of Cotton, and a lot of beef Cattle will come in this afternoon; Cotton and beef will be forwarded, to the River with all despatch. My Scouts from Edwards Station, Champion hill, Halls ferry & Bridgeport ferry report every thing quiet, no enemy has been seen, since the 'soidisant' paroling of the wounded at Champion hill; the paroling officer there only took a list of the men without they giving or Signing the parole; Can such proceeding stand for a parole? All the Wounded are very anxious to get away, but my Means of transportation are not adequate, and, besides I do not consider myself authorized, to cause the transfer! I hope to be able to report to you by to morrow, how I succeeded in the Work of 'laying waste' . . ." ALS, DNA, RG 393, Dept. of the Tenn., Letters Received. *O.R.*, I, xxiv, part 2, 211–12. On May 30 and June 1, Osterhaus wrote to Lt. Col. John A. Rawlins reporting progress in the destruction of the railroad and the results of his patrols. LS and ALS, DNA, RG 94, War Records Office, Dept. of the Tenn. *O.R.*, I, xxiv, part 2, 212–13.

On May 30, Col. Clark Wright, "Big Black Bridge," wrote to Rawlins. "I have just completed a reconnizance on East side of Big Black, and collected the following information. Under cover of secesh captains uniform and Butternut clothing for Ten men to *wit*: South of R. R. in vicinity of Bolton, Raymond, &C I found Col Lyons 8th Kentucky with 250 men (Mounted Infantry,) who Left Vixburgh with 600 men, May 19th via Warrenton, Cayuga, across to crystal spring to meredian (where they mounted their men) then to Jackson, where Gen Loring sent their remaining forces 250 to where I find them to watch roads & collect information, North of R. R. between Bird Song Ferry (B. B. R.) and Brownsville I found Capt Hall with one Company of Cavely and two Companies of mounted Cittizens guarding that road and collecting information. in the vicinity of Brownsville, and two miles beyond there is 400 in camp, for the same purposes. At Mr Rieds Near Balton I met Capt W. J. Bruner, Div Q. M. (Rebel Service) who informes me that Gen Loring night before last (the time Bruner left Jackson) was at Jackson with 5500, and that Johnson was at Canton with 18000, anxiously awaiting reenforcements he said they were not mooving this way nor would not until reinforced, and that they were fearful the Yankeys would moove on them before thier forces arrived. At Wash. Farrs Near Brownsville I met Gen Smead, (Rebel) from whom I learn the same as from Bruner, with the addition, that Johnson said he would not attack with his present force, but within the next ten days he would increase his force to 40,000, then he would advance on the Yankeys. In the course of the interview I learned that when he mooved, he calculated to cross B. Black at Moores Bluffs, and strike Yazoo at Hains Bluff. Detatchments of my command mooving on Raymond, Clinton and Brdgeport roads, at the same time, destroyed a number of Bridges, two R. R. Cares some 2000 Bushels of Corn, some two Hundred Bales of Cotton, and Depot House at Balton. My Comd 6th Mo Cavely is Quite worn down, men & Horses. I send to day for Horse Shoes. we need more Cavely at this point. . . . P. S. Brig Gen Osterhaus has a coppy of this report" ALS, DNA, RG 94, War Records Office, Dept. of the Tenn. On June 1, Wright wrote to Rawlins. "I have Just completed another reconizance on the east Side of Black River. we went South down the River to 14 Mile Creek. All Quiet East Via Champion Hills to a point beyond Balton. All Quiet, North of R. R. to Brownsville All Quiet. The information obtained, Confirms previous reports. The Bridges to the various points indicated, are all distroyed from Black River R. R. Bridge out. dureing the Expedition we burned 825 Bales C. S. A Cotton, 8000 Bushels Corn, 32 Stocks of Fodder and 15000, pounds of Bacon. brought into Camp 8 C. S. A. Steers, 5 mules, and Several Negro men. Coppy of Report sent to Genl. Osterhous" ALS, *ibid.*

On June 2, Lt. Col. Walter B. Scates, adjt. for Maj. Gen. John A. McClernand, wrote to Rawlins. "I have the honor to inform you that a despatch from Genl. Osterhaus has just been received, giving some indications of the approach of the enemy,—though his scouts had been beyond Bolton to Brownsville without meeting any troops. He is informed this morning that a regiment of Cavalry,—he thinks mounted Infantry,—was at Edward's Station at 3 o'clock A. M. this day, and took away one of the prisoners parolled by his Provost Marshal. One of his outpost sentries was wounded last night. He is making every exertion, through his Cavalry, to patrol the country and gain information. A company of mounted rebel Infantry went to the hospital of Genl. Lagan on the Battle ground at Champion Hills, on the 24th inst., and to Genl. Hovey's on the 25th and made a sweeping parole of every body without giving a parole paper or writing to anyone. They returned to Genls. Lagan and Quimby's hospitals yesterday saying they would make the parole good this time. The company was of the 8th Kentucky. Yesterday they said the whole Regt.—1000 strong,—was there. The messenger now in my office,—Lieut. of 11th Inda., detached as Surgeon at Hovey's hospital—says they were expected at that hospital to-day,—and Genl. Osterhaus writes that he thinks it unsafe to send the Ambulance trains on under such escort as he could give it. I received, also, a letter from one of the Clerks of my office—left sick at Champion Hills—who says he has been captured and parolled. He is now at the Church near St. Albans. What shall be done with these wounded?   Shall a flag of truce be sent, —either to bring them away—or to take them rations? They must be fed and cared for. They have provisions,—but they are badly in want of Sanitary goods and shirts, and drawers. 200 or 300 would be able to travel in Ambulances, if sent for them." LS, *ibid.*, RG 393, Dept. of the Tenn., Letters Received.

To Col. John C. Kelton

Head Quarters, Dept. of the Tn.
Near Vicksburg May 21st [*31*]/63

COL. J. C. KELTON
A. A. GN. WASHINGTON,
COL.

Eight men with 200 000 percussion Caps were arrested whilst attempting to get through our lines into Vicksburg. The enclosed Cypher was found upon them. Having no one with me who has the ingenuity to translate it I send it to Washington hoping that some one there may be able to make it out.

Should the meaning of this Cypher be made out I request that a copy be sent to me.

Very respectfully
U. S. GRANT
Maj. Gen

ALS, PPRF; copies (dated May 31, 1863), DLC-USG, V, 6, 8, 24, 94; DNA, RG 393, Dept. of the Tenn., Letters Sent. Dated May 25 in *O.R.*, I, xxiv, part 1, 39. For the enclosure, dated May 25, see *ibid.*, pp. 39–40; *ibid.*, I, xxiv, part 3, 365. On May 30, Brig. Gen. Jacob G. Lauman wrote to USG. "Our pickets arrested a party of men this morning making their way to Vicksburg. The letters enclosed were found upon their persons together with 200.000 percussion Caps. They represent Johnson as being at Jackson in force—The boy who acts as pilot to the party, is one of the boys I let off about three days ago, he is dangerous and should be attended to—He endeavoured to get in by way of the Vicksburg & Warrenton road—you may possibly get some information from the party" ALS, DNA, RG 94, War Records Office, Dept. of the Tenn. *O.R.*, I, xxiv, part 3, 364–65.

On June 16, Col. George Thom, Washington, wrote to USG. "Having in grateful remembrance your present (the pants) recd. through Genl. H., I send you a translation of Joe Johnston's despatch which I *guessed* out in about fifteen minutes—though it may be all *wrong.* I know nothing of the cipher & nothing of the key. What do you think of the translation? We are watching your operations, with full confidence in your success. You have done splendidly thus far, and 'tis well appreciated. We are, all at once, in the midst of most exciting scenes— waiting to hear the progress of the rebel raid now being made into Penn. This is their retaliation for Grierson's & Stoneman's great raids. Please remember me most kindly to Sherman, and McPherson—also to Prime & Wilson, of Engrs.—" ALS, DNA, RG 393, Dept. of the Tenn., Unregistered Letters Received.

On May 28, Lauman had sent to USG Greene S. Douglass, Waul's Tex. Legion, who had surrendered to U.S. forces after leaving Vicksburg with a dispatch from Lt. Gen. John C. Pemberton to Gen. Joseph E. Johnston, dated May 27, giving Pemberton's strength at 18,000. *Missouri Democrat*, June 6, 1863; *Chicago Tribune*, June 7, 1863.

To Maj. Gen. Nathaniel P. Banks

————

Head Quarters. Department of the Tennessee
In rear of Vicksburg Miss. May. 31st 1863

MAJ. GEN. N. P. BANKS.
COMM'D'G DEP'T OF THE GULF.
GENERAL;

Your letters of the 28th and 29th instant by Colonel Riggin, have just been recieved[1]

While I regret the situation in which they left you, and clearly see the necessity of your being reinforced in order to be immediately successful, the circumstances by which I am surrounded will prevent my making any detachments at this time.

Concentration is essential to the success of the general campaign in the West, but Vicksburg is the vital point; our situation is for the first time, during the entire Western campaign, what it should be. We have after great labor and extraordinary risk secured a position which should not be jeopardized by any detachments whatever. On the contrary, I am now, and shall continue to exert myself to the utmost to concentrate. The enemy clearly perceive the importance of dislodging me at all hazards. Genl. Jo. Johnston is now at Canton organizing his forces, and making his dispositions to attack me. His present strength is estimated at 40000, and is known to be at least 20000. The force he took from Jackson was 8000; Loring's Division which has joined him since the battle of Champions' Hill, 3000; Genl. Gist from South Carolina, 6000;[2] stragglers from Pemberton 2000; troops from Mobile, number not known.[3] Besides this, Maj. Gen. Hurlbut writes me he is reliably informed that Bragg has detached three Divisions from his Army, to report to Johnston. Pemberton has himself 18000 effective men.[4]

I have ample means to defend my present position, and effect the reduction of Vicksburg within twenty days, if the relation of affairs which now obtains, remains unchanged. But detach 10000 men from my command and I cannot answer for the result. With activity on the part of the enemy and any increase of his present force, it will become necessary for me to press my operations with all possible dispatch. I need not describe the severity of the labor to which my command must necessarily be subjected in an operation of such magnitude as that in which it is now engaged. Weakened by the detachment of 10000 men, or even half that number, with the circumstances entirely changed, I should be crippled beyond redemption. My arrangements for supplies are ample and can be expanded to meet any exigency. All I want now are men.

> I am, Sir
> Very Respectfully
> Your Obt. Servt.
> U. S. Grant
> Major General.

LS, DNA, RG 94, War Records Office, Dept. of the Gulf. *O.R.*, I, xxiv, part 3, 367; *ibid.*, I, xxvi, part 1, 525–26. Probably on May 31, 1863, USG signaled to Act. Rear Admiral David D. Porter. "Our means for moving the guns are at chickasaw bayou and they are needed at this end of the line. Will you ~~send~~ let me have the *Prise* to send dispatches to Banks? Please ans." Copy (undated), DNA, RG 111, Vicksburg Signal Book. Probably on the same day, Porter replied to USG. "I will do the best I can about the guns. The *Price* has gone below and will be up soon. She is at your com'd—Would a Mortar do" Copy (undated), *ibid.* See *O.R.* (Navy), I, xxv, 63.

On June 4, Maj. Gen. Nathaniel P. Banks wrote to USG. "Colonel Riggin deliverd to me your letter of the 31st May yesterday at 4. P. M.—Appreciating the difficulties of your position I cannot say I was greatly disapponted in learning your inability to send a detachment to our assistance, at the same time I deeply regret it. A little additional strength would carry us through the enemies works without delay. I am confident however that we shall succeed. Our heavy guns are now being placed in position and by tomorrow we shall open a fire that cannot but make a serious impression both upon the works and the garrison of the enemy. There is a force of two or three thousand in our rear, which is being strengthened daily by such additions as can be gathered from the country about us, that will in a short time give us some trouble. Colonel Grierson, had a sharp engagemnt with them yesterday, in which we sustained some loss and the enemy lost heavily. The consideration that gives me most anxiety is what course I should take in joining you. If I abandon Port Hudson, I leave its garrison of 5000. or 6000.—the force of Mouton and Sibley, now in the neighborhood of Brashear City—and the army at Mobile to threaten or attack New Orleans. To detach from my command, troops enough to secure that place, which ought not to be less than 10.000, my support to you would be but trifling, and would not at the same time prevent the enemy's re-inforcing Johnstone by an equal or larger number of men. It seems, to me, that I have no other course than to-carry my object here ~~thus to~~ crippling the enemy, and to join you with my whole strength as soon as possible   This I hope to accomplish in a few days. I believe, if uniterupted by fresh attacks this day week will see our flag floating over the fortifications now occupied by the Enemy. Acting upon the information of Colonel Riggin I shall send my transportation, land and water, for some kinds of ammution, to St. Louis or the nearest depot, for supplies. Major General Halleck writes me, on the 19th May, that he is anxious that I should do all in my power to unite my forces with yours. He can give, he says, neither of us, re-inforcemnts. Both Rosecrans and Burnside are calling loudly for re-inforcemts and he has none for either. With earnest wishes for your success and a determation to join you at the earliest possible moment" ALS, DLC-Robert T. Lincoln. *O.R.*, I, xxiv, part 3, 385–86. On June 8, USG endorsed this letter. "Respectfully forwarded to Head Quarters of the Army, Washington D. C.," ES, DLC-Robert T. Lincoln. On the same day, USG telegraphed to Lincoln. "I send by mail letter from Genl. Banks of June 4th   I am in communication with him. He has Port Hudson closely invested." Telegram received, *ibid.*; DLC-Edwin M. Stanton; DNA, RG 107, Telegrams Collected (Bound); copies, *ibid.*, RG 393, Dept. of the Tenn., Hd. Qrs. Correspondence; DLC-USG, V, 6, 8, 24, 94. *O.R.*, I, xxiv, part 1, 41.

1. See letter to Maj. Gen. Nathaniel P. Banks, May 25, 1863.
2. States Rights Gist, born in S. C. in 1831, graduated from S. C. College

and Harvard Law School, then returned to S. C. to practice law and became state adjt. gen. Appointed C.S.A. brig. gen. on March 20, 1862, he served mostly in S. C. until ordered on May 5, 1863, to take his brigade to join Gen. Joseph E. Johnston.

3. Between May 28 and June 1, Gen. Joseph E. Johnston variously estimated his effective force between 23,000 and slightly over 24,100. *O.R.*, I, xxiv, part 1, 194–95.

4. For the week ending May 26, the army of Lt. Gen. John C. Pemberton was reported as 17,356 present for duty. *Ibid.*, I, xxiv, part 3, 923.

To Maj. Gen. Stephen A. Hurlbut

Near Vicksburg Miss May 31, 1863.

Maj Genl S. A. Hurlbut
Commd.g 16th Army Corps

I send this by Col Hillyer of my staff to insure its reaching you speedily, and that he may urge upon you the necessity of the promptest action. Vicksburg is strong by nature, so well fortified, that a sufficient force cannot be brought to bear against to to carry it by storm against the present garrison. It must be taken by a regular seige, or by starving out the garrison. I have all the force necessary for this if my rear was not threatened. It is now certain that Joe Johnson has already collected a force from 20,000, to twenty five thousand strong, at Jackson and Canton, and is using every effort to increase it to forty thousand. With this he will undoubtedly attack Haines Bluff, and compel me to abandon the investment of the City, if no re-inforced before he can get here. I want your district stripped to the very lowest possible standard. You can be in no possible danger for the time it will be necessary to keep these troops away. All points in West Tennessee North of the Memphis and Charleston road if necessary can be abandoned entirely. Western Kentucky may be reduced to a small garrison at Columbus and Paducah. If you have not already brought the troops to Memphis, to send me, bring Smiths[1] formely, Denvers Division. Add to this all other force you can spare. Send two Regiments of Cavalry also. If you have not received the Cavalry last ordered from Helena, divert them to this place, instead of sending two other Regiments. No boat will be permitted to leave Memphis, going North, until the transportation is fully provided for troops coming this way. The Quarter Master in charge of transportation, and Col Hillyer are specially instructed to see that this direction is fully enforced. The entire rebel force, heretofore against me, are completely at my mercy. I do not want to see them escape by being re-inforced from elsewhere. I hope before this reaches you, troops will be already on the way from your command. Gen'l Dodge can spare enough from his force to garrison La Grange and Grand Junction.

U. S. GRANT Maj Gen'l

Copies, DLC-USG, V, 19, 30; DNA, RG 393, Dept. of the Tenn., Letters Sent; Alcorn Collection, WyU. *O.R.*, I, xxiv, part 3, 368–69. On June 3, 1863, Maj. Gen. Stephen A. Hurlbut wrote to Lt. Col. John A. Rawlins. "Inform Maj Genl Grant that I received his dispatch of 31st to day. Smith's Division has marching orders and will be pushed forward as fast as Oglesby can relieve them   This reduces me to about 20,000 Infantry. I hope in a short time so to clear the country in front as to be able to spare others. I have telegraphed to Washington the situation below and hope heavy reinforcements will come from the East"   ALS, DNA, RG 393, Dept. of the Tenn., Letters Received. *O.R.*, I, xxiv, part 3, 381. On June 8, Rawlins wrote to Hurlbut. "Your Communication of date June 3rd, inst. has been received. Make such disposition of your Infantry and Artillery forces as to be prepared to reduce them to a much greater extent, if possible, than you already have done, at any moment on the receipt of orders. The enemy is collecting a large force at Canton, and some of it is now east of the Big Black River. We must be prepared for any emergency." LS, DNA, RG 94, War Records Office, Military Div. of the Miss. *O.R.*, I, xxiv, part 3, 391. On the same day, Rawlins issued Special Orders No. 154. "Major General C. C. Washburn, is hereby assigned to the command of all the troops of the 16th Army Corps now here and to arrive. He will establish his Headquarters at Haine's Bluffs and prosecute the defense of that place with all possible despatch." Copies, DLC-USG, V, 27, 28; DNA, RG 393, Dept. of the Tenn., Special Orders. *O.R.*, I, xxiv, part 3, 391–92.

1. William Sooy Smith, born in Tarlton, Ohio, in 1830, USMA 1853, resigned from the U.S. Army in 1854 to follow the profession of engineering. Appointed col., 13th Ohio, as of June 26, 1861, and confirmed as brig. gen. on April 15, 1862, he was transferred from the Dept. of the Cumberland to the Dept. of the Tenn. on Dec. 27 and assigned to the 16th Army Corps. *O.R.*, I, xx, part 2, 249.

To Act. Rear Admiral David D. Porter

Near Vicksburg Miss June 2, 1863

Rear Admiral D. D. Porter
Commdg Miss Squadron.

The Expedition under Genl Blair has clearly ascertained the fact that Joe Johnson is collecting an Army at and around Canton Miss. They find also that there is a good ridge road leading between the Black and Yazoo rivers, with cross roads to every ferry on the Black. From Satartia on the Yazoo, it is only about ten miles across to Coxs ferry, on the Black. Mechanicksburg three miles from Satartia, is a key point to the whole neck of land. I have determined to send a garrison up there, using Satartia as a base of supplies. The Infantry will go on Steamers to morrow. I would request that the fleet you keep at Haines Bluff convoy these boats up the Yazoo, and remain at Satartia, whilst troops are kept at Mechanicksburg

U. S. Grant Maj Gen'l

Copies, DLC-USG, V, 19, 30; DNA, RG 393, Dept. of the Tenn., Letters Sent; Alcorn Collection, WyU. *O.R.*, I, xxiv, part 3, 374–75; *O.R.* (Navy), I, xxv, 57–58.

On June 2, 1863, Maj. Gen. Francis P. Blair, Jr., Drumgould's Bluff, wrote to USG. "Since seeing you on yesterday the fifth Illinois Cavalry 750 strong have reached this place, bringing with them carbines for the 4th Iowa cavalry now here. The 5th Illinois is armed with carbines & also the detachment of the 2nd Illinois now here—This gives about 1,2,00 (twelve hundred) well armed cavalry. Col Johnson believes with this force properly supported with Infantry and Artillery he can destroy the Rail Road Bridge over the Big Black north of Canton. The Plan is to move the ~~entirely~~ whole cavalry force towards Mechanicsburg to-morrow morning by the three roads I pointed out to you—the main body moving by the central road with flanking parties on the right & left hand roads and at the same time to send Mowers Brigade with a full battery of Artillery by the Yazoo River to Satartia to land at that point & push out to Mechanicsburg. This will compel Adam's Cavalry, the only force on this side of Black River, to cross the Black River at Kibbys or Cox's Ferry in order to escape capture and prevent them from recrossing that River, while Johnson with his entire force can rush forward & destroy the bridge with little risk or hazard. Nor will Mowers Brigade provided with transports at Satartia convoyed by a gun boat run any risk especially if he keeps out a few cavalry on the different roads to advise him of the enemys movements. As for the cavalry force of Johnsons it cannot be endangered as their are so many roads by which he can retreat and the enemy have no cavalry force sufficient to cut him off from all of them. I think this plan is judicious & feasible and if you will permit it I will issue the necessary orders, and leave one Brigade of troops at this point for greater security during the absence of Mowers Brigade & with the balance of my command return to your lines in rear of Vicksburg to morrow. It will be necessary to send Mower the other two sections of Spore's battery (Iowa battery) of which he now has one, or I can give him a full battery from those now with me   I respectfully submit this plan & await your decision"   ALS, DLC-Blair Family. *O.R.*, I, xxiv, part 3, 373–74. On June 2, Lt. Col. John A. Rawlins endorsed this letter. "Respectfully returned to Maj. Gen. Blair Com'd'g Expeditionary Corps, who will issue orders for the expedition against the Big Black Railroad Bridge north of Canton, in exact accordance with the plan within proposed. He will send one of the Batteries he has with him with this expedition in place of 'Spoors,' which latter he can get when he returns here. Col. Richmonds Brigade has been ordered to debark at Haine's Bluff immediately, and will form the garrison at that place"   ES, DLC-Blair Family. *O.R.*, I, xxiv, part 3, 374. On the same day, Rawlins issued Special Orders No. 148 sending Col. Jonathan Richmond, 2nd Brigade, 3rd Div., 16th Army Corps, to Haynes' Bluff. Copies, DLC-USG, V, 27, 28; DNA, RG 393, Dept. of the Tenn., Special Orders. *O.R.*, I, xxiv, part 3, 376. On June 3, Rawlins issued Special Orders No. 149 assigning Blair to take five brigades to the left of the U.S. position investing Vicksburg, but Special Orders No. 150 of June 4 countermanded this. Copies, DLC-USG, V, 27, 28; DNA, RG 393, Dept. of the Tenn., Special Orders. The first is in *O.R.*, I, xxiv, part 3, 380.

On June 2, Maj. Gen. William T. Sherman wrote to USG. "Admiral Porter, with some of his junior officers, was here, on horseback, the day before yesterday, the same on which I found you complaining of illness. I took the party forward to the trenches, the sun glaring hot, and the admiral got tired and overheated, so that, although we proposed coming to see you, he asked me to make his excuses, and say he would come again to make you a special visit. He took the loss of the Cincinnati in good part, and expressed himself willing to lose all the boats if he could do any good. He wanted to put a battery of heavy guns ashore, and I told him there could be no objection, and, accordingly, Captain Selfridge came up last evening, and said he was prepared to land two 8-inch howitzers—to man and work them—if I would haul these guns out and build a parapet. I can put the party and their guns on Steele's Hill. The hauling will be on a dead-level road till the guns reach the foot of the hill, and the troops can haul them up. I don't think 8-inch howitzers can do any particular good at that point, but they will clear off that hill, and make the enemy suppose it is to be one of our main points of attack. Captain Selfridge is just down from Yazoo and Sunflower. In Sunflower they found the following boats burned and destroyed by the enemy: Dewdrop, Argosy, Sharp, and Argo. In the Yazoo, 15 miles below Greenwood, four boats were sunk across the channel, closing the channel. They, too, were burned to the water's edge, and otherwise destroyed. These were the Scotland, R. J. Lockland, John Walsh, and Golden Era. [S. W.] Ferguson was at Greenwood, with a small force, and it was represented that about fifteen boats remained in the Yazoo above the obstruction and below Greenwood, which the gunboats could not reach." *Ibid.*, p. 372; incomplete in *O.R.* (Navy), I, xxv, 56, 136.

A telegram from Sherman to USG dated only "3" was probably sent on June 3. "I Have been to my Extreme right   two rifle pits almost finished to waters edge   one reaches the mound   a battery is finished & to night a gun will be put in it looking into the upper water battery   putting up navy battery for two (2) Eight 8 inch guns on the right   a pretty sharp artillery fight there this morning but our rifled 30s got the best of it   going to the front with Prime" Telegram received, DNA, RG 94, War Records Office, Dept. of the Tenn. Dated Feb. 3 in *O.R.*, I, xxiv, part 3, 31.

To Brig. Gen. Joseph A. Mower

Near Vicksburg Miss June 2, 1863

Brig Gen'l J. A Mower
Commd'g Advance Forces.

Move your Brigade together with all the Cavalry assigned to your command, to Mechanicksburg. Take with you the Commissary Boat, and one other boat which the Chief Quarter Master is directed to send up to you to-day.[1] Admiral Porter has been directed to send the Gunboats now at Haines Bluff up with you.[2] These with the Steamers, will probably be able to carry your Infantry to Satartia. If not let the transport Steamer make additional trips until your troops are all up. The Cavalry, Artilly, and such land transportation as you want with you, can be moved up by the bottom road. Keep the extra Steamer with you to use in case of need. When your troops are posted at Mechanicksburg, keep the Cavalry actively employed in watching the movements of the enemy. Should a large force get to your rear, move to Satartia and with your transports, move to the west bank of the Yazoo, from which, withdraw to Haines Bluff by land and water as best you can. Whilst stationed in the advance, obstruct all the roads leading to the Black River, in every way you can. Destroy or bring in for your own use, all the forage, provisions and transportation you can. In a few days I will be able to send an entire Division or more to re-inforce you, when I think you will be able to make excursions up through the rich Yazoo bottoms, and keep me well informed, of all information collected

U. S. Grant Maj Gen'l.

Copies, DLC-USG, V, 19, 30; DNA, RG 393, Dept. of the Tenn., Letters Sent; Alcorn Collection, WyU. *O.R.*, I, xxiv, part 3, 375.

On June 3, 1863, noon, USG signaled to Brig. Gen. Joseph A. Mower. "Call on the Gunboats and enquire if they have not received instructions to Convoy you to Satarta" Signal received, ICarbS. On the same day, noon, USG signaled to Act. Rear Admiral David D. Porter. "Has a gunboat been instructed to convoy troops to Satartia on the Yazoo." Signal received, *ibid.* Also on June 3, Porter signaled to USG. "Captain Walker has command at Haines-Bluff, and will give any convoy required. A Deserter just came in, Says they talk of cutting their way out." Signal received, DNA, RG 94, War Records Office, Military Div. of the Miss.; copy (undated), *ibid.*, RG 111, Vicksburg Signal Book. *O.R.*, I, xxiv, part 3, 378; *O.R.* (Navy), I, xxv, 58. On the same day, USG signaled to Porter. "The Gunboats at Hains Bluff Say they have no instructions to convoy troops to Satirtia If one cannot go up and remain there it will not be secure for me to place my surplus troops at Mechanicsburg as I desire." Signal received, ICarbS; copy (misdated April 3), DNA, RG 111, Vicksburg Signal Book. On the same day, Porter signaled to USG. "Written orders have gone up." Copy, *ibid.* On the same day, USG signaled to Mower. "I have asked Admiral Porter to Send a boat to Satirtia and keep her there The request is now reported I think it will be Sent." Signal received, ICarbS.

On June 2, USG had written to Maj. Gen. John A. McClernand, Maj. Gen. James B. McPherson, and Maj. Gen. William T. Sherman. "You will commence firing at 6½—O.clock this evening. Fire ten minutes, Stop twenty, and fire again for twenty minutes more." Copies, DLC-USG, V, 19, 30; DNA, RG 393, Dept. of the Tenn., Letters Sent; *ibid.*, 13th Army Corps, Letters Received. *O.R.*, I, xxiv, part 3, 375. On June 3, Porter wrote to USG. "Six deserters have just come in. One who has been in the trenches says that if you were to fire more at night, it would prevent the Rebels from working and resting—They are moving some heavy guns to the rear which they could not do if the artillery kept at work—I give you the information for what it is worth—We get about fifteen deserters a day who all tell the same story. Shortness of food—and intention to hold out ten or twenty days—Our Mortar Shells have given out, but I hope to have a fresh supply in a day or two—Our Mortars have killed a great many cattle of all kinds, and I am sorry we have no more on hand. The Gunboats tho' keep shelling in direction of the cattle pens—All the cattle drivers (Mexicans) have deserted to us—The Rebels have made a raid upon Perkins landing from Tensas River—1500 of them stood the fire of the Gunboats 'Carondelet' for an hour but finally retreated. The Col. commanding at James Plantation, destroyed all the stores at that place when the Rebels hove in sight, tho' the Gunboat was near at hand—The Captain of the Gunboat thinks he behaved badly—I have sent six 8 inch guns up the Yazoo with men to work them, to be placed where required, and two 9 inch at Warrenton—I will send plenty of hand grenades if you want them. I have sent some already, they work beautifully—Nine Steamers were burnt by the late expedition up the Yazoo. The Rebels set fire to some of them and our men could not put the fire out—Others were aground and we had to burn them, and others up the Sunflower were inside of a bar and could not be got out. they were burned, with a large amount of provisions. I was in hopes of presenting you with some fine transports—I would have been over to see you the other day, but after going over Sherman's works: I was so sick I had not the strength to go further—I will be up in a day or two— . . . P. S. An intelligent black has just come in. He says they talk of cutting their way out. I have just found out where they have moved their cattle to for safety, and am going to shell them with the Gunboats. There are not many troops kept opposite McClernand's front, most of them are in front of McPherson, and Sherman. Your shot and shell are killing a great many—" LS, DNA, RG 94, War Records Office, Dept. of the Tenn. *O.R.*, I, xxiv, part 3, 378; *O.R.* (Navy), I, xxv, 59–60.

1. On June 2, USG wrote to Lt. Col. Judson D. Bingham. "Send one Steamer of good size to Haines Bluff, to move troops from there to Satartia, and to remain subject to the orders of the Commanding Officer of the troops left in that country." Copies, DLC-USG, V, 19, 30; DNA, RG 393, Dept. of the Tenn., Letters Sent; Alcorn Collection, WyU.

2. See preceding letter.

To Brig. Gen. Peter J. Osterhaus

Head Quarters, Dept. of the Ten.
Near Vicksburg, June 2d 1863.

BRIG. GEN. OSTERHAUS,
COMD.G FORCES AT BLACK RIVER,
GEN.

I am sending a force of one Brigade of Infantry, with a Battery, to be stationed at Mechanicsburg, three miles East of Satartia on the Yazoo River. All the Cavalry except what you have and a little with Gen. McClernand go with this command. This Cavalry will watch all the crossings of the Big Black North of Bridgeport and are ordered to obstruct all the roads in every way possible. Your troops should obstruct all roads on both sides of Big Black in every way they can except the roads used by themselves.

Having this force, a Brigade and full 1200 Cavalry, in North of you will relieve you from all danger from a force crossing any place to the North of you.

Very respectfully
U. S. GRANT
Maj. Gen.

ALS, DNA, RG 393, 13th Army Corps, 9th Div., Letters Received.

To Maj. Gen. Henry W. Halleck

Near Vicksburg June 3rd, 1863.

MAJOR GENERAL HALLECK,
WASHINGTON D. C.,

The approaches are gradually nearing the enemy's fortifications. Five days more should plant our batteries on their parapets. Johnston is still collecting troops at Canton and Jackson.
Some are coming over the rail road, and all the country are joining
his standard. The destruction of the enemys artillery and ordnance stores was so complete that all these must be brought in
from a distance. I sent a large force up between the Yazoo and
Black rivers. Forage, beef and bacon, was destroyed by our troops
and the stock brought to Camp. I am now placing all my spare
force on the narrowest part of the land between the rivers, about
forty five miles northeast, with the Cavalry watching all the
crossings of Black River.

We shell the town a little every day and keep the enemy constantly on the alert. We but seldom loose a man now. The best
of health and spirits prevail among the troops

U. S. GRANT
Major General.

Telegram received, DNA, RG 107, Telegrams Collected (Bound); copies, *ibid.*,
RG 393, Dept. of the Tenn., Hd. Qrs. Correspondence; DLC-USG, V, 6, 8, 24,
94. *O.R.*, I, xxiv, part 1, 40–41.

To Maj. Gen. Stephen A. Hurlbut

Head Quarters, Dept. of the Ten.
Near Vicksburg, June 3d 1863

MAJ. GEN. S. A. HURLBUT
COMD.G 16TH ARMY CORPS,
GEN.

Forward as soon as possible three effective batteries from

your command, including one for Helena. In addition to this Gen. Smith should bring with his Division two additional batteries.

All things are progressing here favorably. Every day pushes us a little nearer the enemy. Jo Johnstone is stil threatening us on the other side of the Big Black. What his force is now is hard to tell but all the loose characters in the country seem to be joining his standard besides troops coming over the rail-road daily. I have a strong position front and rear and expect to worry him out if he should come.

Very respectfully

U. S. Grant

Maj. Gen.

ALS, DNA, RG 393, 16th Army Corps, Letters Received. *O.R.*, I, xxiv, part 3, 380. On June 3, 1863, Lt. Col. John A. Rawlins wrote to Maj. Gen. Stephen A. Hurlbut. "Brig General S G. Burbridge, Commanding 1st Brigade, 10th Division, 13th Army Corps, says he has 150 men of his Brigade at Memphis, Tennessee, in the convalescent camp. Your will please order them forward at once, every available man is required to make good in numbers the loss from recent casualities" LS, DNA, RG 393, 16th Army Corps, Letters Received.

On June 5, Hurlbut wrote to USG. "Brig Genl Smiths Division 16 Regiments of Infantry and four Batteries is on the way in & will embark to night and to morrow. My line is singularly reduced by this but nothing worse can happen than a temporary obstruction to the Road. On the 2d I telegraphed to Genl Halleck that at least 10,000 more men than I could safely furnish would be required. I received the following from him late last night. Washington June 4, 1863 Maj Genl S A HURLBUT Memphis Genl. Schofield has sent down the River Eight Regiments and three convoys. Genl Burnside is sending Eight Thousand men. If Vicksbugh falls the latter will be returned to Kentucky wherever they may be at the time H W HALLECK Genl in Chief' You will excuse my venturing to telegraph as above stated but I considered time of importance I have ordered the 2 Wisconsin Cavalry six companies down the River and shall send the 4th Missouri from Columbus" ALS, *ibid.*, RG 94, War Records Office, Dept. of the Tenn. *O.R.*, I, xxiv, part 3, 386–87.

On June 10, Hurlbut wrote three letters to Rawlins. "I have recd to day one letter from Capt Lyfert Chief of Ordnance in relation to sending down 32 lb guns & carriages for 10 inch Columbiads. Col. Kappner 1 Tenn. Heavy Artillery proceeded at once to Columbus and Island 10 to fill this order. In the other from yourself of the 8th you direct the Infantry & Artillery of this command held ready for still further reduction at short notice. The command is ready to be moved as rapidly as can be done and to any extent required by orders from Head Quarters. It now covers the main line of Road from Memphis to Corinth; and covers this very lightly. Had I any disposable infantry force I should move down the Panola Road.—Scout in at LaGrange left Jackson on 7th says they claim 50000 men with Johnston—he thinks not more than 30000. Breckenridge is there with 10000—

forces constantly arriving from Charleston, Savannah & Tenn. The Rail Road was fully repaired on Saturday   Forage & supplies are being forced down from all parts of Mississippi   Jackson & Whitfield with Cavalry reached Jackson on Friday. Hatch has just returned from an Expedition along the Tallahatchie   met nothing but Pickets and light squads. I shall send the whole of my cavalry down as far as they can go to destroy Crops and break up Road & means of Transportation. A portion of the 2d Division of 9th Army Corps arrived this afternoon   the balance will be here in a few hours from Cairo. The divn is in command of Maj Genl Parke. Every thing is being pressed forward as fast as possible—but there is terrible scarcity of Boats and it seems as if Boats that go down to your parts never return. It is impossible to send any thing more until some of the Boats below are returned. Every Boat from St Louis is in service. They should not be kept an hour after they are discharged of their cargoes. I am fully satisfied that Johnston cannot bring more than 35000 men of all arms within the next ten days. Bragg is removing his Stores to Atlanta, but Rosecrans *will not* believe any reports from this quarter and I have ceased communicating with him except through Washington   He could now easily clear Middle Tennessee & open communication with Dodge at Hamburgh." "I received this morning orders thro' Capt Lyfert Ordnance officer to send ten 32 pound Guns—& carriages for 2, 10 inch Columbiads with ammunition. I have sent Col. Kappner 1st Tenn. Heavy Arty to Columbus to procure the same & forward as speedily as possible. They shall be sent as soon as they can be shipped. Maj Genl Parke telegraphs me from Cairo inquiring when first boat of 9th Army Corps arrives   I expect them hourly. Smith has left with his Division   I reiterate my request that the General Commanding will see to it if possible that the Communications north by Rail Road be destroyed. Hatch's Cavalry is now south of the Tallahatchie looking after any proposed advance. Unless it is absolutely necessary I do not desire to move the 4th Mo. Cavalry & on this await orders. The reasons are that Rosecrans is not active near the Tenn; that the abandonment of Jackson lays the whole country open & that active Cavalry movements from Columbus are necessary to cover this open line. Col. Hillyer reported to me with orders from Gen'l Grant to assist in Expediting movements of troops. I am not aware of any assistance rendered by him, although his society was very agreeable when time was allowed to converse with him—I am satisfied that his forte is not in Quarter Master's duty. . . . I have heard incidentally that Col. Duff & Col. Lagow of your Staff have been here—They have not reported to me"   ALS, DNA, RG 393, Dept. of the Tenn., Letters Received. *O.R.*, I, xxiv, part 3, 397–98. "I have the honor to report that 7th June instant, Lieut. Col. Breckinridge, first West Tennessee Cavalry returned to Jackson from expedition across Tennessee River, having destroyed a large amount of property; secured and put on gun boats three thousand sides of leather, and recrossed without any loss except stragglers." LS, DNA, RG 94, War Records Office, Dept. of the Mo. See *O.R.*, I, xxiv, part 2, 445.

To Maj. Gen. John A. McClernand

———

Near Vicksburg Miss, June 3. 1863.

MAJ GEN J. A. McCLERNAND
COMM'DG 13TH ARMY CORPS

I will direct the chief Quartermaster to assign a boat to Col Dunlap.[1] A forage master to one of the Divisions represents that a negro informed him that the enemy were building a bridge over Black river, about Baldwins Ferry. Send your Cavalry to look, after this matter.[2]

U. S. GRANT
Maj Gen.

Copies, DLC-USG, V, 19, 30; DNA, RG 393, Dept. of the Tenn., Letters Sent; *ibid.*, 13th Army Corps, Letters Received; (undated) *ibid.*

On June 3, 1863, USG wrote to Maj. Gen. John A. McClernand. "In addition to the seige guns already furnished by the Navy, they are now furnishing six eight inch guns and two nine inch guns." Copies, DLC-USG, V, 19, 30; DNA, RG 393, Dept. of the Tenn., Letters Sent. On the same day, McClernand wrote to USG. "The enemy opened with Artillery and Infantry from his works this morning but was successfully replied to   I have ordered my Artillery to open at 8 oclock P. M. and to continue fire for fifteen minutes   Shall I send for any of the heavy guns refered to in your telegram?" Copy, *ibid.*, 13th Army Corps, Letters Sent. *O.R.*, I, xxiv, part 3, 378–79.

1. On June 3, USG wrote to Lt. Col. Judson D. Bingham. "Turn over to the Chief Quartermaster of the 13th Army Corps, for the exclusive use of that corps one of the Steamers below Vicksburg." Copies, DLC-USG, V, 19, 30; DNA, RG 393, Dept. of the Tenn., Letters Sent. On the same day, Bingham wrote to USG. "I have the honor to acknowledge the receipt of your order of this date, requiring one of the Boats below Vicksburg to be turned over to the Chief Quartermaster of the 13th Army Corps, for the exclusive use of that Corps. I would respectfully state that all the Boats below Vicksburg were placed at the disposal of the Chief Quartermaster of the 13th Army Corps several days since, for the purpose of ferrying supplies across the River to Warrenton. I have, however, given an order for the transfer of a Boat as directed." ALS, *ibid.*, Letters Received.

2. On June 3, Col. John J. Mudd wrote to Lt. Col. Walter B. Scates, adjt. for McClernand. "In answer to the communication from Grant relating to reported rebel operations near Baldwins Ferry, I have the honor to report that I have to-day had patrols to Hall's Ferry and to a burned bridge half a mile this side of Baldwin's Ferry. Reports from both detachments are that no enemies are in the neighborhood. Major Marsh is yet in the neighborhood of Hall's ferry, but I have report from him down to two o'clock P. M. I think the reported bridge building is entirely unfounded, and originated in some person hearing the pioneers felling

trees there a few days since. My scouts traverse the country as frequently as possible and were, no doubt, at the river on both roads on receipt of General Grants communication. I design going out to Black river to-morrow, and on my return will be able to report the condition of affairs on the line" Copy, *ibid.*, 13th Army Corps, Letters Received. On May 31, Mudd had written to Scates reporting the results of an expedition to destroy bridges and ferry boats along the Big Black River. LS, *ibid.*, Dept. of the Tenn., Letters Received. On the same day, McClernand endorsed this letter. "Respectfully forwardd to Dept Hd Quarters as a report of progress made in obstructing hostile access across Big Black to this Camp   I have ordered Col Whiting Comdg Post at Warenton to obstruct the rear approaches from Big Black to that place" ES, *ibid.*

To Brig. Gen. Nathan Kimball

Head Quarters, Dept. of the Ten.
Near Vicksburg, June 3d 1863,

BRIG. GEN. N. KIMBALL,
COMD.G 3D DIV. 16TH A. C.
GEN.

You will proceed with your command to Satartia on the Yazoo River, thence to Mechanicsburg three miles distant. You will find Gen. Mower there with one Brigade and a force of 1200 Cavalry in addition. Being the Senior you will have command of the whole force.

Instructions have been given for a movement to destroy Black River bridge on the Miss. Central rail-road. Gen. Mower will inform you of the instructions given.

The object of placing troops at Mechanicsburg is to watch the movements of the enemy who are said to be collecting a large force in the vicinity of Canton. With your Cavalry you will watch all the Ferries over Big Black North of Bridgeport. Obstruct all roads leading West from the river not wanted by yourself in every way possible. Collect all the forage, cattle and provisions you can and destroy what you cannot bring away. It is important that the country should be left so that it will not subsist an Army passing over it. Wagons horses & mules should be taken from the Citizens to keep them from being used with the Southern Army.

All negroes coming into your lines send to Hain's Bluff unless their services are required with your command.

One gunboat and one transport besides the Commissary boat should be kept at Satartia at all times.

The Chief Quartermaster at Chickasaw Landing, and Ordnance officer at same place, will supply every thing required for your command from their respective Departments.

It is desirable that all possible information should be acquired of the movements of the enemy and sent promptly to these Hd Qrs. You are authorized to employ Spies and send orders on the Chief Quartermaster, Lt. Col. Bingham, to be approved at Head Quarters, for payment.

> Respectfully &c.
> U. S. GRANT
> Maj. Gen. Com

ALS, Kimball Papers, InU. *O.R.*, I, xxiv, part 3, 379. Nathan Kimball, born in Fredericksburg, Ind., in 1822 or 1823, attended Asbury College in Ind., then practiced medicine in Mo. until he raised a co. for the Mexican War. A physician in Ind. when the Civil War began, he was commissioned col., 14th Ind., on June 7, 1861, and advanced to brig. gen. as of April 15, 1862, following his success in the battle of Kernstown. See Kimball, "Fighting Jackson at Kernstown," *Battles and Leaders of the Civil War*, eds., Robert Underwood Johnson and Clarence Clough Buel (New York, 1887), II, 302–13. On June 4, 1863, 4:00 P.M., Kimball Satartia, Miss., wrote to Lt. Col. John A. Rawlins. "I have the honor to report that I reached here at 11 a. m. to-day, and found General Mower just moving out with his brigade. I immediately debarked the troops with me and moved out, meeting the enemy in force on the hills back of the town. They fell back, skirmishing sharply, until at Mechanicsburg I found them drawn up in line of battle. I attacked them immediately with one brigade, and drove them from their position. The cavalry, coming up just at this time, joined in the pursuit, which at this writing is continued. General Mower behaved with gallantry. . . . P. S.—Send me more artillery. Johnston is massing considerable force at Canton. Please send my remaining infantry forward. We hold Mechanicsburg. I will report as soon as possible." *Ibid.*, I, xxiv, part 2, 436–37.

On June 3, Rawlins wrote to Lt. Col. Judson D. Bingham. "On the arrival of troops at Chickasaw Bayou, information of the fact will be immediately telegraphed to these Head Quarters. They will not be permitted to Disembark until orders to do so are received from the Major General Commanding." Copies, DLC-USG, V, 19, 30; DNA, RG 393, Dept. of the Tenn., Letters Sent. On the same day, Rawlins wrote to Capt. Gilbert A. Pierce, q. m., Chickasaw Bayou.

"The 25th Wisconsin will proceed up the Yazoo to join Gen. Kimball so will all other troops that arrive belonging to Gen Hurlbuts Corps. The four Regiments that were sent from here to Memphis with prisoners, will as they arrive be sent out here to the Corps to which they belong." Copies, *ibid.* On June 4, Pierce signaled to USG. "The 106th Ills Regt passed up without stoping   The 40th Iowa Lt Col Cooper Comdg is here awaiting orders." Signal received, ICarbS. On the same day, USG signaled to Pierce. "The 40 Iowa will proceede up the Yazoo to join Gen Kimball." Signal received, *ibid.*; Tulane University, New Orleans, La.

To Brig. Gen. Peter J. Osterhaus

Head Quarters, Dept. of the Ten.
Near Vicksburg June 3d 1863,

BRIG. GEN. OSTERHAUS,
COMD.G ADVANCE FORCES,
GEN.

A force of the enemy, or their advance, is reported at "Grant's" house. I enclose you notes containing all the information I have relative to the position of this house and the reported movement of rebel troops.

Send your Cavalry out on this side of the river to get full information of any movement of the enemy that may be taking place. Col. Johnson with a battery & about 1200 Cavalry, is now moving out on the Benton road and will probably reach Mechanicsburg tonight.

Respectfully &c
U. S. GRANT
Maj. Gen Com

ALS, DNA, RG 393, 13th Army Corps, 9th Div., Letters Received. *O.R.*, I, xxiv, part 3, 379. On June 4, 1863, Brig. Gen. Peter J. Osterhaus, "Big Black R.r R R bridge," wrote to USG. "I have the honor to acknowledge the receipt of your Favor of yesterday with orders and instructions relative to a rebel force at 'Grants' house. I immediately sent all the available Cavalry forces (3 Comp 6th Mo) in that direction, with orders to proceed as far as practicable with a View to make a connection with Col Johnson's Column and to gather all informations in regard to ferries and fords across B. Black and further in regard to any attempt of the enemy's advance. The party just returns and reports that the Rebel Major Roan with the 20th reg. Miss. Infantry (mounted) 600 Strong had been encamped on the Benton road from Vicksburg, at the bridge across Bear Creek, about 1 Mile east of where General Blair was encamped at Major Harris' place. From a Captain Tom Jones (a dangerous rebel) who is my prisoner, and whom I will forward to the Hd Qrs., we learn, that the above force was the only one in the immediate Vicinity, and that it was the same which was at 'Grant's house. There are several fords north of the Bridgeport ferry, which are now practicable, one ford is between the latter and the Birdsong Ferry, the other below Bush's ferry; from the description of the location of the above mentionned Secesh Camp and the situation of these fords I am inclined to think, that the 20th Miss. which figured a few days ago considerably between Raymond, Bolton & Brownsville, crossed at these fords; and it would be very desirable, to have a flying Column established between 'Bush's ferry (Oak ridge) and Bridgeport ferry, to intercept such raids. I am also informed, that the rebel Genl Walker was crossing his division yesterday at Kibby's Ferry (—I believe it is the same ~~of~~ as Cox ferry); to make a reconnoissance, but that Joe Johnston was not yet prepared to advance. The Party sent out yesterday night did not learn any thing of Col. Johnson. There seem to be a number of rebel Squads running all over the Country in my front and on my right (accross the river); yesterday a patrol of the 3d Mo fell in with about a dozen Men; my men were returning from Championhill and found the rebels on the road east of Edwards; they fired and the rebels turned north, giving my Men the road. Another Patrol under Cptn Millert (6. Mo Cav) ordered to go by Edwards to Bridgeport met about 25 Rebs mounted on Mules, they attacked them and unsaddled one, bringing in Mule and Saddle. From Contraband Source I heard yesterday, that a regiment of Tennesseans were marching towards Baker, or 14 Mile Creek; I at once sent a Company of Cavalry to Baldwins ferry, but on returning the Commander reported every thing quiet in that direction. The 8th Kentucky (rebel) under Lyon marched yesterday morning at 3 oclock through Edwards taking some of the paroled prisoners (rebel) away!—" ALS, DNA, RG 393, Dept. of the Tenn., Letters Received. *O.R.*, I, xxiv, part 2, 214.

On June 4, Col. Clark Wright, "Camp near Black River R R. Bridge," wrote to Lt. Col. John A. Rawlins. "I have just returned from a reconizance up Black River on West Side   I find Major Roan (rebel) with 600 Mounted Infantry (20th Miss) Encamped on the Benton road from Vicksburg where that road Crosses Bear Creek, one mile East of Major Harris, where Genl. Blair Encamped. These are all the rebel forces in That immidiate Vicinity. I learned from Capt. Tom Jones (rebel) who I now have prisoner) under disguise that there was no other in there, that this was the force that was at the Grant House, That Genl. Walker, was Crossing his Division on Yesterday, at Kibbies Old Ferry Big Black   That Joe Johnson was not yet sufficiently reinforced to advance. That Walker was sent down to reconnoiter. I made an effort to Communicate with Col. Johnson, but could not find him or hear of him. There is no force between this point and Oak Ridge. I enclose a rough sketch to give you an Idea of the position of Major Roan,   his Camp is Distant 20 miles up Black River from hear; —a party sent out by me last night to Baldwins Ferry below have returned and report, all Quiet in that Direction. So far as they was able to learn. . . . P. S. The Kibbies Ferry is between Startia an Yazoo Citty. Just below Vernon" ALS, DNA, RG 393, Dept. of the Tenn., Letters Received.

On June 7, Maj. Gen. John A. McClernand wrote twice to Rawlins. "I infer from a conversation with Col. Johnston that both Genl. Grant and myself are possiby mistaken as to the whereabout of Col. Wright, of the 6th Mo Cavy. I understood the Genl's order directing me to garrison the Black river bridge to place at my disposal the 6th Mo. Cavy. If any more than two Companies have been with Genl. Osterhaus there, I am not aware of it. I supposed that the rest of the regiment were under orders in some other direction. It may be, however, that it is now and has been for some days in camp between the Jackson and Bridgeport roads. If this be so, and the regiment can possibly be spared, I wish to send it, immediately, to Genl Osterhaus who is in great need of Cavalry." ALS, *ibid.* "General Osterhaus has just reported that his cavalry force is too small. Colonel Mudd is using the Second Illinois on the Hall's Ferry and Baldwin's Ferry roads and the lateral roads connecting these with Big Black, and cannot well be spared from there. The Sixth Missouri, or some other detachment of cavalry, should be ordered to report to General Osterhaus." *O.R.*, I, xxiv, part 3, 388.

Also on June 7, Osterhaus wrote twice to Rawlins. "Yesterday night by 9½ o'clock my pickets beyond the river on the Edwards Station road were attacked by some rebel force: there was quite lively firing for some time and the commander of my picket considered it prudent to fall back on the Infantry picket at Bayou bridge (in the line of the rifle pits on the other side) the enemy (which I found out since was the 8th Kentucky mounted Infantry, did not follow up and this morning at 4 o'clock my Cavalry was at Edwards' and report, that they were in camp 3 miles beyond. Under instructions of Major General McClernand I sent on friday last a flag of truce into the enemy's line in order to procure from the C. S. commander his consent to remove Gen'l Hovey's wounded from Champion Hill into our lines. Lieutenant Foster, the bearer of the flag returns at this moment; he was within 6 miles of Jackson, when his letter was taken from him to be taken to Jackson: the Lieutenant was then escorted back and an early reply to my request promised. Lieutenant Foster states, that he met no other troops this side of the point where he was halted, except the 8th Kent: mounted: but from all information collected, there seems to be a considerable force at Jackson under general Loring or is the superior of him. The people seem to be in high glee and sanguine, that the rebels will soon be in number strong enough to raise the siege. Of General Johnson I hear he is still at Canton, preparing for an attempt, to break off our river communication north of Vicksburg. I enclose 3 letters: they are rather sweet, but—at least No 3.—is of some interest: they were intercepted by an Orderly of my staff and opened. I believe they were smuggled out by some member of the 7th Kentucky and as appears from one envelope enclosed directed to Yazoo City. There was a rumour near Jackson yesterday that an official telegram from Richmond had arrived, stating that Gen'l Lee had crossed the Rappahannock:" Copy, DNA, RG 393, 13th Army Corps, 9th Div., Letters Sent. *O.R.*, I, xxiv, part 2, 215–16. "A short Time after my despatch of this morning had left, I received reliable information, that the 8th Kentucky Mounted Infantry which attacked us last night, had been reinforced by the 20th and 22d Miss. Mounted Infty and that they were encamped at the Creek (3 Miles) beyond Edwards' Station; large bodies of Negroes appeared at my lines affirming the above report and speaking of more troops approaching. To come to the fact in these informations I ordered so much of the Cavalry, as I could make available,—about 100 Men and 1 Sect Mount. howzrs—to march to the Edwards and beyond and 'feel' the enemy!—They left here by noon under Major Montgomery; and found at the place indicated a rebel Camp; on the approach of my troops though the rebels had left in a southern direction; Contrabands thought, they would go to Bakers or fourteen Mile Creek towards Halls ferry. the Major Montgomery at once returned to Edward's Station and took there a more direct road for Halls ferry; he soon came up with the rebel force, and ordered the attack; after some firing, during which the rebels tried to found, the 6th Mo charged and run them for ca. 4 Miles, when the Confederates dispersed in 2 parties, one taking a by road for Halls Ferry the other the Utica road. Finding that the 'fellows' were better mounted, than anticipated, the Major halted & returned. he arrived here by 6½. p m with two prisoners; they say, that there were 6 Companies in the aggregate at least 300 Strong of the 20. Miss. Mounted Infy in todays skirmish on their side, which were dispersed by 100. of the 6th Mo; they further state, that the 22d Miss. & 8th Kenty Inf were in their Vicinity; but that the 4 Companies belonging to the 20th Miss were detached under Major Roan and operating West of the Big Black; they had left Canton some time ago for Benton and the Yazoo;—you will remember, that this statement corroborates with the information transmitted in my letter of June 4th. The prisoner could or would not tell any thing relative to the movements of other rebel troops; but I will try again to morow morning, to pump them. If I had a little more Cavalry I have no doubt but the surprise and Capture of a number of these Mounted troops were feasible. Awaiting your Orders . . ." ALS, DNA, RG 393, Dept. of the Tenn., Letters Received. *O.R.*, I, xxiv, part 2, 217–18.

On the same day, McClernand wrote to USG. "I have the honor to inform you, in addition to my telegram of this date, that Lt. Foster was sent by Genl. Osterhaus with a flag of truce to bring away the wounded. He went within six miles of Jackson, where he was halted,—and his despatches sent forward. He was told an answer would be sent to the despatch by Genl. Breckenridge, now in command at Jackson,—as soon as a decision was made. The only rebel troops seen by him were the 8th Kentucky mounted Infantry,—which he met three miles east of Edwards' Station, on their return to Bolton's Station from a skirmish with Genl. Osterhaus' pickets yesterday. Their rendezvous is near Bolton. He understood from the people on the route,—who are very sanguine of the result of Genl. Johnsons' attack upon us,—that that Genl. is at Canton having and collecting a large force. He understood that his intention was to break off our line of communication north of Vicksburg. There was also a rumor at Jackson of an official telegram having been received to the effect that Genl. ____ had crossed the Rappahannock. Genl. Osterhaus expressed his very confident opinion that the 8th Kentucky mounted Infty. are the only troops this side of Canton and Jackson. Upon reinforceing his Cavalry, the rebel troops immediately retreated and were followed by his Cavalry as far as Edward's Station" LS, DNA, RG 393, Dept. of the Tenn., Letters Received. On June 8, Osterhaus wrote to Rawlins. "After the hard ride which the 20th Miss was compelled to take yesterday afternoon the 8th Kentucky made its appearance this morning. They formed in sight of my pickets on the Edwards Station road and opened fire, but being unable to make my Videtts fall back they retired on their part again, leaving one man in our hands. He gives almost verbatim the same story of reinforcements arriving to Genl Johnston's Army in the vicinity of Canton as the prisoners yesterday in fact as every body does Coming from beyond Big Black the people is indoubtedly fed upon that hopeful prospect. the present informant adds that an attack would be made simultaneously by Johnston on Snyders bluff and by Brackenridge on the position here and that it was to be looked for soon This morning I visited the

Bridgeport ferry and the macon ford, and I can say that an access from that direction is rather difficult   the roads are very effectualy blocked. There is no ferry and no chance to cross the Big Black between the R Road and Bridgeport no landing and no roads leading to the river between those two points. Macon ford is about 1½ miles North of Bridgeport. I found several boats and ropes there which I have destroyed and taken off. The road leading to the ford—being beyond my rayon is pretty good but a working party will be sent out this night to destroy it—"   Copy, *ibid.*, 13th Army Corps, 9th Div., Letters Sent. *O.R.*, I, xxiv, part 2, 219.

On June 8, McClernand wrote to USG. "By dispatch from General Osterhous Just received I learn—that Maj Montgomery with a detachment of 6 Mo Cavelry found 6 Cos Companys of Mounted Infantry 20th Miss 3 Mile beyond Edwards Station on the Raymond road. They retreated in a southern direction. Learning that they would take the road to Halls Ferry—, he returned to Edwards Station, and took the road to the same ferry on a shorter route. He soon came up with them, and had a skirmish—making a charge their line was broken, & one part ran towards Halls Ferry, and another part, towards Utica. He took two prisoners. These prisoners say that four Companys of their Regiment, Crossed the Big Black some days ago, under Major Roam Near, General Blair's Command, or in that Region—I shall send two Regiments at 3 A. M. today under Col Lindsey to reinforce Genl Osterhous." Copy, DNA, RG 393, Dept. of the Tenn., Letters Received.

To Commanding Officer, Edwards Station, Miss.

Near Vicksburg Miss June 4, 1863.

COMMDG OFFICER CONFEDERATE FORCES
NEAR EDWARDS STATION MISS

I send Asst Surgeon Darrow[1] of the Federal army, in charge of ambulances and supplies for the wounded Soldiers left near that place. I would be pleased to send and get all of my wounded at Bakers Creek, Raymond and Jackson, so that they may be sent to Northern Hospitals for care. Will you please communicate this desire to the General Commanding the Department, with the request that will inform me how these wounded men may be recovered?

U. S. GRANT Maj Gen'l.

Copies, DLC-USG, V, 19, 30; DNA, RG 393, Dept. of the Tenn., Letters Sent. *O.R.*, II, v, 740. See letter to Commanding Officer, Confederate Forces, May 21, 1863.

On June 5, 1863, Maj. Gen. John A. McClernand telegraphed to USG. "I have directed Gen Osterhaus to Send ambulances under escort to Champion Hills hospital to bring away the wounded ~~before~~ but he thinks it best to Send first a flag of truce to ascertain the Situation   I hope this will be Satisfactory"   Telegram received (dated "5"), DNA, RG 393, Dept. of the Tenn., Telegrams Received.

1. Asst. Surgeon William H. Darrow, 5th Iowa, who enlisted on July 1, 1861, from Columbus City, Iowa, as hospital steward.

To Brig. Gen. Nathan Kimball

Near Vicksburg Miss June 4, 1863.

Brig Gen N. Kimball
Comm'dg Advance Forces

I have just received information that a portion of Johnston's force has gone into Yazoo City. In penetrating North, therefore the Cavalry going in advance will be in danger of having their rear cut off, by this force closing in behind them.

The position of the enemy and his numbers must be well ascertained before going much beyond Machanicsburg. I do not want to run any great risk of having any portion of the Army cut off, or defeated. If therefore your judgement is against reaching Black. River Bridge with security and getting back again, you nead not attempt it. Major Marsh of the 2nd Illinois Cavalry who bears this, has been ordered to the front to relieve Col Bush of the same Regiment, who will return to his Army Corps.[1]

U. S. Grant
Maj Gen.

Copies, DLC-USG, V, 19, 30; DNA, RG 393, Dept. of the Tenn., Letters Sent; Alcorn Collection, WyU. *O.R.*, I, xxiv, part 3, 384. On June 4, 1863, USG wrote to Col. Jonathan Richmond, Haynes' Bluff. "General Kimball is at Satartia up the Yazoo or at Machanicsburg, three miles from there. Send the despatches by first Satartia or by Courier to Machanicsburg where Gen Mower is, which ever may be may be most convenient." Copies, DLC-USG, V, 19, 30; DNA, RG 393, Dept. of the Tenn., Letters Sent.

On the same day, USG signaled to Act. Rear Admiral David D. Porter. "Information just Received from Yazoo City. Several Thousand of Johnstons troops went up there on sunday. I will be occupying Mechanicsburg only 19 miles distants from Yazoo" Copy, *ibid.*, RG 111, Vicksburg Signal Book. On the same day, Porter signaled to USG. "I will send every Gun Boat that can ascend the *Yazoo*—" Copy, *ibid.* An undated message from USG to Brig. Gen. Nathan Kimball was probably sent on June 4. "Ad. Porter will send all the Gunboats he has at Yazoo City. Instruct your Cavalry to watch the movements of the Enemy there, and take advantage of any stampeed that may take place among them" Signal received, Kimball Papers, InU.

1. Maj. Benjamin F. Marsh, Jr., 2nd Ill. Cav. On June 3, USG telegraphed to Maj. Gen. John A. McClernand. "Order Maj Marsh to relieve Col. Bush at Haines Bluff and Bush to return. The troops will remain as they are, only change commanders" Copy, DNA, RG 393, 13th Army Corps, Letters Received.

To Brig. Gen. Nathan Kimball

Head Quarters, Dept. of the Tn.
Near Vicksburg, June 5th/63

BRIG. GEN. N. KIMBALL,
COMD.G ADVANCE FORCES,
MECHANICSBURG MISS.
GEN.

Your dispatch is just received. I will renew my instructions not to run any risk of having your forces cut off from the main body. If Mechanicsburg is not safely tenable fall back to Oak Ridge Post Office or Hain's Bluff as necessity may dictate. Should you move back of course you will direct the transports and Gunboats at Satartia to fall back to such position as will be most advantageous to you.

I am exceedingly anxious to learn the probable force of the enemy on the West side of the Black River. Keep me constantly informed of all you may be able to learn.

Very respectfully
U. S. GRANT
Maj. Gen. Com

ALS, Kimball Papers, InU. On June 5, 1863, Brig. Gen. Nathan Kimball, Satartia, Miss., wrote to Lt. Col. John A. Rawlins, then to USG. "I find the enemy in force at Yazoo City—About six miles above here are eight thousand, at Liverpool The whole force on this side the Black River is 20.000 Infantry & Cavalry and twenty five guns—The force between the Yazoo and Black Rivers is under Walker—Johnsons Head quarters are still at Canton where he is massing troops, rumor says sixty thousand My Cavalry penetrated to the Black River yesterday and burned the ferries east of this place but I find it impossible to go further North on the Black as the enemy hold the country in force Genl Mower is ocupying Mechanicsburg and I am doing every thing possible to obstruct an advance should one be made by the enemy—Should it be desired to hold this place in such a case —more force will be required and more artillery Should I not be able to beat or repulse them I shall hold to the very last—" LS, DNA, RG 94, War Records Office, Dept. of the Mo. *O.R.*, I, xxiv, part 2, 437. "Since closing dispatches this mornig I have a prisoner who left Walker command at Yazoo city yesterday he says. Walker has 13000 men—2 Brigades are from Bragg—*Breckenridge* is at Jackson—Johnson has 40.000 at Canton—from all I can gather Walkers Command is all between Yazoo & Big Black I leave to day for Haines Bluff—" ALS, DNA, RG 94, War Records Office, Dept. of the Tenn. *O.R.*, I, xxiv, part 2, 438. On June 5, USG wrote to Kimball. "Your dispatch is just received after 12 O'clock at night. The tenor of it is such that I would direct that you fall back to Oak Ridge Post Office and bring your boats back to Hains Bluff. Keep your Cavalry to the front and off latterally as far as possible Look on Hain's Bluff as the point where you are to make a stand against all odds." ALS, Kimball Papers, InU. An undated message from USG to Kimball may have been sent around June 5. "Leave two Companies of Infantry at Hains Bluff, to report to Lt. Bryant" Signal received, *ibid.*

On June 6, Kimball wrote to Rawlins. "There is in front of me a large force of which I cannot ascertain the exact amount but which is not less than 15000 and in view of the fact that the River is falling rapidly and Gunboats will soon be unable to recross the bar below—I shall today move towards Haynes Bluff starting as soon as I can get ready" LS, DNA, RG 94, War Records Office, Dept. of the Mo. *O.R.*, I, xxiv, part 2, 438.

To Col. Jonathan Richmond

Near Vicksburg Miss. June 3 [5], 1863.

Col J. Richmond,
Comm'dg at Haines Bluff, Miss.

You will please look to the defences of Haines Bluff, and furnish as many men as possible from your command to work on said defences, under the direction of the Engineer Officers in charge of the constructions

You will also furnish to Lieut Z. Bryan[1] Superintendant of the collecting of contrabands for work at Haines Bluff, such details as he may require for guard and other duty. Direct also one of the Medical Officers of your Command to visit and attend to the sick in the contraband camp, near Haines Bluff, until the Medical Director makes other arrangements for their care.

Two Companies of Thielmans Cavalry[2] have been directed to report to you. You will keep them well out towards Machanicsburg and the Big Black River to watch especially any movements that may look to have in view the Crossing of the Big Black between you and our forces at Mechanicsburg.

Report daily any information you may obtain from whatever source, relating to the enemy or his movements.

U. S. Grant
Maj Gen.

Copies, DLC-USG, V, 19 (misdated June 3, 1863), 30; DNA, RG 393, Dept. of the Tenn., Letters Sent; Alcorn Collection, WyU. Col. Jonathan Richmond, 126th Ill., mustered in on Sept. 4, 1862, then commanded a brigade in the div. of Brig. Gen. Nathan Kimball. For his assignment to Haynes' Bluff, see letter to Act. Rear Admiral David D. Porter, June 2, 1863.

1. 1st Lt. Zeph. C. Bryan, 27th Ohio. On June 11, Maj. Gen. Cadwallader C. Washburn, Haynes' Bluff, telegraphed to USG. "There is a very large Negro Camp occupied mostly by women & children at Sniders Bluff & very near where I wish to encamp smiths Division The presence of so many women must be very bad—can they not be removed to millikens Bend or some other point." Telegram received, DNA, RG 393, Dept. of the Tenn., Telegrams Received. On the same day, Lt. Col. John A. Rawlins issued Special Orders No. 157. "Lieut. Z. C. Bryan, of the 27th Regt. Ohio Infty, Vols. will immediately break up the Contraband Camp at Haine's Bluff, and move the old men, women and children to the most valuable of the abandoned plantations within our lines, and put them to work cultivating the Crops growing on said plantations. The able bodied negro men, including both those who have enlisted in companies and those who have not enlisted, will be reported to the Commanding officer of Haines Bluff—for work on the defences of that place and when their services are no longer required for that purpose, those not enlisted will be put out to labor on the plantations, and those enlisted will be subject to such orders as their Commanding Officers may receive from Dept. Headquarters. The Commanding Officers of troops near any of the Plantations, that may be so occupied, will, when necessary, furnish such guards as may be required to protect the occupants of the same from the insults of stragglers and will afford every facility in their power to enable Lieut. Bryan to carry out these instructions without interference or molestation The Quartermasters Department will turn over to Lieut. Bryan for use in tilling of said plantations such of the Captured mules and horses it may have as are unfit for service

in the army." Copies, DLC-USG, V, 27, 28; DNA, RG 393, Dept. of the Tenn., Special Orders.

2. Maj. Christian Thielemann commanded the 16th Ill. Cav. On March 28, Maj. Gen. John A. McClernand, Milliken's Bend, wrote to USG. "I have the honor to state that Major C Thielman was authorized to raise his Squadron to a Regiment and has been engaged some time in recruiting for that purpose. I am informed by him that in addition to his two old companies now in the field in this Department—he has three full Companies mustered into the Service now in Camp Butler Ills. and a fourth nearley full—He is very desirous to be ordered into the field to active duties—I would respectfully request that his Command be ordered forward by the proper authority." Copy, Jacob Ammen Papers, IHi. On March 30, USG endorsed this letter. "Approved, and respectfully forwarded to Head quarters of the Army Washington, D. C." Copy, *ibid.* Cos. A and B, commanded by Capt. Milo Thielemann, were sent to Haynes' Bluff.

To Mary Duncan

Close to Vicksburg Miss.
June 5th 1863

Mrs. Mary Duncan,
233 Fifth Avenue N. Y.

My Dear Madam I have just received your beautiful present of a Cigar Case and will continue to carry and, appreciate it, long after I could have ~~done~~ "smoked" any number of cigars the Express Company are capable of transmitting. Your beautiful note accompanying the present will also be a treasure to me to be preserved.

I wish I could have dated my letter "Vicksburg." I cannot yet. My forces are very near and so far as all the "Pemberton" forces are concerned nothing can keep me from possessing town and troops.

Hoping an honarable and speedy termination to the present rebellion, and a safe, and secure, return to your Husbands possessions in Miss, I remain

yours most truly,
U. S. Grant

ALS, Emerson Opdycke Papers, OHi. Mrs. Mary Duncan was the wife of Henry P. Duncan. Henry P. and Stephen Duncan, Jr., sons of Dr. Stephen Duncan of Natchez, Miss., helped to manage his extensive plantation holdings. Dr. Duncan, born in Carlisle, Pa., in 1787, received a medical degree from Dickinson College in 1808. He then moved to Natchez and soon married Margaret Ellis, the daughter of a wealthy local planter. She died in 1815, and four years later he married Catherine Bingaman, the daughter of another wealthy planter. Duncan was a shrewd investor in cotton and sugar plantations as well as in northern securities. He was president and organizer of the first bank in Miss., and perhaps the wealthiest of all southern planters, with 1,041 slaves and a net income of $150,000 in 1851. Duncan maintained contact with the North, spending his summers in Newport, R. I., and New York City, where he owned homes. The first president of the Miss. Colonization Society and a vice president of the national organization, he donated at least $50,000 for the settlement of blacks in Liberia and fought a lengthy court battle against Miss. statutes preventing the manumission of slaves for the purpose of sending them to Liberia. A former Whig and staunch unionist before and during the Civil War, Duncan finally moved north in Sept., 1863. On Nov. 27, Duncan, New York City, wrote to USG. "Although I well know I ought not to trespass, even for one moment, on your valuable time—I am sustained by my regard for you & all that concerns you,—to offer you, my sincere & warm congratulations, on your recent success—May you never meet with a reverse— For the countrys sake, I could wish, you were on the Potomac. If you were now there, you would be in Richmond, *before congress assembles.*" ALS, USG 3. In spring, 1864, Duncan had assets worth more than $1,000,000 exclusive of land and slaves. Morton Rothstein, "The Antebellum South as a Dual Economy: A Tentative Hypothesis," *Agricultural History*, 41, 4 (Oct., 1967), 373–82; D. Clayton James, *Antebellum Natchez* (Baton Rouge, La., 1968), pp. 150–53; Harold E. Hammond, ed., *Diary of a Union Lady, 1861–1865* (New York, 1962), p. 267; John D. Milligan, ed., *From the Fresh-Water Navy: 1861–64* . . . (Annapolis, 1970), p. 222; Capt. Adam Badeau to Lt. Col. James Harrison Wilson, Nov. 10, 18, 1863, ALS, NjP; Katherine D. Smith, *The Story of Thomas Duncan and His Six Sons* (New York, 1928), pp. 47–48; information on Duncan family genealogy supplied by Margaret Fisher, La. State University Archives, Baton Rouge, La.

On April 28, Maj. Gen. Henry W. Halleck had written to USG. "Mrs Henry Duncan has sent to me letters from Gen Scott and distinguished union men in New York in regard to the family and property of Dr. S. Duncan in Miss. It is represented that all the members of this family have remained staunch unionists, for which they have severely suffered from the rebels, and that their property is now liable to be injured and destroyed by our own troops. It is not only the policy but the duty of our government to give all possible protection to the property of union men in the rebel states. We war against enemies, not against friends. And the line of distinction should be so clearly and strongly drawn as to be obvious to all. Every union man should be protected in person and property, so far as our forces can afford protection. The rebels themselves should be made to *see* and *feel* the distinction. We cannot return to them their slaves, however loyal the former owners may have been, for every slave who enters our lines becomes a free man. This, as well as other individual cases, must be left to your own discretion and judgement in regard to the measures to be adopted to carry out the policy here indicated." ALS (press), DNA, RG 108, Letters Sent.

To Maj. Gen. John A. McClernand

Near Vicksburg, Miss. June 6, 1863.
Maj Gen J. A. McClernand,
Comm'dg 13th Army Corps,

I am going up to Mechanicsburg   cannot be back before to-morrow night. Make all advance possible in approaches during my absence   Communications signaled to Haines Bluff will reach me.

U. S. Grant
Maj Gen.

Copies, DLC-USG, V, 19, 30; DNA, RG 393, Dept. of the Tenn., Letters Sent; *ibid.*, 13th Army Corps, Letters Received. *O.R.*, I, xxiv, part 3, 387. Copies of this letter were sent to Maj. Gen. James B. McPherson and Maj. Gen. William T. Sherman. See letter to Brig. Gen. Nathan Kimball, June 5, 1863.

A telegram from Maj. Gen. John A. McClernand to USG dated "7" was probably sent on June 7. "I am happy to congratulate Admiral Porter through you on the improved & Successfull effects of the fire of this evening   Many of the Shells have exploded over the enemies works   any higher elevation would probably bring them upon my lines   I hope their effect would be increased by lowering their range"   Telegram received, DNA, RG 45, Area 5. Undated in *O.R.* (Navy), I, xxv, 37.

On the same day, McClernand wrote to USG. "I have had a most interesting conversation with Col. Johnson, of the 28th Ill., who has been acting on your staff. As you know, he is lately returned from Mechanicsburg. He says the enemy has already massed a considerable force in front of that place. This is as was expected. The enemy must *soon* attack our rear, or *surrender* Vicksburg and its garrison. Public and official feeling and opinion in the South would not allow the latter without a desperate struggle to prevent it. Both political and military considerations will impel the enemy to make an effort to save Vicksburg at every hazard. In this view, is it not expedient to mass our forces on some point of the Vicksburg works, and try to force it? This is an important question; but probably is the alternative to waiting, and being attacked by the enemy in the rear. So far as my examinations go, I am of opinion that the most vulnerable point in the enemy's works is on his right, near the Mississippi. Attacking him at that point, the gun-boats could efficiently co-operate and assist in covering and holding all the ground gained. These reflections are offered in the interest of our cause, which is my apology for offering them. . . . P. S. The foregoing reflections are based on the idea that your request for reinforcements ~~are~~ is not responded to ~~as~~ promptly and to the necessary extent. If this be otherwise, and a sufficient force can be sent to check the advance of the enemy upon our rear, a second assault by us might not be necessary." ALS, DNA, RG 393, Dept. of the Tenn., Letters Received.

On June 8, McClernand telegraphed to USG. "~~What~~ What does the heavy firing on the right mean ?" Copy, McClernand Papers, IHi. On the same day, USG telegraphed to McClernand. "Enemy trying to put up a heavy gun on Shermans right front trying to prevent it" Copy, *ibid*. Also on June 8, McClernand telegraphed to USG. "Col Whiting reports that twenty five hundred 2500 Negro women & children arrived at Warrenton last night from Grand Gulf the person having them in charge refusing to go on to Youngs point on account of report that the rebels were within two or three miles of it Col Whiting asks what should be done with them at Warrenton they ~~wil~~ soon will eat us out of every thing" Telegram received, DNA, RG 393, Dept. of the Tenn., Telegrams Received. On the same day, Lt. Col. John A. Rawlins wrote to McClernand. "You will direct Col Whitney to send over and ascertain, if there would be any danger in the Negroes marching across to Youngs Point, and if there would be none, send them there without delay, and if they cannot be sent by that route, let them go round by Chickasaw Bayou, travelling at night They cannot be kept at Warrenton. The 108th Ills. and 23d Iowa were to join their Divisions as soon as they could be releived by the 63d Illinois, which went to Youngs-Point yesterday. The disturbed state of that place may delay them there, but they will obey the order as soon as they can be spared from there. No Official report has been received from Gen'l Dennis, one is expected momentarily. Admiral Porter reports the enemy were repulsed yesterday with a loss of 80 left dead on the field" Copies, DLC-USG, V, 19, 30; DNA, RG 393, Dept. of the Tenn., Letters Sent; *ibid*., 13th Army Corps, Letters Received. On the same day, McClernand telegraphed to Rawlins. "The one hundred & Eighth 108 Ill Infy & twenty third 23 Iowa are still at youngs point & have not reported to their Commands." Telegram received, *ibid*., Dept. of the Tenn., Telegrams Received.

On June 6, 1:00 A.M., Rawlins wrote to USG. "The great solicitude I feel for the safety of this army leads me to mention what I had hoped never again to do—the subject of your drinking. This may surprise you, for I may be (and I trust I am) doing you an injustice by unfounded suspicions, but if an error it better be on the side of his country's safety than in fear of offending a friend. I have heard that Dr. McMillan, at Gen. Sherman's a few days ago, induced you, notwithstanding your pledge to me, to take a glass of wine, and to-day, when I found a box of wine in front of your tent and proposed to move it, which I did, I was told you had forbid its being taken away, for you intended to keep it until you entered Vicksburg, that you might have it for your friends; and to-night, when you should, because of the condition of your health if nothing else, have been in bed, I find you where the wine bottle has just been emptied, in company with those who drink and urge you to do likewise, and the lack of your usual promptness of decision and clearness in expressing yourself in writing tended to confirm my suspicions. You have the *full* control of your appetite and can let drinking alone. Had you not pledged me the sincerity of your honor early last March that you would drink no more during the war, and kept that pledge during your recent campaign, you would not to-day have stood first in the world's history as a successful military leader. Your only salvation depends upon your strict adherence to that pledge. You cannot succeed in any other way. As I have before stated, I may be wrong in my suspicions, but if one sees that which leads him to suppose a sentinel is falling asleep on his post, it is his duty to arouse him; and if one sees that which leads him to fear the General commanding a great army is being seduced to that step which he knows will bring disgrace upon that General and defeat to his command, if he fails to sound the proper note of warning, the friends, wives, and children of those brave men whose lives he permits to remain thus imperilled will accuse him while he lives and stand swift witnesses of wrath against him in the day when all shall be tried. If my suspicions are unfounded, let my friendship for you and my zeal for my country be my excuse for this letter; and if they are correctly founded, and you determine not to heed the admonitions and the prayers of this hasty note by immediately ceasing to touch a single drop of any kind of liquor, no matter by whom asked or under what circumstances, let my immediate relief from duty in this department be the result." *New York Sun,* Jan. 23, 1887. On a copy of this letter, Rawlins added an undated endorsement. "This is an exact copy of a letter given to the person to whom it is addressed at its date, about four miles from our Headquarters in the rear of Vicksburg. Its admonitions were heeded, and all went well." *Ibid.* The letter appeared in a lengthy article on Grant's drinking by Washington correspondent Henry Van Ness Boynton, who gave no source. When the Rawlins letter was printed in *Life and Services of Maj. Gen. John A. Rawlins: An Address by John M. Shaw Before John A. Rawlins Post No. 126, G. A. R., Minneapolis, Minn., March 24, 1891* (n.p., 1891), pp. 9–10, Shaw, an antebellum Galena attorney who had known Rawlins since 1853, stated that he had a copy of the letter in his possession with the endorsement in Rawlins's hand. L. B. Crooker claimed to have seen the letter, with both text and endorsement in Rawlins's hand, in the possession of John E. Smith, with whom Rawlins left many of his papers in 1864. *The Nation,* 57, 1481 (Nov. 16, 1893), 370. James Harrison Wilson, *The Life of John A. Rawlins . . .* (New York, 1916), p. 130, indicated that the retained copy was owned by the Rawlins family.

Comments on the Boynton article included an interview with Dr. Edward D. Kittoe of Galena in the *Chicago Tribune,* Jan. 27, 1887, which tended to support Boynton, and a letter from William C. Carroll, Feb. 4, 1887, which discussed his relations with USG at Cairo and provided a lengthy account of the interview with C.S.A. officers at Lucas Bend in 1861, about which Boynton had made allegations of drinking. *Baltimore American,* Feb. 7, 1887. See *ibid.,* Feb. 11. In addition, newspaper correspondent Sylvanus Cadwallader wrote an article, "Grant and Rawlins," which stressed the role of Rawlins in furthering USG's career. *St. Louis Globe-Democrat,* Feb. 11, 1887. On Feb. 4, 1887, Gen. William T. Sherman wrote to Col. John E. Tourtellotte. "The Newspaper Clipping you sent I had seen here in the Sun—It fell still-born. Boynton is a Coyote, a hyena, scratching up old forgotten scandals, publishing them as something new—We all knew at the time that Genl Grant would occasionally drink too much—He always encouraged me to talk to him frankly of this & other things and I always noticed that he could with an hours sleep wake up perfectly sober & bright—and when any thing was pending he was invariably abstinent of drink—After Vicksburg, you must remember that a deligation of preachers waited on President Lincoln to Complain of Grants habit—Mr Lincoln heard them patiently and enquired—'Do you know where Grant buys his whiskey? I would like to present some to other Generals not so successful.' Mr. Lincoln knew all that Boynton now reveals & more—but Mr Lincoln wanted success, and had more sense than a thousand Boyntons—Halsted &c who from their safe places in the rear knew how to fight battles, and to hold the Generals responsible, for high water crowded camps and the consequent pestilence which we tried to hide from the Country, and even from the men —I well remember when the high water of the Mississippi drove us to the Levees which were also the only burial places, when the living & dead lay with but a foot of damp earth between, when Grant & his army demonstrated the largest measure of patience and Courage and perseverance, whilst Halsted in Cincinati ~~was~~ by just such articles as the one here displayed, was trying to create panic, mistrust and failure. It is not my office to defend General Grant, for time has stamped his fame as real—not accidental or meretricious, and I only refer to this publication of Boynton because you sent it to me, and may think it is something new—No it is as old as that most wonderful series of events which began with the Mexican War, 1846. Grants whole character was a mystery even to himself—a combination of strength and weakness not paralleled by any of whom I have read in Ancient or Modern History—The good he did lives after him—let his small weaknesses lie buried with his bones—and shame on the Curs and Coyotes who arise to rake them up again. . . ." ALS, University of Iowa, Iowa City, Iowa. See Ronald L. Fingerson, "A William Tecumseh Sherman Letter," *Books at Iowa*, 3 (Nov., 1965), 34–38.

In presenting the letter of June 6 in his biography of Rawlins, Wilson (p. 128) tied it to a statement of Charles A. Dana that USG was "ill" while on board a steamboat bound for Satartia, near Mechanicsburg. *Recollections of the Civil War* (New York, 1898), p. 83. The publication of Benjamin P. Thomas, ed., *Three Years with Grant as Recalled by War Correspondent Sylvanus Cadwallader* (New York, 1955), amplified Dana's statement by providing (pp. 102–10) a lengthy account of USG's drinking during the trip to Satartia, during which Cadwallader portrayed himself as shielding USG from discovery but informing Rawlins of the spree as soon as they returned. For the controversy provoked by publication of the Cadwallader manuscript, see letter to Maj. Gen. William T. Sherman, Aug. 8, 1862. A reporter for the *Chicago Times*, presumably Cadwallader, sent a dispatch from Satartia on June 6, 10:00 P.M., and could have accompanied USG downriver. *Chicago Times*, June 15, 1863.

The date on the Rawlins letter, June 6, 1:00 A.M., establishes that it was written before USG left Vicksburg, since Dana wrote on June 6, 7:00 P.M., that USG had just started for Satartia. *O.R.*, I, xxiv, part 1, 94. Nor could this be a matter of accidental misdating by one day, since Cadwallader's account would not place USG at his hd. qrs. the next day. Furthermore, the Rawlins letter does not discuss events of the trip to Satartia, and the endorsement contradicts Cadwallader. See Bruce Catton, *Grant Moves South* (Boston and Toronto, 1960), pp. 463–64, 535–36. Wilson and Cadwallader began to correspond in the late 1880s. After Cadwallader told Wilson the Satartia story, Wilson wrote to Dana. On Jan. 18, 1890, Dana replied that "Cadwallader was not along." ALS, DLC-Cadwallader. After reading Dana's letter, Cadwallader noted that there must have been two trips by USG to Satartia, with Cadwallader on the first. AES, *ibid*. But there was only one, and this lame explanation discredits Cadwallader as a witness to the events of the day.

On Jan. 28, 1887, the *New York Sun* printed an editorial, "Gen. Grant's Occasional Intoxication," undoubtedly written by Dana, then its editor, which defended President Abraham Lincoln's decision to retain USG in command despite his drinking. "Gen. GRANT's seasons of intoxication were not only infrequent, occurring once in three or four months, but he always chose a time when the gratification of his appetite for drink would not interfere with any important movement that had to be directed or attended to by him. In the particular case to which the letter of Gen. RAWLINS refers—we mean the letter brought out by Gen. BOYNTON—we were alone with Gen. GRANT at some distance from his headquarters near Vicksburg when Gen. RAWLINS rode up and delivered that admirable communication. It was a dull period in the campaign. The siege of Vicksburg was progressing with regularity. No surprise from within the doomed city or from without was to be apprehended; and when GRANT started out in drinking, the fact could not imperil the situation of the army or of any member of it except himself. After putting RAWLINS's missive in his pocket he wound up by going on board a steamer, which he had ordered for an excursion up the Yazoo River, and getting as stupidly drunk as the immortal nature of man would allow; but the next day he came out as fresh as a rose, without any trace or indication of the spree he had passed through. So it was on two or three other occasions of the sort that we happened to know of. The times were chosen with perfect judgment, and when it was all over, no outsider would have suspected that such things had been."

Wilson had noted in his diary for June 7, 1863, "Genl. G. intoxicated." Historical Society of Delaware, Wilmington, Del. Before meeting USG, Wilson had already described him as drinking constantly. John D. Hayes, ed., *Samuel Francis Du Pont: A Selection from his Civil War Letters* (Ithaca, 1969), II, 22. In Nov., 1862, Wilson met Rawlins, who told him that liquor threatened USG's career. Wilson, *Rawlins*, p. 100; Wilson, *Under the Old Flag* (New York and London, 1912), I, 136–37. On first reading Cadwallader's Satartia story, Wilson responded on Nov. 8, 1889, that he had already heard it from Dana and William M. Dunn. ALS, DLC-Cadwallader. Whatever happened on the trip to Satartia seems to have been discussed at USG's hd. qrs.—where Cadwallader might have heard it—and to have been the subject of gossip for years afterward.

To Maj. Gen. Henry W. Halleck

Near Vicksburg
June 8: 1863.

MAJ. GEN. H. W. HALLECK
GENL-IN-CHF

Vicksburg is closely invested. I have a spare force of about thirty thousand (30.000) with which to repel anything from the rear. This includes all I have ordered from west Tennessee. Johnston is concentrating a force at Canton, and now has a portion of it west of Black River. My troops have been north as far as Sartartia, and on the ridge back to that point there is no force yet.

I will make a waste of all the Country I can between the two Rivers.

I am fortifying Haines' Bluff, and will defend the line from here to that point at all hazards.

U. S. GRANT

Major Genl.

Telegram received, DNA, RG 107, Telegrams Collected (Bound); copies, *ibid.*, Telegrams Received in Cipher; *ibid.*, RG 393, Dept. of the Tenn., Hd. Qrs. Correspondence; DLC-USG, V, 6, 8, 24, 94. *O.R.*, I, xxiv, part 1, 41. On June 8, 1863, USG again telegraphed to Maj. Gen. Henry W. Halleck. "It is reported that three divisions have left Bragg's army to join Johnston. Breckinridge is known to have arrived" Telegram received, DNA, RG 107, Telegrams Collected (Bound); copies, *ibid.*, Telegrams Received in Cipher; *ibid.*, RG 393, Dept. of the Tenn., Hd. Qrs. Correspondence; DLC-USG, V, 6, 8, 24, 94. *O.R.*, I, xxiv, part 1, 41.

To Brig. Gen. Elias S. Dennis

Near Vicksburg Miss June 8th, 1863

BRIG GEN'L. E. S DENNIS
COMMDG DIST' OF N. EASTERN LA

I have ordered Genl Mowers Brigade over to re-inforce you.[1] He is sent merely for temporary service to repel any threatened attack. With the force you will have with this accession, I think you can drive the enemy beyond the Tensas river. If, however you think more force is required, let me know, and it will be promptly sent. If the enemy is in the neighborhood of Richmond, he should be driven from there, and our troops should push on to Monroe. Every vestige of an enemy's camp ought to be shoved back of that point. I am not fully advised of the force you are likely to meet, but cannot think it large. No such blind move could be made by an intelligent foe, as to send more than a force for a raid into such a pocket. Let me hear what intelligence you have from the rebel forces concentrating on the peninsula

U. S. GRANT Maj Gen'l

P. S. You understand that all the troops in the District of North Eastern La, both black and white, are subject to your orders. At Lake Providence you have two White Regiments that can join you in any movement towards Monroe.

U. S. G.

Copies, DLC-USG, V, 19, 30; DNA, RG 393, Dept. of the Tenn., Letters Sent; Alcorn Collection, WyU. On June 7, 1863, Brig. Gen. Elias S. Dennis signaled to USG. "The enemy three thousand strong have attacked Millikens Bend. I have sent all my available force there; also, a Gun boat." Copy, DNA, RG 94, Letters Received, 56S 1864; copy, *ibid.*, RG 111, Vicksburg Signal Book. On June 8, Dennis, Young's Point, wrote to Lt. Col. John A. Rawlins. "The enemy 2.500 Strong under Genl McCullough attacked our forces at Millekens Bend Yesterday morning about daylight, and were repulsed with heavy loss. I learned the evening before that the enemy were advancing upon that point, and immediately sent the 23d Iowa Infantry and a Gun Boat to their assistance. Yesterday morning I also sent the 120th and 131st Ill Infy to reenforce them, but they arrived too late to take part in the engagement. The loss of the 9th and 11th Louisiana Vols. A. D. was about 60 killed and 100 wounded, and that of the 23d Iowa, 26 killed and 44 wounded. The loss of the enemy, I think, exceeds ours. I will send a full report as soon as possible, in the mean time, the following I have gleaned from a deserter, and consider it reliable. That the force of the enemy consisted of 9 regiments of Infantry, of 600 men each, and one battery of Artillery, all in command of General's McCollough, Randall, and Walker. Walker threatened Young's Point, while McCollough engaged the forces, at Millekens Bend; The artillery was left back at Tensas Bayou. The enemy expected to form a junction with General Price at Richmond.   the enemy have retreated to Richmond." LS, *ibid.*, RG 94, War Records Office, Union Battle Reports.

On June 7, Act. Rear Admiral David D. Porter signaled and wrote to USG. "The enemy attacked Millikens-Bend. Commenced driving the Negro regiments, and killing all they captured. This infuriated the negroes who turned on the 'Rebs' and slaughtered them like sheep, and captured two hundred prisoners. I also hear they captured five peices artillery. The Choctaw and Levington were there." Signal received, *ibid.*, Military Div. of the Miss.; copies, *ibid.*, Letters Received, 56S 1864; *ibid.*, RG 393, 13th Army Corps, Letters Received; *ibid.*, RG 111, Vicksburg Signal Book. *O.R.*, I, xxiv, part 2, 453. "Last night, or early this morning, the Rebels, supposed to amount to 3000 or 4000 strong, attacked Milliken's Bend and nearly gobbled up the whole party, fortunately I heard of it in time to get the 'Choctaw' and Lexington up there just as their attack commenced—The Rebels got into our Camps and killed a good many negroes, and left about 80 of their number killed on the levee—Our troops (mostly negroes) retreated behind the banks near the water's edge, and the Gunboats opened so rapidly on the enemy that they scampered off, the shells chasing them as far as the woods, they got nothing but hard knocks—The moment I heard of it I went up in the 'Black Hawk' and saw quite an ugly sight, The dead negroes lined the ditch inside of the parapet, or levee, and were mostly shot on the top of the head, in front of them: close to the levee, laid an equal number of rebels stinking in the sun—Their Knapsacks contained four days provisions.   they were miserable looking wretches. I had no sooner got there, than the despatch boat brought me a letter from the General Commanding here, informing me that the Rebels had appeared near the Canal in force. I hurried back and found all the Vessels h[a]ving guns ready to receive them, and heard nothing of the rebels.   it was a false alarm, but the steamers had all gone off for Young's point—There are about 300 troops here in all, not counting the 'blacks.' I think we should have a thousand men near the Canal and at Young's Point—and I recommend moving everything from Milliken's Bend to the latter place. We can defend it much better. Those fellows will be scouting about here for some time, and it is no longer safe to run teams across to the Vessels on the other side. I think the Rebels are in force there. When, the Brigade comes I will land them, but I hear they are at Memphis waiting for troops—The 29th Iowa, (I think it was) behaved so well to-day—It stood its ground against great odds, and kept the enemy out of the Camps until the men could form and get into some kind of order—I think we want more force here—and everything at Young's Point, moved over on the the the opposite side of the River, near the mouth of the Yazoo, where there is a good landing—"   LS, DNA, RG 393, Dept. of the Tenn., Letters Received. *O.R.*, I, xxiv, part 2, 453–54; *O.R.* (Navy), I, xxv, 164–65. Also on June 7, Rawlins signaled to Porter and to Dennis. "Genl Grant not yet having returned from Mechanicksburg ~~this~~ yr communication is refered to to Maj Genl Sherman who will give Such orders as in his judgement the case may require"   Copy, DNA, RG 111, Vicksburg Signal Book. On the same day, Rawlins wrote to Maj. Gen. John A. McClernand. "It is supposed that everything is safe at Millikens Bend. Genl Dennis is there in command, and nothing further has been heard from him." Copies, DLC-USG, V, 19, 30; DNA, RG 393, Dept. of the Tenn., Letters Sent; *ibid.*, 13th Army Corps, Letters Received. On the same day, Rawlins wrote to Maj. Gen. James B. McPherson. "Has the 63d Ills. gone to Youngs Point, as per orders of the 5th inst? If not send them at once, as they are needed there, the enemy three thousand strong, having attackted Millikens Bend." Copies, DLC-USG, V, 19, 30; DNA, RG 393, Dept. of the Tenn., Letters Sent. Also on June 7, John Macfeely, "Yazoo River," telegraphed to Rawlins. "Col Macfeely is now at Youngs point—We have no reliable information of the fight at Millikens Bend Boat from Youngs point is expected every minute   will let you know on its arrival   Gen Grant has just left this for Hd Qrs—"   Telegram received, *ibid.*, Telegrams Received. On the same day, Col. George E. Bryant, 12th Wis., Grand Gulf, wrote to Rawlins. "I am *positively* informed, that *Seven Transports* Crowded with Rebels, under McCullough, Taylor & Walker—a part of whom attacked the force at Pirkins, a week ago—are making their up '*Tansas*' and that they intend to attack Milikins Bend, or failing in that to Capture—a Steam Boat & cross to Miss—'The force is 'Six Thousand Strong' estimated at *10'000*—*Harrison* was Ordered to join them. . . . I shall be away from him in 4 Transports more—" ALS, *ibid.*, RG 94, War Records Office, Dept. of the Tenn. Incomplete in *O.R.*, I, xxiv, part 3, 388.

On June 16, USG wrote to Brig. Gen. Lorenzo Thomas. "Herewith I have the honor of enclosing Brig. Gen. E. S. Dennis' report of the 'Battle of Millikin's Bend, La. fought on the 7th day of June 1863 together with list of casualties. In this battle most of the troops engaged were Africans who had but little experience in the use of fire arms. Their conduct is said however to have been most gallant and I doubt not but with good officers they will make good troops." ALS, DNA, RG 94, War Records Office, Union Battle Reports. *O.R.*, I, xxiv, part 2, 446.

On June 12, Dennis prepared a detailed report of the battle of Milliken's Bend addressed to Rawlins. LS, DNA, RG 94, War Records Office, Union Battle Reports. *O.R.*, I, xxiv, part 2, 447–48. For further reports, see *ibid.*, pp. 455–70; *O.R.* (Navy), I, xxv, 162–66.

On May 28, Rawlins issued Special Orders No. 143. "All that portion of the State of Louisiana, now in the occupancy of the 'Army of the Tennessee,' will constitute the District of North Eastern Louisiana, and be commanded by Brig. Genl J. C. Sullivan,   During the absence of Brig. Gen'l J. P. Hawkins, all troops of African descent in the District of North Eastern Louisiana, will be under the immediate command of Colonel Isaac T. Shepard. Troops, especially those of African Descent, will be so disposed as to afford the best possible protection to plantations leased by Government" Copies, DLC-USG, V, 27, 28; DNA, RG 393, Dept. of the Tenn., Special Orders. *O.R.*, I, xxiv, part 3, 357. On June 1, Brig. Gen. Jeremiah C. Sullivan, Young's Point, wrote to USG's hd. qrs. "States that his health is such as to render him unable to pay the required attention to his command. Has but two Regts at Young's Point and in his opinion neither could be trusted in an engagement. The rebels made a dash on Perkins Hospital and our men destroyed a large amount of Hospl' Stores. Commissioners are asking for Guards, and he has no more men than are necessary for fatigue and Picket Asks a reply soon" DLC-USG, V, 22; DNA, RG 393, Dept. of the Tenn., Register of Letters Received. On June 2, Rawlins issued Special Orders No. 148 assigning Dennis to replace Sullivan. Copies, DLC-USG, V, 27, 28; DNA, RG 393, Dept. of the Tenn., Special Orders; *ibid.*, District of Northeast La., Letters Received. On June 2, Sullivan signaled to USG. "Rumers of an attack on this place. I can defend everything here, but have not sufficient force to move on to meet them. If they should attempt to come in. The Rebels are still parolling our men and sending them across. I have ordered the new boat to be seized and destroyed, and the men to be held as prisoners." Signal received, *ibid.*, RG 94, War Records Office, Military Div. of the Miss.; ICarbS. *O.R.*, I, xxiv, part 3, 375. On June 3, Sullivan signaled to USG. "The large number ~~of~~ of Deserters coming in to my lines raises my suspicion all is not right   on investigation I find nearly all are persons incapable of military duty or convalescents   by getting rid of these kind of men they can make their provision last longer   shal I not hold these as prisoners of war and had ~~not~~ not admiral Porter better ~~not~~ allow his Gun Boat to receive no more deserters." Copy, DNA, RG 111, Vicksburg Signal Book. On the same day, Sullivan wrote to Rawlins. "Large numbers of *Contrabands*, women and children, have collected at this point. Their condition is such that immediate action is needed—No one seems to take charge of them, to feed them, or to attend properly to their sanitary or moral condition. Our soldiers are rapidly becoming demoralized by being thrown in contact with them, and the contrabands are becoming depraved, vicious and unruly. I have been of the opinion that the commissioners were obliged to see that all negroes who came into our lines were provided with food—a proper camp selected for them, and necessary rules and restrictions placed upon them. Captain Breeze, of the U. S. Navy informs me that his *personal application* was met with a refusal to receive a number of contrabands that the Navy had to turn over to them—and that consequently, he having no means to provide for them, would be compelled to turn them on the 'bank.' The Government is now feeding, at a heavy expense, a large number of dissolute and idle negroes, most of which might be saved if they were ordered to be 'corralled' near the present encampment of the African regiments, and the undrawn rations, or company savings turned over to them. Their Husbands, Brothers and Sons, have enlisted in these regiments, and should be compelled to aid in their support. I submit the following plan, which I hope, with improvements, may be issued: 1. Contrabands may be assembled, and, after being divided into families, ascertain the whereabouts of their Sons, Husbands, Brothers and Fathers. 2. That each Colonel be directed to ascertain from his recruits the number of persons in the family of each dependent on him for support—and their whereabouts. 3. That families be furnished with tickets certifying that they have Sons, Brothers, or Husbands serving in these regiments. 4. That such soldiers shall have placed opposite their names on their Pay Rolls, an amount, carefully proportioned, which shall be called an allotment, and be subject to the draft of the Commissary Dept. 5. That a Chief Commissary be appointed for the African Dept, who shall be furnished semi-weekly with a complete list of tickets issued and allotments made. 6. That all details for fatigue work made to the q. m. or Commissary Dept. be furnished with tickets, which, presented in the aggregate, may be issued on by the Commissary nearest the place of work—provided that such tickets shall not exceed in value per day, for each one, the daily pay of a private soldier—rations included." LS, *ibid.*, RG 393, Dept. of the Tenn., Letters Received. Also on June 3, 1:00 P.M., USG signaled to Sullivan. "Send Steamer Courier to Chickasaw Landing Imeadietly"   Signal received, ICarbS.

1. On June 8, Rawlins wrote to Brig. Gen. Joseph A. Mower. "You will move with your Brigad including your artillery, to Youngs Point La, and report to Brig Gen'l Dennis, Commanding District of Northeaster La. The Quarter-Masters Dept has been directed to send Steames to Haines Bluff Landing to transport you to night." Copies, DLC-USG, V, 19, 30; DNA, RG 393, Dept. of the Tenn., Letters Sent; Alcorn Collection, WyU. On the same day, USG wrote to Capt. Gilbert A. Pierce. "Send transports to Haines Bluff to move a Brigade of troops to Youngs Point. Send immediately"   Copies, DLC-USG, V, 19, 30; DNA, RG 393, Dept. of the Tenn., Letters Sent. On June 9, USG signaled to Dennis. "two Boats Loaaded with troops have just Gone down"   Copy, *ibid.*, RG 111, Vicksburg Signal Book. On the same day, Dennis signaled to USG. "Please hury forward Brigade.   indications of enemy in vicinity"   Copy, *ibid.* See letter to Brig. Gen. Elias S. Dennis, June 11, 1863.

To Brig. Gen. Jacob G. Lauman

Near Vicksburg Miss June 8, 1863.

BRIG GEN'L. J. G. LAUMAN
COMMD'G 4TH DIV, 16TH ARMY CORPS.

Move your left Brigade to the right, so as to leave one Regiment, on the left of Halls Ferry road. As you now have your troops disposed, there is great danger of having them picked up in detail. When your other Brigade arrives, you will be able to occupy the position now held by Col Hall.[1]

U. S. Grant Maj Gen'l.

Copies, DLC-USG, V, 19, 30; DNA, RG 393, Dept. of the Tenn., Letters Sent; Alcorn Collection, WyU. On June 8, 1863, USG again wrote to Brig. Gen. Jacob G. Lauman. "Admiral Porter having kindly permitted Capt Crowell, and his party, of the coast survey, to assist in the operations against Vicksburg, you will please see that while in your front, they are provided with horses, men and subsistence, and that every facility for the Speedy acomplishment of this work, is afforded them." Copies, DLC-USG, V, 19, 30; DNA, RG 393, Dept. of the Tenn., Letters Sent. On June 5, USG had signaled to Act. Rear Admiral David D. Porter. "Have you an *engineer Officer* or two you can spare for a few days? I am much in need of such Officers" Copy, *ibid.*, RG 111, Vicksburg Signal Book. On June 6, Porter wrote to USG. "I send you three gentlemen who, I think are good and competent engineers. Will you please order them provided with such things as are necessary for their comfort, as I send them unencumbered with anything, save their necessary instruments." LS (press), *ibid.*, RG 45, Correspondence of David D. Porter, Mississippi Squadron, General Letters.

1. Col. Cyrus Hall, 14th Ill., then commanded the 2nd Brigade, 4th Div., 16th Army Corps.

To Samuel L. Casey

Near Vicksburg Miss June 8, 1863.

Hon. S Casey
Chickasaw Bayou Landing

In reply to your note I would state that I have telegraphed to the President and to the General in chief. The enemy are accumulating a force North of me, and may get more troops than I can manage with my present force. A dispatch just received from Gen'l Halleck states that he is doing all in his power to strengthen me, and I feel no doubt but that every thing possible will be done to secure a victory here. Feeling under many obligations for your interest in the success of this campaign.

U. S. Grant Maj Gen'l.

Copies, DLC-USG, V, 19, 30; DNA, RG 393, Dept. of the Tenn., Letters Sent. See letter to Brig. Gen. Lorenzo Thomas, April 14, 1863, note 3.

To Julia Dent Grant

—————

June 9th 1863.

DEAR JULIA,

I wrote to you by every courier I was sending back up to the Capture of Jackson. Having written to you to start for Vicksburg as soon as you heard the place was taken, and thinking that would be before another letter would reach you, I wrote no more.

You may start down as soon as you receive this letter. If Vicksburg is not in our hands then you can remain on board the steamer at the landing with the prospect of my calling to see you occasionally. I have enjoyed most excellent health during the campaign, so has Fred. Fred. has enjoyed his campaign very much. He has kept a journal which I have never read but suppose he will read to you.

The Pony, "Little Rebel," which I have got for Miss & Jess. is the smallest horse I ever saw. I want you to get saddles for both the children. The saddle I had for Jess was a very old one and being rode by persons too large for it it broke to pieces and had to be thrown away.

I can tell you but little about matters here. We are up close to the enemy's forts and so far as the present force is concerned we must capture them. The enemy however may make a desperate effort to get a force outside of me to relieve the present garrison. If they do I occupy one of the strongest imaginable positions. I have ordered all the troops from West Tennessee that can possibly be spared from there. In addition to this other troops are coming from Kentucky and Mo. With the whole of them there is but little doubt but that I can hold out against anything likely to be brought against me.

I want to see you very much dear Julia and also our dear little children.

Good bye
ULYS.

ALS, DLC-USG.

To *Act. Rear Admiral David D. Porter*

Head Quarters, Dept. of the Ten.
Near Vicksburg June 10th 1863.

ADMIRAL D. D. PORTER
COMD.G MISS. SQUADRON,
ADMIRAL,

I send you a dispatch, by signal, requesting you to send a gunboat to meet transports known to be on their way here loaded with troops.[1] I have been informed of thirteen of them being loaded at Memphis and expected them here last night.[2] Their nonarrival causes me much uneasiness lest they may be interupted some place by a battery of the enemy.

I have information of 19 000 troops being on their way here besides those already arrived and would request that until they all get here a gunboat ply about Island 6[5] and other dangerous points below[.]

I am aware Admiral that h[eavy] drafts have been made on your fleet above Vicksburg but hope you will still be able to comply with the request made herein.

I am fortifying Hains Bluff and expect to hold it. At present I do not think the enemy are near there. All the forces coming to me now are being sent to Hain's Bluff and I need not tell you how anxious I feel for the arrival of those I know to have started.

Very Truly your obt. svt.
U. S. GRANT
Maj. Gen.

ALS, MdAN. *O.R.*, I, xxiv, part 3, 396; *O.R.* (Navy), I, xxv, 67–68.

On June 9, 1863, Maj. Gen. William T. Sherman telegraphed to USG. "About Sunset I heard a good deal of musket firing apparently in Vicksburg I was at my extreme right where ~~not~~ we have used up one of the water batteries Can you explain the firing of musketry" Telegram received, DNA, RG 393, Dept. of the Tenn., Letters Received. On the same day, Sherman telegraphed to Lt. Col. John A. Rawlins. "Capt Selfridge says heavy Eight inch navy guns was landed at the steamboat landing for McClernand and are now in danger of loss by the caving of the bank—~~Mc~~McClernand should send for them or they should be put" Telegram received (incomplete), *ibid.* On June 9, Act. Rear Admiral David D. Porter, *Black Hawk,* wrote to USG. "I attempted to move the guns at Haynes' Bluff, down to the beach, in case of any change in our present position to have them completely under the guns of the vessels. If it should turn out so unfortunate that Johnson obliged you to move away, we should lose them all and have them be used against us once more, while if taken away we can always hold Haynes' Bluff. I don't see how the rebels ever get them into some of their places. If you will order a detail of men, Capt Walker will supply tackles and other appliances, and superintend getting them down. I will in the mean time send for gun carriages and they can be mounted where you may like to have them. I think this a safe arrangement, and one that prudence would suggest." LS, *ibid.* On June 10, USG wrote to Maj. Gen. John A. McClernand. "Capt Selfridge says heavy eight inch guns were landed at Chickasaw Bayou Landing for you, and that they are in danger of being lost from the caving in of the bank.   you will please send for them at once. Musketry fireing was heard from here about sunset around towards the left.   was there anything unusual occurred. ?" Copies, DLC-USG, V, 19, 30; DNA, RG 393, Dept. of the Tenn., Letters Sent; Alcorn Collection, WyU. On the same day, USG wrote to Capt. Gilbert A. Pierce. "Move those eight inch guns left by the Navy for Gen'l McClernand, from the landing to a position where they will safe from the caving in of the river bank." Copies, DLC-USG, V, 19, 30; DNA, RG 393, Dept. of the Tenn., Letters Sent.

On June 9, Porter wrote to USG. "I am much hampered just at this moment for want of teams to haul coal over to the vessels on the other side. I have in consequence to suspend operations, which is very unfortunate at this moment, as our co operation with the army is expected, while we have not coal enough with which to move the vessels. Admiral Farragut is also calling on us for coal for his vessels below, and we cannot get it to him. You will, I feel comprehend the necessity of our being placed in a condition to move when called upon, and I beg that you will give an order so that we can be supplied with a sufficient quantity of teams, without interruption." LS, *ibid.,* Letters Received. On June 10, USG wrote to Porter. "I will give the Quarter Master directions to turn over to you all the teams he can spare, to haul coal. A limited number of teams are required to take across the point supplies of ammunition and provisions for those troops drawing their supplies from Warrenton. All the remainder at Youngs Point, can be taken to haul coal." Copies, DLC-USG, V, 19, 30; DNA, RG 393, Dept. of the Tenn., Letters Sent.

On June 11, USG wrote to Pierce. "Turn over to the Navy all the wagons that can possibly be spared at Youngs Point, to haul coal across for the Gunboats. Direct Gen'l Dennis by my order, to give every facility to getting over coal for the Navy." Copies, *ibid.* On the same day, Pierce telegraphed to Rawlins. "The orders of the Genl regarding the removal of Cannon on the bank to a place of safety & the turning over of teams to the navy to haul coal across the point have been obeyed" Telegram received, *ibid.,* Telegrams Received. On June 13, Pierce telegraphed to Rawlins. "Please Send me an order by telegraph for Commanding officer at Youngs Point,—To furnish a detail of Negroes or soldiers to drive the teams fitted up for the navy—They appear for some reason to have a vast amount of confusion" Telegram received, *ibid.* On June 14, USG wrote to Pierce. "There is great complaint of scarcity of Boats up the river. Release them as fast as possible." Copies, DLC-USG, V, 19, 30; DNA, RG 393, Dept. of the Tenn., Letters Sent.

On June 10, Porter wrote to USG. "The commanding officer at White River has orders to convoy all the vessels that come down, and I expect the detention of the troops is owing to the head vessels waiting until the stern ones come up. I gave the officer in charge there, orders not to *permit* any vessel to pass *without* a convoy. I have 4 vessels at Young's Point—2 here—one (the Lexington) at Milliken's Bend—one 20 miles above Milliken's Bend—one at Providence—2 at Greenville—3 between Greenville and White River—one at Island 65, and three or four scattering, so that transports will always be warned of dangerous places. The enemy have no artillery, though a party are on their way here from Harrisonburg with six or seven pieces—I think we can manage them. I will have to take 2 gunboats from Hayne's Bluff, but will leave the 'De Kalb' there, and the 'Forest Rose' and 'Rattler.' I heard that Ellet was at Memphis three days ago, but no troops on board yet. I will keep a bright lookout on the river, and do all I can to prevent any accident happening to the transports   The Rebels will soon have here 12000 men, which Banks might as well have kept employed on the Red River —had he taken my advice he would have saved us this trouble—taken Harrisonburg, and been here with twenty thousand men—leaving fifteen thousand to keep Port Hudson quiet—as it is he has done nothing; had two repulses, and is no further ahead than before. . . . P. S. I send you a letter I received from Gen'l Banks in answer to one, I wrote him advising him to come here to help you, taking Harrisonburg on his way. You see how well he promised; had he done as he said he would, we would have had all the party that have been annoying us here, with their guns." LS, *ibid.*, Letters Received.

On June 11, Porter signaled to USG. "A Col. a Capt & three privates escaped from Vicksburg last night in a Skiff and landed above Willow Bayou above the Cincinatia   they expect to return in A day or two   with dispatches and Percusion Caps   they Crossed over one Mile above Mouth of yazoo"   Copy, *ibid.*, RG 111, Vicksburg Signal Book.

1. On June 10, USG signaled to Porter. "I had notice two days ago of, thirteen boats loaded with troops being on their way here. They have not yet arrived and I fear have been blockaded on the river. Would it not be advisable to send a Gunboat to convoy them? These boats will be followed by as many more from St Louis, and the Ohio river, which should also have convoys." Copies (dated June 9), DLC-USG, V, 19, 30; DNA, RG 393, Dept. of the Tenn., Letters Sent; (dated June 10) *ibid.*, RG 111, Vicksburg Signal Book. On June 10, Porter signaled to USG. "There is eleven Gun-boats between this and Helena. All ordered to convoy.   the river is perfectly quiet. I will send a special one." Signal received, *ibid.*, RG 393, Dept. of the Tenn., Letters Received; copy, *ibid.*, RG 111, Vicksburg Signal Book.

2. George W. Graham, Yazoo River, telegraphed to USG a message dated only "10." "No troops yet arrived—Captains of steamers arriving two days ago are positive to their information that thirteen steamers are detained for troops Cannot ~~vouch for troops cannot~~ truth vouch for the truth   the statement came from good authority   I will telegraph you particulars on arrival of first boat" Telegram received, *ibid.*, RG 393, Dept. of the Tenn., Telegrams Received.

To Maj. Gen. Cadwallader C. Washburn

Near Vicksburg Miss June 10th 1863,

MAJ GEN'L C. C. WASHBURN
COMMD'G DETACHMN'T 16TH ARMY CORPS,

Your note of this date is just received. I am looking every day for the arrival of Gen'l W. S. Smith with Sixteen Regiments of Infantry, and three batteries to re-inforce you. They will be sent to Haines Bluff on their arrival. A still larger force is coming down, which could also be sent immediately to Haines Bluff, when it becomes known than an attack is to be made on that place. My instructions have been more particularly, to blockade the roads leading to the different ferries on the Black river. The Valley and ridge roads, should both be kept open, and only closed against an advancing army. Telegraph instruments and an operater have been sent from here to you.

U. S. GRANT Maj Gen'l.

Copies, DLC-USG, V, 19, 30; DNA, RG 393, Dept. of the Tenn., Letters Sent; Alcorn Collection, WyU. On June 10, 1863, Maj. Gen. Cadwallader C. Washburn, "Haines Bluff," wrote to USG. "I have had the country between the Yazoo & Big Black very thoroughly explored, and we have been able to discover no enemy. The force of mounted rebels which Gen. Osterhause spoke of in his letter to you of yesterday we have not been able to hear of anywhere nearer than in the region of Mechanicsburgh, and the report that the Cavalry of Gen Osterhouse having met them yesterday must b[e] a mistake. A detachment of Cavalry, scouted through to near BirdSongs ferry on the Black yesterday, and fell in about 5 oclk P. M, with, a detachment of about 100 from the 6th Mo, but they did not report having seen any enemy during the day. The entire country between the Yazoo & Black is very broken except in the valley along the Yazoo. A large army can only approach with great difficulty except down the Yazoo Valley between the bluffs & the river. I shall obstruct all the roads leading across to Black River, as soon as I can obtain axes—I sent a boat to Youngs Point for them yesterday, but it came back & reported none to be had either there or at Chicasaw Landing. This fact I notified you of this morning & I hope to recieve some tonight, as I feel that we are losing valuable time for want of tools. You are aware that the force now here is but small, numbering all told Infantry Artillery & Cavalry only about 6.000. There is but one Battery here. The place I regard as very easily defended, and [6].000 men can hold it against 30.000—I hear that Gen Osterhouse has pretty effectually blockaded the road leading to Bridgeport. It is worthy of consideration as to how far the business of blockading roads should be carried on. Should it become necessary for us to make a sudden aggressive movement we might find our obstruction seriously interfering with our own movements. I however shall proceed to blockade as soon as I can procure axes, all the roads, except that up the valley, which cannot be easily obstructed. I have sent out yesterday & today four spies, who if not picked up will visit Canton, Jackson & Yazoo City before they return, and as fast as I can find suitable scouts I propose to send them into the enemies lines to obtain information. I call your attention to the fact that the telegraph is not yet in operation. . . . P. S. I am just advised of the arrival of axes &c" ALS, DNA, RG 393, Dept. of the Tenn., Letters Received. See *Morningside Bookshop Catalogue Number Seven* [1975], p. 46.

On June 9, Maj. Gen. John A. McClernand wrote to USG. "Genl. Osterhaus reports that the enemy are crossing at Macon Ford, seven miles north of Bridgeport ferry,—that his pickets with two companies of cavalry have momentarily checked him,—that he must be reinforced by all available cavalry. I have sent all my cavalry. This movement is far to my right. Cant McPherson and Sherman send reinforcements? Should not a mobile force be immediately thrown between Bridgeport and Oak ridge ferries? Please immediately send to Genl. Osterhaus the balance of the 2nd Ills. Cavalry and as much more as you can. Genl. Osterhaus suggests that a Cavalry force moving down from Haine's Bluff to the Messenger ford, will cut off any rebel force on this side the Big Black." LS, DNA, RG 94, War Records Office, Dept. of the Tenn. *O.R.*, I, xxiv, part 3, 393–94. On the same day, McClernand telegraphed to USG. "Osterhaus reports that the Eighth Kentucky Mounted Infantry attacked his pickets on Edwards Station road, but, failing to drive it, retired, leaving a prisoner, who says, as the prisoners taken the day before, that General Johnston is rapidly collecting at Canton, and that Johnston will soon attack Snyder's Bluff and Breckinridge Big Black Bridge. Can't you send Osterhaus the detachment of the Second Illinois Cavalry ordered from me? Ought not communication to be opened between Osterhaus and Kimball, and each be ready to succor the other?" *Ibid.*, p. 393. On the same day, Lt. Col. John A. Rawlins wrote to McClernand. "There is a Division of troops at Haines Bluff under Command of Maj Gen'l Washburn; he has been directed to send out a sufficient force in the direction of the Macon ford to cut off the enemy, or drive him beyond the Big Black, also to open communication with Gen'l Osterhaus. The 2nd Ill Cavalry are ordered to report as you request." Copies, DLC-USG, V, 19, 30; DNA, RG 393, Dept. of the Tenn., Letters Sent; *ibid.*, 13th Army Corps, Letters Received. *O.R.*, I, xxiv, part 3, 394. On the same day, McClernand telegraphed to USG. "I have just ordered that Part of the 2d Ills cavalry under command of Lt Col Bush to report forthwith to Genl. Osterhauss   Can you send that part at Haines Bluff   he was sent there to releif Maj Bush Some days since" Telegram received, DNA, RG 393, Dept. of the Tenn., Telegrams Received. Also on June 9, 6:30 P.M., Washburn signaled to USG. "Dispatch received and orders sent to second Ills Cavalry to report to ~~you~~ Osterhaus at once" Signal received, *ibid.*, RG 94, War Records Office, Military Div. of the Miss.

On June 9, Brig. Gen. Peter J. Osterhaus, "Big Black," twice wrote to Rawlins, the second time at 1:00 P.M. "I just receive information that some rebel forces were crossing the river at Messenger or Macon ford north of Bridgeport; about 10 or 12 miles from here; I reinforced my picket in that direction by 2 strong Companies of Cavalry and 1 Sect. of Moutnain howitzers; this is all I possibly could spare, and it leaves me only a very few Cavalry Men here; it would be very well, to have a force established in the Vicinity of the above fords and two others further north; as there is no doubt, that in any advance, the rebels may attempt, they will avail themselves of these crossing places.—My Cavalry is, from this very hard service, getting Overly worn out; and a strengthening in numbers would be very desirable. As soon, as I learn from the troops sent out, I will report." ALS, *ibid.*, RG 393, Dept. of the Tenn., Letters Received. "Major Montgomery who is in Command of the detachment of Cavalry and Mount. howitzers, sent out to the ford north of Bridgeport (as stated in my dispatch of this morning) reports, that he fell in with a pretty large force of Rebel mounted troops and that he took a position, where he thinks he, he can hold his own; about 150 Rebles attempted to flank. But the Major succeeded in repelling them; he sent through for all the Cavalry left here, and I canplied with his request which gives him not over 150 men besides his 2 Mtn howitzrs   At the same time I forward 1 Regiment of Infantry to the Bovina-Bridgeport road and took the necessary steps to guard against an attack on my left flank; My patroles to Edwards Just returned, found no sign of any enemy there, and it strikes me that the concentration of the mounted rebel forces, which were in my front yesterday, is very likely at the fords where they can cross the river without molestation; A force sent out from Haynes bluff could cut off the retreat of any rebel on this side of the river;" Copy, *ibid.*, 13th Army Corps, 9th Div., Letters Sent. *O.R.*, I, xxiv, part 2, 220. On the same day, Rawlins wrote to Osterhaus. "Your communication of this date, relating to a force of the enemy being on this side the Big Black is received, and has been referred to Maj. Gen. C. C. Washburne Com'd'g at Haines Bluff, with directions to send out a force sufficient, and cut off, if possible, their return to the other side of the river. Gen Washburne is also instructed to establish and keep communications with you at the Big Black Railroad Bridge. You will please aid in carrying out these latter instructions. The 2nd Illinois Cavalry has been ordered to report to you." LS, DNA, RG 393, 13th Army Corps, 9th Div., Letters Received.

Also on June 9, Col. Clark Wright, "Camp near Black River Bridge," wrote to Rawlins. "Immediately after the departure of my despatch of the 7th my scouts reported the 20th Miss Mounted Infty, Maj Boan was crossing from the west to east side of Black River at the Messenger Ford some three miles above bridgeport. I at once sent a Detachment of my Command under Maj Montgomery in direction of Edwards Depot with orders to intercept and disperse them at or near Edwards, drove in their skirmishers.   both Parties formed line of Battle, during which time some fifty shots were exchanged without effect. Montgomery ordered the charge, and the Rebels dispersed in every direction scattering like sheep. Montgomery followed them some four or five miles and captured three prisoners.   he learned that they had been joined by a portion of the 8th Kentucky. This morning the 20th Miss recrossed to the west side of the River at a ford below ~~bridgeport~~ Bird Song Ferry. I at once sent a Detachment in pursuit.   they have not yet returned. A messenger just in from there informed me that the Rebels when last heard from were moving up in the direction of the benton Road, then formed encampment. My information is that there is still no advance movement from Jackson or Canton.   an additional force of Cavalry, at this point would be desirable   the vast amount of labor, intense hot weather, with no forage but Corn is fast consuming our Horses.   the Command is in good spirits—Except the loss of Horses" ALS, *ibid.*, Dept. of the Tenn., Letters Received. On the same day, Lt. Col. James H. Wilson signaled to Rawlins. "No news of the enemy here. One brigade of troops on the Valley road six miles to the Northward of this place.

Think we can make this place very strong with little work. The line located by Maj Tweedle covers the lower landing or Sniders Bluff. I have selected one to cover both landings. Will locate it definitely tomorrow and make arrangements to have the work begun. I think we can so obstruct the ridge road that an army will find difficulty in passing—" Signal received, *ibid.*, RG 94, War Records Office, Military Div. of the Miss.

On June 10, Osterhaus wrote to Rawlins. "Your despatch of yesterday was received in due time, and I feel very much obliged for your kind and immediate attention to my request! A small detachment of 3d Illinois and a Comp. of 1. Indiana (escort Companies) arrived in the night; and the 2d Illinois Cavalry is reported in the vicinity, they will be here this evening. Major Montgomery in command of the 6th Mo sent out in pursuit of the rebel force, returns just now— 2 oclock p m—and reports, that they were the same companies of the 20th Miss. who were at Grants house and in the Oakridge region for some time:—after having received the reinforcements, Major Montgomery advanced and followed up the enemy as far up as Birdsong ferry, at which crossing only the fords near by he lost sight of them. the Major is most positive, that there is no rebel left on the west side of the river between Birdsong and this point;—Of course I ordered the escort Companies mentioned above, to return to their resp head-quarters; and I feel very certain, that with the addition of the 2d Illinois to my Cavalry force and with the detachment of Genl. Washburns Cavalry north of Bridge port, we are perfectly able, to keep the rebels on the other side of big Black. The Information, brought in by Major Montgomery, is that General Johnston is not moving and not even expected to move forward soon, that on the contrary some of his forces had been withdrawn;—I believe though, that their news ought to be received 'cum grano Salis'! I enclose a letter, brought in by flag of truce; the request seemed to me an extraordinary one, and I refused to grant it; promising though, to lay it before the Major General Comg the depart-ment for his action.—In doing so I request to give me his decision for communi-cation to Col Lyon, if the General should not approve of my denial. By the way I have to state, that this Colonel Lyon is desribed an overbearing & towards our wounded at Championshill a very rude character." ALS, *ibid.*, RG 393, Dept. of the Tenn., Letters Received. *O.R.*, I, xxiv, part 2, 221. On the same day, USG wrote to Osterhaus. "Your communication enclosing one from Col H. B. Lyon, conveyed to you, under Flag of Truce, is just received. You did just right not to entertain so absurd a proposition for a single moment." Copies, DLC-USG, V, 19, 30; DNA, RG 393, Dept. of the Tenn., Letters Sent. For the letter of Col. Hylan B. Lyon, 8th Ky., C.S.A., see *O.R.*, II, v, 761.

On June 12, Osterhaus wrote to Rawlins. "I ordered the Commander of my picket at Bridgeport this morning, to communicate with the Cavalry stationed above Bridgeport, in order to perfect the guarding the river;—Cptn Morris— 6th Mo Cavalry—who is in Command of the post there just now reports as fol-lows: 'Sergt. Robinson—in charge of the patrol—went to the widow Hills, 9 miles from this point (Bridgeport picket Station); he heard from all, that Col Swan was there last night, blockading the road, & left about dark, intending to go to camp at Haynes bluff; he has not come back to day—' On the Sergeants return, he run into a squad of about 15 rebels at Birdsong ferry; they exchanged shots, and the rebels retired across the river, where there are larger forces. the Ser-geant had one of his men (9.) slightly wounded and took two prisoners; I will send them to your Hd. Qrs. to morrow morning, as they are very talkative; they say, that General Forrest with his rebel Cavalry is at Mechanicsburg, and that another part of his force was exspected to day to form junction with him at or near the said town. the whole command is estimated at 4000 men.—The prisoners of course repeat the story, that Johnston with 30/m is moving on Yazoo river. Big Black in consequence of the last rains, was swollen considerably, but is receding rapidly again, so much so, that in the opinion of Cptn Morris the fords at Messenger's and near Birdsongs ferry are practicable again; Therefor I reinforced the Captain by another Company in the exspectation though, that some of Genl. Washburns Cavalry will relieve my men there to morrow. I learn from my Edwards Station, patrol that 2 new mounted regiments the 16th and 3d Miss are in the vicinity of Bolton or Raymond;—this seems to corroborate ~~with~~ the above statement, that the rebel Cavalry force had been increased. To meet emergencies I am constructing some breastworks defending the crossing of the river here; I will lay the plan before you in a day or two; having but a very limited number of contrabands here for that kind of work, I would be very glad, to have about 100 more Negroes from the organizing regiments temporarily detailed to assist my working party; if such a detail could be granted, the men had to bring tools along." ALS, DNA, RG 94, War Records Office, Dept. of the Tenn. *O.R.*, I, xxiv, part 2, 221–22. On the same day, Wright wrote to Rawlins. "I have Quite reliable information that Johnson is moving Via Yazoo City with five Divisions or about 30.000 Troops, his reinforcements are from Braggs Army. The Cavalry on East Side of River To *wit* 8th Kentucky 150 men 20th Miss 300 men; Vandornes Old Command 1.000 men are at Bolton Depot, some 2,000 Cavalry Said to be Forests are at or near McChenecksburgh. There has been about one Hundred prowling about the River Bank from Birdsongs to Bridge-Port Ferrys since Daylight this morning. a Detatchmet of my Command, has been Nine Miles above Bridgeport up on West Side of Black River To day and failed to find any Federal Cavalry within that distance, but engaged and drove back 25 Rebels to the East side at Birdsong. The Fords on the river are Fordable this evening again. my Command is Quite worked down." ALS, DNA, RG 94, War Records Office, Dept. of the Mo. *O.R.*, I, xxiv, part 3, 405.

On June 13, McClernand telegraphed to USG. "Company A 2d Ill Cavalry is not in my command nor do I know where it is" Telegram received, DNA, RG 393, Dept. of the Tenn., Telegrams Received.

On June 14, Osterhaus wrote to Rawlins. "Every thing remained here in statu quo as at the time of my last despatch. the C. S. Cavalry force on the East Side of the river at Bridgeport and north of it, is still there, but since the 11th they have not been seen on this side of the big Black; yesterday they came close up to the bank at Bridgeport, where my picket fired on them; the rebels returned the fire; one of theirs was mortally wounded and rolled down the bank.—The river is getting quite low again and is fordable at many places not only above the R R. bridge, but also as far down as Halls Ferry!—I have no report yet of any of our cavalry north of Bridgeport, which was to cooperate and connect with my pickets there; my Patrols have still to go 10 to 12 miles beyond Bridgeport, which renders that part of the duties here very severe. The telegraph wire along the J. & V R R I ordered to be put up again from the bridge to the Hd. Qrs of 13th A. C. where it will be connected with the Wire to your hd Qrs.; I think, the constructing party will get to the point of connection by tomorrow night; If it meets the Generals approval and he considers it of necessity, I should like to get a battery and an operator;—" ALS, *ibid.*, Letters Received. On the same day, Rawlins wrote to Osterhaus. "The chief Telegraph operator here will be ordered at once to procure and furnish a battery and the necessary telegraph operators, for an Office at your Head Quarters, Haines Bluff, and your position will then be in telegraphic communication via these Head Quarters. The operator will have to be detailed, from the ranks   perhaps you can find one in your Division." Copies, DLC-USG, V, 19, 30; DNA, RG 393, Dept. of the Tenn., Letters Sent.

On June 17, Osterhaus wrote to Rawlins. "Since my last the complexion of things on my front has not changed. Rebel cavalry is appearing at every point permitting access on the eastern river bank, occasionally exchanging shots with my pickets. Yesterday a large force attempted to drive in the vedettes on the Edwards Station road, but was readily repulsed by the reserve pickets. In general, there is no menacing attempt made as yet. This morning a very intelligent contraband, George McCloud, came into our lines, who had left Demopolis, Ala., on the 14th, Meridian on the 15th, and arrived in Jackson that same day. Yesterday morning he left Jackson for our lines. The negro was employed in the arsenal at Demopolis, and understands the making of all wood work connected with the ordnance department. He can read and write. This man states that the whole force at Jackson does not exceed 3,000 men, and the army collected and collecting by Johnston at Canton he heard estimated by leading officers at 15,000 effective men at the outside, with no prospect to swell it beyond 20,000. He describes the people and soldiers, including officers, in very low spirits as to the success of the Southern cause. The theme of raising the siege of Vicksburg is freely discussed on all sides, but no hopes are entertained that their forces will be in condition or in number equal to meet the Federal army. Notwithstanding these doubts, the negro says that great preparations are made for the relief of General Pemberton. Large quantities of ammunition and ordnance stores were forwarded from Demopolis to General Johnston, and from the general run of conversation he thinks that an attack will be made within a very few days on the right flank of our lines, with a view to give Pemberton a chance to break through the investing army. I will send the negro to your headquarters to-morrow morning, deeming him an interesting, perhaps a useful, man—perhaps a rogue. I had telegraphic communication with the wires to your headquarters and everything ready for the expected operator, when this morning some officer of another corps, passing Mount Alban with a squad of cavalry, cut down the wire and the poles. The citizens informed the officer that the telegraph was put up only the day before by our soldiers, but he would not listen to any such stuff. I hope to have the line up again by to-morrow night. The railroad track between here and Vicksburg is also repaired again, and a flat car constructed from the ruins on the east side of the river is put on the track. Four mules, in lieu of locomotive, form an essential addition to my transportation." *O.R.*, I, xxiv, part 2, 223–24.

To *Abraham Lincoln*

Near Vicksburg Miss,
June 11th 1863.

HON. A. LINCOLN
PRESIDENT OF THE UNITED STATES,
SIR:

Enclosed herewith I send report of Chaplain J. Eaton, Gen. Supt. of Contrabans for this Department, embracing a very complete history of what has been done for, and with, this class of people within my command to the present time.[1]

Finding that negroes were coming into our lines in great numbers, and receiving kind or abusive treatment according to the peculiar views of the troops they first came in contact with and not being able to give that personal attention to their care and use the matter demanded I determined to appoint a General Superintendent over the whole subject and give him such Assistants as the duties assigned him might require. Mr. Eaton was selected for this position. I have given him such aid as was in my power by the publication from time to time of such orders as seemed to be required, and generally at the suggestion of the Supt.

Mr. Eatons labors in his undertaking have been unremitting and skillful and I fear in many instances very trying. That he has been of very great service to the blacks in having them provided for when otherwise they would have been neglected, and to the government in finding employment for the negro whereby he might earn what he was receiving, the accompanying report will show, and many hundreds of visiters and officers and soldiers near the different camps can bear witness to.

I commend the report to your favorable notice and especially that portion of it which would suggest orders regulating the subject of providing for the government of the contraband subject which a Department commander is not competant to issue.

I have the honor to be
very respectfully
your obt. svt.
U. S. GRANT
Maj. Gen. Vols.

ALS, DLC-Robert T. Lincoln. On July 23, 1863, Chaplain John Eaton, Jr., Washington, wrote to USG. "I have had one interview with the Secy of War & two with the President. Every one in the Gove't & many out of it appear to be thinking strongly towards this subject but as yet it seems likely to be accomplished only by pieces, &, in the Secy's office there would appear to be lack of well defined system in what has already been undertaken. The Secy understands that he has an officer to attend to such subjects but the office does not understand that his instructions embrace them :—simply the organisation of colored troops :—yet all matters connected with these organisations in you Dept. are now determined by Ajt. Genl. Thomas—refered to him as they arrive. His health though better is such that he is kept away at lighter duty. It would have gratified me could I have placed before Mr. Stanton a more general & comprehensive view of the facts in the Dept in regard to these people. He asked me who appointed me to the charge of these people as if he did [*not*] know anything had been done for them save through the Commissioners. He is evidently well disposed towards you. Bothe interviews with the Prest. were full of interest—the last very lengthy. He spoke with great freedom of his difficulties, so much so as to charge me with silence & perhaps as I send this by the customary mail, I had better omit the details. He remarked that it gratified him to know the observation of so many facts in your Dept. had suggested plans which agreed in the main with the outline ideas in his own mind. He is pleased that you have made them so useful to the army, and that your management of them meets present exigencies without attempting to determine impossibilities. He has heard that Mr. Dana has said that you had remarked that you could not have taken Vicksburg had it not been for the proclamation; but as he was not assured that Mr. Dana had said it he doubted somewhat whether you made so strong a statement. The order that you prepared to issue I am confident will give satisfaction here. I think the President would prefer these people should be called freed-men or freed people though he is not so particular as Mr. Chase who said to me he would not read a doccument that had the term contraband in it. It appears several prominent gentlemen have been directed to gather matter upon the whole subject of the management of these people & the Prest. has directed me to go to N. York & see two of them Hon. Messrs. Owen & McKay. Mr. Lincoln with every body of loyal sentiments is taking great satisfaction in the issue of your operations. He was full of it, repeated your last despatches, laughed over your capture of cattle, read his letter to you. He had a map of your operations on a tripod in his room. Those who made such effort to interfere with you, now are ashamed to aver it. Mr. Washburne's course in support of you is greatly commended. Genl. Sherman is being strongly vindicated. At Cincin. I met the two Societies that have been furnishing us supplies; at Columbus among others Ex Gov. Dennison, Gov. Todd, Ajt Genl. Hill, Judge Swayne—every where I am unable to say enough. I hope my visit will not only result in good at W. but in various ways in other directions—I enclose some of the many straws which indicate how the wind blows. Hoping your health is good & that your efforts will be crowned with every success." ALS, DNA, RG 94, War Records Office, Dept. of the Tenn. See Lincoln, *Works* (*Supplement*), p. 195.

1. On April 29, Eaton, Memphis, prepared a lengthy report addressed to Lt. Col. John A. Rawlins. Copy, DNA, RG 94, Letters Received, 328 0 1863. For a summary account, see John Eaton, *Grant, Lincoln and the Freedmen* (New York, 1907), pp. 63–70.

To Maj. Gen. Henry W. Halleck

Near Vicksburgh June 11—[*1863*]

H. W. HALLECK
GENL. IN CHIEF—

Reinforcements other than from my own command are beginning to arrive. There is every indication that they may be required. The enemy occupy Yazoo City and Canton with an entire division of Cavalry in the ridge between the two rivers— I am fortifying Haines' [Bluff] and will have a garrison there of thirteen thousand troops besides the ability to throw an Equal amount more there in case of an attack and still keep up the investment of Vicksburg   Kirby Smith is showing signs of working to this side of river either to operate against Gen Banks or myself. He may find difficulty in crossing the river but the great number of bayous & little lakes within a short distance of shore in this region afford such facilities for concealing boats that the means of crossing an army may still be left the rebels particularly may this be the case about Natchez—

I now fear trouble on the opposite side of the river between [Lake] Providence and Millikens Bend.

U. S. GRANT
[Major General]

Telegram received, DNA, RG 107, Telegrams Collected (Bound); copies, *ibid.*, Telegrams Received in Cipher; *ibid.*, RG 393, Dept. of the Tenn., Hd. Qrs.

Correspondence; DLC-USG, V, 6, 8, 24, 94. *O.R.*, I, xxiv, part 1, 42. Transmitted from Cairo on June 16, 1863, this telegram reached Washington at 10:00 A.M. the same day.

On June 12, 11:30 A.M., Maj. Gen. Henry W. Halleck telegraphed to USG. "I hope you fully appreciate the importance of *time* in the reduction of Vicksburg. The large reenforcements sent to you have opened Missouri & Kentucky to rebel raids. The seige should be pushed night & day with all possible despatch." ALS (telegram sent), DNA, RG 107, Telegrams Collected (Bound); copy, *ibid.*, RG 108, Telegrams Sent. *O.R.*, I, xxiv, part 1, 42. On the same day, Maj. Gen. Stephen A. Hurlbut wrote to USG. "I forward with this Telegram received to day from Genl Halleck. In this connection I would state that I am informed that Price left Little Rock a week since with four Brigades and two Batteries and has effected a junction with Marmaduke. As he has not been heard from at Helena. I think he has moved up toward South Eastern Missouri and will be heard from there in a few days. No news here" ALS, DNA, RG 94, War Records Office, Dept. of the Mo.

To Maj. Gen. Henry W. Halleck

Behind Vicksburg
June 11. 1863.

MAJ GEN H W HALLECK
GENL-IN-CHF

I have reliable information from the entire interior of the South. Johnston has been re-inforced by three thousand troops from Mobile & other posts of Georgia, by McGown's & Breckenridge's Divisions[1] 9,000 troops, & 4,000 of Forrest's Cavalry from Bragg's army. 9,000 troops from Charleston & 2,200 from Port Hudson. Orders were sent to evacuate Port Hudson the very day Gen Banks invested garrison there, now 8,000.

Lee's army has not been reduced Bragg's troops, now 46,000 Infantry & artillery & 15,000 Cavalry. Everything not required for daily use has been removed to Atlanta Ga. His army can fall back to Bristol or Chattanooga at a moments notice, which places it is thought, he can hold, & spare 25.000 troops, Mobile, & will then move all west[2] entirely without garrison further than men to manage large guns. No troops left in the interior to send any place All further re-inforcements will have to come from one of the great armies. There are above 32,000 west of the Mississippi, exclusive of the troops in Texas. Orders were sent them one week ago by Johnston, the purport of order ~~of~~ not known. Herron has arrived here[3] & troops from Gen. Burnside looked for tomorrow.

U. S. GRANT. M G

Telegram received, DNA, RG 107, Telegrams Collected (Bound); copies, *ibid.*, Telegrams Received in Cipher; *ibid.*, RG 393, Dept. of the Tenn., Hd. Qrs. Correspondence; DLC-USG, V, 6, 8, 24, 94. *O.R.*, I, xxiv, part 1, 42. Transmitted from Memphis on June 14, 1863, this telegram reached Washington at 6:00 P.M., June 16.

1. Since C.S.A. Maj. Gen. John P. McCown had recently been court-martialed, Maj. Gen. John C. Breckinridge took to Miss. his own div. and that of McCown.

2. In USG's letterbooks "Savannah are now almost" appears instead of the five words following the ampersand in the telegram received.

3. Francis J. Herron, born in Pittsburgh in 1837, moved to Dubuque, Iowa, in 1855 to join three brothers in establishing a bank. Commissioned capt., 1st Iowa, as of May 14, 1861, he rose to lt. col., 9th Iowa, for his services at Wilson's Creek, and to brig. gen. as of July 16, 1862, after the battle of Pea Ridge where he was taken prisoner. Confirmed as maj. gen. on March 9, 1863, to rank from Nov. 29, 1862, Herron was then the youngest officer of that rank in the U.S. Army. On June 4, 1863, Capt. Richard McAllister, St. Louis, wrote to Lt. Col. John A. Rawlins. "Major General Herron, with two Divisions of Infantry and several batteries leaves hear to-day to join your army. You know Frank. Herron well. He commands some of the best troops in the west and they have unbounded confidence in him. I believe he ranks all the Commanders in your army except Corps Commanders. Cannot an army Corps be given to Major General Herron? I know he likes Genl. Grant and an army Corps upon Genl. Grant's recommendation would attach him to Genl. Grant with hooks of steel. No man here or in Iowa is so popular as Herron. Various reports are in circulation here as to the probable success of your operations before Vicksburg. You have a gigantic work to accomplish but I tell every one that Grant never was whipped and never means to be." ALS, DNA, RG 393, Dept. of the Tenn., Letters Received. On June 5, Maj. Gen. John M. Schofield, St. Louis, telegraphed to USG. "I send you (yesterday and to-day) eight regiments of infantry and three batteries—about 5,000 men—under command of Major-General Herron." *O.R.*, I, xxiv, part 3, 387.

To Act. Rear Admiral David D. Porter

June 11th 1863,

DEAR ADMIRAL,

Gen. Ellet has just r[e]ported to me the fact of having a number of persons aboard of his vessels who have been sent from St. Louis on account of disloyalty who it was intended should be debarked at Greenville.

Feeling that a Flag of Truce might not be respected sending these people to the interior in ambulances but two ways suggest themselves to me for geting rid of them. One is to send them on a Steamboat, convoyed by a gunboat as high up the Yazoo as possible, say to Satartia. The other is to transfer them across the point, at Young's Point, and send them to Natchez.

I have no official knowledge of these people being sent South by any proper authority but finding them here I suppose they must be treated as suspicious persons who it will not do to have passing through our lines any more than is necessary in getting clear of them. Any disposition you may make of them, or anything you can suggest for me, will gladly acknowledged.

Very Truly
your obt. svt.
U. S. GRANT
Maj. Gen. Com

ADMIRAL D. D. PORTER
COMD.G MISS. SQUADRON,

ALS, MdAN.

To Maj. Gen. Stephen A. Hurlbut

Head Quarters, Dept. of the Ten.
Near Vicksburg, June 11th/63

MAJ. GEN. S. A. HURLBUT,
COMD.G 16TH ARMY CORPS,
GEN.

Yours of the 8th is just received. The Artillery with Smith's Division will make the supply here sufficient, supposing of course that all reinforcements to arrive will have their quota of Artillery with them.

I do not hear of the enemy runing cars North of Water Valley. If this is so they cannot send any large force against you without your Cavalry being able to give timely notice of their approach.

Should Johnstone disappear from my flank I will have a much larger force than is required and would at once relieve you either by sending troops back by way of the river or sending them up in the rear of any force that might be advancing on you, or both. I may however be deceived by the enemy showing all the time a force at Yazoo City and across to Canton whilst he will have the main body moving North. You will have to keep a good lookout for this with your Cavalry and through Scouts.

It is now evident the enemy have brought large reinforcements from Braggs Army and I cannot think it is with any other design than to raise the siege of Vicksburg. It would only be after dispairing of sucsess here that they would attempt a Northern move.

Keep me well informed of all you learn of the movements of the enemy.

Very Respectfully,
your obt. svt.
U. S. GRANT
Maj. Gen. Com

ALS, DNA, RG 393, 16th Army Corps, Letters Received. *O.R.*, I, xxiv, part 3, 404–5. On June 8, 1863, Maj. Gen. Stephen A. Hurlbut, Memphis, wrote to USG.

"Your personal letter of 3rd June is received this morning. Smith's Division is embarking in great confusion from the inefficiency of the Quarter Masters Department but will be off to day. They take five Batteries one of which will be left at Helena for Prentiss. I cannot very well cut down the artillery of Oglesby's command with the space he is required to hold, especially as the enemy's light troops shew in considerable force near the Tallahatchie and Coldwater. There are now but two light batteries here with the Division around Memphis. Herron and Van Dorn with two Brigades and two Batteries to the Brigade are here and on the way down. Eight thousand men from Burnside's force are also on the way. It is important for this command that a close watch be kept on any northerly movement of the force under Johnston." Copy, DNA, RG 393, 16th Army Corps, Letters Sent. *O.R.*, I, xxiv, part 3, 391.

On June 7, Hurlbut had written to Lt. Col. John A. Rawlins. "I ask leave through you to suggest to the Major General Commanding the necessity as soon as may be done of an Expedition which shall destroy the Rail Road or Rail Road Transportation below Granada. I cannot reach Wall's Station where the Rail Road crosses the Big Black the highest & most important bridge on the Route and now well guarded nor can I reach the Engines & Cars at Canton or Vaiden. They may be reached from the Army below. Johnston has 25 good Engines 15 in poor order and at least 400 cars. With these he may run to Panola without my Knowledge and if he becomes desperate as to Vicksburgh it would be eminently a good movement to strike Memphis. The City Guard duty here is enormous and I cannot safely reduce it. With the reduction of the force on this line will of course again spring up Guerilla Bands which must be suppressed by hard riding and some severe examples. I propose tomorrow to start my best spy from this place to pass down the entire line and bring you all the information he can gather and send you as a means of identifying one of his Reports in his own hand writing. If he gets through you may rely upon his statements, as he is a man of sharp observation and of capital judgment and about as effective a scamp as the 19th Ills ever had on their Rolls . . . P. S. He goes by the name of C. S. Bell   His name is *Spencer*"   ALS, DNA, RG 393, Dept. of the Tenn., Letters Received. *O.R.*, I, xxiv, part 3, 389. The report of C. Spencer is in DNA, RG 393, Dept. of the Tenn., Letters Received.

On June 13, Hurlbut wrote to USG. "As the Continental is about to leave soon I write a short letter by her. I expect a good deal of trouble on the left of my line. Genl. Wood has moved up to Bear Creek with a considerable force not precisely known. I shall know to day the amount. Cavalry have crossed the Tennessee at Cumberland and are now above Jackson. I have ordered the 3d Mich. to watch them. Whether this is only a system of annoyance or something more serious I can not tell. Rosecrans does not seem to press forward his right which I think he should do, & this leaves my flank & rear open to any attacks by way of Tenn. River & it will not be difficult for them as they contract their lines to send a force of 6. to 10,000 in rear of Corinth. The demonstrations in that quarter have compelled me to countermand a strong expedition intended to operate below the Tallahatchie. I hope in a few days to clear that part of the line & reach below" ALS, *ibid*. *O.R.*, I, xxiv, part 3, 408–9.

On June 16, Hurlbut wrote to Rawlins. "Nineteen Hundred Cavalry left LaGrange this morning to go by Wyatt South of Tallatchie, break the Rail Road south of Panola, turn on Chalmers, sweep the Country of Horses mules Negroes & the new crop of wheat and work back with the results. Immediately after this

I shall send a force to Okalona on the same errand. Biffles crossed the Tennessee at Cumberland and has broken the R. Road & Telegraph wires for miles beyond Bolivar. Cornyn is after him. The late expedition of Col. Cornyn across the Tennessee at & near Florence was very brilliantly successful and the loss inflicted very heavy. I will send official report when you have time to read it" ALS, DNA, RG 94, War Records Office, Union Battle Reports. *O.R.*, I, xxiv, part 2, 485.

On June 20, Hurlbut wrote to Rawlins. "I wrote some days since of my intention of sending a Cavalry force below the Tallahatchie. In pursuance of this Mizner with (1900) nineteen hundred mounted men left Lagrange on Tuesday with instructions to cross at Wyatt, break the Railroad below Panola sweep round, and break up Chalmers forces at Panola and Belmont Having learned on Wednesday that a force with Two pieces of Artillery had moved from Panola to Commerce I ordered Major Henry 5th Ohio Cavalry Volunteers to proceed with about (400) Four Hundred Cavalry south on Hernando and Coldwater to divert the force from our boats, threaten their lines, and communicate with Mizner if the Country was clear. He left on Wednesday since that time I have no Official report from him. on yesterday stragglers from the command came and are still coming in who report that Major Henry allowed himself to be surrounded, and surprised in Camp three miles below Hernando. If the facts are as stated great criminality attaches to the Commanding Officer who went deliberately into Camp, unsaddled, and acted as if at his ease. I fear that nearly all of the command has been cut off. I moved out Infantry last night fifteen miles to form a rallying point for the broken Cavalry. I have not strength to pursue them further and keep my hold on Memphis Owing to the strange apathy of Rosecrans my entire rear and left is open and the rebel cavalry cross the Tennessee almost at will, They are only hindered by the Gunboats which they avoid. Dodge and Cornyn, by superhuman exertions keep their range of Country clear, but with the force about Panola, and near Okolona, it requires about all we can do to keep the front clear. These bands in our rear are picking up deserters, conscripting, and carrying off cattle for Bragg. I do not think they will try to cross in force, although Three Regiments and a battery are reported trying to cross at Double Island. I will do the best I can under these circumstances but cannot repel or punish as I would wish raids within my command which must be looked for. If Mizner has been successful it will go far toward relieving us for a time. This irregular force below keeps close lines, and it is very difficult to ascertain the movements of the main force below. I therefore request that as far as possible the movements of General Johnston looking North may be watched from your force." Copy, DNA, RG 393, 16th Army Corps, Letters Sent. *O.R.*, I, xxiv, part 2, 485–86.

To Maj. Gen. John A. McClernand

Near Vicksburg Miss June 11, 1863.

MAJ GENL. J. A. McCLERNAND
COMMD'G 13TH ARMY ARMY.

Genl Herron will cross at Warrenten tomorrow   Eight

thousand more troops now on the way will cross the same place, and occupy South of the City. This will enable Lauman to close up up on you and if necessary take some of the front occupied by your left.

U. S. GRANT Maj Gen'l

Copies, DLC-USG, V, 19, 30; DNA, RG 393, Dept. of the Tenn., Letters Sent. On June 11, 1863, Maj. Gen. John A. McClernand twice telegraphed to USG. "I have sent my escort out tonight to reconnoitre towards Halls ferry" "A Negro teamster reports that a Negro girl told him today that Johnston was to have crossed the big black at Covingtons bluffs between Hankersons & baldwins ferries I have sent word to Lauman & to whiting to Mudd the two latter to look into the matter" Telegrams received, *ibid.*, Telegrams Received.

Also on June 11, George W. Graham telegraphed to Lt. Col. John A. Rawlins. "Sixteenth 16th Army Corps gone to Haines Bluff Genl Herrons to Shermans Landing for Warrenton as directed by you they say fifteen thousand 15.000 more from Cairo from burnside will be here soon" Telegram received, *ibid.*

To Maj. Gen. William T. Sherman

Near Vicksburg Miss June 11, 1863.

MAJ GENL. W. T. SHERMAN
COMMD'G 15TH ARMY CORPS

Washburn who is in command at Haines Bluff, reports that a Division of rebel cavalry is encamped two miles beyond Mechanicksburg, and Walker with an Infantry force is at Yazoo City.[1]

Gen'l W. S. Smiths Division from West Tennessee is begining to arrive, and I suppose will all be here today. This force goes to Haines Bluff, and will make a force of from thirteen to fourteen thousand at that place.

I have also received confirmation that two Brigades from Missouri, are on their way, and have passed Memphis, and 8,000 are coming from Burnsides Dep't.

These latter I propose to land at Youngs Point, and send across to Warrenton to close up the south side of Vicksburg.

With the Cavalry we have at Haines Bluff, when required, two Brigades from your Corps, and three from McPhersons, to be further releived if it should become absolutely necessary, by taking all the troops to the left of McClernand. In case this has to be done, you will be detached temporarily from the command of your Corps here., to take command at Haines Bluff whilst it may be beseiged.

The order then intended to be conveyed is, that two Brigades from the 15th Army Corps, be held in readiness to March to Haines Bluff, at the shortest notice.

U. S. Grant Maj Genl

Copies, DLC-USG, V, 19, 30; DNA, RG 393, Dept. of the Tenn., Letters Sent; Alcorn Collection, WyU. *O.R.*, I, xxiv, part 3, 402. On June 11, 1863, Maj. Gen. William T. Sherman, Walnut Hills, wrote to Lt. Col. John A. Rawlins. "I have the honor to acknowledge receipt of General Grant's letter of this date, and to answer that I will be prepared to move, on the shortest notice, to Haynes' Bluff. I will make immediate orders to place Blair's three brigades to the front, and draw back Tuttle's two brigades, to be ready to move to Haynes' Bluff, viz., Buckland's and J. J. Woods'. One of Buckland's regiments (Judy's) is now on picket at Templeton's, a point common to both Haynes' and this place. The other brigade has but three regiments, and Colonel Gresham, commanding a regiment of Indiana troops, in Johnson's brigade, of Lauman's division, has just been here, and is very anxious to come to my corps. He is one of my Kentucky colonels, and, if he could be transferred to me, I could give him command of a brigade. I told him General Lauman should consent before a written application should be made. He has gone to procure it. If this transfer could be made, it would complete an imperfect brigade, and would give Tuttle twelve regiments, four of which are now absent with Mower. I would like also to get another battery for this division, which now has only two four-gun batteries, and, I am informed, Lauman has six batteries, two to each brigade. I have only three batteries to two of my divisions, and two for Tuttle. Supposing, of course, that provisions are delivered at Snyder's by boat, and that rifle-pits are in course of construction, I take it the force indicated by the general will be ample for all contingencies. I would like to reconnoiter the ground from Milldale to the Bald Ground before an enemy makes his appearance from the direction of Yazoo City, on the ridge back of Haynes', and therefore will be prepared for further orders at once." *Ibid.*

Also on June 11, Rawlins wrote to Maj. Gen. James B. McPherson. "The Enemy is reported by Maj Gen Washburne as having a force of ten Regiments of Cavalry under Jackson, encamped two miles beyond Mechanicsburg, and a force of Infantry, under Walker at Yazoo City. Gen W. S. Smiths Division of Gen Hurlbuts Corps which is now on the way here, under orders to go to Haines Bluff, which with Genl Kimballs Division now there will make a force of between twelve and fourteen thousand as the Garrison, but in the event of a movement of the enemy in this direction it may become necessary to strengthen the force there. Gen Sherman has been directed to hold two Brigades in readiness to move to the reinforcement of Haines Bluff on receipt of orders. Mowers Brigade of Shermans Corps has been sent to Young's Point to Strengthen that place   You will hold three Brigades of your Corps in readiness to move to the reinforcement of Haines Bluff on receipt of orders. Maj Gen Herron is now here with a Division from Gen Schofields Army and has orders to proceed to Warrenton, and take up a position to the left of Gen Lauman. Eight thousand men from Gen Burnsides' Army are reported to be *en-route* for this place, which will also be ordered to a position on the left, if nothing occurs between this and the time of their arrival, to change the present phase of affairs; but should any further reinforcements for Haines Bluff be required they will be taken from the left of General McClernand." LS, DNA, RG 94, War Records Office, 17th Army Corps. *O.R.*, I, xxiv, part 3, 403.

1. On June 11, Maj. Gen. Cadwallader C. Washburn, "Haines Bluff," wrote to USG. "I send you the statements of ten Captured rebel Pickets taken last night about six miles this side of Mechanicsburgh. I am inclined to think that the most of Johnsons forces have crossed the Big Black & are between it & Yazoo City. The arrival of Gen. Smith with his Division, I think renders our position pretty secure. With the troops of Burnside, ~~4000~~ 8.000 of whom I hear are now on their way, & 10.000 from the rear of Vicksburgh, we can move aggressively & successfully in pursuit of Johnson. In three days I hope to have our defences in such a state of forwardness as to defy any force they can bring." ALS, DNA, RG 94, War Records Office, Dept. of the Tenn. The statements are *ibid.* William H. T. Walker of Ga., USMA 1837, resigned as maj. as of Dec. 20, 1860, having been on sick leave for the previous four years. Appointed C.S.A. brig. gen. in 1861, he resigned later that year for reasons of health, but on March 2, 1863, was again confirmed as brig. gen. On May 5, Gen. Pierre G. T. Beauregard, Charleston, S. C., sent Walker's brigade to Miss. *O.R.*, I, xxiv, part 3, 833. On June 10, Walker's div., hd. qrs. Yazoo City, had 12,158 men present for duty. *Ibid.*, p. 958.

To Brig. Gen. Elias S. Dennis

————

Near Vicksburg Miss June 11, 1863.

Brig Gen'l E. S. Dennis
Commdg Dist N. E. La.

In view of present danger of attack upon your command, it is advisable that every precaution should be taken to hold all government stores, and the troops at least secure from capture. If the government farms can be held, they should be held also, but not at the expense of sacrificing government troops and stores first, and the plantations afterwards in detail[1]   Not being on the ground myself, I cannot say exactly how your troops should be located. A general direction, I would say occupy and fortify three points. One of these should be Lake Providence and one Millikens Bend. At Lake Providence direct Gen'l Reid to fortify close to the river, where he can protect his troops and public stores, at least until he can notify you of his necessities for more troops. All the Black troops should be got as much to themselves as possible, and required to fortify. Millikens Bend will be the proper place for them. You want to keep Youngs Point and the road across the point perfectly protected. This can be done with a very small force, the distance across being short, and Gun boats at both ends of the road. Gen'l Mowers Brigade was sent to you merely for an emergency. As soo as the emergency ceases, I want them returned to their Division. With the Cavalry you have, the mounted men Gen'l Reid has, and by mounting part of one negro Regiment, they can scout out every road from Lake Providence to Youngs Point so as to keep you advised of the approach of any force in time to prepare for them. Have you learned what has become of the force that attacked you a few days since? They should not be allowed to remain about Richmond.

U. S. GRANT Maj Genl

Copies, DLC-USG, V, 19, 30; DNA, RG 393, Dept. of the Tenn., Letters Sent; Alcorn Collection, WyU. *O.R.*, I, xxiv, part 3, 403–4. On June 11, 1863, Lt. Col. John A. Rawlins wrote to Brig. Gen. Elias S. Dennis. "You will direct all troops that arrive from Major Genl Hurlbuts command, to proceed without delay on the transports on which they are now embarked to Haines Bluff, and report to Maj Gen'l C C Washburn Commdg for orders. All troops from other points, will be directed to debark at Youngs Point, and proceed across the peninsula to Warrenton. Maj Gen'l Herrons Divisions on its reaching Warrenton will take up a position as close on Brig Gen'l Laumans left, as possible. As soon after their arrival as possible, procure and forward to these Head Quarters, the organization of said forces by Regiments, Batteries, Brigades and Divisions, with the names of Commanding officers." Copies, DLC-USG, V, 19, 30; DNA, RG 393, Dept. of the Tenn., Letters Sent.

On June 13, Dennis, Young's Point, wrote to Rawlins a report of the C.S.A. attack on Lake Providence, June 9. LS, *ibid.*, RG 94, War Records Office, Union Battle Reports. *O.R.*, I, xxiv, part 2, 448–49. On June 13, USG wrote to Dennis. "Drive the enemy from Richmond. Reinforce Mower all you can, and send him to do it." Copies, DLC-USG, V, 19, 30; DNA, RG 393, Dept. of the Tenn., Letters Sent; *ibid.*, RG 111, Vicksburg Signal Book. On the same day, Brig. Gen. Joseph A. Mower signaled to Rawlins. "The dispatch from Gen Grant to Gen. Dennis has been received. Gen Dennis is absent. I will move on to Richmond in the morning" Signal received, *ibid.*, RG 94, War Records Office, Military Div. of the Miss.; copy, *ibid.*, RG 111, Vicksburg Signal Book. See *O.R.*, I, xxiv, part 2, 451–53.

On June 16, Act. Rear Admiral David D. Porter wrote to USG. "Rather than be idle; and thinking it a good plan not to let the Rebels be enjoying themselves too much at Richmond, I dispatched Gen'l Ellet to the Commanding officer to see if he would not lend a hand to drive the Rebels away. So they started yesterday morning at early daylight with about two thousand men all told, and found the Rebels strongly posted at Richmond with 4000 men and six pieces of artillery. After an hours fight in which nobody was badly hurt (I believe) on our side, the Rebels cleared out and Richmond was burned in the row. Eleven prisoners fell into our hands, from them we learn that there are 6000 men at Delhi; but without transportation, They left their Wagons in Alexandria. From all I can learn they expect more troops to join them, more field pieces, and their Wagons. They have Signals going on all around here. I have the names of a number of houses where the signals are made from, and Ellet's cavalry will go out to morrow and arrest them all. My idea is that this force is intended to co-operate with Vicksburg at the proper time. With the boats, flats, and coal barges they have; they can transport their whole force to this side from Vicksburg in six hours, and if this party should suddenly seize the Point we could not prevent it. I am keeping a strong force of Gun boats here, and shall keep the Brigade ready to land at a moments notice. The 'Benton' will be above the Canal every night and the other boats when they return up the River—I shall also have the 'Osage' in time to dash down amongst them if they try anything of the kind. Still with all that the thing can be done. I do not know what else would bring these fellows here in such a hurry and why they avoid a fight so. They lost 98 killed at Milliken's Bend according to their own account, and a proportional number of wounded, also some horses. I tell you what I suppose to be their plans. You may see something else in the movement. I caught a messenger from Vicksburg night before last slipping out in a Canoe. I keep a picket boat out; on the Mississippi side, above the Canal, and the fellow was floating by, lying down—He would tell nothing, we only know that he threw his package overboard and we could not get it. He says there is 60 days provisions in Vicksburg which we know cannot be so. Says we have killed nobody and done no damage, which is bosh. I have told Capt. Walker to supply 32 pounder guns if you want any at Haine's Bluff. Will have carriages in a day or two for those there if you want them, tho' the guns are very heavy and will be difficult to transport—Everything is quiet up the River, hearing that Price was advancing on Helena I sent a force of Gunboats there." LS, DNA, RG 94, War Records Office, Dept. of the Tenn. *O.R.*, I, xxiv, part 2, 454–55; *O.R.* (Navy), I, xxv, 176–77. See *ibid.*, pp. 175–76.

1. Brig. Gen. Lorenzo Thomas had instituted a policy of leasing abandoned and confiscated plantations to loyal white men who agreed to pay wages to the former slaves who worked them. Thomas appointed George B. Field, Chaplain Lark S. Livermore, 16th Wis., and Commissary Capt. Abraham E. Strickle as commissioners of plantations. Louis S. Gerteis, *From Contraband to Freedman* (Westport, Conn., 1973), pp. 123–81. On April 17, the commissioners wrote to USG. "We the undersigned commissioners of Plantations for the U. S. Government, Have the honor to request The detail of one Regiment of about five hundred men to protect the property on plantations between Millikens Bend & Lake provi-

dence until such time as The negro regiments now forming shall be able to relieve them.   we also desire the occupation of the Mansion on the Morancy estate for offices of our board. . . . P. S. our office is at present on board steamer Rocket" LS, DNA, RG 393, Dept. of the Tenn., Letters Received. On April 18, by Special Orders No. 108, Dept. of the Tenn., USG granted these requests. Copies, DLC-USG, V, 26, 27; DNA, RG 393, Dept. of the Tenn., Special Orders. On April 23, Rawlins issued General Orders No. 27 which provided army protection for and assistance to plantation lessees. Copies, DLC-USG, V, 13, 14, 95; DNA, RG 393, Dept. of the Tenn., General and Special Orders; (printed) USGA. See letter to Brig. Gen. Lorenzo Thomas, July 11, 1863.

To Brig. Gen. Lorenzo Thomas

Head Quarters, Department of the Tennessee,
Near Vicksburg, Miss., June 12. 1863.
Brig. Gen. L. Thomas,
Adjutant General of the Army,
General:—

Paragraph 13. of Special Orders No. 187, current Series, ordering Surgeon John Moore to report to this Department to relieve Surgeon M. Mills, as Medical Director, is recieved. I regret that this order was ever issued. This Department has probably suffered more than any other from frequent changes in Medical Directors, and from the incompetency of some of those serving as such. Surgeon Mills has brought up his department from a low standard to a very high one. He has been with the Army through a trying campaign, and no officer has ever attended more strictly to his duties, or shown greater ability to stand all the fatigue of a campaign.

It will be manifest injustice to Surgeon Mills to order him before a Retiring Board, and greater injustice to the service to have such Board retire him.

I do not think it injustice to the balance of the Medical Corps of the Army to say, that none of them could surpass Surgeon Mills in his administration of his duties in this Department, and but few equal it.

I deem it a duty to the troops under my command to suspend that portion of Special Orders No. 187, or the operation of it, so far as it effects any change in Medical Director here, until the end of the present Siege, unless otherwise specially directed.[1]

I am, General,
Very Respectfully,
Your Obed't Servant
U. S. GRANT
Major General

LS, DNA, RG 107, Letters Received, Irregular Series. On June 25, 1863, Brig. Gen. William A. Hammond, surgeon gen., endorsed USG's letter. "It was officially reported to this office by a Medl. Inspector sent West by the Secretary of War, that Surg. Mills was unfit for field duty, and recommended that he should be retired under Sec. 6 of an Act of Congress published in Gen'l Orders 43, A. G. O. Apr. 19, 1862. In this report & recommendation Surg. Mills himself concurred. The detail of Surg. Moore to relieve Surg Mills as Medl. Director, Dept: of the Tennessee, was made after full consideration both of the importance of the position, and the abilities of Surg. Moore. While it is grateful to me to learn that the faithfulness & labor of Surg. Mills are recognised by Major General Grant, I do not think it would be for the good of the service to modify par. 13. Special Orders 187, current Series." ES, *ibid*. On July 2, Brig. Gen. Edward R. S. Canby wrote to USG. "Your communication of the 12th ultimo, to the Adjutant General of the Army, has been submitted to the Secretary of War, by whom I am instructed to say, that the change in the Medical Director of your Army, was based upon the report of Medical Inspector Vollum, a copy of which is enclosed, and was believed to be necessary, in consequence of the failing health of Surgeon Mills, an opinion in which that officer concurred. The Secretary of War is gratified to learn, that this necessity does not exist now, and authorizes you to suspend the execution of the order, until the change can be made without embarrassment to the Service." LS, *ibid*., RG 94, Staff Papers. He enclosed a copy of a letter from Lt. Col. Edward P. Vollum, medical inspector, to Hammond, April 14, recommending that Surgeon Madison Mills "be ordered to appear before a Board of Examiners for retirement from the service, on account of physical disability. . . . I am satisfied that a paralytic affection of long standing and recent attacks of neuralgia, are so rapidly undermining his health, as to render him unable to perform the duties of his office,—in which he fully concurs." Copy, *ibid*.

1. See letter to Brig. Gen. William A. Hammond, July 10, 1863.

To Maj. Gen. John A. McClernand

Near Vicksburg Miss June 12, 1863,

MAJ GEN'L. J. A. MCCLERNAND
COMMD'G 13TH ARMY CORPS,

With Hairrons force, and 8000 more that are to be pushed into the left, the enemy can be so enclosed as to have all of Herrons force free either to act with the extreme left, or with you or Lauman as circumstances may require. Lauman is on the same general line with your Corps, and has commenced his advances, and I do not like to move him. If you desire however, I will as soon as all the forces come in, put one Division to occupy the position of your left Division, and releive it from reserve for your Corps.

U. S. GRANT Maj Gen'l

Copies, DLC-USG, V, 19, 30; DNA, RG 393, Dept. of the Tenn., Letters Sent; *ibid.*, 13th Army Corps, Letters Received.

On June 12, 1863, Maj. Gen. John A. McClernand wrote to USG. "I send you W. L. Newman, a deserter. He was at Canton some eight days since. Then Johnson had concentrated there about 7000 men from Ga. and S. C.—He also met three brigades, on his way to Jackson, going to Johnson. Breckenridge had 3000 men at Jackson, about seven days ago. He heard that Johnson would advance between the Yazoo and Black,—and that Breckenridge would cross the Big Black at the Rail Road Bridge, or some point between there and the rear of Warrenton, but that the attack would not be made until the enemy were 40,000 strong. He thinks it was their expectation to attack about this time." Copy, *ibid.*, RG 94, War Records Office, Dept. of the Tenn. On the same day, McClernand wrote to Lt. Col. John A. Rawlins. "During the day yesterday the second parallel trench in front of Genl. Smith was nearly completed. It is now of sufficient width to allow troops to march through in two ranks without difficulty. Last night 100 negroes were employed in working on a trench still further in advance, on the right hand side of the road and within 75 yards of a large fort on the left hand side of the road. This last is our most advanced work. Three hundred men from Genl. Smith's Division were employed during the night on a trench still further to the right, and on the same line as the one last referred to. This was cut to a width of six feet and to a depth sufficient to afford a strong parapet. In Genl. Carr's Division 200 men worked upon a zig-zag trench which is being pushed a cross the ravine in front of his center. They also worked on his left, on a work which is being prepared for the two 30 pdr Parrotts, which are to be removed to give place to the 8 inch guns as soon as the latter arrive. In Genl. Hovey's Division little was done but to cut drains to draw off the water from the trenches at such points as the rain had shown this to be necessary. Work still continues on the mine in Genl. Smiths front, though from the toughness of the clay and the difficulty of removing it, progress is less rapid than was anticipated" Copy, *ibid.*, RG 393, Dept. of the Tenn., Letters Received.

On June 13, McClernand wrote to Rawlins. "Last night the trench on the right of the road in Genl. Smith's extreme front was extended by running a flying sap toward the road in front of the enemy's salient. It was also extended to the left some distance. The second parallel trench in the same front was improved by placing sand bags on top of the parapet. In Genl. Carr's front a boyaux was run from the railroad to the left towards the bottom of the ravine. The one in front of his center, commenced night before last,—was extended to the bottom of the ravine. Genl. Hovey was employed in improving his trenches." LS, *ibid.* On the same day, Capt. Joseph B. Gorsuch, provost marshal, 13th Army Corps, wrote to USG reporting information derived from C.S.A. deserters. ALS, *ibid.*, RG 94, War Records Office, Dept. of the Tenn. *O.R.*, I, xxiv, part 3, 407.

On June 14, McClernand wrote twice to Rawlins. "Col. Mudd, from Hubbord's Mill, reports,—'a negro from the other side says that Johnson is said to be seven or eight miles beyond Brownsville, and had at last date (some time since) 11000 men.' " "On yesterday and last night Genl. Smith was employed in opening the flying sap towards the road in his extreme front. He also commenced a defensive arm in the right of the same, which, when completed, will open communication with the extreme in the second parallel. The boyaux in Genl. Carr's front was pushed forward,—the one to the left, across the stream. In Genl. Hovey's front the trenches are still being improved. To-day a detail is employed preparing the advance trenches of Genl. Smith, with loopholes made by placing sand bags on the top of the parapet." LS, DNA, RG 393, Dept. of the Tenn., Letters Received. On the same day, McClernand telegraphed to USG. "Only a sharp skirmish between opposite lines of infantry & artillery ending in the enemies quitting" Telegram received, *ibid.*, RG 94, War Records Office, Dept. of the Tenn.

To Maj. Gen. Cadwallader C. Washburn

Near Vicksburg Miss June 13, 1863.

MAJ GEN'L. C. C WASHBURNE
COMMDG DETACHM'T 16TH ARMY CORPS.

Directions were given General Kimball to station his Cavalry at Oak Ridge P. O. I find from Maj Wilson[1] of the Cavalry that no force is kept

It seems to me that a force should be kept well advanced on the Ridge road, either at the P. O. or some other suitable place. All the roads north and east, should be scouted frequently, and no chance left the enemy of coming near from any direction. The enemys Cavalry above you, should be driven out by all means, and made to feel that it is not safe to venture too near Haines Bluff. I am particularly desirous to learn if there is a large force of the enemy at Yazoo City: If Johnson has crossed Black River with the bulk of his army: If any troops have crossed the Yazoo and gone West.

U. S. GRANT Maj Gen'l

Copies, DLC-USG, V, 19, 30; DNA, RG 393, Dept. of the Tenn., Letters Sent; Alcorn Collection, WyU.

On June 13, 1863, Maj. Gen. Cadwallader C. Washburn, "Haines Bluff," wrote to USG. "Before leaving Memphis I secured by personal application Six Mountain Howitzers for the use of the Cavalry in West Tenn. They were consigned to me at Memphis but did not arrive there until a day or two after I left. Previous to leaving, but while still Commanding the Cavalry there, I approved requisitions for the 2nd Wis Cav for two of the pieces, & for the 2nd Iowa for two pieces. The Second Wis. Cav. was under orders to report to me here when I left Memphis, and I had no doubt but they would bring the Howitzers with them. The Regt. has just arrived here, but reports that Genl. Hurlbut would not allow them to bring the guns. We want these guns very much for the Cavalry here, and I wish you would order four of them to be sent here at once. . . . P. S. Our defences are proceeding here rapidly, and Gen. Johnson can come whenever he gets ready. We shall want some more artillery, and if you have any that you can spare I wish you would send it up." ALS, DNA, RG 393, Dept. of the Tenn., Letters Received.

1. James Grant Wilson, born in Edinburgh in 1832, raised in Poughkeepsie, N. Y., a journalist in Chicago before the Civil War, was appointed maj., 15th Ill. Cav., as of Dec. 25, 1862. Just before entering the service, Wilson wrote *Biographical Sketches of Illinois Officers* . . . (Chicago, 1862), which included (pp. 12–16) what was probably the earliest printed biography of USG other than newspaper accounts.

To Col. John C. Kelton

Head Quarters Department of the Tenn.
Before Vicksburg, Miss. June 14th 1863.
Colonel J. C. Kelton
Asst. Adj't. General,
Washington D. C.
Colonel,

I have the honor to acknowledge the communication of William Swift and other enlisted men of the Army of the Potomac and prisoners at Cairo, Illinois, referred to me by your endorsement of date May 17th 1863 and for report I would respectfully state:

That the order, a true copy of which is set out in said communication, I published after consultation with Rear Admiral, (then Flag Officer) Foote, Commanding the Mississippi Gun Boats, but from the fears manifested by Regimental Commanders, because of so many of their men desiring to be transferred to the Naval Service and my own doubts as to whether my action would meet the approval of higher authority the order was immediately recalled, and not to exceed ten men were transferred under it, and these were cases where their commanding officers were anxious to procure their transfers, and thus the matter of transfers from the Land to the Naval Service stood, until the 27th day of January 1862, when the following communication was received from the General in Chief then commanding the Department of the Missouri.

"Head Quarters Dept. of the Missouri.
St. Louis Mo. Jany. 27th 1862.
Brig. General U. S. Grant,
Commanding &c:
General,

"Authority is just received from Washington to permit volunteers who desire it, to be discharged and recruited by Com. Foote for Navy Service on the Gun Boats, but this must be so distributed among the regiments as not to destroy the efficiency of any organized Company.

"Please inform Com. Foote that if he can send a recruiting officer here a considerable number of river men can be obtained from the regiments here. Keep me informed of the progress made in their supplying the Gun Boats.

Very respectfully
(signed)   H. W. HALLECK
Major General."

Regarding this authority as ample and sufficient for my action, I discharged from 70 to 100 men stating in the discharge by what authority it was made made and also the purpose of it. The greater number of those discharged belonged to the 4th Regt. Illinois Cavy, and 17th Regt. Illinois Infy.

I know nothing of the circumstances of the imprisonment of the men whose names are signed to the communication referred to me nor of the conditions of their enlistment or transfer to the Navy. They were not at the date of their going on the Gun Boats in my command, nor have they been since, nor do I know that previous to their going on board the Gun Boats they had ever seen the order set out in the communication, or if they had seen it, whether it was any inducement to their action. The men discharged by me were enlisted in the Naval Service for one year at the expiration of which time they have been duly discharged by the naval commanders.

I am Colonel,
Very respectfully,
Your obedt servt
U. S. GRANT
Major General

Copies, DLC-USG, V, 6, 8, 24, 94; DNA, RG 393, Dept. of the Tenn., Hd. Qrs. Correspondence; *ibid.*, Army of the Potomac, Miscellaneous Letters Received (Woodruff File). In an undated petition, William Swift and twenty-five others wrote to Maj. Gen. Henry W. Halleck. "The undersigned Prisoners in the Guard House at Cairo, Illinois, would respectfully state that in the Month of February A. D. 1862, they were soldiers in the Union Army and connected with the Army of the Potomac   That when the call was made for a detail of River and Seafaring men, for the Western Gun Boat service, they were solicited to join said service and were then promised, that they should be discharged from this service at the expiration of one year if not sooner discharged. That about the time they came to Cairo Illinois, to enter upon the said service Brig Genl U. S. Grant issued the Order, of which the following is a true Copy   'Hd. Qrs, District of Cairo   Cairo Illinois   Commanders of Regiments will report to these Headquarters without delay the names of all River and Seafaring men who are willing to be transferred from the Military to the Gunboat Service. Seeing the importance of fitting out our Gun boats as speedily as possible it is hoped there will be no objections raised by Regimental or Company commanders, in responding to this call; Men thus volunteering will be discharged at the end of one year or sooner should the War terminate. By Order U. S. GRANT Brig General   Jany. 20th 1862'   They would further represent that they have served out their time honestly and faithfully in said Gun Boat service for the space of one year, and while they were in the face of the enemy they expressed a willingness to remain under the Command of Admiral Porter, but as soon as an early prospect of a battle before Vicksburg had ceased, Your Petitioners respectfully asked that they might be discharged by reason of the expiration of their time of service; but said Admiral Porter refused to release them. Your Petitioners then respectfully protested against further duties except in case of an emergency and in the face of the enemy. That after said Protest said Admiral Porter sent your Petitioners to Cairo in the charge of the officers of the Receiving Ship 'Clara Dolsen' and from there without just cause or provocation they were sent to the Guard House at Cairo Illinois, where they are now unjustly detained   They therefore ask that they may have a speedy and impartial trial if any charges are preferred against them for any unsoldierlike conduct. If not they ask that they may be respectively exhonerated and discharged from said service. While they respectfully protest against being detained beyond the limit of their time of service, without their consent, as well as the ill treatment from the officers of the Gun Boat Service, they are willing to rejoin their respective Regiments in the Army of the Potomac if the exigencies of the Service require it. In the meantime they confidently await the decision of the Commanding General, and hope he will grant such speedy relief as to Justice appertains"   Copy, *ibid.* See letters to Capt. John C. Kelton, Jan. 20, 1862, and to Flag Officer Andrew H. Foote, Jan. 29, 1862.

General Orders No. 36

Headquarters Department of the Tennessee
In field near Vicksburg, Miss., June 15th, 1863
GENERAL ORDERS, No. 36.

I . . . So much of General Orders, No. 5, of date Memphis, Jan. 16th, 1863, from these Headquarters, as requires Provost Marshals to collect for the secret service and Hospital Fund, fees for permits to buy cotton at Military Posts, and for permits to trade at Military Posts, where trade is not regulated by civil authorities,[1] and all existing orders within this Department "conflicting or inconsistent with the orders in respect to the regulating of intercourse with the insurrectionary States the collection of abandoned property, &c.," published for the information and government of the Army, and of all concerned, in General Orders, No. 88, of date April 3d, 1863, Adjutant Generals Office, or which permit or prohibit, or in any way or manner interfere with any trade or transportation conducted under the Regulations of the Secretary of the Treasury, prescribed March 31st, 1863; and all permits heretofore granted to persons to trade or ship goods to this Department, by the Major General Commanding, or by his order, are hereby revoked.

II . . . The shipment of goods for sale south of Helena, in this Department, by any person other than sutlers regularly and duly appointed in pursuance of existing law is positively prohibited. Upon the approval of Army Corps Commanders, or the Commanders of Posts, or of forces detached from their respective Army Corps, and on compliance with the Treasury Regulations and orders, regularly appointed sutlers, may be permitted to ship to their Regiments, for sale within their *camp* lines, such sutler goods as are specifically designated and permitted to be sold by them, under the act of March, 19th, 1862, published in General Orders, No. 27., A. G. O., series 1862, and the articles added thereto, as published in General Orders, No. 35, of date February 7th 1863, Adjutant Generals Office, and they will be allowed to sell only the articles designated in said law and orders, and none others, and at such prices, and not exceeding such, as may be affixed to said articles by a Board of Officers, in pursuance of the provisions of said act. The Board of Officers upon whom the duty of establishing and fixing the prices exceeding which the articles permitted to be sold by sutlers shall not be sold, is impowred by said act, will immediately proceed to establish and affix said prices in all cases where it has not already been done.

III . . . All traders not regularly authorized sutlers, with their stocks in trade, will be required to remove at once, to Helena, or north of that place.

IV . . . No spirituous vinous or malt liquors will be permitted to pass south of Cairo, Illinois, except such as belong to the Commissary and Medical Departments.[2]

V . . . Any violation, or non-compliance with this order, directly or indirectly, will work a forfeiture of all the goods the person or persons guilty of such violation or non-compliance, may have in his or their possession, and subject such offenders to imprisonment in the Military Prison at Memphis, Tenn., at the discretion of the General Commanding the Department.

VI . . . The enforcement of General Orders No. 88, current series, Adjutant Generals Office, of the Treasury Regulations herein referred to, and of this order is especially enjoined upon all Military Commanders and the respective Provost Marshals in this Department.

VII . . . All property seized for violations of this order will be disposed of and accounted for in accordance with existing orders.

VIII . . . No applications for the shipment of goods, or for permits to trade, within this Department, will be entertained at Department Headquarters.

By order of Maj. Gen. U. S. Grant
Jno. A. Rawlins
Asst. Adjt. General.

Copies, DLC-USG, V, 13, 14; DNA, RG 393, Dept. of the Tenn., General and Special Orders; (printed) USGA. *O.R.*, I, xxiv, part 3, 412–13.

1. On Jan. 16, 1863, Lt. Col. John A. Rawlins issued General Orders No. 5. "Hereafter, there shall be collected, by Provost Marshals, for secret service and Hospital Fund, the following fees: For each permit to buy cotton at any Military Post, whether as principal or agent, one hundred dollars. For each permit to trade at any Military Post, where trade is not regulated by the civil authorities, one hundred dollars. The amount thus collected shall be reported and paid over by each local Provost Marshal to the Provost Marshal of his District, at the time of making his weekly report; and by District Provost Marshals, reported and paid over to the Provost Marshal General, at the time of making their semi-monthly reports. The Provost Marshal General will pay over said fund to the Chief Quartermaster of the Department, who will hold the same subject to the

order of the General Commanding the Department. Each local Provost Marshal will keep a duplicate of all permits granted under this order, and will state in his report the name, and residence of the party obtaining the permit, and the date thereof. All permits heretofore granted will be considered revoked and the parties required to comply with the terms of this order. This order is not to be construed to remove any restrictions imposed by previous orders." Copies, DLC-USG, V, 13, 14, 95; DNA, RG 393, Dept. of the Tenn., General and Special Orders. *O.R.*, I, xvii, part 2, 569. On Feb. 5, Brig. Gen. Mason Brayman reported that traders in Memphis who had paid the fee had been prevented from shipping goods by the special agent of the Treasury Dept. On Feb. 16, USG endorsed this letter. "Money once taken up and accounted for to the credit of the Government cannot be returned to parties from whom received without liability of the officer ordering the return being held responsible. I cannot see however why the Treasury agent interferes in the remarkable manner which he does with trade in this Dept. There is probably a greater Military necessity of putting an end to trade in Memphis than in any other part of the Department. From Memphis the most of the smuggling is done" Copies, DLC-USG, V, 25; DNA, RG 393, Dept. of the Tenn., Endorsements.

On Feb. 22, USG endorsed a letter of G. F. Robb, a merchant of Paducah, asking if General Orders No. 5 covered Paducah. "Referred to Provost Marshal. Genl. Order No. 5 should not apply to the state of Ky. that state having never seceded" Copies, *ibid*. On March 6, Judge George C. Hallet, Hickman, Ky., wrote to USG arguing that "old resident merchants" should be exempt from the terms of General Orders No. 5. ALS, *ibid*., 16th Army Corps, Letters Received. On March 20, Rawlins endorsed this letter. "The within construction of the order referred to, is correct: it was never intended to apply to resident merchants and legimate traders of Kentucky, in places where the state and municipal laws is in force. It only applies to cotton speculators and traders, where the Civil law is suspended in states in rebellion against the federal government. District and local Provost Marshals will be governed by this decision." Copy, *ibid*. On April 14, Hallet wrote to USG that the fees had been collected anyway. ALS, *ibid*. On April 26, Rawlins endorsed Hallet's second letter with a reaffirmation of his earlier statement. ES, *ibid*.

On April 27, M. Weil, Mayfield, Ky., wrote to USG. "I am a Merchant of Mayfield Ky. have been doing business here for years. Not long since Major Gibson Provost Marshal at Paducah Ky called upon me for One hundred dollars as a Military License to buy Cotton in Mayfield Ky. claiming it under an order issued by yourself. We believe he has misconstrued the intention of your order, as having reference to those who bought Cotton in Kentucky, and especially in the place where they have lived and done business for years. I am told that the money has been refunded to some who paid the tax; if it is not lawful, and in accordance with your order, I respectfully ask that you will order the same paid back to me.—" Copy, *ibid*., RG 109, Union Provost Marshals' File of Papers Relating to Individual Civilians.

2. On June 25, U.S. Treasury Agent Thomas H. Yeatman wrote to USG's hd. qrs. asking that General Orders No. 36 "be modified so as to allow liquor to brought to Memphis, and asks that malt liquors and catawba wine be excepted in the order, stating 'that they are actually necessary for the comfort of the inner man,' and that they promote temperance." DLC-USG, V, 25; DNA, RG 393, Dept. of the Tenn., Endorsements. On July 3, USG's adjt. endorsed this letter. "General Orders, No. 36, was issued on due reflection, based upon past experi-

ence, and will be adhered to without modification." Copies, *ibid.* On Aug. 26, Maj. Gen. Stephen A. Hurlbut, Memphis, wrote to USG. "Many applications are daily made to me in relation to the shipment to this place of Wines Ales & Beer—I decline them constantly unless you choose to give discretion in the matter —Wines & Malt Liquors I consider there should be some discretion—I do not desire that any others should be permitted" ALS, *ibid.*, 16th Army Corps, Letters Received. On the same day, USG endorsed this letter. "Discretion will be allowed the Commanding Officer of the 16th A. C. as to what liquors are to be imported into his Command." AES, *ibid.*

On June 28, USG wrote to Brig. Gen. Elias S. Dennis. "I understand some one is selling Ale at the Point. If so confiscate their entire stock in trade, turn it over to the Sanitary commission, arrest the parties and send them North by first boat." Typescript, Walter Trohan, Silver Spring, Md. On July 7, Henry W. Warriner, U.S. Sanitary Commission, wrote to USG. "Understanding from General Dennis that a lot of contraband ale was at Youngs Point, and that he received orders from you to turn it over to the Sanitary Commission I have the honor to report that no such article has yet come to me and that I have heard nothing further from it since my last interview with Gen. Dennis some four days since" ALS, DNA, RG 393, Dept. of the Tenn., Letters Received. On July 7, Rawlins endorsed this letter. "Respectfully referred to Brig.-Gen'l. E. S. Dennis, Commd'g. District N. E. La., who will please comply with the order within mentioned, or report reasons for non-compliance to these Headquarters." ES, *ibid.* On July 8, Dennis referred the matter to Lt. Col. John W. Jefferson, post commander at Young's Point, who endorsed the letter on July 10. "The enclosed paper will explain" AES, *ibid.* On July 5, Jefferson had written to Dennis that he had seized a shipment of liquor on board the steamer *Gladiator* ten or fifteen days before but upon investigation was satisfied that the parties involved had not knowingly violated General Orders No. 36. LS, *ibid.* Rawlins endorsed this letter on July 6. "These Parties will be allowed to take their Liquors north, but will not sell them here, contrary to existing orders. If they have been seized, release them" AES, *ibid.* Jefferson endorsed this letter on July 10. "The above orders of Gen Grant July 6th have been complied with. The Liquors &c have been released" AES, *ibid.*

On Aug. 8, Yeatman wrote to USG. "Letter of information to Major General U. S. Grant in relation to Steamer Gladiator which cleared from St Louis on the 17th of June, and had on as appeared by her manifest 1625 packages of Wines, Liquors and fruits which goods were permitted by the Surveyor to pass Memphis, in violation of G. O. No. 36, from Dept Hd. Qrs. It appears the wine was not allowed to land at Vicksburg. Capt of Gladiator put said packages on Steamer J C. Swan June 27, at Chickasaw Bayou or at least a portion of them. Viz. 216 cases wine & 50 half Bbls ale, Several cases of the wine was in the hold of the Boat as she passed up, and reported by the aid as not appearing on the manifest. this wine and other not regulary permitted goods I have ordered to be seized at Cairo, hopes the General Command'g will make an Example by ordering the seizure of the Gladiator and the Liquor now on J. C. Swan Understands the wine is owned by one M. Powers, who has been strongly suspected for smuggling goods through the lines" DLC-USG, V, 99. On Aug. 19, Rawlins endorsed this letter to Col. Loren Kent, provost marshal. Copy, *ibid.* On Sept. 15, Kent endorsed this letter. "Respectfully returned. I am informed by Mr. W. P. Mellen, Treasury Agent, that the Liquor within mentioned came down the river by authority of the Treasury Agent, Mr Howard at Saint Louis upon the request of Major Genl F P. Blair, who represented that he wanted this large amount, (amounting to from $6,000$\frac{00}{100}$ to 8,000$\frac{00}{100}$ in value) for himself and Officers with him. Mr. Mellen further says that Mr Howard has been reported for violation of orders, and that he thinks the Captain of the Steamer Gladiator acted in good faith. The Steamer is now in port, but I have thought proper to submit the additional information before arresting the Captain upon the State-ment of Mr. Yeatman, which would probably fail to convict him before a Military Commission" Copy, *ibid.* On Sept. 16, Rawlins endorsed this letter. "Respect-fully returned to Lieut Col Kent Pro. Mar. Genl. I view of the statement of Mr. Mellan and also the difficulty of conviction in the case the Capt. of said Steamer will not be arrested" Copies, *ibid.*, V, 25; DNA, RG 393, Dept. of the Tenn., Endorsements. This matter later received an extensive investigation by a special committee of the U.S. House of Representatives, which reported that Maj. Gen. Francis P. Blair, Jr., and his staff had placed a moderate order for liquor for private use on June 3 which had been altered by Michael Powers to authorize the large amount actually brought down. *HRC*, 38-1-61. See *Missouri Democrat*, Oct. 26, 27, 30, Nov. 3, 1863.

To Maj. Gen. John A. McClernand

Head Qrs. Dept. of the Ten.
Near Vicksburg, June 15th 1863.

MAJ. GEN. J. A. MCCLERNAND
COMD.G 13TH ARMY CORPS,
GEN.

A portion of the 9th Army Corps, about 8000 strong, have now arrived and will take position on the South side of the city thus making the investment complete.[1]—This will release Gen. Herron who is instructed to move to Gen. Hovey's place thus contracting your front to the ground occupied by Smith & Carr.

Should the enemy attack Hains' Bluff in such force as to make it necessary to detach a greater force than has already been desig-nated, i e the six Reserve Brigades of McPhersons's & Sherman's Corps, I will have to entirely uncover on the South side of the city. This will necessarily involve an exposure of our Left flank from the Garrison of Vicksburg.—We should hold, and fight the enemy wherever he presents himself, from the extreme right to your present extreme left. That is all the ground taken by the three Army Corps on first investing the city should be held. Your left Division is, or will be, replaced by one numerically stronger. By replacing it thus it gives you a reserve of three Brigades. Lauman, with near 6000 men will also be there to strengthen you still further in this imergency.

I do not want to give up the front occupied by Lauman unless it should become absolutely necessary to do so but give this as plan to be adopted in case of the greatest presure on the left.

The idea then is that two lines should now be selected for runing perpendicular to our present line, one from Laumans left or along Halls Ferry road and one from Hoveys present left.— Should Parks command, the 9th Corps, be removed your reserve should at once be thrown on to the first line chosen or the Halls Ferry road. Should they be so hotly pressed as to make it necessary for them to fall back on to the second line then Lauman's Division should be brought on to it also. The very moment an order goes for the removal of the 9th Army Corps you will be notified. You will then assume command of all the forces to the left of you, in addition to your own Corps. Everything in the shape of extra Ammunition, Com.y stores and other public property not required should be got back to within what may possibly become our most contracted line. Should the enemy attempt to get past your left with the view of forming a junction with Johnstone's forces he must be defeated.—An attempt to leave his lines however I do not look upon as probable. This would give us the city and leave my whole force to act directly against the enemy, and as a last resort fall into his lines and act on the defensive behind works of his own building. This is given only as a general plan to be adopted under certain contingencies. The movements of an enemy necessarily determine countermovements.

After writing the foregoing, and after Gen. Parks had moved one Division of his command to opposite Warrenton I had to change my plan and send him to Hains' Bluff. From information received the enemy have 12000 Infantry & Artillery at Yazoo with orders to move south, Four thousand Cavalry already between the Yazoo and Black rivers, and Loring ordered to cross. This made it necessary to send the extra force up the Yazoo river.

You will assume command of Lauman's Division at once. Heron taking up a part of the ground occupied by Lauman the latter can better spare a regiment to garrison Warrenten than any one els. I would not take a regiment from you for the Garrison of Warrenten but Herron has a long line to hold and but eight regiments to do it with.

Lauman will be directed to report to and receive orders from you.

> Very respectfully
> your obt. svt.
> U. S. GRANT
> Maj. Gen. Com

ALS, McClernand Papers, IHi. *O.R.*, I, xxiv, part 3, 409–10.

On June 15, 1863, Maj. Gen. John A. McClernand wrote to Lt. Col. John A. Rawlins. "The advance trenches in Genl. Smith's front were pushed forward,— yesterday by a party of negroes, and last night, by a detail from Genl. Smith's division. The work at this point is so close to the enemy's line that it has to be prosecuted with great caution. The enemy brought a gun to bear upon the gabioned parapet at this place yesterday, and fired three shots doing no damage. In Genl. Carr's front, the advance trench on his left was pushed forward to the top of the hill beyond the ravine. Genl. Hovey's left was advanced 200 yards. The front of two regiments was thus moved forward and established by digging a trench sufficient to enable our men to hold the position. This last trench will be finished as quickly as possible" LS, DNA, RG 393, Dept. of the Tenn., Letters Received. On the same day, Col. John E. Whiting, 87th Ill., Warrenton, wrote to McClernand. "I find that there is very heavy fatigue duty to be done at this place and more particularly so at this time,—as all of the boats are entirely out of fuel we are therefore compelled to go to the woods and cut and haul wood,— as coal can not be had in sufficient quanties. Both of the colored Regiments have been taken away from this point, and with them about 80 who were organized by me into a working party, and who were allowed to go into the 3rd Miss, with the understanding that they were going to remain here, and the promise that they should continue work as formerly. Now, General, it is a hard case to require the soldiers (white) to do heavy military duty and also heavy fatigue duty, I have several times suspended work, for a short time, on the fortifications, (even against my own judgment.) in order to fill very pressing orders. I hardly know how I am to get along unless I can have some more Contrabands. Of course I will try,—and not only so but will keep up the work, but still if we had a colored Regt. we could get along much better" Copies, *ibid.*; *ibid.*, 13th Army Corps, Letters Received. On the same day, McClernand endorsed this letter. "Respectfully referred to Maj. Genl. Grant. I have two regiments at Young's Point,—one at Warrenton and seven at Big Black. I respectfully renew my application for the return of the regiments at Young's Point and Warrenton, including Col. Whiting. Genl. Herron can more conveniently garrison Warrenton than I can. He is more directly interested in Warrenton than I am. My orderlies and reconnoitering parties have to pass him in going to and fro." ES, *ibid.*, Dept. of the Tenn., Letters Received.

On June 16, McClernand wrote to Rawlins. "Last night the advance approach in front of Genl Smith was extended to the left, across the road and partly up the bank. It was also extended to the right, as far as possible. In Genl Carr's front the zig-zag apprach, near the Railroad, was pushed forward to the stream in the ravine, in front of the 1st Missouri Battery. The one on the left, was pushed to the crest of the ridge, upon which Genl Lawler advanced to the assault on the 22d ult. At this point considerable opposition has been experienced, the enemy throwing out each night, a strong line of pickets, and at times openening a small gun on our working party. Genl Hovey continued to strengthen the position, to which his left was thrown forward night before last." LS, *ibid.*

Also on June 16, Rawlins telegraphed to McClernand. "will have line built. No operators or Instruments on hand now, expected every Boat" Copy, *ibid.*, 13th Army Corps, Letters Received. On the same day, USG telegraphed to McClernand. "Several telegraph operators with Instruments will be down from Memphis by first boat, and as soon as they arrive Genl. Osterhaus shall be supplied" Copy, *ibid.*

On June 17, McClernand wrote to Rawlins. "Yesterday and last night the advance trench across the road in Genl. Smiths front, was widened and otherwise improved. The two advance trenches in front of Genl Carr, wer each pushed about fifty yards. Genl. Hovey was employed in improving and strengthening his position. He also had men employed in building furnaces to heat shot for the 24 pdrs. The Pioneers are working on platforms for the 8 inch navy guns, which I hope soon to have mounted and in position." LS, *ibid.*, Dept. of the Tenn., Letters Received.

On June 18, McClernand wrote to Rawlins. "Yesterday and last night, in Genl. Smiths front, the left of the extreme advance trench was extended some ten or fifteen feet. Communication was opened with this trench and one still further to the right. On the left of the road the a defensive rifle pit has been started and is well under way, to protect the advance from a sortie on the left. In Genl. Carr's front the right approach was extended, and will by tomorrow be across a small run that passes the foot of the hill, parallel to our line. Considerable difficulty is experienced at this point as the ground is somewhat marshy. The left approach is extended twenty yards. In front of Genl. Hovey, the advance trench and the batteries were improved. Furnaces were completed and hot shot thrown into the city." LS, *ibid.* On the same day, McClernand wrote to USG. "It is reported that some officer, professing to act by authority of Genl. Sherman, has taken down and away a considerable portion of the wire of the line I had just restored between here and Big Black. Please have it restored and further interference stopped." LS, *ibid.* On the same day, Sherman endorsed this letter. "In answer to the within I have to report that the Pioneer Companies have been in the habit of using Telegraph wire to tie Fascines. Not knowing that orders had been made to repair the Line to Black River it seems that Capt Ashmead sent a Lieutenant John Adams with a wagon to bring in wire. I enclose his Report, by which you will see he asserts that he went to the very place he had been before, and had no idea that the Line was being repaired. Of course personally I knew nothing of the Matter till this letter was received. It is now too late to mend it." AES, *ibid.*

1. John G. Parke, born in Chester County, Pa., in 1827, USMA 1849, served in the Topographical Engineers before the Civil War. Appointed brig. gen. as of Nov. 23, 1861, and maj. gen. as of July 18, 1862, Parke served under Maj. Gen. Ambrose E. Burnside in the N. C. expedition and in the Army of the Potomac. Ordered to send 8,000 men from the Dept. of the Ohio to USG, Burnside sent two divs. of the 9th Army Corps commanded by Parke. *O.R.*, I, xxiv, part 3, 383–84. On June 14, Rawlins telegraphed to Parke. "Your despatch received. Maj Genl Grant is out to the extreme left, near Warrenton, and will not be back until toward evening. Orders have been ~~send~~ Telegraphed to Chickasaw Landing, to Col. Macfeely, chf. Com, who is now on the road to that place, to take immediate steps to supply you with rations, and land transportation. He will see you there." Telegram received, DNA, RG 94, War Records Office, Dept. of the Ohio; copies, *ibid.*, RG 393, Dept. of the Tenn., Letters Sent; DLC-USG, V, 19, 30.

On June 15, USG signaled to the commanding officer, Young's Point. "If Gen Parks troops have not started across the Point, Ha~~u~~lt them unti~~ll~~ further orders.—" Copy, DNA, RG 111, Vicksburg Signal Book. On the same day, Lt. Col. Nicolas Bowen, adjt. for Parke, signaled to USG. "Gen. Parke's troops are now opposite Warrenton where they are waiting further orders." Signal received, *ibid.*, RG 94, War Records Office, Military Div. of the Miss.; copy, *ibid.*, RG 111, Vicksburg Signal Book. On the same day, Rawlins telegraphed to Parke. "The order for you to move to Warrenton is countermanded. You will move your entire command to Haines Bluff with as little delay as possible" Copies, DLC-USG, V, 19, 30, 101; DNA, RG 393, Dept. of the Tenn., Letters Sent. On the same day, Parke telegraphed to USG. "Dispatch Recd—The three 3 brigades left this morning to cross the peninsula but have not started across to Warrenton. the baggage had not started at last advices owing to the delay in the wagons Shall I stop the movement & order the troops back the two additional briga[des] have not yet reported" Telegram received, *ibid.*, Telegrams Received. Also on June 15, USG telegraphed twice to Parke. "Has your command started over from Youngs Point? If they have not, move on Haines Bluff. I do not ~~to~~ want to turn them back after having started, but will move troops from here instead." Telegram received, *ibid.*, RG 94, War Records Office, Dept. of the Ohio. "A division of troops have been sent to Haines Bluff since I was there. I cannot say whether you should go above or below them. Col. Wilson Inspector General is going up this evening and will have your place designated and will be there when you arrive" Copies, *ibid.*, RG 393, Dept. of the Tenn., Letters Sent; DLC-USG, V, 19, 30, 101.

To Maj. Gen. Cadwallader C. Washburn

·Near Vicksburg Miss June 15, 1863.

Maj Gen'l. C. C. Washburne
Commdg Detach'mt. 16th Army Corps.

I did not think it advisable to Send Sergeant Hall and party on the expedition marked out for them. It would be of vast importance to us if accomplished, but with the small force taken by Sergeant Hall, every neighberhood could raise a force to follow them and insure his capture. If captured they would certaily be hung, if not shot when taken.

The information given by McBerney does not look to me like an intention to attack Haines Bluff, immediately, but a disposition to get and hold a footing on the ridge as near to it as possible, while they are collecting their forces for an attack. Their intention ividently is to come down suddenly, when they do move, and for that reason they will endeavour to get a position as near us as possible. It is not necessary for me to say to you, that great vigilance should be shown by our Cavalry. I have directed Hall to scout through the country from the Sun. Flower to Greenville. I want to discover if the enemy are collecting stores apparantly to be used on the Mississippi river, or if they are all to be east of the Yazoo. They may possibly design their present movement to cover the crossing of troops to the west bank of the Yazoo. I hold here Six Brigades in readiness to move at a moments notice, should an attack become inevitable. If more artillery can be got to send you, I will send it, but troops will not be sent at present. They cannot be sent without changing lines here, or without taking the Reserve Brigades from one of the army Corps.

U. S. GRANT Maj Gen'l.

Copies, DLC-USG, V, 19, 30; DNA, RG 393, Dept. of the Tenn., Letters Sent; Alcorn Collection, WyU. *O.R.*, I, xxiv, part 3, 410–11. On June 14, 1863, Maj. Gen. Cadwallader C. Washburn, Haynes' Bluff, twice wrote to USG. "I send you Mr. McBirney a Spy that I sent five days ago to Yazoo City. The information he gives is valuable and I believe perfectly reliable. If the enemy is moving this way, it might be well to send him another division. At all events we should have more artillery at once. I assured McBirney that if he would make this trip he should receive big pay, and I request that you will see that he receives pay in proportion to the hazard incurred   Mr. McBirney can give you information that may enable you to capture some of their couriers. I send in the morning 225 Cavalry across the Yazoo. They will proceed up the west side of Deer Creek about 20 miles & cross & pass up between Deer Creek & Sunflower, & drive out parties that I hear are in there in pursuit of stock for Johnsons Army." "A Citizen has just come to my quarters who left Rolling fork yesterday morning. He says parties of Secesh Soldiers crossed the Sunflower river while he was there who had been sent in to gather up Stock for Johnsons army. He says that there are immense amounts of Cattle Corn & hogs on Deer Creek. He thinks they will be able to secure several thousand head if they are allowed time. They will gather it up about the Rolling fork & above on Deer Creek & drive it up so as to cross the Sunflower & Yazoo beyond the reach of our GunBoats. We have no Gun Boats here now that can go above Yazoo City. The DeKalb is the only Iron Clad & she draws too much water. The Sunflower & Yazoo are both rising a little   One of the tin clads can probably get up to the Sunflower. If we could land three or four hundred Cavalry at Greenville, and let them dash down between Deer Creek & Sunflower they can readily get back to this point, & bring in I have no doubt a large amount of Stock & probably some prisoners, & will interfere largely with Johnsons supplies." ALS, DNA, RG 393, Dept. of the Tenn., Letters Received. On the same day, Washburn telegraphed to USG. "I shall send two hundred & fifty cavalry across the Yazoo & up between Deer Creek & Sunflower to drive out the secesh who are gathering up stock & to drive the stock into our lines— Capt Walker will Send a gunboat up Sunflower at same time"   Telegram received, *ibid.*, RG 94, War Records Office, Dept. of the Tenn. Misdated [May 24] in *O.R.*, I, xxiv, part 3, 346.

On June 15, Washburn wrote to USG. "My pickets brought in this forenoon Seven deserters from the 8th Kentucky Mounted Infantry, Lorings Division. I send you one of the most intelligent, for you to interrogate   He was at Jackson five days ago, & saw Breckenridge there. His information confirms the impressions I have recd. from other quarters that the enemy is concentrating, between Big Black & Satartia. Our defences are progressing finely, but we are very short of artillery." ALS, DNA, RG 393, Dept. of the Tenn., Letters Received.

To Brig. Gen. Elias S. Dennis

Near Vicksburg Miss June 15, 1863.

BRIG. GEN'L. E. S DENNIS
COMMDG DIST. N. E. LA.

My letter to you was not intended as an order, but simply advising on my part, as to the points you should garrison.[1] In speaking of fortifying three points, Youngs Point was not included. I merely spoke of that as a point that must be held for Military purpose. There being always transient troops passing, and Gun boats on both sides of the point; no troops are necessary there, except as a guard for public property. The three points then, to be fortified, are from Millikens Bend to Lake Providence. It seems to me Lake Providence, Millikens Bend and an intermediate point, should be the places to fortify, you however as

Commander of the District, must exercise your own judgement as to where troops should be stationed, and where how used. I repeat what was before given as instructions. Public property must be protected first, after that, all the protection you can give to Plantations leased by goverment, must be given. Negro troops should be kept aloof from White troops, especially in their camps, as much as possible. Wherever the movements of the enemy require a concentration of your forces, bring them together without regard to color.

U. S. GRANT Maj Gen'l.

Copies, DLC-USG, V, 19, 30; DNA, RG 393, Dept. of the Tenn., Letters Sent; Alcorn Collection, WyU. *O.R.*, I, xxiv, part 3, 411–12.

On June 18, 1863, Brig. Gen. Joseph A. Mower signaled to Lt. Col. John A. Rawlins. "I am ordered to rejoin my Division—Gen. Tuttle's   is it in the rear of Vicksburg or at Haine's Bluffs"   Copy, DNA, RG 111, Vicksburg Signal Book. On the same day, USG signaled to Mower. "You will remain where you are untill Further Orders"   Copy, *ibid.* Also on June 18, Brig. Gen. Elias S. Dennis signaled to USG. "Gen Mowers Brigade were about to rejoin their division. Your Despatch to him Recd. about sending a Regt. to Providence." Signal received, *ibid.*, RG 94, War Records Office, Military Div. of the Miss.; copy, *ibid.*, RG 111, Vicksburg Signal Book. On the same day, Rawlins signaled to Dennis. "Mowers Command will remain in your command untill further orders"   Copy, *ibid.*

1. See letter to Brig. Gen. Elias S. Dennis, June 11, 1863.

To Jesse Root Grant

Walnut Hills, Miss
June 15th 1863,

DEAR FATHER,

I have received several letters from Mary and yourself but as I have to do with nineteen twentyeths of those received have neglected to answer them.

All I can say is that I am well. Have the enemy closely hemed in all round. My position is naturally strong and fortified against an attack from outside. I have been so strongly reinforced that

Johnstone will have to come with a mighty host to drive me away. —I do not look upon the fall of Vicksburg as in the least doubtful. If however I could have carried the place on the 22d of last month I could by this time have made a campaign that would have made the state of Mississippi almost safe for a solitary horseman to ride over. As it is the enemy have a large Army in it and the season has so far advanced that water will be difficult to find for an Army marching besides the dust and heat that must be encountered. The fall of Vicksburg now will only result in the opening of the Miss. river and demoralization of the enemy. I intended more from it. I did my best however and looking back can see no blunder committed.

ULYSSES.

ALS, PPRF.

To *Julia Dent Grant*

Walnut Hills, Miss.
June 15th 1863.

DEAR JULIA,

When I last wrote I told you that you might come down. I thought then I would write no more expecting that you would leave before another letter would reach you. But you may remain long enough to get another letter. If you should come down before Vicksburg falls you would hardly see me until the place is taken however. My Hd Qrs. are six miles from the landing with the road always blocked with wagons bringing supplies for our immense army. My duties are such that I can scarsely leave.—I have continued well except an attack of Dysentery which now has entirely left me. Fred. has been complaining a little for a few days. His Uncle Lewis[1] was down this morning and I let him go back with him to spend a short time. I have proposed to Fred. to go to St. Louis several times but he objects. He wants to see the end of Vicksburg. Everything looks highly favorable here now. I have the town closely invested and our Rifle Pitts up so close to the enemy that they cannot show their heads without being shot at at short enough range to kill a squirrel. They dare not show a single gun on the whole line of their works. By throwing shells every few minuets the people are kept continuously in their caves. They must give out soon even if their provisions do not give out. Some of the rebels are escaping to our lines every night. They all unite in discribing every thing inside as in a deplorable condition. Troops are on less than half rations and many poor people without anything. I decline allowing any of them to come out.

I want to see you and the children very much. Miss and Jess I know will be delighted with their pony. He is so small that Fred can ride him with one foot draging on the ground. You must not neglect bringing a little saddle for both Jess & Miss, and a small bridle. I sent up to Memphis and got all the clothing I wanted except cravats. You may bring me two black ones and half a dozen light ones.—I paid Lewis the $500 still due on Wish ton Wish. No one on my staff has resigned except Hillyer and he remained one month after the acceptance of his resignation.[2] Lagow has gone home sick and I expect never to recover. He may get up so as to return but will never be well. All my staff are well. Why did you not stop and see Nelly on your way down?[3]

Remember me to all. Kisses for yourself and children.

ULYS.

ALS, DLC-USG.

1. The brother of Julia Dent Grant. On April 15, 1863, USG wrote to Maj. Gen. Frederick Steele. "Turn over to the bearer Lewis Dent, lessee of Plantation, under regulations established by the Government, One hundred (100) mules and such plow harness as may be collected from abandoned plantations, to be appraised by the commissioners duly appointed and now here." Copies, *ibid.*, V, 19, 30; DNA, RG 393, Dept. of the Tenn., Letters Sent. On the same day, Lt. Col. John A. Rawlins issued Special Orders No. 105. "By direction of Brig. Gen'l L. Thomas, Adjutant General of the Army, the Chief Commissary of this Department, will turn over to Judge L. Dent, Government lessee of a plantation on the Mississippi River, ten Bbls of Pork, and one Bbl. Molasses, which Pork and Molasses will be replaced by Judge Dent, as soon as the same can be procured

from Memphis, Tennessee." Copies, DLC–USG, V, 26, 27; DNA, RG 393, Dept. of the Tenn., Special Orders. See letter to Julia Dent Grant, July 1, 1863.

2. On April 10, by Special Orders No. 100, Dept. of the Tenn., Lt. Col. Loren Kent, 29th Ill., replaced Col. Addison S. Norton, 17th Ill., as provost marshal of the army before Vicksburg, while Col. William S. Hillyer, provost marshal, Dept. of the Tenn., was recalled from Memphis. Copies, DLC–USG, V, 26, 27; DNA, RG 393, Dept. of the Tenn., Special Orders. On June 16, Rawlins issued General Orders No. 37, announcing Kent as provost marshal, Dept. of the Tenn. Copies, DLC–USG, V, 13, 14; DNA, RG 393, Dept. of the Tenn., General and Special Orders; (printed) Oglesby Papers, IHi; (printed) USGA.

3. On June 4, Dr. Alexander Sharp, Louisiana, Mo., husband of Ellen Dent Sharp, wrote to USG. "From day to day from week to week & from month to month I have been thinking I would write to you for months now past. And, now that I am writing I feel that your time must be entirely too valuable to consume in reading any thing that I might say. Of one thing you may be certain that although no letters have passed between us, I have not ceased to watch your upward & onward march from one hight to still another, & higher one of glory & renown and tho, I have said nothing to you I often feel my heart—to use a common expression—to swell with proud satisfaction & delight when I as I do daily see your quick & rapid strides to highest honors. I suppose you are now in the daily receipt of many very many congratulatory letters—Your last brilliant campaign from Grand Gulf to Vicksburg as far surpasses the Donelson campaign & it did any other since this war commenced. This seems to be the common verdict of the whole country. I feel very anxious to read a well written detailed account of the operations from the time you left Grand Gulf up to the present time. What little I have seen only whets the appetite for more. Let me say to you that Grant stock stands high in this market. If you can take Vicksburg in 30, 60 or 90 days even with heavy losses you will have done the biggest & best job that has been done since this war commenced, & will thereby do more to end the Rebellion than all that has been done else lumped together. If you can do it with small loss of men, so much the better even if it takes longer time. But take the place if you have to dig a big hole under it & blow it to atoms. Especially to Missouri is this important & to the whole west. But I will not trouble you any further. I only wanted to offer my hearty congratulations on your recent victories & to wish you God speed to newer fresher & greater ones soon. I am proud to say that we have a 3 months old boy that we have named Grant whom I think you will not be ashamed to own as a namesake, if he keeps improving as fast as he has thus far We feel much disappointed that Sis & family should pass within 100 yards of our door & not stop to see us—We would be muc[h] pleased to have her come & sta[y] some time with us. We have most excellent Schools here & plenty of them, & room in our house. Nellie got a letter from Sis from Galena. If you have time write to me, wont you? . . . I forward a letter from my Bro. Thomas at his request." ALS, USG 3.

To George G. Pride

———

Walnut Hills Miss.
June 15th 1863.

Dear Pride,

I received your very welcom letter and should have answered it sooner but find my time very much taxed. —I will avail myself of your offer should there be another movement made under my command. I missed you wonderfully in geting our wagons, baggage and everything over the river with the limited means at hand. I felt that you would have expedited matters one half. All is going on here now just right. We have our trenches pushed up so close to the enemy that we can throw Hand Grenades over into their forts. The enemy do not dare show their heads above the parapets at any point so close and so watchful are our sharpshooters. The town is completely invested. My position is so strong that I feel myself abundantly able to leave it so and go out twenty or thirty miles with force enough to whip two such garrisons. If Johnstone should come here he must do it with a larger Army than the Confederacy have now at any one place. This is what I think but do not say it boastingly nor do I want it repeated or shown.

Yours Truly
U. S. Grant

ALS, MoSHi.

To Brig. Gen. Lorenzo Thomas

Headquarters Department of the Tennesse
Near Vicksburg Miss. June 16th 1863

BRIG GENL L. THOMAS
ADJUTANT GENERAL OF THE ARMY,
WASHINGTON D. C.

GENERAL:

I have the honor to acknowledge the receipt of the communication of Col. B. L. E. Bonneville, U. S. A., Superintendent Recruiting Service Missouri Militia, of date March 26th, 1863, enclosing copies of orders detailing six enlisted men and one Commissioned Officer from Engineer Regiment of the West on recruiting Service, also a copy of an order issued from these Headquarters on which said details were made, by Col. J. W. Bissell of said Regiment and referred from your office to me, and for report would respectfully state: —

That Special Orders No. 22, of date La Grange, Tenn. Nov. 18, 1862, from these Headquarters, of which a copy is herewith enclosed, authorizing Col. Bissell to make the recruiting details therein mentioned was made so far as the sending of them to the States of Iowa, Illinois and Missouri, upon the authority of the letter (a copy of which is herewith enclosed) of Brig. Gen. George W. Cullum, Chief of Staff and Engineers of the Staff of the General in Chief.[1] The consent of the Governers of said states was considered as a matter of course, said Regiment being composed of men pretty equally from these states, although it was organized as a Missouri Regiment.

So far as the order authorizes Colonel Bissell to detail two Commissioned Officers or detail one and go himself, as he might deem advisable, and one enlisted man from each Company of said Regiment, it was made upon the representations of Colonel Bissell that men of his Regiment frequently received letters from their homes, stating that recruits might be had, and giving the names of such persons as desired to enlist; that if he had such authority as was given him in said order, he would send only those who had reliable assurances of obtaining at least five recruits, and returning at once with them to the Regiment, but under no circumstances was more than one man to be absent from the Company on this Service. He also represented that he could greatly facilitate the filling up of his Regiment, if permitted to go himself, and while I knew him to be an active and enterprising man, suited to such service—I felt also that his Regiment would not suffer from his absence, but on the contrary be more available for any duty required of it. His proposed action was plausible, and having confidence that he would not abuse the authority he asked for, the order was made.

I would further invite attention to Colonel Bissell's endorsement on said communication of Col. Bonneville.

Colonel Bissell's tender of resignation has been received and accepted which I trust, together with this report, will be satisfactory to the Secretary of War.

> I am General
> Very respectfully
> Your Obt Servt
> U. S. GRANT
> Major General

LS, DNA, RG 94, Vol. Service Div., Letters Received, M326 (VS) 1862.

1. On Nov. 1, 1862, Brig. Gen. George W. Cullum wrote to USG. "A general order will be published in a few days authorizing the following organization of Volunteer Engineer Regiments & Companies. . . . Permission is granted by the Secretary of War to enlist recruits for Col Bissell's Engineer regiment in Illinois, Iowa and Missouri, provided the consent of their Governors be obtained. The General-in-Chief has no objections to the issue of Commissions regimentally to Col Bissell's regiment, if Gov. Gamble is willing to do so." LS, *ibid.*, RG 108, Letters Sent (Press).

On Aug. 12, Brig. Gen. James B. McPherson had written to USG. "The undersigned a Brigadier General of Vols. at present commanding the 'Engineer Brigade' respectfully represents—That the '*Engineer Reg't. of the west*' at present numbers Eight hundred and thirty (830) men of all grades, and that it is for the Public interest that it be filled to the Maximum number. He therefore respectfully requests [that] the Commissions to its Officers be issued directly by the President of the U. S. as Volunteers, and that its ranks may be recruited from any of the

Western States and that all such recruits be credited to each state from which they may be enlisted towards its proportion of any call upon such state for Volunteers." ALS, *ibid.*, RG 94, Vol. Service Div., Letters Received, M326 (VS) 1862. McPherson enclosed a statement of Aug. 10 in which Col. Josiah W. Bissell described the organization of the Engineer Regt. of the West. ADS, *ibid.* On Aug. 13, USG endorsed this statement. "Respectfully forwarded to Hd Qrs. of the Army, Washington, D. C." AES, *ibid.*

On Sept. 15, Bissell, Jackson, Tenn., wrote to McPherson. "I arrived here yesterday afternoon in consequence of letters recd from my Adjutant about the troubles in Cos. C & G—I had those two companies assembled in the presence of the Regiment & read to them the oath they had taken & part of the articles of war, then told them they would certainly all be punished for what they had done, but that if any one wished to return to his duty & put himself on his good behavior he could do it, that they must consider it as a favor from me to them & not from them to me, they had sworn to do their duty & I certainly should do mine   Every man stepped forward & all are at work   It is nearly two months since the passage of the law relating to Engineer Rgts was passed & about 6 weeks since I left in your hands the communication to the Secretary of War relative to this Rgt— Would it be proper to write a telegraph to Genl. Halleck asking that a decision may be rendered as the men naturally feel very unsettled in the present state of the case rendering it easy for evill disposed persons to keep up a ferment?" ALS, *ibid.* On Sept. 22, USG endorsed this letter. "Respectfully forwarded to Headquarters ~~Dist.~~ of the Army Washington, D. C." ES, *ibid.* On Oct. 11, Maj. Gen. Henry W. Halleck endorsed this letter. "The 20th Section of the Act of July 17, 1862 authorizes an increase of the rank and file of the companies of this regiment to make each 150 men. Being a state organization, no change can be made in the manner of recruiting the regiment or appointing its officers   A portion of the regiment having received pay as 'extra-duty men' to May 31, 1862, I would recommend that *all* be paid in the same way to the same time, and from June 1, 1862 as engineer soldiers." AES, *ibid.*

To Maj. Gen. Henry W. Halleck

Near Vicksburg
June 18th [*16*] 1863

MAJ GEN H W HALLECK
GENL IN CHIEF

Everything progresses well here. Johnstons forces are at Yazoo City, Benton, Brownsville and Clinton   I am fortifying Haines Bluff to make my position certain, but believe I could go out with force enough to drive the Rebels from between the two Rivers

Deserters come out daily—All report rations short. We scarcely ever lose a man now. Health and condition of troops most excellent

U. S. Grant, M G Comdg

Telegram received, DNA, RG 107, Telegrams Collected (Bound); copies, *ibid.*, Telegrams Received in Cipher; (dated June 16, 1863) *ibid.*, RG 393, Dept. of the Tenn., Hd. Qrs. Correspondence; DLC-USG, V, 6, 8, 24, 94. Dated June 18 in *O.R.*, I, xxiv, part 1, 43. This telegram, sent via Cairo on June 23, arrived in Washington on June 24, 1:45 A.M.

To Maj. Gen. Francis J. Herron

Head Quarters, Dept. of the Ten.
Near Vicksburg, June 16th 1863.

Maj. Gen. Heron,
Comd.g Left Investing Forces,
Gen.

Your position on the line will not now be changed Gen. Parke having been sent to Hain's Bluff with his command. You will push forward therefore as rapidly as possible towards the enemy's lines establishing your batteries on the most commanding positions as you advance.

As soon as you have gained a position giving you a range beyond the Rifle Pitts of the enemy with Artillery, and Infantry commanding every part of your front, inform me of the fact. It is my intention then to shell the town for two hours.[1]

Very respectfully
U. S. Grant
Maj. Gen. Com

ALS, NHi.

1. On June 13, 1863, Act. Rear Admiral David D. Porter wrote to USG. "In case you should want any blowing up of works done—one of the officers I sent you, Mr. Kroehl, has been engaged in that kind of business for some years, and that is his duty in the Squadron. You will find him very expert in all such matters. The Guard, General Sherman sent out, found the boat the rebel officers

escaped in—it was hid in the spot I indicated. I have put the officer on the track of the parties and hope that we may catch them all and perhaps some others. I am going to keep a picket boat about there. I sent out the cavalry of the Brigade to-day, to see if I can hear anything of the rebels. I think they are hovering about Richmond, and having been disappointed in their attack on Milliken's Bend and Young's Point don't know what to do. The rebels are in force 3000 at Island 65, but I am looking out for them. I have ordered Capt Phelps down there with all the vessels that cannot navigate the Tennessee River. I shall open in the morning on the works in front of steele and in that gorge below heavily with a ten inch gun I have mounted on a mortar boat. I intend to place it under the point, 400 yards off from the enemys water battery—please inform General Steele, and let me know by signal how the gun fires. If he will direct the firing from his position I can rake the whole valley where the rebels have their tents." LS (press), DNA, RG 45, Correspondence of David D. Porter, Mississippi Squadron, General Letters. On June 14, USG signaled to Porter. "Yours of the 13th just reched me." Copy, *ibid.*, RG 111, Vicksburg Signal Book. On June 14, Porter signaled to USG. "Three hundred Nine-inch-Shell now ready for you, and waiting transportation" Signal received, *ibid.*, RG 94, War Records Office, Military Div. of the Miss.; copy, *ibid.*, RG 111, Vicksburg Signal Book.

On June 15, Lt. Col. John A. Rawlins telegraphed to Maj. Gen. John A. McClernand, Maj. Gen. James B. McPherson, and Maj. Gen. William T. Sherman. "Fire your artillery as little as possible until you receive orders from here, it being desirable when there is Artillery firing to have it all round the line and continuous for certain periods of time." Copies, DLC-USG, V, 19, 30, 101; DNA, RG 393, Dept. of the Tenn., Letters Sent; (misdated June 16) *ibid.*, 13th Army Corps, Letters Received.

On June 16, USG signaled to Porter. "Can you furnish me with some Sulphur, Nitre and Meal powder. If so I can burn such of Vicksburg as may be desirable." ALS, ViHi. On the same day, Porter signaled to USG. "I have no sulphur or nitre and no powder there is ten at barls at Chickasaw bayou morter powder sent to blow up forts. I am fireing incendiary shells and burn a house now and then" Copy, DNA, RG 111, Vicksburg Signal Book. Also on June 16, USG telegraphed to McClernand. "If you can get furnaces built for heating shot I wish you would do so. Gen. Hoveys position and his 24 pound guns are well adapted to their use" Copies, DLC-USG, V, 19, 30, 101; DNA, RG 393, Dept. of the Tenn., Letters Sent; *ibid.*, 13th Army Corps, Letters Received.

To Maj. Gen. John A. McClernand

Near Vicksburg Miss June 17th 1863

MAJOR GENERAL MCCLERNAND
COMMANDING 13TH ARMY CORPS.
GENERAL:

Enclosed I send you what purports to be your Congratulatory Address to the 13th Army Corps.

I would respectfully ask if it is a true copy. If it is not a correct copy furnish me one by bearer as required ~~to do~~, both by Regulations, and existing orders of the Dept.

> Very respectfully
> U. S. GRANT.
> Maj. General.

Copies, DLC-USG, V, 19, 30, 101; (2—one misdated July 17, 1863) DNA, RG 108, Letters Received; *ibid.*, RG 393, Dept. of the Tenn., Letters Sent; (misdated July 17) *ibid.*, 13th Army Corps, Letters Received; (dated June 17) McClernand Papers, IHi. *O.R.*, I, xxiv, part 1, 102, 159. For General Orders No. 72, issued by Maj. Gen. John A. McClernand on May 30, see *ibid.*, pp. 159–61.

On June 18, Lt. Col. Walter B. Scates, adjt. for McClernand, wrote to Lt. Col. John A. Rawlins. "I have the honor to acknowledge the receipt of Maj. Genl. Grant's despatch to Genl. McClernand in relation to his Address to the Officers and Soldiers of the 13th Army Corps. The Maj. Genl. Comdg. was absent at the time of its receipt and has not yet returned. I hasten to comply with the order of Genl. Grant by enclosing a correct copy of the address." LS, DNA, RG 94, War Records Office, Dept. of the Tenn. Misdated June 13 in *O.R.*, I, xxiv, part 1, 161. On June 18, McClernand telegraphed to USG. "I have Just returned—the newspaper slip is a correct copy of my congratulatory Order No 72   I am prepared to maintain its statements   I regret that my adjt did not Send you a copy promptly as he ought & I thought he had"   Telegram received, DNA, RG 393, Dept. of the Tenn., Telegrams Received. *O.R.*, I, xxiv, part 1, 103; (misdated June 13) *ibid.*, p. 162.

Also on June 18, Rawlins issued Special Orders No. 164. "Major General John A. McClernand is hereby relieved from the command of the 13th Army Corps. He will proceed to any point he may select in the State of Illinois, and report by letter to Head Quarters of the Army, for orders. Major General E. O. C. Ord is hereby appointed to the command of the 13th Army Corps, subject to the approval of the President, and will immediately assume charge of the same." DS, McClernand Papers, IHi. *O.R.*, I, xxiv, part 1, 103, 164–65. On the same day, McClernand wrote to USG. "Your order relieving me and assigning Maj. Genl. Ord to the Command of the 13th Army Corps is recd. Having been appointed by the President to the Command of the Corps, under a definite act of Congress, I might justly challenge your authority in the premises, but forbear to do so, at present. I am quite willing that any statement of fact in my Congratulatory order to the 13th Army Corps, to which you think just exception may be taken, should be made the subject of investigation, not doubting the result." ALS, DNA, RG 94, War Records Office, Dept. of the Tenn. *O.R.*, I, xxiv, part 1, 103, 166.

On June 19, USG telegraphed to Maj. Gen. Henry W. Halleck. "I have found it necessary to relieve Maj Genl. McClernand particularly at this time for his publication of a congratulatory Address calculated to create dissention and ill feeling in the Army. I should have relieved him long since for general unfitness for his position. Maj Gen Ord is appointed to his place subject to the approval of President"   Telegram received, DNA, RG 107, Telegrams Collected (Bound); copies, *ibid.*, Telegrams Received in Cipher; *ibid.*, RG 393, Dept. of the Tenn.,

Hd. Qrs. Correspondence; DLC-USG, V, 6, 8, 24, 94. *O.R.*, I, xxiv, part 1, 43. See letter to Brig. Gen. Lorenzo Thomas, June 26, 1863.

On July 10, Col. Edward D. Townsend, "By direction of the President of the United States," issued AGO Special Orders No. 305 appointing Maj. Gen. Edward O. C. Ord to command the 13th Army Corps as of June 18. *O.R.*, I, xxiv, part 3, 497. On May 25, Townsend had issued Special Orders No. 234 sending Ord to USG. Copy, DLC-USG, V, 105. *O.R.*, I, xxiv, part 3, 351. Ord arrived at Vicksburg on June 18 and assumed command of the 13th Army Corps the next day. *Ibid.*, I, xxiv, part 1, 102; *ibid.*, I, xxiv, part 3, 419.

On June 19, Charles A. Dana telegraphed to Secretary of War Edwin M. Stanton. "Though the congratulatory Address in question is the occasion of Gen McClernands removal, it is not its cause as McClernand intimates, where he says incorrectly that Gen Grant has taken exceptions to this address   That cause as I understand it is his repeated disobedience of important orders—his general insubordinate disposition, and his palpable incompetency for the duties of the position as I learned by private conversation   It was in Gen Grants judgement also necessary that he should be removed for the reason above all, that his relations with other Corps and Commanders rendered it impossible that the Chief Command of this Army should devolve upon him, as it would have done were Gen Grant disabled, without most pernicious consequences to the cause. . . ." Telegram received, DLC-Edwin M. Stanton. *O.R.*, I, xxiv, part 1, 103.

On June 4, McClernand had written to USG. "What appears to be a systematic effort to destroy my usefulness and reputation as a commander, makes it proper that I should address you this note. It is reported among other things, as I understand, that I attacked the enemy's works on the 22nd inst. without authority; again, that I attacked too late; again, that I am responsible for our ~~great~~ failure and losses; again that I am arrested and being sent North; again that my command is turned over to another officer; and again that you have, personally, assumed command of it. These reports are finding their way from the landing, up the river, and are a poor requital for the chief part taken by my Corps and myself in the advance from Millikens Bend to Bruin's Landing; Port Gibson, Champion Hill; Edwards Station and Big Black. I hardly need say to you that all these reports are false—that I obeyed orders in attacking on the 22nd—that my attack was prompt and in a larger measure successful than any other—that the ultimate failure of the general attack and the losses attending it were, under the circumstances, unavoidable consequences of obstacles found to be insurmountable and of a determined effort, at least on my part, to carry and hold the enemy's works in obedience to your express and peremptory order. I may add that I am not yet under arrest or being sent away, or superseded in my Command. All these things being known to you, and these false reports being brought to your notice it remains for you to determine whether truth, justice and generosity do not call on you for such a declaration as will be conclusive in the matter." ALS, DNA, RG 94, War Records Office, Dept. of the Tenn. *O.R.*, I, xxiv, part 1, 165–66.

On June 9, McClernand wrote to USG. "The inaccuracy of the accompanying newspaper slip leads me to believe it is not official; yet, as it purports to be, I have deemed it proper to refer it, together with the accompanying letter from General Hovey and the reports of his brigade commanders, to you, as affording reliable means for all needful correction in the premises. That General Hovey's division, of my corps, bore the brunt at Champion's Hill; that both it and the re-enforcement from General McPherson's corps were temporarily forced back;

and that General Hovey's artillery, which had been massed for that purpose, aided by Captain Dillon's Wisconsin battery, of General McPherson's corps, retrieved and secured the fortune of the day in that part of the field, is susceptible of the clearest and most conclusive proof. After the above, I hardly need say that I am not the author of the newspaper slip referred to." *Ibid.*, I, xxiv, part 2, 48. For the enclosure, see *ibid.*, pp. 47–48.

To Maj. Gen. William T. Sherman

Near Vicksburg June 17th 1863.

MAJ. GEN. SHERMAN

To build the detached works spoken of in your note of last evening I see no way but to divide the work between the 15th and 17th Army Corps   All other troops are too far off

A heavy detail can be got to do the work by collecting Stragglers and working them constantly under guard, and without reference to the Corps they may belong to.

I will have the ground examined with reference to locating these works, and will be glad to have ~~the ground~~ all the information you can gather by having the ground further reconnoitred

Very resply
U. S. GRANT
Maj Gen

Copies, DLC-USG, V, 19, 30, 101; DNA, RG 393, Dept. of the Tenn., Letters Sent. On June 16, 1863, 8:00 P.M., Maj. Gen. William T. Sherman, Walnut Hills, had written to Lt. Col. John A. Rawlins. "Last night in company with Col Wilson I rode up to Snyders Bluff, and this morig examined the Line of pits & Batteries in course of construction. They appear to me well adapted to the end in view and will enable the two Divisions of Kimball and Smith to hold any force comig from the North & North East. I examined in company with Generals Washburn, Kimball & Smith also Col Wilson the vally of the Skillet Goliah and have advised that General Parke dispose his force along that valley, its center near the Church at Mill dale, Left near Snyders, and Right up toward Templetons, where I have a strong Picket. General Parke had not arrived at the hour of my starting back 4 P M, but I saw Steamboats comig which I think contained his troops. The accounts of the enemy brought in from the front were very conflicting, and my inference was that Lorig is feelig his way cautiously down with cavalry and a moderate force of Infantry as far as Post oak Ridge. It seems the cavalry picket drew in from that point last night, but Genl Washburn assured me he would replace them today The 4th Iowa Cavalry have moved by my orders to Wixons, with orders to watch the approaches from Bush's & Birdsongs Ferries. With arrangments now completed the enemy cannot come down the Valley Road, or the Ridge Road via Snyders. If he comes he must come across the head of Clear Creek debouching near Marshalls. That ground cannot well be obstructed, but is advantageous to us and could be rendered more so, by constructing two or three detached Forts, one near Marshalls another at the point where the Bridgeport Road leaves the Benton Road, and another intermediate. If you deem it prudent I will cause the ground to be more closely examined, and works laid off & begun. As you know my Corps has done much labor, but I will do anything and Evything in human power to achieve final success." ALS, *ibid.*, RG 94, War Records Office, Dept. of the Tenn. *O.R.*, I, xxiv, part 3, 415.

To Col. John C. Kelton

———

Headquarters Department of the Tennessee
In Field, Near Vicksburg. Miss. June 18, 1863.

Col. J. C. Kelton
Asst. Adjnt General
Washington, D. C.

Colonel:

I have the honor to acknowledge the receipt, this day, of your communication of date June 8th, asking for a copy of General Orders No 13 from these Headquarters, and stating that no copies of General Orders issued by me this year are on file at the War Department.

I herewith enclose a file of the General Orders issued by me this year, and also beg to state that in each case the orders were mailed to the Adjutant General of the Army, immediately after their publication.

A complete file of my General Orders for 1863, will this day be sent to the War Department

I am, Colonel,
Very Respectfully
Your Obt Serv't
U. S. Grant
Major General

LS, DNA, RG 108, Letters Received. On June 8, 1863, Col. John C. Kelton wrote to USG. "The General in Chief directs me to call for a copy of your General Order No 13 of this year, promulgating the proceeding of a Court Martial in the case of a citizen &c. and to state that no General Orders, issued by you this year, have been received at the War Department." ALS, *ibid.*, RG 393, Dept. of the Tenn., Unregistered Letters Received.

To Act. Rear Admiral David D. Porter

Head Quarters, Dept. of the Ten.
Near Vicksburg, June 18th 1863.

ADMIRAL D. D. PORTER,
COMD.G MISS. SQUADRON,
ADMIRAL.

Your letter of yesterday places the possible intentions of the rebels in a light I had never thought of before. There appears to be a movement of Price's forces to get with Kirby Smith and all must have some bearing upon the siege of Vicksburg. In what way they propose to help Pemberton I do not exactly see but they might, as a last resort, place themselves to facilitate the escape of the men of Pemberton's Army in the way you suggest. The men only could escape. The Artillery and munitions of war would necessarily be left behind.

I have a very reliable man now in Louisian for no other purpose than to discover what orders Smith Price &c. are now executing. I know that orders left Jackson two weeks ago to-day from Jo Johnstone to Kirby Smith and Dick Taylor. I have rather suspected they were to act against Banks whilst Price was to gain a lodgement on the river some place below the Arkansas to interrupt our communications. As soon as I learn anything definite I will let you know.

I regret the stupidity, of the picket in preventing you getting out to camp yesterday. The propensity of officers as well as men to loaf off to the Steamboat landing makes it necessary to give strict orders against persons passing without permits. But the guard could have called his officer who would have passed you without any trouble. I will give orders that Naval officers are to be passed without permits so that the same difficulty will not occur again.

I intended going down to see you to-day but have too much to do to get off.

I hope Admiral you will not be detered by your experiance of yesterday from making us another call.

In a day or two, probably on Saturday,[1] I will be ready to bombard the town from all points. I want to get the batteries well closed up on the left first and think by that time all will be ready.

I will inform you in time.

Very Truly Yours
U. S. GRANT
Maj. Gen.

ALS, MdAN. On June 18, 1863, Act. Rear Admiral David D. Porter wrote to USG. "In two days more I hope to have a hundred pound Rifle, a nine inch and a ten inch gun, well supplied with ammunition and powder, on a Mortar boats under the Point, and within 1400 yards of the water batteries near Gen'l Sherman. By that time I also expect a further supply of Mortars and powder, and I think we will, when your batteries open, get a good cross fire on the Rebels. I sent Gen'l Ellet down to the Point yesterday with a rifle 12 pounder, to try and destroy their boats on the landing. He had it all his own way for a time, but this morning they opened on the Point with every thing they had in the shape of a gun. I am sorry not to have been able to get out to your camp yesterday—I hope Joe Johnson may have as hard a time as I had. You need not apologize for the pickets; for I think they saved my neck, my horse had been dancing about and standing on his hind legs for some time, and it was very uncertain how long it would be before he landed me in Chickasaw Bayou. Capt. Breese who was with me says he thinks I was glad of an excuse to turn back, he admits that he was; as his horse was rather more frisky than suited the habits of a sailor. The next time I start I will go better prepared—I think Price is aiming at Helena to get that and cut off your supplies. He will not get it if Gun boats will stop him. I expect Gen'l Prentice was rather surprised when he found the Gun boats crowding in there. If they should not be wanted, so much the better. all points on the River are well guarded—The Rebels may get possession of this point for a little while, but I think with the arrangements I have made, they will lose half the army if they attempt to cross over—still many could escape. it would soothe their pride to do so—I landed two more shell guns at Warrenton for Gen'l Herron, and sent an officer to attend to them—I hope they will be up by this evening. he thinks he can silence the guns in front of him with them. We will open on them at the same time with the

'Benton.' The 'Benton' unfortunately dropped some shell out over our works yesterday; thinking the Rebs were there, but fortunatly did no damage, and found it out in time to prevent any mishaps. It shows that Gen'l Herron is getting ahead, as the Rebels have been there up to yesterday—" LS, DNA, RG 393, Dept. of the Tenn., Letters Received.

1. June 20.

To Maj. Gen. John G. Parke

Head Quarters, Dept. of the Tenn
Near Vicksburg June 18th 1863

MAJ GEN. J. G. PARKE
COMDG FORCES, HAINES BLUFF.
GENERAL:

No instructions have been sent you heretofore, nor do I deem it specially necessary to send them now, knowing that a vigilant watch will be kept on the movement of the enemy, and any advance he may attempt checked in time.

I want the work of entrenching your position pushed with all dispatch ready to receive an attack if one should be made and to leave the troops free to move out should the enemy remain where he is.

My information now is that Loring's Division is a very strong one consisting of four Brigades is at Benton, or between that and Black River. Walker with his Division is at or near Yazoo City and Evans[1] is near Brownsville. The enemy also have full 4000 Cavalry. These forces if attacked could all be collected on the ridge near Benton before they could be reached from Hain's Bluff. Breckenridge is also at Clinton, too far off to join the Benton force on the first day of Battle should we march on them. I hear no information of any other rebel forces than those named above.

Keep your Cavalry well out and collect all the information you can of the movements of the enemy. Report all that you learn promptly.

No order has been published assigning you to the command of all the forces at Hains Bluff, but being isolated from the general command, and being the senior officer, you necessarilly command the whole.

> I am with great respect
> Your Obt Servt
> U. S. GRANT
> Maj. General

Copies, DLC-USG, V, 19, 30, 101; DNA, RG 393, Dept. of the Tenn., Letters Sent. *O.R.*, I, xxiv, part 3, 418. On June 18, 1863, Maj. Gen. John G. Parke, "Mill Dale," telegraphed to USG. "Your dispatch recd I have issued orders Sending four brigades to occupy the line Extending from A Greens on the Benton Road by way of McCalls to Tiffins on the bridgeport road Can Gen Osterhaus Connect with my troops at Tiffins" Telegram received, DNA, RG 94, War Records Office, Dept. of the Tenn. *O.R.*, I, xxiv, part 3, 418.

Also on June 18, USG telegraphed to Parke. "Can you spare Col Babcock for a few days. If so send Him to Report to me as soon as possible" Telegram received, DNA, RG 94, War Records Office, Dept. of the Ohio. On the same day, Parke, Snyder's Bluff, telegraphed to USG. "Col Babcock & I are making an examination of our front and will be able to locate a good line of defense Extending from Genl Washburn to Gen Sherman I would like to keep Col Babcock until the line is staked out & parties put to work Shall I do so I consider it important that Col Babcock should remain" Telegram received, *ibid.*, RG 393, USG Letters Received 1862. On the same day, USG telegraphed again to Parke. "Of course Keep Col. Babcock I[t] was only if you could spare Him that I wanted His Services" Telegram received, *ibid.*, RG 94, War Records Office, Dept. of the Ohio.

1. Nathan G. Evans, born in Marion, S. C., in 1824, USMA 1848, resigned as capt. from the U.S. Army in 1861. He received praise for his conduct at First Bull Run and his commission as brig. gen. dated from his victory at Leesburg (or Ball's Bluff) on Oct. 21. His entire brigade had arrived to join Gen. Joseph E. Johnston by May 25, 1863, and was assigned to the div. of Maj. Gen. William W. Loring. *O.R.*, I, xxiv, part 1, 222; *ibid.*, I, xxiv, part 3, 937.

To Commanding Officers, Edwards Station and Raymond

————

Head Quarters, Dept. of the Ten.
Near Vicksburg, June 19th 1863,

COMD.G OFFICERS
CONFED. FORCES, EDWARDS STATION & RAYMOND,
SIRS:

The bearer of this, Asst. Surgeon J. J. Whitney of the Federal Army goes to Bakers Creek and Raymond for the purpose of removing such wounded Federal soldiers as will bear transportation and for taking supplies, Medical stores &c. for those whos condition requires them to remain where they are for a longer time.

I have been humanely permitted thus far to furnish supplies to the wounded necessarily left in hospital near the field of battle. It will always be my pleasure to reciprocate should it be in my power hereafter to do so.

Very respectfully
your obt. svt.
U. S. GRANT
Maj. Gen.

ALS, DNA, RG 109, Documents Printed in *O.R. O.R.*, I, xxiv, part 3, 419. On June 22, 1863, Brig. Gen. Peter J. Osterhaus, "Big Black," transmitted to Lt. Col. John A. Rawlins a message from C.S.A. Brig. Gen. John W. Whitfield to Asst. Surgeon Joshua J. Whitney, 18th Wis. "In obedience to instructions from Genl Johnstone I must not allow you to enter our lines but will deliver to you at the outer chain of videttes all wounded Federals in hospital within our lines who will bear transportation Any Supplies of medicines &c which you may have brought for such of your wounded as cannot be moved will be received & disposed of in accordance with your wishes" Telegram received, DNA, RG 393, Dept. of the Tenn., Telegrams Received. See *O.R.*, I, xxiv, part 3, 969, 975. On June 22, USG wrote to Osterhaus. "Send the Medicines and Supplies to be used for the use of Federal wounded within Confederate lines, who will not bear removal. All our wounded who may be returned, will be received at our outer lines." Copies, DLC-USG, V, 19, 30, 101; DNA, RG 393, Dept. of the Tenn., Letters Sent.

General Field Orders

———

[June 19th 1863]

GEN. FIELD ORDERS,

At 4 O'Clock a. m on the 20th inst a general cannonading will be commenced from all parts of the line on the city of Vicksburg. Firing will continue until 10 a. m. unless otherwise directed.

Care must be taken to retain for emergency ~~present in camp or with the gun~~ at least 100 rounds each for all the Field Artillery, and twenty Rounds per gun for the siege guns.

All the Rifle pitts will be filled with as many men as can be accommodated in them. Troops will be held under arms from 6½ a. m. ready to take advantage of any signs the enemy may show of weekness or to repel an attack should one be made.

It is not designed to assault the enemy's works but to be prepared. Should Corps Commanders believe a favorable opportunity ~~had~~ presented~~s~~ itself for possessing themselves of any portion of the lines of the enemy, without a serious battle, they will avail themselves of it, telegraphing immediately to HdQrs. ~~what the~~ of other Corps and to Gen. HdQrs. what ~~they had were~~ [they are] doing and suggesting any assistance or cooperation they ~~might~~ [may] require.

ADf, CSmH. Bracketed words not in USG's hand. Issued as Special Orders No. 165 on June 19, 1863, by Lt. Col. John A. Rawlins. Copies, DLC-USG, V, 27, 28; DNA, RG 393, Dept. of the Tenn., General and Special Orders; *ibid.*, Special Orders. *O.R.*, I, xxiv, part 3, 418–19. On June 19, USG signaled to Act. Rear Admiral David D. Porter. "I Shal bombard Vicksburg from four A. M. to ten tomorrow" Copy, DNA, RG 111, Vicksburg Signal Book. On June 20, Porter wrote to USG. "I was sorry not to be able to [assist] in the way of bombarding, this morning, but the enclosed letter will [ex]plain the reason. Unless you come to my assistance my gunboat will be laid up. I obtained [. . .] thirty five wagons for one day only in obedience to your order. I presume the demand for them here very great and the officers cannot supply [them]. If you would send me 30 wagons from Chickasaw Bayou and place them entirely under my control with orders for forage &c I would in a short time with hard work get my lower fleet in order again. As it is they are quite helpless." LS (press), *ibid.*, RG 45, Correspondence of David D. Porter, Mississippi Squadron, General Letters. On June 20, USG signaled to Porter. "I will have 50 wagons for you to-morrow to be used expressly for hauling coal" Copy, *ibid.*, RG 111, Vicksburg Signal Book. On June 22,

USG signaled to Porter. "On the 20th before Receiving your letter, I orderd Quarter Master 50 wagons to ~~be~~ be exclusively for hauling coal for the use of the navy" Copy, *ibid*. On June 23, USG signaled to Porter. "The quartermaster reported to me yesterday that 40 wagons were hauling coal I have repeated my orders however that coal must be hauled" Copy, *ibid*.

To Abraham Lincoln

Headquarters Department of the Tennessee,
Near Vicksburg, June 19, 1863.

Hon. A. Lincoln,
President of the United States:

Sir: I beg leave very respectfully to call your particular attention to the inclosed letter from Maj. Gen. W. T. Sherman to me on the subject of filling the old regiments of the Army from the contemplated draft. I would add that our old regiments, all that remains of them, are veterans equaling regulars in discipline, and far superior to them in the material of which they are composed. A recruit added to them would become an old soldier, from the very contact, before he was aware of it.

Company and regimental officers, camp and garrison equipage, transportation and everything are already provided. He would cost Government nothing but his pay and allowances, and would render efficient services from the start. Placed in a new organization all these things are to be provided. Officers and men have to go through months of schooling, and, from ignorance of how to cook and provide for themselves, the ranks become depleted one-third before valuable services can be expected.

Taken in an economic point of view, one drafted man in an old regiment is worth three in a new one.

I am, sir, with great respect, your obedient servant,

U. S. Grant,
Major-General.

O.R., III, iii, 386. On June 2, 1863, Maj. Gen. William T. Sherman, Walnut Hills, wrote to USG. "I would most respectfully suggest that you use your personal influence with President Lincoln to accomplish a result on which it may be the ultimate peace and security of our country depends. I mean his use of the draft to fill up our old regiments. I see by the public journals that a draft is to be made, and that 100,000 men are to be assigned to fill up the old regiments, and 200,000 to be organized as new troops. I do not believe that Mr. Lincoln, or any man, would, at this critical period of our history, repeat the fatal mistakes of last year. Taking this army as a fair sample of the whole, what is the case? The regiments do not average 300 men, nor did they exceed that strength last fall. When the new regiments joined us in November and December, their rolls contained about 900 names, whereas now their ranks are even thinner than the older organizations. All who deal with troops in fact instead of theory know that the knowledge of the little details of camp life is absolutely necessary to keep men alive. New regiments, for want of this knowledge, have measles, mumps, diarrhea, and the whole catalogue of infantile diseases; whereas the same number of men, distributed among the older regiments, would learn from the sergeants and corporals and privates the art of taking care of themselves, which would actually save their lives and preserve their health against the host of diseases that invariably attack the new regiments. Also recruits, distributed among older companies, catch up, from close and intimate contact, a knowledge of drill, the care and use of arms, and all the instructions which otherwise it would take months to impart. The economy, too, should recommend the course of distributing all the recruits as privates to the old regiments, but these reasons appear to me so plain that it is ridiculous for me to point them out to you, or even to suggest them to an intelligent civilian. I am assured by many that the President does actually desire to support and sustain the army, and that he desires to know the wishes and opinions of the officers who serve in the woods instead of in the 'salon.' If so, you would be listened to. It will take at least 600 good recruits per regiment to fill up the present army to the proper standard. Taking one thousand as the number of regiments in actual existence, this would require 600,000 recruits. It may be the industrial interests of the country will not authorize such a call. But how much greater the economy to make an army and fight out this war at once? See how your success is checked by the want of prompt and adequate re-enforcements to guard against a new enemy gathering to our rear. Could your regiments be filled up to even the standard of 700 men for duty, you would be content to finish quickly and well the work so well begun. If a draft be made, and the men be organized into new regiments, instead of filling up the old, the President may satisfy a few aspiring men, but will prolong the war for years, and allow the old regiments to die of natural exhaustion. I have several regiments who have lost honestly in battle and by disease more than half their original men, and the wreck, or remainder, with colonel, lieutenant-colonel, major, ten captains, &c., and a new squad of men, reminds us of the army of Mexico—all officers and no men. It would be an outrage to consolidate these old, tried, and veteran regiments, and bring in the new and comparatively worthless bodies. But fill up our present ranks, and there is not an officer or man of this army but would feel renewed hope and courage to meet the struggles before us. I regard this matter as more important than any other that could possibly arrest the attention of President Lincoln, and it is for this reason that I ask you to urge it upon him at this auspicious time. If adopted, it would be more important than the conquest of Vicksburg and Richmond together, as it would be a victory of common sense over the popular fallacies that have ruled and almost ruined our country." *Ibid.*, I, xxiv, part 3, 372–73; *ibid.*, III, iii, 386–88.

On July 14, Maj. Gen. Henry W. Halleck wrote to USG. "Your letter to the President of June 19th, forwarding one from Genl Sherman to you of June 2d, in regard to filling up old regiments with drafted men, has been sent to me for reply. The course you recommend was determined on by the War Dept some time ago, and will be carried out as soon as the draft is made. Permit me to call your attention to the propriety of sending such communications through the proper military channels. They will in that way recieve an earlier attention, for there is always much delay in in referring them back. Moreover, that course will be in compliance with Army Regulations and the usages of service." ALS, DNA, RG 94, War Records Office, Dept. of the Tenn. *O.R.*, III, iii, 487.

To Maj. Gen. Edward O. C. Ord

Near Vicksburg, June 19th 1863

GEN. ORD:

The island referred to by Contraband must be where Jeff and Joe Davis' plantations are. Of course no such rumor as a large force being there can be true. You had better send your Cavalry to Hankersons Ferry to Scout down Black River, from there to the Miss and up by Warrenton to see if they can discover anything. Hines County is beyond Black River. Get batteries as well advanced as possible during the day and night. We want a general cannonading tomorrow. Gen. Lauman you know is attached to your corps.

U. S. GRANT
Maj Gen'l.

Copies, DLC-USG, V, 19, 30, 101; DNA, RG 393, Dept. of the Tenn., Letters Sent; *ibid.*, 13th Army Corps, Letters Received. On June 19, 1863, Maj. Gen. Edward O. C. Ord telegraphed to USG. "Col Whiting at Warrenton writes that a contraband tells him he heard his Master, that Genl Johnston is on an Island in Hines County Miss with one hundred & fifty thousand men & is going to attack us also Warrenton   Col Whiting is about to arrange Signal to all the Gunboats to his aid if necessary   I find Genl Smith pretty well advanced   he can mine the parapet of a redoubt tonight or tomorrow   Is now in the ditch   Shall I tell him to mine or Shall I get Batteries well advanced on every approach"   Telegram received, *ibid.*, Dept. of the Tenn., Telegrams Received.

Also on June 19, USG telegraphed to Ord. "There is a citizen living about four miles from your Headquarters, who I understand is scouting about the county very suspiciously. He rides a very fine brown stallion, and may be known by the Provost Marshal 13th Corps. Arrest him and have the horse kept by some one of your staff until it is determined what should be done with him." Copies, DLC-USG, V, 19, 30, 101; DNA, RG 393, Dept. of the Tenn., Letters Sent; *ibid.*, 13th Army Corps, Letters Received; *ibid.*, Letters Sent.

Also on June 19, Lt. Col. John A. Rawlins wrote to Ord. "There is a partially organized regiment of Colored troops in your corps. Please order them together with their women and children to proceed at once to Chickasaw Bayou Landing, where they will go into Camp and furnish such details for fatigue duty as may be required in the Commissary, Ordnance and Quartermaster's Department at that place; and at the same time complete their organization." Copies, DLC-USG, V, 19, 30, 101; DNA, RG 393, Dept. of the Tenn., Letters Sent; *ibid.*, 13th Army Corps, Letters Received. On the same day, 8:30 P.M., Ord telegraphed to USG. "Capt Haines reports that the fourth Miss Col Ourd is very necessary working by day in the trenches   Cannot I keep them for that work a few days longer & thus save the men of other regts" Telegram received, *ibid.*, Dept. of the Tenn., Telegrams Received.

To Act. Rear Admiral David D. Porter

Head Quarters Dept of the Tennessee
Near Vicksburg June 21st 1863

ADMIRAL D. D. PORTER
COMDG MISS SQUADRON.
ADMIRAL:—

Information received from Vicksburg last night confirms your theory of the probable method Pemberton will take for escaping in the last extremity. One of our Pickets and one of the enemy by mutual consent laid down their arms, met half way and had a long conversation. The rebel said that our cannonading killed and wounded a great many in the rifle pits, otherwise done no great damage. They fully counted upon an assault as being intended and were prepared for it. Finding that no assault was made, the feelings of the troops was canvassed to see if they could be got out to attack the Yankees   They not only declined this, but those on the right and left almost mutinied because their officers would not surrender. They were only reassured and persuaded to continue on duty by being told that they had provisions enough on hand to last seven days. In that time they would have

2000 boats finished, and they could make their escape by the river. The rebel said they were tearing down houses to get the material out of which to build boats.

I will direct Mower (Gen) to keep a strong Picket in the river in front of Vicksburg at night, to place his battery behind the levees or hold it in some good position to be used if an attempt should be made to escape in that way. If possible fix up Material to light and illuminate the river should a large number of boats attempt to cross.

I will direct Gen Mower to call on you, and consult as to the best plan for defeating this method of escape. You will find Gen Mower an intelligent and gallant officer, capable of carrying out any plan that may be adopted

> Very truly your Obt Servt
> U. S. GRANT
> Maj. Genl.

Copies, DLC-USG, V, 19, 30, 101; DNA, RG 393, Dept. of the Tenn., Letters Sent. *O.R.*, I, xxiv, part 3, 423–24; *O.R.* (Navy), I, xxv, 85–86. On June 22, 1863, Act. Rear Admiral David D. Porter wrote to USG. "I have received yours in relation to the movements of the enemy and have been prepared for it for some-days. I have three rifled guns right in front of the town under charge of Col' Ellet and fifty sharp-shooters   All the rest of the Brigade are stationed on the lower end of the canal and in the woods with six pieces of Artillery. The Gun boats all have their orders if they get coal but I am sorry to say that no attention has been paid to your orders about carts   A System of signals has been established all along the levee—and and with the Gun boats which are ordered to rush on regard-less of every thing and swamp the boats with their wheels   I would recommend that two of your best side wheel steamers transports be got ready with about two hundred soldiers on each to destroy the boats as they try to escape. I know they have many skiffs and every man is making a paddle—so a deserter tells us —The De Kalb and Forrest Rose are at Haines Bluff—I will have three gun boats at Millikens Bend, three at Youngs Point, three from the head of the canal stretching along the River and one covering this point—Look out strong the Rebels dont come up stream in the eddy, and escape by the Bayou where the Cincinatti is—I have sixty (60) bbls tar with which I will illuminate the River—I will look out—only I wish I had coal—it makes me very helpless without it" LS, DNA, RG 393, Dept. of the Tenn., Letters Received.

On June 22, Lt. Col. John A. Rawlins rewrote USG's letter to Porter in the form of a letter to Brig. Gen. Elias S. Dennis, with some detailed instructions at the end. Copy, DLC-USG, V, 101. Entered as written by USG *ibid.*, V, 19, 30. *O.R.*, I, xxiv, part 3, 426. On June 22, USG wrote to Dennis. "There is some probability of an attack here by Jo Johnston within the next twenty four or forty eight hours. In such case an attack upon you is not at all impossible. You will therefore exercise unusual vigelence in your preparations to receive an attack. Keep your cavalry out as far as possible to report any movements of the enemy, and confer with Admiral Porter that their may be unanimity in your action." Copies, DLC-USG, V, 19, 30, 101; DNA, RG 393, Dept. of the Tenn., Letters Sent. *O.R.*, I, xxiv, part 3, 427; *O.R.* (Navy), I, xxv, 90–91. On the same day, Dennis wrote to USG. "I have the honor to acknowledge the receipt of dispatches from you of this date. A Cavalry reconnoisance that I ordered in the direction of Richmond returned night before last, and report that they proceeded as far as Richmond, and found no force there, or any indications of an enemy in that vicinity. The enemy in their retreat burned the bridge over Tensas Bayou, and are undoubtedly beyond Delhi. From what I can learn the Rebels are unquestionably building Skiffs and flat boats at Vicksburg. You may rest assured, General, if they intend an attack upon us, they will not catch us napping." LS, DNA, RG 94, War Records Office, Union Battle Reports. *O.R.*, I, xxiv, part 3, 427.

To Maj. Gen. Richard Taylor

Near Vicksburg Miss. June 22. 1863

BRIG. GEN. R. TAYLOR,
COMD'G CONFED. FORCES,
DELHI, LA.

Upon the evidence of a white man, a citizen of the south, I learn that a white Captain and some negroes, captured at Millikens Bend, La, in the late skirmish at that place, were hanged soon after at Richmond. He informs me that a white Sergeant, captured by Harrison's Cavalry at Perkins' plantation, was hung.

My forces captured some six or eight prisoners in the same skirmish who have been treated as prisoners of war notwithstanding they were caught fighting under the "Black Flag of "No Quarter"

I feel no inclination to retaliate for the offences of irresponsible persons, but if it is the policy of any General entrusted with the command of troops to show "no quarter," or to punish with death prisoners taken in battle, I will accept the issue.

It may be you propose a different line of policy towards Black troops and Officers commanding them to that practiced towards

White troops? If so I can assure you that these colored troops are regularly mustered into the service of the United States. The Government and all Officers under the Government are bound to give the same protection to these troops that they do to any other troops.

Col. Kilby Smith of the United States Volunteers service and Col. John Riggin A. A. D. C. U. S. Army go as bearers of this and will return any reply you may wish to make.

Hoping there may be some mistake in the evidence furnished me, or that the act of hanging had no official sanction and that the parties guilty of it will be duly punished, I remain &c.

U. S. Grant.

Maj. General.

Copies, DLC-USG, V, 19, 30, 101; (2) DNA, RG 108, Letters Received; *ibid.*, RG 393, Dept. of the Tenn., Letters Sent. *O.R.*, I, xxiv, part 3, 425–26. Richard Taylor, born near Louisville in 1826, graduated from Yale, managed the plantation of his father, President Zachary Taylor, in Miss., and then established his own sugar plantation in La., where he served in the state senate (1856–61). Appointed col., 9th La., on July 6, 1861, he was appointed brig. gen. as of Oct. 21, promoted to maj. gen. as of July 28, 1862, then assigned to command the District of West La.

On June 16, 1863, Lt. Commander Elias K. Owen, U.S.S. *Louisville*, Grand Gulf, wrote to Act. Rear Admiral David D. Porter. "The following persons were received on board this vessel—June 14—1863—James Henry—and William D Shoemaker, deserters from 12th Arkansas Regt. Sharp Shooters—Thomas Cormal, deserter from Major Harrisons Battery Light Artillery—also his wife June 15 —1863—George Ferris, from Rodney, Jeff Co Miss.—deserter from Capt Powers detachment of Sharp Shooters—Thomas Cormal witnessed the hanging at Richmond La. of the white Captain and negroes, captured at Millikens Bend—Gen Taylor and Command were drawn up to witness the execution—It is also reported by this man, that the Sargent who commanded a company of Contrabands, and who was captured by Harrisons Cavalry some weeks ago was also hung at Perkins Landing" Copy, DNA, RG 108, Letters Received. *O.R.*, I, xxiv, part 3, 425. On June 19, Porter wrote to USG. "I enclose you a letter from Capt Owens, in relation to the hanging of one of your Officers by G[en] Taylor who also should be hung himself on the spot if ever taken—or any of his gang—It appears he is at the head of the troops at Delhi—" LS (press), DNA, RG 45, Correspondence of David D. Porter, Mississippi Squadron, General Letters. On June 22, USG wrote to Brig. Gen. Lorenzo Thomas. "Enclosed herewith please find copy of letter from Admiral Porter to me and one sent by me to Gen. Taylor of the Confederate Army. As soon as a reply is rec'd I will send that also to Hd Qrs. of the Army." ALS, *ibid.*, RG 108, Letters Received. *O.R.*, I, xxiv, part 3, 425; *ibid.*, II, vi, 32. For Taylor's reply, see letter to Maj. Gen. Richard Taylor, July 4, 1863.

To Act. Rear Admiral David D. Porter

Head Quarters, Dept. of the Ten.
Near Vicksburg, June 22d 1863.

ADMIRAL PORTER,
COMD.G MISS. SQUADRON,
ADMIRAL,

There is every indication of Jo Johnstone making an attack within the next forty eight hours. I have given all the necessary orders to meet him some twenty-five miles out, Sherman commanding. As Johnstone undoubtedly communicates with the garrison in Vicksburg, and the troops West of the Miss, there is probably an understanding by which there may be a simultaneous attack upon Youngs Point, our lines here and by Johnstone on the outside.

I will direct Gen. Dennis to be vigilent and not allow the enemy to approach without timely notice to his troops. Millikin's Bend in such case may come in for a visit also. I would think it advisable therefore to keep one Gunboat there.

My hands will be very full here in case of an attack. I will direct Gen. Dennis therefore to consult with you in all matters relating to defences on the West side of the river.

Very Truly your obt. svt.
U. S. GRANT
Maj. Gen.

ALS, MdAN. *O.R.*, I, xxiv, part 3, 429; *O.R.* (Navy), I, xxv, 90.

On June 22, 1863, USG signaled to Act. Rear Admiral David D. Porter. "I am Sending a Cavalry force to Bruinsburg on important Service   Can you furnish a Convoy." Copy, DNA, RG 111, Vicksburg Signal Book. On the same day, Porter signaled to USG. "The Louisville is at Grand-Gulf and will accompany the Officer on your Order. Please state how long the vessel will be needed." Signal received, *ibid.*, RG 94, War Records Office, Military Div. of the Miss.; copy, *ibid.*, RG 111, Vicksburg Signal Book. On the same day, USG signaled to Porter. "As Soon As the troops debark the vessel can return"   Copy, *ibid.* Also on June 22, Porter signaled to USG. "Do the troops for 'Bruinsburg' embark at 'Warrenton'"   Copy, *ibid.*; (intercepted) *ibid.*, RG 109, Pemberton Papers. On the same day, USG signaled to Porter. "Yes, they embark at warrenton" Copy, *ibid.*, RG 111, Vicksburg Signal Book.

To Maj. Gen. Francis J. Herron

———

June 22d 1863.

GEN. HERRON.

Be ready to move with your Division at the shortest notice with two days cooked rations in haversacks. Your wagon trains should follow with Ammunition and what rations they can carry as soon as possible. Be prepared to leave neither Ammunition or provisions in case of being ordered off.

U. S. GRANT
Maj. Gen.

ALS, ICHi.
On June 22, 1863, Maj. Gen. Francis J. Herron telegraphed to USG. "I need more heavy guns have you any objections to my calling on Admiral Porter for the use of two 42 pdr rifles" Telegram received, DNA, RG 393, Dept. of the Tenn., Telegrams Received. On the same day, USG wrote to Herron. "You need not call on the Navy for guns just now. An attack from Johnston within forty-eight hours is not improbable. Should the forces at present indicated be insufficient to cope with him, your Division will be withdrawn and sent to reinforce them." Copies, DLC-USG, V, 19, 30, 101; DNA, RG 393, Dept. of the Tenn., Letters Sent. *O.R.*, I, xxiv, part 3, 427. Also on June 22, Herron wrote to USG. "Have pushed my left farther up, and occupy a position within 200 yards of their left works. Have taken two rifle-pits and 10 prisoners alive and 1 wounded. No loss on our side." *Ibid.*, I, xxiv, part 2, 317.

To Maj. Gen. James B. McPherson

———

Near Vicksburg June 22, 1863

GEN McPHERSON:

There is indication that Johnston will attack within forty-eight hours; Notify McArthur to be in readiness to move at a moments notice on Sherman's Order. Sherman goes out to meet Johnston if he comes. The greatest Vigilance will be required on the line, as the Vicksburg Garrison may take the same occasion for an attack, also. Batteries should have a good supply of grape and canister.

U. S. GRANT
Maj. Genl

Copies, DLC-USG, V, 19, 30, 101; DNA, RG 393, Dept. of the Tenn., Letters Sent. *O.R.*, I, xxiv, part 3, 427.

To Maj. Gen. Edward O. C. Ord

June 22 1863

There is now every probability of an attack from "Johnston" within 48 hours   Osterhaus' should be reinforced immediately with the remainder of his Brigade ~~in~~ to enable him to withstand a Cavalry attack—The attack will come from the Black river from above Bridgeport—instruct Osterhaus in case it becomes nescessary to abandon his position to effectually destroy the Bridge and join Sherman who goes out to meet the Enemy about Bear Creek —Your forces should have strong Pickets to the rear to guard against a Cavalry dash

U S GRANT
Maj. Genl. Vol.

Telegram received, DNA, RG 94, War Records Office, 16th Army Corps; copies, *ibid.*, RG 393, Dept. of the Tenn., Letters Sent; DLC-USG, V, 19, 30, 101. *O.R.*, I, xxiv, part 3, 427–28. On June 22, 1863, Maj. Gen. William T. Sherman telegraphed to USG. "I have seen your telegraph to genl ord   will come to my Hd Qrs at once prepared for any orders or instructions" Telegram received, DNA, RG 94, War Records Office, Dept. of the Tenn.

On June 22, Maj. Gen. Edward O. C. Ord telegraphed to USG. "Shall I send the batteries belonging to Osterhaus brigade which was left here   One of them is a 20 pdr battery the other ~~of~~ three inch Rodman" Telegram received, *ibid.*, RG 393, Dept. of the Tenn., Telegrams Received. On the same day, USG twice wrote to Ord. "Send such guns to Osterhaus as you can spare. You need not send any that are in position unless he is with out cannon." "Hold A. J. Smith's Division in readiness to move out to Shermans' assisstance Should it prove necessary with two days rations cooked in havrsacks. He should take his light batteries and ordnance train; and two or three days rations in wagons should follow as soon as possible. In case of taking Smith away, his rifle pits must be manned from Divisions to his left." Copies, DLC-USG, V, 19, 30, 101; DNA, RG 393, Dept. of the Tenn., Letters Sent. On the same day, Ord telegraphed to USG. "Piquets in A J Smiths front report firing by volleys about Eleven 11 oclock last night among the rebels behind works near them they could not see the flash It was not at our line & the sound come from the Nor west ~~there~~ three volleys at intervals of twenty minutes with Scattering Shots the vollys appeared too Strong to come from details executing Sentences" Telegram received, *ibid.*, Telegrams Received.

To Maj. Gen. John G. Parke

Near Vicksburg June 22d 1863

MAJ. GEN PARKE.

Loring has crossed a portion of his troops below Vernon.[1] An attack is contemplated evidently by way of Bear Creek and that within two days. Move out four Brigades of your command to Support your cavalry and obstruct their advance as near Black River as possible until all the forces to Spare can be brought against them. Travel with as little baggage as possible, and use your teams as an ordnance and Supply train to get out all you may want from the River. The enemy once fixed upon any ground, all the forces from Hain's Bluff can be taken to the attack and a large number from here also. Move out early tomorrow morning or sooner if you can

U. S. GRANT
Maj. Genl.

Copies, DLC-USG, V, 19, 30, 101; DNA, RG 393, Dept. of the Tenn., Letters Sent. *O.R.*, I, xxiv, part 3, 428.

On June 20, 1863, USG wrote to Maj. Gen. John G. Parke. "Have all the boats you can unloaded and discharged as soon as possible." Copies, DLC-USG, V, 19, 30, 101; DNA, RG 393, Dept. of the Tenn., Letters Sent. On the same day, USG telegraphed to Parke. "Relieve Shermans Picket station at Templetons with one equally strong from your command Notify Sherman by Telegraph when it is done" Telegram received, *ibid.*, RG 94, War Records Office, Dept. of the Ohio; copies, *ibid.*, RG 393, Dept. of the Tenn., Letters Sent; DLC-USG, V, 19, (misdated June 22) 30, 101. On June 22, Parke telegraphed to USG. "I have moved one 1 brigade out to Templeton another will go out to Hoges Mrs Campbells on the benton road & the other two will move early in the morning I now go to meet Gen Sherman at Templetons" Telegram received, DNA, RG 94, War Records Office, Dept. of the Tenn.; copy, *ibid.*, RG 393, 9th Army Corps, Letters Sent.

On June 21, Parke telegraphed to USG. "I have been informed that batty L & M 3rd U S artillery while en route to Join my command was detained by Gen Asboth at Columbus & ordered to be disembarked" Telegram received (misdated June 22), *ibid.*, Dept. of the Tenn., Telegrams Received; copy, *ibid.*, 9th Army Corps, Letters Sent. On June 22, Lt. Col. John A. Rawlins wrote to Maj. Gen. Stephen A. Hurlbut. "Maj. Gen. J. G. Parke, Commanding 9th Army Corps, represents that Brig Gen. Asboth, stopped Batteries "L" and "M," 3d U. S. Artillery, belonging to his Corps, while en route for this place, and ordered them to debark at Columbus. You will please inquire into this matter at once, and direct Gen. Asboth to send forward these Batteries without delay." LS, *ibid.*, RG 94, War Records Office, Military Div. of the Miss. On June 29, Brig. Gen. Alexander Asboth, Columbus, Ky., wrote an explanation of the detention of the batteries and on June 30 reported that they had left for Memphis. DLC-USG, V, 22; DNA, RG 393, Dept. of the Tenn., Register of Letters Received.

1. On June 22, USG wrote to Brig. Gen. Peter J. Osterhaus. "Loring is reported South of Vernon, along Black River. Try and ascertain if any preparations are making to cross the river." Copies, DLC-USG, V, 19, 30, 101; DNA, RG 393, Dept. of the Tenn., Letters Sent. On the same day, Osterhaus, "Big Black," telegraphed to USG. "A pretty smart Contraband Just comes into our lines   he left Mobile on Tuesday the 9th inst passed through Jackson thence he went to Raymond Utica & to our lines on the Edwards Station road   there were but very few troops at Mobile & at Jackson either   at the latter place not over two thousand five hundred men   in his very circuitous route from Jackson he only met small patrols from at Raymond   nobody at Utica" Telegram received, *ibid.*, Telegrams Received. Also on June 22, Osterhaus wrote three times to USG. "A dispatch from Bridgeport, come in at this moment, reports that 125 men of the Fourth Iowa Cavalry, stationed near Messinger's, were attacked by 500 rebel cavalry and badly cut up, and about 40 men of the Iowa cavalry were either killed, wounded, or captured; also one small gun was taken by the enemy. Our cavalry were blockading the road when they were surprised." "The commanders of the different pickets have just reported all quiet on the Jackson road. My patrol found a rebel cavalry squad near Edwards Station; fired at it and drove it to Baker's Creek, where the officer considered it prudent to desist the chase, the woods being reported full of rebels. There is no regular camp this side of Champion's Hill. Yesterday a regiment of rebels passed Edwards Station, going south. It has not yet returned. It is undoubtedly the same troops which were observed by my patrols on the Baldwin's Ferry road, on east side of river. Nobody living any more between here and Champion's Hill who could give any information; even negroes are secesh." "Colonel Wright, commanding the Missouri cavalry now opposite Bridgeport, [reports] in relation to the fight this p. m. as follows: The fight of the Fourth Iowa was near the junction of Bridgeport and Vicksburg and Jones' Ferry roads. Four companies of Fourth Iowa were blockading Vicksburg and Jones' Ferry road when some 600 or 800 rebels charged on them. The rebels crossed the river at Jones' or Birdsong crossing. My men have reconnoitered 2 miles up the river, and found all quiet at present. My impression is that the rebels have recrossed the river. I anticipate no trouble to-night, but may have

to-morrow. I shall be on the alert.['] The Forty-second Ohio and four companies of Twenty-second Kentucky Infantry, under Colonel Lindsey, have just arrived." *O.R.*, I, xxiv, part 2, 225–26.

On June 25, Osterhaus wrote to USG. "All quiet. Scouts from the east side of river report a picket (60 men) near Bridgeport, and a camp 2 miles back of Messinger's. Other cavalry is stationed at Queen's Hill Church, and north and south of Bolton. This statement is corroborated by that of a deserter of the Sixth Texas Cavalry, who came into my line yesterday, and gives the cavalry force in this vicinity as follows: First Texas Legion, 160 strong; Third Texas Cavalry, 300 strong; Sixth Texas Cavalry, 250 strong; Ninth Texas Cavalry, 250 strong; total 960 men, under General [J. W.] Whitfield. There is another cavalry brigade (Mississippians), about 2,000 strong, stationed near Big Black, on the direct road from Canton to Haynes' Bluff. Vernon east [north?] of this. Two brigades, one rifled 6-pounder gun and one 12-pounder howitzer with it. I don't anticipate attack at present. The section of artillery has reported, and is stationed at Bovina." *Ibid.*, pp. 226–27.

To Maj. Gen. John G. Parke

June 22d 1863

GEN. PARKE

Sherman goes out from here with five Brigades and Osterhaus Division subject to his order besides. In addition to this another Division 5000 strong is notified to be in readiness to move on notice. In addition to this I can spare still another Division 6000 strong if they should be require[d.] We want to whip Johnstone at least fifteen miles off—if possible.

U. S GRANT
Maj. Gen.

ALS (telegram sent), NN; telegram received, DNA, RG 94, War Records Office, Dept. of the Ohio. *O.R.*, I, xxiv, part 3, 428.

On June 22, 1863, Maj. Gen. John G. Parke, Milldale, Miss., twice telegraphed to USG. "One of the Cavalry men sent out this morning on patrol has returned and reported that a detachment of the 4th Iowa Cav on beyond Bear Creek blockading roads were attacked by a force of 1000 Cavalry and driven back to this side of the Creek   Two hundred of our men are reported missing   The Rebels have not yet Crossed   Reinforcements have been sent out." Copy, DNA, RG 393, 9th Army Corps, Letters Sent. *O.R.*, I, lii, part 1, 363. "Can I use the negroes now with Gen Washburn a few days" Telegram received, DNA, RG 393, Dept. of the Tenn., Telegrams Received; copy, *ibid.*, 9th Army Corps, Letters Sent. On the same day, USG wrote to Parke. "Certainly use the negroes and everything with in your command to the best advantage." Copies, DLC–USG, V, 19, 30, 101; DNA, RG 393, Dept. of the Tenn., Letters Sent.

To Maj. Gen. William T. Sherman

Head Quarters, Dept. of the Tenn.
Near Vicksburg June 22. 1863

Maj Gen'l W. T. Sherman.

Information just received indicates that the enemy are crossing Black River, and intend marching against us by way of Bear Creek. They probably will start out tomorrow. I have ordered Parke to move out with four Brigades to support his Cavalry and hold the enemy as near Black River as possible until their position is clearly defined when we can draw all our forces from Snyders Bluff and the forces previously indicated here to their support. Tuttles Division should be marched out within supporting distance of Parke at once. You will go and command the entire force. Your wagon train can move from wherever you may be to Lakes Landing or Snyders Bluff whichever may be the most convenient for supplies and Ordnance stores. When on the ground you can draw troops from Snyders Bluff, and the three Brigades designated from McPhersons Corps directly without communicating through Headquarters. Should any force become necessary I can take them from our left, by leaving that in the same condition it was before the arrival of Lauman & Herron.

Yours &c
U. S. Grant
Maj Genl

Copies, DLC–USG, V, 19, 30, 101; DNA, RG 393, Dept. of the Tenn., Letters Sent. *O.R.*, I, xxiv, part 3, 428.

To Maj. Gen. Francis J. Herron

Near Vicksburg June 23. 1863

Gen'l. Herron:

Heavy firing is reported on our left. Is it in your front? What are the indications?

U. S. Grant
Maj. Genl.

Copies, DLC-USG, V, 19, 30, 101; DNA, RG 393, Dept. of the Tenn., Letters Sent.

On June 23, 1863, 2:00 A.M., Maj. Gen. Francis J. Herron wrote to USG. "Have just taken another rifle-pit and 13 prisoners in moving up my right line of skirmishers. Will be ready for your final orders to move. I believe I can go into the enemy's works from this position to-morrow night." *O.R.*, I, xxiv, part 2, 317.

On June 24, Herron twice wrote to USG. "Nothing of special importance has occurred on my front since yesterday. I am still working up my sharpshooters, having them within 150 yards on the left. This morning my right was advanced to within 400 yards of the heavy works. We are constructing deep rifle-pits at every advance, to make the positions perfectly safe. To-night I will finish a heavy battery within 400 yards of the works." "We had a sharp little skirmish this evening while moving farther, but succeeded in gaining the desired position, and captured a lieutenant and 9 men. Our loss, 1 killed and 1 wounded. Several of the enemy were killed and wounded, in addition to those captured. The enemy used light artillery and musketry from their first line of works." *Ibid.*, pp. 317–18.

To Maj. Gen. James B. McPherson

Near Vicksburg June 23d 1863

Gen. McPherson.

Genl Ord reports the firing on his left, as if a Sally were being made. Have your forces in readiness for any action

U. S. Grant
Maj. Genl

Copies, DLC-USG, V, 19, 101, 103; DNA, RG 393, Dept. of the Tenn., Letters Sent. On June 23, 1863, Maj. Gen. James B. McPherson wrote to USG. "Heavy and rapid musketry and artillery firing on the left and center apparently of General Ord's corps. What does it purport?" *O.R.*, I, xxiv, part 3, 430.

On June 23, USG telegraphed to Maj. Gen. Edward O. C. Ord. "You need only fire when you see something to fire at. it is not necessary to keep up a constant fire—" Copy, DNA, RG 393, 13th Army Corps, Letters Received. On the same day, Ord wrote to USG. "Pretty lively firing on my left, as if a sally. I have sent to Lauman and Hovey, if an attack occurs on either side of them, to re-enforce the point attacked." *O.R.*, I, xxiv, part 2, 208.

Also on June 23, Ord telegraphed to Lt. Col. John A. Rawlins. "I understand those ~~are~~ six 6 thirty 30 pounder parrott guns have arrived at Chickasaw Landing   Cannot I get three for this Corps   Gen McPherson has three 3 belonging to me. We need thim very much"   Telegram received, DNA, RG 393, Dept. of the Tenn., Telegrams Received.

On June 23, Rawlins wrote to Ord. "The enclosed extracts of Special Orders No 169, prohibiting communications between ours and the enemys Pickets, is not intended to interfere with the Arrangements you and the General Commanding was speaking of today, nor with any future arrangements you may desire to make, with a view of obtaining information from the enemy that you think can be obtained through his pickets"   Copies, DLC-USG, V, 19, 101, 103; DNA, RG 393, Dept. of the Tenn., Letters Sent. On the same day, Rawlins issued Special Orders No. 169. "All talk conversation exchanging of Papers or other friendly intercourse between our pickets and those of the enemy is hereby positively prohibited, and any violation of this order by officers or men will be summarily punished." Copies, DLC-USG, V, 27, 28; DNA, RG 393, Dept. of the Tenn., Special Orders.

On June 24, Ord telegraphed to USG. "Shall I direct Gen Smith to return his light guns into position or put others in their places"   Telegram received, *ibid.*, Telegrams Received. On the same day, Ord wrote twice more to USG. "The firing last night was a sortie on Lauman's front, resulting in the loss of 1 man killed and 4 slightly [wounded]. The enemy was driven back and the work continued. Report just come in." "Colonel Bush, Second Illinois Cavalry, reports, 'Our pickets report that the rebels were at work at Baldwin's Ferry last night.' I shall ascertain whether it is true or not. If they are preparing to cross, I will send notice." *O.R.*, I, xxiv, part 2, 208–9.

To Maj. Gen. William T. Sherman

Head Quarters, Department of the Tenn
Near Vicksburg June 23, 1863

GENERAL:

In addition to the troops with you, and at Snyders, I have notified Herron's, and A. J. Smiths Divisions, to be in readiness to move at a moments notice. In addition to this two more Brigades can be taken from your corps with out breaking the line investing Vicksburg. Should Johnston come, we want to whip him if the Seige has to be raised to do it.

Use all the forces indicated above as you deem most advantageous, and should more be required, call on me and they will be furnished to the last man here and at Young's Point.

Yours &c

U. S. GRANT

Maj Genl

To MAJ GENL W. T. SHERMAN

COMDG EXPEDITION

Copies, DLC-USG, V, 19, (dated June 22, 1863) 30, 101; DNA, RG 393, Dept. of the Tenn., Letters Sent. *O.R.*, I, xxiv, part 3, 430–31. On June 23, 11:00 A.M., Maj. Gen. William T. Sherman, "At McCalls," wrote to USG. "Parke with Smith's Division and one Brigade of his Yankee troops is on the Ridge Road from Neelys to Post Oak Ridge, with orders to feel forward to the Bridge across Bear Creek 6 miles beyond P O Ridge. My cavalry is now down at Little Bear Creek on the Birdsong Road. Tuttles Division is close up to the Cavalry, and McArthur is now here and we are waiting for his troops to come up   I will put them on this Birdsong Road. Parke & I can communicate by the Ridge from McCall's to Neelys. After nooning I propose to go forward to the Black. I hear nothing of Johnson at all, no traces of him or signs of his approach. The Country is ill adapted to Large masses. It is cut up by impracticable Ravines and all the Roads are on Narrow Ridges where a Regimt will find difficulty in forming a Front. A small force can oppose a large one, and as to getting at Johnson unless he crosses to this side of Big Black I think it cannot be done. If he crosses Big Black and comes by any Road I shall of course meet him and oppose him, calling for all the help I may deem necessary. If he crosses Big Black I think this is the place to fight him.—Order Osterhaus to be certain to Blockade all Roads from Black towards Vicksburg, between Clear Creek and this Road. After satisfying myself that there is, or is not a purpose on his part to cross over I will communicate the fact, but no matter what his strength he must come by narrow Roads, and I have as many men as can be handled on such ground. If I conclude he does not design to come in by Birdsongs Ferry or the Ford above I will blockade it so as to force him to come on the Main Ridge within striking distance of Haines Bluff, so that we would care if he comes or not. Yesterday 4 companies of my Cavalry 4th Iowa had gone to Black River on the Road to obstruct it. They had felled many trees and must have been off their Guard, when their pickets came in from three directions giving notice of the approach of the enemy. Quite a fight ensued, in which our men got the worst, and were forced to fly. As soon as ~~Col Swan~~ the news Reached Camp, Col Swan went to the ground with his Regiment and found 8 dead, 12 wounded and about 20 missing. From the People he heard the attack came from Wirt Adams Cavalry, which had gone off in the direction of Mechanicsville. Col Swan buried the dead & brought off all wounded except one who was left well cared for at a house.   he could hear of but about 12 prisoners in the hands of the enemy, so that he expects some 8 more will have gone down to Osterhaus, and will come in today.—The party lost that 2 lb gun we captured at Jackson but before abandning it they disabled it by taking out the Breech pin. The fact of our comig out today is attributed by the secesh ~~that it is~~ to our purpose to punish the perpetraters of this action. I will send you positive inteligence tonight if Johnson be comig or not this side of Black River. On the best evidence now procurable he is not coming this way or at this time   I take it for granted you do not want me to attempt to follow him *across* that River unless after a defeat   If he crosses to this side I can hold him till reinforced, and then I know we can whip him. In the mean time look out toward Baldwins & Hankensons, though I do not believe he will put himself in such a pocket." ALS, DNA, RG 94, War Records Office, Dept. of the Tenn. *O.R.*, I, xxiv, part 2, 245–46.

Also on June 23, Lt. Col. John A. Rawlins wrote to Maj. Gen. Edward O. C. Ord. "Dispatches just received from Gen Sherman on Bird's Song ferry Road. Had heard nothing of Johnson up to 11 A. M. Dont think he is this side of the Big Black. You will order Gen. Osterhaus to immediately blockade all roads leading from the Big Black River towards Vicksburg between Clear Creek and the Bird's Song Ferry road. Let him send competent ~~officers~~, and reliable officers in command of the blockading parties, who will see that the work is speedily and effectually done. The utmost vigilance should be observed in watching the crossings of the Big Black, South of the Railroad Bridge." Copies, DLC-USG, V, 19, 101, 103; DNA, RG 393, Dept. of the Tenn., Letters Sent. *O.R.*, I, xxiv, part 3, 429–30. On the same day, Ord telegraphed to Rawlins. "You heard Col Bushes report of where his cavalry was patrolling road to the ferries   I have sent him word to use renewed vigilance where he was   shall I send him my escort & Hoveys & Smiths escort to go to the ferries tonight" Telegram received, DNA, RG 393, Dept. of the Tenn., Telegrams Received. Rawlins drafted his reply at the foot of this telegram. "You will exercise your own jugement. It would perhaps be well to send the Cavalry as you propose to the Ferries tonight, ~~or at least~~ or at an early hour in the morning" ADfS, *ibid*.

Also on June 23, Maj. Gen. Cadwallader C. Washburn telegraphed to USG. "I have Just returned from the front   all is quiet" Telegram received, *ibid*. On the same day, Brig. Gen. Peter J. Osterhaus, "Big Black," wrote to USG. "A large body of cavalry appeared in front of position across Big Black, on and near Smith's plantation." *O.R.*, I, xxiv, part 2, 226.

To Act. Rear Admiral David D. Porter

Head Quarters, Dept. of the Ten.
Near Vicksburg, June 24th 1863,

ADMIRAL D. D. PORTER
COMD.G MISS. SQUADRON,
ADMIRAL,

I have just received information that the Rebel Bledsow[1] has gone from Yazoo City to a point on the Miss. where the channel runs near the Mississippi shore about six miles above Greenville. He has with him about 150 Cavalry and a battery of Light Artillery. My Cavalry and spare troops are now out with Sherman looking for Johnston so that I cannot well attend to him. Can you send the Marine Brigade up to clear Bledsow out? They might land at Greenville and dash in behind them so as to secure the Artillery if nothing more.

Please answer by bearer so that I may fit out an expedition for Greenville in case the Marine Brigade cannot go.

Respectfully yours

U. S. GRANT

Maj. Gen.

ALS, MdAN. *O.R.*, I, xxiv, part 3, 435; *O.R.* (Navy), I, xxv, 198. On June 24, 1863, Act. Rear Admiral David D. Porter wrote to USG. "The major part of the Marine Brigade have gone out to Delhi—I sent them out to try and get some information about Gen'ls Taylor, and McCulloch. They will not be in until day after tomorrow. The rest are working a battery right in front of the town; and doing most excellent service, and a party are acting as a reserve to Gen'l Moway. It will take some time for them to get ready, and I am afraid there would be a loss of time in getting them all on board, under the circumstances I would advise a separate expedition to Greenville—I have two Gun-boats there; and will send a convoy if you will telegraph me—The enemy have erected a battery of six (6) guns at Catfish Point: opposite Greenville, and are going to put six (6) more in a battery at the same place. I have sent the 'Lexington' up, and Capt. Selfridge goes up tomorrow in the 'Manitou.' This party for Greenville intend to get a cross fire on us. I am sure the Brigade would not get there in time to prevent anything being done—" LS, DNA, RG 393, Dept. of the Tenn., Letters Received.

On June 24, Maj. Gen. Cadwallader C. Washburn wrote to USG. "McBirney arrived this morning from an Exploration in rear of Greenville. The princepal information of importance he brings is that Bledsoe has crossed from the Yazoo over to a point Six miles above Greenville with a Battery of Guns & about 150 men, with the object of firing into our transports. Would it not be well to send about 300 Cavalry by boats to Greenville supported by about the same amount of Infantry to land at Greenville & get in their rear and capture them. After doing that the Cavalry could return by land to this point between Deer Creek & Sunflower driving down what stock they can find, & destroying the corn & such articles of subsistence as cannot be brought away—Our transports are being so much annoyed by ~~that~~ river batteries, and they have become so bold about it, it seems to me that they ought to be cleaned out. I recd. your despatch in regard to the capture of Port Hudson which causes general rejoicing. I ~~having~~ have nothing new from our front. I was along the whole front line yesterday, and all was quiet when I left. . . . P. S. I send McBirney down with the bearer of this." ALS, *ibid*.

On June 22, Brig. Gen. Hugh T. Reid, Lake Providence, La., wrote to USG discussing information provided by deserters from the army of C.S.A. Maj. Gen. Sterling Price in Ark., and reporting a C.S.A. battery at Catfish Point, Ark., near Greenville, Miss. LS, *ibid.*, RG 94, War Records Office, Dept. of the Mo. *O.R.*, I, xxiv, part 3, 431–32. See letter to Lt. Col. Samuel J. Nasmith, June 25, 1863.

1. Capt. Hiram M. Bledsoe commanded a Mo. battery.

To Brig. Gen. Lorenzo Thomas

Head Quarters, Dept. of the Ten.
Near Vicksburg, June 25th 1863,

BRIG. GEN. L. THOMAS
ADJ. GEN. OF THE ARMY,
GEN.

Some time since recommendations were forwarded for the appointment of Ely S. Parker for the appointment of Asst. Adj. Gen. to be assigned to the staff of Brig. Gen. J. E. Smith.[1]

Gen. Smith commands a Division and is without an Asst. Adj. I am personally acquainted with Mr. Parker and think eminently qualified for the position. He is a full blooded Indian but highly educated and very accomplished. He is a Civil Engineer of conciderable eminence and served the Government some years in superintending the building of Marine Hospitals and Custom Houses on the upper Miss. river.

The recommendation of Mr. Parker passed through these Hd Qrs. on the 2d of April.

Very respectfully
your obt. svt.
U. S. GRANT
Maj. Gen.

ALS, DNA, RG 94, ACP, 731 1887. Born into the Seneca tribe in 1828, Ely S. Parker, educated at Rensselaer Polytechnic Institute, worked on a number of government engineering projects including those at Galena before the Civil War.

First rejected for U.S. Army service as an Indian, Parker had already been appointed capt., asst. adjt. gen., as of May 25, 1863. David William Smith, "Ely Samuel Parker, 1828–1895 . . ." (M.A. Thesis, Southern Illinois University, 1973).

1. On April 13, USG endorsed a letter of April 2 of Brig. Gen. John E. Smith to Brig. Gen. Lorenzo Thomas recommending the appointment of Parker as asst. adjt. gen. on his staff. "Respectfully forwarded to Head qrs. of this Army, Washington, D. C. and recommended. There is no A. A. G. in this Depart. unassigned" ES, DNA, RG 94, ACP, 731 1887.

To Maj. Gen. Francis J. Herron

Near Vicksburg June 25th 1863, 12 M.

MAJ. F. J. HERRON.

One of our mines in Gen'l McPhersons front will be exploded at three P. M. today. Have your rifle pits well filled with men, and the remainder of your ~~remainder~~ line, and when you hear the explosion, open with all your artillery that is in position for fifteen or twenty minutes; and should you discover any signs of the enemy moving troops towards McPherson, you will make such demonstrations as to lead him to believe you intend to attack him

U. S. GRANT
Maj Genl

Copies, DLC-USG, V, 19, 101, 103; DNA, RG 393, Dept. of the Tenn., Letters Sent. *O.R.*, I, xxiv, part 3, 441. On June 25, 1863, USG wrote to Maj. Gen. Edward O. C. Ord. "McPherson will Spring the mines in his front between 2 & 4 o.clock to-day, and will try to take possession of the main fort. Hold your troops in readiness to threaten an assault to keep the enemy from massing on McPherson. As soon as you hear the explosion open with artillery lively for about fifteen minutes." Copies, DLC-USG, V, 19, 101, 103; DNA, RG 393, Dept. of the Tenn., Letters Sent. *O.R.*, I, xxiv, part 3, 438. On the same day, Maj. Gen. James B. McPherson wrote to USG and Ord. "The mine will be exploded about three P. M. (3) to-day." Copy, DNA, RG 393, 13th Army Corps, Letters Sent. *O.R.*, I, xxiv, part 3, 438.

To Maj. Gen. Edward O. C. Ord

Near Vicksburg June 25, 1863

GEN'L ORD.

McPherson secured the Crater made by the explosion. The cavity made is sufficiently large to shelter two Regiments. The enemy made an effort to drive our troops away. Our loss about thirty killed and wounded; some ten of them officers, and three field officers. Guns will be in battery in the crater by morning, with rifle pits to the left to defend it. If we can hold the position until morning it evidently will give us possession of a long line of rifle pits to the right, and a fair way of advancing to enfilade to the left.

U. S. GRANT
Maj Gen'l.

Copies, DLC–USG, V, 19, 101, 103; DNA, RG 393, Dept. of the Tenn., Letters Sent. *O.R.*, I, xxiv, part 3, 441. A copy of this letter went to Maj. Gen. Francis J. Herron. On June 25, 1863, Maj. Gen. Edward O. C. Ord telegraphed to USG. "How is McPherson doing holding his own   Shall I hold men ready to move that way   if so how many"   Telegram received, DNA, RG 393, Dept. of the Tenn., Letters Received. On the same day, Ord telegraphed to USG. "A colored man got in last night from Vicksburg   Started night before   re [*he*] was servant to staff officers to Gen Lee   confirms other statement about provisions & Sick inside   thinks the men wont stand it a week longer"   Telegram received, *ibid.*, Telegrams Received.

To Maj. Gen. Edward O. C. Ord

June 25th 63

GEN. ORD

McPherson occupies the crater made by the explosion. He will have guns in battery there by morning. He has been hard at work running rifle Pitts right and thinks he will hold all gained. Keep Smiths Division sleeping under arms to-night ready for an

The Siege of Vicksburg. Representing the Position of Maj. Gen. John A. Logan's Division of Maj. Gen. J. B. McPherson's Army Corps. Lithograph from a sketch by Alfred E. Mathews. *Courtesy Ohio Historical Society.*

The Siege of Vicksburg. Representing the Position of Gen. A. P. Hovey's Division. Lithograph from a sketch by Alfred E. Mathews. *Courtesy Ohio Historical Society.*

The Siege of Vicksburg. Representing the Position of the Seventh Division of Maj. Gen. J. B. McPherson's Army Corps. Lithograph from a sketch by Alfred E. Mathews. *Courtesy Ohio Historical Society.*

The Siege of Vicksburg, The Fight in the Crater of Fort Hill, after the explosion, June 25 63. Gen. Logan's Division, Gen. McPherson's Army Corps. Lithograph from a sketch by Alfred E. Mathews. *Courtesy Ohio Historical Society.*

imergency. Their services may be required particularly about daylight to morrow morning. There should be the greatest vigelence on the whole line.

U. S. Grant

Maj. Gen.

ALS (facsimile), P. C. Headley, *The Life and Campaigns of General U. S. Grant* ... (New York, 1868), pp. [14–15]. *O.R.*, I, xxiv, part 3, 441. On June 25, 1863, Lt. Col. William T. Clark, adjt. for Maj. Gen. James B. McPherson, telegraphed to Lt. Col. John A. Rawlins. "Find it impossible to hold point without great Sacrifice of life   have withdrawn men & have opened with artillery   think we shall yet hold it"   Telegram received, DNA, RG 94, War Records Office, Dept. of the Tenn. *O.R.*, I, xxiv, part 3, 441.

On the same day, Maj. Gen. Edward O. C. Ord telegraphed to USG. "I ~~doubted~~ doubled my piquets a few days ago   if there is no enemy in force South of their road near Big Black can I not bring in the extra piquet force"   Telegram received, DNA, RG 393, Dept. of the Tenn., Telegrams Received. On the same day, USG wrote to Ord. "Keep a heavy picket force south of the Railroad, in the direction of the big Black, and have the cavalry visit all fords on the river daily. With the force we have north, the enemy will not attempt to come in that direction." "The telegraph operator at Genl. Herron's Headquarters, reports that the rebels have driven in Herrons pickets. Notify Genl Lauman, to be in readiness all night to afford any assistance necessary." Copies, DLC-USG, V, 19, 101, 103; DNA, RG 393, Dept. of the Tenn., Letters Sent. On June 26, Ord telegraphed to USG. "I recd from Halls ferry last P M a prisoner who represented that he had left Vicksburg the night before by going down the levee   that he met no piquets   The other information he gives is only corroborative   Shall I send the man to you"   Telegram received, *ibid.*, Telegrams Received.

To Maj. Gen. William T. Sherman

Near Vicksburg, June 25. 1863

Maj. Genl. W. T. Sherman, Comdg &c.

The only news of importance from Port Hudson, Garrison still holds out, and have nothing but parched corn to live on. Kirby Smith is trying to releive them, by attacking the point opposite. Banks had two repulses,—lost heavily. Rebels have about 3000 men in the fort, so say deserters. The report that Port Hudson was in Banks possession, came from a despatch from Gen. Herron, which was founded on Misinformation. A deserter just in from the other side of the Black River, says: Johnson's left is at Bolton, 3 Regts of Cavalry in vicinity of Champion Hill. No force south of Rail Road. His statements are deemed reliable.

U. S. Grant

Maj. General

Copies, DLC-USG, V, 19, 101, 103; DNA, RG 393, Dept. of the Tenn., Letters Sent. *O.R.*, I, xxiv, part 3, 439–40.

On June 24, 1863, USG signaled to Act. Rear Admiral David D. Porter. "Have you any off. news from 'Port Hudson' Is it captured When Was the Garrison Captured" Copy, DNA, RG 111, Vicksburg Signal Book. On June 24, Porter signaled to USG. "There is no news of importance from Port-Hudson. Garrison still holds out, and have nothing but parched corn to live on. Kirby Smith is trying to relieve them by attacking the point opposite Banks had two repulses. Loss in killed and wounded, four-thousand. The rebels have about three thousand in the fort; so say the Deserters" Signal received, DNA, RG 94, War Records Office, Military Div. of the Miss.; copy, *ibid.*, RG 111, Vicksburg Signal Book. *O.R.*, I, xxiv, part 3, 435.

To Maj. Gen. William T. Sherman

———

Headquarters, Dept of the Tennessee

Near Vicksburg, June 25. 1863

Maj. Genl. W. T. Sherman
Comdg. Expedition &c:
General:—

Your note is just received. This morning a deserter, the Hospital Steward of the 6th Texas Cavalry, a young man from Indiana, but who moved to Texas in /58, came in. He reports having come as far as Mechanicsburg between the two Rivers when their Cavalry first arrived; Since that they have fallen back across Black River, and now his Brigade, Whitfield commanding are at Bolton. The enemy have no body of troops south of the railroad. Johnston has his Headquarters between Brownville and Canton about 15 miles from Bolton. The deserter says he hears the men say that Johnston has 35000 men. They estimate our force as 90.000 but thinks Pemberton can detain most of them. They are anxious to attack, relieve the suspense.

Col. Blood[1] captured a rebel courier coming out of Vicksburg last night. He had with him quite a number of private letters for the Mail outside. The most important among them is one from M. L. Smith[2] to his wife and one from Withers.[3] The former said their fate must be decided in the next ten days. If not releived in that time he expects to go North but calculates on a speedy exchange, when he will be restored to the bosom of his family. A number of the letters speak of getting 4 ounces of bacon per day, and bread made of rice and flour mixed Corn $40.00 per Bushel, and not to be had at that. Strong faith is expressed by some in Johnston's coming to their relief. Withers particularly cannot believe they have been so wicked as for Providence to allow their loss of the strong hold of Vicksburg   Their principle faith seems to be in Providence & Jo Johnston

Dana will probably go out this evening and will carry you any news we may have up to that time.

There is no truth in the rumor that Port Hudson has fallen. I believe a vessel has come up from Port Hudson but no word for me. Admiral Porter informs me that Banks has lost severely. That Kirby Smith is attempting to relieve the Garrison from the opposite side of the River.

McPherson will spring the mine in his front this afternoon He will try then to secure a place within the fort now in his front. The mines are run about thirty five feet in, and will go up with a blast of 1000 pounds of powder. I think it advisable to keep your troops out until Jo Johnton evinces a design to move in some other direction. Continue to obstruct roads to confine his advance on as far and as narrow passes as possible. Should you discover a change of plan on his part, move to counteract it

Respectfully yours

U S. Grant

Maj Genl

Copies, DLC-USG, V, 19, 101, 103; DNA, RG 393, Dept. of the Tenn., Letters Sent. *O.R.*, I, xxiv, part 3, 439. On June 24, 1863, Maj. Gen. William T. Sherman, Bear Creek, telegraphed to USG. "Not the sign of an enemy from Post Oak ridge P. O. to Birdsongs ferry   Every point has been examined today & nothing seen No sign of an intention to cross any where near Bear Creek. I hear Port Hudson is taken   please telegraph me the whole truth   the bearer of this note will wait an answer at the Bluff   I am now with Gen Park at Post Oak P. O. But will return to my Extreme right near Youngs"   Telegram received, DNA, RG 94, War Records Office, Dept. of the Tenn. *O.R.*, I, xxiv, part 2, 246.

    1. Col. James H. Blood, 6th Mo.
    2. Martin L. Smith, born in Danby, N. Y., in 1819, USMA 1842, served in the Topographical Engineers, largely in the South, before the Civil War. Appointed C.S.A. maj., Corps of Engineers, to rank from March 16, 1861; col., 21st La., from Jan. 30, 1862; brig. gen. on April 11; and maj. gen. as of Nov. 4, Smith commanded a div. during the siege of Vicksburg. For his report, see *ibid.*, pp. 397–99.
    3. Col. William T. Withers, 1st Miss. Light Art., chief of field art. at Vicksburg. See *ibid.*, p. 336.

To Maj. Gen. Frederick Steele

Headquarters, Dept of the Tennessee
Near Vicksburg June 25, 1863

MAJ. GENL. F. STEELE
COMD'G 15TH ARMY CORPS.
GENERAL:

You will please detail a light battery from the 15th Army Corps, to proceed immediately to Chickasaw Landing, to go with an expedition to Greenville Miss., and Catfish Point, Ark. to capture or drive out some batteries established at those places by the rebels.

The commander of the battery will call on the Quartermaster for transportation.

There will be Infantry and cavalry accompanying the expedition.

All instructions will be given to the commander of the expedition, and from him the Artillery will receive orders. Let me know immediately if it interferes with batteries in position to comply with these directions. If so, a battery can probably be taken from the 17th Corps.

Respectfully Yours

U. S. Grant

Maj Genl

Copies, DLC-USG, V, 19, 101, 103; DNA, RG 393, Dept. of the Tenn., Letters Sent.

To Maj. Gen. Cadwallader C. Washburn

Near Vicksburg, June 25, 1863

Gen'l. Washburn,

Snyders.

The Marine Brigade cannot go to Greenville. Detail one good Regiment of Infantry, and about 200 cavalry, if they can be raised, to start immediately. They should take seven day's rations. I will send artillery from here.

U. S. Grant

Maj. Genl

Copies, DLC-USG, V, 19, 101, 103; DNA, RG 393, Dept. of the Tenn., Letters Sent. On June 25, 1863, USG again wrote to Maj. Gen. Cadwallader C. Washburn. "In the detailing of the regiment for the expedition to Greenville, make the detail with reference to the competency of the Colonel who will command the expedition. He must be a live and an active man. Telegraph his name and when selected, that the necessary instructions may be sent him to Chickasaw Bayou landing." Copies, *ibid.* On the same day, Washburn telegraphed to USG. "The expedition will be Commanded by Lt Col N A Smith 25th Wisconsin who is regard as a live man   the telegraph is now at Gen Parkes Hd Qrs two miles from mine which will account for any delay in answering any despatches"   Telegram received, *ibid.*, Telegrams Received.

To Lt. Col. Samuel J. Nasmith

Head Quarters Dept. of the Tenn.
Near Vicksburg, June 25. 1863

Comd'g Officer
Ex. Against Greenville Miss.
Sir:

As soon as the troops brought by you, from Snyders Bluff, and the battery of artillery sent from here, are embarked, you will proceed to the mouth of the Yazoo River, where you will find two gunboats lying, under the command of Capt Selfridge[1] of the Navy, ready to accompany you. You will report to Capt Selfridge and as soon as he can get off you will proceed to Greenville Miss

It is reported that the enemy have moved a battery & about 250 men from Yazoo City, to a point some 6 miles above Greenville. The object of expedition you command is to capture this battery, and troops if possible. Specific directions how to do it are not necessary, but use every effort to effect the object of the expedition. Should they retreat, and your force prove sufficient to compete with them, follow them as long as there is a hope of capture. On your return in case of pursuit, destroy all bridges and corn cribs. Bring away with you all negroes disposed to follow you, and teams of rebels to haul them, and their plunder Keep your men out of the houses of citizens, as much as possible, and prevent plundering. Give the people to understand if their troops makes raids necessary, all their crops and means of raising crops will be destroyed.

After breaking up the Rebels on the Miss, then proceed to Catfish Point Ark, where there is also said to be a battery established by the enemy. The same general directions apply to them.

Should any negroes accompany you they will be left at one of the Camps established either at Millikens bend or Youngs Point

Respectfully yours
U. S. Grant
Maj Genl

Copies, DLC-USG, V, 19, 101, 103; DNA, RG 393, Dept. of the Tenn., Letters Sent. *O.R.*, I, xxiv, part 3, 437–38; (incomplete) *O.R.* (Navy), I, xxv, 199. On June 25, 1863, USG signaled to Act. Rear Admiral David D. Porter. "I will Send a force from here to Greenville will let you know when they are ~~redy~~ ready to Start" Copy, DNA, RG 111, Vicksburg Signal Book. On the same day, Porter twice signaled to USG. "Three (3) gunboats will be ready at mouth of Yazoo to Convoy the troops to Greenville. Please have Convoy Communicate with them. There are also 3 (three) gun boats at Yazoo, and 6 or 7 a Short distance above." Signal received (intercepted), *ibid.*, RG 109, Pemberton Papers; copy, *ibid.*, RG 111, Vicksburg Signal Book. "I have been able to raise one-hundred cavalry out of the brigade which will join your troops as they come out of the Yazoo Part of the Cavalry returned on the other side of Richmond. They report the enemy had returned to Monroe after the attack of Generals Mower & Ellett. Nothing seen of them on the road to Delhi" Signal received, *ibid.*, RG 94, War Records Office, Military Div. of the Miss.; (intercepted) *ibid.*, RG 109, Pemberton Papers. *O.R.*, I, xxiv, part 3, 437; *O.R.* (Navy), I, xxv, 198. On June 25, USG again wrote to Lt. Col. Samuel J. Nasmith, 25th Wis. "If you can make room for 100 more cavalry, Admiral Porter will furnish them at Young's Point as you go by. When you call on Capt Selfridge, you will be able to ascertain where this cavalry will be found" Copies, DLC-USG, V, 19, 101, 103; DNA, RG 393, Dept. of the Tenn., Letters Sent.

On June 26, Porter wrote to USG. "I heard last night that you had the big fort, and sent off the news this morning by our mail boat. There is no news here, of consequence, we are ready for any thing; the troops for Greenville got off with 4 Gun boats and 100 of Ellets Cavalry. We had (not I) a big scare last night. It was reported to me at 2. a. m. that Genl. Price (!) was advancing on Milliken's Bend with a large Army!! and Gun boats were wanted. I had 6 there in a short time, and all of Ellet's brigade, except about 200 who were left in charge of the batteries. When day broke the big army had vamosed into ~~their~~ thin air, and nothing was heard of them. The remainder of Ellet's Cavalry are out now as far as Richmond looking for them. There was signaling between Vicksburg and opposite Warrenton last night and I hope to night that we may catch the parties. Genl. Herron has some intimation of a move on the part of the enemy, and requested the co-operation of the Gun boats. What this move is I dont know. I instructed Capt. Woodworth to attend to it. If the Rebels try the escaping game they will be very much surprized at what they will see. I have tar barrels enough along the Rivers to beat any illumination *they* ever made. The Gunboats from below says Banks was badly repulsed twice, but that he will get in the next time, having found a soft spot. The Rebels are only 3200 strong in Hudson, and have only parched corn. I have been able to keep you pretty well supplied with Ammunition and shall have another boat tomorrow—They use it up very fast. There is no news from Vicksburg except the old story of 6 days provisions 13.000 sick and wounded; and 600 barrels of flour on hand, which is all they have to eat, the corn meal all gone and the cats getting too cunning to be caught. I have 23 Gunboats between this and Helena, not counting those here, so I think our folks will be able to get down safely." LS, *ibid.*, Letters Received.

On July 1, Nasmith wrote an extensive report of the expedition to Lt. Col. John A. Rawlins. *O.R.*, I, xxiv, part 2, 516–18; (incomplete) *O.R.* (Navy), I, xxv, 199–200.

1. Thomas O. Selfridge, Jr., born in Mass., graduated from the U.S. Naval Academy in 1854. Confirmed as lt. commander on Feb. 21, 1863, to rank from July 16, 1862, he commanded naval guns placed on shore during the siege of Vicksburg and apparently did not accompany the expedition to Greenville.

To Brig. Gen. Lorenzo Thomas

Headquarters Department of the Tennessee
In Camp, near Vicksburg, Miss., June 26, 1863
BRIG. GEN. L. THOMAS
ADJUT. GEN'L OF THE ARMY,
WASHINGTON, D. C.
GENERAL:

Inclosed, I respectfully transmit the letters of Maj. Gen. W. T. Sherman, Com'd'g 15th Army Corps, and, Maj. Gen. J. B. McPherson, Commanding 17th Army Corps, of date respectively the 17th and 18th inst., relative to the congratulatory order of Maj. General John A. McClernand to his troops, a copy of which order is also herewith transmitted, together with copies of the correspondence relating thereto, and my order relieving. Gen. McClernand from the Command of the 13th Army Corps, and assigning Maj. Gen. E. O. C. Ord to the Command thereof, subject to the approval of the President.

A disposition and earnest desire on my part to do the most I could with the means at my command, without interference with the assignments to command which the President alone was authorized to make, made me tolerate Gen. McClernand long after I thought the good of the service demanded his removal. It was only when almost the entire Army under my command seemed to demand it, that he was relieved. The enclosed letters show the feelings of the Army Corps serving in the field with the 13th Corps.

The removal of Gen. McClernand from the Command of the 13th Army Corps has given general satisfaction, the 13th Army

Corps sharing perhaps, equally in that feeling with the other Corps of the Army.

My action in the relieving of Maj. Gen. John A. McClernand from the command of the 13th Army Corps, and the assignment of Maj. Gen. E. O. C. Ord. to that command, I trust will meet the approval of the President.

> Very Respectfully
> Your O'b't. Serv't
> U. S. GRANT
> Major General.

LS, DNA, RG 108, Letters Received. *O.R.*, I, xxiv, part 1, 158–59. See letter to Maj. Gen. John A. McClernand, June 17, 1863.

On June 17, Maj. Gen. William T. Sherman wrote to Lt. Col. John A. Rawlins. "On my return last evening from an inspection of the new Works at Snyders Bluff, General Blair, who commands the 2d Division of my Corps, called my attention to the enclosed publication in the Memphis Evening Bulletin, of ~~May~~ June 13th inst., entitled: 'Congratulatory Order of General McClernand'— with a request, that I should notice it, lest the statements of facts and inference countained therein might receive credence from an excited public.—It certainly gives me no pleasure or satisfaction to notice such a catalogue of nonsense, such an effusion of vain glory and hypocrisy;—nor can I believe, General McClernand ever published such an Order, officially to his Corps.—I know too well, that the brave and intelligent Soldiers and Officers, who compose that Corps, will not be humbugged by such stuff.—If the order be a genuine production, and not a forgery, it is manifestly addressed, not to an Army, but to a constituency in Illinois, far distant from the scene of the events, attempted to be described, who might innocently be induced to think Genl. McClernand the sagacious leader and bold hero, he so complacently paints himself.—But it is barely possible, the order is a genuine one, and was actually read to the Regiments of the 13th Army Corps, in which case a Copy must have been sent to your Office for the information of the Commanding General.—I beg to call his attention to the requirements of General Orders No. 151 of 1862 which actually forbids the publication of all Official Letters and Reports, and requires the name of the writer to be laid before the President of the United States for dismissal.—The document under question is not technically a Letter or Report, and though styled an Order, is not an Order.— It orders nothing, but is in the nature of an address to Soldiers, manifestly designed for publication, for ~~ultimate~~ ulterior political purposes.—It perverts the Truth, to the ends of flattery and Self-glorification;—and contains many untruths, among which is one of monstrous falsehood.—It substantially accuses General McPherson and myself, with disobeying the orders of General Grant in not assaulting on the 19th and 22d of May, and allowing on the latter day the enemy to mass his forces against the 13th Army Corps alone,—Genl. McPherson is fully able to answer for himself, and for the 15th Army Corps I answer, that on the 19th and 22d of May it attacked furiously, at three distinct points the enemys works, at the very hour and minute fixed in General Grants written orders;—that on both days

we planted our Colors on the exterior slope, and kept them there till nightfall;—
that from the first hour of investment of Vicksburg, until now, my Corps has at
all times been far in advance of General McClernand's;—that the General-in-
Chief by personal inspection knows this truth, that tens of thousands of living
witnesses beheld and participated in the attack,—that General Grant visited me
during both assaults, and saw for himself, and is far better qualified to judge,
whether his orders were obeyed, than General McClernand, who was near three
miles off;—that General McClernand never saw my Lines, that he then knew,
and still knows nothing about them, and that from his position he had no means
of knowing, what occured on this Front. Not only were the assaults made at the
time and place, and in the manner prescribed in General Grants written Orders—
but about 3. P. M. five hours after the assault on the 22d began,—when my Storming party lay against the exterior slope of the Bastion on my Front, and Blair's
whole Division was deployed close up to the parapet, ready to spring to the
assault, and all my field Artillery were in good position for the work—General
Grant shew me a note from General McClernand—that moment handed him by
an Orderly, to the effect that—'he had carried three of the enemy's Forts—and
that the Flag of the Union waved over the stronghold of Vicksburg—' asking that
the enemy should be pressed at all points, lest he should concentrate on him;—
Not dreaming, that a Major General would at such a critical moment make a mere
buncombe communication, I ordered instantly Giles A. Smith's, and Mower's
Brigades to renew the assault, under cover of Blairs Division, and the Artillery,
deployed, as before described, and sent an Aid to General Steele, about a mile to
my Right, to convey the same, mischievous message, whereby we lost needlessly
many of our best Officers and men.—I would never have revealed so unwelcome
a truth, had General McClernand in his process of Self-flattery, confined himself
to Facts in the reach of his own observation, and not gone out of his way to charge
others for results, which he seems not to comprehend.—In cases of repulse and
failure congratulatory addresses by subordinate Commanders are not common,
and are only resorted to by weak and vain men, to shift the burden of responsibility from their own, to the shoulders of others.—I never make a practice of
speaking or writing of others, but during our assault of the 19th, several of my
Brigade Commanders were under the impression, that McClernands Corps did
not even attempt an assault.—In the congratulatory Order I remark great silence
on that subject.—Merely to satisfy inquiring parties, I should like to know, if
McClernands Corps did—or did not assault at 2 P. M. of May 19th, as ordered.
—I don't believe it did, and I think General McClernand responsible.—With
these remarks I leave the matter, where it properly belongs,—in the hands of the
Commanding General, who knows his plans and orders, sees with an eye, single
to success, and his Countrys honor and not from the narrow and contracted circle
of a subordinate Commander, who exaggerates the importance of the events, that
fall under his immediate notice, and is filled with an itching desire for 'Fame—
not earned.—'" LS, DNA, RG 108, Letters Received. *O.R.*, I, xxiv, part 1,
162–63. On June 18, Maj. Gen. James B. McPherson wrote to USG. "My attention has just been called to an order, published in the Missouri Democrat, of the
10th inst, purporting to be a congratulatory order from Maj Gen'l Jno A. McClernand, to his command. The whole tenor of the order is so ungenerous, and the
insinuations and criminations against the other Corps of your Army, are so manifestly at variance with the facts, that a sense of duty to my command as well as
the verbal protest of every one of my Division and Brigade commanders, against

allowing such an order to go forth to the Public unanswered, require that I should call your attention to it. After a careful perusal of the Order, I cannot help arriving at the conclusion, that it was written more to influence Public Sentiment at the North, and impress the Public mind with the magnificent strategy, Superior Tactics, and brilliant deeds of the Major Gen'l commanding the 13th Army Corps, than to congratulate his troops, upon their well merited successes. There is a vaingloriousness about the Order, an ingenious attempt to write himself down, the hero, the master mind, giving life and direction to Military operations in this Quarter, inconsistent with the high toned principles of the Soldier, 'Sans peur, et Sans reproche.' Though 'born a Warrior,' as he himself stated, he has evidently forgotten one of the most essential qualities, viz: that elevated, refined sense of honor, which, while guarding his own rights with jealous care, at all times, renders justice to others. It little becomes Major General McClernand to complain of want of cooperation on the part of other Corps, in the assault on the enemy's works on the 22d ult, when 1218 men of my command were placed 'hors de combat' in their resolute and daring attempt to carry the positions assigned to them, and fully one third of these from Gen'l Quimby's Division, with the gallant and accomplished Co'l Boomer at their head, fell in front of *his own lines,* where they were left, after being sent two miles to *support him,* to sustain the whole brunt of the battle, from 5 P. M. until after dark, *his own men being recalled.* If Gen'l McClernand's assaulting columns, were not immediately supported, when they moved against the enemy's intrenchments, and few of the men succeeded in getting in, it most assuredly was his *own fault,* and *not* the fault of *any other* Corps commander. Each Corps commander, had the positions assigned to him, which he was to attempt to carry, and it remained with him to dispose his troops in such a way as to support promptly and efficiently, any column, which succeeded in getting in. The attack was ordered by the Maj Gen'l, commanding the Department, to be simultaneous at all the points selected, and precisely at the hour, the columns moved, some of them taking a little longer, than others to reach the Enemy's works, on account of the natural and artificial obstacles to be overcome, but the difference in time was not great enough to allow of any changing or massing of the enemy, from one part of the line to the other. The assault failed, not in my opinion from any want of cooperation or bravery on the part of our troops, but from the strength of the works, the difficulty of getting close up to them under cover, and the determined character of the assailed." LS, DNA, RG 108, Letters Received. *O.R.,* I, xxiv, part 1, 163–64.

To Maj. Gen. Henry W. Halleck

Near Vicksburg June 26, 1863—

H. W. HALLECK
GENL. IN CHIEF—

Yesterday a mine was sprung under the enemy's work, most commanding the fort, producing a crater sufficient to hold two regiments of infantry. Our men took immediate possession and still hold it. The fight for it has been incessant, and thus far we have not been able to establish batteries in the br[ea]ch—Expect to succeed. Joe Johnston has removed east of the Big Black. His movements are mysterious and may be intended to cover a movement from his rear into East or West Tennessee or upon Banks —I have Gen. Sherman out near his front on the big black, with a large force watching him. I will use every effort to learn any move Johnston may make, and send troops from here to counteract any change he may make, if I can

U. S. GRANT
Maj. Genl.

Telegram received, DNA, RG 107, Telegrams Collected (Bound); copies, *ibid.*, Telegrams Received in Cipher; *ibid.*, RG 393, Dept. of the Tenn., Hd. Qrs. Correspondence; DLC-USG, V, 6, 8, 24, 94. *O.R.*, I, xxiv, part 1, 43. This telegram was received in Washington on July 1, 1863, 1:00 P.M.

To Maj. Thomas Hendrickson

Headquarters Dep't of the Tennessee
Near Vicksburg Miss., June 26. 1863

MAJOR T. HENDRICKSON.
3RD REGT. U. S. INFANTRY
COMMD'G MILITARY PRISON
ALTON, ILLINOIS.
MAJOR:

Your communication of date April 5, 1863, to Colonel W Hoffman Commissary General of Prisoners, relative to the confinement in the Military prison at Alton, Illinois of prisoners from the various Volunteer forces serving in the West, has been referred to me.[1]

You will confer upon me an especial favor by having made out, and forwarded to me, a list of all enlisted men, whom you may have confined, giving their names, Company and Reg't, that

I may have the respective cases of those of my command inquired into, and the proper orders and descriptive lists sent you, and in case of sentences to hard labor, when it is practicable and not inconsistent with orders and Military law, have them transferred to the Military Prison at Memphis, Tennessee.

I am compelled to request this favor of you, from the fact that in many cases, men have been tried by Court Martial, and the sentence promulgated by Division and Army Corps Commanders, without coming to me, and consequently I have no record of them, and in others, where I have approved them, they have been ordered to be carried into execution by the immediate commdg officer, and I cannot in all cases know whether they done all the Regulations and orders required.

> I am Major
> very respectfully
> Your Obt. Servt.
> U. S. Grant
> Maj. Genl.

Copies, DLC-USG, V, 19, 101, 103; DNA, RG 393, Dept. of the Tenn., Letters Sent. Thomas Hendrickson, born in Pa., had first entered the U.S. Army in 1819. In March, 1863, as maj., 3rd Inf., he was assigned as commandant of the military prison at Alton, Ill. On Aug. 11, he relinquished this command, preparatory to retirement. On July 15, Hendrickson wrote to USG. "In compliance with your request as contained in your communication of June 26, 1863, received here a few days since, I have the honor to forward, herewith, a list of enlisted men belonging to the Volunteer forces serving in your Department, now in confinement in this prison, under sentence by General Court Martial for various periods of service, a large portion of them for the remainder of thier term of enlistment." ALS, *ibid.*, Letters Received. Hendrickson enclosed a list of sixty-nine enlisted men.

1. On April 16, Hendrickson wrote to Col. William Hoffman, commissary gen. of prisoners. "I have to report that deserters and other prisoners, from the various Volunteer forces serving in the West, are being sent to this prison every few days for confinement and punishment. There are about sixty of these men in confinement here now, all of whom are under sentence to hard labor, with ball and chain, forfeiture of pay, &c, &c, for a longer or shorter period. In scarcely one instance has a proper descriptive roll been sent here with these men, and in some cases not a scratch of a pen, of an official character, has been received to show the nature of the offence charged, or by what tribunal they were tried and sentenced. In the case of two men recently received here, who appear to have been tried by General Court Martial, the Court sentenced each of them to a forfeiture of part of their pay and 'to be reprimanded by the commanding officer of

their regiment.' This sentence was disapproved by the Division Commander Brig. General Logan, and the two men was each ordered by him 'To be confined in the Military Prison at Alton, Ill. until the expiration of his term of enlistment, at which time he shall be dishonorably discharged, with the forfeiture of all pay and allowances now due him, or which may become due.' Another case is that of a man purporting to be a private of Company C of the 24th Ohio Volunteers, received here yesterday from Nashville, Tenn (nineteen others came from Corinth, Miss, a few days previous) and the only thing to show that he was a prisoner under sentence, was the following remark upon a paper which came with him, and which is altogether unofficial 'sentenced by General Court Martial to twenty years confinement in the Alton Penitentiary.' As all these men are soldiers of the United States forces, and not prisoners of war, my object in writing you about them, is to know if I am to be held responsible for the carrying into effect of these sentences, or if I am responsible for these prisoners at all. There is no kind of hard labor within the prison walls at which prisoners can be employed neither are there any balls and chains under my control. Being soldiers of the United States, these prisoners should, I think, be under the management and control, as far as practicable, of the Commander of the Post, and be accounted for on his return of troops at the post." Copy, *ibid.* On April 22, Hoffman endorsed this letter. "Respectfully referred to the Genl in chf whose attention is particularly called to the action of Gen Logan in the cases mentioned. It is very objectionable that convicts belonging to the Army should be sent for punishment to a prison appropriated to prisoners of War, and I respectfully suggest that some other disposition be made of them." Copy, *ibid.*

To Maj. Gen. Henry W. Halleck

———

Near Vicksburg
June 27. 1863,

MAJOR GEN H W HALLECK
GENL-IN-CHF

Joe Johnston has postponed his attack until he can receive ten thousand re-inforcements now on their way from Bragg's army.

They are expected early ~~next week~~ next week. I feel strong enough against this increase & do not despair of having Vicksburg before they arrive. This latter however I may be disappointed in. I may have to abandon protection to the leased plantations from here to Lake Providence to resist a threat from

Kirby Smith's troops. The location of these leased Plantations was most unfortunate & against my judgment.

I wanted them put north of White River.

U. S. Grant
Major Genl

Telegram received, DNA, RG 107, Telegrams Collected (Bound); *ibid.*, Telegrams Collected (Unbound); copies, *ibid.*, Telegrams Received in Cipher; *ibid.*, RG 393, Dept. of the Tenn., Hd. Qrs. Correspondence; DLC-USG, V, 6, 8, 24, 94. *O.R.*, I, xxiv, part 1, 43–44. This telegram was received in Washington on July 3, 1863, 9:40 a.m.

To Maj. Gen. Stephen A. Hurlbut

Head Quarters, Dept. of the Ten.
Near Vicksburg, June 27th 1863.

Maj. Gen. S. A. Hurlbut
Comd.g 16th Army Corps,
Gen.

Your idea of massing as many troops as possible at the important bridges, in case of an attack, is right. If it should become necessary you can go further and hold only Memphis & Corinth. As much of the road should be held as possible however.

The troops from Braggs Army that are threatning you are probably doing so to cover a further movement from his army to reinforce Johnston. I have information that Johnston expects 10,000 men from there in a few days. There is scarsely a shadow of doubt but I will be attacked by next Wednesday[1] or Thursday unless Vicksburg should fall in the mean time. It will be impossible for me to send troops from here in the mean time.

Should I learn that Johnston was moving off I will send all my surplus force to counteract his movement whether it be to East or West Tennessee.

Should more troops become absolutely necessary for the

maintainance of your position, before I can send them, telegraph directly to the Gen. in Chief for them.

> Very Respectfully
> Your obt. svt.
> U. S. GRANT
> Maj. Gen. Com

ALS, DNA, RG 393, 16th Army Corps, Letters Received. *O.R.*, I, xxiv, part 3, 444–45. On June 23, 1863, Maj. Gen. Stephen A. Hurlbut, Memphis, wrote to Lt. Col. John A. Rawlins. "Ruggles, Inge, Roddy & Biffles are endeavoring to effect a junction in force from Okalona to Bear Creek, either to attack the M & C. R. Road or for some other purpose. They will have when united about 14 pieces of artillery and probably from 8 to 10,000 men. Chalmers force is also reported to be under the same orders. Col Phillips with 700 men has had a severe skirmish with them below Rocky ford. Mizener's command crossed the Tallahatchie at Wyatt moved down below Panola, burned the Yockna bridge and all the Trestles to Senatobia, destroyed the ripe grain (wheat) for miles, took Panola, destroyed all public property and a good deal of private there and at Senatobia and when last heard from the 2d Iowa & 3d Michigan were in sharp pursuit of the party which captured Major Henry & 75 of his Cavalry. I trust they will be able to strike a severe blow upon this band. No final report has been had from them. In the peculiarly exposed condition of this line I have ordered Genl. Oglesby to send in all Sick from LaGrange to this place, and to make Pocahontas & Moscow his points of concentration. It will not be possible to hold LaGrange against an attack in force   The Bridges & the situation of the Country make the points selected most vital to the Road. As soon as the men are rested from their trip south I shall direct an attack to be made by the entire mounted force supported by a Brigade of Infantry on Okalona. My whole reliance now to defend the Road is upon active movements of Cavalry   I am weary of looking to Rosecrans   I think my Rail Road will be broken up, but there will be a comfortable list of killed & wounded when the thing is done. I have repeatedly mentioned to the Maj. Genl. Co'm'g Dept that I have not force to hold the line intact. I shall do my best & leave the consequences where they belong"   ALS, DNA, RG 94, War Records Office, Union Battle Reports. On the same day, Hurlbut again wrote to Rawlins. "From the best information I can gather Gen'l. Price is at Jacksonport. His whole command since brought together is about 6,000. The Artillery which fired on the Platte Valley was one 6 & one 4 prdrs   They have sent for and expect two twelve pounders & will put them in position about Island 35—If they get these I will strike them   The admiral should send Gunboats to protect the travel from Island 10 to Helena. Three would do." AL (signature clipped), *ibid.*, RG 393, Dept. of the Tenn., Letters Received. *O.R.*, I, xxiv, part 3, 432.

On June 25, Hurlbut wrote to Rawlins. "I forward herewith Telegraphic Report of Col. Mizner's Expedition South. It has been an eminent success. By breaking up the Rail Road, destroying crops and bringing off Horses Mules and Negroes he has succeeded in placing a wider belt of difficult country between the head of the Rail Road and my line, and in depriving the enemy of large supplies of wheat now just harvested. The only misfortune attending the movement was the loss of men, horses and arms of the party from Memphis commanded by Major Henry 5th O. V. C Col Mizner was detained one day in crossing the Tallahatchie or he would have prevented or punished this. As it is Chalmers barely escaped him by taking to the swamps & bottoms near Commerce. I shall move them as soon as the weather and roads admit in the direction of Okalona. Now by the terrific rains of the last two days the Country is impassable. All the streams ponds & bayous are full to overflowing. Asboth reports a force across the Tennessee and is very much disturbed about it. He is in direct communication with Washington and I think will get himself into serious trouble as an Alarmist. Genl Halleck has directed that in case of a movement in force on New Madrid, Asboth shall throw his whole force there even to the abandonment of Columbus & Fort Pillow. I dread to trust him with such discretion. He has very little judgment. In the endeavor to cover the line of the Tenn as well as my front I am breaking down my cavalry and were it not for the superior qualities of the Officers' charged with this harassing duty, I should not be able to do as much. I have repeatedly mentioned the ~~superior~~ singular activity & courage of Dodge ably supported as he is by Cornyn and Philips. The Centre Cavalry Brigade under Mizner & Hatch is doing splendidly and with them are associated on all heavy Expeditions the 3d 4th & 9th Ills from Germantown & Collierville. The only mode in which I can at all protect this Road is by Cavalry movements well to the front, But meantime by the inactivity of the Army of the Cumberland my rear is open and it is extremely difficult to cover both sides with the force I have. However I am weary of writing about Rosecrans as it does no good and only desire by this repetition to put it distinctly on record in case of disaster. There is no doubt that an attempt will be made by Price's force on the Arkansas side and such force as can get over the Tenn. to close the Mississippi. This movement I expect to be made near Island 35. In case Asboth should abandon Fort Pillow under an apprehension of attack on New Madrid without positive assurance of force there, it will be occupied no doubt. It is of prime necessity to the safety of your supplies that three Gunboats be held in readiness—one to cruise from Island No 10 to Memphis, one from Memphis to Helena and one in reserve here. Capt Pennock will do nothing without orders from the admiral. There is no doubt but the taking of Vicksburgh will be a virtual abandonment of Miss and will be followed by rapid movements by Johnston toward Bragg either directly North or by falling to the line of the Tombigbee River." ALS, DNA, RG 94, War Records Office, Union Battle Reports. *O.R.*, I, xxiv, part 2, 487–88. On June 29, USG endorsed this letter. "Respectfully forwarded to Headquarters of the Army Washington, D. C." ES, DNA, RG 94, War Records Office, Union Battle Reports. For the enclosure, see *O.R.*, I, xxiv, part 2, 489–90.

On June 28, Hurlbut wrote to Rawlins. "The rise in the Tennessee caused by recent rains and the probable advance of Rosecrans on Bragg, have caused the recall of the flying parties North of me & west of the Tenn. It is reported on pretty good authority that Marmaduke has occupied the crossing of the L'Aroguille River 35 miles N. W. of Helena, and that Price's whole force from Jackson port is on its way down, threatening Helena but as I think to come in at or near Milliken's Bend, and either unite with Pemberton's force escaping from Vicksburgh by skiffs &c which my scouts inform me they have prepared or effecting a crossing and joining Johnstone. One of our best spies just from Jackson reports that unless Johnstone is reinforced by Kirby Smith and Price he will not be in condition to attack Genl. Grant. The feeling throughout Miss is despondent and they all talk of the line of the Tombigbee as the next last ditch. Vicksburgh and Port Hudson seem to be given up by every body. Nothing now looks dark except the movement of Lee into Maryland & Penn. This would seem from the papers to be in very heavy force, and may be productive of very serious consequences. It is affirmed by the Rebels at Jackson that a large part of Hunter's So. Ca. force are with Banks. The damage done by the recent Cavalry movement of Mizener has been very serious & deprived Johnstone of supplies which are limited enough The Mississippi Militia men do not respond well to the urgent calls for them. I am delayed in striking for Okalona from want of proper ammunition for the Revolving Rifles of 3d Mich & 2d Iowa. That which has been furnished is too large and bursts the bands. I hope to have it by the time that the Roads & Rivers will permit. Will you do me the favor of requesting Maj. Genl. Washburne to obtain and send forward Reports from my Divisions with you. Every thing is quiet here—my lines not interrupted and no force nearer than Ruggles at Okalona. I learn from spies that a heavy force under Genl Sherman moved out to look for Johnston but hear of no results." ALS, DNA, RG 393, Dept. of the Tenn., Letters Received. *O.R.*, I, xxiv, part 3, 448.

    1. July 1.

To Brig. Gen. Elias S. Dennis

Headquarters, Dept. of the Tennessee

Near Vicksburg, June 27th 1862 [*1863*]

BRIG. GEN'L E. S. DENNIS
COMD'G. DIST. N. E. LA.
GENERAL.

There is now a probability that Smith will come into the point opposite Vicksburg, for the purpose of aiding the rebel Garrison in their escape, or to furnish them supplies. Should you discover any attempt of the kind, concentrate your whole force, black and white, from Lake Providence down at Young's Point, or the most suitable place for resisting them. With Johnston in my rear, I cannot detach troops for this purpose.

Should such a move become necessary, notify the Negro Commissioners of the fact, so that they can warn the planters in time to drive in their stock and hands, within our lines for safety.

You had better notify the Commissioners at once, that such a course may become necessary.

Respectfully
U. S. Grant
Maj Genl

Copies, DLC-USG, V, 19, (misdated June 27, 1862) 101, 103; DNA, RG 393, Dept. of the Tenn., Letters Sent. *O.R.*, I, xxiv, part 3, 444.
      On June 30, 1863, Capt. Embury D. Osband telegraphed to Lt. Col. John A. Rawlins. "Yesterday the rebels reported six thousand 6000 strong with eight pieces artillery attacked Lake Providence La   were repulsed with small loss both sides   they are proceeding to Millikins bend burning & destroying every thing on the road   Skirmishing with them was taking place late last evening fifteen miles this side providence   Gen Grants brother & five friends are here awaiting transportation to camp   Send to Steamer"   Telegram received, DNA, RG 393, Dept. of the Tenn., Telegrams Received. On the same day, Brig. Gen. Elias S. Dennis wrote to USG's hd. qrs. "Contradicts the rumor that our forces has been captured at Goodrich's Landing and the Steamer Jacob Strader' burned. Col. Weber of the 11th Mo V. I. was killed by being struck on the head with a piece of shell   Rebels are burning cotton Gins between Goodrichs Landing and Lake Providence"   Copies, DLC-USG, V, 22; DNA, RG 393, Dept. of the Tenn., Register of Letters Received. See *O.R.*, I, xxiv, part 2, 450, 466.

To Maj. Gen. Francis J. Herron

Near Vicksburg, June 28th 1863

Genl. Herron.

A prisoner brought to these Headquarters, and who was arrested near Black River, reports having passed down the levee, from Vicksburg, expecting to encounter pickets to give himself up to, but meeting none he walked on to Black River, where the Cavalry arrested him. This was the first place, he encountered armed soldiers.

Pickets should run to the River bank, and as close to the enemy as possible. A reconnoisance under the bluffs might disclose a weak place, where troops can be got into the City without loss. I wish you would have such reconnoisance made.

U. S. Grant
Maj. Genl.

Copies, DLC-USG, V, 19, 101, 103; DNA, RG 393, Dept. of the Tenn., Letters Sent.

On June 28, 1863, Maj. Gen. Francis J. Herron wrote to USG. "Six deserters just been brought in. They are from Nineteenth Arkansas, stationed near [the] center, and deserted under the impression that the town would be surrendered in a few days. They report a further reduction in rations and great dissatisfaction among men. General Green, commanding the brigade in which their regiment was, was killed yesterday by a musket ball. They say next Saturday will settle the question. I shall be engaged all night with my advanced battery, and will not get over to your headquarters until day after to-morrow. My picket arrangements on river are complete." *O.R.*, I, xxiv, part 3, 447–48. On the same day, Act. Rear Admiral David D. Porter signaled to USG. "A vessel will go down in about four days. I will notify you in time. Two deserters came over yesterday. They say the town will surrender on the 4th of July after the rebels fire a salute. Six days ¼ rations left yesterday"   Signal received, DNA, RG 94, Letters Received. *O.R.*, I, xxiv, part 3, 447; *O.R.* (Navy), I, xxv, 98. An intercepted copy of this message is *ibid.*, p. 119.

To Maj. Gen. Edward O. C. Ord

Near Vicksburg, June 29th 1863

GENL ORD.

Now that the nights are light, it is more important that the Cavalry should be on the watch at Hall's Ferry and North from there during the night than at any other time. I think it would be advisable to send one or two Regiments of Infantry out near Black River Between Halls Ferry & Baldwins Ferry roads with a Light Battery with instructions to reconnoiter all the crossings of Black River between the two ferries and to obstruct the two roads in every possible way.

Johnston finding such preparations to receive him North of the railroad, may try a dash South of it.

U. S. GRANT. Maj Genl

Copies, DLC-USG, V, 19, 101, 103; DNA, RG 393, Dept. of the Tenn., Letters Sent.

On June 28, 1863, Maj. Gen. Edward O. C. Ord telegraphed to USG. "Maj Fullerton of Cav. reports from Hackersons ferry that our pickets there heard drums some distance off yesterday a m about six oclock & cannonading heard in the direction of Grand Gulf continuing from about sunset yesterday till one oclock this morng. sent scout down the river this morng who heard nothing twenty Rebel cavalry at Baldwins Ferry yesterday morng exchanged shots with our pickets" Telegram received, *ibid.*, Telegrams Received.

On June 29, USG wrote to Ord. "Genl Lauman was ordered when he took his present position to keep two regiments to the left of Halls Ferry road. It will give Genl. Herron too extended a line if Lauman keeps less." Copies, DLC-USG, V, 19, 101, 103; DNA, RG 393, Dept. of the Tenn., Letters Sent. A copy of this letter was sent to Maj. Gen. Francis J. Herron. On the same day, USG wrote to Herron. "You can place a regiment in the bottom if you deem it advisable." Copies, *ibid.* On June 30, Herron wrote to USG. "Deserters in to-day report provisions exceedingly scarce and a bad feeling among the troops. Mules were killed this morning and the meat distributed to the troops. They confirm the report of General Martin [E.] Green's death. He commanded the Second Brigade of Bowen's division." *O.R.*, I, xxiv, part 3, 452.

On June 29, USG wrote to Ord. "I would like to see you at Headquarters at 10 A. M. tomorrow to meet other corps commanders." Copies, DLC-USG, V, 19, 101, 103; DNA, RG 393, Dept. of the Tenn., Letters Sent. On the same day, Ord sent three telegrams to USG. "Camp near Black River 29th Halls Ferry to COL BUSH Comdg 2d Ill Cav.—Sir I have the honor to report that four of Capt Gallaghers men discovered a canoe in Black River this mornig one of the men swam over & brought the canoe over ~~and brought~~ to this side the four men crossed over without orders from their comdg officer went back five miles into country to a plantation house where they gained information that twelve hundred (1200) mounted Infy with two pieces of artiley passed down the river yesterday claiming that they intended crossing Black River at Hackersons ferry the four men can be relied on These men saw a no. of staggles Yours Respy signed THOS J JONES Comdg Det. A true Copy W B MOORE Adjt 2d Ill Cav The above just recd from Capt Jones Is it of sufficient importance to warrant a detachment of a Regt there is one at Warrenton I can send out if necessary" Telegram received, *ibid.*, RG 94, War Records Office, Military Div. of the Miss. "In consideration I have determination I have concluded to send one regt to Baldwins & one to Hankinsons Baldwins & Halls are well obstructed The roads to the two latter report impassable for Arty & the two roads with 2 miles of each other to near the river" "I have two Companies of Cav. under a maj at Hankersons Ferry two Regts & section of arty at Warrentenon Shall I send word to latter place to be on his guard the Country from Hankersons ferry to Warrenton is open & unobstructed & facilities for bridges near the ferry shall I send there & have faculites destroyed" Telegrams received, *ibid.*, RG 393, Dept. of the Tenn., Telegrams Received. Also on June 29, USG wrote three more times to Ord. "Word should be sent to troops at Warrenton to be on their guard. All facilities for building bridges should be destroyed at Hankersons & Halls ferries. Buildings on this side of the river need not be destroyed, but should on the other." "It may possibly be the intention of these men to make a dash into Warrenton. There is other danger from them. Warrenton should be made secure against an attack from them. Some cavalry should watch Hankersons Ferry to report if any rebels cross." "There is no necessity for sending a regiment to Hankersons Ferry. It is too far down the river for the enemy to think of using it, more than for a small reconnoitering force. It would take the enemy too heavy days march to reach it from the railroad." Copies, DLC-USG, V, 19, 101, 103; DNA, RG 393, Dept. of the Tenn., Letters Sent.

To Maj. Gen. William T. Sherman

———

Headquarters Dept. of the Tenn
Near Vicksburg June 29. 1863

MAJ. GENL. W. T. SHERMAN.
COMDG 15TH ARMY CORPS
GENERAL:

Your General Order blank No. is received.[1] The dispositions you have made are excellent. It will be impossible for Johnston to cross the Black River North of the Railroad without being discovered and your troops ready for him. My only apprehensions are that Johnston finding us so ready, may cover a movement South, and dash in at Baldwins and South of that before troops can be got out to meet him. A move of this kind certainly could not be intended for anything more than a diversion to relieve the Vicksburg Garrison. It does not look to me as if Johnston would ever think of bringing his wagon train across Black River South of us.

I had but little confidence in the blockading the roads South of the Jackson road. Something has been done however and will help a little if Johnston should attempt to come in that way.

Ord's cavalry watch all the ferries south of Baldwins and though they sometimes see rebel cavalry east of the River, yet they discover no signs of an attempt to cross.

I sent out a scout who travelled for some distance east from Black River Bridge, and South of the Railroad. He says no troops have gone South of the Railroad. The same statement is made by a deserter from one of the Texas Regiment, stationed at Bolton Station, but this information is several days old. In the mean time Johnston may have changed his plans, and the position of his troops half a dozen of times.

You need not fear General, my tender heart getting the better of me, so far as to send the secession ladies back to your front. On the contrary I rather think it advisable to send out every living being from your lines, and arrest all persons found within, and who are not connected with the army

Very truly yours

U. S. GRANT

Maj. Genl

Copies, DLC-USG, V, 19, 101, 103; DNA, RG 393, Dept. of the Tenn., Letters Sent. *O.R.*, I, xxiv, part 3, 449. On June 29, 1863, Maj. Gen. William T. Sherman, Camp at Bear Creek, wrote to Lt. Col. John A. Rawlins. "It was my purpose to have come to Head Qrs yesterday, but the importance of knowing the ground in this quarter so broken and complicated, induced me to continue what I had begun, that I continued my exploration. Black River is so easy passable at many points that I am forced to extend my Lines, to watch all, and the result of my personal observations are contained in an order made last night which is now beig carried into effect   I found the enemy watching with Cavalry on every ford at Messengers House. The family consisting of many women whose Husbands are out, are evidently serving an easy purpose of keeping up communications so I moved them all by force, leavig a fine house filled with elegant furniture & costly paintings to the Chances of war. Also the family of Hill with other War Widows at a place on the Birdsong Road is removed to a harmless place within our Lines. These may appeal to the tender heart of our Commanding General but he will not reverse my decision when he knows a family accessible to the enemys Keen scouts can collect & impart more information than the most expert spies—Our volunteer pickets & patrols reveal names & facts in their innocence, which if repeated by these women give the key to our points. As a General thing the valley of Black River above the Bridge has a wide fertile valley on this side, the hills comig down rather abrupt from the other. The ground slopes easily & gradually from the Ridge marked on Wilsons map from Oak Ridge, Neillys, McCall, Wixons & Tiffin town. Innumerable roads & Cross Roads intersect the country which cannot be obstructed but which runig on narrow ridges with narrow corn fields admit of easy defence. It is only by familiarity with the country, its ugly ravines, its open narrow ridges all comig to a common Spur that a comparativly small force can hold in check a large one. If the enemy crosses at one point he must take some days to get over his men & material & then would have to feel his way, as he knows full well that many of them have been made impassable to his wagons & Artillery   This will give us time to fall on him, or await his attack.   should he cross at several points our tactics would be to hold small forces in observation at the several points named in my order, and a heavy force fall on one or other of his detachmts. If the enemy forces us back Wixons will be the grand Battle field, or somewhere on Clear Creek. I think unless General Grant thinks my services more useful elsewhere I had better remain as naturally all look to me for orders. Please ask the Genl to read the enclosed order carefully and if any part is open to objection to state it that I may modify in time. I sent 800 cavalry under Col Russy up the Ridge Road towards Mechanicsville last night to sweep back by the lower Benton Road, they will return to P. O Ridge & have not yet reported. Yesterday our pickets skirmished a little at Messengers. I was there & did not see more than 15 or 20 men on horseback as curious to watch us as we them. One man near Hills was shot through the hand by a scamp from the bushes, who could not be

found—As usual my cavalry is not bold, but the Infantry go in without any hesitation. Not a sound, sylable or Sign to indicate a purpose of crossig Black River
towards us, but I still enjoin on all, that our enemy is too wary to give us notice
a minute too soon. Evry possible motive exists for them to come to the relief of
V Burg and we should act on that supposition rather than the mere signs of
movemts which are known only to Johnson and will not be revealed even to his
own troops till the last momnt. In order that you may understand any future
communication, mark your map as follows,—1½ miles East of Youngs, where
the Road comes in from Markhams mark 'Hills.' 1½ miles south east of Hills
Jones Plantation   2 miles below Birdsongs Ferry, Jones Ford. 1½ miles S. E. of
Camerons   Messingers Plantn & Ford. 1 mile east of Fox—mark Parson Fox.
3 miles east of Tiffin on the Bridgeport Road, Brooks   All these points may
become of note. I still regard the country at Tiffin, Brant, Cowans, W. Wixon,
and Hardaway as the key points of this Region. I still have my Head Qrs by the
Roadside in front of Tribbs where the Road fork to Youngs and Markham. When
this letter is read please send it to my adjt to be copied in my Letter Book &
returned to you for file." ALS, DNA, RG 94, War Records Office, Dept. of the
Tenn. Dated June 27 in *O.R.*, I, xxiv, part 2, 246–48.

Also on June 29, Brig. Gen. Peter J. Osterhaus telegraphed to USG through
Maj. Gen. Edward O. C. Ord. "Gen McArthurs are exchanging shots with rebels
across the river at Messengers ford and my pickets at Bridge port have been also
fighting since 10 a m   no attempt made as yet by enemy to Cross the river   my
pickets are still on the river bank" Telegram received, DNA, RG 94, War
Records Office, Dept. of the Tenn. *O.R.*, I, xxiv, part 2, 227. On June 30, Sherman, Big Black, telegraphed to USG. "I am at Gen Osterhaus on a visit   All
quiet along the black River   A Cavalry force under Col Bussey went yesterday
15 Miles up the ridge & returned along Black River down as far as Mouth of
Bear Creek   Saw nothing of interest   the Cavalry of the enemy Can be seep
seen opposite Messengers but quite immediately on a few rounds of parrotts
Shell   All the troops are now in position   Please telegraph me if nothing new.
I feel uneasy about the affair about Washington   Have seen the st Louis papers
of the 24th   Have you anything later" Telegram received, DNA, RG 94, War
Records Office, Dept. of the Tenn. *O.R.*, I, xxiv, part 2, 248.

1. See *ibid.*, I, xxiv, part 3, 449–50.

To Julia Dent Grant

———

June 29th 1863

DEAR JULIA,

During the present week I think the fate of Vicksburg will
be decided. Johnston is still hovering beyond the Black river and
will attack before you receive this or never. After accumulating

so large an army as he has, at at such risk of loosing other points in the Confederacy by doing it, he cannot back out without giving battle or loosing prestige. I expect a fight by Wednsday or Thursday. There may be much loss of life but I feel but little doubt as to the result.—Saturday[1] or Sunday next I set for the fall of Vicksburg. You can come down then and bring the children with you. We will have to make some arrangement for them to go to school as soon as schools open after vacation. You will have to stay with them as a general thing but by selecting a good place for you and them to board you can visit me a part of the time, when I am still. I do not expect to be still much however whilst the war lasts.

Fred. has returned from his uncles. He does not look very well but is not willing to go back until Vicksburg falls. I think I will send him a trip as far North as St. Paul after the fall of Vicksburg.[2] Remember me to all at home. You do not say whether you have leased the farm or not. I do not want White to hold it.

Kiss the children for me.

ULYS.

ALS, DLC-USG.

1. July 4, 1863.
2. On July 11, Silas A. Hudson, Memphis, wrote to Brig. Gen. Grenville M. Dodge, that he was "on my way home with Master Fred, the Generals son, who will remain sometime North for the benefit of his health." ALS, Dodge Papers, IaHA. See "Frederick Dent Grant at Vicksburg," *USGA Newsletter*, VII, 1 (Oct., 1969), 1–10.

To Absalom H. Markland

Headquarters Department of the Tennessee,
Near Vicksburg, June 29, 1863.

A. H. MARKLAND, SPECIAL AGENT,
POST-OFFICE DEPARTMENT:
DEAR SIR:

Yours of yesterday, stating that an effort was being made to change the plan of distributing the mails for the Department of the Tennessee from Memphis to Cairo, is received.

The mails for this department are carried by Government through their own agents, I believe, as far as Memphis. From that point they are distributed by agents detailed by me. Nearly the entire mail for the department must come to Memphis, whether distributed elsewhere or not, and, in my opinion, should be gotten to that point with as little delay as possible. The distribution at Cairo would necessarily involve some delay, at least for those letters and public documents intended for the commander of the District of West Tennessee, and would not hasten the delivery of one single letter within the department. I have, therefore, to request that no change be made in the present satisfactory postal arrangement.

Very truly, yours,
U. S. Grant.

O.R., I, xxiv, part 3, 448–49.

To Maj. Gen. Nathaniel P. Banks

Head Quarters, Dept. of the Ten.
Near Vicksburg, June 30th 1863.

Maj. Gen. N. P. Banks,
Comd.g Dept. of the Gulf,
Gen.

Feeling a great anxiety to learn the situation at Port Hudson I send Col. Kilby Smith to communicate with you. Col. Smith has been here during the entire siege of Vicksburg and can inform you fully of the position of affairs at this place.

I confidantly expected that Vicksburg would have been in our possession before this, leaving me able to send you any force that might be required against Port Hudson.—I have a very large force, much more than can be used in the investment of the rebel works, but Johnston still hovers East of Black River. Whether he will attack or not I look upon now as doubtful. No doubt he would however if I should weaken my force to any extent.

I have sent into Louisiana to learn the movements of Kirby Smith but as yet hear nothing definite.

Should it be my good fortune Gen. to get into Vicksburg whilst you are still investing Port Hudson I will commence immediately shipping troops to you, and will send such number as you may indicate as being necessary.

The troops of this command are in excellent health and spirits. There is not the slightest indication of dispondency either among officers or men.

Hoping to hear favorable news from your field of opperations by the return of Col Smith, I remain

> Very respectfully
> your obt. svt.
> U. S. Grant
> Maj. Gen.

ALS, CSmH. *O.R.*, I, xxiv, part 3, 451–52; *ibid.*, I, xxvi, part 1, 49.

On June 30, 1863, USG signaled to Act. Rear Admiral David D. Porter. "If I send an officer by you to Port Hudson, how is he to get back again?" Signal received (intercepted), DNA, RG 109, Pemberton Papers.

To Maj. Gen. Francis J. Herron

Near Vicksburg July 1st 1863

Gen Herron,

It seems certain from reports just in to Gen Ord that the enemy in some force are crossing at Hankerson's Ferry. Ord moves one Brigade out to night to resist them should they come. Hold one Brigade of your command in readiness to move to their support, should they be required   If one Brigade is moved, their present front should still be occupied as long as possible.

> U. S. Grant
> Maj. Genl.

Copies, DLC–USG, V, 19, 101, 103; DNA, RG 393, Dept. of the Tenn., Letters
Sent. On July 1, 1863, Maj. Gen. Francis J. Herron twice wrote to USG. "Nothing
especially new on my front to-day. I opened this morning with my advanced battery of 42-pounder rifle guns, and used the enemy's works badly. The enemy's
mortar was fatally brought to bear on the battery and exploded one shell between
the two guns, killing 2 and badly wounding 4 men, but not interfering with the
further work of battery." "Colonel Logan, commanding at Warrenton, informs
me by messenger that Major Wilson, commanding cavalry pickets on Big Black
River, has just come in, and reports that he was attacked by 60 of the enemy's
cavalry, and fought them some time, when a force of about 200 infantry attempted
to flank him, and he fell back. The rebel cavalry crossed at Hankinson's Ferry,
and negroes report a force of 2,000 men with artillery crossing at same place.
Major Wilson also states that the cavalry sent to examine the crossings between
Hankinson's Ferry and Grand Gulf have arrived, and report no signs of enemy
below. Colonel Logan desired to have this forwarded to General Ord, and I also
send copy to you." *O.R.*, I, xxiv, part 2, 318.

To Maj. Gen. James B. McPherson

Near Vicksburg July 1 1863

GEN. McPHERSON.

Explode the mine, as soon as ready. Notify Ord the hour, so
that he may be ready to make a demonstration, should the enemy
attempt to move towards you. You need not do more than have
rifle pits filled with Sharpshooters. Take all advantage you can
after the explosion of the breach made, either to advance guns or
your Sharpshooters.[1]

U. S. GRANT
Maj. Genl.

Copies, DLC–USG, V, 19, 101, 103; DNA, RG 393, Dept. of the Tenn., Letters
Sent. *O.R.*, I, xxiv, part 3, 456. On July 1, 1863, Maj. Gen. James B. McPherson
telegraphed three times to USG. "The mine on Logans front is ready & the enemy
appear to be digging in towards it   Shall I explode it & what disposition do you
desire me to make of my troops anything more than having the rifle pits filled
with sharpshooters"   "The mine will be exploded about three *3* P M today"
Telegrams received, DNA, RG 94, War Records Office, Dept. of the Tenn. *O.R.*,
I, xxiv, part 3, 456. "The mine was successfully Exploded today damaging the
enemy's works considerably & killing & wounding a number of their men   Six
men were blown out on our side of the defensive four of them killed one mortally
wounded & one a negro slightly hurt   the seige guns a portion of Logans &

Ransoms arty opened on them with good effect as well as Ransoms Sharp shooters Ransom who was in a position to see the inside of the works says the rebels must have lost a good many men   it has just been reported to me by Lt Branigan 1st infy in chg of 30 pdr parrotts that three rebel regts were seen crossing the bottom running towards our right Shermans Command beyond the range of any of our guns except the 30 pdrs from which he fired as long as they could be seen . . . P. S. The explosion today evidently took the rebels by Surprise"   Telegram received, DNA, RG 393, Dept. of the Tenn., Telegrams Received.

Also on July 1, USG telegraphed to McPherson. "Cant you take possession of the ground gained by the explosion today, after dark; and hold it without much sacrifice of life?" Copies, DLC-USG, V, 19, 101, 103; DNA, RG 393, Dept. of the Tenn., Letters Sent. On the same day, McPherson telegraphed to USG. "Will go over & see you"   Telegram received, *ibid.*, Telegrams Received.

1. On the same day, 11:00 A.M., McPherson informed Maj. Gen. John A. Logan that he planned no assault after the mine detonation. *O.R.*, I, xxiv, part 3, 456–57.

To Maj. Gen. Edward O. C. Ord

Near Vicksburg July 1st 1863

GEN. ORD.

Exercise your own judgement about paroling the citizen prisoners. Move your troops on Black River to such points as you may deem most threatened. Gen. Herron reports presence of troops at Hankersons Ferry now crossing.

U. S. GRANT
Maj. Genl

Copies, DLC-USG, V, 19, 101, 103; DNA, RG 393, Dept. of the Tenn., Letters Sent. On July 1, 1863, Maj. Gen. Edward O. C. Ord telegraphed to USG. "One of the men who gave himself up is confined here   here is about three miles from here   his wife is sick expected to die   he is poor & without Servants   the man has behaved well & is anxious to give his parole & be with his wife   can I parole him as I should do if it was left with me   all quiet on Black river this Eve"   Telegram received, *ibid.*, Telegrams Received. On the same day, Ord wrote to Lt. Col. John A. Rawlins. "I have the honor to send to Head Qrs. two prisoners captured with a black boy near the mouth of Big Black,—by Maj. Jas. Grant Wilson, 15th Ills. Cavalry,—while attempting to cross the river in a canoe. Maj. Wilson found a few letters in the possession of the prisoners, which are enclosed for the information of the Major General Commanding. If the statements in the letters of the amount of rations,—and the black boy says it has been but ¼ pound of bacon and meal each for ten days past,—can be relied on, the information is valuable. It is strongly corroborated by the statements of deserters for some days past." ALS, *ibid.*, RG 94, War Records Office, Dept. of the Tenn. *O.R.*, I, xxiv, part 3, 457.

To Maj. Gen. Edward O. C. Ord

[*July 1, 1863*]

Have you any information besides what I sent you? If it is really true that the enemy have 2000 troops at Hankersons ferry they should be met. I will telegraph Gen. Herron to ascertain more fully.[1]

U. S. GRANT
Maj. Gen.

ALS (telegram sent), DNA, RG 94, War Records Office, Dept. of the Tenn. *O.R.*, I, xxiv, part 3, 457. On July 1, 1863, Maj. Gen. Edward O. C. Ord twice telegraphed to USG. "Shall I send out a brigade with arty to the south to meet the reported march" Telegram received, DNA, RG 94, War Records Office, Dept. of the Tenn.; copies, *ibid.*, RG 393, Dept. of the Tenn., Letters Sent; DLC-USG, V, 19, 101, 103. *O.R.*, I, xxiv, part 3, 457. "Nothing further than the dispatch from Herron which came from Logan & Maj Wilson via Warrenton Wilson was stationed near Hankersons ferry I think it is likely the enemy have shown some force there perhaps as a feint I have two brigades ordered to be ready to march for the country between Warrenton & Halls ferry Shall I send them off" Telegram received, DNA, RG 94, War Records Office, Dept. of the Tenn. *O.R.*, I, xxiv, part 2, 209. USG drafted a reply on the bottom of Ord's second telegram. "A cavalry picket to give notice if crossing is attempted will be sufficient. Only move troops after it is known there is a force to oppose." ALS (telegram sent), DNA, RG 94, War Records Office, Dept. of the Tenn.

On July 1, Ord telegraphed to USG twice more. "I have positive intelligence from cavalry just in & from the report of Maj Wilson that the enemy have crossed at & near Hankersons ferry. I have ordered Lawler with a brigade to move down east of Warrenton & occupy the ground between Warrenton & Hankerson ferry he will be off in half an hour if you do not direct otherwise" Telegram received, *ibid. O.R.*, I, xxiv, part 2, 209. "I have just recd the following from Maj Wilson Warrenton 1st 7 P M Genl—Have this moment arrived here with my Command from Hankersons ferry after an obstinate conflict & a loss of several killed wounded & prisoners the enemy have crossed with infy but how many I cannot say. Can only state that while engaged with their cavalry whom we drove back about 200 infy made an attack on us we fell back ab a mile & there remained until we found the enemy were flanking us when I determined to fall back to this

point where I shall wait further orders   have given Col Logan all the facts before
leaving the neighborhood of the ferry   I dispatched messengers to Maj Fullertons
to Halls ferry also to Lt Cary in command of the Co sent out this morning to
watch crossings below   To the latter I sent orders to fall back on Warrenton
loss one man & one horse killed 4 wounded & 3 taken prisoners"   Telegram
received, DNA, RG 94, War Records Office, Dept. of the Tenn. On the same
day, USG answered Ord. "Major Wilson's report looks as if it would be prudent
to move out troops. They had better be sent to Big Bayou tonight, and tomorrow
take a strong position, whilst the Cavalry reconnoitre the enemy. We can tell
better then what to do." Copies, DLC-USG, V, 19, 101, 103; DNA, RG 393,
Dept. of the Tenn., Letters Sent. On July 2, Ord telegraphed to USG. "Maj
Fullerton at Halls Ferry started me word late last night 12 oclock that he hadd
of the Rebels crossing at Hankinsons   that he found the reserve Cavalry at Halls
& Harris ferris had fallen back to Jas Gibsons   he ordered them to return to
bout places   states 'I will leave a strong picket there & with about fifty men
reconniter to Hankersons or as near as possible & report"   Telegram received
(misdated June 2), *ibid.*, Letters Received. "I just recd the following   Hankersons ferry July 2d 6 a m   TO MAJ GEN ORD COMDG &C   SIR: all right here
no signs of the enemy nor the least preperation for crossing the river here   I will
return to Halls ferry this morning   Signed HUGH B FULLERTON Maj 2d
Ill Cav. It seems the enemy simply dashed at the outpost & returned   Shall I
call in Lawlers brigade or keep part of it as reserve for Cavalry at the ferries"
Telegram received, *ibid.* On the same day, Ord transmitted to USG a telegram
from Brig. Gen. Michael K. Lawler. "I have crossed over Big Bayou & taken the
Halls Ferry road with view of going to Red Church as ordered but find the road
so blockaded with fallen timber that further advance with artillery is impossible
I shall recross the Bayou & take road leading down to the two Gibsons & try to
reach the vicinity of the church from that direction   I have sent a communication
to Col Logan at Warrenton making known my whereabouts & situation . . . I
have halted at Big Bayou for two hours to allow my men to breakfast & rest   shall
send out scouts to scour the country in ever direction"   Telegram received, *ibid.*

    1. On July 1, USG wrote to Maj. Gen. Francis J. Herron. "Do you regard
it as reliable that the enemy are at Hankersons Ferry? If so telegraph Gen. Ord,
and he will send a Brigade to meet them." Copies, DLC-USG, V, 19, 101, 103;
DNA, RG 393, Dept. of the Tenn., Letters Sent. On the same day, Herron wrote
to USG. "I do not place any confidence in the report of the infantry being at
Hankinson's Ferry, but think it probably a scout of their cavalry crossed. I have
telegraphed fully to General Ord." *O.R.*, I, xxiv, part 3, 457.

To Maj. Gen. Edward O. C. Ord

Near Vicksburg, July 1st 1863

GENL. ORD.

    Genl. Lauman is only required to picket his own front. He

was directed to leave two regiments South of Hall's Ferry road. Gen. Herron reported these men being withdrawn, and would leave his front too extended. It was only compliance with first orders that was required.

U. S. GRANT
Maj. Genl.

Copies, DLC-USG, V, 19, 101, 103; DNA, RG 393, Dept. of the Tenn., Letters Sent.

To Maj. Gen. Edward O. C. Ord

Near Vicksburg July 1st 1863

GEN ORD.

Sherman has had a Scout out to Bolton. He can discern no indication of troops having passed South. Johnston must be watched at all points however. Big Bayou should be obstructed as high up as possible, except where we use the crossing

U. S. GRANT
Maj. Genl.

Copies, DLC-USG, V, 19, 101, 103; DNA, RG 393, Dept. of the Tenn., Letters Sent. On July 1, 1863, Brig. Gen. Peter J. Osterhaus, "Big Black," telegraphed to USG through Maj. Gen. Edward O. C. Ord. "A mounted Infy patrol sent out this morning on Edwards Station road was fired into near that place   men dis dismounted & attacked the enemy was about 50 strong Infy & some mounted men & drove them beyond Edwards Station   Lt Sample of 118th Ills Mounted Infy was severely & 2 men wounded   the enemies loss not known"   Telegram received, DNA, RG 94, War Records Office, Dept. of the Tenn. *O.R.*, I, xxiv, part 2, 227–28.

To Maj. Gen. William T. Sherman

Near Vicksburg July 1, 1863

GEN. SHERMAN.

The enemy have shown some force this side the Black at Hankerson's Ferry. Ord sends out one Brigade to night to watch them. They may try a direction to the South of the City, with the view of drawing as much force in that direction as possible.

I will let you know all that takes place as early as possible.

U. S. GRANT

Maj. Genl.

Copies, DLC-USG, V, 19, 101, 103; DNA, RG 393, Dept. of the Tenn., Letters Sent. *O.R.*, I, xxiv, part 3, 457. On July 1, 1863, USG again wrote to Maj. Gen. William T. Sherman. "Our Cavalry report on information received from citizens east of the river, that 12.000 of Johnston's troops have passed south of Baldwins Ferry. I place no great reliance in the information, but it may prove true. Do you learn anything from Johnston?" Copies, DLC-USG, V, 19, 101, 103; DNA, RG 393, Dept. of the Tenn., Letters Sent. *O.R.*, I, xxiv, part 3, 458. On the same day, Sherman telegraphed to USG. "I am just in ~~front~~ from a ~~circular~~ circuit all is absolutely silent along Black River   One of your best Scouts Tuttle is just in from Bolton where I sent him to see if he could learn if any part of Johnsons Army had passed south of the R R especially to watch the course of army wagons   he could see nor hear nothing to show that a movement south was in progress   I will send him out to Auburn tonight   Osterhaus watches Baldwins & Hills Ferries   It might be well to send a small force to the Red church between Warrenton & Hankinsons to make a show   my troops are in such a position that they could reach Noland or Whitales in five hours. Big Bayou should made impassable   I am at one bridge as high up as possible shortening the neck between it & the branch   see your map & I have a good ~~to~~ road to run between the R R via Tiffin ~~Bovina~~ Bovina & Noland   I think Johnstone may feint to the south but do not think he will risk chances in the pocket of of Black River   Still we must watch him close. I will have a scout out on an old road from Rosley Springs & Auburn & can tell quick if anything is afloat. Every body still reports a few rebel force at Mechanicsburg Vernon ~~Browns Hill~~ Brownville & Bolton. Militia Collecting at Jackson   Johnson vibrating between Jackson & Canton. All well" Telegram received, DNA, RG 94, War Records Office, Dept. of the Tenn. *O.R.*, I, xxiv, part 2, 248–49. On July 2, Sherman, Oak Ridge, telegraphed to USG. "I do not believe Johnson will come in by Haninkson but will be ready to move in that direction on short notice   My scout to Auburn will ~~dep~~ develope the truth & I had him make speed" Telegram received, DNA, RG 94, War Records Office, Dept. of the Tenn. *O.R.*, I, xxiv, part 2, 249.

To Julia Dent Grant

July 1st 1863,

DEAR JULIA,

When you come here you need not bring a saddle & bridle for Jess. Some one has thought enough of him to send him a present of a very fine set of pony equipments.

Lewis Dent,[1] [an]d the Governme[nt] lessees of plantation[s ge]nerally, have been burned out. I have received no
official report of the result yet but believe the negro troops
whipped the rebels wherever they met but were not able to follow on foot fast enough to keep their cavalry from burning cotton
gins and plantation houses.

I see Lagow has gone with Lewis again! I suppose he will
insist on you coming down with him. You remain where you are
until I write to you to come, or you know I am in Vicksburg.

U<small>LYS</small>.

ALS, DLC-USG.

1. See letters to Julia Dent Grant, June 15, and to Col. William Hoffman,
Aug. 11, 1863.

To Act. Rear Admiral David D. Porter

———

Near Vicksburg July 2, 1863

A<small>DMIRAL</small> P<small>ORTER</small>.

Brig. Genl Hovey informs me, that the firing from the mortar
boats this morning has been exceedingly well directed on my
front. One shell fell into the large fort and several along the lines
of the rifle pits. Please have them continue firing in the same
direction and elevation.

U. S. G<small>RANT</small>
Maj. Genl.

Copies, DLC-USG, V, 19, 101, 103; (intercepted) DNA, RG 109, Pemberton
Papers; *ibid.*, RG 393, Dept. of the Tenn., Letters Sent. *O.R.*, I, xxiv, part 3,
458; *O.R.* (Navy), I, xxv, 99–100.

To Lt. Gen. John C. Pemberton

———

Head Quarters, Dept. of the Ten.
Near Vicksburg, July 3d 1863

Lt. Gen. J. C. Pemberton,
Comd.g Confed. Forces &c.
Gen.

Your note of this date is just received, proposing an armistice for several hours for the purpose of arranging terms of capitulation through commissioners to be appointed, &c.

The useless effusion of blood you propose stopping by this course can be ended at any time you may choose, by an unconditional surrender of the city and garrison. Men who have shown so much endurance and courage as those now in Vicksburg, will always challenge the respect of an adversary, and I can assure you will be treated with all the respect due to prisoners of war.

I do not favor the proposition of appointing commissioners to arrange terms of capitulation, because I have no terms other than those indicated above.

I am Gen. Very respectfully,
your obt. svt.
U. S. Grant
Maj. Gen. Com

ALS, DNA, RG 109, Documents Printed in *O.R. O.R.*, I, xxiv, part 1, 60, 283–84. On July 3, 1863, C.S.A. Lt. Gen. John C. Pemberton wrote to USG. "I have the honor to propose to you an armistice for __ hours, with a view to arranging terms for the capitulation of Vicksburg—To this end if agreeable to you, I will appoint three commissioners, to meet a like number to be named by yourself, at such place and hour to day as you may find convenient—I make this proposition to save the further effusion of blood which must otherwise be shed to a frightful extent, feeling myself fully able to maintain my position for a yet indeffinite period—This communication will be handed you under flag of truce by Maj. Genl. J. S. Bowen" ALS, DNA, RG 94, War Records Office, Union Battle Reports. *O.R.*, I, xxiv, part 1, 59, 283. At the suggestion of C.S.A. Maj. Gen. John S. Bowen, USG agreed verbally to meet with Pemberton at 3:00 p.m. on July 3 between the lines to discuss the situation. USG described the meeting in *Memoirs*, I, 558–59. See Adam Badeau, *Military History of U. S. Grant* (New York, 1868), I, 380–81; Charles A. Dana to Secretary of War Edwin M. Stanton,

July 4, 1863, *O.R.*, I, xxiv, part 1, 114–15. Pemberton's first account of the meeting is *ibid.*, p. 284. A more detailed account is in his letter to John P. Nicholson, June 12, 1875. ALS, CSmH. See John C. Pemberton, *Pemberton: Defender of Vicksburg* (Chapel Hill, 1942), pp. 226–30, 281–85. After the meeting, USG called a conference of his commanders, which he termed "the nearest approach to a 'council of war' I ever held," to discuss the terms to be offered. Against the judgment of his commanders, he then sent his second letter of the day detailing his own terms. *Memoirs*, I, 560.

On July 3, 1863, anticipating the surrender of Vicksburg, USG wrote to his corps commanders and Maj. Gen. Francis J. Herron. "No more deserters will be received from Vicksburg as deserters, all coming out hereafter will be treated as prisoners of war." Copies, DLC-USG, V, 19, 101, 103; DNA, RG 393, Dept. of the Tenn., Letters Sent; *ibid.*, 9th Army Corps, Letters Sent; *ibid.*, 13th Army Corps, Letters Sent; *ibid.*, 13th Army Corps, Letters Received; *ibid.*, RG 94, War Records Office, Dept. of the Ohio.

On July 3, USG wrote twice to Herron. "Order firing to cease along your front until further orders. Capitulation is being concidered." "Your Artillery will be at liberty to fire tonight or in the morning, if you hear firing on the right, otherwise not." Copies, DLC-USG, V, 19, 101, 103; DNA, RG 393, Dept. of the Tenn., Letters Sent. On the same day, Lt. Col. John A. Rawlins wrote to Herron. "Direct your pickets to watch closely the enemy tonight, lest he may attempt to get out by your front. Permit no person to pass your lines from Vicksburg. General Pemberton proposed capitulation to day if suitable terms could be agreed upon, and in view of all the circumstances, the General Commanding offers to parole the garrison here and let them proceed to their homes. This offer you may permit some discreep persons to communicate to their pickets." Copies, *ibid. O.R.*, I, xxiv, part 3, 467.

On July 3, Maj. Gen. Edward O. C. Ord telegraphed to USG. "Gen Lauman reports rebels very busy at work in their trenches in front of us" Telegram received, DNA, RG 94, War Records Office, Dept. of the Tenn. USG drafted his reply on Ord's telegram. "We must work in the trenches also. I have given the same direction on the right." ADfS, *ibid.* Ord telegraphed to USG four more times that day. "Last night came in an Irish deserter whose story is straight he says that he heard the Commissary sergt in town say day before yesterday that there was no more flour in town it had all been issued three days rations to the army & thirty days to hospital I think this important they still get a little bacon the ration of beans has been reduced one half" "Capt Mcalister has just stated that he would like to make himself & have his engineers make a reconnoissance of the enemies line during any temporary cessation of hostilities which an interview between you & Genl P would necessitate shall I tell him to do so" Telegrams received, *ibid.*, RG 393, Dept. of the Tenn., Telegrams Received. "In reply to your intimation that if Genl Pemberton wished an interview he would show a white flag at some specified point Genl Bowen stated to Genl Smith that he knew Genl Pemberton would be glad to meet Genl Grant & Genl Bowen on the return of Genl Smith from you appointed the point where the Jackson & Vicksburg Road crosses the rebel trenches as the place where the white flag would be raised at three (3) oclock P M—This point is in front of Gen McPhersons— The rebel time is forty eight (48) minutes faster than mine I will send you my time" Telegram received, *ibid.*, RG 94, War Records Office, Union Battle Reports. *O.R.*, I, xxiv, part 3, 460. "Shall I notify my men of the enemys offer it will renew their energy after the momentary relaxation by indicating the hold we have on the enemy" Telegram received, DNA, RG 393, Dept. of the Tenn., Telegrams Received. A copy of USG's reply to the last message was noted on the telegram. "Certainly let them know it" Copy, *ibid.* On the same day, Rawlins wrote to Ord and Maj. Gen. James B. McPherson. "Permit some disrceet men on picket tonight to communicate to the enemy's pickets, the fact that General Grant has offered in case Gen. Pemberton surrenders, to parole all the officer and men, and permit them to go home from here." Copies, DLC-USG, V, 19, 101, 103; DNA, RG 393, Dept. of the Tenn., Letters Sent. *O.R.*, I, xxiv, part 3, 460.

To Lt. Gen. John C. Pemberton

Head Quarters, Dept. of the Ten
Near Vicksburg, July 3d 1863.

Lt. Gen. J. C. Pemberton,
Comd.g Confed. Forces,
Vicksburg Miss.
Gen.

In conformity with agreement of this afternoon, I will submit the following proposition for the surrender of the city of Vicksburg, public stores &c. On your accepting the terms propo[sed] I will march in one Division as a guard and take possession at 8 a. m. to-morrow. As soon as rolls can be made out and paroles signed by officers and men you will be allowed to march out of our lines the officers taking with them their side arms and clothing, and the Field, Staff & Cavalry officers one horse each. The rank & file will be allowed all their clothing but no other property.

If these conditions are accepted any amount of rations you may deem necessary can be taken from the stores you now have, and also the necessary cooking utensils for preparing them. Thirty wagons also, counting two two horse or mule teams as one, will be allowed to transport such articles as cannot be carried along.

The same conditions will be allowed to all sick and wounded

officers and soldiers as fast as they become able to travel. The paroles for these latter must be signed, however, whilst officers are present authorized to sign the roll of prisoners.

> I Am Gen. Very respectfully
> your obt. svt.
> U. S. GRANT
> Maj. Gen.

ALS, ICHi. *O.R.*, I, xxiv, part 1, 60, 284. On July 3, 1863, C.S.A. Lt. Gen. John C. Pemberton wrote to USG. "I have the honor to acknowledge the receipt of your communication of this date proposing terms of capitulation for the garrison and post—In the main your terms are accepted; but in justice both to the honor and spirit of my troops manifested in the defense of Vicksburg, I have to submit the following amendments, which if acceded to by you, will perfect the agreement between us. At 10 'o'clock A. M. tomorrow I propose to evacuate the works in and around Vicksburg, and to surrender the city and the garrison under my command by marching out with my colors and arms, stacking them in front of my present lines, after which you will take possession—Officers to retain their side arms, and personal property, and the rights and property of citizens to be respected—" ALS, DNA, RG 94, War Records Office, Union Battle Reports. *O.R.*, I, xxiv, part 1, 60–61, 284–85. See letter to Lt. Gen. John C. Pemberton, July 4, 1863. According to S. H. Lockett, "The Defense of Vicksburg," *Battles and Leaders of the Civil War*, eds., Robert Underwood Johnson and Clarence Clough Buel (New York, 1887), III, 492, information gained by C.S.A. interception of signal messages between USG and Act. Rear Admiral David D. Porter enabled Pemberton to negotiate for parole of the garrison. See following letter.

To Act. Rear Admiral David D. Porter

Near Vicksburg July 3. 1863

ADMIRAL PORTER:

The enemy have asked Armistice to arrange terms of Capitulation. Will you please cease firing until notified or you hear our batteries open. I shall fire a national salute into the city at daylight if they do not surrender[1]

> U. S. GRANT
> Maj. General

Copies, DLC–USG, V, 19, 101, 103; DNA, RG 393, Dept. of the Tenn., Letters Sent. *O.R.*, I, xxiv, part 3, 459; *O.R.* (Navy), I, xxv, 102. On July 3, 1863, USG twice telegraphed to Act. Rear Admiral David D. Porter. "There is a cessation of hostilities. You will please cease firing till you hear from me" Copy, DNA, RG 94, Letters Received. *O.R.*, I, xxiv, part 3, 460; *O.R.* (Navy), I, xxv, 102. "I have given the rebels a few hours to consider the proposition of surrendering. All to be paroled here. The officers only to take side arms. My own feelings are against this but all my officers think the advantage gained by having our forces and transports for immediate purposes more than counterbalance the effect of sending them north" Copies, DNA, RG 94, Letters Received; (intercepted, incomplete) *ibid.*, RG 109, Pemberton Papers. *O.R.*, I, xxiv, part 3, 460; *O.R.* (Navy), I, xxv, 102. On July 4, 4:30 A.M., USG ordered Lt. William C. Magner, Signal Corps, to flag Porter. "The enemy has accepted in the main my terms of Capitulation and will surrender the city, works, & garrison at 10 A M. The firing now going on arises from misapprehension." Facsimile in J. Willard Brown, *The Signal Corps, U. S. A. in the War of the Rebellion* (Boston, 1896; reprinted, New York, 1974), p. 516; copies, DNA, RG 94, Letters Received; (intercepted) *ibid.*, RG 109, Pemberton Papers. *O.R.*, I, xxiv, part 3, 470; *O.R.* (Navy), I, xxv, 103. On the same day, Porter responded. "I congratulate you in getting Vicksburg on any honorable terms. You would find it a troublesome job to transport so many men and I think that you will be left so free to act it will counterbalance any little concession you may seem to make to the garrison. I see they are taking a blow out to night" Copies, DNA, RG 94, Letters Received; (intercepted) *ibid.*, RG 109, Pemberton Papers. *O.R.*, I, xxiv, part 3, 470; *O.R.* (Navy), I, xxv, 103.

1. On July 3, Lt. Col. John A. Rawlins issued Special Orders No. 179. "Army Corps Commanders and Major General Herron, Commanding extreme left Division, will fire a national salute of 34 guns from each Battery (not from each gun) they may have in position on tomorrow the 87th Anniversary of American Independence, at 5 o'clock, A. M., after which they will only fire at living objects or batteries, until such times as they may receive special directions from these Headquarters Should white flags be displayed upon the enemy's lines and forts in their immediate fronts they will move up and take possession of such lines and hold them until further orders." Copies, DLC–USG, V, 27, 28; DNA, RG 393, Dept. of the Tenn., Special Orders. *O.R.*, I, xxiv, part 3, 467. Probably on the same day, USG telegraphed to his corps commanders and Maj. Gen. Francis J. Herron. "The salute ordered to be fired at 5 Oclk tomorrow morning will not be fired until further orders." Copies, DLC–USG, V, 19, 101, 103; DNA, RG 393, Dept. of the Tenn., Letters Sent. On July 4, 1:45 A.M., Lt. Col. James H. Wilson telegraphed to Maj. Gen. James B. McPherson. "Genl. Grand directs that ~~without~~ unless you receive further notice from him, you will begin the national salute according to previous orders." Telegram received, *ibid.*, Telegrams Received. At the same time, Wilson telegraphed to Maj. Gen. Edward O. C. Ord. "Genl. Grant directs that in case you should hear firing from McPherson's batteries at 5 o'clock, you begin the national salute, in accordance with previous orders." Telegram received, *ibid.* At 4:00 A.M., Wilson telegraphed again to McPherson. "Don't open fire till further orders—Genl. Pemberton accepts the terms but makes a wry face, and one or two unimportant amendments." Telegram received, *ibid.*

To Maj. Gen. William T. Sherman

Grant's Hd. Qrs.
July 3d 1863.

GENERAL SHERMAN—

I judge, Johnston is not coming to Vicksburg, he must be watched though. I judge from the fact, that I have just received a proposition from Pemberton to appoint three Commissioners to arrange terms of Capitulation to save effusion of blood &c.— I reply, that the appointment of Commissioners is unnecessary, because he could put an end to it by surrender—and be treated with all the respect due prisoners of War.—When we go in, I want you to drive Johnston from the Mississippi Central Rail Road,—destroy bridges as far as Grenada with your Cavalry, and do the enemy all the harm possible—You can make your own arrangements and have all the Troops of my Command, except one Corps—McPhersons—say.—I must have some Troops to send to Banks to use against Port Hudson.—

U. S. GRANT.

Telegram, copies, DLC-USG, V, 19, 101, 103; DNA, RG 94, War Records Office, Union Battle Reports; *ibid.*, RG 393, Dept. of the Tenn., Letters Sent. *O.R.*, I, xxiv, part 3, 461. On July 3, 1863, Maj. Gen. William T. Sherman telegraphed to USG. "All well & quiet with me   I have now an infantry picket near Hookers so that Col Clark Wrights reports will not be so troublesome   I think your scout Tuttle is valuable   the others not much   If you have some of un-doubted courage send me one man   I have Tuttle watching the road at Cayuga I want another between Brownville & Vernon   Our redouts at Oakridge McCalls & Tiffin are progressing   my pickets are up to Black river from Birdsongs to Baldwins & all report quiet excepting some enemys Cavalry at Messengers & Hookers   should Johnson break through any where between Tiffin & Railroad I would of course attack by Tiffin & Hookers   Should I call for a force it should come out by Edward & williamsons to Clear Creek—nothing indicates such a move & I only refer to it as a chance   If Johnson is deterred ~~in~~ by the signs of our preparations here & chose Hankinsons I would want good reconnoisance from To Whitels & Gibsons   Shall I make it or will you   [This] hot weather is harder on" Telegram received (incomplete), DNA, RG 94, War Records Office, Dept. of the Tenn.

On July 3, Sherman wrote to USG introducing Mrs. R. A. Wilkinson. *Personal Memoirs of Gen. W. T. Sherman . . .* (4th ed., New York, 1891), I, 358.

To Maj. Gen. William T. Sherman

——————

Near Vicksburg, July 3rd 1863

Maj. Gen. Sherman,

Pemberton wants conditions to march out paroled &'c   The conditions wanted are such as I cannot give. I am to submit my proposition at 10 to night. I have directed Steele and Ord to be in readiness to move as you suggested, the moment Vicksburg is surrendered. I want Johnston broken up as effectually as possible, and roads destroyed. I cannot say where you will find the most effective point to strike. I would say, move so as to strike Canton and Jackson, whichever might seem most desirable.

U. S. Grant
Maj. Genl.

Copies, DLC-USG, V, 19, 101, 103; DNA, RG 393, Dept. of the Tenn., Letters Sent. *O.R.*, I, xxiv, part 3, 460. On July 3, 1863, Maj. Gen. William T. Sherman, "Parkes," telegraphed to USG. "I am this momos   m [*moment in*] & have your despatch   telegraph me the moment you have vicksburg in possession & I will secure all the crossings of Black River & move on Jackson or Canton as you may advise   I want my own Corps & Ords with Park in reserve train small all of which will be arranged   I know for certain that you are in absolute possession If you are in Vicksburg Glory Hallelujah the best fourth of July since 1776   Of course we must not rest idle only dont let us brag too soon   I will order my troops at once to occupy the forks of big black & await with anxiety your further answer"   Telegram received, DNA, RG 94, War Records Office, Dept. of the Tenn. *O.R.*, I, xxiv, part 3, 461. On July 3, USG again telegraphed to Sherman. "There is but little doubt, but the enemy will surrender to night or in the morning —make your calculations to attack Johnston—destroy the Road North of Jackson. The Country from Baldwins to Hankersons is picketed and patroled every day by Ord's force.—" Copies, DLC-USG, V, 19, 101, 103; DNA, RG 94, War Records Office, Union Battle Reports; *ibid.*, RG 393, Dept. of the Tenn., Letters Sent. *O.R.*, I, xxiv, part 3, 461. On the same day, Sherman, "Oak Ridge," again telegraphed to USG. "I have your dispatch   I have sent forces to make a bridge at Messengers as soon as the surrender is ~~as~~ certain   Order my Corps to march by the bridgeport road to Tiffin Ords Corps to the Railroad Cross at Rail road bridge & I will order Parkes Corps to cross at Birdsongs all to concentrate north of Bolton to move direct on Johnston where ever he may be   the ~~Railroad~~ railroad should be broken east to Meridian & north to Grenada   Order all troops to move light with ten 10 days rations of bread Salt Sugar & Coffee. If Rawlins will send Condit Smith an approximate return of the troops I think he will have the rations provided & hauled   I will concentrate at Bolton and strike from there   Pemberton will probably ~~f~~ have advised Johnston of his purpose to surrender   The enemy's pickets on the other side are shy but are there   I propose to bridge at once tonight   Only the ~~will~~ move will only be made in force when I know my own corps & Ords are crossing" Telegram received, DNA, RG 94, War Records Office, Dept. of the Tenn. *O.R.*, I, xxiv, part 2, 249. On the same day, Sherman, "near Bear Creek," wrote to Lt. Col. John A. Rawlins. "I am in receipt of two despatches from General Grant, telling me of the opening of negotiations for the surrender of Vicksburg, and ordering me to move against Johnson and to destroy the Central Road as far north as Grenada, and generally to do the enemy as much damage as possible. I have heard some considerable heavy firing at Vicksburg this afternoon which I do not understand, and am this moment, (sundown) in receipt of a letter from Clark Wright, which I enclose. I have so little faith in Col Wright that I would heed his messages very little only I feel assured that every motive that could influence Johnson is at work to make him attempt to relieve Vicksburg, that I am willing to believe he is concentrating at Bolton. If so well, and better still if Vicksburg has surrendered. I send these papers in for the information of General Grant, who tonight will have arrived at some real conclusion and will be prepared to act. If Vicksburg is ours it is the most valuable conquest of the War, and the more valuable for the stout resistance it has made, if complete we should follow up rapidly but should leave nothing to chance. Of course we should instantly assume the offensive as against Johnson. I now have the Bridge at Osterhaus position   I have five Regimts and a Battery at Messengers 3½ miles above Bridgeport with orders to hold the opposite Bank, and tonight to collect log houses for piers, and materials for a double Bridge to be built the moment I know that Vicksburg has surrendered. I have my Cavalry in possession of a ford above Bear Creek & below—Birdsongs—Now Johnson may have under the pressure have collected a force of some 30 000. He has his old force, that of Loring, Breckenridge & McCowns Divisions from Bragg and a considerable force from Charleston & Mobile. If we have Vicksburg we should start with as large a force as possible and as soon as Johnson is met and his forces developed, the balance of the plan of destroying Road could be carried out by a smaller force. I propose that Ord move out to the RRoad Bridge, My Corps, to Messengers Parke's in reserve to cross at same point, and W. S. Smiths Division with the Cavalry not exceeding 1000 men to cross at the Ford below Birdsong, that all meet on the Bridgeport Road about 8 miles out & move on Bolton,— then direct on Jackson, and if necessary to Meridian, destroying of course the Railroad and doing all manner of harm, then return to Jackson whence I could send back to Vicksburg all troops not absolutely needed for the trip up to Grenada & back. Port Hudson is now well invested and an increased force there could do less good than the destruction of the only army that can afford them relief viz Johnstons   But as soon as Johnston is met and either defeated or dispersed, a force could go to Banks. I think the fall of Vicksburg when known will parallyze the confederates West of the Mississippi, for Port Hudson was only used in connection with Vicksburg, ~~with~~ to make the intervening space a 'Mare Clausum' to which these Forts gave the enemy absolute title. If these my views meet the information of General Grant, Generals approval, I ask the issuance of a special Order from your Head Qrs. that Ords Corps move to RR Bridge provided with 5 ds rations & 150 rounds of cartridges—~~has~~ve the 15th to be ordered to come forward provided in like manner with the same rations & ammunition and order J Condit Smith to organize a train of 200 wagons with bread, salt, sugar, & coffee, to come forward in two trains by the same road, behind the troops,—for all my staff to come forward at once, and generally all orders that will initiate the movemt. As you see I must still watch Johnston, and these preparations can be made better at your end—This would leave McPhersons Corps at Vicksburg Herrons Division disposable, one Brigade of which could hold the works at the RR Bridge and Kimballs Division at Haines Bluff. Indeed in the movemt against Johnston we should risk nothing, provided Vicksburg is surely surrendered. The news is so good I can hardly believe it and I am confused by the sound of cannon at Vicksburg this P M. I keep a staff officer at the Telegraph office 3 miles back to bring me the earliest inteligence.—If all is right & Vicksburg is surrendered, after ordering troops to move as suggested, it may be well to order my Qr. Mr J. Condit Smith to ride out quick to see me, after ordering 200 wag[ons] to load as before recited. Also send me plenty of the best maps Wilson has.—I have left mine behind, and must depend on Wilson." ALS, DNA, RG 94, War Records Office, Union Battle Reports. *O.R.*, I, xxiv, part 3, 461–63.

On July 3, Maj. Gen. John G. Parke, Oak Ridge, telegraphed to USG. "General Sherman desires me to ask what means the heavy firing at Vicksburg." *O.R.*, I, xxiv, part 3, 463. On the same day, USG replied to Sherman and Parke. "Flag of truce only covered the bearer of dispatches, Firing was continued to the balance of the line" Copies, DLC-USG, V, 19, 101, 103; DNA, RG 393, Dept. of the Tenn., Letters Sent. *O.R.*, I, xxiv, part 3, 463.

On July 3, Brig. Gen. Peter J. Osterhaus, "Big Black," telegraphed three times to USG. "Col Wright reports the following I caught one of Breckenridges men today & learn from him him that Breckenridge arrived at Bolton last night with seven thousand 7000 troops and large supply train Johnston is moving from above to form junction with 'B' the prisoner thinks in my front & will arrive at or near the river tonight Whitfields Cavalry, Moved from Bolton last night as Breckenridge arrived the prisoner thinks they moved to the right but but does not know" Telegram received, DNA, RG 94, War Records Office, Dept. of the Tenn. *O.R.*, I, xxiv, part 2, 228. "Col Wrights reports as follows Rebel pickets tonight are immediately on the Bank of the river at Bridgeport their line of pickets extend down to Croc[ke]rs Commands are distinctly heard from this side indicating that the advance at least has arrived Evidently there is considerable force in our immediate front My pickets are on the river bank & will be kept there unless driven in by superior force I communicate the above to Gen McArther him to support Col Wrights Cavalry" "Scout Lorraine Ruggles just returns & reports only one detachment of cavalry not over four hundred (400) strong south of Edwards station on the road on the 14 mile creek He could not learn of any general movement further down" Telegrams received, DNA, RG 393, Dept. of the Tenn., Unregistered Letters Received. Osterhaus also wrote to USG on July 3. "I send you the Prisoner wherein I mentioned in my telegraphic dispatch at this p. m.: he was a lieutenant in a Louisiana regiment, and was to be mustered out in consequence of the consolidation of his regiment and be drafted again as a Private!! Such is the story he gives for the cause of his desertion; He reports Breckenridge 7000 Strong (5 brigades, each with 1–6 gun battery) of the Whereabouts and Strength of Johnstons Armey he knows nothing reliable; of the time of the contemplated attack he is also ignorant" Copies, *ibid.*, 15th Army Corps, 9th Div., Letters Sent; *ibid.*, Letters Received. *O.R.*, I, xxiv, part 2, 228. On the same day, USG wrote to Osterhaus. "You can do as desired in your dispatch, but hold yourself in in readiness to move, if your Division should be ordered tomorrow." Copies, DLC-USG, V, 19, 101, 103; DNA, RG 393, Dept. of the Tenn., Letters Sent.

Special Orders No. 180

Head Quarters, Dept. of the T[en]
Near Vicksburg, July 4th 1863,

SPL. ORDERS, NO 180

~~H H~~ 1 ~~Immediately~~ On the surrender of ~~the City~~ of Vicksburg Maj. Gen. Herron will advance one Brigade of his Division to within the fortifications of the enemy. He will ~~immediately~~ throw out guards to prevent all persons, ~~from~~ soldiers or citizens, from entering or leaving the city.

~~The Division of Maj. Gen. J. A. Logan will march in and take cha~~

2 H Maj. Gen. J. A. Logan is assigned temporarily to the command of the city of Vicksburg, and ~~He~~ will march his Division ~~immediately~~ within the entrenchments of the enemy to a suitable camp ground. He will ~~ta~~ furnish all the guards necessary to prevent the escape of citizens or prisoners from ~~the~~ Vicksburg or the entrance of soldiers and all out side parties into the city.

One regiment will be immediately placed on guard in the city to preserve order and to prevent pillaging and other destruction of property.

Five companies, commanded by a competant Field Officer, will report at once to Lt. Col. Bingham, Chief Quartermaster, to ~~guard a~~ collect and guard all captured property, and to superintend working parties of such negroes as may be collected and employed in discharging boats and other~~wise~~ labor in the Quartermaster's Dept.

3 No citizens will be permitted to land from steamers until authority may hereafter be given.

4 All able bodied negro men in the city will be immediately collected and organized into working parties under suitable officers ~~& non-commissioned officers~~. They will at once be set at policing the city and ~~all~~ the grounds within the entrenchments.

5. Capt. Comstock,[1] Chief Eng. will ~~superintend~~ direct the destruction of the outside approaches made to the enemy's

works. All necessary details will be made for this purpose by the Comdr of the 17th Army Corps, either from his ~~Py~~Pioneer Corps, negroes collected, or by details from the ranks. All heavy Artillery will be moved into the entrenchments and properly located for defence. Division Engineer officers, or in their absence, Division Qr. Mrs. will collect and save all mining tools belonging to their respective commands.

ADf, CSmH. *O.R.*, I, xxiv, part 3, 477.

On July 4, 1863, Lt. Col. James H. Wilson wrote to USG. "I have the honor to recommend, that in justice to the endurance, discipline and valor displayed by the Army throughout the campaign, ending with the capture of Vicksburg, such regiments as may have borne an honorable part in any of the various battles, be allowed to inscribe upon their banners the names of those battles and that for the purpose of ascertaining, which regiments are entitled to this honor, the Generals Commanding the different Army Corps and detached divisions, constituting the Army of the Tennessee, be directed to order a board of Officers, consisting of three membres, the corps Commander or Division commander in each case being the President. These boards should meet at once and report without delay," LS, DNA, RG 393, Dept. of the Tenn., Letters Received. On July 12, Maj. Theodore S. Bowers issued a circular ordering each army corps and div. commander to convene a board of three officers to list the battles participated in by each regt. so that they might be inscribed on their banners. Copies, DLC-USG, V, 19, 103; DNA, RG 393, Dept. of the Tenn., Letters Sent; (dated Aug. 1) *ibid.*, 16th Army Corps, 1st Div., 1st–2nd Brigades, Letters Received. On Aug. 12, the "Board on Inscriptions," 15th Army Corps, submitted its report, which Maj. Gen. William T. Sherman endorsed: "Approved and forwarded to Dept Hd. Qrs. for orders in the Case." DS and AES, *ibid.*, Dept. of the Tenn., Miscellaneous Letters Received. On Sept. 25, Sherman telegraphed to Brig. Gen. John A. Rawlins. "You remember thet Report of the board determined the battles each regt of my command could inscribe on their colors do you understand that the order for such inscription is made by the War Dept by you or by me I want to bring up the records to date in case I have to [*go to*] Chattanooga I hear from interior merly a rumor that Rosecrans advanced from the Tenn but was compelled to ~~put the~~ fall back to Chattanooga The flag of truce which goes out today can bring back more definite news" Telegram received, *ibid.*, RG 94, War Records Office, Dept. of the Tenn.; copy, *ibid.*, RG 393, Dept. of the Tenn., Telegrams Sent. *O.R.*, I, xxx, part 3, 842–43. See telegrams to Maj. Gen. Henry W. Halleck, Sept. 25, 1863, note 3, and to Maj. Gen. William T. Sherman, Sept. 30, 1863, note 1. On Sept. 26, Rawlins telegraphed to Sherman. "The report of the board will be forwarded to Washington with proper remarks endorsed thereon for the orders of Gen'l in Chief." Copies, DLC-USG, V, 19, 103; DNA, RG 393, Dept. of the Tenn., Letters Sent. On Oct. 15, Bowers issued General Orders No. 64 listing the battles which regts. of the 15th Army Corps were entitled to inscribe on their colors and guidons. Copies, DLC-USG, V, 13, 14; DNA, RG 393, Dept. of the Tenn., General and Special Orders; (printed) Lawler Papers, ICarbS. On Oct. 6, Rawlins wrote to Maj. Gens. Stephen A. Hurlbut,

James B. McPherson, and Edward O. C. Ord, noting that no report had been received pursuant to the inscriptions circular. Copies, DLC-USG, V, 19, 103; DNA, RG 393, Dept. of the Tenn., Letters Sent.

On Sept. 2, Maj. Thomas M. Vincent, AGO, wrote to USG, noting certain regts. for which the Ordnance Bureau had received no "Company histories" as required by War Dept. General Orders No. 19, Feb. 22, 1862, and threatening to stop the pay of officers who remained delinquent in obeying this order. LS, *ibid.*, Letters Received. On Sept. 21, USG endorsed a copy of this letter. "Respectfully referred to Major. Genl. E. O. C. Ord Comd'g 13th Army Corps who will please have the within letter of instructions complied with and take such steps as will hereafter insure prompt compliance with 'Regulations' and 'Orders' in the making out of reports and returns required for the Ordnance Department at the time they are due" Copies, DLC-USG, V, 25; DNA, RG 393, Dept. of the Tenn., Endorsements. On the same day, Rawlins similarly endorsed other copies of Vincent's letter to Hurlbut, McPherson, and Sherman. ES, *ibid.*, Letters Received; copies (3), *ibid.*, Endorsements; DLC-USG, V, 25. On Sept. 23, Vincent wrote to USG, seeking compliance with his letter of Sept. 2. Copy, DNA, RG 393, Military Div. of the Miss., War Dept. Correspondence. On Oct. 5, USG endorsed this letter. "Respectfully referred to Major Genl. N. P. Banks comd'g Dept. of the Gulf, in whose command the 7th Kentucky is now serving" Copies, DLC-USG, V, 25; DNA, RG 393, Dept. of the Tenn., Endorsements. On Oct. 12, Col. Edward D. Townsend, AGO, wrote to USG, listing regts. still remiss in furnishing co. histories. LS, *ibid.*, Unregistered Letters Received. On Oct. 17, Bowers endorsed copies of this letter to Hurlbut, McPherson, and Sherman. AES (3), *ibid.*; *ibid.*, 16th Army Corps, Letters Received.

1. Cyrus B. Comstock of Mass., USMA 1855, served in the Corps of Engineers and as asst. professor, USMA, before the Civil War. After assignment to construction of the defenses of Washington, D. C., early in the war, he served in various engineering capacities in Va. Promoted to capt., March 3, 1863, he was ordered on June 8 to report to USG. On June 20, Rawlins issued Special Orders No. 166. "Major General T. J. Herron, Commanding Herrons Division and Brig. General J. G. Lauman, Commanding 4th Division, 16th Army Corps, will furnish from their respective Commands all the men that may be required by Capt. Cyrus B. Comstock, Engineer in charge of the work in their front, to push forward the work laid out by him to rapid Completion, and also the necessary guards to protect the men in said work." Copies, DLC-USG, V, 27, 28; DNA, RG 393, Dept. of the Tenn., Special Orders.

To Lt. Gen. John C. Pemberton

Hd Qrs. Dptmt of the Tenn:
Before Vicksburg July 4th 1863

Lieut Genl J. C. Pemberton
Comdg Confederate Forces
Vicksburg
General

I have the honor to acknowledge the receipt of your communication of 3rd July

The amendments proposed by you cannot be acceded to in full. it will be necessary to furnish every officer and man with a parole signed by himself which with the completion of the rolls of the prisoners will nescessarily take some time.

Again I can make no stipulations with regard to the treatment of citizens and their Private Property—While I do not propose to cause them any undue annoyance or loss, I cannot consent to leave myself under any restraint by stipulations

The property which officers can be allowed to take with them will be as stated in my proposition of last evening, that is, officers will be allowed their Private Baggage and sidearms and mounted officers one horse each

If you mean by your proposition for each brigade to march to the front of the lines now occupied by it and stack arms at ten o'clock a. m. and then return to the inside and there remain as prisoners until properly paroled I will make no objections to it

Should no notification be recieved of your acceptance of my terms by nine o'clock a. m., I shall regard them as having been rejected and shall act accordingly

Should these terms be accepted white flags will be displayed along your lines to prevent such of my troops as may not have been notified, from firing upon your men.

I Am Gen. Very respectfully
your obt. svt.
U. S. Grant
Maj. Gen

LS, DNA, RG 109, Pemberton Papers; Df, *ibid.*, RG 94, War Records Office, Union Battle Reports. *O.R.*, I, xxiv, part 1, 61, 285. On July 4, 1863, Lt. Gen. John C. Pemberton wrote to USG. "I have the honor to acknowledge the receipt of your communication of this date; and in reply to say that the terms proposed by you are accepted—" ALS, DNA, RG 109, Documents Printed in *O.R. O.R.*, I, xxiv, part 1, 61, 285; *O.R.* (Navy), I, xxv, 102. Since Pemberton was from Philadelphia, his motives for surrendering Vicksburg on Independence Day were questioned throughout the South. Sensitive to doubt of his loyalty, he answered that he could secure better terms on July 4 due to "the vanity of our foes." *O.R.*, I, xxiv, part 1, 285. USG believed, however, that Pemberton "knew his men would not resist an assault, and one was expected on the fourth." *Memoirs*, I, 565.

To Maj. Gen. Richard Taylor

Headquarters Dept. of the Tenn
Near Vicksburg, July 4th 1863.

MAJ. GENERAL R. TAYLOR
COMD'G. CONFED FORCES
ALEXANDRIA, LA.
GENERAL.

Your letter of the 27th of June, disclaiming the act of hanging Union soldiers who were taken prisoners by your forces near Milliken's Bend on the 7th of June is just received. I could not credit the story although told so straight, and I am now truly glad to have your denial. The prisoners taken by our forces have not been subjected to any harsh treatment in consequence of the statements detailed in my former letter.

In the matter of treatment of Negro soldiers taken prisoners, I do not feel authorized to say what the government may demand in regard to them, but having taken the responsibility of declaring slaves free and having authorized the arming of them, I cannot see the justice of permitting one treatment for them, and another for the white soldiers   This however is a subject I am not aware of any action having been taken upon.

I am, General
Your Obt Servt
U. S. GRANT
Maj Genl Comd'g.

Copies, DLC-USG, V, 19, 101, 103; DNA, RG 393, Dept. of the Tenn., Letters Sent. *O.R.*, I, xxiv, part 3, 469. On June 27, 1863, C.S.A. Maj. Gen. Richard Taylor, Alexandria, La., wrote to USG. "Your communication of the 22d inst attributing to the troops of my command, upon evidence furnished you by 'a *white man*,' certain acts disgraceful alike to humanity and to the reputation of soldiers, has just reached me. In reply I beg to say that I remained at Richmond and in its vicinity for several days after the skirmish to which you allude, and had any officer or negro been hung the fact must have come to my knowledge, and the act would most assuredly have met with the punishment it deserved. The hanging of a white sergeant by Col Harrison's cavalry is I am satisfied likewise a fabrication. I shall however cause this matter to be thoroughly investigated and should I [disco]ver evidence of such acts having been perpetrated the parties shall meet with summary punishment. My orders at all times have been to treat all prisoners with every consideration. As regards negros captured in arms the officers of the Confederate States Army are required by an order emanating from the general government, to turn over all such to the civil authorities to be dealt with according to the laws of the state wherein they were captured." LS, DNA, RG 94, War Records Office, Dept. of the Tenn. *O.R.*, I, xxiv, part 3, 443–44. See letters to Maj. Gen. Richard Taylor, June 22, 1863; to Maj. Gen. Henry W. Halleck, Aug. 29, 1863.

To Maj. Gen. Henry W. Halleck

Near Vicksburg
July 4th 10 30 A. M 1863

MAJ GEN H. W. HALLECK
GEN IN CHIEF

The Enemy surrendered this morning.[1] The only terms allowed is their parole as prisoners of war[2]   This I regarded as of great advantage to us at this juncture. It saves probably several days in the capture term—leaves troops and transports ready for immediate service. Gen Sherman with a large force will face immediately on Johnstone and drive him from the state. I will send troops to the relief of Gen Banks and return the ninth Corps to Gen Burnside

U. S. GRANT
Maj Genl

Telegram received, DNA, RG 107, Telegrams Collected (Bound); copies, *ibid.*, Telegrams Received in Cipher; *ibid.*, RG 393, Dept. of the Tenn., Hd. Qrs.

Correspondence; DLC-USG, V, 6, 8, 24, 94. *O.R.*, I, xxiv, part 1, 44. On July 3, 1863, USG wrote to George W. Graham. "Have a fast boat ready to send up the river, whenever it it is required, and let no boat go up without orders." Copies, DLC-USG, V, 19, 101, 103; DNA, RG 393, Dept. of the Tenn., Letters Sent. On July 3, Graham telegraphed to Lt. Col. John A. Rawlins. "Will you permit the steamboat men to celebrate the fourth of July. By the firing of cannon from their respective steamers at sunrise & sunset holding a meeting reading of Declaration of independence &c" Telegram received, *ibid.*, Telegrams Received. USG's reply, "Yes," was noted on the bottom of this telegram. Copy, *ibid.* Probably on the same day, Graham telegraphed again to Rawlins. "Can you send me early in the morning Copy of declaration of Independence not one Copy here" Telegram received, *ibid.* Rawlins drafted his reply on the bottom of this telegram. "I will if I can find one" ADfS, *ibid.* On July 4, Graham telegraphed to Rawlins. "Boys very uneasy along the river cannot you send me glad tidings something that I can depend upon for fourth of July." Telegram received, *ibid.* Rawlins again drafted his reply on the bottom of the telegram. "Vicksburg will probably be surrendered at 10 oclock today. the terms have not yet been fully settled, will be by nine oclock, will send you word. Dont go off half cocked" ADfS, *ibid.*

On July 4, USG wrote to Graham. "If any boat is ready for Memphis, or getting ready, hold it until you receive orders from here." Copies, DLC-USG, V, 19, 101, 103; DNA, RG 393, Dept. of the Tenn., Letters Sent. On the same day, Graham telegraphed to USG. "Boat in readiness & will leave on arrival of despatches" Telegram received, *ibid.*, Telegrams Received. Rawlins's reply was copied on the telegram. "Hold the boat until Mr. Dana arrives" Copy, *ibid.* Graham responded to Rawlins on the same day. "Boat Gone an hour ago no boat here can overtake her" Telegram received, *ibid.* Rawlins's reply was copied on the bottom of the telegram. "All right—" Copy, *ibid.*

1. On July 7, Maj. Gen. Stephen A. Hurlbut, Memphis, wrote to USG. "I send you the inclosed copy of dispatch from the Admiral received by Lieut. Comg Pattison U. S. N, early in the morning of the 6th *with instructions* to keep it quiet for some hours after the dispatch Boat left. It reached me indirectly about 1. P. M. I cannot conceive the object of this" ALS, *ibid.*, 16th Army Corps, Letters Received. Enclosed was a copy of Act. Rear Admiral David D. Porter's telegram of July 4 to Secretary of the Navy Gideon Welles announcing the surrender of Vicksburg. Copy, *ibid. O.R.* (Navy), I, xxv, 103. Porter's message arrived in Washington on July 7, 12:40 P.M., one day before USG's telegram to Maj. Gen. Henry W. Halleck. However, the Memphis telegraph operator, Albert J. Howell, sent his own message first to Col. Anson Stager, general manager, Military Telegraph: "Pemberton surrendered July 4." This enabled Secretary of War Edwin M. Stanton to spread the news before Welles. William R. Plum, *The Military Telegraph during the Civil War in the United States* (Chicago, 1882), I, 321.

2. On July 8, Halleck telegraphed to USG. "I fear your paroling the garrison at Vicksburg without actual delivery to a proper agent as required by the 14th article of the cartel may be construed into an absolute release & that these men will be immediately placed in the ranks of the enemy. Such has been the case elsewhere. If these prisoners have not been allowed to depart, you will retain them till further orders." ALS (telegram sent), DNA, RG 107, Telegrams Col-

lected (Bound); telegram received, *ibid.*, RG 393, Dept. of the Tenn. *O.R.*, I, xxiv, part 1, 62; *ibid.*, II, vi, 92–93. On July 10, 10:00 A.M., Halleck telegraphed to USG. "On a full examination of the question, it is decided that you as the commander of an Army was authorized to agree upon the parole and release of the garrison of Vicksburgh with the Genl commanding the place." ALS (telegram sent), DNA, RG 107, Telegrams Collected (Bound); copies, *ibid.*, RG 108, Telegrams Sent; *ibid.*, RG 249, Letters Received. *O.R.*, I, xxiv, part 1, 62; *ibid.*, II, vi, 97. On July 19, Col. William Hoffman, commissary gen. of prisoners, wrote to USG. "I have the honor to communicate herewith for your information a copy of a telegram, addressed by the Gen'l in Chief to Major Genl Meade and other Commanders. 'Washington D. C. July 10. 1863. MAJOR GEN'L MEADE, Army of the Potomac. It has been understood and agreed, between Col. Ludlow and Mr Ould, agents for exchange of prisoners, that paroles not given as prescribed in section seven of the cartel, after May 22d are to be considered as Null and void, and that the officers and men of the respective parties paroled not in accordance with that section of the cartel, will be returned to duty without exchange. They will be so returned to duty. (Signed) H. W. HALLECK. Gen'l in Chief." LS, DNA, RG 94, War Records Office, Dept. of the Tenn. See *O.R.*, II, vi, 97.

To Maj. Gen. Nathaniel P. Banks

Head Quarters, Dept. of the Ten.
Near Vicksburg, July 4th 1863.

MAJ. GEN. N. P. BANKS,
COMD.G DEPT. OF THE GULF,
GEN.

The garrison of Vicksburg surrendered this morning. Number of prisoners as given by the officers is 27000, Field Artillery 128 pieces and a large number of siege guns, probably not less than Eighty. The other stores will probably not amount to any great deal.

I held all my surplus troops out on Black River and between there and Hain's Bluff. Intending to assault in a few days I directed that they be kept in readiness to move on the shortest notice to attack Johnston. The moment the surrender of Vicksburg was agreed upon the order was given and troops are now in motion. Gen. Sherman goes in command of this expedition. His force is so heavy I think it cannot fail.—This move will have the effect of keeping Johnston from detaching a portion of his force for the relief of Port Hudson.

Although I had the garrison of Vicksburg completely in my power I gave them the privilege of being paroled at this place, the officers to retain their side arms, and private baggage, and Field, Staff & Cavalry Officers to take with them one horse each. I regard the terms really more favorable than an unconditional surrender   It leaves the transports and troops free for immediate use. At the present juncture of affairs in the East, and on the river above here, this may prove of vast importance.

I hope General, and from what Admiral Porter tells me, this probably will find you in possession of Port Hudson.

> I am Gen. Very respectfully
> your obt. svt.
> U. S. Grant
> Maj. Gen.

ALS, DNA, RG 94, War Records Office, Dept. of the Gulf. *O.R.*, I, xxiv, part 3, 470–71; (incomplete) *ibid.*, I, xxvi, part 1, 53. On July 7, 1863, 11:00 A.M., Maj. Gen. Nathaniel P. Banks, "Before Port Hudson," wrote to USG. "Your most gratifying despatch has just been received, announcing the surrender of Vicksburg. I beg you to accept my hearty congratulations. It is the most important event of the war, and will contribute most to the re-establishmt of the Governmt. The freedom of the Mississppi, puts an end to the Rebellion, so far as an independent Confedeacy is concerned. There is no room for an indepenet Governmt between the Mississppi and the Atlantic. Port Hudson will be in our possession before the close of this week. The Army of the Gulf sends its congratulates to the Gallant & Successfull troops of your Comnd. Salutes will be fired at noon, from the batteries on the Right, Left, and Center, of our Lines in honor of the Fall of Vicksburg." ALS, DNA, RG 94, War Records Office, Dept. of the Tenn. *O.R.*, I, xxvi, part 1, 619–20.

On July 4, Act. Rear Admiral David D. Porter signaled to USG. "What prospect ~~of a~~ is ~~Surrender~~ there of a Surrender to day.   the rebels under McCullock are building bridges over the tensas River and advancing on Goodriches landing again in force   I have sent two Gun Boats there   Stil the rebs will ravage the plantations and carry off the Blacks unless you Soon have a force to Spare to check them" Copy, DNA, RG 111, Vicksburg Signal Book. On the same day, USG answered. "The enemy surrendered at 10 A-M–" Copy, *ibid.* On the same day, Porter signaled to USG twice more. "When can the vessels ~~move~~ come do[wn] & when are yo[u] going to moove ~~to~~ in" Copy, *ibid.* "I will have a Steamer ready to carry dispatches to Gnl Banks and the fleet below. what time will you wish to send, and will you take up your Hd Qrs in the city at once" Copy, *ibid.*; *ibid.*, RG 94, War Records Office, Military Div. of the Miss. *O.R.*, I, xxiv, part 3, 470; *O.R.* (Navy), I, xxv, 105. On taking possession of the city, USG met Porter briefly at the river to exchange congratulations. USG did not move his hd. qrs. into the city until July 6. Admiral Porter, *Incidents and Anecdotes of the Civil War* (New York, 1885), p. 200; *Memoirs*, I, 566–67.

On July 4, USG signaled to Brig. Gen. Elias S. Dennis. "Send Battery of light Artilery to lake Providence as soon as practible"　Copy, DNA, RG 111, Vicksburg Signal Book.

To Maj. Gen. Francis J. Herron

Headquarters Dept of Tennessee
Near Vicksburg July 4, 1863

Gen Herron.

The object of moving your troops in, was to help guard the city, to prevent ingress and egress.[1] Gen. McPherson's corps moves inside and forms what you fail to of the investment. If the ground is suitable for an encampment inside, you had better move in your entire Division　Collect together all the arms accoutrements and colors on your front, and hold them for the ordnance officer to get when he calls. None of the colors are to be taken by any individual. They are all to be sent to Washington. Gen Logan commands the remainder of the city Guard, and you will connect with him as nearly as possible.

U. S. Grant
Maj. Genl.

Copies, DLC-USG, V, 19, 101, 103; DNA, RG 393, Dept. of the Tenn., Letters Sent. On July 4, 1863, 4:45 A.M., Lt. Col. James H. Wilson issued a circular. "Should white flags be displayed upon the enemy's works, at 10 this morning, it will be to signify the acceptance of the terms of Capitulation. The enemy will be permitted to move to the front of his works, and after stacking flags and arms, will then return to his camps. The works will be occupied only by such troops, as may afterwards be selected. Those troops not designated for the purpose, will not occupy the enemy's line, but remain in their present camps." Copies, *ibid*. On July 4, USG wrote to Maj. Gen. Francis J. Herron, Maj. Gen. James B. McPherson, and Maj. Gen. Edward O. C. Ord. "The enemy will march outside their works, stack arms and return inside as prisoners. No troops except those specified in special orders will enter the city for the present." Copies, *ibid*. *O.R.*, I, xxiv, part 3, 472; *O.R.* (Navy), I, xxv, 105. On the same day, Ord telegraphed to USG. "There are no guards along the rebel works to keep either party from crossing, . . . The town is full of our men plundering & the rebels are straggling out. The troops occupying Vicksburg should stop this." Quoted in Bernarr Cresap, "The Career of General Edward O. C. Ord to 1864," Ph.D. Dissertation, Vanderbilt University, 1949, p. 287. Also on July 4, USG wrote to McPherson. "Gen. Ord reports rebels slipping through our lines on his front. He leaves tonight, and cannot keep up guards. Has Gen Smith moved in, and established lines on Ord's front." Copies, DLC-USG, V, 19, 101, 103; DNA, RG 393, Dept. of the Tenn., Letters Sent. On the same day, McPherson telegraphed to Lt. Col. John A. Rawlins. "If one regt goes in in advance to the court house to take ~~ad~~ possession I respectfully request that it be the 45th Ills   this regt has born the brunt of the battle oftener than any other in my Command & always behaved nobly" Telegram received, *ibid.*, RG 94, War Records Office, Dept. of the Tenn. *O.R.*, I, xxiv, part 3, 476. Rawlins drafted his answer on the bottom of the telegram. "~~You will designate~~ It is left for you to designate such Regt as you may ~~want~~ see proper to go forward & take possession of the Court house" ADfS, DNA, RG 94, War Records Office, Dept. of the Tenn. *O.R.*, I, xxiv, part 3, 476. On the same day, McPherson telegraphed to USG. "In case Logans Division marches into the city as one of ~~it~~ his brigades is absent cannot I ~~detach~~ attach Ransoms Brig to Logans Division temporarily to march in   It will suit both parties" Telegram received, DNA, RG 393, Dept. of the Tenn., Telegrams Received. USG's answer, "Yes," was noted on the telegram. Copy, *ibid.*

1. See Special Orders No. 180, July 4, 1863.

To Maj. Gen. Edward O. C. Ord

———

Vicksburg July 4—63—

Gen Ord.—

Prepare to march this evening.—Five (5) days rations of Bread &c will be sufficient to take, sherman has made arrangements for two hundred (200) wagons of a supply train   in addition, take one hundred fifty (150) rounds of ammunition in addition to that in Boxes.   leave a guard for Stores, and public property left behind—

U. S. Grant
Maj Gen

Telegram received, Ord Papers, CU-B; copies, DLC-USG, V, 101; (incomplete) *ibid.*, V, 19; DNA, RG 393, Dept. of the Tenn., Letters Sent. On July 4, 1863, USG telegraphed to Maj. Gen. Edward O. C. Ord. "take as many rations as you can   five (5) days is given as the minimum" Telegram received, Ord Papers,

CU-B; copies, DLC-USG, V, 19, 101, 103; DNA, RG 393, Dept. of the Tenn., Letters Sent. On July 4, Ord telegraphed to USG. "Shall I designate the troops of my corps to occupy the enemys works   if so what force"   Telegram received, *ibid.*, Telegrams Received. On the bottom of the telegram, USG's reply was noted. "None of your forces will occupy the Enemys Works"   Copy, *ibid.* On the same day, Ord telegraphed to USG twice more. "Shall I let working parties rest today & order men to clean up & give them a drink all around"   Telegram received, *ibid.* "Genls Smith & Carr are here   their Divisions are as much in hand as any & in reply to the order Gen Carr states he can get off by tonight by working the men all day   Gen Smith states he can't get his guns & men into marching order before tomorrow morning   Benton takes Carrs place   I have set them to work   Shall I order the Siege arty to move with the columns   Am of opinion many men broke by the guards & went into town"   Telegram received, *ibid.*, RG 94, War Records Office, Dept. of the Tenn. *O.R.*, I, xxiv, part 3, 471. On the same day, USG telegraphed to Ord. "None but light artillery need be taken with you. I have given orders for bringing the Siege Artillery into rebel works. Get your troops of as soon as possible, including Lauman's Division" Copies, DLC-USG, V, 19, 101, 103; DNA, RG 94, War Records Office, 17th Army Corps; *ibid.*, RG 393, Dept. of the Tenn., Letters Sent. On the same day, Ord telegraphed to USG. "I have ordered in my cavalry from Baldwins Halls & Hankersons ferries   this leaves that front exposed to adams & Barnes Texas Cavalry which I hear by reliable intelligence are at Rocky springs   should not some piquets replace mine"   Telegram received, *ibid.*, RG 94, War Records Office, Dept. of the Tenn. *O.R.*, I, xxiv, part 3, 471. USG drafted his reply on the bottom of the telegram. "All the Cavalry belonging to this Army goes with Sherman except what you have. Leave ~~your~~ all but two Companies to Picket Black River." ALS, DNA, RG 94, War Records Office, Dept. of the Tenn. *O.R.*, I, xxiv, part 3, 471.

Also on July 4, USG telegraphed to Ord. "Gen Hovey's Division will have to go. If Gen Hovey is sick, Gen. Sullivan can be sent to command it. I will send Gen. Sullivan out in the morning to join the command if he is required. Gen. Hovey's staff will be required with the Division." Copies, DLC-USG, V, 19, 101, 103; DNA, RG 393, Dept. of the Tenn., Letters Sent.

To Maj. Gen. Edward O. C. Ord

Near Vicksburg July 4th 1863

GEN ORD.

The route travelled by your corps on coming to Vicksburg, is exactly the route they will travel back. They come by Black River Bridge, Edward's Station and Champion Hill. That is the route they now go. If they leave that route after passing Champion Hills, all will be equally ignorant of the route, none of our troops having been North of that road. Haines[1] can tell you all about the route.

U. S. GRANT
Maj. Genl

Copies, DLC-USG, V, 19, 101, 103; DNA, RG 393, Dept. of the Tenn., Letters Sent. *O.R.*, I, xxiv, part 3, 471. On July 4, 1863, Maj. Gen. Edward O. C. Ord telegraphed to USG. "I have telegraphed Gen Sherman for instructions in detail no answer can you send me one in my ignorance of country north, routes I cant issue an order for my different divisions none of my staff know anything of Route all come via Edwards ferry & champion hills" Telegram received, DNA, RG 393, Dept. of the Tenn., Telegrams Received.

1. Peter C. Hains of N. J., USMA 1861, 1st lt., Corps of Engineers, served as chief engineer, 13th Army Corps, during the Vicksburg campaign. His report is in *O.R.*, I, xxiv, part 2, 180–87.

To Maj. Gen. William T. Sherman

Headquarters Dept of the Tennessee
Near Vicksburg July 4th 1863

GEN. SHERMAN.

Your note is received. Propositions have been sent in for the surrender of Vicksburg. Pemberton's reply is momentarily expected If he does not surrender now, he will be compelled to by his men within two days no doubt. The orders will be made as you suggest, the moment Vicksburg is ours. Ord and Steele have both been notified to move the moment Vicksburg falls. Ordered to take ten days hard bread, salt coffee and sugar. I will change this to five, in view of the provision train you expect to take. I will let you know the moment Pembertons answer arrives.

U. S. GRANT
Maj. Genl

Copies, DLC-USG, V, 19, 101, 103; DNA, RG 393, Dept. of the Tenn., Letters Sent. *O.R.*, I, xxiv, part 3, 469–70. On July 4, 1863, to expedite supplies to Maj. Gen. William T. Sherman, USG telegraphed to the commanding officer, Chickasaw Bayou. "Use all the force you have, and all that can be picked up in loading teams, until all are got off. Boats will all be sent to Vicksburg tomorrow, and your troops relieved from their present arduous duties." Copies, DLC-USG, V, 19, 101, 103; DNA, RG 393, Dept. of the Tenn., Letters Sent. On the same day, Lt. Col. John A. Rawlins also telegraphed to the commanding officer, Chickasaw Bayou. "You will furnish all necessary details for loading wagons tomorrow expeditiously." Copies, *ibid.* On July 5, Maj. George R. Clarke, 113th Ill., "Chickasaw," telegraphed to Rawlins. "Whose orders shall I obey Genl Grants thro. you as per telegraph or Gen Blair   you order me to fill details here to load teams &c which I am now doing   Gen Blair orders me to march with my Brigade   please answer immediatly   We have but ninety men" Telegram received, *ibid.*, Telegrams Received.

To Maj. Gen. William T. Sherman

Near Vicksburg July 4, 1863

GEN. SHERMAN.

Ord will only get off a Division of his troops to night, and balance in the morning. Steele will get off before day in the morning. I have just returned from a visit to the Admiral at Vicksburg landing. The number of prisoners as given by the rebels is 27,000. There is much more artillery than we thought. The field pieces are given at 128, and about 100 seige guns.

U. S. GRANT
Maj. Genl

Copies, DLC-USG, V, 19, 101, 103; DNA, RG 393, Dept. of the Tenn., Letters Sent. *O.R.*, I, xxiv, part 3, 474. On July 4, 1863, USG telegraphed to Brig. Gen. John McArthur, "Black River." "Can you forward dispatches for us from Black River to Gen. Sherman." Telegram received, DNA, RG 94, War Records Office, Dept. of the Tenn.

On July 4, Maj. Gen. John G. Parke, "Oak Ridge," telegraphed to USG. "Gen Sherman desires me to tender his warmest congratulations   please accept —my own   Gen Sherman will hold the R R Bridge for Ord Messengers for the fifteenth 15 Corps & Birdsongs for the 9th   orders are Issued for the movement" Telegram received, *ibid. O.R.*, I, xxiv, part 3, 471. On the same day, Maj. Gen. William T. Sherman, "Camp on Bear Creek," wrote to USG. "The telegraph has just announced to me that Vicksburg is ours; its garrison will march out, stack arms, and return within their lines as prisoners of war, and that you will occupy the city only with such troops as you have designated in orders. I can hardly contain myself. Surely will I not punish any soldier for being 'unco happy' this most glorious anniversary of the birth of a nation, whose sire and father was a Washington. Did I not know the honesty, modesty, and purity of your nature, I would be tempted to follow the examples of my standard enemies of the press in indulging in wanton flattery; but as a man and soldier, and ardent friend of yours, I warn you against the incense of flattery that will fill our land from one extreme to the other. Be natural and yourself, and this glittering flattery will be as the passing breeze of the sea on a warm summer day. To me the delicacy with which you have treated a brave but deluded enemy is more eloquent than the most gorgeous oratory of an Everett. This is a day of jubilee, a day of rejoicing to the faithful, and I would like to hear the shout of my old and patient troops; but I must be a Gradgrind—I must have facts, knocks, and must go on. Already are my orders out to give one big huzza and sling the knapsack for new fields. Tuttle will march at once to Messinger's, Parke to Birdsong, and I will shift my head-quarters to Fox's. McArthur will clear the road of obstructions made against the coming of the unseen Johnston, and as soon as Ord and Steele's columns are out, I will push ahead. I want maps, but of course the first thing is to clear the Big Black River and get up on the high ground beyond, when we move according to developments. I did want rest, but I ask nothing until the Mississippi River is ours, and Sunday and 4th of July are nothing to Americans till the river of our greatness is free as God made it. Though in the background, as I ever wish to be in civil war, I feel that I have labored some to secure this glorious result." *Ibid.*, p. 472. Also on July 4, Sherman, "Fox's," telegraphed to USG. "Your dispatch announcing the magnitude of the capture of vicksburg is most gratifying   the importance of the place in our case cannot be exaggerated   I have left Kimballs Division at Haines Bluff with instructions to picket at Oak Ridge   I will order Gen McArthur to relieve Osterhaus at the bridge tomorrow so that Osterhaus may report to Gen Ord. Three 3 bridges will be built tomorrow at Birdsong Messengers & the R R Crossing tomorrow   I suppose Ord & Steele will be up so that next day I will cross & move in force on Bolton   The enemy showed one gun opposite Messingers   this place I am willing he should meet us at once the nearer on river the better   If he declines I will follow promptly at Clinton then I can discover of Johnstone is scattered or concentrated when I will act accord-ingly   I have not yet heard if the prisoners are to be parolled here or sent northe the farmer & farmless out here acknowledge the magnitude of this loss & now beg to know their fate. All crops are destroyed & cattle eaten up   you will give their case your attention as soon as more important business is disposed of at least I promise them this   I advise them if you find a locomotive that you run cars out to Black River & make that a depot   please tell Wilson or Maj Matz about the maps east of Black River   I am without any   I feel an intense curiosity to see Vicksburg & its people but recogniz importance of my present task & think of nothing else   I will keep few orderlies at Osterhaus which is now my nearest telegraph office"   Telegram received, DNA, RG 94, War Records Office, Dept. of the Tenn. *O.R.*, I, xxiv, part 3, 474. On the same day, Sherman, "Oak Ridge," telegraphed to Lt. Col. John A. Rawlins. "Dont forget to send Mowers brigade along with my Corps   Tuttle division is very imperfect without it"   Telegram received, DNA, RG 94, War Records Office, Dept. of the Tenn. USG apparently drafted his answer to Sherman's letter on the bottom of the telegram. "The senti-ments expressed in your letter do credit alike to yo"   AN, *ibid*. On July 5, Brig. Gen. Peter J. Osterhaus telegraphed to USG. "I have report from all points from Halls & Baldwins ferries to Messengers Ford   There is not a single rebel any where except very small squad on the other side of Edwards station   Genl. Shermans scout Tuttle just in from a trip up the river from Hankinsons ferry to the Bridge here on the east side of the river cooperating the above statement   He further reports that the whole train of Genl Breckenredge was ordered back to Jackson & the other side of Pearl river"   Telegram received, *ibid.*

To Maj. Gen. William T. Sherman

Near Vicksburg July 4, 1863

Gen. Sherman.

Ord and Steele will leave this evening, the former for Black River Bridge, the latter for Bridgeport. They will take 150 rounds of amunition, besides that in cartridge boxes, and all the rations they can, not less than five days. Your leaving the 9th corps as a reserve is just right. Inform me the moment you know it will not be required, and I will send it back to Burnside. I have no suggestions or orders to give. I want you to drive Johnston out in your own way, and inflict on the enemy all the punishment you can. I will support you to the last man that can be spared.

U. S. Grant
Maj. Genl

Copies, DLC-USG, V, 19, 101, 103; DNA, RG 393, Dept. of the Tenn., Letters Sent. *O.R.*, I, xxiv, part 3, 473. On July 6, 1863, Maj. Gen. William T. Sherman, "Big Black," telegraphed to USG. "Troops all in position but somewhat disordered by Vicksburg 4th July and the terrible heat & dust   my new Bridges interrupted some what by a rise of four feet in black River making ford impassable but I expect to Cross this afternoon and move out almost of Edwards Station tomorrow noon at Bolton & next day Clinton by which time I will know the purposes of the enemy & act accordingly"   Telegram received, DNA, RG 94, War Records Office, Dept. of the Tenn. *O.R.*, I, xxiv, part 2, 520–21. On the same day, Maj. Gen. Edward O. C. Ord, "Big Black," telegraphed to USG. "The Big Black is up   Bridge here is damaged   are repairing it   hope to cross today   Osterhaus cavalry went as far as Bridgeport yesterday but a small detachment"   Telegram received, DNA, RG 94, War Records Office, Dept. of the Tenn. On July 7, Sherman, "Bolton," telegraphed to USG. "The 13th 15th army corps Crossed Black river yesterday at 4 P M & moved out four miles today   Marched to Bolton   Day Excessively hot & troops suffered exceedingly from heat & dust. From some unexplicable cause the 9th corps is not yet up & I have as no assurance that it is on this side of Black River   I tonight to Genl Parke to stop work on his bridge & follow by Messengers from Evidence collected it appears Johnstone intended to have crossed black River during the 4th or 5th of July with four hundred 400 wagons but he heard of the capitulation on the 3d He was in person opposite Birdsong with one division three 3 divisions were opposite Messengers & one opposite Bridgeport all provided with pontoon trains all commenced falling back toward Jackson yesterday. Breckenridge did not leave Bolton until Midnight last the whole country is marked with their encampments especially Bolton. Tomorrow I will feel toward Clinton with Cavalry but a wait Parks arrival before moving farther" Telegram received, *ibid.*; copy, *ibid. O.R.*, I, xxiv, part 2, 521.

To Maj. Gen. Henry W. Halleck

Head Quarters Dept of the Tenn
Vicksburg Miss, July 5th 63.
Respectfully forwarded to Head Quarters of the Army Washington and recommended, This officer on receiving a very slight wound immediately availed himself of a leave of absence & on his way north actually gave circulation to the report that our losses in the assault on the Enemys works before Vicksburg, on the 22nd of May: 1863. was from 10.000 to 20.000 in killed and wounded, thereby creating undue excitement north and tending to increase the Hopes of the enemy, Our loss, in that assault in fact but little exceeded three thousand in killed and wounded.

U. S. GRANT
Major General.—

ES, DNA, RG 94, Vol. Service Branch, T426 VS 1863. On June 28, 1863, Lt. Col. James H. Wilson wrote to Lt. Col. John A. Rawlins. "I have the honor to inform you that Lieut. Col. Warmouth of Genl. McClernand's staff, permitted to go north on insufficient grounds, for twenty days, has overstayed his time two weeks. He should be mustered out of service for absence without leave." ALS, *ibid.* USG's recommendation was approved by Maj. Gen. Henry W. Halleck on July 20. AES, *ibid.* On June 23, Lt. Col. Henry C. Warmoth, Rolla, Mo., had written to Rawlins. "Enclosed I send certificate to be filed in your office, or though, you forwarded to the War Dept or Ajt Genl. I am not familiar with the Late order. My Health is very poor and I seem to sink under the Heat of the Sun, I am thank god better than I was. Remember me kindly to the Genl. & Lagow Wilson, Bowers & all our friends." ALS, *ibid.* On July 9, USG endorsed the letter. "Respectfully forwarded to the Adjutant General of the Army. This certificate was received here to day. The envelope is marked Pacific, Mo., July. 1st,

1863. On the 5th inst, a communication was forwarded from these Headquarters to the A. G. O. recommending his dismissal." ES, *ibid.* Warmoth, protesting that he had been unjustly charged by USG and Wilson, solicited testimonials to his veracity from numerous prominent civilian and military officials. He then traveled to Washington and succeeded in bringing his case to the attention of President Abraham Lincoln, who endorsed the testimonials on Aug. 30. "Judge Advocate General please examine and report upon this case." AES, *ibid.* In a letter of Sept. 1 to Lincoln, Col. Joseph Holt, judge advocate gen., argued that "Upon returning to his post, as he did, two or three days before his last extension had expired, Lt. Col. Warmoth made a written report to Maj. Gen. Ord, who had succeeded Gen. McClernand in Command—setting forth the circumstances of his absence, upon which Gen. Ord—endorses—'*respectfully returned—satisfactory.*' Evidently the matter should have ended here. It is seen that the Lt. Col. was permitted to leave the field upon a regular & formal leave of absence, and upon quite sufficient grounds—that his term of absence is properly accounted for ~~on~~ according to the rules of the service: and that his explanation of all the circumstances of this absence was entirely satisfactory to his corps commander. The report of Lt. Col. Wilson therefore was, as has been said, '*extra-official, officious, & not true.*' As to the charge of *Circulating false reports in reference to the losses of the Army*, it is first to be remarked that it ~~is first to be remarked~~ nowhere appears in what way Genl. Grant became informed of these reports; and that this charge could be answered or disproved only indirectly by Lt. Col. Warmoth—This Officer has filed a number of letters relating to conversations had by him with different individuals—during his absence—which have an important bearing upon the question of the truth of this charge. . . . In view of all these facts, presented by the Lieut. Col. by way of defence to the second charge made against him, it is difficult to arrive at any conclusion other than that Genl. Grant was mistaken or misled in reference to the subject of this charge. . . . Lt. Col. Warmoth has fortified his case by an array of testimonials from military and state officials and members of Congress. His character as a gentleman, and as an officer of efficiency, gallantry and courage in the field, are amply vouched for. His conduct at the actions of Port Gibson, Champion Hills, and the Big Black—is spoken of with high praise. It will be sufficient to quote the language of Brig. Gen. Carr—who says of him—'he possesses in an eminent degree the qualities of bravery, intelligence, zeal, energy and untiring endurance;' and also the remark of Brig. Gen. Benton, who calls him—'an ornament to the service—' His services at the commencement of the rebellion are especially commemorated. Here he was 'faithful among the faithless'—was appointed Brig. Gen. of the state militia, and was one of the first to organize troops for the defence of the state and the country. He is said to have raised nearly the whole of the regiment to which he belongs. In short it is believed that few young men in the service can present a fairer or more honorable record. In view of the manifest injustice which has been done Lieut. Col. Warmoth, and of his evident value to the service—it is recommended that the Special Order dismissing him be at once revoked, so that he be placed, as to his rank, pay &c.,—in precisely the position which he would have occupied, had he not been dismissed," LS, *ibid.* On Sept. 9, Lincoln endorsed Holt's report. "The report of the Judge Advocate General is approved. Let the special order by which Lt. Col. Warmoth was dismissed be at once revoked, so that he be placed as to his rank and pay, in the same position that he would have occupied had he not been dismissed." ES, *ibid.*

On Aug. 22, 1871, Wilson wrote to USG about Holt's report enclosing a story from the *New Orleans Republican*, Aug. 17, recounting Wilson's role in the episode. "As I was the Inspector General of your troops at that time and made the report in question, or caused it to be made, and am not conscious of having misrepresented, or been privy to a misrepresentation of the facts in that or any other case, I am unwilling to believe that Genl. Holt could have characterized my official conduct by any such language as that just quoted, and particularly, not without having taken the usual official steps of referring the case to your head quarters for further report." ALS, *ibid.* Horace Porter endorsed Wilson's letter on Aug. 23. "Respectfully referred to the Sec. of War who is requested to furnish Gen. Wilson with a copy of Gen. Holt's letter." AES, *ibid.* A typescript copy of Holt's report is in Wilson's papers, Bender Collection, Wy-Ar. See Henry Clay Warmoth, *War, Politics and Reconstruction: Stormy Days in Louisiana* (New York, 1930), pp. 17–25.

To Maj. Gen. James B. McPherson

Head Quarters, Dept. of the Ten.
Near Vicksburg, July 5th 1863,

MAJ. GEN. MCPHERSON,
COMD.G 17TH ARMY CORPS,
GEN.

Where families of Officers or citizens wish to leave the city, either with or after the Confederate Army leaves, and have private carriages of their own they may be permitted to do so and take their carriages with them.

Col. Dockery[1] having no horse but one captured from our Army at Champion Hill, and he having been reclaimed since the surrender of Vicksburg, you may direct your quartermaster to deliver him another from any of the captured animals in your Corps.

Very respectfully
U. S. GRANT
Maj. Gen. Com.

ALS, Mr. and Mrs. Philip D. Sang, River Forest, Ill.

1. Thomas P. Dockery, born in N. C. in 1833, shortly thereafter moved with his family to Ark., where his father established a prosperous plantation. Ap-

pointed col., 19th Ark., early in the war, he commanded a brigade during the Vicksburg campaign. In later years, Dockery's wife recounted seeking out USG on July 5 to inquire about the fate of her husband. According to her account, USG immediately sent an inquiry to Lt. Gen. John C. Pemberton, who replied that Dockery had survived the siege in good health. See *USGA Newsletter*, III, 4 (July, 1966), 25–27.

To Maj. Gen. James B. McPherson

Head Quarters, Dept. of the Ten.
Near Vicksburg, July 5th 1863

Maj. Gen. J. B. McPherson,
Comd.g 17th Army Corps.
Gen.

No enlistments of the negroes captured in Vicksburg will be allowed for the present. All the Male Negroes we want collected and organized into working parties for the purpose of policeing the grounds around the city, unloading Steamers and fitting up the fortifications for our use.

In regard to rebel officers taking their servants with them that is one of the conditions I expressly refused them. After the city was surrendered however one of the officers on Gen. Pemberton's Staff asked me what I was going to do about servants who were anxious to accompany their masters, remarking that many of them had been raised with their servants and it was like severing families to part them. I remark that no compulsory measures would be used to hold negroes.

I want the negroes all to understand that they are free men. If they are then anxious to go with their masters I do not see the necessity of preventing it. Some going might benefit our cause by spreading disaffection among the negroes at a distance by telling that the Yankees set them all free.

It is not necessary that you should give yourself any trouble about negroes being enticed away from officers. Every one who looses a negro will insist that he has been enticed off because otherwise his negro would not leave. As I said before it was possitively refused that the privilege of carrying off private servants should be granted. Because I said afterwards coertion would not be used to retain servants it is no reason that the strength of the garrison should be used in preserving a neutrality between our men and the negroes that would enable the Confederate officers to carry off their negroes by force.

Forage cannot be issued, at least not more than for one day, to Pembertons forces when they leave. A thousand horses too looks like much more than they could reasonably take under the terms of the Capitulation.

Very respectfully
U. S. GRANT
Maj. Gen

ALS, James S. Schoff, New York, N. Y. *O.R.*, I, xxiv, part 3, 479. On July 5, 1863, Lt. Col. John A. Rawlins issued Special Orders No. 181. "Major General James B. McPherson, Commanding 17th Army Corps and troops garrisoning Vicksburg, and guarding prisoners of war, will take immediate charge of the paroling of the capitulating Confederate States Forces, and hurry the same forward with all possible dispatch. Every printing press that can be had, he will put into requisition for the printing of the necessary blanks. Lieut. Colonel Kent, Provost Marshal General will report him for orders. Not one of the capitulated garrison must be allowed to escape, but all must be paroled, and duplicate lists certified by the proper officers retained." Copies, DLC-USG, V, 27, 28; DNA, RG 393, Dept. of the Tenn., Special Orders. *O.R.*, I, xxiv, part 3, 478.

To Maj. Gen. Henry W. Halleck

———

Vicksburg. Miss, July 6. 1863.

MAJOR GENERAL H. W. HALLECK
WASHINGTON, D. C.,

The number of prisoners and pieces of Artillery taken with Vicksburg is greater than was at first supposed. The number proves to be over thirty thousand (30,000) prisoners and over one hundred and seventy pieces of Artillery. We have found

considerable ammunition and about four days rations of flour
and bacon and two hundred and fifty thousand (250,000) pounds
of sugar. The small arms are of good quality and over fifty
thousand (50,000) in number.

Sherman is after Johnston but no news from him to day.

U. S. GRANT
Major General

Copies, DLC-USG, V, 6, 8, 24, 94; DNA, RG 393, Dept. of the Tenn., Hd. Qrs.
Correspondence. *O.R.*, I, xxiv, part 1, 62.

To Col. John C. Kelton

———

[*July 6, 1863*]

COL. J. C. KELTON
ASST. ADJ. GEN.
WASHINGTON, D. C.
COL.

I have the honor to submit the following report of the opperations of the Army of the Ten. from the time of leaving Millikins
Bend La. to the investment of Vicksburg, Miss.

From the moment I took of taking command of the "Army
in the Field," in person, I became satisfied that Vicksburg could
only be sucsessfully turned from the South side of the City. I
therefore prossecuted the work on the south si Canal across the
isthmus opposite on the Louisiana side of the river with all viger,
hoping to make a channel which would pass transports [enough]
for moving the army and bringing supplies to the new base of
opperations thus provided. The task was a much more Hurculian
than it at first appeared and was made much more so by the
almost continuous rains which fell during the whole of the time
this work was prossecuted. The river too continued to rise during the whole of the time making a large expenditure of labor
necessary to keep the water out of our Camps and the Canal.
Finally on the   of February the rapid rise and consequent

great presure upon the dam of the canal caused it to give way and let through the low lands back of the camps a torrent of water that separated the North & South shores of the peninsula as effectually as if the Mississippi had flowed between them. ~~This When~~ This occured when the enterprise promised success within a short time.

There was some delay in trying to repair damages. Finding however that at the stage of water then existing, and the "oldest inhabitant" predicting a continuance until the middle of June; some other plan had to be adopted for geting below Vicksburg with transports.

Capt. F. E. Prime, Chief Eng. in this Dept. and Col. G. G. Pride who was acting on my Staff, prospected the route through by the bayous which run from near Millikins Bend on the North and New Carthage on the South, through Roundaway Bayou, into the Tensas River. Their report of the practicability of this route determined me to commence ~~it~~ work upon it.—Having three Dredge boats at the time the work of opening this route was executed with great rapidity. One small steamer and a number of barges were taken through the channel opened by this route, but the water commencing to fall very rapidly about the middle of April, and the roads becoming passable between Millikins Bend & New Carthage, made it impracticable to open water communication between these two points, and altogether unnecessary.

Soon after commencing the first Canal spoken of I caused a channel to be cut from the Miss. river into Lake Providence. ~~and~~ Also one from the Mississippi into Coldwater by way of Yazoo Pass.—I had no great expectation of results from the former of these. But having more troops than could be employed at Youngs Point, and knowing that Lake Providence was connected with Bayou Macon, ~~did~~ a navigable stream ~~through~~ to the ~~Tensas thence by the Washita & Black rivers~~ to the Mississippi did not know but a route might be opened which would enable me to co-operate with Gen. Banks ~~in the~~ opening ~~of lower Mississippi~~ on Port Hudson.

By Yazoo Pass I only expected at first, with some of the lighter gunboats, and a few troops, to get into the Yazoo River and destroy the enemy's transports on that stream, and some gunboats which I knew were being built. The navigation ~~through~~ proved so much better than had been expected however that I thought for a time of the possibility of making this a route for obtaining a foothold on high land above Hain's Bluff Miss. Accordingly small class steamers were ordered for transporting an ~~large Ar~~ Army. Gen. McPherson was directed to hold his Army Corps in readiness for taking this route, and one Division from each the 13th & 15th Army Corps were collected near the entrance of the Pass to be added to this command.

It soon became evident that boats sufficient, of the right class, could not be collected for the enterprise. The enemy too worked dilligently in closing one end of the Pass whilst the Federal troops were opening the other. In this way they succeeded in gaining time to fortify Greenwood, ~~sufficently strong~~ below the junction of the Tallahatchie & Yalobush, strongly.

~~I have had no official report from Gen. L. F. Ross who com-manded the Expedition during the greater part of the time it was near Greenwood, nor from Gen. I. F. Quinby who reinforced him and commanded at the time of its abandonment. In justice to Gen. Quinby I must state that shortly after he reached Green-wood I ordered the withdrawel of the expedition under his charge.~~ The expedition however succeeded in reaching Cold-water on the   of Feb.y. after much difficulty and the partial disabling of most of the boats. From the entrance into Coldwater to Fort Pemberton, at Greenwood Miss. no great difficulty of navigation was experianced nor interruption of magnitude by the enemy.

Fort Pemberton ~~t~~ extends from the Tallahatchie to the ~~Yalo-bush~~ Yazoo at Greenwood. Here the two rivers come within a few hundred yards of each other. The land around the fort is low and at the time of the attack was entirely overflown. Owing to this fact no movement could be made by the army to reduce it but all depended on the ability of the Gunboats to silence the guns of the enemy and ~~to~~ enable the transports to run down and land troops immediately on the fort itself. ~~The accompanying report from Brig. Gen. Ross, who commanded the expedition~~ Brig. Gen. Quinby reached the Yazoo Expedition on the   of Feb.y and being senior to Gen. Ross assumed command on the same day. On the   of Feb.y I sent orders for the return of the expedition This I regarded as advisable because to continue was exposing my command to the danger of being beaten in detail.

On the 14th of March Admiral Porter informed me that he had had a reconnoisance made up Steeles Bayou and partially through Black Bayou towards Deer Creek and so far as explored these water courses were reported navigable for the smaller ~~Iron Clads~~ Iron clads. Information given mostly by the negroes of the country I believe was that Deer Creek could be navigated to Rolling Fork and from there, through the Sunflower to the Yazoo River there was no question about the navigation. On the following morning I accompanied Admiral Porter on the Ram Price, several Iron clads preceeding us, up through Steele's Bayou to near Black Bayou.—At this time our forces were at a dead lock at Greenwood and I looked upon the success of this enterprise as of vast importance. It would, if sucsessful, leave Greenwood between two forces of ours and would necessarily have caused the immediate abandonment of that stronghold. About thirty steamers of the enemy would have been ~~between~~ cut off from further use to the enemy and must have been destroyed or fallen into our hands. Seeing that, the great obsticles to navigation, so far as I had gone, was from overhanging trees, I left Admiral Porter near Black Bayou and pushed back to Young's Point for the purpose of sending forward a Pioneer Corps to remove all difficulties of navigation. Soon after my return to Young's Point Admiral Porter sent back to me for a co-operating Military force. Gen. Sherman was promptly sent, with one Division of his Corps The number of steamers suitable for the navigation of these bayous being limited the most of ~~this~~ his force was sent up the Miss. River to Eagle Bend, a point where the river runs with one mile of Steele's Bayou, ~~and probably thirty miles from~~ thus saving an important part of this difficult navigation.

This expedition failed probably more from want of a previous knowledge ~~of~~ as to what would be required to open this route than from any impracticability in the navigation of the streams & bayous through which it was proposed to pass. Want of this knowledge led the expedition on until the difficulties were encountered and then it would become necessary to send back to Young's Point for the means of removing them. This gave the enemy time to move forces to effectually checkmate any further progress, when the expedition was within but a few hundred yards of free and open navigation to the Yazoo. All this may have been providential in driving us ultimately [to a line of operations which has proven eminently successfull.]

~~As soon as the roads became practicable~~

As soon as the roads became practicable for passing troops and Artillery from Millikins Bend to New Carthage, the first point below Vicksburg that could be reached by land at the stage of water then existing, the 13th Army Corps, Maj. Gen. McClernand Commanding, was ordered to take up their line of march for that place, moving no faster than supplies and Ammunition could be transported for them. The roads though level were intolerably bad and the movement necessarily slow. Arriving at Smith's Plantation, two miles from New Carthage, it was found that the levee of Bayou Videl was broken in several places thus leaving New Carthage an Island. All the boats that could be were collected from the different bayous around and others built. But the transportation of an Army in this way was found exceedingly tedious. Another rout had to be found. This was done by making a further march around Videl to Perkin's plantation, a distance of Twelve miles more making the whole distance to be marched from Millikins Bend to reach water communication on the opposite side of the point Thirty-five miles. Over this distance, with bad roads to contend against supplies of ordnance store and provisions had to be hawled with which to commence a Campaign on the opposite side of the river. In fact, owing to the limited number of transports below Vicksburg, it was found necessary to extend this line of ~~commun~~ land travel to Hard Times La. which by the sircuitous route it was necessary to take is about seventy miles.

The transports used had all to be run past the batteries of Vicksburg. Three of these, the Forest Queen, Silver Wave & Henry Clay, started on the night of the   April. The boilers were protected as well as possible by packing the guards and bows with hay, cotton & forage. More or less Com.y stores were put in each.—All these boats were struck more or less frequently whilst runing the enemy's batteries, and the Henry Clay, by the explosion of a shell or from some other cause, was set on fire and entirely consumed. The other boats were somewhat injured but not seriously disabled. Not a sole on board of either was hurt.

Finding that these boats got by so well I ordered six more to be prepared in like manner and sent past the Vicksburg batteries. These left Millikins Bend on the night of the ~~15~~ [22]th of April. Five got by in a somewhat damaged condition but the sixth, the Tigress, received a shot which passed through the bottom and caused her to sink ~~soon~~ on the Louisiana shore soon after passing the last battery. Two men were mortally wounded in runing these last boats by and several more or less injured. The number sustaining injury I do not know.

The crews of steamers runing the blockade, in every instance except with the Forest Queen, and the Capt. of the Silver Wave, Capt. D. Conway commanding the first,[1] and   McMillen[2] commanding the second, backed out and their places had to be suppled by volunteers from the Army. No sooner was volunteers called for for this dangerous enterprise than officers and men presented themselves by the hundred, all anxious to undertake the trip. The names of those whos services were accepted will be given in a separate report.

It is a striking feature of the present volunteer Army of the United States that there is nothing which men are called upon to do, Mechanical or Professional, that accomplished adebts cannot be found to perform in almost every regiment.

The boats runing the blockade were much injured in runing the blockade, but the Navy being supplied with the most of the material required for repairs, and Admiral Porter being ever ready to give all the assistance in his power for the furtherance of the cause of the Union, in a few days five of the eight boats were ready to get up steam and the remainder were in condition to be used as barges.

Each of the last six boats runing the blockade of Vicksburg started with two barges in tow about half of which got through in a condition to be used afterwards.

The 13th Army Corps being all through to the Mississippi, and the 17th well on the way, so much of the 13th as could be got aboard of the transports & barges in navigable condition were put aboard and moved to the front of Grand Gulf on the 29th of April.

The[plan]here was that the Navy should silence the guns of the enemy and the troops land under the cover of the gunboats and carry the place by storm.

At 8 O'Clock a. m. the Navy made the attack and kept it up for more than five hours in the most gallant manner. I ~~witness was in~~ [From] a tug out in the stream [I] witnessed the whole engagement. Many times it seemed to me the gunboats were within pistol shot of the enemys batteries. It soon became evident that the guns of the enemy were too elevated, and their fortifications too strong to be taken from the land side.—The whole range of hills to the water side were known to be lined with Rifle Pitts besides the Field Artillery could be moved to any position where it could be made useful in case of an attempt at landing. This determined me to again run the enemy's batteries and turn their position. Accordingly orders were immediately given for the troops to debark, at Hard Times La. and march across the point to immediately below Grand Gulf. At dark the gunboats again engaged the enemy's batteries and all the transports run by, ~~with the Artillery on board~~, receiving but two or three shots in the passage, and these without injury. The original plan was to go to Rodney. The work of ferrying the troops to Bruinsburg was commenced at daylight in the morning, the gunboats as well as transports being used for the purpose. As soon as the 13th Army Corps were landed and could draw three days rations to put in their haversacks, (no wagons were allowed to be taken across until the troops were all over) they were started on the road to Port Gibson. I deemed it a matter of vast importance that the high lands should be reached without resistince.

The 17th Army Corps followed as rapidly as they could be put across the river.

About 2 O'Clock a. m. on the 1st of May the advance of the enemy was met some ~~six~~ [(8) eight] miles from ~~Port Gibson~~ [Bruinsburg], on the road to ~~Bruinsburg~~ [Port Gibson]. They were forced to fall back but ~~being~~ as it was dark, they were not pursued far ~~much~~ until daylight. Early in the morning of the 1st I went out with two or three members of my Staff and found Gen. McClernand ~~with three Divisions of~~ [with] his, the 13th Army Corps, engaging the enemy ~~at what I believe is known as Thompson's Hill, and~~ about four miles from Port Gibson. At this point the roads branched in exactly opposite directions both however leading to Port Gibson. The enemy had taken position on both branches thus, as they fell back, dividing the pursuing forces.

The nature of the ground in that part of the country is such that a very small force could retard the progress of a much larger one for many hours. The roads usually run on [narrow &] elevated ridges with deep and impenitrable ravines on either side.

On the right were the Divisions of ~~Carr~~ Hovey [Carr & Smith] and on the Left the Division of Osterhaus. The former two succeeded in driving the enemy from position to position back towards Port Gibson steadily all day.

Osterhaus however did not move the enemy from the position occupied by him, on our left when I arrived upon the field, until Logan's Division of the 17th Army Corps arrived.

Gen. McClernand, who was with the right, in person, sent repeated messages to me before the arrival of any portion of the 17th Army Corps, to send Logan's and Quinby's Divisions to him. I had been on that as well as all other parts of the field and could [not] see how they could be used to advantage. However as soon as ~~they arrived~~ the advance of the 17th Army Corps, Logans Division, arrived I sent one Brigade to [Gen McClernand on] the Right and sent one Brigade, Gen. J. E. Smith Comd.g to the Left to the assistance of Osterhaus. By a judicious disposition made of this Brigade, under the immediate supervision of Gens. McPherson & Logan, a position was soon obtained giving an advantage which soon drove the enemy from that part of the field to make no further stand south of Bayou Pierre. The enemy was repulsed here with a heavy loss in killed, wounded and prisoners.

I will leave it to Division & Corps Commanders to make ~~up~~ mention of those who specially distinguished themselves making only such comments upon their representations as my own observation enables me to make.

The repuls of the enemy on our Left took place late in the afternoon. They were pursued towards Port Gibson but ~~clos~~ night closing in, and the enemy making the appearance of another stand the troops slept upon their arms until daylight. In the morning it was found that the enemy had ~~all left~~, [retreated] across~~ing~~ Bayou Pierre on the Grand Gulf and Hankerson Ferry roads, distroying the bridges behind them. ~~The enemy placed some~~ [with] Artillery and sharpshooters ~~behind rear a slight~~ he made a show of force in entrenchment on the North side of Bayou Pierre, on the Grand Gulf road, ~~which~~ A Brigade of Logan's Division ~~covered~~ divert his attention whilst a floating bridge was being built across ~~North~~ South ~~Fork of~~ Bayou Pierre immediately at Port Gibson. This bridge was completed, eight miles marched by the 17th Army Corps to North Fork of Bayou Pierre, that streams bridged and the advance of ~~the~~ [this] ~~troops~~ [Corps commenced passing] over it ~~before daylight~~ [at 5½ oclock] the following morning.

On the 3d the enemy were pursued to Hankerson's Ferry with slight skirmishing all day, during which we took ~~prisoners~~ quite a number of prisoners, stragglers from the enemy.

Finding that Grand Gulf had been evacuated and the advance of my troops were already fifteen miles ~~on their way~~ out from there ~~over there, the road~~ and on the road too they would have to take to reach either Vicksburg, Jackson or any intermediate point on the rail-road between the two places, I determined not to march them back. Taking a small escort of Cavalry, some fifteen or twenty men, I went on to the Gulf myself and ~~pas~~ made the necessary orders for changing my base of supplies from Bruinsburg to Grand Gulf.

In moving from Millikin's Bend the 15th Army Corps, Maj. Gen. Sherman Comd.g, was left to be the last to start. To prevent heavy reinforcements from Vicksburg going to the assistance of the Grand Gulf forces I directed Gen. Sherman to make a demonstration on Hains Bluff and to make all the show possible. From information since received ~~this was~~ from prisoners captured this ruse succeeded most admirably.

It had been my intention up to the time of crossing the Miss. river to collect all my forces at Grand Gulf and get on hand a good supply of provisions and Ordnance stores before moving. In the mean time to detach an Army Corps to Co-opperate with Gen. Banks on Port Hudson and effect a junction of our forces. About this time a letter was received from Gen. Banks[3] giving his position West of the Miss. and stating that he could return to Baton Rouge by the 10th of May. That by the reduction of Port Hudson he could join me with 12 000 men.—I learned about the same time that troops were expected at Jackson from the Southern Cities with [Gen] Beaurigard to command. To delay until the 10th of May, and for the reduction of Port Hudson after that the accession of 12 000 men would not leave me relatively so strong as to move promptly with what I had.

Information received from day to day of the movements of the enemy also impelled me to the course ~~I~~ pursued. Whilst laying at Hankinsons Ferry waiting to get ~~transportation over the river~~, wagons, supplies ~~and~~ and Gen. Sherman's Corps, which had come forward in the mean time, over the river demonstrations were made, successfully I believe, to induce the enemy to ~~believe~~ think that route, and by Hall's Ferry above were objects of much solicitude with me.

Reconnoisances were made North of the Black to within six miles of Warrenton.

On the 7 of May an advance was made McPhersons Corps keeping the road nearest Black River, to Rocky Springs McClernands Corps keeping the Ridge road from Willow Springs and Sherman following with his Corps divided on the two roads. All the ferries were closely guarded until our troops were far past.

It was my intention here to hug the Black River as closely as possible with McClernand's & Sherman's Corps and get them on to the rail-road [at] some place from between Edwards Station to and Bolton. McPherson was to move by the way of Utica to Raymond and from there into Jackson, destroy the rail-road, telegraph and public stores &c. and push West to rejoin the remainder of the main forces   Orders were given to Gen. McPherson accordingly. Sherman was moved forward on the Edwards ferry station road crossing 14 mile creek at Dillon's Plantation. McClernand was moved acrossed the same creek, further West, sending one Division of his Corps by Baldwins Ferry road as far as the river   At the crossing of Fourteen Mile Creek both McClernand & Sherman had conciderable skirmishing with the enemy to get possession of the crossings. McPherson met the enemy three or four thousand strong near Raymond, on the same day, engaged him and after several hours hard fighting drove him with much loss in killed, wounded, prisoners, and stragglers who [many] threw down their Arms and deserted.

My position at this time was with Sherman's Corps, some seven miles from the battle field [East of Raymond], and about the center of the army.

On the morning [night] of the 12th of May, after orders had been given for the Corps of McClernand & Sherman to march upon the rail-road by paralld roads to   hearing the order was changed and both were directed to move towards Raymond. This was in consequence of information received that reinforcements were arriving daily at Jackson and Gen. Jo. E. Johnstone was hourly expected to take command in person. I determined to take make shure of that place and leave no enemy in my rear. It might be the

McPherson moved on this day, the 13th, to Clinton, destroyed the rail-road and telegraph and captured some important dispatches from Pemberton to Gen. Gregg who had commanded in the battle of Raymond the day before. Sherman moved to a parallel position with McPherson on the Mississippi Springs & Jackson road. McClernand moved forward to near Raymond. On the 14th the entire force moved forward towards Jackson. The rain fell in torrents from early in the morning until about noon making the roads at first slippery then myery. Notwithstanding this the troops marched in excellent order, without straggling, and in the best of spirits, about ten [14?] miles and engaged the enemy outside of Jackson before 12 O'Clock M. This was two Divisions of each ~~of~~ the ~~Corps~~ 15th & 17th Army Corps. McClernand occupied that day Clinton with one Division, Miss. Spring's with one, Raymond with a third and [had] his fourth Division and one Division of Shermans Corps with a wagon train still in the rear. It was not the intention to move these forces any nearer Jackson, but to have them in a position where they were in supporting distance if the resistance at Jackson should prove more obstinate than there seemed to be reason to ~~suspect~~ [expect].

The enemy marched out the bulk of his force on the Clinton road and engaged McPherson's Corps, about 2½ miles from the city. A small force of Artillery and Infantry took a strong position in front of Sherman about the same distance out. By a determined advance of a few skirmishers these latter were soon driven back to within their Rifle Pitts just outside of the City. It was impossible to ascertain the strength of the enemy at this part of the line ~~immediately~~ in a few minuets. Consequently McPherson's two Divisions engaged the main bulk of the Rebel Garrison of Jackson without further aid than the Moral support given it by the knowledge the enemy had of a force at the South side of the City and the few Infantry and Artillery detained there to impede [our] progress.

The weakness of the enemy was soon discovered by Gen. Sherman sending a reconnoitering party to ~~the~~ his right which also had the effect of causing the enemy to retreat from this part of his line. A few Artillerests stood to their places however firing upon Sherman's troops until the last moment, evidently instructed to do so with the expectation of being captured in the end.—Marching into the city it was found that the main body of the enemy had retreated North after a brisk engagement with the 17th Corps of more than two hours ~~engagements~~ in which he was handsomly beaten. Some of the troops pursued until near night but without capturing troops or Artillery other than what was left by the enemy in the city.

~~When~~ During the evening it was ascertained that Johnstone, as soon as he had satisfied himself to a certainty that Jackson was to be attacked, had ordered Pemberton peremptorily to march out from Vicksburg and attack our rear. Taking advantage of this information orders were immediately issued for McClernand to face his troops towards Edward's station and march upon different roads converging ~~at that~~ near that place. His troops were admirably located for such a march. McPherson was ordered to retrace his steps on the Clinton road. Sherman was left [in Jackson] to destroy the rail-roads, work shops, arsenals and every thing valuable in support of the Rebel Army. This was done in the most effectual manner.

On the afternoon of the 15th I proceeded as far West as Clinton, McPhersons Corps having passed on through and up to within supporting distance of Gen. Hovey's Division which had moved on the same road.—~~At a ear~~

At an early hour on the 16th two employees on the Southern rail-road were brought to my quarters. They had passed through the rebel army and said their force concisted of eighty regiments with ten batteries of Artillery, the whole force estimated at 25000 men. ~~the regiments being reduced in numbers and probably heavy details left behind~~. They gave me the position being taken up by the enemy also. I had determined to leave Sherman one day longer in Jackson but this information determined me to bring him forward at once. Accordingly I dispatched [to] him to move forward as soon as possible and at Clinton to take the Bridgeport road. My dispatch was taken back to Jackson, ten miles, and at 10 a. m. ~~the~~ [Sherman's] advance Division was in motion.

At an early hour I left for the advance. Arriving at the crossing of the Vicksburg & Jackson road with the road from Raymond to Bolton, I found ~~Gen~~. McPherson's advance and his Pioneer Corps engaged in rebuilding a bridge on the former road that had been destroyed by our troops. The train of Hovey's Division was at a halt and blocked up the road from further advance on the Vicksburg road. I ordered all Quartermasters & Wagon Masters to draw their teams to one side and make room for the passage of troops. ~~Gen~~. McPherson was brough ~~forward~~ [up] by this road. Passing to the front I found Hovey's Division of the 13th ~~Army~~ Corps at a halt, with the enemy's pickets and his skirmishers near each other. ~~Gen~~. Hovey was bringing his troops into line ready for battle and could have brought on an engagement at any moment.

The enemy had taken up a very strong position on a narrow ridge, ~~their~~ his left resting on a hight where the road makes a sharp turn to the left, ~~advancing~~ towards Vicksburg. The top of the ridge and ~~down~~ the precipitous hillside to the left of the road ~~i~~ [are covered by] a dense forest and undergrowth. To the right of the road the timber extends ~~a short~~ [about half a mile] distance down the hill, and then opens into cultivated fields on a gentle slope and into a valley extending for a conciderable distance. On the road and into the wooded ravine, and hillside Hovey's Division was disposed for the attack. McPherson's two Divisions, all of his Corps with him on the march from Millikin's Bend until we arrived at Black River, were thrown to the right of the road, properly *speaking* the enemy's rear. I would not permit any attack to be commenced by our troops until I could hear from ~~Gen~~ McClernand who was advancing ~~by two other road~~ with four divisions, two of them on a road intersecting the Jackson road about one mile from where the troops above described were placed, ~~the other two Divisions still~~ and about the center of the enemy's line, the other two Divisions on a road still South and near[ly] the same distance off.

I soon heard from ~~Gen.~~ McClernand through members of his Staff [and my own whom I had sent to him early in the morning] and found that he was 2½ miles ~~off~~ [distant]. I sent several messages to him to push forward with all rapidity. There had been continuous firing between Hovey's skirmishers and the Rebel advance which by [11] O'Clock grew into a battle. For some time this Division bore the brunt of the ~~battle~~ [conflict] but finding the enemy too strong for them, at the instance of Gen. Hovey I ~~sent~~ directed first one and then a second brigade from Crockers Division to reinforce them. All this time Logans Division was working upon the enemy's rear and weakened his front attack most wonderfully. The troops here opposing us evidently far outnumbered ours. Expecting ~~Gen.~~ McClernand, with four Divisions, momentarily, I never felt a doubt of the result. ~~They never~~ [He did not] ~~arrived~~ however until the enemy had been driven from the field, after a hotly contested battle of hours with a heavy loss of killed wounded & prisoners, [on his part] and a number of pieces of Artillery.

It was found afterwards that the Vicksburg road, after following the ridge in a southerly direction for about one mile, and to where it intersected one of the Raymond roads, turned almost to the West, down the hill and across the valley, in which ~~Gen.~~ Logan was opperating ~~to~~ ~~their~~ on the rear of the enemy. One Brigade had, uncontious of the important fact, penetrated nearly to this road and thus compelled a retreat to prevent capture. As it was, much of the [enemy's] Artillery was cut off and all of Lorings Division, besides the prisoners captured.[4]

~~Gen.~~ Hovey still calling for more reinforcements, just before the route of the enemy commenced, I ordered ~~Gen.~~ McPherson to move what troops were left with him by a left flank around to the front of the enemy. ~~Gen.~~ Logan riding up at this time told me that if Hovey could make another dash at the enemy he could come up from where he then was, and capture most of their force. I immediately rode forward and found the troops that had be so gallantly engaged for so many hours withdrawn from their advanced position and engaged [in] filling their Cartridge boxes.

I directed their commander to ~~expedite~~ use all dispatch in getting cartridges and push forward as soon as possible, explaining the position of ~~Gen.~~ Logan's troops. I then rode forward expecting every moment to see the enemy. Passing along what had been their line I found they were retreating. Arriving at the Raymond road I saw to my left, and on the next ridge, a column of troops moving towards me in fine order. Awaiting their arrival I found it to be Carr's Division and ~~Gen.~~ McClernand with it. The situation was soon explained. ~~and Gen.~~ I then ordered Gen. Carr to pursue the enemy with all speed, to Black River and across if he could.—Some of Logan's troops had already got into the road, in advance, but having marched and engaged the enemy all day they were fatigued and gave the road for Gen. Carr's troops to pass.—The pursuit was continued until after dark and resulted in the capture of a train of cars, loaded with Ordnance stores, and of other property.

The delay in the advance of the ~~enemy the~~ troops immediately with Gen. McClernand no doubt was caused by the enemy presenting a front of Artillery and Infantry where it was impossible, from the nature of the ground, and density of the forest, to discover their numbers. As it was the Battle of Champion's Hill, or Baker's Creek, was fought by Hovey's Division of the 13th Army Corps, and Logan's & Quinby's, Commanded then by Gen. Crocker, of the 17th Army Corps.

~~On th~~ At daylight on the 17th the pursuit was renewed with the 13th Army Corps in the aavance. The enemy were found strongly posted on both sides of the Black River. The bluffs extend to the waters edge ~~from~~ on the West bank at this point on Black River. The East side is an open cultivated bottom of near one mile in width, surrounded by a narrow bayou from the river above the rail-road to the river below. Following the ~~crest~~ [line] of this bayou the enemy had sunk Rifle Pitts leaving a ~~sluggish~~ stagnant ditch of water, from two to three feet in debth and from ten to twenty feet wide, ~~as a~~ outside. Carrs Division occupied the right in investing this place and Lawlers Brigade the right of his Division. After skirmishing for a few hours Gen. Lawler, on his own volition I believe, finding an opportunity to charge gave the command. ~~S~~ Notwithstanding the level ground to pass over affording no cover to his troops, and the ditch in front of the enemy's works ~~affording~~ being a great obsticle, the charge was gallantly made and in a few minuets the entire garrison, with seventeen pieces of Artillery, were the trophies of this brilliant dash. The enemy on the West bank of the river immediately set fire to the rail-road bridge and retreated, thus cutting off all chance for escape for any portion of their forces ~~from~~ [still remaining on] the East bank.

Sherman by this time had arrived at Bridgeport on the Black River above. The only Pontoon train with the expedition was with him. By [the] morning of the 18th his command had crossed the river and were ready to march on Walnut Hills by daylight.

McClernand and McPherson each built floating bridges during the night and had them ready for crossing Artillery by 8 a. m. on the 18th. The march was commenced by Sherman at an early hour by the Bridgeport & Vicksburg road turning to the right when within three & a half miles of the city to get possession of Walnut Hills and the Yazoo river. This was sucsessfully accomplished before night of the 18th. McPherson, with ~~his Corps~~ the 17th Corps, crossing Black river above the Jackson road come into the same road with Sherman but to his rear. He arrived after night fall with his advance where Sherman turned to the right. McClernand moved with the 13th Army Corps by the Jackson and ~~Mt. Alb~~ Vicksburg road to Mt Albans, ~~At that~~ where he turned to his left and got on to the Baldwin's Ferry road. By this arrangement the three Army Corps covered all the ground their strength would admit of. By the night of the 19th the investment was made as complete as our numbers would admit of. A landing was secured on the Yazoo river from which to draw supplies. Sherman had sent some of his Cavalry to Hain's Bluff to take possession of that place [which they did successfully]. By the night of the 20th supplies were begining to arrive from the river.

During the day there was continuous skirmishing, and I was not without hope of carrying the enemys works.—Relying upon the demoralization of the enemy in ~~his~~ consequence of repeated defeat outside of Vicksburg I ordered a general assault at 2 P. M. on this day. The 15th Army Corps from having arrived in front of the enemy's works in time on the 18th to get up a good position were enabled to make the assault vigerous. The 13th & 17th Corps succeeded no further than to gain advanced positions covered from the fire of the enemy ~~The 15th & 17th Army Corps executed the order with much viger but succeeded no further than to gain ground much closer to the enemy's works than they before held and where they were covered from his fire.~~—The 20th & 21st were spent in perfecting communications with our supplies. Most of the troops had been marching and fighting battles for twenty days on an average of about five days rations drawn from the Commissary Department. Though they had not suffered from short rations, up to this time, the want of bread to accompany the other ration was begining to be much felt. On the 21st my arrangements for drawing supplies of every discription being complete I determined to make another effort to carry Vicksburg by assault. There were many reasons ~~why~~ to determine me to adopt this course. First: I believed an assault from the positions gained by this time could be made sucsessfully. It was known that Johnstone was at Canton with the force taken by him from Jackson, reinforced by other troops from the East and more reaching him daily. With the force I then had a short time must have enabled him to attack me in the rear and possibly succeed in raising the ~~blockade~~ siege. Possession of Vicksburg ~~then~~ at that time would ~~have~~ enabled me to have turned upon Johnstone and drive him from the state, and possess myself of all the rail-roads, and practical Military highways, thus effectually securing to ourselves all territory West of the Tombigbee. This before the season was too far advanced for campaigning in this latitude. It would have saved Government sending large reinforcements, much needed elswhere, and finally the troops themselves were impatient to possess Vicksburg and would not have worked in the trenches with the same zeal, believing it unnecessary, they did after their failure to carry the enemy's works. Accordingly on the 21st orders were issued for a general assault, to on the whole line, to commence at 10 a. m on the 22d. All the Corps Commanders set their time by mine that there should be no difference between them in the moment of Assault. Promptly at the hour designated the three Army Corps then in front of the enemy's work commenced the Assault. I had taken a commanding position near Gen. McPherson's front and from which I could see all the advancing columns from his corps and a part from each Sherman's and McClernand's. A portion of the commands of each one succeeded in planting their flags on the outer slopes of the enemy's bastions and maintained them there until night. Each Corps had many more men than they could possibly be use in the assault;, over the such ground as intervened between them and the enemy. More men could only avail in case of breaking through the enemy's line, or in repelling an assault [a sortie]. The assault was gallant in the extreme on the part of all the troops. But the enemy's position was too strong both naturally and artificially to be taken in that way. At every point assaulted, and at all of them at the same time, the enemy was able to show all the force their works would cover. The assault failed, I regret to say, with much loss on our side in killed and wounded, but without weakening the confidance of the troops in their ability to ultimately succeed.

No troops succeeded in entering any of the enemy's works with the exception of a Sgt. Griffith[5] of the 21st Iowa vols. and some eleven privates of the same regiment. Of these none returned except the Sgt. and possibly one man. The work entered by him, from its position, could give us no pratical advantage unless others to the right and left of it were carried and held at the same time. About   O'Clock a dispatch from Gen. McClernan was received stating (Here copy dispatchs one, two, & three with my replies)[6]

The position occupied by me during most of the time of the assault gave me a better opportunity of seeing what was going on in front of the 13th Army Corps than I believed it possible for the Commander of it to possibly have. I could not see his possession of forts, ~~and~~ nor necessity for reinforcements, as represented in his dispatches. [up to the time I left it which was between 12 M & 1 P. M.] and I expressed doubts ~~as to of~~ of their correctness; which doubts ~~the fact so~~ the facts subsequently ~~confirmed~~ but too late confirmed. At the time I could not disregard his reiterated statements ~~then~~ for they might possible be true ~~But~~ and that no possible opportunity of carrying the enemy's stronghold should be allowed to escape, through fault of mine I ordered Quinbys Division which was ~~all~~ all ~~g~~ of McPherson's Corps, then present, but four Brigades to report to Gen. McClernand, and notified ~~McClernand~~ of the ~~same~~ order ~~and~~ I shewed his dispatches to ~~Gens~~ McPherson ~~&~~ as I had to Sherman to satisfy ~~them~~ him of the necessity of an active diversion on ~~their his~~ their part ~~in favor of~~ to hold as much force in ~~their his~~ their front as possible. The diversion was promptly and vigorously made and resulted in the increase of our mortality list full fifty per cent, without advancing our position or giving other advantage.

The assault of this day proved the quality of the soldiers of this Army. Without entire success, and with a heavy loss, there was no murmuring or complaining, no falling back nor other evidence of demoralization.

After the failure of the 22d I determined upon a regular siege. The men now being fully awake to the necessity of this worked dillegently and cheerfully. The work progressed rapidly and satisfactorily until the 3d of July, when all was about ready for a final assault.

There was ~~a~~ great scarsity of Engineer officers in the begining but under the skilful superintendence of Capt. F. E. Prime, of the Engineer Corps, Lt. Col. Wilson of my staff and Capt. Comstock of the Eng. Corps, who joined this command during the siege, such practical experiance was gained as would enable any Division of this Army, hereafter, to conduct a siege ~~with a great deal~~ with conciderable skill in the absence of ~~an~~ a regular Engineer officer.

On the ~~evening~~ afternoon of the 3d of July a letter was received from Lt. Gen. Pemberton proposing the appointment of Commissioners to arrange the terms ~~of the~~ for the surrender of the place. The correspondence resulted in the surrender at 8 O'clock a. m. on the morning of the 4th, as I regarded it, on terms more favorable to the Government than an unconditional surrender. A copy of the correspondence is herewith accompanying.[7] The particulars and incidents of the siege will be contained in the reports of Division and Corps Commanders, which will be forwarded as soon as received.

All maps showing the march from Millikin's Bend to the rear of Vicksburg, the different battle fields &c. not accompanying this report will be forwarded as fast as completed.

During the siege I was reinforced by three Divisions from the 16th Army Corps, Maj. Gen. Washburn Comdg one Division, Maj. Gen. Herron Comd.g from the Dept. of the Mo. and two Divisions from the 9th Army Corps, Maj Gen. Parks Comd.g. This gave me a force which enabled me to make the investment of Vicksburg most complete and at the same time left a large reserve to watch the movements of Johnstone.

Gen. Herrons Division was placed south of the city and Gen. Lauman's Division of the 16th Army Corps was placed between that and the 13th Army Corps. All the other reinforcements were sent to Snyders Bluff. This place was ~~fortified~~ fortified to the land side and every preparation made to resist a heavy force. Johnstone crossed Big Black River with a portion of his force and every thing indicated an attack from him about the 25th of June. The work done by the troops engaged in the siege of Vicksburg having made their positions about as strong against a sortie from the enemy as their works were against an assault, I placed Maj. Gen. Sherman in command of all the troops left to look after Johnstone. I added to his command one Div. from his own Corps and one from McPhersons and authorized him in addition to command the whole of the 13th Corps, including Gen. Lauman Division of the 16th Corps, in case of necessity. Johnstone did not attack however.

Determining to attack Johnstone the moment Vicksburg was

in our possession I notified Gen. Sherman on the   of July that I should carry the place at day light on the 6th ~~of July~~ For him to have up supplies of all discriptions ready to move the moment I notified him of our success. Preparations were at once made and when the place surrendered on the 4th, two days earlyer than I had intended the attack, Gen Sherman was found ready—I ~~acted~~ and moved at once. In addition to what he had previously notified would be subject to his orders I sent the remainder of the 15th Army Corps.

Gen. Sherman is still absent on this expedition which will be the subject of a separate report.

In ~~this~~ the march from Bruinsburg to Vicksburg, covering a period of twenty days before supplies could be obtained from Government stores, but about five days rations were issued, and three days of those were taken in haversacks at the start and soon exhausted. The balance was drawn from the country through which we passed. The march was also commenced without a single wagon except such as could be picked up through the country. The delay in ferriage with the small and disabled steamers at command would have been ~~to~~ so great as to have defeated the expedition had wagons been crossed before moving.

The country was found abundantly supplied with corn, bacon, beef & mutton. The troops enjoyed excellent health and no army was ever know to appear in better spirits or to feel more confidant of success.

~~Whilst the~~

In accordance with previous instructions Maj. Gen. [S. A.] Hurlbut started Col. (now Brig. Gen.) B. H. Grierson, with a Cavalry force from Lagrange, Ten. to make a raid through the Central portion of the state of Miss. to destroy rail-roads and ~~destroy~~ other public property for the purpose of creating a diversion in favor of the Army moving to the attack on Vicksburg. On the 17th of ~~March~~ April this expedition started and arrived at Baton Rouge on the   of June thus having successfully traversed the whole state of Miss. This expedition was skilfully conducted reflecting great credit on Gen. Grierson and all ~~the~~

of his command. The notices given this raid by the Southern press show the importance it has been to us and that in their estimation, as well as our own, ~~this~~ it has been one of the most brilliant Cavalry exploits of the war and will be handed down in history as an example to be imitated. ~~by others in future wars.~~ ~~—For particulars see Gen. Grierson's report herewith accompanying~~.

For ~~casualties~~ details of the different battles fought, and casualties, see accompanying reports.

The number of prisoners captured and sent North exceeds 6000. Besides these 2000 or more wounded, and their attendants, left in hospital, have been paroled.

I cannot close this report without expressing ~~my thankfulness~~ thanfulness ~~for~~ at being placed in cooperation with an officer of the Navy who never throws obsticles or objections in the way of any move, but gives it ~~his~~ whatever it may be an efficient and active support. Admiral Porter, and the ~~very efficient~~ officers under him, have ever shown the greatest readiness in their cooperation no matter what was to be done or what risk to be taken, either by their men or their vessels. Without this hearty support my movements might have been much embarassed, and especially in effecting the first landing on the East bank of the Miss.

Running the blockade all the transports were more or less disabled. The Navy at once took hold of them and with their material and Mechanics repaired them with the greatest promptness. Capt. Shirk, Commanding Gunboat Tuscumbia, unasked, in fact before my arrival at New Carthage, took the matter of repairs in his own hands and pushed it night and day. When the river was to [be] crossed all the gunboats, including the Flag ship, were volunteered, and used, to ferry the troops over.

The result of this Campaign has been the defeat of the enemy in five battles outside of Vicksburg, the capture of Vicksburg with all its garrison and munitions of war, the loss to the enemy of Thirty-seven thousand prisoners and at least thirteen thousand ~~men~~ in killed & wounded, ~~to the enemy~~ beside many hundreds, and it may be thousands, who have straggled from their commands and have been lost to the ~~Confederacy~~ enemy. Arms sufficient for an Army of 60 000 men have fallen into our hands and no doubt the enemy have lost many that we have not got.

Our loss in the series of battles has been _____ thousands.[8] Of this many were only slightly wounded and continued on duty. Many more were slightly hurt requiring but a few days or weeks for their recovery thus reducing the actual loss of killed and perminantly disabled to probably not one half of the number given above.

In all former reports I have failed to make mention of Company "A" 4th Ill. Cavalry Capt. E. Osband Commanding. This Company started with me as Escort Company at Cairo the Fall of 1861. They have been with me from that time to the present. Every engagement I have been in they have been in also doing excellent service. This company have attracted general attention for their exemplary conduct, soldierly bearing and promptness. I do not think I overstate the merits of this company when I say that a Cavalry regiment could be well officered, from the Captains up, from this Company alone.

ADf, DLC-USG, III. Apparently before July 4, 1863, USG drafted the first twenty-six pages of his report of the Vicksburg campaign, covering the period through the investment of the city. Lt. Col. John A. Rawlins later copyedited the report, adding dates, names, inserting correspondence or figures where indicated by USG, and correcting errors of fact. Material added or altered in USG's draft —largely by Rawlins—appears in brackets. A nearly complete copy of the report is dated July 16. Copy, USG 3. Some time between July 18 and 22, USG signed the final version of the report, still dated July 6, as maj. gen. in the U.S. Army. He had learned of his promotion on July 18, and Rawlins left for Washington with the final version of the report on July 22. LS, DNA, RG 94, War Records Office, Union Battle Reports. *O.R.*, I, xxiv, part 1, 44–59. See letters to Brig. Gen. Lorenzo Thomas, July 18, 1863, and to Abraham Lincoln, July 20, 1863. The report was soon published. See *Army and Navy Official Gazette*, I, 6 (Aug. 11, 1863), 82–87; *New York Times*, Aug. 13, 1863.

James Harrison Wilson later asserted that Rawlins was largely responsible for the writing of USG's report. *The Life of John A. Rawlins* . . . (New York, 1916), pp. 147, 157–58. In 1876, USG presented the original draft of the Vicksburg report to his son, Frederick Dent Grant, proving his authorship. AN, DLC-USG. USG refers in the draft to numerous other reports of the Vicksburg campaign. Most of these reports can be found in *O.R.*, I, xxiv, parts 1 and 2. The expanded and revised report USG sent to Washington follows.

"I have the honor to submit the following report of the operations of the Army of the Tennessee and co-operating Forces, from the date of my assuming the immediate Command of the Expedition against Vicksburg, Miss., to the reduction of that place. From the moment of taking Command in person, I became satisfied, that Vicksburg could only be turned from the south side, and in accordance with this conviction, I prosecuted the work on the Canal, which had been located by Brig Genl: Williams, across the peninsula, on the Louisiana side of the river, with all vigor, hoping to make a channel, which would pass transports for moving the Army, and carrying supplies to the new base of operations thus provided. The task was much more herculean than it at first appeared, and was made much more so, by the almost continuous rains that fell during the whole of the time this work was prosecuted. The river, too, continued to rise, and make a large expenditure of labor necessary, to keep the water out of our camps and the canal. Finally on the 8th of March, the rapid rise of the river, and the consequent great pressure upon the dam across the canal, near the upperend, at the Main Mississippi Levee, caused it to give way, and let through the low lands back of our camps, a torrent of water that separated the North and South shores of the peninsula as effectually, as if the Mississippi flowed between them. This occured when the enterprise promised success within a short time. There was some delay in trying to repair damages. It was found, however, that with the then stage of water, some other plan would have to be adopted, for getting below Vicksburg with transports. Captain F. E. Prime, Chief Engineer, and Col G. G. Pride, who was acting on my staff, prospected a route through the Bayous which ran from near Millikens Bend on the north and New Carthage on the south, through Roundaway Bayou into the Tansas river. Their report of the practicability of this route, determined me to commence work upon it. Having three dredge boats at the time, the work of opening this route was executed with great rapidity. One small steamer and a number of barges were taken through the channel thus opened, but the river commencing about the middle of April to fall rapidly, and the roads becoming passable between Millikens Bend and New Carthage, made it impracticable and unnecessary to open water communication between these points. Soon after commencing the first canal spoken of, I caused a channel to be cut from the Mississippi river into Lake Providence; also one from the Mississippi river into Coldwater, by way of Yazoo Pass. I had no great expectations of important results from the former of these, but having more troops than could be employed to advantage at Youngs Point, and knowing that Lake Providence was connected by 'Bayou Baxter' with 'Bayou Macon,' a navigable stream through which transports might pass into the Mississippi below, through Tansas, Wachita and Red rivers, I thought it possible that a route might be opened in that direction, which would enable me to cooperate with Genl: Banks on Port Hudson. By the Yazoo Pass route I only expected at first to get into the Yazoo by way of Coldwater and Tallahatchie with some of lighter Gun-boats and a few troops and destroy the enemy's transports in that stream, and some Gunboats which I knew he was building. The navigation, however, proved so much better than had been expected, that I thought for a time of the possibility of making this the route for obtaining a foothold on high land above Haines Bluff Mississippi, and small class steamers were accordingly ordered, for transporting an army that way. Maj Genl: J. B. McPherson commanding 17th. Army Corps, was directed to hold his Corps in readiness to move by this route; and one Division from each the 13th and 15th Corps were collected near the entrance of the Pass, to be added to his command. It soon became evident, that a sufficient number of boats of the right class could not be obtained for the movement of more than one Division. Whilst my forces were opening one end of the Pass, the enemy was diligently closing the other end, and in this way succeeded in gaining time, to strongly fortify Greenwood, below the junction of the Tallahatchie and Yallobusha. The advance of the expedition, consisting of one Division of McClernands Corps from Helena, commanded by Brig. Genl: L. F. Ross and the 12th and 17th Regiments Missouri Infantry from Shermans Corps, as sharp-shooters on the Gunboats, succeeded in reaching Coldwater, on the 2d day of March, after much difficulty, and the partial disabling of most of the boats. From the entrance into Coldwater to Fort Pemberton at Greenwood, Miss., no great difficulty of navigation was experienced, nor any interruption of magnitude from the enemy. Fort Pemberton extends from the Tallahatchie to the Yazoo at Greenwood. Here the two rivers come within a few hundred yards of each other. The land around the Fort is low, and at the time of the attack was entirely overflowed. Owing to this fact, no movement could be made by the Army to reduce it, but all depended upon the ability of the Gunboats to silence the guns of the enemy, and enable the transports to run down and land Troops immediately on the Fort itself. After an engagement of several hours, the Gunboats drew off, being unable to silence the Batteries. Brig. Genl: I. F. Quimby commanding a Division of McPherson's Corps, met the expedition under Ross, with his Division, on its return near Fort Pemberton, on the 21st of March, and being the senior, assumed Command of the entire Expedition, and returned to the position Ross had occupied.—On the 23d day of March I sent orders for the withdrawal of all the Forces operating in that direction, for the purpose of concentrating my Army at Milliken's Bend. On the 14th day of March, Admiral D. D. Porter, Commanding Mississippi Squadron, informed me that he hade made a reconnoisance up 'Steeles Bayou,' and partially through Black Bayou, towards 'Deer Creek,' and so far as explored these water courses were reported navigable for the smaller Iron-clads. Information given mostly, I believe, by the Negroes of the country, was to the effect, that Deer Creek could be navigated to Rolling Fork, and that from there through the Sunflower to the Yazoo river, there was no question about the navigation. On the following morning I accompanied Admiral Porter in the ram 'Price,' several iron-clads preceeding us, up through Steele's Bayou, to near Black Bayou. At this time our Forces were at a deadlock at Greenwood, and I looked upon the success of this enterprise as of vast importance.—It would, if successful, leave Greenwood between two Forces of ours, and would necessarily cause the immediate abandonment of that stronghold. About thirty steamers of the enemy would have been destroyed or fallen into our hands. Seeing that the great obstacles to navigation, so far as I had gone, was from overhanging trees, I left Admiral Porter near Black Bayou, and pushed back to Young's Point, for the purpose of sending forward a Pioneer Corps, to remove these difficulties. Soon after my return to Young's Point, Admiral Porter sent back to me for a co-operating military Force. Sherman was promptly sent with one Division of his Corps. The number of steamers suitable for the navigation of these Bayous being limited, most of the Force was sent up the Mississippi river, to Eagle's Bend, a point where the river runs within one mile of Steele's Bayou, thus saving an important part of this difficult navigation. The Expedition failed, probably more from want of knowledge as to what would be required to open this route, than from any impracticability in the navigation of the Streams and Bayous through which it was proposed to pass. Want of this knowledge led the expedition on until difficulties were encountered, and then it would become necessary to send back to Young's Point, for the means of removing them. This gave the enemy time to move Forces to effectually checkmate further progress, and the Expedition was withdrawn, when within a few hundred yards of free and open navigation to the Yazoo. All this may have been Providential, in driving us ultimately to a line of operations which has proven eminently successfull. For further particulars of the Steele's Bayou Expedition, see report of Maj. Genl: W. T. Sherman, forwarded on the 12th of April. As soon as I decided to open water communication from a point on the Mississippi near Milliken's Bend, to New Carthage, I determined to occupy the latter place, it being the first point below Vicksburg, that could be reached by land at the stage of water then existing, and the occupancy of which, while it secured to us a point on the Mississippi river, would also protect the main line of communication by water. Accordingly, the 13th Army Corps, Maj. Genl. J. A. McClernand, Commanding, was directed to take up its line of march on the 29th day of March for New Carthage, the 15th and 17th Corps to follow, moving no faster, than supplies and ammunition could be transported to them. The roads though level, were intolerably bad, and the movement was therefore, necessarily slow. Arriving at Smith's plantation, two miles from New Carthage, it was found that the levee of 'Bayou Vidal' was broken in several places, thus leaving New Carthage an Island. All the Boats that could be, were collected from the different Bayous in the vicinity, and others were built; but the transportation of an Army in this way was found exceedingly tedious. Another route had to be found. This was done by making a further march around Vidal to Perkin's plantation, a distance of twelve miles more, making the whole distance to be marched from Milliken's Bend to reach water communication on the opposite side of the point, thirty five miles. Over this distance with bad roads to contend against, supplies of Ordnance stores and provisions had to be hauled by wagons, with which to commence the campaign on the opposite side of the river. At the same time that I ordered the occupation of New Carthage, preparations were made for running transports by the Vicksburg Batteries, with Admiral Porter's Gunboat Fleet. On the night of the 16th of April, Admiral Porter's Fleet and the Transports, 'Silver Wave' 'Forest Queen' and 'Henry Clay' ran the Vicksburg Batteries. The boilers of the Transports were protected as well as possible with hay and cotton. More or less Commissary stores were put on each. All three of these boats were struck more or less frequently while passing the enemy's batteries, and the 'Henry Clay' by the explosion of a shell, or by some other means, was set on fire, and entirely consumed. The other two boats were somewhat injured, but not seriously disabled. No one on board of either was hurt. As these boats succeeded in getting by so well, I ordered six more to be prepared in like manner for running the batteries. These latter viz: 'Tigress,' 'Anglo Saxon,' 'Cheeseman,' 'Empire City,' 'Horizonia,' and 'Moderator,' left Millikens Bend on the night of the 22d of April, and five of them got by but in a somewhat damaged condition. The 'Tigress' received a shot in her hull, below the water line, and sunk on the Louisiana shore soon after passing the last of the batteries. The crews of these steamers, with the exception of that of the 'Forrest Queen' Capt. D. Conway, and the 'Silver Wave' Capt. McMillan, were composed of Volunteers from the Army. Upon the call for Volunteers for this dangerous enterprise, Officers and men presented themselves by hundreds, anxious to undertake the trip. The names of those, whose services were accepted will be given in a separate report. It is a striking feature, so far as my observation goes, of the present Volunteer Army of the United States, that there is nothing which men are called upon to do, mechanical or professional, that accomplished adepts cannot be found, for the duty required, in almost every Regiment. The Transports injured in running the blockade, were repaired by order of Admiral Porter, who was supplied with the material for such repairs as they required, and who was and is ever ready to afford all the assistance in his power, for the furtherance of the success of our arms. In a very short time five of the Transports were in running order, and the remainder were in a condition to be used as barges in the moving of troops. Twelve barges loaded with forage and rations were sent in tow of the last six boats that ran the blockade. One half of them got through in a condition to be used. Owing to the limited number of transports below Vicksburg, it was found necessary to extend our line of land travel to Hard Times La, which, by the circuitous route it was necessary to take, increased the distance to about seventy miles from Milliken's Bend our starting point. The 13th Army Corps being all through to the Mississippi, and the 17th Army Corps well on the way, so much of the 13th as could be got on board of the transports and barges, were put aboard and moved to the front of Grand Gulf, on the 29th of April. The plan here was, that the Navy should silence the guns of the enemy, and the troops land under the cover of the Gunboats, and carry the place by storm. At 8. o. clock A. M. the Navy made the attack, and kept it up for more than five hours in the most gallant manner. From a tug out in the stream, I witnessed the whole engagement. Many times it seemed to me the Gunboats were within pistol shot of the enemy's batteries. It soon became evident, that the guns of the enemy were too elevated, and their fortifications too strong, to be taken from the water side. The whole range of hills, on that side, were known to be lined with rifle pits, besides the Field Artillery could be moved to any position where it could be made useful in case of an attempt at landing. This determined me to again run the enemy's batteries, turn his position by effecting a landing at Rodney or at Bruinsburg, between Grand Gulf and Rodney. Accordingly orders were immediately given for the troops to debark at 'Hard Times,' La. and march across to the point immediately below Grand Gulf. At dark the Gunboats again engaged the batteries, and all the Transports run by, receiving but two or three shots in the passage, and these without injury. I had sometime previously, ordered a reconnoisance to a point opposite Bruinsburg, to ascertain if possible, from persons in the neighborhood, the character of the road leading to the highlands back of Bruinsburg. During the night I learned from a Negro man, that there was a good road from Bruinsburg to Port Gibson, which determined me to land there. The work of ferrying the troops to Bruinsburg was commenced at daylight in the morning, the Gunboats as well as Transports being used for the purpose. As soon as the 13th Army Corps was landed, and could draw three days rations to put in haversacks, (no wagons were allowed to cross, until the troops were all over,) they were started on the road to Port Gibson. I deemed it a matter of vast importance that the highlands should be reached without resistance. The 17th Corps followed as rapidly as it could be put across the river. About 2 o'clock on the 1st: of May the advance of the enemy was met eight miles from Bruinsburg, on the road to Port Gibson. He was forced to fall back, but as it was dark, he was not pursued far until day-light. Early on the morning of the 1st, I went out, accompanied by members of my staff, and found McClernand, with his Corps, engaging the enemy about four miles from Port Gibson. At this point the roads branched in exactly opposite directions, both, however, leading to Port Gibson. The enemy had taken position on both branches, thus dividing, as he fell back, the pursuing forces. The nature of the ground in that part of the country is such that a very small force could retard the progress of a much larger one for many hours. The roads usually run on narrow, elevated ridges, with deep and impenetrable ravines on either side. On the right were the Divisions of Hovey, Carr and Smith, and on the left the Division of Osterhaus, of McClernands Corps. The three former succeeded in driving the enemy from position to position, back towards Port Gibson, steadily all day. Osterhaus, however, did not move the enemy from the position occupied by him on our left, until Logan's Division of McPherson's Corps arrived. McClernand, who was with the right in person, sent repeated messages to me, before the arrival of Logan, to send Logan's and Quimby's Divisions, of McPherson's Corps, to him. I had been on that, as well as all other parts of the Field, and could not see how they could be used there to advantage. However, as soon as the advance of McPherson's Corps (Logans Division) arrived, I sent one Brigade to McClernand on the right, and sent one brigade, Brig. Genl. J. E. Smith Commanding, to the left, to the assistance of Osterhaus   By the judicious disposition made of this Brigade, under the immediate supervision of McPherson and Logan, a position was soon obtained, giving us an advantage which soon drove the enemy from that part of the Field to make no further stand south of Bayou Pierre. The enemy was here repulsed with a heavy loss in killed, wounded and prisoners. The repulse of the enemy on our left, took place late in the afternoon. He was pursued towards Port Gibson, but night closing in, and the enemy making the appearance of another stand, the troops slept upon their arms until daylight. In the morning it was found, that the enemy had retreated across Bayou Pierre, on the Grand Gulf road, and a Brigade of Logan's Division was sent to divert his attention, whilst a floating bridge was being built across Bayou Pierre, immediately at Port Gibson. This bridge was completed, eight miles marched by McPherson's Corps, to the north fork of Bayou Pierre, that stream bridged, and the advance of this Corps commenced passing over it at 5 o'clock the following morning. On the 3d: the enemy was pursued to Hankinson's Ferry with slight skirmishing all day, during which we took quite a number of prisoners, mostly stragglers, from the enemy. Finding that Grand Gulf had been evacuated, and that the advance of my Forces was already fifteen miles out from there, and on the road, too, they would have to take to reach either Vicksburg, Jackson or any intermediate point on the Rail-Road, between the two places, I determined not to march them back, but taking a small escort of Cavalry, some fifteen or twenty men, I went to the Gulf myself, and made the necessary arrangements for changing my base of supplies, from Bruinsburg to Grand Gulf. In moving from Milliken's Bend, the 15th Army Corps, Maj. Genl: W. T. Sherman, Commanding, was left to be the last to start. To prevent heavy reinforcements going from Vicksburg to the assistance of the Grand Gulf Forces, I directed Sherman to make a demonstration on Haines Bluff, and to make all the *Show* possible. From information since received from prisoners captured, this ruse succeeded admirably. It had been my intention, up to the time of crossing the Missippi river, to collect all my Forces at Grand Gulf and get on hand a good supply of provisions, and Ordnance stores before moving, and in the meantime, to detach an Army Corps to co-operate with Genl: Banks on Port Hudson, and effect a junction of our Forces. About this time I received a letter from Genl: Banks giving his position west of the Mississippi river, and stating that he could return to Baton Rouge, by the 10th of May; that by the reduction of Port Hudson he could join me with 12,000 men. I learned about the same time, that Troops were expected at Jackson from the southern cities, with Genl: Beauregard in Command. To delay until the 10th of May, and for the reduction of Port Hudson, after that, the accession of 12,000 men, would not leave me relatively so strong, as to move promptly with what I had. Information received from day to day of the movements of the enemy also impelled me to the course pursued. Whilst lying at 'Hankinsons Ferry' waiting for wagons, supplies and Sherman's Corps, which had come forward in the meantime, demonstrations were made, successfully, I believe, to induce the enemy to think that route, and the one by, 'Halls Ferry' above, were objects of much solicitude to me. Reconnoisances were made to the west side of the Big Black, to within six miles of Warrenton. On the 7th of May an advance was ordered, McPherson's Corps keeping the road nearest Black river to Rocky springs, McClernand's Corps keeping the Ridge road from Willow Springs, and Sherman following with his Corps divided on the two roads. All the Ferries were closely guarded until our troops were well advanced. It was my intention here to hug the Black river as closely as possible with McClernand's and Sherman's Corps, and get them to the Rail-Road, at some place between Edwards Station and Bolton. McPherson was to move by way of Utica to Raymond, and from there into Jackson, destroying the railroad, telegraph, public stores &c. and push west to rejoin the main force. Orders were given to McPherson accordingly. Sherman was moved forward on the Edward's Station road, crossing Fourteen Mile Creek at Dillon's plantation, McClernand was moved across the same creek, further west, sending one Division of his Corps by the Baldwins Ferry road, as far as the river. At the crossing of Fourteen Mile Creek, both McClernand and Sherman had considerable skirmishing with the enemy, to get possession of the crossings. McPherson met the enemy near Raymond, two Brigades strong under Gregg and Walker on the same day, engaged him and after several hours hard fighting, drove him with heavy loss in killed wounded and prisoners. Many threw down their arms and deserted. My position at this time was with Shermans Corps, some seven miles west of Raymond, and about the Centre of the Army. On the night of the 12th of May, after Orders had been given for the Corps of McClernand and Sherman to march toward the Rail Road by parrallel roads, the former in the direction of Edward's Station, and the latter to a point on the Rail Road between Edward's Station and Bolton, the order was changed, and both were directed to move towards Raymond. This was in consequence of the enemy having retreated towards Jackson after his defeat at Raymond, and of information that reinforcements were daily arriving at Jackson, and that Genl: Joe Johnston was hourly expected there to take Command in person. I therefore determined to make sure of that place, and leave no enemy in my rear. McPherson moved on the 13th to Clinton, destroyed the Rail Road and Telegraph and captured some important dispatches from Genl: Pemberton to Genl: Gregg, who had commanded the day before in the Battle of Raymond. Sherman moved to a parrallel position on the Mississippi springs and Jackson road; McClernand moved to a point near Raymond. The next day Sherman and McPherson moved their entire force towards Jackson. The rain fell in torrents all the night before and continued until about noon of that day, making the roads at first slippery and then miry. Notwithstanding, the Troops marched in excellent order, without straggling, and in the best of spirits, about fourteen miles, and engaged the enemy about 12' o clock M. near Jackson. McClernand occupied Clinton with one Division, Mississippi Springs with another, Raymond with a third, and had his fourth Division and Blair's Division of Sherman's Corps, with a wagon train, still in the rear near

New Auburn, while McArthur with one Brigade of his Division, of McPherson's Corps, was moving towards Raymond on the Utica road. It was not the intention to move these forces any nearer Jackson, but to have them in a position, where they would be in supporting distance, if the resistance at Jackson should prove more obstinate, than there seemed reason to expect. The enemy marched out the bulk of his force on the Clinton road, and engaged McPhersons Corps about 2½ miles from the city. A small force of Artillery and Infantry took a strong position in front of Sherman, about the same distance out. By a determined advance of our skirmishers, these latter were soon driven within their rifle-pits just outside the city. It was impossible to ascertain the strength of the enemy at this part of the line, in time to justify an immediate assault, consequently McPherson's two Divisions engaged the main bulk of the rebel garrison at Jackson, without further aid than the moral support given them by the knowledge the enemy had of a force to the south side of the city, and the few Infantry and Artillery of the enemy posted there to impede Sherman's progress. Sherman soon discovered the weakness of the enemy, by sending a reconoitering party to his right, which also had the effect of causing the enemy to retreat from this part of his line. A few of the Artillerists, however, remained in their places, firing upon Shermans Troops, until the last moment, evidently instructed to do so, with the expectation of being captured in the end. On entering the city it was found, that the main body of the enemy had retreated north, after a heavy engagement of more than two hours with McPherson's Corps, in which he was badly beaten. He was pursued until near night, but without further damage to him. During that evening I learned that Genl: Johnston, as soon as he had satisfied himself that Jackson was to be attacked, had ordered Pemberton peremptorily to march out from the direction of Vicksburg and attack our rear. Availing myself of this information, I immediately issued Orders to McClernand, and Blair of Sherman's Corps, to face their Troops towards Bolton, with a view to reaching Edwards Station, marching on different roads converging near Bolton. These Troops were admirably located for such a move. McPherson was ordered to retrace his steps early in the morning of the 15th on the Clinton road. Sherman was left in Jackson to destroy the Rail Roads, Bridges, Factories, Workshops, Arsenals and every thing valuable for the support of the enemy. This was accomplished in the most effectual manner. On the afternoon of the 15th, I proceeded as far west as Clinton, through which place McPherson's Corps passed to within supporting distance of Hoveys Division of McClernands Corps, which had moved that day on the same road to within one and a half miles of Bolton. On reaching Clinton at 4:45. P. M., I ordered McClernand to move his command early the next morning towards Edwards Depot, marching so as to feel the enemy, if he encountered him, but not to bring on a General Engagement, unless he was confident he was able to defeat him, and also to order Blair to move with him. About 5 o'clock on the morning of the 16th two men, employees on the Jackson and Vicksburg Rail Road, who had passed through Pemberton's Army the night before, were brought to my Headquarters. They stated Pemberton's force to consist of about eighty Regiments with ten batteries of Artillery, and that the whole force was estimated by the enemy at about 25,000 men. From them, I also learned the positions being taken up by the enemy, and his intention of attacking our rear. I had determined to leave one Division of Sherman's Corps one day longer in Jackson, but this information determined me to bring his entire Command up at once, and I accordingly dispatched him at 5:30 A. M. to move with all possible speed until he came up with the main force near Bolton. My dispatch reached him at 7:10 A. M., and his advance Division was in motion in one hour from that time. A dispatch was sent to Blair, at the same time, to push forward his Division, in the direction of Edwards Station, with all possible dispatch. McClernand was directed to establish communication between Blair and Osterhaus of his corps, and keep it up, moving the former to the support of the latter. McPherson was ordered forward at 5:45 A. M., to join McClernand, and Lieut: Col: Wilson, of my staff, was sent forward to communicate the information received, and with verbal instructions to McClernand as to the disposition of his forces. At an early hour, I left for the advance, and on arriving at the crossing of the Vicksburg and Jackson Rail Road with the road from Raymond to Bolton, I found McPherson's advance and his Pioneer Corps engaged in rebuilding a bridge on the former road, that had been destroyed by the Cavalry of Osterhaus's Division that had gone into Bolton the night before. The train of Hovey's Division, was at a halt, and blocked up the road from further advance on the Vicksburg road. I ordered all Quartermasters and Wagon masters to draw their teams to one side, and make room for the passage of troops. McPherson was brought up by this road. Passing to the front, I found Hovey's Division of the 13th Army Corps, at a halt, with our skirmishers and the enemy's pickets near each other. Hovey was bringing his troops in, to line, ready for battle, and could have brought on an engagement at any moment. The enemy had taken up a very strong position on a narrow ridge, his left resting on a hight where the road makes a sharp turn to the left, approaching Vicksburg. The top of the ridge, and the precipitous hillside to the left of the road are covered by a dense forest and undergrowth. To the right of the road the timber extends a short distance down the hill, and then opens into cultivated fields on a gentle slope and into a valley, extending for a considerable distance   On the road and into the wooded ravine and hillside, Hovey's Division was disposed for the attack. McPherson's two Divisions, all of his Corps with him on the march from Milliken's Bend (until Ransom's Brigade arrived that day after the battle,) were thrown to the right of the road, properly speaking the enemy's rear. But I would not permit an attack to be commenced by our troops until I could hear from McClernand, who was advancing with four Divisions, two of them on a road intersecting the Jackson road, about one mile from where the troops above described were placed, and about the centre of the enemy's line; the other two Divisions on a road still north, and nearly the same distance off. I soon heard from McClernand, through members of his staff, and my own whom I had sent to him early in the morning, and found that by the nearest practicable route of communication, he was two and a half miles distant. I sent several successive messages to him to push forward with all rapidity. There had been continuous firing between Hovey's skirmisher's and the rebel advance, which by 11 o'clock grew into a battle. For some time this Division bore the bront of the conflict, but finding the enemy too strong for them, at the instance of Hovey, I directed first one and a second Brigade from Crocker's Division to reinforce him. All this time Logan's Division was working upon the enemy's left and rear, and weakened his front attack most wonderfully. The troops here opposing us evidently far outnumbered ours. Expecting McClernand momentarily with four Division's, including Blair's, I never felt a doubt of the result. He did not arrive, however, until the enemy had been driven from the field, after a terrible contest of hours, with a heavy loss of killed, wounded and prisoners, and a number of pieces of Artillery. It was found afterwards that the Vicksburg road after following the ridge in a southerly direction for about one mile, and to where it intersected one of the Raymond roads, turns almost to the west, down the hill and across the valley in which Logan was operating on the rear of the enemy. One Brigade of Logan's Division had unconscious of this important fact, penetrated nearly to this road, and compelled the enemy to retreat, to prevent capture. As it was, much of his artillery and Lorings Division of his Army, was cut off, besides the prisoners captured. On the call of Hovey for more reinforcements, just before the route of the enemy commenced, I ordered McPherson to move what troops he could by a left flank around to the enemy's front. Logan rode up at this time and told me that if Hovey could make another dash at the enemy, he could come up from where he then was, & capture the greater part of their force. I immediately rode forward & found the troops that had been, so gallantly engaged for so many hours, withdrawn from their advanced position, and were filling their cartridge boxes. I directed them to use all dispatch and push forward as soon as possible, explaining to them the position of Logan's Division. Proceeding still further forward, expecting every moment to see the enemy, and reaching, what had been his line, I found he was retreating. Arriving at the Raymond road I saw to my left, and on the next ridge, a column of troops, which proved to be Carr's Division, and McClernand with it in person; and to the left of Carr, Osterhaus' Division soon after appeared with his skirmishers well in advance. I sent word to Osterhaus that the enemy was in full retreat, and to push up with all haste. The situation was soon explained, after which I ordered Carr to pursue with all speed to Black river, and across it if he could, and to Osterhaus to follow. Some of McPhersons troops had already got into the road in advance, but having marched and engaged the enemy all day, they were fatigued and gave the road to Carr, who continued the pursuit until after dark, capturing a train of cars loaded with Commissary and Ordnance stores and other property. The delay in the advance of the troops, immediately with McClernand, was caused no doubt by the enemy presenting a front of Artillery and Infantry, where it was impossible, from the nature of the ground and the density of the forest, to discover his numbers. As it was the battle of Champions Hill or Bakers creek was fought mainly by Hovey's Division of McClernand's Corps and Logan's and Quimby's Divisions (the latter commanded by Brig. Gen. M. M. Crocker) of McPherson's corps. Ransome's Brigade of McPherson's corps, came on to the field where the main battle had been fought immediately after the enemy had began his retreat. Word was sent to Sherman, at Bolton, of the result of the days engagement, with directions to turn his Corps towards Bridgeport, and to Blair to join him at this latter place. At daylight on the 17th, the pursuit was renewed, with McClernand's Corps in the advance. The enemy was found strongly posted on both sides of the Black river. At this point on Black river the bluffs extend to the water's edge on the west bank. On the east side is an open, cultivated bottom of near one mile in width, surrounded by a Bayou of stagnant water, from two to three feet in depth, and from ten to twenty feet in width, from the river above the Rail Road to the river below. Following the inside line of this Bayou the enemy had constructed rifle pits, with the Bayou to serve as a ditch on the outside and immediately in front of them. Carr's Division occupied the right in investing this place, and Lawler's Brigade the right of his Division. After a few hours skirmishing Lawler discovered that by moving a portion of his Brigade under cover of the river bank, he could get a position from which that place could be successfully assaulted, and ordered a charge accordingly. Nothwithstanding the level ground over which a portion of his troops had to pass without cover, and the great obstacle of the ditch in front of the enemy's works, the charge was gallantly and successfully made, and in a few minutes the entire garrison, with seventeen pieces of Artillery, were the trophies of this brilliant and daring movement. The enemy on the West bank of the river immediately set fire to the Rail Road bridge, and retreated, thus cutting off all chance of escape for any portion of his forces remaining on the east bank. Sherman by this time had reached Bridgeport on Black river above. The only Pontoon Train with the expedition was with him. By the morning of the 18th he had crossed the river, and was ready to march on Walnut Hills. McClernand and McPherson built floating bridges during the night, and had them ready for crossing their Commands by 8. A. M. of the 18th. The march was commenced by Sherman at an early hour by the Bridgeport and Vicksburg road, turning to the right when within three and a half miles of Vicksburg, to get possession of Walnut Hills, and the Yazoo river. This was successfully accomplished before the night of the 18th. McPherson crossed Black river above the Jackson road, and came into the same road with Sherman, but to his rear. He arrived after nightfall with his advance to where Sherman turned to the right. McClernand moved by the Jackson and Vicksburg road to Mount Albans, and there turned to the left to get into Baldwin's Ferry road. By this disposition the three Army Corps covered all the ground their strength would admit of, and by the morning of the 19th the investment of Vicksburg was made as complete as could be, by the Forces at my command. During the day there was continuous skirmishing, and I was not without hope of carrying the enemy's works. Relying upon the demoralization of the enemy in consequence of repeated defeats outside of Vicksburg. I ordered a general assault at 2 P. M. on this day. The 15th Army Corps from having arrived in front of the enemy's works in time on the 18th to get a good position, were enabled to make a vigerous assault. The 13th and 17th Corps succeeded no further than to gain advanced positions, covered from the fire of the enemy. The 20th and 21st were spent in perfecting communications with our supplies. Most of the Troops had been marching and fighting battles for twenty days, on an average of about five days rations, drawn from the Commissary Department. Though they had not suffered from short rations up to this time, the want of bread to accompany the other rations was beginning to be much felt. On the 21st my arrangements for drawing supplies of every description being complete, I determined to make another effort to carry Vicksburg by assault. There were many reasons to determine me to adopt this course. I believed an assault from the position gained by this time could be made successfully. It was known that Johnston was at Canton with the force taken by him from Jackson, reinforced by other troops from the East, and that more were daily reaching him. With the Force I then had, a short time must have enabled him to attack me in the rear, and possibly succeeded in raising the seige. Possession of Vicksburg at that time would have enabled me to have turned upon Johnston and driven him from the State, and possess myself of all the rail roads and practical military highways, thus effectually securing to ourselves all territory west of the Tombigbee, and this before the season was too far advanced for campaigning in this latitude. I would have saved Government sending large reinforcements, much needed elsewhere; and finally, the troops themselves were impatient to possess Vicksburg, and would not have worked in the trenches with the same zeal, believing it unnecessary, that they did after their failure to carry the enemy's works. Accordingly on the 21st, orders were issued for a general assault on the whole line, to commence at 10. A. M., on the 22d. All the Corps Commanders set their time by mine, that there should be no difference between them in movement of assault. Promptly at the hour designated, the three Army Corps, then in front of the enemy's work, commenced the assault. I had taken a commanding position near McPherson's front, and from which I could see all the advancing columns from his Corps, and a part of each of Sherman's and McClernand's. A portion of the Commands of each succeeded in planting their flags on the outer slopes of the enemy's bastions, and maintained them there until night. Each Corps had many more men than could possibly be used in the assault, over such ground as intervened between them & the enemy. More men could only avail in case of breaking through the enemy's line, or in repelling a sortie. The assault was gallant in the extreme on the part of all the troops, but the enemy's position was too strong, both naturally and artificially to be taken in that way. At every point assaulted, and at all of them at thes ame time, the enemy was able to show all the force, his works would cover. The assault failed, I regret to say, with much loss on our side in killed and wounded; but without weakening the confidence of the troops in their ability to ultimately succeed. No troops succeeded in entering any of the enemy's works, with the exception of Sergeant Griffith, of the 21st Regiment Iowa Volunteers, and some eleven privates of thes ame Regiment. Of these, none returned except the Sergeant, and possibly one man. The work entered by him, from its position, could give us no practical advantage, unless others to the right and left of it, were carried and held at the same time. About 12. M., I received a dispatch from McClernand that he was hard pressed at several points, in reply to which I directed him to reinforce the points hard pressed from such troops as he had that were not engaged. I then rode round to Sherman, and had just reached there, when I received a second dispatch from McClernand stating positively & unequivocally, that he was in possession of and still held two of the enemy's forts—that the American flag then waved over them, and asking me to have Sherman and McPherson make a diversion in his favor. This dispatch I showed to Sherman, who immediately ordered a renewal of the assault on his front. I also sent an answer to McClernand, directing him to order up McArthur to his assistance, and started immediately to the position I had just left on McPherson's line, to convey to him the information from McClernand by this last dispatch that he might make the diversion requested. Before reaching McPhersons I met a messenger with a third dispatch from McClernand, of which the following is a copy:

> Head Quarters 13th Army Corps
> In the Field, near Vicksburg Miss.
> May 22d: 1863.

GENERAL:

    We have gained the enemys entrenchments, at several points, but are brought to a stand. I have sent word to McArthur to reinforce me if he can. Would it not be best to concentrate the whole or a part of his Command on this point.

> (signed)   JOHN A. McCLERNAND
> Major Genl. Comd'g.

To MAJ GENL. U. S. GRANT

    P. S.: I have received your dispatch. My troops are all engaged, and I cannot withdraw any to reinforce others

> (signed)   McC.

The position occupied by me during most of the time of the assault, gave me a better opportunity of seeing what was going on in front of the 13th Army Corps, than I believed it possible for the Commander of it to have. I could not see his possession of forts, nor necessity for reinforcements as represented in his dispatches, up to the time I left it, which was between 12. M. and 1 P. M, and I expressed doubts of their correctness, which doubts the facts subsequently, but too late, confirmed. At the time, I could not disregard his reiterated statements, for they might possibly be true, and that no possible opportunity of carrying the enemy's stronghold should be allowed to escape through fault of mine, I ordered Quimby's Division, which was all of McPhersons Corps then present, but four Brigades, to report to McClernand, and notified him of the order. I showed his dispatches to McPherson, as I had to Sherman, to satisfy him of the necessity of an active diversion on their part to hold as much force in their fronts as possible. The diversion was promptly and vigerously made, and resulted in the increase of our mortality list full fifty per cent, without advancing our position, or giving us other advantages. About 3:50. P. M., I received McClernand's fourth dispatch, as follows:

> Head Quarters 13th Army Corps
> May 22d 1863.
>
> GENERAL:
>
> I have received your dispatch in regard to Genl: Quimby's Division and Genl: McArthurs Division. As soon as they arrive I will press the enemy with all possible speed, and doubt not I will force my way through. I have lost no ground, My men are in two of the enemy's forts, but they are commanded by rifle-pits in the rear. Several prisoners have been taken, who intimate, that the rear is strong. At this moment I am hard pressed.
>
> (signed)   JOHN A. McCLERNAND
>   Major Generall Commanding
>
> MAJ GEN. U. S. GRANT
> DEPART. OF THE TENN.

The assault of this day proved the quality of the soldiers of this Army. Without entire success, and with a heavy loss, there was no murmering or complaining, no falling back, nor other evidence of demoralization. After the failure of the 22d, I determined upon a regular siege. The troops now being fully awake to the necessity of this, worked diligently and cheerfully. The work progressed rapidly & satisfactorily until the 3d of July, when all was about ready for a final assault. There was a great scarcity of Engineer Officers in the beginning, but under the skillful superintendence of Capt. F. E. Prime, of the Engineer Corps, Lieut. Col: Wilson of my staff, and Captain C. B. Comstock of the Engineer Corps, who joined this Command during the siege, such practical experience was gained as would enable any Division of this Army, hereafter, to conduct a siege with considerable skill in the absence of regular Engineer Officers. On the afternoon of the 3d of July, a letter was received from Lieut. General Pemberton, commanding the Confederate Forces at Vicksburg, proposing an Armistice and the appointment of Commissioners to arrange terms for the capitulation of the place. The correspondence, copies of which is herewith transmitted, resulted in the surrender of the city and garrison of Vicksburg at 10 o'clock A. M. July 4th, 1863, on the following terms: The entire garrison, Officers and men, were to be paroled not to take up arms against the United States until exchanged by the proper authorities; Officers and men each to be furnished with a parole signed by himself, Officers to be allowed their side-arms and private baggage, and the Field, Staff and Cavalry Officers one horse each; the rank and file to be allowed all their Clothing but no other property; rations from their own stores sufficient to last them beyond our lines; the necessary cooking utensils for preparing their food; and thirty wagons to transport such articles as could not well be carried. These terms I regarded more favorable to the Government than an unconditional surrender. It saved us the transportation of them north, which at that time would have been very difficult, owing to the limited amount of river transportation on hand, and the expense of subsisting them. It left our Army free to operate against Johnston, who was threatening us from the direction of Jackson; and our river transportation to be used for the movement of troops to any point the exigency of the service might require. I deem it proper to state here, in order that the correspondence may be fully understood, that after my answer to Genl: Pemberton's letter of the morning of the 3d, we had a personal interview on the subject of the capitulation. The particulars and incidents of the siege, will be contained in the reports of Division and Corps Commanders, which will be forwarded as soon as received. I brought forward during the siege in addition to Lauman's Division and four Regiments previously ordered from Memphis, Smith's and Kimball's Divisions, of the 16th Army Corps, and assigned Maj. Genl: C. C. Washburn to Command of same. On the 11th of June, Maj. Genl: F. J. Herron's Division, from the Department of the Missouri, arrived, and on the 14th two Divisions of the 9th Army Corps, Maj. Genl: J. G. Parke, commanding arrived. This increase in my force enabled me to make the investment most complete, and at the same time left me a large reserve to watch the movements of Johnston. Herron's Division was put into position on the extreme left, south of the city, and Lauman's Division was placed between Herron and McClernand. Smith's and Kimball's Divisions, and Parke's Corps were sent to Haines Bluff. This place I had fortified to the land side, and every preparation made to resist a heavy force. Johnston crossed Big Black river with a portion of his force, and everything indicated that he would make an attack about the 25th of June. Our position in front of Vicksburg having been made as strong against a sortie from the enemy as his works were against an assault, I placed Maj. Genl: Sherman in Command of all the Troops designated to look after Johnston. The Force intended to operate against Johnston, in addition to that at Haines Bluff, was one Division from each of the 13th 15th, and 17th Army Corps, and Lauman's Division. Johnston, however, not attacking. I determined to attack him the moment Vicksburg was in our posession, and accordingly notified Sherman that I should again make an assault on Vicksburg at daylight on the 6th, and for him to have up supplies of all descriptions, ready to move upon receipt of orders, if the assault should prove a success. His preparations were immediately made, and when the place surrendered on the 4th, two days earlier than I had fixed for the attack, Sherman was found ready and moved at once, with a force increased by the remainder of both the 13th and 15th Army Corps, and is at present investing Jackson, where Johnston has made a stand. In the march from Bruinsburg to Vicksburg, covering a period of twenty days, before supplies could be obtained from Government stores, only five days rations were issued, and three days of these were taken in haversacks at the start, and were soon exhausted. All other subsistence was obtained from the country through which we passed. The march was commenced without wagons except such as could be picked up through the country. The country was abundantly supplied with corn bacon, beef and mutton. The Troops enjoyed excellent health; and no Army ever appeared in better spirit, or felt more confident of success. In accordance with previous instructions, Maj. Genl: S. A. Hurlbut, started Col (now Brig. Genl:) B. H. Grierson, with a Cavalry force, from La Grange, Tenn., to make a raid through the central portion of the State of Mississippi to destroy rail roads and other public property, for the purpose of creating a diversion in favor of the Army moving to the attack on Vicksburg. On the 17th of April this expedition started, and arrived at Baton Rouge, on the 2d of May, having successfully traversed the whole state of Mississippi. This expedition was skillfully conducted, and reflected great credit on Col: Grierson and all of his Command. The notice given this raid by the Southern press confirm our estimate of its importance. It has been one of the most brilliant Cavalry exploits of the war and will be handed down in history as an example to be imitated. Col Grierson's report is herewith transmitted. I cannot close this report, without an expression of thankfulness for my good fortune in being placed in co-operation with an Officer of the Navy, who accords to every move that seems for the interest and success of our arms, his hearty and energetic support. Admiral Porter, and the very efficient Officers under him, have ever shown the greatest readiness in their co-operation, —no matter what was to be done—or what risk to be taken—either by their men or their vessels. Without this prompt and cordial support my movements would have been much embarrassed, if not wholly defeated. Captain J. U. Shirk, commanding the 'Tuscumbia' was especially active and deserving of the highest commendation for his personal attention to the repairing of the damage done our Transports by the Vicksburg batteries. The result of this campaign has been the defeat of the enemy in five battles outside of Vicksburg; the occupation of Jackson the capital of the State of Mississippi, and the capture of Vicksburg and its garrison and munitions of war; a loss to the enemy of thirty seven thousand (37,000) prisoners, among whom were fifteen General Officers; at least ten thousand killed and wounded, and among the killed Generals Tracy, Tilghman and Green; and hundreds and perhaps thousands of Stragglers, who can never be collected and reorganized. Arms and munitions of war for an Army of sixty thousand men have fallen into our hands, besides a large amount of other public property, consisting of rail roads, locomotives, cars, steamboats, cotton &c, and much was destroyed to prevent our capturing it. Our loss in the series of battles may be summed up as follows:

Port Gibson	130 killed,	718 wounded,	5 missing
Fourteen mile creek (skirmish)	4 ",	24 "	—
Raymond	69 ",	341 "	32 missing
Jackson	40 ",	240 "	6 "
Champions Hill	426 ",	1842 "	189 "
Big Black R. R. Bridge	29 ",	242 "	2 "
Vicksburg	545 killed	3688 wounded	303 missing.

Of the wounded many were but slightly wounded and continued on duty, many more required but a few days or weeks for their recovery. Not more than one half of the wounded were permanently disabled. My personal staff and Chiefs of Departments have in all cases rendered prompt and efficient service. In all former reports I have failed to make mention of Co: A: 4th Regiment Ills. Cavalry Vols, Capt. E. D. Osband, commanding. This Company has been on duty with me as an Escort Company since Novbr 1861., and in every engagement I have been in since that time, rendered valuable service, attracting general attention for their exemplary conduct, soldierly bearing and promptness. It would not be over-stating the merits of this Company to say that many of them would fill with credit any position in a Cavalry Regiment. For the brilliant achievements recounted in this report, the Army of the Tennessee—their Comrades of the 9th Army Corps, Herrons Division of the Army of the Frontier, and the Navy co-operating with them, deserve the highest honors their Country can award." LS, DNA, RG 94, War Records Office, Union Battle Reports. *O.R.*, I, xxiv, part 1, 44–59.

On Aug. 1, 9:45 A.M., Maj. Henry W. Halleck telegraphed to USG. "Your report dated, July 6th of your campaign in Mississippi, ending in the capitulation of Vicksburg, was recieved last evening. Your narrative of this campaign, like the operations themselves, is brief, soldierly, and in every respect ceditable & satisfactory. In boldness of plan, rapidity of execution, and brilliancy of results, these operations will compare most favorably with those of Napoleon about Ulm. You and your army have well deserved the gratitude of your country, and it will be the boast of your children that their fathers were of the heroic army ~~of Grant~~, which reopened the Mississippi River." ALS (telegram sent), DNA, RG 107, Telegrams Collected (Bound). *O.R.*, I, xxiv, part 1, 63.

1. On Dec. 3, 1864, Capt. C. Dan Conway, Madison, Ind., wrote to USG. "the Steamer Forest Queen had the following officers on her while she run the Blockade of Vicksburg on the night of the 16th April 1862 also at Grand Gulf Apl. 29th 1864 and was on board during the Sige untill Aug 28th. Dan Conway Captain   John L Conway Pilot   Jas. M Miller Pilot   Billy Blanker Clerk   Wilson Johnson Engineer   Jos. Aust. Engineer   L. Gale Engineer   B. Brad-ford Engineer   Lewis Noble Mate   Owin Conly. Watchman   Z. Lamb. Car-penter (who died by getting Scalded after our steam pipe was shot away)   the above officers where men of family & made their living by daily Labor.   the Str. Forest Queen was burned at St. Louis and the Capt Conway Billy Blanker clerk John L Conway Pilot Lewis Noble Mate Owin Conly Watchman are on the Steamer Brilliant and has been running from Cincinnati to New. Orleans. and Capt. Conway & his Crew. are allways willing to try it again for the Good of our. Country. and we also congratulate Genl. Grant. & army. also our old Friend Maj Genl. W. T. Sherman for all the Victorys that both armys have Gained. & hope that our Army & Navey may always prove successfull." ALS, DNA, RG 393, Dept. of the Tenn., Miscellaneous Letters Received. Other documents relating to the running of the Vicksburg batteries are *ibid.*

2. See letters to Brig. Gen. Robert Allen, July 25, 1863, and Brig. Gen. Montgomery C. Meigs, Aug. 10, 1863.

3. See letter to Maj. Gen. Nathaniel P. Banks, May 10, 1863.

4. The div. commanded by Maj. Gen. William W. Loring was not captured.

5. On May 29, 1863, USG endorsed a letter of Brig. Gen. Michael K. Lawler recommending Sgt. Joseph E. Griffith, 22nd Iowa, for promotion for bravery on May 22. "Respectfully forwarded to his Excellency Governor Kirkwood of the State of Iowa, and recommended. Conduct in the line of duty so marked and gal-lant as was displayed by Sergeant Joseph E Griffith of Company I. 22nd Iowa Vols, in the assault on Vicksburg on the 22nd inst. is so worthy of recognition, by immediate promotion, that I feel that His Excellency need only be made acquainted with the facts to secure his promotion and commission to date from the 22nd inst." Copies, DLC-USG, V, 25; DNA, RG 393, Dept. of the Tenn.,

Endorsements. Griffith was commissioned 1st lt. as of May 22. See *O.R.*, I, xxiv, part 2, 142, 243; letter to Brig. Gen. Lorenzo Thomas, Aug. 11, 1863.

    6. See letter to Maj. Gen. John A. McClernand, May 22, 1863.

    7. See letters to Lt. Gen. John C. Pemberton, July 3, 4, 1863. *O.R.*, I, xxiv, part 1, 59–61.

    8. On July 19, USG telegraphed to Lt. Col. Walter B. Scates. "Please telegraph me by 12 oclock to morrow an official Statement of the aggregate killed, the aggregate wounded, the aggregate missing of the 13th Army Corps, each engagement seperately in which it participated during the late Campaign up to the Capitulation of Vicksburg." Copies, DLC-USG, V, 19, 101, 103; DNA, RG 393, Dept. of the Tenn., Letters Sent; *ibid.*, 13th Army Corps, Letters Received. On July 20, Scates wrote to Rawlins. "All the reports of killed, wounded and missing up to the Capitulation of Vicksburg are at the old Head Quarters, of this Corps near Vicksburg. These reports were all sent you before we left that place. My Clerk Walter Sherwood there will furnish the statement required, upon application direct to him. I have not the dates to make it here." Copy, *ibid.*, Letters Sent. On the same day, Maj. Gen. James B. McPherson wrote to Rawlins. "I have the honor to transmit herwith statement of the loss killed wounded and missing suffered by this command in the several engagements of Port Gibson Raymond, Jackson Champion Hills and in the seige of Vicksburg. . . ." Copy, *ibid.*, 17th Army Corps, Letters Sent.

To Jesse Root Grant

Vicksburg, July 6th 1863

DEAR FATHER,

    Vicksburg has at last surrendered after a siege of over forty days. The surrender took place on the morning of the 4th of July. I found I had continuously underestimated the force of the enemy both in men and Artillery. The number of prisoners surrendered was Thirty-~~two~~ thousand & two hundred. The process of parolling is so tedious however ~~and~~ that many who are desirous of getting to their homes will escape before the paroling officers get around to them. The Arms taken is about 180 pieces of Artillery and over 30 000 stand of small arms. The enemy still had about four days rations of flour & meat and a large quantity of sugar.

    The weather now is excessively warm and the roads intolerably dusty. It can not be expected under these circumstances that the health of this command can keep up as it has done. My troops were not allowed one hours idle time after the surrender but were at once started after other game.

My health has continued very good during the campaign which has just closed.—Remember me to all at home.

ULYSSES

ALS, NN.

Calendar

———

1863, April 1.   Col. Edward D. Townsend, AGO, to USG. "There will be made, on the 10th of April, or as soon thereafter as practicable, a general Muster of all troops in the service of the United States, wheresoever they may be. The muster rolls will be immediately sent to the Adjutant General of the Army for the use of the Provost Marshal General in making drafts to fill up regiments, and batteries to the proper complement."—LS (telegram sent), DNA, RG 107, Telegrams Collected (Bound); telegram received, *ibid.*, RG 393, Dept. of the Tenn., Telegrams Received. The same telegram was sent to nine other commanders. On April 6, Lt. Col. John A. Rawlins issued General Orders No. 24 concerning the muster.—Copies, DLC-USG, V, 13, 14, 95; (2) DNA, RG 393, Dept. of the Tenn., General and Special Orders.

1863, April 2.   Maj. Robert Williams, AGO, to USG. "Please telegraph to this office any information you may possess concerning 2d Lt Chas K Kershaw 2d U S Cavalry   he was Commissioned on the 17th of July last & his Commission was sent to the Comdr of Co C 2d U S Cavalry at Pitts landing   On the rolls of Co C 2d Cavalry He is reported as having deserted June 14th 1862"—ADfS, DNA, RG 107, Telegrams Collected (Unbound); copies, *ibid.*; *ibid.*, RG 94, Letters Sent. On April 23, Maj. Gen. Stephen A. Hurlbut telegraphed to Brig. Gen. Lorenzo Thomas. "In reply to telegraph rec'd, from your office to Gen. Grant & referred to me as whereabouts of Lieut Kershaw second U. S. caval'y—I report the company on its way to join Reg't, by order of Secy. of War—Lieut. Kershaw has not been within limits of this command since I assumed command"—Telegram received, *ibid.*, Letters Received; copy, *ibid.*, RG 393, 16th Army Corps, Letters Sent.

1863, April 4.   Col. Edward D. Townsend, AGO, to USG. "In consequence of a note addressed by Lord Lyons to the Department of State, I am directed by the Secretary of War to invite your attention to General Orders, No. 82. of July 21. 1862. in relation to administering oaths of allegiance to aliens. The Secretary enjoins the observance of the spirit as well as of the letter of this order, that foreigners arrested on suspicion, as well as those engaged in traffic, may not be exposed to unnecessary hardship, merely because they, as aliens, decline to rescue themselves from difficulty by taking the oath of allegiance to the United States when tendered to them."—LS, DNA, RG 393, Dept. of the Tenn., Unregistered Letters Received.

1863, April 4. Col. Josiah W. Bissell, Young's Point, La., to USG. "In reply to a communication from Nancy E. Tolleson to Maj Genl. Hurlbut referred to me from Department Head Quarters on the 2d inst for report   I beg leave respectfully to report   That I have never taken any cotton under any circumstances without immediately reporting the same & turning it over to the proper officer—The cotton referred to by Mrs. Tollison was seized at Memphis, a day or two after the day it was claimed to have been purchased by an Agent of the Treasury Department—I was applied to soon afterwards by an attorney for my deposition in the case & I was then informed by that attorney and also by the Treasury Agent that Mrs Tolleson had filed her claim before the United States Court—"—ALS, DNA, RG 393, 16th Army Corps, Letters Received. On March 28, Nancy E. Tolleson, Memphis, wrote to Maj. Gen. Stephen A. Hurlbut. "The following charges are respectfully submitted for your adjudication against Col Bissell. On the 4th of Sep 1862, he took 18 Bales Cotton & 800 lbs in bags from me at Cat Island, Arkansas, with the apparent intention of appropriating it. That he has done so, is evident from the fact that the Cotton has not been accounted for at the proper office here. When I claimed my Cotton he said it was purchased from somebody, a negro as I would infer. I had a letter written to Segt Armstrong then in command of the pickets at my landing informing him that I had the cotton concealed, & that I would pay him handsomely for having it shipped for me, as all my hands had run off, & I had none to haul it to the landing. On the same day a neighboring negro found the cotton & sold it to Col Bissell as I was informed. I have done nothing against the government, & therefore request that you will investigate the matter, & reinstate me in my rights. These charges against Col Bissell I can fully sustain & am ready to do so at your pleasure. . . . You Will Pleas Answer   Eye Will Wait for it"—LS, *ibid.* On March 28, Hurlbut endorsed this letter. "Col Bissell not being within this Command this charge is respectfully forwarded to Dept. Head Qrs for action"— AES, *ibid.* On April 2, Lt. Col. John A. Rawlins endorsed the letter to Bissell for a report, then on April 4 endorsed both letters to Hurlbut. —ES, *ibid.*

1863, APRIL 6. USG endorsement. "Respectfully forwarded to Maj. Gen. S. R. Curtis Comd.g the Dept. of tne Mo."—AES, DNA, RG 109, Union Provost Marshals' File of Papers Relating to Individual Civilians. Written on a letter of March 30 from Heloise Gibson, St. Louis, to USG. "Will you please excuse the liberty I take in addressing you, and may you grant this request of an afflicted and desolate Mother. My Son George now my only support in my old age is in Prison now six weeks and I will give you a true and candid statement of the case. A number of letters came through the Post Office addressed to George, G. Gibson. without his knowledge or authority and destined for the South he having never given permission to anyone to use his name for such a purpose, a few of those letters he took out of the office and on discovering that they were for the South and not knowing what to do with them handed them to his sister whose husband was in the upper part of the state from whence those letters came and who has had for five years a great and personal grudge against George and would do anything to get him where he now is. George had a trial and at the time his sister's evidence was against as she had received these letters which however she very prudently destroyed by burning, and George at the time of his trial under embarrassment and perplexing questions particularly as he has never befor been on trial. Court contridicted his statement, and found guilty of a crime for which he is to recieve an awful sentence now in the course of this week. Now General Grant I appeal to you by all that you hold most dear on earth your own beloved wife who is a Cousin of my poor unfortunate Son to intercede with those in high authority here in behalf of my son my *only Stay* one word from you dear General would be as a Command oh do not overlook this matter but at the earliest opportunity please interest yourself for him. I must here remark that George has always been loyal to our Government, and so his brothers, one of ~~his~~ whom has been with General Curtis's Staff train while in Helena, and also here in St Louis until his health became so much impaired since the Helena Campaign that he had to come home and is now an invalid likely however to have lost his health With strong hope that you will do something for the release of my son, I remain with sentiments of respect . . . P. S. George is willing to take the oath they will prescribe and also to give bond but that was refused by one of the three Militaries before whom he was examined"—ALS, *ibid.*

On July 31, Maj. William M. Dunn, St. Louis, wrote to Julia Dent

Grant. "I received, yesterday, a letter from my Son. Lieut. Dunn, informing me that you, requested the release of George G. Gibson now confined in the Alton Military Prison. I communicated your desire to Major General Schofield, and I have the pleasure of enclosing to you a copy of his order for the release of Gibson."—Copy, *ibid.*, RG 393, Dept. of the Mo., Letters Sent by the Judge Advocate Gen.

1863, April 6.   S. D. Beloate, Memphis, to USG. "Knowing how much your time and attention is required to things of more importance, I would not trespass upon your patience if justice to myself and country did not demand it. It is now six weeks since I presented to Gen Hurlbut your Special order No. 56   He has not Sent a Commission under Him an offical copy or notice of it—Hence my authority is not recognized by any of them   it has been impossible for me to get the approval of any requisition which I have yet made—as soon as I returned from youngs point in February—I applied officially to Gen. Hurlbut for a House to use as an office for recruiting. He re[fus]ed and told me that if I wanted one to Hire it. and it was not until Saturday last that I was able to get one. He on that day sent for me, and gave me an order on the quarter master for one   He held at the Same time my last official communication to you. He Has refused every detail asked by me of Him and made none which you Have granted   in fact Gen Grant He has done every thing He could do to throw impediments in my way and prevent my Success—and done nothing to encourage or forward it   Adgt Gen Thomas was Here a few days ago—He sent for me to See him at Gen Hurlbut's Head quarters   He told me that I was not capable of raising a Brigade of Troops and that He would advise the Secretary of War to revoke the order of the 12th of Feb—*Some one* had pregudiced Him against me   *who was it*   Those Alabama troops He terms as a part of Gen Dodges command. He Says that I did not raise *them*   it is true that Cpt Cameron of Yates Sharp Shooters enlisted the most of them while I was on my way from Washington to youngs point and Corinth but he only completed what Lieut Hurley and myself had begun previous to my visit to Washington. As it is Gen my hands are tied   until I hear from You I can do nothing. Gen Veach (whome I Highley respect) has informed me that He cannot Sign any requisitions until the matter is untangled   Had I funds of my own I would press forwards but I have not   I have allready in this war, (as it is well known) sacrificed a plantation and Fifty three negroes. I have made my Family and myself Homeless—but if my country is Successful I Shall not regret it—Gen if you think it best, I will resign my position as recruiting Officer   if not, will you issue the necessary order to enable me to carry out your Special Order No. 56 of the date of Feb 25th 1863   Hoping to hear from you soon   I have the Honor to remain"—ALS, DNA, RG 109, Union Provost Marshals' File of Papers Relating to Individual Civilians. On April 11, Lt. Col. John A. Rawlins endorsed this letter. "Respectfully referred to Major General S. A. Hurlbut, Comm'dg 16th Army Corps, for report."— ES, *ibid.* On April 15, Maj. Gen. Stephen A. Hurlbut wrote to Rawlins. "A letter of S. D. Beloatte forwarded with your indorsement has come to me for Report. I have the honor to state that I received Special Order 56 date Feby 25. on Feby 28. 1863. Dr S. B. Beloate reported to me in charge of recruiting service. He applied for money for recruiting expenses which I did not have and was not authorized to pay to him if I had. He applied for Quarters for which I referred him to Capt A. R. Eddy Depot Q. Master. I directed him to proceed to Jackson & Corinth and to report to me when he had any recruits to be mustered or rationed or otherwise provided for   He has never reported a recruit nor to the best of my information and belief raised one. He claimed to have raised 5 companies of Alabamians—I have the best reasons for saying that he had no influence nor part in so doing—For they have been long borne on Genl. Dodge's reports before his advent in the Department. He has never made a requisition of any kind upon me, nor offered one to be signed. He has applied for details for orderlies which I refused upon the ground that he had no use for them. He has applied for an Adjutant of a Regiment to assist him, which I declined until he showed me he had something to do.—He has abandoned the only field where he could by possibility recruit and established himself in the City of Memphis where he can do nothing but mischief. Both by examination and by his own confession he is wholly ignorant of Military affairs and he has not a particle of influence among the Refugees. Lieut. Hurley of whom he speaks is an active brave man, but has now & will have nothing to do with Beloate   The men can be recruited best at our outstations, but it can only be done by somebody in whom these people have confidence. They have none in him. He is simply an ambitious ignorant man & I concur completely in Genl Thomas' estimate of him. His desire to be relieved from this service is the first glimmer of sense I have seen about him, and I have no hesitation in recommending it. For four weeks he has lounged about the streets and Theatre of Memphis and has not taken one single step toward the performance of the duties to which he was assigned. I am and always have been ready to receive ration and equip his recruits but he reports none and in my judgment never will, but I do not propose to assist him in living in idleness at the expense of the U. States"—ALS, *ibid.*, RG 393, Dept. of the Tenn., Letters Received. On April 6, Secretary of War Edwin M. Stanton telegraphed to Brig. Gen. Lorenzo Thomas. "You will make an order revoking all authority in Dr Beloit for raising troops for the U. S. service and direct the Commanding General of the Department in case he should undertake [*to r*]aise troops under color of Authority from the U. S. to take means to prevent his acting without Authority and against your own. My belief is no authority was given him by this Dept, but that he was referred to Genl Grant to give it if the Genl thought proper. You will call upon him to produce his authority and if he does not do so, direct the Commanding Genl to Proceede against him as one usurping a dangerous power against the authority of the Govt"—Copy, *ibid.*, RG 109, Union Provost Marshals' File of Papers Relating to Individual Civilians.

1863, APRIL 7.   To Maj. Gen. William T. Sherman. "Fifteen hundred men will be required tomorrow instead of one thousand. They will go by Lancaster and Lacon"—Signal received, ICarbS.

1863, APRIL 7.   To Lt. Murdock. "You will not move your boat untill further orders. The Paymasters must not be discommoded in their necessary transactions of business   Another Steamer will be assigned them"—Signal received, ICarbS. On the same day, an unidentified paymaster had signaled to USG. "What Shall we do for Quarters. Lieut Murdack Says he will move up the river in the morning. Your attention is directed to Maj Hazletons letter of this date in the hands of Col Kowlands"—Signal received, *ibid.*

1863, APRIL 9.   USG endorsement. "The recommendation of Lt. W. W. How, 7th Kansas Cavalry for promotion to Asst Adj. Gen. and assignment to the Staff of Brig. Gen. A. L. Lee is heartily concured in by me and respectfully recommended."—AES, DNA, RG 94, ACP, L63 CB 1863. Written on a letter dated April 10 from Charles A. Dana to President Abraham Lincoln. "Gen. A. L. Lee has applied for the appointment of 1st Lieut W. W. Howe of the 7th Kansas cavalry as his Assistant Adjutant General. Lieut Howe has already been detailed by Gen. Grant to act in that capacity, but he desires a regular appointment to the post. Having known Mr. Howe for several years, I can cordially recommend him as possessing every qualification both of capacity & character for the commission which Gen. Lee wishes to have conferred upon him."—ALS, *ibid.* No appointment followed.

1863, April 9.   Col. William Hoffman, commissary gen. of prisoners, to USG. "Please inform me if the crew of the Queen of the west belongs to Ellets brigade"—Telegram received, DNA, RG 107, Telegrams Collected (Unbound); copy, *ibid.*, RG 249, Telegrams Sent. *O.R.*, II, v, 457. On April 22, USG endorsed this telegram. "Respectfully returned to Colonel Hoffman, commissary-general of prisoners, and attention invited to report of Lieutenant-Commander Breese, Mississippi Squadron, accompanying for the information desired."— *Ibid.*, p. 458. On April 20, Lt. Commander K. Randolph Breese wrote to Lt. Col. John A. Rawlins. "Your communication of yesterday has been received. The crew of the Queen of the West do belong to Ellet's brigade, although not soldiers, being hired men for a specified time as master, pilots, mates, deck-hands, &c. The crew proper work the vessel, in addition to which they have soldiers who fight her."— *Ibid.*, p. 499.

1863, April 10.   Maj. Gen. Stephen A. Hurlbut to Lt. Col. John A. Rawlins. "I have the honor to transmit herewith the written statement of Capt Danl Bradley in reference to Cotton Transactions at Collierville in January last. Neither Capt Bradley nor Col. Marsh are within my command. I accordingly refer the matter to Hd Qrs Dept for such action as may be deemed advisable. I arrested Capt Bradley & he has paid voluntarily to Mr A. Strauss the amount obtained from him withheld. I make no remarks upon the transaction"—ALS, DNA, RG 393, Dept. of the Tenn., Miscellaneous Letters Received. On April 7, Capt. Daniel Bradley, 20th Ill., wrote to Hurlbut. "In compliance with your instructions I proceed to give a statement of such knowledge as I possess in relation to any and all transactions in cotton in which Col Marsh has been implicated. While the Brigade commanded by Col Marsh was stationed at Colliersville, Tenn, in January last, some cotton which had been hauled to the depôt for defensive purposes, was by his order, confiscated. I do not remember the exact date of the order, but it was in the neighborhood of the 20th day of Jany. The number of bales at first seized, was, if I remember rightly, thirty-nine; but there was a good deal of question as to the ownership, and the number of bales it was finally determined to hold was, I believe, twenty-eight. I cannot be positive as to numbers and dates; because, at the time of which I am writing, I had no idea that I would ever be called upon to give any evidence or statement in the matter whatsoever. Oweing to the number and persistent efforts of some speculators who were in and about Colliersville at the time, Col Marsh determined, so he informed me, ~~determined~~ to sell the cotton on government account, provided, it could not be got through to Memphis. He authorized me, by order, to sell it to one A. Strauss. Strauss advanced Fifteen-hundred dollars; this, as I understood it, was rather ~~and~~ advance to *secure* the purchase of the cotton from the Government when it should have been brought to Memphis, than an actual advance upon the purchase. Col Marsh rec'd Five-hundred of the fifteen-hundred dollars so advanced, the balance remaining in my possession. I remained in Colliersville some two days after the Brigade left, but, failing to get the cotton shipped, reported at Memphis. I arrived here the evening before Col Marsh left for the North; he had just been wounded, and I had but little opportunity of conversing with him upon business matters. He left, retaining the five-hundred dollars; I soon became uneasy, for I had but a portion of the money then, and did not know what questions might arise; in this emergency I laid the facts of the case before Col W. S. Hillyer, who advised the rendition of the money, in order to do away with even the color of wrong. But, before I saw Col Marsh, or could communicate with him by letter, our Division was ordered down the river; it is but about ten-days since Marsh returned to his command, and from him I first learned of the condition in which the matter stood. I eagerly seized upon an opportunity which presented for me to come up the river, and was ordered by Genl. McPherson to do so. Col Hillyer came up on the same boat, and I again spoke of the matter to him; his opinion was that the money had better be held for the Government. And now, General, comes the most unpleasant part of my duty; the money, or a portion of it, remaining in my possession, and we having been long without pay, I, from time to time, have used of it what my circumstances required, but I have nevertheless always considered myself, as I do now, responsible for the amount, I think that the fact of my having stated the circumstances to the Provost Marshal General will be to you sufficient evidence of this. I was going to Cairo, where my order carries me, and thought that there I might put myself in position to meet all my obligations. My arrest prevented my going, and I respectfully ask that I be released from duress, confident, at least, that my motives and intentions were good. It may be proper for me to state that I know Col Marsh to be ready and anxious to turn over the amount he received."—ALS, *ibid.*

1863, April 11. Lt. Col. James A. Hardie, AGO, to USG. "I am directed to request you to furnish a list of all the Staff Officers on duty with Army Corps divisions & brigades or Otherwise under your Command where assigned list to date April fifteenth (15) 1863."— Telegram received, DNA, RG 393, Dept. of the Tenn., Telegrams Received; copy, *ibid.*, RG 94, Commissions and Returns, Letters Sent. On May 6, Hardie telegraphed to USG. "Have the list of Staff Officers asked for on the Eleventh (11th) Ult been forwarded they are much needed"—Telegram received, *ibid.*, RG 393, Dept. of the Tenn., Telegrams Received; copy, *ibid.*, RG 94, Commissions and Returns, Letters Sent.

1863, April 11. Act. Rear Admiral David D. Porter to USG. "I inclose you a letter from General Sherman relative to some hay I made a request for. Will you be so good as to furnish the necessary order referred to in the within communication and oblige"—LS, DNA, RG 393, Dept. of the Tenn., Letters Received. The enclosed letter of April 11 from Maj. Gen. William T. Sherman to Porter discussed the proper procedure for transferring hay from the Army to the Navy.— ALS, *ibid.*

1863, April 12. USG pass. "Pass Morgan Griffin & family to Cairo free on any Government or chartered boat going up the river. Also pass baggage free."—ANS, Parsons Papers, IHi. On the same day, Maj. Gen. William T. Sherman favorably endorsed to USG a letter of Col. Charles H. Abbott, 30th Iowa, introducing Morgan Griffin.— Copy, DNA, RG 393, 15th Army Corps, Endorsements.

1863, April 13. USG endorsement. "Respectfully forwarded to Head Quarters of the Army, Washington, D, C., for an authoritative construction of Section, 35, of an Act entitled an Act for enrolling and calling out the National Forces, and for other purposes; In my opinion said section, 35, does not effect the extra Duty pay allowed by Army Regulations to enlisted men for extra Duty, but simply prohibits the payment to enlisted men detailed on a special service, of a greater amount than is allowed other enlisted men on extra Duty, by the Army Regulations. There is no question in my mind, that enlisted men on extra Duty are justly entitled to pay therefor. For the same services many of them perform especially as clerks in the several Departments of the Army, the employment of Civilians would cost the Government from one hundred to one hundred and fifty dollars per month, besides many of these positions should be regarded as in the light of promotions to which competent enlisted men are entitled"—Copies, DLC-USG, V, 25; DNA, RG 393, Dept. of the Tenn., Endorsements. Written on a letter of Capt. J. Condit Smith concerning rations and pay of troops assigned to clerical duties.—*Ibid.*

1863, APRIL 16.   To commanding officer, Richmond, La. "Send a party of from 20 to 50 in boats [. . . .] Roundaway and Tensas to clear out a party of cotton burners said to be in that neighborhood. Send 3 days rations."—Signal received, DLC-James M. McClintock.

1863, APRIL 16.   Capt. John W. DeFord, U.S. Signal Corps, to USG. "I have the honor to enclose a small sketch of the stations at present occupied by the officers and men of this command. Should you now, or hereafter, desire a different disposition of them, I would respectfully request to be informed of your wishes at the earliest convenient moment."—ALS, DNA, RG 393, Dept. of the Tenn., Letters Received. The map is *ibid.* On April 3, Lt. Col. John A. Rawlins issued Special Orders No. 93 assigning DeFord as chief of the signal corps for USG's army.—Copies, DLC-USG, V, 26, 27; DNA, RG 393, Dept. of the Tenn., Special Orders. On April 8, DeFord sent to Washington a requisition for six "Electric Signal Trains" which bore the signature of USG.—DS, *ibid.*, RG 111, Letters Received. On April 22, Capt. Leonard F. Hepburn, signal officer, Washington, wrote to USG. "I have the honor to state that the six (6) Signal Telegraph Trains and appurtenances for which Capt. De Ford made requisition, will be ready in a very short time; in the mean time I have to request that you will cause to be detailed Four Lieuts and Twelve Sergeants with orders to report in person to the Signal officer of the Army at Washington,

D. C. This course is necessary that the officers and non-commissioned officers may be thoroughly instructed, and that the Trains upon entering the field may be in charge of skilled operators."—Copy, *ibid.*, Letters Sent. During the Vicksburg campaign, DeFord fell ill and was replaced by Capt. Lucius M. Rose.—*O.R.*, I, xxiv, part 1, 131, 133. On May 27, 1:00 P.M., Rose signaled to USG. "The line is now open and ready to transmit Messages."—Signal received, DNA, RG 94, War Records Office, Military Div. of the Miss.

1863, April 16. Capt. W. H. B. Hoyt, signal officer, to USG. "The flag of truce Gun has been fired at Vicksburg."—Signal received, ICarbS.

1863, April 17. Capt. John W. Cornyn, Richmond, La., to USG. "The bayou has risen here two inches from ten oclock A. M yesterday to seven and a half today" "I have not been out to get boats yet, May by to morrow, if so shall I send to tensas bayou. I have a small force—it is kept busy and worked hard"—Signals received, DLC-James M. McClintock.

1863, April 18. To Col. James B. Fry. "I have the honor to transmit, herewith, lists of Deserters from the following Regts, and Detached Companies of this Department: . . ."—Copy, DLC-USG, V, 94. On April 26 and 27, USG wrote similar letters to Fry.—Copies, *ibid.* On June 2, USG wrote a similar letter to Fry.—LS, Goodspeed's Book Shop, Inc., Boston, Mass. On June 22, USG wrote a similar letter to Fry.—LS, IHi. On June 26, USG endorsed a list of deserters sent to Fry.—Kingston Galleries, Catalogue No. 7, No. 76.

1863, April 18. Brig. Gen. Lorenzo Thomas to USG. "I respectfully request a return of the troops under Your Command by Corps, Divisions & Brigades with the names of Commanders. It need not be minute in its details of men, I only wishing numbers for duty, sick, absent, Total & Aggregate present and absent"—Copies, DLC-USG, V, 105; DNA, RG 393, Military Div. of the Miss., War Dept. Correspondence Received.

1863, April 18. [P. T. Bisse] to USG. "I have Six cases of Small Pox I Would like to Send them to the Pest Hospital"—Signal received, ICarbS.

1863, April 19.   Maj. Gen. John A. McClernand to USG. "Finding that the relations between Lieutenant Reynolds and myself have become unpleasant and unsatisfactory, I have relieved him from duty on my Staff and ordered him to report to his Regiment. I hope you will approve what I have done."—DfS, McClernand Papers, IHi; copy, *ibid.*; DNA, RG 393, 13th Army Corps, Letters Sent.

1863, April 19.   A. R. Stoner, Memphis, to USG. "On the 19th of Febuary last my house, situate on south side of Jefferson St and between Main and Second Sts was seized by the military authorities—myself placed under arrest with heavy bonds to answer charges. Two months have now passed and, nothing done in premises beyond renting out my building to tradesmen and other strangers   I am also informed by Provost Marshal Col D E Anthony and Provost Marshal Genl Col W. S. Hillyer that no charges have been filed against me and that they are unable to find any grounds upon which to predicate them   As my house never fell under any of the classes announced by you or Genl Sherman as coming under the jurisdiction of the Rental Office—and is not now used or needed, excepting two rooms for any public purposes, and as I am myself a loyal citizen, having taken the oath soon after the occupation of Memphis, ever endeavouring to conform my conduct to all military orders and regulations I respectfully submit that justice requires that I should be placed in possession of the same and permitted to collect rent from such portions of the house as are now leased to private parties or remain vacant. So far as any part of the building may be occupied or required for any public necessity I make no complaint, being always willing to contribute, to the extent of my means, whatever will subserve the cause of the General Government. I would not make this appeal to you, Genl, or intrude upon your valuable time, had I not utterly failed after repeated efforts, to obtain any satisfaction or redress from the authorities at this City."—ALS, DNA, RG 109, Union Provost Marshals' File of Papers Relating to Individual Civilians. On April 22, Lt. Col. John A. Rawlins referred this letter to Maj. Gen. Stephen A. Hurlbut, who replied that Stoner was a "common gambler."—ES, *ibid.*

1863, April 20.   Maj. Robert Williams, AGO, to USG. "I am directed to request that you will cause the Descriptive Lists and accounts of pay and clothing of the men, whose names follow, to be forwarded to this Office as soon as practicable. . . ."—LS, DNA, RG 393, Dept. of the Tenn., Miscellaneous Letters Received. On April 21, Williams wrote to USG requesting similar information about another private.—Copy, DLC-USG, V, 105. On April 22, Williams wrote another such letter to USG.—LS, DNA, RG 94, Letters Received.

1863, April 20. Lt. Commander K. Randolph Breese, U. S. S. *Black Hawk*, to USG. "We have here in the Squadron two Rebel Prisoners of War taken on the Tallahatchie whom the Admiral requested me to ask you to receive. Will you grant the necessary permission for your Provost Marshal to receive them?"—LS (press), DNA, RG 45, Mississippi Squadron, Letters Sent by K. Randolph Breese.

1863, April 21. To Col. John C. Kelton. "Col Jackson J. Wood 12th Regt Iowa infantry Vols. Col Danl H Brush 18th Regt Ills Infantry Vols [C]ol Francis H Mantie 32nd Missouri"—Telegram received (dated April 24), DNA, RG 107, Telegrams Collected (Bound); copies (dated April 21), *ibid.*, RG 393, Dept. of the Tenn., Hd. Qrs. Correspondence; DLC-USG, V, 5, 8, 24, 94. On April 6, Kelton had written to USG. "In each state a Deputy Provt Marshall General is to be appointed. Selection will be made from among the field officers appd from the respective states, to fill this position. As these officers will report directly to, and will be controlled exclusively by orders from the War Dept, they should be men of much address and discretion so as to gain the hearty cooperation of state and military authorities. They will be required to decide many questions without reference to the Provt Marshall General. Please designate several field Officers serving in your Dept from Illinois, Missouri & Iowa, with sufficient health and ability to perform the duties of the position named. The duty will be temporary. If you will telegraph me the names only, I will understand what is meant."—ALS, DNA, RG 393, Dept. of the Tenn., Letters Received; *ibid.*, RG 108, Letters Sent by Gen. Halleck (Press).

1863, April 21. Col. William Hoffman, commissary gen. of prisoners, to USG. "I beg leave again to call your attention to the incomplete rolls of prisoners of war which are forwarded from the Dpt of the Tennesee to this office. Some of them give neither the time or place of capture nor what disposition has been made of the prisoners, and are wholly useless either for the records of this office or for purposes of exchange I have the honor to enclose herewith one roll as a specimen. There is nothing upon it to show where it was made, or by whom, nor whether the prisoners are Federal or rebel except by the designation of the regiments Other rolls were more complete but still defective in parts. They should show at what place prisoners were held if still retained in our hands or at what point delivered if sent beyond our lines"—Copy, DNA, RG 249, Letters Sent. *O.R.*, II, v, 501.

1863, APRIL 23. Maj. Samuel Breck, AGO, to USG. "The application of Owen McNulty of Dodge county, Wis, for the discharge of his son Robt McNulty, 17th Wisconsin Vols on the ground of family matters having been approved by the General-in-chief I am directed to instruct you to discharge him from the Military service of the United States upon receipt of this communication"—Copies, DLC-USG, V, 105; DNA, RG 94, Enlisted Branch, Letters Sent.

1863, APRIL 23. Maj. Gen. Henry W. Halleck to USG. "Prisoners sentenced to hard labor, &c., in your Dept. should not be sent to Alton Prison, where there is no labor to be performed, but should be made to work on fortifications, &c., in your Dept. Moreover, Alton is not capable of accommodating the prisoners sent there."—LS, DNA, RG 393, Dept. of the Tenn., Letters Received; ADfS, *ibid.*, RG 94, Generals' Papers and Books, Drafts of Letters Sent by Gen. Halleck. *O.R.*, II, v, 508.

1863, APRIL 27. Maj. Gen. Ambrose E. Burnside, Cincinnati, to USG. "owing to certain movements soon to take place in this Dept I am very anxious to retain Col Droury here for a time his health is such as should render him for arduous service in his own dept. at present & shall be glad if you he can be retained please answer"— Telegram received, DNA, RG 393, Dept. of the Tenn., Telegrams Received; copy, *ibid.*, Dept. of the Ohio, Telegrams Sent. The officer involved was Col. John F. De Courcy, 16th Ohio.

1863, MAY 1. Maj. Oliver D. Greene, AGO, to USG. "I am directed to request that you will cause the discharge papers, final statements and Descriptive List of Sergeant William H Wright 1st U. S. Cavalry formerly a private in Co "A" 47th Ohio Volunteers, to be forwarded to this Office as soon as practicable."—Copy, DNA, RG 94, Letters Received. On June 30, USG endorsed this letter. "Respectfully returned to Headquarters of the Army, Washington, D. C, with Descriptive Roll, Descharge and final statements, as required."—ES, *ibid.*

1863, MAY 2. Col. John C. Kelton to USG. "Please direct that two copies of al[l] General Orders and printed Sp. Field Ord[ers] issued by you since your assignment to command of the Dept. of the Tenn., and als[o] two copies of all orders that may be hereafter issued, be forwarded to Head Quarters of the Army."—LS, DNA, RG 108, Letters Sent (Press).

1863, MAY 2. John W. Leftwich, Memphis, to USG. "This will introduce to you Dr P. M Dickinson Recorder of the City of Memphis who I can testify has been an Unflinching Union man All the time and indeed about the only one among us who had nerve enough to openly express his sentiments under all circumstances"—ALS, DNA, RG 45, Subject File, RV 587.

1863, MAY 4. Maj. Gen. Francis P. Blair, Jr., to USG protesting the arrest of George P. Deween and H. B. Rooker, charged with improper dealings in cotton.—ADf, DLC-Blair Family.

1863, MAY 6. USG endorsement. "Respectfully forwarded to the Adj. Gen. of the Army approved & urgently recommended."—AES, DNA, RG 94, ACP, W825 CB 1863. Written on a letter of the same day from Brig. Gen. Michael K. Lawler to Brig. Gen. Lorenzo Thomas. "I would respectfully recommend and request that 1st Lieutenant Bluford Wilson Adjutant 120th Regiment Illinois Volunteers be promoted to the position of Assistant Adjutant General United States Volunteers and that he be ordered to report to me for duty"—LS, *ibid.* Bluford Wilson, brother of Lt. Col. James Harrison Wilson and Maj. Henry S. Wilson, 18th Ill., was appointed capt., asst. adjt. gen., as of May 6.

1863, MAY 7. USG pass. "Mrs. Bagnun will be protected from further impressments of provisions and supplies by the Federal Army. . . . Should they desire it they may be permitted to go out of our lines

Southward . . ."—James F. Drake, *Catalogue of Autographs* 66 (1913), p. 18.

1863, MAY 7.   Secretary of War Edwin M. Stanton to USG. "The President and General-in-Chief have just returned from the Army of the Potomac. The principal operation of General Hooker failed but there has been no serious disaster to the organization & efficiency of the Army. It ~~The Army~~ is now occuping its former position on the Rappahannock having recrossed the river without any loss in the movement   Not more than one third of General Hookers force was engaged. ~~In consequence of the nature of f field not advisable a general engagement~~. General Stonemans operations have been a brilliant success, a part of his force advanced to within two miles of Richmond and the enemies communications have been cut in every direction. The Army of the Potomac will speedily resume offensive operations."—ADfS (telegram sent), DNA, RG 107, Telegrams Collected (Bound); telegram received, *ibid.*, Telegrams Collected (Unbound); *ibid.*, RG 393, Dept. of the Tenn., Unregistered Letters Received. *O.R.*, I, xxv, part 2, 437–38. The same telegram went to five other gen. officers and to governors of states.

1863, MAY 9.   William G. Fuller, asst. superintendent, U.S. Military Telegraph, Memphis, to Maj. Theodore S. Bowers. "I have just received a Letter from J. C. Sullivan, Telegrapher with Genl. Grant, stating that the Party sent down some ten days since to construct a Telegraph Line from Millikens Bend to New Carthage were unable to obtain the necessary transportation to enable them to proceed with the work. The Quarter Masters here all state that everything in the shape to transportation here, has been sent below, and Genl. Hurlbut refers me to you as the proper Officer to apply to at Millikens Bend. This Line was ordered by Genl. Grant and I supposed it was near completion. Please furnish Sol. Palmer my foreman of builders with the transportation he requires. I understand there is a shorter route than the one we were at first ordered to build upon,   If so please direct the line to be built upon the best route & very much oblige . . . N. B. I will be responsible for proper receipts being returned for any memorandum receipts Mr Palmer may give for the Articles necessary to do his work. Do what you can for us & very much oblige"—ALS, DNA, RG 393, Dept. of the Tenn., Letters Received.

1863, MAY 11.   Col. William Hoffman, commissary gen. of prisoners, to USG. "I am instructed by the Genl-in-Chief, to say that when
a person is arrested charged with being a spy, or the commission of
any other specific offence, requiring a trial, an immediate investigation
must be had before a military tribunal at the place where the offence
was committed, and when the witnesses are within reach. Many persons have been arrested as spies and sent to interior prisons, and after
months of detention, it has been found that the charges had neither
specifications, nor evidence to sustain them. In cases where arrests are
made on a general charge of disloyal conduct, it is necessary that full
details in each case, with the character of the person should be given,
in order to a proper disposal of it. Please give the necessary instructions to insure compliance with the foregoing in your Department."—
LS, DNA, RG 94, War Records Office, Dept. of the Tenn. *O.R.*, II,
v, 592–93. An identical letter went to five other commanders.

1863, MAY 11.   Maj. Thomas M. Vincent, AGO, to USG. "I have
the honor to enclose herewith copies of communications from this
Bureau the originals of which are supposed to have been destroyed,
recently by the burning of the Mail Steamer."—Copies, DLC-USG,
V, 105; DNA, RG 393, Military Div. of the Miss., War Dept. Correspondence.

1863, MAY 12.   Brig. Gen. Hugh T. Reid, Providence, La., to USG
conveying information about C.S.A. strength on the Yazoo River and
reporting skirmishes at Caledonia and Pin Hook, La.—ALS, DNA,
RG 94, War Records Office, Dept. of the Tenn. *O.R.*, I, xxiv, part 3,
301–3. See *ibid.*, I, xxiv, part 1, 694–700.

1863, MAY 13.   Brig. Gen. Edward R. S. Canby, AGO, to USG.
"The Secretary of War introduces and commends to your consideration and courtesies Major General Fogliardi of the Army of Switzer-
land and his Staff. The General visits this country on a tour of observation and the Secretary of War desires that you will extend to him any
necessary facilities and assistance in visiting such points of interest
within the limits of your command, as he may desire to visit, if the
circumstances of the service at the time are such that it may be done
without embarassment to the service."—Copies, DNA, RG 107, Vol.
Branch, Letters Sent; *ibid.*, Vol. Branch, Orders Sent. Identical letters
went to Maj. Gens. Ambrose E. Burnside and William S. Rosecrans.

1863, MAY 13. Maj. Samuel Breck, AGO, to USG. "I have the honor to request that you will furnish to this Department a report of the Composition of your command, giving accurately the Corps, Divisions, Brigades, Detached commands &c with their present Stations and commanding officers : this Report is espically required at this time, that missing returns required by the Department from troops in your command may be written for. Your attention is called also to the fact that the Different Corps returns frequently report the same officer, for instance on the Tri-monthly report of the 15th Corps (April 10. 1863) Brig Genl. J. C. Veitch is reported as commanding the District of Memphis, Tenn; this Officer is also reported on the return of the 16th Corps for April 10th '63 at the same station, leaving the Dep't. in doubt as to which Corps he is attached. Please give the Report your early attention, and extend a supervision over the different Returns so far as possible, that accurate ones may be forwarded to this Office."—LS, DNA, RG 393, Dept. of the Tenn., Unregistered Letters Received.

1863, MAY 15. Judge Advocate Gen. Joseph Holt to USG. "On Deer Creek in Washington County Miss is a plantation known as the Henry Vick estate! Its late owner Co.l. Henry Vick died two years ago, as he had lived, *faithful to the union.* The property now belongs to his only surviving child a young girl who lives with her aunt Mrs Pindell in Louisville Ky, where she has resided since she was eight years old. Her aunt & all her relatives in Ky. are thoroughly loyal. This young girl has had no connection with the rebellion & could have no sympathy with it, & I have ventured to bring her case to your notice, only for the purpose of asking in the name of humanity & justice, that, so far as may be consistent with the success of your military operations her estate may be spared from the ravages of war."—ALS, USG 3.

1863, MAY 15. Maj. Gen. Daniel Butterfield, "Camp near Falmouth Va," to USG enclosing documents concerning methods of supplying troops in the field with a minimum of wagon trains.—LS, DNA, RG 393, Dept. of the Tenn., Letters Received.

1863, MAY 16. Maj. Gen. Samuel R. Curtis, St. Louis, to USG. "The bearer Mr E A. Whipple goes south within our lines on business. Mr Whipple is a particular friend of mine and eminently a loyal and reliable man. Any assistance or kindness shown him will be remem-

berd as a personal favor by me"—LS, DNA, RG 366, Second Special
Agency, Trade Applications.

1863, MAY 21.   Maj. Samuel Breck, AGO, to USG. "I have the
honor to request that you will direct the Corps commd'rs in your
Department to report the letter of companies of the Regular Regiments serving in their commands, on all returns to this Office"—LS,
DNA, RG 393, Dept. of the Tenn., Letters Received.

1863, MAY 21.   Maj. Samuel Breck, AGO, to USG. "I have the
honor to acknowledge the receipt of the papers in the case of M. H. B.
Cunningham 18th Wis. with the request that he be send to his Regt
from U. S. A. Genl. Hospital, Chester Pa., and to inform You that he
was sent to the Convalescent Camp near this City and on April 7th he
was ordered to report to Camp Distribution to await transportation
to his Regt., this he failed to do and he is reported on the records of the
Convalesent Camp as a 'Deserter' April 7th 1863."—Copies, DLC-
USG, V, 105; DNA, RG 94, Enlisted Branch, Letters Sent; *ibid.*, RG
393, Military Div. of the Miss., War Dept. Correspondence.

1863, MAY 22.   Maj. Thomas M. Vincent, AGO, to USG. "You are
authorized by the Secretary of War to select your own time as to the
consolidation of Regiments under General Orders No. 86, Current
Series, War Department. You are not required to make them until
you find it convenient to do so."—LS, DNA, RG 393, Dept. of the
Tenn., Letters Received.

1863, MAY 23.   USG endorsement. "Respectfully forwarded to
Headquarters of the army, Washington, D. C., and urgently recommended. The inefficiency in the Quartermasters Department in this
army is owing to the inexperience of the assistant Quartermaster's,
who have been appointed and assigned to duty to duty here. The
within named officers, whose appointments are asked for, have been
and are now on duty as acting assistant Quartmasters and have proven
themselves well qualified for the position"—ES, DNA, RG 94, ACP,
334B CB 1863. Written on a letter of May 23 from Lt. Col. Judson D.
Bingham, Yazoo River, to Lt. Col. John A. Rawlins. "I have the honor
to request that application be again made for the appointment of the
following named officers to the rank of Captain and Asst Qr Master,

and that they be assigned to duty in this Department without delay. Viz:—Lieut Chas. H. Irvin. 9th Mich vols   Lieut H. W. Janes, 55th Ills vols   Lieut J. T. Conklin 14th Wis vols.   Lieut W. C. Hurlbut 56th Ills vols   I desire these officers to replace Capt Greene Durbin A. Q. M. and others who have not performed their duties in a satisfactory manner. I also respectfully request that an earnest protest may be entered against the assignment of any more inexperienced Quarter Masters to this army in the field. Five asst Qr Masters have been assigned to duty in this army during the last thirty days, and not one had ever performed one days service in the Department previous to arrival here."—LS, *ibid.* On April 23, Bingham, Milliken's Bend, had written to Brig. Gen. Lorenzo Thomas recommending 1st Lt. Charles H. Irvin for appointment as asst. q. m.—LS, *ibid.,* 264½B CB 1863. On April 26, USG endorsed this letter. "Approved and respectfully recommended to Gen. Thomas Adj. Gen. of the Army."—AES, *ibid.*

1863, MAY 24.   To Brig. Gen. Lorenzo Thomas. "Two of the young men nominated for my Staff, Capts. O. H. Ross & Peter Hudson, have received no official notice of their confirmation. I would respectfully ask for information whether they have been confirmed."—ALS, DNA, RG 94, ACP, G154 CB 1863. See letter to Edwin M. Stanton, Nov. 27, 1862.

1863, MAY 25.   USG endorsement. "Respectfully forwarded to Brig. General L. Thomas. Adjutant General of the Army,   These applicants have been informed of the manner in which officers are selected for the Regiments of African descent, to be recruited in this Department, viz: by the immediate Division Commanders when called on by your orders. They have now I am informed about 250 recruits at Perkins Plantation, which I have ordered for the present to Youngs Point, under the charge of the applicant for the position of Colonel."—ES, DNA, RG 94, Colored Troops Div., Applications, G8 CT 1863. Written on a group of five applications for commissions.—*Ibid.*

1863, MAY 29.   USG endorsement. "Respectfully refered to the Sec. of War. Augustus S. Montgomery seems to occupy no official position and as he is an entire stranger to me I deem it my duty to forward this for the action of the War Dept."—AES, DNA, RG 393, Dept. of the Tenn., Letters Received. Written on a letter of May 13 from Augustus

S. Montgomery, Washington, to USG. "A *plan* has been adopted for
a simultaneous movement to sever the rebel communications throughout the whole South, which is now disclosed to some general in each
military department of the seceded states in order that they may act in
concert and thus insure success. The *plan* is to induce the *blacks* to make
a concerted & simultaneous movement or rising on the *Night of the
1st of August* next, over the entire states in rebellion. To arm themselves with any and every kind of weapon that may come to hand and
commence operations by burning all railroads and country bridges,
and tear up railroad tracks and cut and destroy telegraph wires—and
when this is done take to the woods, the swamps, or the mountains,
whence they may emerge as occasion may offer for provisions and for
further depredations. No blood is to be shed except in self defence.
The Corn will be in roasting ears about the *1st of August*, and upon
this and by foraging on the farms at night, they can subsist. This is the
plan, in substance and if we can obtain a concerted movement at the
time named it will be successful, and the rebellion will suddenly come
to an end. To carry the plan into effect in the department in which you
have a command, it is requested that you select one or more intelligent
contrabands and after disclosing to them the *plan* and the *time* (*Night
of the 1st of August*) you will send them into the interior of the country,
with instructions to communicate the *plan* and the *time* to as many
intelligent slaves as possible, and requesting of each to circulate it far
and wide over the whole country. By adopting this plan in every military department of the South, nothing will be easier than to make the
fact known throughout every state in rebellion by the *1st of August*,
and thus cause the movement to be general and simultaneous. When
you have made these arrangements please enclose this letter to some
other general commanding in the same department with yourself—
some one whom you know or beleive to be favorable to such movement
—and he in turn is requested to send it to another, and another, until
it has traveled the entire rounds of the department, and thus each
command and *post* will be acting in concert, and employing negroes to
carry the *plan* into effect at the same *time*. When this circular letter
has gone the rounds in your department please send it to some general
in the next department to yours, and they in turn will send it to the
next; until it has gone the rounds of all the military departments in
the south;—when it is requested of the last person possessing it, to
enclose it to my address that I may know and communicate that the

plan is being carried out at the *time* named. In this way the *plan* will be adopted at the same *time* and in concert over the whole south; and yet no one of all engaged in it will learn the names of his associates, and will only know the number of generals acting together in the movement. To give this last information, and before enclosing this letter to some other general; put the numeral 1 after the word '*Approved*' at the bottom of this sheet. Be assured General that a similar letter to this has been sent to every military department in the rebellious states, that the *plan* and the *time* may be adopted in concert over the whole South."—ALS, *ibid.* On June 17, Maj. Gen. Henry W. Halleck endorsed this letter. "Respectfully returned. I have no knowledge of this man or any of his plans."—AES, *ibid.* A copy of this letter addressed to Maj. Gen. John G. Foster in N. C. fell into C.S.A. hands. *O.R.*, I, xviii, 1067–69, 1072–73; *ibid.*, I, li, part 2, 736–38.

1863, MAY 31.   Maj. Gen. John A. McClernand to Lt. Col. John A. Rawlins. "Capt Ballinger who has the command of the 1st Mississippi Regiment of african decent—stationed at Grand Gulf wishes to move them up to Warenton   is 1000 strong and armed.   they can be made useful at Warenton in fortifying the place if that would become nessessary and could be drilled better than at grand gulf   Could also be used to defend Warenton and in forwarding Army stores to this Corps. If they can be moved up to Warrenton I will send an officer to muster them into the service. This Regiment was raised in this Army Corps and should like to complete the orginaztion of them"—LS, DNA, RG 393, Dept. of the Tenn., Letters Received.

1863, MAY 31.   Col. Thomas S. Mather to USG. "I am directed by Maj. Genl. McClernand, to inform you, that Capt. Tittman, A. C. S. 9th Division, who has just returned from Grand Gulf; reports that last evening about 10-o clock, the boat from Grand Gulf, bound to Warrenton, when opposite to Perkins Plantation; was hailed by Col. Owen's. 60th. Ind. Vols. Comdg. the Post, who stated, that a force of Rebels said to number 1500 men with artillery, were approaching that place; Capt. Tittman also reports, that subsequently a Gun boat, went down with a transport to protect the embarkation of our troops and to drive away the rebel forces, who he says made their appearance. I am also directed, by the General, to advise you, that Col. Whiting

Comdg. the Post, at Warrenton, has addressed him a communication, expressing his desire to have reinforcements sent him, and requests as he has but 500. men, composed in part of a regiment from this corps, and a part of his own, that four companies of his regiment now stationed near Genl. Logans. Head Quarters be immediately sent him. The General also directs me to say, that he strongly recommend's the granting of this request. The General thinks, that in view of these facts, that the enquiry naturally suggests itself whether the forces at Warrenton and at or in the vicinity of the landing on the Louisiana side above Warrenton are sufficient to hold those points."—ALS, DNA, RG 393, Dept. of the Tenn., Letters Received. On the same day, Lt. Col. John A. Rawlins issued Special Orders No. 146 directing the commanding officer at Grand Gulf to move his troops and supplies to Warrenton.—Copies, DLC-USG, V, 27, 28; DNA, RG 393, Dept. of the Tenn., Special Orders. *O.R.*, I, xxiv, part 3, 368. Also on May 31, Col. Richard Owen, 60th Ind., Warrenton, wrote to Brig. Gen. Jeremiah C. Sullivan. "Not knowing the name of your A Adjt. Genl. I take the liberty of addressing you personally to inform you that my Regt. had an engagement with a large (at least comparatively large) rebel force, which *may* march over from Perkins Plantation to Young's Point or Milliken's Bend. They came up the Tensas River in 4 boats, the largest called the Louis D'or all sidewheel steamers & the rebels were said to number 5000; but I think not over three thousand, as we saw only 4 stand of colors & 3 pieces of Artillery. I think one of the colors was the standard borne by the Cavalry Regt., perhaps Harrisons Tensas Cav. Fortunately I had a strong picket force out & a breastwork, on the levee of cottonbales, forming 3 sides of a square our rear resting on the Miss. river. The Carondolet very promptly arrived on my notifying the Forest Queen of the Expected attack & shelled the Enemy, while we used about 300 negroes, (who had taken refuge with me) for loading our stores & finally embarked without any serious loss, having we think killed a good many by the shells from the gunboat. I thought it advisable to give you the earliest intimation of these facts, lest they should press round in your direction before you were apprised We are ordered to the front, otherwise I should have much pleasure in again aiding to hold them in check, although my present available force is not over 300. . . . P. S. I send the negroes by Capt Goelzer, of my Regt., who is authorized by Genl. Grant to raise a negro Regt. & will probably soon receive his Commission as Colonel"—ALS,

DNA, RG 393, Dept. of the Tenn., Letters Received. On June 1, Sullivan endorsed this letter to USG's hd. qrs.—AES, *ibid.*

1863, [JUNE 1?].   Unknown signal officer to USG. "An officer on picket below Vicksburg says from one Thousand to Fifteen hundred ded Horses & mules floated down the river during the last twenty four Hours"—Copy (undated), DNA, RG 111, Vicksburg Signal Book.

1863, JUNE 2.   Maj. Gen. John A. McClernand to USG. "I have sent Lt Jayne of my staff to the several Hospitals at Youngs Point and Millikens Bend and the floating hospitals—with directions to Collect all Covalescents soldiers of the 13th Army Corps fit for duty and bring them forthwith to their Regiments. Beleving that great numbers of soldiers fit for duty are detained as nurses or for other duties under pretences of details of which regimental nor other higher Commanders have any knowledge or notice, I would most respectfully ask that you give Lt Jayne a peremptory order to surgeons of hospitals, to deliver up all Covalescents fit for duty to him"—Copy, DNA, RG 393, 13th Army Corps, Letters Sent.

1863, JUNE 3.   Col. William Hoffman, commissary gen. of prisoners, to USG. "I have the honor to inform you that the following declaration of exchanges of prisoners of War was made on the 30th Ult. viz. . . . 3d. All the officers and enlisted men, captured and paroled at Holly Springs, Mississippi, in December 1862. . . . All officers and men whose exchange is announced in the above declaration will be ordered to join their proper commands as soon as practicable."—LS (forged), DNA, RG 94, War Records Office, Dept. of the Tenn.; copy (signed by Capt. Wilson T. Hartz), *ibid.*, RG 249, Letters Sent. *O.R.*, II, v, 738–39.

1863, JUNE 3.   Maj. Gen. Stephen A. Hurlbut, Memphis, to Brig. Gen. Jacob Ammen, Springfield, Ill. "I am ordered by General Grant to cause the immediate arrest of Alfred Spink formerly assistant cashier in the Marine Bank of Chicago, who left Memphis Tenn, last week supposed to be on way for Chicago. Please order his arrest. An officer from Vicksburgh will follow this:"—Copy, DNA, RG 393, 16th Army Corps, Letters Sent.

1863, JUNE 4. Asst. Adjt. Gen., Washington, D. C., to USG. "I have the honor to ~~report~~ acknowledge the receipt of the application of George Brown, Pay Master, U. S. A, for the discharge of Private John R. Young 64th Illinois Volunteers from the Mitary service of the U. S., that he may receive the position of Paymasters Clerk   I am directed to inform you in reply, that the present exigencies of the service will not permit the granting of his request"—Copy, DNA, RG 393, Military Div. of the Miss., War Dept. Correspondence Received.

1863, JUNE 5. USG pass. "Capt. P. F. Schliecker a Loyal Citizen of the United States is authorized to pass south to Bayou Sara in any Government Transport that may be plying below Vicksburg, and is commended to the Commander of the Dept. of the Gulf, for authority to visit New Orleans"—Copies, DLC-Robert T. Lincoln; DNA, RG 109, Union Provost Marshals' File of Papers Relating to Individual Civilians. On Sept. 10, Maj. Gen. Stephen A. Hurlbut wrote to Brig. Gen. John A. Rawlins. "I am told one P. F. Schlicker formerly of Memphis is at Vicksburgh. He is an unmitigated Scoundrel banished from this place by forging a pass for a Smuggler. He will bear watching & I recommend it"—ALS, *ibid.* On Sept. 19, Rawlins endorsed this letter. "Respectfully referred to the Provost Marshal General who will have this man arrested & sent out of the Department at once"— ES, *ibid.* On Nov. 7, 1866, P. F. Schliecker swore before a notary public in Norfolk, Va., that he was fifty-two years of age, had been born in Baltimore, raised in Norfolk, and had moved to Columbus, Ky., in 1852, where he contracted to carry mail to and from Cairo, Ill. On Aug. 1, 1861, he was arrested by rebels and eventually spent one and one-half years in C.S.A. prisons. After moving to Norfolk, he swore, he had been continually persecuted by C.S.A. sympathizers. —*Ibid.*

1863, JUNE 5. Act. Rear Admiral David D. Porter to USG. "Will you please give me an Order for Fifty Wheel Barrows, to wheel Coal" —Copy, DNA, RG 111, Vicksburg Signal Book. On the same day, USG signaled to Capt. Benjamin F. Reno, Young's Point. "Furnish the Navy all the *Wheel Barrows* they require. If~~f~~ not in your ~~power~~ Charge instruct the Officer having them"—Copy, *ibid.* On the same day, USG signaled to Porter. "the Q m is instructed to Furnish you all the wheel Barrows you want   any thing you require and the army

has call uppon the officer having the articles and I will give such
instructtions that you will always be accommodated."—Copy, *ibid.*

1863, June 5. Maj. Gen. Stephen A. Hurlbut, Memphis, to Lt. Col.
John A. Rawlins. "I have ordered Lt. Col M. Smith to his Regiment
as directed from your Head Quarters. It is a peculiarly unfortunate
time to remove him. The office has been brought from Chaos into
shape & form and I know no officer whom I could as ill spare as Col.
Smith. If the change has been ordered for any but military reasons it
is an error of judgment and on mistaken information. Every loyal man
in Memphis will regret it, and the smugglers disloyalists and secret
abetters of rebellion will and do rejoice. So far I have found no fault
with Lt Col Smith, on the contrary I have seen much to praise. As soon
as he can close his accounts make up his property & prison lists and
turn over to his successor in office (Col. Howe 32d Wisconsin) he will
rejoin his command"—ALS, DNA, RG 94, War Records Office, Dept.
of the Tenn. On the same day, F. H. Clark and twenty-two others,
Memphis, wrote to USG. "Unless in your better informed judgment
the presence elsewhere of Col Smith is more essential to the welfare
of the service we earnestly request his continuance as Provost Marshal
of Memphis   We have no personal preference for Col Smith nor do
we know whether it is his desire to remain here or join his Regt. but
we *do* know that his upright prompt and energetic course has done and
is doing more to enlist the earnest and active cooperation of the *real*
Union Men of Memphis than we can hope for from any new man
There is now we can assure you a more united determination on the
part of the Loyal Citizens of Memphis to sustain and cooperate with
the Military Authorities than has ever existed heretofore and in our
judgment it is attributable to the life and energy infused into his
department by Col Smith who knows no cliques nor favorites and
nothing but his duty and has a happy faculty of showing to all that
there is a legitimate diference between the truly Loyal and the cringing
and fawning quasi secessionists   He is now in the midst of the vigilant
excution of Genl Hurlbut's Order No 65 which promises most satisfactory and salutary results if rigidly enforced to accomplish which
requires a knowledge of Memphis and its citizens not to be acquired
without time as well as industry and talent   Our request eminates
from no dictatorial or presuming spirit but from the single desire to
advance the interests of our common cause   Hoping you may grant

it and *above all* that our ears may continue to be delighted with news
of your Glorious Victories . . ."—DS, *ibid.*, RG 393, Dept. of the
Tenn., Letters Received. On June 11, Rawlins wrote to Hurlbut.
"Your communication of date June 5, 1863, relating to the order
releiving Lieut Col M. C Smith, of the 45th Ills Infty Vols from duty
as Provost Marshal at Memphis, is received. Major Luther H Cowen,
late of said Regiment, was killed in the assault on Vicksburg on the
22d ult which leaves in the absence of Lt Col Smith, but one Field
Officer with the Regiment, and the Col. of the Regiment expressed a
desire to have him with it, and supposing his place as Provost Marshal,
might be filled by some one of the many officers who have been disabled from active duty in the field, the order referred to was made.
But as you seem of opinion, (and you should know best) that it will
be difficult to find one to discharge the duties of Provost Marshal of
Memphis so ably and satisfactorily, as Lt Col Smith, the order releiving him, and directing him to join his Regiment is revoked."—Copies,
DLC-USG, V, 19, 30; DNA, RG 393, Dept. of the Tenn., Letters Sent.

1863, JUNE 6. Col. William Hoffman, commissary gen. of prisoners,
to USG. "I have the honor to enclose herewith lists of deserters from
several Corps of your Army, who have been paroled and delivered at
City Point by the rebel authorities, and are now in the Old Capitol
Prison in this City. Please have their respective Company Comd'rs
notified of the apprehension and delivery of these deserters, and direct
descriptive rolls to be furnished to this office. It will probably be impossible to try them by a Court Martial before their return to their
regiments and they will therefore be held subject to your orders."—
LS, DNA, RG 393, Dept. of the Tenn., Miscellaneous Letters Received.

1863, JUNE 6. Maj. Gen. William T. Sherman, Walnut Hills, Miss.,
to USG. "In reviewing and submitting the report of General Blair,
I can only say the facts are so fully and clearly stated that nothing can
be added. I take great pleasure in indorsing all he says of the conduct
of his men and officers during both assaults of May 19 and 22, for,
from my position on both days, I had this division in full view. If any
troops could have carried and held the intrenchments of Vicksburg,
these would. I recommend to the notice of the President the names
enumerated by General Blair as worthy of promotion in their line of

profession; and the storming party that volunteered to scale the works, and did do so, and remain on the exterior slope amid that fierce conflict, merit not only the medal of honor, but more substantial reward. In justice to Col. T. Kilby Smith, who commanded the Second Brigade, the absence of whose report is noticed by General Blair, I explain that I know he prepared a report, and showed it to me about May 24, at the time General Blair was absent, detached toward Yazoo City, and, now that General Blair has returned, Colonel Smith happens on detached duty at Milliken's Bend, by order of General Grant. His report will be sent in to department headquarters with this, if Colonel Smith can be heard from, and the officers and men named by him as worthy of special notice will be entitled to the same honors as are accorded to those of the other brigades. In making special mention of Col. Giles A. Smith, commanding First Brigade, I but repeat former expressions of praise. An officer who is always present with his command, who carries a severe wound without a flinch or the loss of a minute's duty, and who takes a pride in studying his chosen profession, deserves the special notice of his commanders, without a just cause for the envy of any other. Being in command of a brigade, and worthy of it, he should have the rank."—*O.R.*, I, xxiv, part 2, 261. For the report of Maj. Gen. Francis P. Blair, Jr., see *ibid.*, pp. 254–60.

1863, JUNE 8.   To Brig. Gen. Lorenzo Thomas. "I have the honor to transmit herewith the reports of the investigation of claims of French subjects, together with the original papers, referred to me from your office in the following cases, to wit: . . ."—Copies, DLC-USG, V, 6, 8, 24, 94; DNA, RG 393, Dept. of the Tenn., Hd. Qrs. Correspondence.

1863, JUNE 8.   [Lt. Col. John A. Rawlins] to Maj. Gen. Stephen A. Hurlbut. "The report required by the Secretary of War in the case of one William Miller, claiming to be a British subject, arrested by the Provost Marshal at Jackson, Tenn, Maj. Smith, on the 24th February last, on complaint of C. S. Ridgway, that said Miller had defrauded him in a cotton transaction in which they were partners, on which he was held to bail in the sum of $5000. to report to said Provost Marshal three times a day until the sum claimed was paid, has just been received through you. You will immediately direct the release of said William Miller, from said bond. The transaction was purely a private one, and the parties must settle it among themselves, without any interference by the Military authorities."—L (unsigned), DNA, RG 94, War Records Office, Military Div. of the Miss. On the same day, USG endorsed a letter of Lord Lyons. "Respectfully forwarded to Head Quarters of the Army Washington D. C., and attention invited to accompanying reports. Upon the receipt of this report, which was the first information on the subject that came to my knowledge, I directed Major General Hurlbut, Comdg 16th Army Corps, to at once release the said William Miller. The matter being one in which the Military should not have interfered."—Copies, DLC-USG, V, 25; DNA, RG 393, Dept. of the Tenn., Endorsements. The letter, dated March 31, enclosed a letter of William Miller, "claiming to be a British Subject and stating that he is required to report to military authorities at Jackson Daily or forfeit $5000.00   That he is prevented from moving with his family to Ills. and demands his trial or or the privelege of changing his residence. Requests that the matter be examined with a view, towards redress"—DLC-USG, V, 21; DNA, RG 393, Dept. of the Tenn., Register of Letters Received. On June 16, USG endorsed a second letter from Lyons on the same matter. "Respectfully returned. A similar communication has been previously received in this case, on investigation of which, an order, of which the enclosed is a copy, was made and sent to Major General Hurlbut, Memphis, Tenn., for execution. Said communication with report of investigation in the case, was forwarded to Head Quarters, of the Army Washington, D. C., on the 8th day of June '63."—Copies, DLC-USG, V, 25; DNA, RG 393, Dept. of the Tenn., Endorsements.

1863, June 11.   Maj. William W. Burns, Milwaukee, to USG. "I want to recommend to your care and for your benefit my former Adjt Genl—Capt Geo. A. Hicks—1st Division 9th Corps—I can vouch for him as for myself   I gave him the benefit of all I know in his Dept and can assure you of his success with me for more than a year—do for him as for me—for auld lang syne—Glory for you my old friend!—You have outlived and ought fought Political and Partisan feuds—Old West Point and all lovers of the Country who are so, per se—swell with pride at your success—No Ephemeral fame is yours   go on & win—"—ALS, USG 3. Burns, USMA 1847, served as brig. gen. of vols. Sept. 28, 1861–March 20, 1863, then resumed his position in the Subsistence Dept.

1863, JUNE 12.   USG endorsement. "I have little personal acquaintance with Capt. Pierce to warrant me in speaking of him but officially
I have known him for more than eighteen months. He has given the
highest satisfaction to commanders under whom he immediately served
throughout. Maj. Gen. C. F. Smith was one of Capt. Pierce's first
commanders and I know was by him held in high esteem. My confidance in those whose testamonials precede this, and that of Gen. Smith
who I know if living would add his also, is such that I do not hesitate
to endorse the recommendation for Capt. Pierces promotion."—AES,
DNA, RG 94, ACP, P1040 CB 1864. Written on a document composed of statements of five gen. officers recommending Capt. Gilbert
A. Pierce for promotion.—AES, *ibid.* No promotion followed.

1863, JUNE 12.   Maj. Samuel Breck, AGO, to [USG]. "I have the
honor to acknowledge the receipt of the communication of Geo M
Woodridge referring to the case of Jessie B Marshall, 63d Ohio Volunteers alleged to have been improperly discharged. It appears from
the rolls of that command, on file in this Office, that Jessie B. Marshall,
Co "G" 63d Ohio Vols was discharged Feb 15 '63 on account of disability existing when enlisting. This in addition to the fact that he
never rendered any service, confirms the statements of his Commanding Officer, that he is not entitled to pay."—Copies, DNA, RG 393,
Military Div. of the Miss., War Dept. Correspondence; (misaddressed
to Maj. Gen. Ambrose E. Burnside) DLC-USG, V, 105.

1863, JUNE 12.   W. B. Dickerman, East Hampton, Mass., to USG.
"I have the honor to inform you in behalf of the Adelphi Society of
Williston-Seminary that at its last regular meeting you was elected to
an honorary membership of said Literary Organization—Hoping that
you will accept this office—"—ALS, USG 3.

1863, JUNE 13.   To Paymaster Edwin D. Judd. "You need not return
to Memphis. I will order payments made now."—Copies, DLC-USG,
V, 19, 30; DNA, RG 393, Dept. of the Tenn., Letters Sent. On June 12,
Lt. Col. John A. Rawlins issued Special Orders No. 158. "Major E. D.
Judd, Paymaster in charge of paying troops in this Department, owing
to the impracticability of making payments to the troops engaged in
the seige of Vicksburg, at this time, will return with his Corps, of
Paymasters, to Memphis, Tenn., and pay off the troops in the District

of West Tennessee, prior to making payments here. In view of the fact that in a short time the troops engaged in the seige of Vicksburg, will have two additional months pay due them it is desired that Major Judd will make every effort to provide means to make payment to this Army to include the 30th of June. at as early a day as it will be practicable to make payments."—Copies, DLC-USG, V, 27, 28; DNA, RG 393, Dept. of the Tenn., Special Orders. On June 14, Judd telegraphed to USG. "Shall I attack the whole Army at once or certain portions which you may designate. And will you issue a General Order to the Army to Send the pay rolls for March and April on board some steamer here to be designated"—Telegram received, *ibid.*, Telegrams Received.

1863, JUNE 14.   To Lt. Col. Loren Kent, provost marshal. "Do not permit the Steamer 'City of Alton' to leave until authorized by the Medical Director."—Copies, DLC-USG, V, 19, 30; DNA, RG 393, Dept. of the Tenn., Letters Sent.

1863, JUNE 16.   USG endorsement. "Respectfully forwarded to his Excellency, Richard Yates, Governor of the State of Illinios"—ES, Records of 61st Ill., I-ar. Written on a letter of May 24 from Maj. Simon P. Ohr, 61st Ill., Bolivar, Tenn., to Brig. Gen. Mason Brayman. "I have the honor to forward proceedings of the officers of this Regiment, expressing their views as to existing vacancies in the Field Offices thereof, viz:—We certify that at a meeting of the Field, Staff, & Line Officers of the 61st Illinois Volunteer Infantry held on the 23d day of May ~~May~~ 1863, Major *Simon P. Ohr* was unanimously elected *Lieut Colonel* of said Regiment—and Captain *Daniel Grass* of Company "H" was by a majority of votes elected *Major.* B. B. HAMILTON Chaplain 61st Ill   GEO. H. KNAPP. Asst Surgeon   Tellers   Be pleased to forward recommendations to the Governor of Illinois in accordance with the above expression, and oblige"—ALS, *ibid.* The appointments requested were made as of May 14.

1863, JUNE 16.   R. M. Thomas, Centralia Station, Ill., to USG. "being Compelled to wait here for the train North Some two Hours I got in Conversation with a soldier who is just from Prison in the South—having effected his escape by the aid of a union man and directed on his way by negroes in the night—wishing to do all that lies in my power for my Country I hasten to lay before you the news that this man brings—states that he was one of Col Straights men—was taken prisoner & was also very ill and near the point of death that he was imprisoned and with no attention shown him covered with vermin & filth he gave himself up to die—but an officer of the Prison who proved to be a union man Connived at his escape after he had grown convalescent,   he was dressed in a Confederate Soldier garb & effecting great lameness started out on his perilous journey telling those that he met that he was discharged on account of wounds & sickness & showing his counterfeit Papers to that effect, stating that he lived near Memphis tennessee.   states that Sometimes he was allowed to ride on the trains & at others not, states that evry R road was crowded with troops for Johnson, thousands & tens of thousands any amt of artillry & it accompanied by the best artillerist in the rebel army, that he overheard the rebel officers state that Johnson had written or telegraphed that he had recd a message from Pemperbton that he could hold out until the 10th of July, that he had provisions hid away from his men—that Johnson must be ready to act by the 25 of this month.   also heard the officers say that they would have at least 100.000 men with Johnson by the 25.   this man states that he knows that he saw himself over 20.000 that trains were crowded & loaded down.—Now General whether these things are so or not is for you to determine,   this mans name is—Robert Powell.   his home is in OshKosh.—Said he would not tell me the name of the officer who got him out of prison.—you know your own business but but if Johnson is going to have even 50.000 men & he attacks you you will loose more than by storming Vicksburg.—"—ALS, DNA, RG 393, Dept. of the Tenn., Letters Received.

1863, June 17.   J. W. Merrill, vol. aide and provost marshal, 3rd Div., 15th Army Corps, "On Board Steamer Platte Valley Near Columbus Ky," to USG. "On the 16th day of June I took passage on steamer Platte Valley at Memphis for Cairo—we left Memphis at Six Oclock P M.   when opposite Bradleys Landing we were met by a heavy Fire from a Battery Planted on the Bank and also by a Sharp Volly of Musketry—Killing three Men and wounding Two—the Pilot House was Completely Riddled Two Shots explodeing in it.   the Boat was Struck by over one Hundred Shot.   at the time of the attack the Boat was Rounding in for the Purpose of taking on Ten Bales

Cotton, under a Permit Issued by R Hough 'Special agent of the Treasury Dept.' This Permit was obtained by S. B. Lane of Memphis and G. B. Bransford of Shelby County Tenn. these Men were on the Boat at the time of the Attack and with a man named C. S. Kane of Memphis stood together on the Hurricane Roof Foward, and Pointed out the Place where they wished the Boat to Land and where they said the Cotton was Piled up. there were no Shot struck the Part of the Boat where these men were standing and there was no Cotton in sight; we had—seventy five Confederate Prisoners on Board, and taking all the Circumstances into Consideration, namely—the Pointing out of this *Particular Spot to Land*—the *Batteries Ready Planted*, and the absence of the Cotton which was said to be there, I felt Convinced that it was a *Preconcerted* Plan to Capture the Boat and Liberate the Prisoners, and after Consulting with Col Hilliar of your Staff who was confined to his Room by sickness, I arrested the Men *Lane, Bransford* & *Kane* and shall leave them with Genl. Buford at Cairo to be held Prisoners Subject to your Order. (By Col Hilliars Directions) the Captain and Pilot of the Steamer, deserve much credit for their coolness and Presence of Mind, the Pilot never Leaving the wheel—and the Captain standing by him and Refuseing to surrender his Boat while she could Float a Plank—Lieut Blake in Command of the guard for Prisoners, Replied Promptly to the Gurrilla Fire, with forty Muskets as long as the Boat was within Range—I placed a guard of Discharged Soldiers and a few *Civillians that I knew*, over the Prisoners and used the Entire guard for the Defence of the Boat (Col Hilliar thought that Cairo would be the Safest Post to leave there men as Prisoners)"
—ALS, DNA, RG 393, Dept. of the Tenn., Letters Received. See Merrill to Brig. Gen. Napoleon B. Buford, June 18, *ibid.*, RG 109, Union Provost Marshals' File of Papers Relating to Two or More Civilians; *O.R.*, I, xxiv, part 2, 507; *O.R.* (Navy), I, xxv, 187.

1863, JUNE 18. USG pass for W. H. Keene.—*ABPC*, 1900, 1904.

1863, JUNE 18. Chaplain John Eaton, Jr., "Yazoo River," to Lt. Col. John A. Rawlins. "~~May~~ I have made proposed Examination Suggested all changes Expedient for contrabands across the river in accordance with the Generals instructions They will now have medical care I propose to hasten to Memphis Keeping in mind a man for this place do business there & be back in season for any changes here—My

Examinations assure me that the right man with these plantations this opportunity for woodcutting these flowing logs & saw mills at hand & cast off soldiers clothing can greatly relieve the government in Supporting these people"—Telegram received, DNA, RG 393, Dept. of the Tenn., Telegrams Received.

1863, JUNE 18.　Eliza D. Gerrish, West Creek, Lake County, Ind., to USG. "I address you in behalf of my son, James L. Gerrish, who enlisted August 1862, Co. A. 99 Reg. Ind. Vol. Being from a child of delicate constitution, & never able to perform hard labors; his physician & friends felt that he could not endure the exposure of the camp. So it has proved. Before he left the state, at South Bend he was in the hospital. Very soon after the Reg. went south, he was obliged to go into the hospital at Memphis & staid untill the first day of Feb. then went to the Reg. In a few days was sick again, & went into the hospital at La Grange Tenn. His last last letter was dated April 22, he was then able to sit up half of the day. My request to you Sir, is, that he may be discharged & returned to his anxious mother"—ALS, USG 3.

1863, JUNE 19.　USG endorsement. "Respectfully forwarded to his Excellency the Governor of Illinois"—ES, Records of 18th Ill., I-ar. Written on a letter of June 12 from Capt. Peter McGowan, Co. E, 18th Ill., to Ill. AG Allen C. Fuller recommending promotions in his co.—LS, *ibid.*

1863, JUNE 20.　USG endorsement. "Approved and respectfully forwarded. Gen. Dodge is one of the most valuable officers we have and ablest Dist. Commanders. I would ask therefore that the date of his leavig his command be subject to my orders."—AES, DNA, RG 94, Letters Received. Written on a letter of June 8 from Brig. Gen. Grenville M. Dodge, Corinth, to Lt. Col. Henry Binmore, adjt. for Maj. Gen. Stephen A. Hurlbut, asking sixty days leave to attend to personal business.—LS, *ibid.* On July 10, Maj. Gen. Henry W. Halleck approved the request.—AES, *ibid.*

1863, JUNE 20.　USG endorsement. "Respectfully forwarded to Hd Qrs. of the Army and recommendation concured in."—AES, DNA, RG 94, ACP, 340H CB 1863. Written on a petition of June 13 addressed to President Abraham Lincoln signed by Brig. Gen. Eugene

A. Carr, Brig. Gen. Michael K. Lawler, Maj. Gen. John A. McClernand and Maj. Gen. Frederick Steele. "We beg leave respectfully to recommend Col Charles L Harris, 11th Wis Infy Vols. for promotion, for gallant & meritorious services in the present, as well as former campaigns. Col Harris, was the first man to volunteer in Wisconsin, in response to your Excellencys call for 75,000 men in April 1861; was Lieut. Col. of the 1st Wis Infy, performed efficient service in Va. during the three months of his term & returned home to raise & command the 11th Wis Infy, at the head of which he gallantly charged the Enemys works at Big Black River Bridge on the 17th & at Vicksburg on the 22d ult;—For 6 months Col Harris commanded a Brigade with great satisfaction to the men & officers of his command. He is a thorough soldier, a brave and patriotic man, who deserves promotion, and we respectfully ~~ask~~ ~~that~~ recommend him for the office of Brig Gen'l of Vols:"—DS, *ibid.* Col. Charles L. Harris, 11th Wis., was not promoted until after the war.

1863, JUNE 20. USG endorsement. "Respectfully forwarded to the Governor of Illinois"—ES, Records of 28th Ill., I-ar. Written on a petition of May 8 of officers of the 28th Ill. to Governor Richard Yates of Ill. asking the promotion of Dr. John Kemper from asst. surgeon to surgeon.—DS, *ibid.* Kemper, however, was not promoted until July 26, 1864.

1863, JUNE 20. Capt. Charles C. Gilbert, Cincinnati, to USG. "My appointment as Brigadier General not having been confirmed by the Senate, I shall join my company I presume at the end of my present leave of absence—Just before leaving Murfreesboro, Gen'l Thomas suggested to me the idea of joining the part of the 1st Infy now with your army and thus endeavor to have it turned into a corps of sappers —If you have not already organized ~~an~~ a body of Engineer troops, may I ask you to consider the foregoing—The war as it progresses will involve the necessity of a few well trained engineer troops in every army—Debarred as I now consider myself from the command of troops in the line—I seek an opening which offers distinction if not military rank"—ALS, USG 3.

1863, JUNE 22. Maj. Thomas M. Vincent, AGO, to USG. "I have the honor to acknowledge the receipt of your endorsement on the letter of Brigadier General S. G. Burbridge, dated May 29th, asking that the date of the resignation of Captain A. N. Keigwin, 26th Kentucky Volunteers, may be changed. In reply, I am directed to inform you that the request cannot be considered until it is shown why the Commanding Officer of his regiment did not inform him, at the proper time, of his resignation having been accepted. Captain Keigwin appears to have neglected his duty in not having kept himself informed of the station of his regiment and in not making inquiry to ascertain whether his resignation had been accepted when he knew it had been tendered."— LS, DNA, RG 393, Dept. of the Tenn., Letters Received.

1863, June 22. John B. McFadden, Pittsburgh, to USG. "A. stranger to you,—allow me to avail my self of the opportunity, politely tendered by my friend Asst. Surgeon White (who is now ordered to report at your Head Quarters) of sending a small package to your address containing the photographs of two of your old Army friends, Lieuts. Farrelly and Hays of the 4th Infantry   My gallant step son Farrelly was killed by a fall from his horse, near Fort Waschita I. T. August 1854—he was then in command of a company of the 5th Infantry. (Capt Morays)   My son in Law Hays is now a Brigadier of Vol, and is in command, in the outer line of defences of Washington— near Bull Run. Abercrombie is his division Commander. Hays distinguished him self during the present war, and was promoted for Gallent conduct on the field, he was badly wounded at Chantelly. The larger photograph is from a daguerotype taken at Natchtoches La. 1845, which you kindly sent to Mrs Hays—You will recognise in the picture the form of your old friend and admirer, Hays—familarly called 'Old Red'   The Artist aided by your modesty placed you in the back ground when the picture was taken—now the people with a much better appreciation of your worth, have placed you in the fore ground, where you ought to have been long since   With the best wishes for your success and a speedy termination of this unholy War . . ."— ALS, USG 3. For a reproduction of the daguerreotype, see Lawrence A. Frost, *U. S. Grant Album* (Seattle, 1966), p. [21].

1863, June 23. C.S.A. Maj. N. G. Watts, agent for the exchange of prisoners, to USG concerning the exchange of hostages.—ALS, DNA, RG 94, War Records Office, Dept. of the Tenn. *O.R.*, II, vi, 37. See letter to Lt. Gen. John C. Pemberton, Dec. 15, 1862, note 1.

1863, JUNE 23. C. L. Davis, Metropolis, Ill. "States that there is a secret plot formed by leading rebels in Ky, having for its object the taking of Maj Genl' Grant's life   He has been acting for a spy, is now under arrest   Asks to be released."—DLC-USG, V, 22; DNA, RG 393, Dept. of the Tenn., Register of Letters Received.

1863, JUNE 23. Charles Evans, Jr., Washington, Iowa, to USG. "I have seen thirteen months hard service   I have been in the Battles of Belmount and Fort Donelson under you   now I should like to go into the service again but I should like to go as a scout under you   I am 21 years of age shrewd quick and active   if you find it suitable to give me that position or any other dangerous position under you should like to hear from you"—ALS, USG 3.

1863, JUNE 24. Lt. Col. John A. Rawlins endorsement. "Respectfully referred to Col. Isaac F. Shepard Commanding Colored Troops. The General Commanding deems it inexpedient to attempt the organizing of any more regiments of colored troops, until those that have already been ordered by General Thomas have been recruited and mustered in. Should there be any vacancies in the regiments authorized to be raised, in any of the respective grades for which there are applicants in the inclosed applications they might be given them. As you (in the absence of General Hawkins) have charge of the organization of these colored troops, you will please take such steps or make such recommendations in reference to the enclosed applications as you may deem best, under your instructions from General Thomas."—Copies, DLC-USG, V, 25; DNA, RG 393, Dept. of the Tenn., Endorsements. Written on the application of Capt. Charles During and others for appointments in the U.S. Colored Troops.—*Ibid.* On July 3, Col. Isaac F. Shepard, "Steamer 'Fanny Bullitt,' " wrote to Rawlins. "I entirely approve of Gen. Grant's decision, as conveyed on cover of applicants for position, to put a stop to the *quasi* formation of African Regiments by unauthorized parties. The 8th, 9th, 10th, 11th, and 12th Louisiana, and the 1st, 2d and 3d Mississippi,—besides the 1st & 2d Arkansas, are *all* that Gen. Thomas has authorized—the last two at Helena. All others are forming without *proper* authority, and it seems to me the men *should be ordered* to some one of the others to fill up, and the acting officers recruiting be returned to their respective companies. This I hear has been done in some instances, but not in all. Gen. Thomas writes me he will issue Rosters for the 4th & 5th Miss.—the 13th, and higher Louisiana Regiments, '*when the the others are filled.*' Then it will be time enough for officers to commence recruiting, and it is mischievous to do so before, as colored men aggregated for an *expected* Regiment are so worked upon they are disinclined to join others. Sometimes direct prejudice is inspired in them against particular organizations. This is all wrong. No one of the *authorized* Regiments is yet full, and by losses in battle and from disease some have lost half they had. The following schedule will very accurately show the number of recuits needed as well as the number on the rolls at this date. . . . The 12th La.—and the 2d Miss. are recruiting with your army, and their state I know nothing of. But *they need 2020 men more* than is noted above, making a demand for nearly *five thousand recruits* to fill up as the Regiments *ought to be filled.* This is a large number, perhaps more than there is material for, and therefore everything should be used in making it up. Cannot an order issue *to all* collected bodies to ~~either~~ report to some one of these Regiments?—the 1st Mississippi and 9th Louisiana especially? Capt. Wolf, the bearer, will give information of nearly 300 held by Gen. Osterhaus' authority—can you not give him an order to take them at once for the 1st Miss.?—Or,—if it be thought better, let them be sent forward for *general* distribution, and I will see them equitbly disposed. I regret to trouble you, but am very anxious to get these troops *into useable condition,*—and I think these statements and suggestions will convey just the information you may desire from me. . . . P. S.—Judge Dent is safe and well. I landed him at his plantation 36 hours since. He wishes me to inform Gen. Grant. His *house* stands,—gin and out buildings all burned. Negroes mostly saved."— ALS, DNA, RG 393, Dept. of the Tenn., Letters Received. See letter to Col. William Hoffman, Aug. 11, 1863.

1863, JUNE 24. Maj. Gen. Stephen A. Hurlbut to Lt. Col. John A. Rawlins. "I send herewith statements in relation to the unwarrantable seizure of property of Mr E. E. Clark and Dr Peters by troops under command of Maj Genl Prentiss. The facts are sufficiently set forth in the papers. It appears to me that this was a Raid to procure Negroes to fill up a Regiment and that they have been forced into the service unwillingly. It is a very gross violation of your safeguard and is of very dangerous consequence. It is out of my jurisdiction & I simply report it"—ALS, DNA, RG 109, Union Provost Marshals' File of

Papers Relating to Two or More Civilians. Hurlbut enclosed letters of June 23 from E. E. Clarke and George B. Peters, Memphis, addressed to USG, complaining that on June 2 cav. landed by the steamboat *Pike* seized Negroes and supplies at their plantations.—ALS, *ibid.* On June 29, Rawlins endorsed Hurlbut's letter. "Respectfully referred to Maj. Gen'l. B. M. Prentiss, Com'd'g Dist N. E. Ark. for report. Mr. Clarke was vouched for to the General Commanding, in Memphis, as a Union man. As such he received protection papers. It is understood that he was cultivating his plantation by hiring his hands, exactly in accordance with the policy shadowed out by the President in his proclamation and in accordance with the plan, since established by leasing plantations, and hiring the Negroes   Violating the safeguard given by the General Commanding the Department was a gross violation of military propriety, whether the facts upon which the safe guard was given were true or not. If deception has been practiced, it was the duty of the officer knowing the fact to report it, with the evidence so that it might be withdrawn. Gen Prentiss will make an early and full report in this case, showing all the facts. These papers to be returned to these Headquarters with report."—ES, *ibid.* On July 8, Maj. Gen. Benjamin M. Prentiss wrote to Rawlins. "I have the honor to return herewith, as directed, Major General Hurlbut's letter of the 24th ultimo and the papers therein referred to,—I also send copies of Capt. Clammers report and of the papers I gave Mr. Clarke and can only add in addition to the information contained in them that the negroes taken from Clarke's plantation explicitly deny that they were hired by Clarke or that any arrangement was made whereby they were to receive any compensation for their labor. I beg leave to state also that while I refused to put the negroes back as Mr Clarke requested, I told him that he might freely confer with them and if he could find any of them willing to return I would furnish them transportation. Mr Clarke did have frequent and lengthy interviews with them, but could not pursuade them to return—The same is true in Dr Peters case.—I am satisfied that the negroes came away voluntarily, and therefore Mr Clarke has no claim against the Government for the loss of an expected crop of cotton. Capt. Clammers denies all knowledge of your safe-guard until meeting ~~his~~ Clarke's son just as the boat was preparing to leave. I think that Mr Covington may have been arrested but not on Clarke's plantation—but was immediately released on the ground that he was a Brittish subject. During Mr. Clarke's interview with me I proposed to put back all his property that could be found, but when he failed to pursuade the negroes to return he did not wish the property returned."—ALS, *ibid.*

1863, JUNE 26.   USG endorsement. "Gen. Oglesby has been a valuable officer to Government and his present unfitness for further service originates from a wound received whilst gallantly serving the cause of the Union. It seems a pity that Gen. Oglesby should be compelled to resign his position because in serving faithfully he has rendered himself unfit for further serving and possibly from following his profession in civil life. I recommend a leave of absence for six months with permission to resign at the expiration if he then desires to do so."—AES, DNA, RG 94, ACP, O6 CB 1863. Written on a letter of June 23 from Maj. Gen. Richard J. Oglesby, La Grange, Tenn., to Brig. Gen. Lorenzo Thomas resigning for reasons of health.—ALS, *ibid.* On July 6, President Abraham Lincoln endorsed this letter. "I wish Gen. Oglesby to be obliged—by a leave of absence, rather than an acceptance of his resignation, if that would be a greater kindness—excepting always, that if the service requires his commission to be given to another, it must be done."—AES, *ibid.* On the same day, Secretary of War Edwin M. Stanton endorsed this letter. "Ninety days leave of absence is given to Major General Oglesby with permission to visit Washington if so disposed—action on the resignation is in the meantime Suspended"—AES, *ibid.* On June 27, Lt. Col. John A. Rawlins wrote to Oglesby. "Inclosed please find a copy of the indorsement of the Major General Commanding on your letter of resignation, indicating the action he is desirous the authorities at Washington should take relative thereto. You will also find inclosed herewith an order granting you leave of absence to go beyond the limits of this Department to await notification of the action of the President on your letter of resignation."—LS, Oglesby Papers, IHi. On June 22, Maj. Sheridan Wait, adjt. for Oglesby, wrote to Thomas resigning because of Oglesby's resignation.—ALS, DNA, RG 94, ACP, 518S CB 1863. On June 26, USG endorsed this letter. "Approved and respectfully forwarded to Hd Qrs. of the Army."—AES, *ibid.* Wait's resignation was accepted as of July 10; Oglesby remained in service until May 26, 1864.

1863, JUNE 26.   A. F. Lamb, Lake Providence, La., to Lt. Col. John A. Rawlins. "I was arrested at this place on the 19th inst and have been

held till the present time. No Charges have been made known to me
nor any reason except as stated in my statement. My private papers
have been taken from me and are still retained by them. I have been
offered my release if I wished to go up the river   I am a contractor to
get out cotton, have also a general authority to ship cotton belonging
to loyal persons. My character has been assailed by this, I consider,
unwarrantable arrest and detention and I most respectfully ask that a
full and complete investigation may be had immediately concerning
both my own act & the reason for my detention   I have just learned
that a communication has been sent to Adj Sabine on Gen McArthur's
staff mentioning among other matters my arrest and detention here
and by permission of the author I refer you to it. I know nothing of its
contents   All I ask if there is anything laid to my charge is a speedy
investigation for I am responsible for all my acts and perfectly willing
to take the consequences of them. Your early attention to this affair
will much oblige,"—ALS, DNA, RG 109, Union Provost Marshals'
File of Papers Relating to Individual Civilians. On July 5, Rawlins
endorsed this letter. "Respectfully referr[ed] to Brig General Reed,
Comdg at Lake Providence fo[r] report"—ES, *ibid.* On July 12, Brig.
Gen. Hugh T. Reid wrote to Rawlins. "I have the honor to report
that A F Lamb came here some time since, probably at the time stated
by him, from below but had no pass, but having a paper from Mr
Yeatman, Special Treasury Agent at Memphis Authorizing him to
pick, gin, and bale cotton in Desha County Arkansas, and wishing to
remain only a few days for the return of Mr Munson with whom he
had business, he was permitted to remain for some days, but left, going
up the river before Mr Munsons return. The day after he left, an
officer arrived from below for the purpose of arresting Mr. Lamb, on
suspicion of being a Spy, as the Provost Marshal Maj Reynolds was
informed. A few days after this Lamb returned with additional papers
from Mr Yeatman authorizing him to ship cotton for loyal persons to
Mr Yeatman to be held subject to the orders of Lamb, approved by the
Sec of the Treasury. I was credibly informed and am still well satisfied
of the fact, that Lamb had been ordered out of the lines when our army
was in front of Corinth, and he admits the fact of being ordered as far
as Cairo. With this information before me and the suspicious circumstances of his getting authority to pick, gin, and bale cotton in Arkansas
where we had no troops, I ordered Mr Lamb to report twice a day until
something more could be heard from below, and as Lieut Foster Asst

Pro. Marshal was here and promised to investigate the matter and report here, Mr Lamb was still required to report but never had any permission whatever either from myself or the Provost Marshal to go up the river, neither was he informed as to the suspicions of his being a spy, as he was detained for the purpose of ascertaining the fact   No report of his case has as yet been recd from below. I returned his papers, with a letter to Mr Yeatman informing him of the supposed character of the man, stating that the papers would be delivered to Lamb or returned to him, (Mr Yeatman) as he might desire and only yesterday received an answer from Mr Yeatman which I herewith enclose marked A. B. and C.   Much of Lambs statement in relation to my conduct and that of the Provost Marshal is but a tissue of false hood and I shall send his papers to Mr Yeatman and him away from this Post, believing him to be one of a gang who wish to rob the Government and Loyal citizens, under the pretense of serving both unless other wise ordered from your Head Quarters"—ALS, *ibid.*

1863, JUNE 27.   Brig. Gen. Peter J. Osterhaus, Big Black, to Lt. Col. John A. Rawlins. "Permit me, to lay the enclosed request of Mrs. Elmira J. Kelley before you for your decision; I am at a loss, what to do—Mrs. Kelley is a 'Southern' woman, but rather of a mild species. There is another 'lady' in the vicinity of my Camps a Mrs. Faulkes whose husband is in the rebel army; she is the hottest rebel firebrand around but that is not the reason for my mentioning her; if I had no cause to believe her a dangerous Spy;—She has been at all Hd. Quarters near Vicksburg and seems to be well posted; yesterday on an inspecting Tour to Baldwins and Halls ferries I was informed, that this Mrs. Faulkes attempted to cross the river same day last Week at Hall's, but unsuccessfull there—really did cross at a private ferry at a little distance from Hall's, and returned on this side again. I have her closely watched now and find her already under a kind of a Parole to Major Genl. McPherson. Some paroled Rebel officers have so far recovered from their wounds, that I considered it prudent, to forward them to the river; they are prowling around constantly and make themselves obnoxious generally. Every thing remains quiet here, my connections with General Sherman's troops are getting perfect.   a very strict system of patrols in connection with the stationary pickets and videttes guards the river bank, wherever accesible, from Bridgeport to Baldwins ferry. I enclose again my former application for detail of Lt. Wm.

E. Wangelin (3d Miss Inf A. d.) and hope, that the endorsement of Col. Ballinger, you required, will be satisfactory."—ALS, DNA, RG 109, Union Provost Marshals' File of Papers Relating to Two or More Civilians. On June 28, Elmira J. Kelley wrote to Osterhaus. "I am desirous of obtaining a passport to Cincinatti for my son George Kelly, for the purpose of attending grammar school. His eduacation has been neglected for two years past and at his age 15 yrs I feel it essential to pay attention to his education. George has an uncle (John Kelley) residing at Cincinatti."—ALS, *ibid.* On June 27, Rawlins wrote to Osterhaus. "Your communication of this date relating to the request of Mrs. Kelley to send her son North, and Mrs. Faulkes and the wounded rebel officers is received. There is no objection to granting Mrs Kelleys request. Mrs Faulkes should be closely watched, and if necessary put in arrest. She must not be permitted to pass our lines, nor any one else, at present, not connected with our Army, no matter whose pass they may have, unless they present at the same time letters from the General Commanding explanatory of the same. There are some persons who obtained passes some time ago to pass our lines, but have not yet availed themselves of them. These persons will not now be allowed to go, but their passes you will take up, until such time as it may be deemed safe to let them pass. All wounded Rebel Officers who can be moved without endangering their lives, you will have sent in at once to the Provost Marshal General at these Headquarters, to be sent to our Hospitals if they have not entirely recovered."—LS, *ibid.*, RG 393, 13th Army Corps, 9th Div., Letters Received.

1863, JUNE 28.   To Act. Rear Admiral David D. Porter. "Enclosed I send you, letter of surgeon Izpell [*Azpell*], endorsed by my Medical Director, on the subject of the detention of Hospital boats for convoy. To the present time boats carrying the Hospital Flag have not been interfered with, and as they are required to get the sick and wounded from the field to comfortable hospitals, with as much promptness as possible, I would suggest that the river guards be instructed to let all such boats pass without awaiting convoy."—ALS, MdAN.

1863, JUNE 29.   USG endorsement. "I am cognizant of the stand taken by Col. Manter in Mo. when the rebellion first broke out and of his continued services in the cause of the Union since. He is a man of intelligence and influance and by those officers who have served immediately with him is represented to be a most efficient soldier. I therefore take pleasure in recommending Col. Manter for promotion for gallant and meritorious conduct."—AES, DNA, RG 94, ACP, 814M CB 1863. Written on a letter of May 4 from Maj. Gen. Frederick Steele and Maj. Gen. Francis P. Blair, Jr., to President Abraham Lincoln recommending Col. Francis H. Manter, 32nd Mo., for appointment as brig. gen.—LS, *ibid.* No appointment resulted.

1863, JUNE 29.   Col. Edward D. Townsend, AGO, to USG. "Maj. Gen Hooker has been relieved and Maj. Gen. Mead assigned to command army, of Potomac by the President."—Telegram received, DNA, RG 107, Telegrams Collected (Unbound).

1863, JUNE 29.   Act. Rear Admiral David D. Porter to USG. "The vessel is not at all Suited for carrying horses. She is one of Faragot's vessels, very high out of water."—Signal received (intercepted), DNA, RG 109, Pemberton Papers.

1863, JULY 1.   USG endorsement. "Respectfully forwarded to his Excellency Richard Yates, Governor of the State of Ills."—ES, Records of 106th Ill., I-ar. Written on a letter of June 19 from Maj. John M. Hurt, 106th Ill., Snyder's Bluff, Miss., to Governor Richard Yates of Ill. recommending promotions.—ALS, *ibid.* On July 3, Hurt again wrote to Yates recommending promotions.—ALS, *ibid.* On July 7, USG endorsed this letter. "Respectfully forwarded to his Excellency, Richard Yates Governor of the State of Illinois"—ES, *ibid.*

1863, JULY 3.   USG endorsement. "Respectfully forwarded to Hd Quars of the Army. Washington. D. C. I have directed Maj. Genl. S. A. Hurlbut, Commanding 16th Army Corps, Memphis. Tennessee to carry into effect the recommendations of the Commission"—ES, DNA, RG 108, Letters Received. Written on the report of a commission headed by Col. Warren L. Lothrop, Memphis, to Lt. Col. Henry Binmore, April, 1863, making recommendations concerning the art. of Fort Pickering, Memphis.—DS, *ibid.*

1863, JULY 5.   USG endorsement. "Approved and respectfully forwarded to Headquarters of the Army, Washington, D. C. Lieut Col. Schwartz is a brave, and when in health, an efficient officer. He has rendered valuable services to his Country in the field, but from wounds received at the battle of Shiloh he has never recovered, and is consequently unable for field service."—ES, DNA, RG 94, ACP, 545S CB 1863. Written on a letter of June 23 from Lt. Col. Adolph Schwartz, Springfield, Ill., to Lt. Col. Walter B. Scates, adjt., 13th Army Corps, requesting an honorable discharge on account of wounds.—ALS, *ibid.*

Index

All letters written by USG of which the text was available for use in this volume are indexed under the names of the recipients. The dates of these letters are included in the index as an indication of the existence of text. Abbreviations used in the index are explained on pp. xvi–xx. Individual regts. are indexed under the names of the states in which they originated.